8th Annual Edition
KNIVES '88

Edited by
Ken Warner

DBI BOOKS, INC.

STAFF

EDITOR
Ken Warner

ASSOCIATE EDITORS
Robert S.L. Anderson
Harold A. Murtz
Deborah Warner

ASSISTANT TO THE EDITOR
Lilo Anderson

COVER PHOTOGRAPHY
John Hanusin

MANAGING EDITOR
Pamela J. Johnson

PUBLISHER
Sheldon L. Factor

DBI BOOKS INC.

PRESIDENT
Charles T. Hartigan
VICE PRESIDENT & PUBLISHER
Sheldon L. Factor
VICE PRESIDENT—SALES
John G. Strauss
TREASURER
Frank R. Serpone

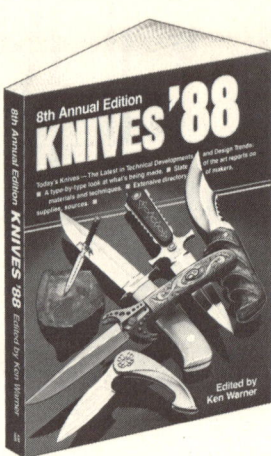

THE COVER KNIVES

Our flamboyant centerpiece is an all-titanium locking folder by the team of Michael and Patricia Walker—the colors are anodized, not applied. At bottom, we show a tour-de-force of another kind in Ray Appleton's fully machined folder—that starburst is the lock release. Across the top from the left you can see Earl Witsaman's tiny dagger-in-a-crystal, a George Herron ivory-handled fighter of classic shape, a fancy dagger by A.J. Hubbard, and another, albeit low-keyed, example of the unusual in Larry DiTommaso's carved and sculptured—with hand-held tools, mind you—short skinning knife. In all, a fine display, elegantly photographed by John Hanusin.

Copyright © MCMLXXXVII by DBI Books Inc., 4092 Commercial Ave., Northbrook, IL 60062. Printed in the United States of America. All rights reserved. No part of this book may be reproduced, stored in a retrieval system or transmitted in any form or by any means, electronic, mechanical, photocopying, recording or otherwise, without prior written permission of the publisher.

The views and opinions of the authors expressed herein are not necessarily those of the publisher, and no responsibility for such views will be assumed.

Arms and Armour Press, London, G.B., exclusive licensees and distributors in Britain and Europe; New Zealand; Nigeria, South Africa and Zimbabwe; India and Pakistan; Singapore, Hong Kong and Japan. Capricorn Link (Aust.) Pty. Ltd. exclusive distributors in Australia.

ISBN 0-87349-015-0   Library of Congress Catalog Card #80-67744

CONTENTS

Introduction 5

FEATURES

50 Years of Randall Knives
    by Ken Warner 6

There Is No Best Sword
    by Hank Reinhardt 14

Bowie and Black: Fiction or Fact?
    by B. R. Hughes 22

Hollow Handle History
    by Bernard Levine 26

More About Richtig
    by Harlan Suedmeier 30

Knives of The Gaucho
    by Abel A. Domenech 37

Handmade Knives in Argentina Today
    by Abel A. Domenech 44

TRENDS

Bowies 48
Movie Knives 53
The Working Straight Edge 56
Straight Standards 58
Leather and Other Stuff 77
Knives in the Kitchen 81
The Folding Standards 84
Simple Knives 96
Carving Sets Anyone? 99
Single-Edged Fighters 101
Trout and Bird Knives 103
The Return of the Sabertooth 106

50 Years of Randall Knives

The main knife, the Randall No. 1 All-Purpose fighter.

FOR FIVE DECADES, Walter Doane Randall, Jr. has been producing handmade knives of his design, and has thereby created a worldwide name for himself and for his knives. Along the way, "Bo" Randall showed all the other knifemakers in the U.S. how the craft should be carried on.

That doesn't mean that Bo Randall showed everybody how to make knives. He did a lot more than that. He showed everybody how to be a knifemaker; how to be a person who made a knife right in the first place and stood behind it in the second place; how to be, in short, a master craftsman answering within the terms of his craft only to himself. Next to those things, making the knives took mere technical skill.

A fellow like Randall, raised up in the idea that his function was to manage capital, capital expenditures and the ventures they produced, had to be a knifemaker as an avocation. He simply brought to it the right management attitude to make it self-sufficient as an activity. In order to make it go, he successively hired trainees; he tried manufacturing out from under his own roof; eventually he hired a real cutler, an Englishman named Bill Platts. Together, Bo Randall and Bill Platts and, later, Gary Randall, Bo's son, made Randall knives what they have become.

Randall was not then and never has been a mere dabbler, mind you. He made those first knives himself; he continued making knives when he felt like it for a long, long time; many of the thousands of knives in the Randall collection were personally chosen by Bo Randall. He bought one or two collections, but, he also bought a lot of knives because there are very few of us more interested in knives than W.D. Randall, Jr.

Once the Randall knife was launched, Bo Randall saw little reason to tamper with success. The knives are all forged in Randall's shop; carbon steel knives are oil-hardened and stainless steel knives are air-hardened. Except for details and his half-tang combat models developed in the '50s, every step of the narrow-tang handle construction, brass furniture manufacture, and all the other steps in the manufacture of the Randall knife are essentially as Bo Randall first developed them a half-century ago. They are refined, but they are just about the same.

(Opposite page) This is the main man in handmade knives, W.D. Randall, Jr., himself.

by KEN WARNER

The Randall No. 2 is a straightforward double-edged and stout dagger as it has been for 50 years.

If this hunting knife pattern looks familiar it's because a lot of people make knives that look like Randall's No. 3.

The Smithsonian Bowie has made its mark as well. For a long time it was *the* big American knife.

This is the Bushmaster, a short, stout do-anything design. The false edge is usually grooved for chopping. Bo Randall has pointed out it's really only a very stubby No. 1.

The departure from Randall's original narrow tang design was with his Attack series—it has a half-tang along the back of the handle.

If you wanted a drop-point hunter, you could have had this one from Randall before anyone else was specializing in the design.

Probably the most-used photo ever of the Randalls, this one shows Gary and Bo looking over their astronaut's knife.

Here it is, the toothpick that went with so many Randall Bowies as the other half of a pair. (Zelones photo)

It is true there are now 18 people making Randall knives. They work in a now-crowded shop 100 yards or so from Randall's Florida home in Orlando. The guys who make the knives hang around there a lot. They have an archery range and a shooting range, with chronograph, and they are there at 7:00 in the morning, turning the switches on and getting on with it. Very likely, this crew makes more Randall knives a day than any earlier crew has.

Before we get into a short trip through some of the landmarks in knife design for Randall, we might note that there is one almost universal change between latter day knives and earlier ones. In a half-century, Americans have had an ample opportunity to get bigger and so have their hands and so Randall knives today have fatter handles than they used to have. That is a deliberate improvement in the breed and it is a little startling to an old Randall fan who has not been watching carefully, but nevertheless that is the reason why Randall handles are bigger these days.

The first landmark is appropriately called the Randall No. 1 All-Purpose Fighting Knife. In terms of handmade knives, this is one of the two or three most-copied designs ever made. Most of the single-edge fighting knives made even today owe some percentage of their layout or profile or balance or feel to this trail Bo Randall personally blazed as far back as World War II.

You're entitled to say, "Who says so?"

Well, for one, I do. I am not a collector, but there is one Randall No. 1 I would cherish. It was carried by R.C. Albritton of Sarasota, Florida, during distinguished service in the parachute infantry in a very difficult series of campaigns through the mountains of Italy, culminating in a combat jump into the south of France. Bob bought his No. 1 and a No. 2 for $25 each in 1942 in a jewelry store in Venice, Florida. By subsequent standards, this is a rough old cob of a knife, but it was one of those that set that world standard when carried by fighting men like Bob Albritton.

The current 27th printing of the catalog and knife manual for Randall-made knives, carrying a date of June 17, 1987, declares that deliveries would normally

This crew just about had the building broken in when this photo was made. That's Bill Platts in the back row.

be scheduled for June 1989 to those who order from this catalog. The catalog contains descriptions of 32 Randall designs, ranging from the Model 8 trout and bird to the Model 12 Smithsonian Bowie, which is, together with the Model 13 Arkansas toothpick and Model 12 Raymond Thorpe Bowie, the most expensive knife in the catalog at $330. The least expensive knife, apart from the Model 9 Pro Thrower and the Model 10 fisherman and household utility knife, is the Model 21 Little Game knife at $140. It is possible, by exercising options, to get any of these knives a great deal more expensive than that, but when you consider that a Model 1 All-Purpose Fighter is $160, and most of the common using designs are in this general price bracket, it is obvious that a Randall knife is tuned more closely to the hunting and fishing public than to the collector and armchair user.

Randall's shop foreman points out, in fact, "There is no better credit deal around than the one we offer."

That is, you can order a Randall knife for later delivery and simply send $10. You can pay for it along and along, or you can wait until it's ready, but any time along the way to the finished knife if you want all your money back, Randall will send it to you. And chances are that when you accept delivery of your knife, the same model will sell for more money in the Randall catalog. Come to think of it, that *is* a little difficult to beat.

There are all sorts of other landmarks. The knife that went to space was one; and the hollow-handled survival knife and a couple of early drop-point designs were, too. The profiles of tens of thousands of knives made in imitation of the unmistakable Randall look are testimony to the landmark nature of the whole enterprise.

There are those bales of correspondence (one bale per war) from military people—a scad of generals, and a man who claimed scores of combat kills for his Randalls, and a Captain named Ronald Reagan—and hunters and novelists. And there was all that publicity—not much per year, but a *lot* in a decade and a *whole* lot in 50 years.

Considered carefully, after 50 years, the story is virtually a textbook for building a legend. The knives were soon legendary; the rest of it took a while. The rest of it included keeping the knives as good as ever. Gary Randall says today's Randalls are the best ever.

Here's how it's done today—the tang is forged from the bar, the blade is then forged to shape, ground and tempered and polished and assembled—all hand held all the time.

In celebration of the five decades and in tribute to Scagel, the Randall shop is turning out a limited number of special knives. (Weyer photo)

(Below left) Steve Alexander from Ramrod Knife and Gun likes to sell special Randalls, and here holds one such. (Warner photo)

This is the crew that does the work today. You couldn't call any of them puny.

Made to suit a USAF survival instructor, this Randall brush knife was never made a regular model. (Warner photo)

For decades, Bo Randall has bought knives (or swapped for them) from other makers. Mike Leach says this one was personally ordered by and personally delivered to Bo at Orlando. (Weyer photo)

Jack Crider is one of the top Randall collectors. He has a lot of very special knives *and* a lot of regular Randalls.

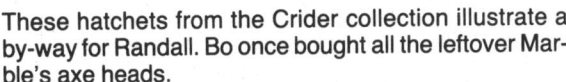

These hatchets from the Crider collection illustrate a by-way for Randall. Bo once bought all the leftover Marble's axe heads.

If there's an unusual Randall big knife, Jack Crider has it or is trying to buy it to go with all these.

This is not the place to argue technique and fit and finish in all those myriad details. There are knifemakers out there working to higher finished standards than the Randall shop does; there are knifemakers out there working very hard at balance and fit in the hand; there are people working in shiny new alloys and radical heat treatments and incredible surface treatments and all of that high-tech and low-tech effort at creating the ultimate knife. There are people out there who find a ready market for knives at higher prices than Randall-priced knives. There just don't seem to be any people out there making knives functionally superior to the general run of the Randall line.

That's one thing.

The other thing is that every Randall knife is a Randall. Bo Randall's knifemaker inspiration was William Scagel, but the Randall line—that S-curve that repeats throughout—is Randall's own. Every Randall knife is a Randall knife, and you can tell it from across the room.

That stamp in the Randall blades shows scimitars and the words "Randall-made, Orlando, Florida." The world-famous Randall enterprise has been buried now, in the virtual metropolis that Orlando has become. There are 40-story buildings and Disney World and Epcot Center and Sea World and 30 miles of city, a major airport with little trains to tote folks from terminal to plane, and there is a great deal of bustle going on as folks from out of town charge back and forth between all of that and the 20,000 hotel rooms Orlando now boasts. And, sad to relate, there are probably not three cabdrivers in town who could find Randall's place, there on the Orange Blossom Trail, by the sign with the scimitars. So the only world-class stuff Orlando has is about to celebrate its 50th anniversary and Orlando isn't looking, let alone celebrating.

The world has changed a lot in 50 years, but fighting men still belt on Randalls to go to whatever wars we are having at the time, and Randalls are still good buys and it looks as if, so long as we are an identifiable culture, there may be new Randall knives. Then for a few more centuries, there will still be Randall knives, and maybe that was worth 50 years of effort, which is something Walter Doane Randall, Jr. must think about these days. A lot of the rest of us do.

EIGHTH ANNUAL EDITION **13**

The rapier and its kindred were civilian arms for civilian fights—very romantic.

There Is No Best Sword

If there were no firearms, they'd still be designing new swords.

ALL THIS new interest in swords is both gratifying and greatly frustrating. It gives me a chance to share an interest and hobby I have had for many years, but now I encounter more and more mistakes, misunderstandings, and just plain stupid ideas.

Frequently, I hear this stuff from people who should know better. I know a collector of custom knives who is a fanatic in the care of his blades. He will buy a very fine and well-made knife and take superb care of it. The edge will never be abused. He was stunned, recently, to find out that swords will nick when struck edge to edge. He frankly didn't think I knew what I was talking about, I guess because they do it in the movies all the time. When I suggested he try it with a couple of his knives, he got the idea.

I once had a guy pick up one of my swords, a *schiavona*. I warned him that it was quite sharp, but he assured me that he was quite familiar with swords and actually was quite expert in their use. He then proceeded to go into some *katas* designed for the katana. Before I could say anything he had drawn the back edge of the sword along his shoulder, cutting a 6-inch gash in his deltoid and arm.

On another occasion I watched a young guy pick up a large two-hand claymore. He immediately assumed some of the stances made popular by Arnold Schwarzenegger as Conan—stances also based on katas for the katana. After manfully trying to whirl the heavy sword one-handed, he handed it back to the owner, said "Nice balance" and strutted off, obviously convinced the people watching were impressed. Alas, most of them were giggling. It was obvious he couldn't handle the sword; it was simply too big for the way he was trying to use it.

Because of the popularity of Oriental martial arts and the Japanese sword, what I see the most are people trying to handle one-handed broadswords like katanas. But I have also had fencers pick up the same sword and tell me it is impossible to fight with, as you can't even hold it in a proper guard position.

There is not just one type of sword, nor is there just one way to use a sword. A specific technique requires a specific sword, and a specific type of sword requires a specific technique. Rapiers do not cut near as well as katanas. Katanas do not penetrate near as well as rapiers. Neither is very good against plate armor.

At the risk of repeating myself I want to point out that swords are designed with specific uses in mind. They should be judged this way.

I have heard people argue over which is the better sword, the rapier or a Viking type for instance. This is foolish. What they are actually talking about are fighting styles, not swords. Any sword should be discussed only in the context of what it was designed to do.

This is not a chicken or egg question. Sword designs came first, and practical styles evolved around them. The first sword design was dependent on the skill of the maker, and the material from which it was made—copper, then bronze. Then sword and technique in Europe entered into a constantly whirling and evolving dance that didn't end until the development of the repeating firearm. Swords and technique in many parts of the world evolved very slowly; in some places they never arrived; and in some places they took directions that were strange to say the least.

Wooden swords edged with shark's teeth, drawcuts, pulling cuts, slashes—all of these are understandable, but there has always been one type of sword and fighting technique that fills me with . . . well, I'm not sure what. You decide: The Abyssinian *shotel* is a long curved double-edged sword. At first glance, it looks like a Near Eastern scimitar, but on closer inspection you realize that the curve is a full half circle. And it is, I repeat, double-edged. The blade, generally, is a flattened diamond cross section and quite stiff.

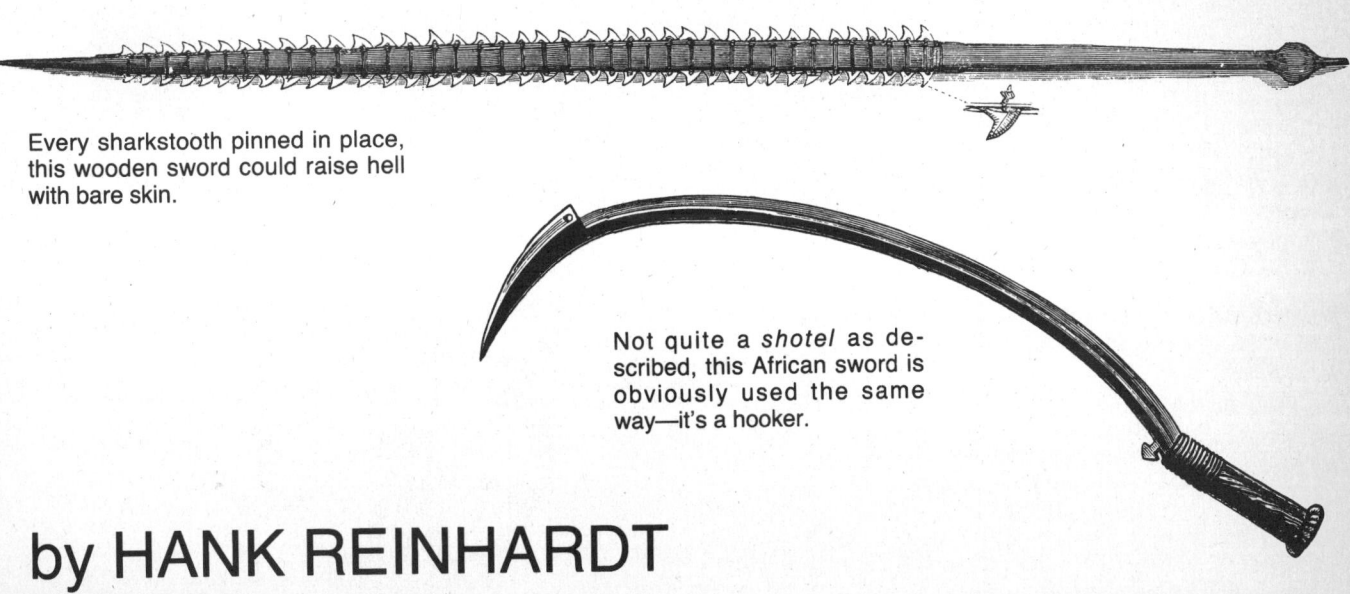

Every sharkstooth pinned in place, this wooden sword could raise hell with bare skin.

Not quite a *shotel* as described, this African sword is obviously used the same way—it's a hooker.

by **HANK REINHARDT**

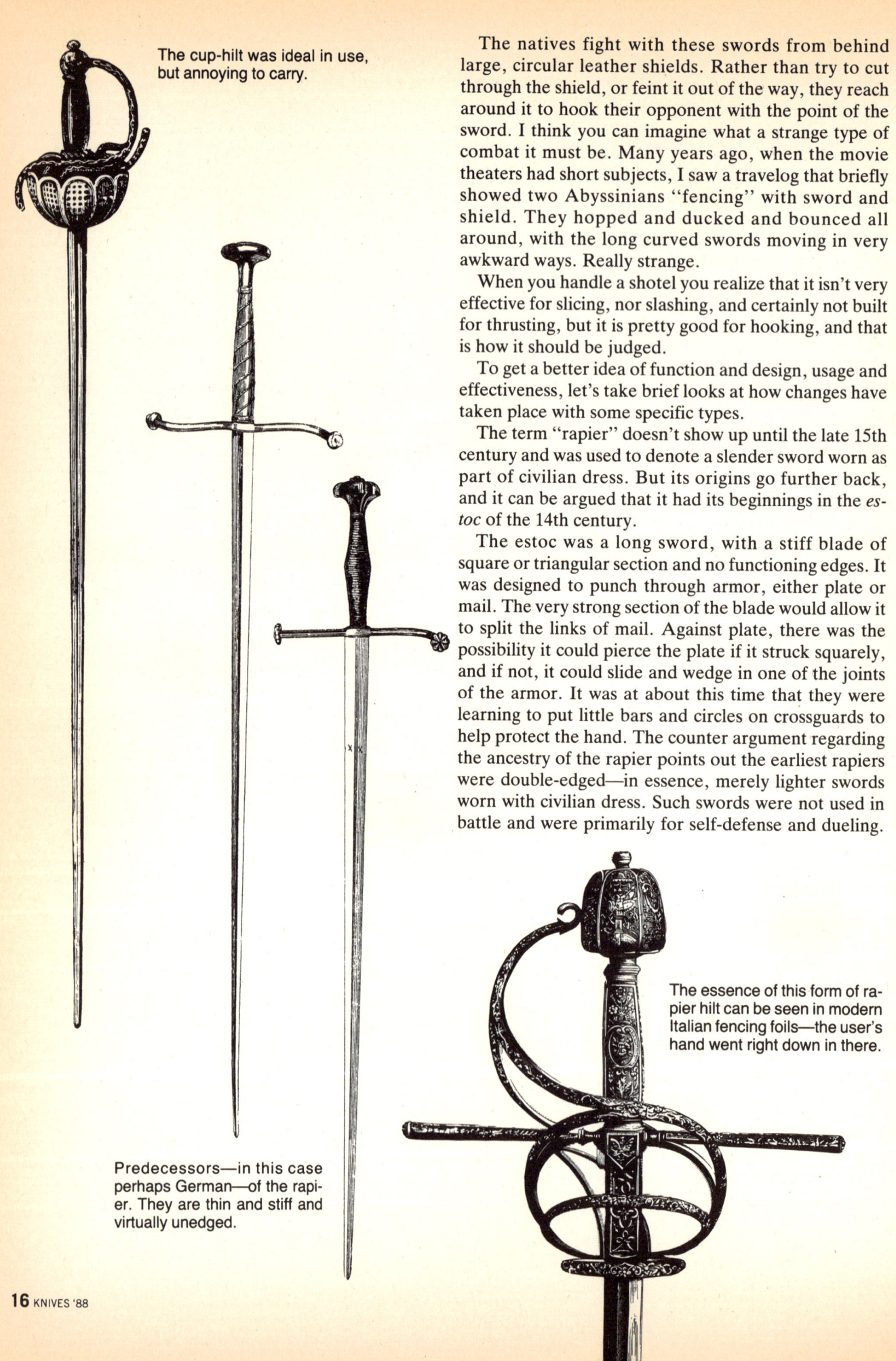

The cup-hilt was ideal in use, but annoying to carry.

Predecessors—in this case perhaps German—of the rapier. They are thin and stiff and virtually unedged.

The essence of this form of rapier hilt can be seen in modern Italian fencing foils—the user's hand went right down in there.

The natives fight with these swords from behind large, circular leather shields. Rather than try to cut through the shield, or feint it out of the way, they reach around it to hook their opponent with the point of the sword. I think you can imagine what a strange type of combat it must be. Many years ago, when the movie theaters had short subjects, I saw a travelog that briefly showed two Abyssinians "fencing" with sword and shield. They hopped and ducked and bounced all around, with the long curved swords moving in very awkward ways. Really strange.

When you handle a shotel you realize that it isn't very effective for slicing, nor slashing, and certainly not built for thrusting, but it is pretty good for hooking, and that is how it should be judged.

To get a better idea of function and design, usage and effectiveness, let's take brief looks at how changes have taken place with some specific types.

The term "rapier" doesn't show up until the late 15th century and was used to denote a slender sword worn as part of civilian dress. But its origins go further back, and it can be argued that it had its beginnings in the *estoc* of the 14th century.

The estoc was a long sword, with a stiff blade of square or triangular section and no functioning edges. It was designed to punch through armor, either plate or mail. The very strong section of the blade would allow it to split the links of mail. Against plate, there was the possibility it could pierce the plate if it struck squarely, and if not, it could slide and wedge in one of the joints of the armor. It was at about this time that they were learning to put little bars and circles on crossguards to help protect the hand. The counter argument regarding the ancestry of the rapier points out the earliest rapiers were double-edged—in essence, merely lighter swords worn with civilian dress. Such swords were not used in battle and were primarily for self-defense and dueling.

After a short period of time, it became quite obvious that additional guards were needed to protect the hand.

At this time, the blades were generally double-edged, but somewhat slim, and used for both the cut and thrust. The Art of Fence was quite rudimentary. The sword had always been considered an offensive weapon; one blocked or parried only in dire emergencies. Soon, however, the sword was used as a defensive weapon as well. Of course, this tore the edges up pretty badly, but they also quickly learned to parry with the flat, and, anyway, the point was more deadly.

As this style of combat took over, the sword began to change again. The hilt began to acquire more elaborate rings in order to protect the hand, and the blade began to lengthen and narrow. By the middle of the 16th century, the sword had become the swept-hilt rapier. The blade had gotten quite long, and the edge was no longer important. Indeed, there was one blade that was square in section and flattened for the last inches, so that it was sharp there. This point was used for slashing cuts, usually at the face and eyes. The blade was excessively long, up to 60 inches in some cases. It was felt, incorrectly, that the longer blade gave advantage.

It must have been awkward walking around with a 60-inch sword blade banging into things and tripping people. It got to be such a nuisance in England Queen Elizabeth issued an edict, and every sword over a yard long was broken.

The Art of Fence was getting better and better, and by the turn of the century, the lunge was developed. This really put an end to excessively long blades, and they rapidly shrank to about 36-39 inches. In the meantime, the hilt had been acquiring a few shells and plates and finally, in the early 17th century, acquired the form known as a cavalier hilt. It is very similar to the slightly earlier dish hilt, and both are frequently confused with the cup hilt, which did not come into play until about 1640-50. The cup hilt, which is a superb hilt form offering almost complete hand protection, is a pain to wear. It has a tendency to bounce about and proved annoying. Besides, they didn't think it looked very dressy. I do, but I also realize that to me it looks romantic as hell.

And so the sword continued to change. The guard became smaller; the crossguard, wherein one once looped his fingers for a very secure grip, was now merely decorative. The blade continued to shrink until at last the final form of the smallsword was reached—triangular blade, very light and fast, from 30 to 33 inches long.

They look like beautiful and deadly little toys, smallswords do. They are light and slim and very attractive. Many consider them the ultimate sword and the most deadly of all the dueling weapons. Personally, I strongly disagree. They are *quite* deadly when used within the limitations now taken for granted. That is, one is not supposed to grab the blade. However, grabbing the blade was an honorable and valued tactic, even if it is now illegal in sport fencing. I can assure you it is not difficult to slap a blade aside with your off hand or even seize it if the missed thrust is even the tiniest bit slow. This is not a feasible tactic if the blade is well edged, but with a triangular blade it is quite possible.

We have not really studied the development of the rapier here, but it is hoped we have shown something of the dynamics of the design progression from beginnings to the peak in the 1670s and then to its final and (my opinion) degenerate form. The purpose of this sort of sword at this time was to provide civilian protection. As more was learned the sword changed to take advantage of this knowledge. Fashion and changing social conditions worked on the rapier, but even in its final form it never strayed from its intended purpose as a thrusting weapon, designed to be used with one hand, and to provide protection from a similar weapon. In none of these forms was it intended to be used against armor or in the

The author in one of his sword-toting get-ups. He is not often allowed into modern swordplay because he cheats and wins.

It got pretty grim on the old battlefields, but it probably never actually looked like this.

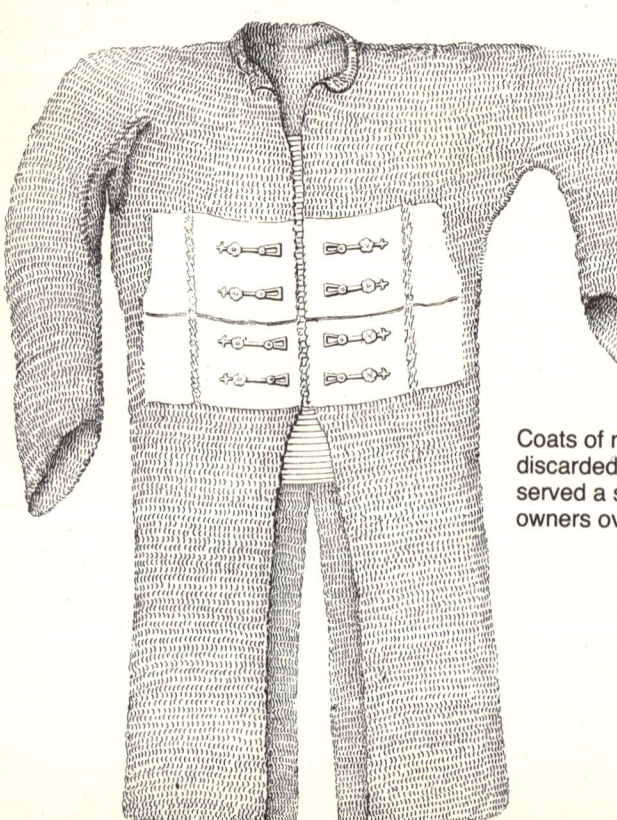

Coats of mail were rarely discarded and, once made, served a succession of owners over the centuries.

An early cruciform sword—not very far from the Viking's blunter sword.

18 KNIVES '88

heavy heat of battle.

Another sword that needs to be looked at is the medieval knightly cruciform sword that is always incorrectly referred to as a broadsword. This sword can easily be traced back to the beginning of the Iron Age. For our purposes, we can start with the Vikings.

The early Viking sword in general use was long—about 33-34 inches—broad—2-2½ inches—with a single fuller. The blade had parallel sides, with little or no taper. Steel was quite valuable, and at this time making large quantities was quite difficult. As a result, the swords were made by a process called pattern welding.

In this process, steel bars containing a good deal of carbon were welded to iron bars, then all were twisted and rewelded to produce the patterns we refer to as Damascus. A high-carbon edge was then welded on, the sword was filed, ground, tempered and polished. The end result was a light and fast blade, capable of delivering a terrible shearing cut. A good Viking sword was flexible, yet had a very hard edge.

This sword was designed to be used in conjunction with a wooden shield. It would be facing, more than likely, another wooden shield, and a foe wearing an iron helmet and armored with leather. If that opponent were very rich he would be wearing a mail shirt.

The sword, therefore, had to be flexible. It needed to take a lot of shock when hitting a shield, and cutting into a torso or even a leg—the most likely target—put a lot of strain on the sword. If it wasn't flexible, then it would bend easily. Of course, the sword could have been made thicker, but then the weight would be too great for combat. Swords at this time weighed between 2 and 3 pounds, tops. One wins an encounter with swords by cutting the other fellow first. In the 14th century, given the state of defensive armor, that meant leg cuts. Of the hundreds of corpses piled at Visby in 1361, 70 percent had leg wounds, most of them deep enough to be seen in the bones 500 years later.

The edge, we see, had to be hard. Bone is tough, so is a steel rimmed shield. And there was always the likelihood of hitting mail. One tried to avoid this by cutting at the neck, the hands and arms and, particularly, the legs.

Sometimes you got an opening and just had to take a cut. Mail is tough, composed of iron wire. It was not tempered and is somewhat soft. Tempered mail is not a good idea—under a blow, such mail will break, giving free rein to the edge. Soft mail will bend and deform, resisting the cut a long way. Any mail will nick the edge, but if the blow is delivered accurately, at the proper angle and with a great deal of force, this sword can and will cut mail.

That is the sword in general use in Europe at the beginning of the Viking Age.

Around 900 AD, a new sword appeared. The blade was slightly shorter—32 inches average—but with the same width. It tapered much more acutely, and ended in a good serviceable point. The change in blade shape makes this a much faster sword in both the cut and the recovery. By throwing the weight closer to the hand, the sword becomes easier to maneuver.

Those features weren't the big difference. The real biggie was that the whole sword was made of steel. No matter how good the smith, a pattern-welded sword was an expensive and slow production. With large pieces of steel, the whole process is speeded up, the sword is cheaper, and just as good. But the new sword had to be better because the armor had also started to improve. Actually, the armor was pretty much the same, except there was now more of it, and mail was more likely to be encountered because it was accumulating, generation by generation.

The next 200 years saw more changes. Mail now covered the whole body. Fighting on foot was left to the peasant. The knight, fully armored, held a good solid wooden shield and the lance was the main weapon. The sword became secondary, a back-up, and was used against lightly armored foot soldiers.

The sword had changed again. Its shape reverted and the two edges were more nearly parallel. Speed was not quite as important now as the weight of the blow. The blade had become slightly longer to give greater impetus to the blow, and to give the horseman greater reach.

The next 200-year jump brings us to 1300 AD, and even more changes.

At this time, armor was beginning to win the eternal fight with arms. Mail was slightly thicker and stronger, and strenghtened with plates and splints of steel. These changes brought about changes in sword design and new types of swords appeared.

The most prominent of these swords was the Great Sword or War Sword. This is a long-bladed sword, and blades average about 40 inches in length. The sword is not particularly heavy, weighing 4 to 5 pounds. It is light enough to be swung one-handed in conjunction with a shield, but the grip is long enough to accommodate another hand, so that the sword can be used two-handed. The great length increases velocity and cutting power. Along with the long-bladed Great Sword, a shorter weapon appears, with a blade shape similar to the later Viking swords, but more exaggerated. These are big swords, with very wide blades tapering sharply. The wide blade increases the cutting power of the sword, while the strong taper makes the point a most important part of the sword. Flexibility is now sacrificed for rigidity to strengthen the thrust.

Even a third sword achieved new use. The falchion had always been around, but with the increase in protective capability of armor the Falchion became a most useful weapon. With a short very wide blade, single-edged, it is capable of delivering a terrible blow. Shaped like a modern Shriner's scimitar, it became popular not only with knights, but with archers and men-at-arms.

From here until the 1650s the changes in arms and ar-

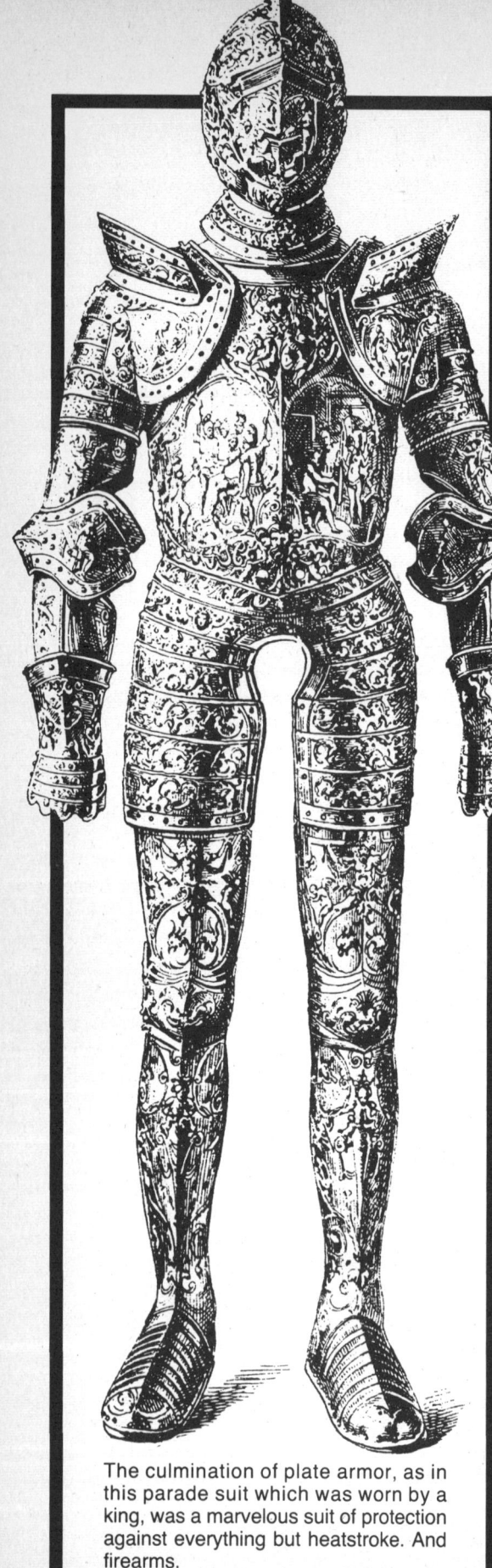

The culmination of plate armor, as in this parade suit which was worn by a king, was a marvelous suit of protection against everything but heatstroke. And firearms.

mor became more rapid.

Mail, that most ancient and honored form of denfense, was discarded in favor of plate. The skill of the armorer reached heights that have never been, and never will, be equalled. Plate armor is a light, rigid defense that allows a man to move quite freely, and yet gives great protection. The only real drawback is that it is extremely hot. Ventilation is almost nil, and this can cause exhaustion. Fighting on horseback, when the main body parts used are the arms, is OK. One can do this for a rather long while. However, on foot, when the legs are used, much more heat is generated and more oxygen required and plate is less useful.

Swordmakers made one last attempt to overcome the new armor.

Light and flat cutting blades were abandoned. The sword profile with a blade wide at the top and tapering very sharply, stayed pretty much the same. However, the cross-section became a thick, flattened diamond, and the sword became quite rigid. Weight varied a great deal. Some blades stayed light, weighing 2 to 3 pounds, while others went upwards of 5 pounds. These heavy swords became nothing but sharpened bars of steel. Both the heavy and light versions were attempts to punch through the armor, and it could be done if the blow was heavy and square. In a slightly off-center blow, there was a chance the sword would slide into a crevice or chink and wound the man. And the heavy swords also tried to "break" the armor by sheer weight and force.

This was the last attempt of the sword to overcome armor and that fight was abandoned. There was simply no way that a sword was going to cut through steel plate. Axes, maces and war hammers became the weapons of armored combat.

The sword was by no means abandoned. It simply was not used when fighting armored knights. The sword was too important socially and traditionally to be cast aside. Civilian swords became important items of dress. In combat, the flat, light cutting sword came back and was carried to fight men at arms and other lightly armed troops.

This is, of course, a quick and simplified view of the whole thing. Obviously, the bow and the pike were to render armor almost obsolete, and gunpowder administered the coup de grace. However, we can see here that swords are all shaped to achieve specific goals while overcoming specific obstacles. Each new type of sword was a response to a new development in armor or fighting style.

Let's look at a modern example where sword and style conflict mightily.

Japanese arms and armor were fully developed by the 1200s, and stayed pretty much the same for several hundred years. The katana is an excellent sword, and quite well designed for the type of fighting for which it is intended. The fencing techniques are excellent. Regardless of other styles you may consider superior—sword and shield, rapier fencing, Turkish and Iranian swordplay—Japanese fencing and the katana are perfectly matched.

In fighting with a katana, many of the moves are drawcuts, and many of the attacks are designed to be struck with the front 16 inches of the blade. The katana is well suited for this, as the blade is strong, thick and well curved.

In a recent movie, the hero uses a wide, straight and heavy sword. All his moves and posturing, however, are for the katana in attacks that simply would not work with such a sword. A blow with the front 6 inches would set up vibrations that could jar your teeth. And it wouldn't cut very deep. Now you could stop the vibrations by making the blade extremely thick, but then you also increase the weight and lessen the cutting power even more. In short, the movie sword was simply wrong for the type of fighting shown. About the only thing more ludicrous would have been using it like a rapier. Of course, the movie's hero was a sort of superhero who could handle a heavy sword. The actor, however, was swinging an aluminum blade. Don't ever try those moves with a sharp 6-pound steel sword, let alone one of those 9-pounders some guys make.

On the subject of modern swords, I am told some of them are hung on the wall in anticipation of defense against intruders. The merits of this as an idea should be debated in some other forum; we can discuss the new swords, however.

Most of them are well-made of good materials. I believe some of them are a little too hard for the shocks a sword blade must take. Almost all are far too heavy. A 6-pound sword is laughable, and a 4-pounder is only worth a chuckle. A sword is not a long knife; it must be, for its size, more lightly constructed.

Only a 2- to 3-pound sword should be considered for modern use; nothing heavier will achieve the velocity needed, nor will a heavier sword maneuver, parry or recover fast enough. It should be relatively short and quite sharp and straight enough for a serious thrust. The straight wakizashi sold as a "ninja" sword, the hanger or European hunting sword, and shorter 19th century foot officers swords are all useful models, but 12-pound knightly swords? Never.

One sword that provides quite interesting material for such speculation is the saber. It can also show the relationship between fighting styles, perceived fighting styles and design.

Most people will tell you that the curved cavalary saber was tried for a number of years, was found wanting, and the final, most efficient cavalry sword was the straight one. They will point to both the British and U.S. cavalry swords of this century. Both were straight-bladed thrusting weapons. They were, however, the last designs only because the machine gun had rendered cavalry obsolete. The question as to which was the best was never fully answered.

The fight was bitter for a century or more, and the thrusting sword won only by very narrow margins. Here is some of the argument employed over the efficiency of the two styles:

The curved sword has been the sword of the mounted warrior in many places and for many years. A curved slashing blow is very damaging, and even if it does not kill, it can render its victim unable to continue the fight. Against infantry, the curve allows the cavalryman to strike a strong and effective blow that does not imprison the blade and cause it to be wrenched from the hand. Against other mounted troops it provides effective offense and defense. Sitting astride a horse, the sword is easier to handle in cutting motions than the unnatural thrusts that a straight blade requires.

Opponents pointed out the many times that soldiers had been struck repeatedly on the head with curved sabers and continued to fight. They also cite times when swords have been driven deep into the body, and wrenched from the grasp as the horse swept past. After pointing out the horrors and inadequacies of the curved saber, they launch on the merits of the straight blade.

It can reach an infantry soldier lying flat on the ground. The horse won't willingly step on a man, and you need to lean too far out of the saddle to cut someone lying flat. However, with a straight blade you can reach the ground with the point, which means you can thrust through. A most valid point is that when someone is stabbed, he isn't likely to continue to fight. As for fighting other mounted troops, with proper training you can learn to stab. As for holding on to the weapon, with the proper wrist motion the sword can be pulled from the body of the enemy, either by the cavalryman himself, or he can let the motion of the horse do it. And it was claimed the thrust was hard to dodge or parry.

One can see that both swords have their merits, and both have their flaws. One of the most serious flaws of the curved saber was one that could have most easily been corrected. You see, most military sabers were never sharpened. They just had flats and no real edge. They made nasty surface wounds by splitting the flesh, but did not cut deeply. Had they been sharpened—ahh, then things would have been quite different. On the other hand, the thrust of a 40-inch blade at the end of an outstretched arm, urged along by 800 pounds of moving horse, provides a serious problem and certainly no easy answers.

That, in a nutshell and with different problems and different swords, is the story of sword design. Most well-made swords did their jobs well, but there never was an all-around sword. Judge them that way, each in its own context—there is no best.

This is the 1960 restoration of James Black's smithy in Washington, where legend says the orginal Bowie knife was made during the winter of 1830-1831.

BOWIE AND BLACK: Fiction or Fact?

New evidence may tip the scales the Arkansawyer's way.

I STRAINED to read the fading and quaint columns of print, and my heart skipped a beat when the impact of what I was reading hit me. Here was evidence I had been seeking for over two decades, the evidence many acknowledged authorities maintained did not exist. It was the most positive proof yet discovered to support the belief that James Black, a Washington, Arkansas, blacksmith and cutler, sold a knife to James Bowie, *the* James Bowie.

The story that Black made a knife for the immortal Bowie is readily accepted in many quarters, yet summarily rejected in others. Much of what we know about Black can be traced to an account by Daniel Webster Jones, published in 1903. Jones, who served Arkansas as governor from 1897 until 1901, lived most of his life in Washington, and Black lived as a ward of the Jones family from 1842 until his death in 1872.

Black had been blinded as a result of a beating administered by his father-in-law in 1839. Black was gravely ill when he was struck a number of times with a walking stick. This left him almost blind, and what little sight remained was destroyed by a "doctor" in Ohio, who, for his trouble, also took what little money Black had left.

The future governor of Arkansas was born in 1839 and was a toddler when the blind Black moved in with the family. It does not require a great deal of imagination to realize that Black probably improved the story of how he made a knife for Bowie, and he may well have seized far more credit than that to which he was entitled. But, and this may well be the crux of the matter, the credit does belong to Black, if we limit ourselves to the premise that once upon a time in the small city of Washington, Arkansas, he sold a knife to Jim Bowie. Or so I now firmly believe.

Washington in 1830 was one of the major cities on the American frontier, the jumping off place to Texas for many settlers and adventurers. Rezin Bowie, James' older brother, owned a plantation at Walnut Hill, Arkansas, less than 50 miles as the crow flies from Washington.

Most of the Black detractors base their case upon the belief that Jones' story was the first published account crediting Black with being the maker of "the Bowie knife." This position is easily outflanked with some research:

Fay Hempstead, a noted historian, wrote in his monumental *Pictorial History of Arkansas*, published in 1890, "A matter of interest concerning the town of Washington . . . the Bowie knife . . . was originally made in that town by a man named James Black." It may be interesting for some readers to learn that Hemp-

by
B.R. HUGHES

The author is shown with two employees of the Arkansas Parks Commission preparing a display of Bowie knives in Washington, Arkansas, in 1971.

stead was a man, not a woman, as one detractor once wrote. The title of the book is somewhat misleading because, while there are illustrations, it is made up primarily of text.

One year before the Hempstead book was published, the Goodspeed Publishing Company printed *Historical Memoirs of Northeast Arkansas,* and this also credits Black as having made a knife for Bowie.

In 1895, *Early Days in Arkansas,* authored by William F. Pope, was published, and this tome credited Black as having made a knife for Rezin Bowie. Perhaps he did or perhaps Pope simply got his Bowies mixed up.

For all of this, it is evident all these references could have been inspired by Jones' story. Perhaps it had not yet been published, but Jones was a prominent citizen of Arkansas by the 1880s, elected attorney-general in 1884.

But what of the *Arkansas Gazette* story that was printed September 1, 1872? The editor of the *Gazette* felt that the news that "James Black, the maker of the first Bowie knife, died at Hempstead, Texas, a few days ago" was important enough to put on the front page.

This was only 36 years after the death of James Bowie, and there were countless men and women living in 1872 who had personally known Bowie, and it seems unreasonable to believe that none of them saw this article. If there was any reader who questioned Black's claim to fame, no subsequent issue of the *Arkansas Gazette* contained any type of rebuttal or counterclaim. This silence speaks volumes.

If that were the sum total of the evidence for James Black, it would represent enough to make a strong case, but please consider the following excerpt from a letter I received in 1982 from Mrs. Gwendolyn M. Burks, who at that time was 87 years of age and whose grandfather was none other than Rezin P. Bowie:

> Many times, we have heard the tale of the reason for the making of the Bowie knife. My grandmother told me she was present when Bob Snowden and grandfather attempted to kill a heifer. Grandfather held the knife, which struck a bone and the blade was driven back through his hand. It almost amputated two fingers. He remarked to Bob later that if the blade had a guard that never would have happened. So, to the shop they went, and Bob fashioned a knife from an old file. When Jim saw the knife, he exclaimed that it would make a fine hunting knife and he would go to Arkansas and have one made for himself. We have all grown up with the understanding that was what he did. I can offer you no better proof than that.

I will readily concede that Mrs. Burke did not mention James Black by name, but she did indicate that James Bowie went to Arkansas to have his knife made. This does nothing to weaken the case for Black.

Now, permit me to return to the opening lines of this narrative. During the spring of 1987, I was spending some time in Washington in the company of old friend Kent Biffle, who writes a fascinating column for the *Dallas Morning News* on the facts and fictions of Texas and the Southwest. Washington is no more than 40 miles from my home, and there is a great deal of evidence there that James Black was an active member of the Washington community during the 1830s: He served on a jury, he paid taxes, he got married, and so on. Looking at some old copies of the *Washington Telegraph,* a weekly newspaper that was operating in the 1840's but which is now out of business, we found the issue of December 8, 1841, and on the front page was the following story:

During the Civil War, when Federal troops captured Little Rock, Washington served the Confederates as the Arkansas state capitol for the remainder of the war. Washington was bigger than we think!

THE BOWIE KNIFE

This far famed deadly instrument had its origin we believe in Hempstead County. The first knife of the kind was made in this place by Mr. James W. Black for a man named James Bowie who was killed at the Alamo, in Texas, and hence it is sometimes called the Black knife, sometimes the Bowie knife. The small dagger usually worn, in former times, has given place to this more formidable invention, and the Bowie knife, throughout the West is now the most common weapon of attack or defense. Could each of these knives speak for itself, what a catalogue of bloody deeds would be unfolded! One would tell of assassinations, and lawless assaults—another of murders committed in secret, to gratify revenge or avarice, and another of unavoidable voilence and unfortunate rencountres. What acts of infamy and moral degradation; what seens [sic] of domestic sorrow and heartrending distress would be exhibited! One would inform us how it was plunged, at the dead hour of night, into the bosom of its sleeping victim, and another tell us how it leaped forth to take sudden satisfaction for some fancied insult. Some would point to the Penitentiary and gallows—others to mourning and afflicted families and friends and exclaim—"We have been the instruments of men's passions—behold the fruits!

But terrible as have been the uses of the Bowie knife, we cannot say that if it had not been invented, the dark consequences of the passions of men would have been, in any great degree, prevented. As long as these passions are unsubdued, they will be liable to outbreaks, and would have found other instruments of vengence if there had never been a Bowie knife; and when we have improved our minds, and learned to govern our passions, and to confine them in their proper channels, we will have no use for Bowie knives and pistols.

Whilst on this subject we cannot forbear mentioning the sad dispensation with which Mr. James W. Black, the inventor of this knife has been visited. Several years since he lost his eyesight, and the green earth and shining heavens are to him alike, unchangeably dark. The events of the past must give employment to his mind, nor do we imagine that the thought of his having invented the Bowie knife will not for a moment disturb his bosom's lonely quietude; for whilst the manufacture of the article afforded the means of a comfortable subsistence, its appearance did not create, nor would its suppression have destroyed, the stormy passions of the soul.

(EDITOR'S NOTE: This excerpt is from a Xerox of a paper called the TELEGRAPH, datelined WASHINGTON, December 8, 1841, edited by JAMES P. JET. Writer Hughes furnished the Xerox. Editor)

The article is a delightful example of the journalistic style of the 1840s, and I distinctly recall that I felt a sense of amusement at the very idea of the editor's feeling obliged to explain to his readership who James Bowie was and where the Alamo was located. It has since occurred to me that both Bowie and the Alamo are probably more famous today than they were in 1841.

Please go back and check the date of this article—December 8, 1841. At that time, Daniel Webster Jones was 2 years old, so not even the most fervent Black detractor can attribute this story to Jones' account.

For the time being at least, this represents my case on behalf of James Black. It is not a flimsy case. It is, to me at least, important to note that, as time goes by, more and more evidence has been produced to support Black's claim and nothing new has come to light which would discredit him. Barring the disclosure of some evidence to the contrary—something more tangible than saying, "I don't believe it!"—it now seems relatively safe to say with more conviction: "James Black made a knife for Jim Bowie."

HOLLOW HANDLE HISTORY

Rambo wasn't the First!

by BERNARD R. LEVINE

SO THERE was Rambo, Sylvester Stallone's anti-hero who just wanted the world to let him be. When the world would not oblige, Rambo single-handedly took on the police, the National Guard, and, symbolically, all of bureaucratic official society. Armed only with his wits, his hands, and, of course, his Jimmy Lile *First Blood* hollow-handle survival knife, Rambo triumphed over the forces of dullness and conventionality.

In the process of defeating the bureacracy, Rambo gave left-wing media a handy new epithet to hurl at the Reagan administration and he gave custom knife-makers and cutlery manufacturers a whole new product line to improve their year-end financial statements. The first of the makers to benefit was, of course, Mr. Lile himself, but plenty more have followed suit.

Among the manufacturers, the best known of the Rambo imitators is Buck with their popular Buckmaster. Others range from the elegant sophistication of Timberline to the rugged no-nonsense (and no hollow handle) approach of Gerber's BMF and LMF, to the light-weight practicality of Case's little Model 369 "Outlander" hollow-handled survival knife, to the comical 5-dollar survival knives advertised in magazines and on television (actually, for the price they are not bad).

To tell the truth, it is only in the popular mind that Rambo was the first to use a hollow-handle survival knife. All us knife types know that W.D. "Bo" Randall of Florida was making and selling hollow-handle Model 18 Attack-Survival and Model 17 Astro knives for nearly a quarter of a century before Rambo first crashed through the woods onto the silver screen.

Randall's Model 18 (which inspired the *First Blood* knife), was based on a sketch submitted from Viet Nam by U.S. Army Medical Corps Captain George Ingraham in January, 1963. Ingraham wanted a saw-back blade that could quickly cut through the skin of a downed helicopter.

As a medical man, Captain Ingraham intended the hollow handle of the knife to hold three necessities of short-term post-crash survival: water purification tablets, pain killer (Demerol), and a strong stimulant (Dexedrine). Ingraham figured that it was better to have these basic first-aid necessities packed inside a knife one always wore, than it was to have lots of sophisticated survival equipment packed in a crash kit that was stowed somewhere inside a wrecked and probably burning helicopter. Captain Ingraham's original sketch is reproduced here from page 359 of my book, *Levine's Guide to Knives and Their Values,* published by DBI Books.

Although Rambo and Jimmy Lile were the popularizers of the hollow-handle survival knife, they were not its inventors. In point of fact, however, neither were Captain Ingraham and Bo Randall its real originators.

From the mid-1930s through the 1940s, both W.R. Case & Sons of Bradford, Pennsylvania, and Union Cutlery Company (Ka-Bar) of Olean, New York, offered their customers several styles of hollow-handled hunting knives. These knives did not have saw teeth on the back of the blade, I guess because the helicopter had not yet been perfected. However, they did include a little French-made compass set into the inside of the aluminum or composition pommel threaded into the end of the handle.

According to the companies' catalog listings, the hollow handles of these knives were intended to serve as match safes, obviating the need to carry a separate match safe. Marble's of Gladstone, Michigan, made the standard match safe of that period, and perhaps the Case and Ka-Bar people were concerned that if a sportsman bought a Marble's match safe, he might decide to go all the way and buy a Marble's knife, too. Both of the Warner knives here had old matches in the handles when he found them.

Union/Ka-Bar offered at least five models of hollow-handled knives. In addition, I have observed variations of marking and decoration in some of these models.

The first one of these knives I actually saw in person

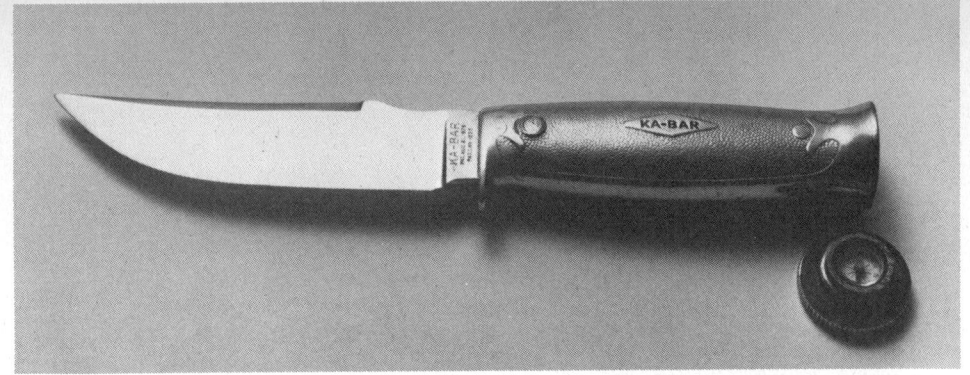

UNION/KA-BAR early Model 2000 with aluminum handle, patent designation on blade, "DR.A.W.A./12-25-34" scratched on pommel. Compass with beveled glass cover was made in France. (B. Levine photo)

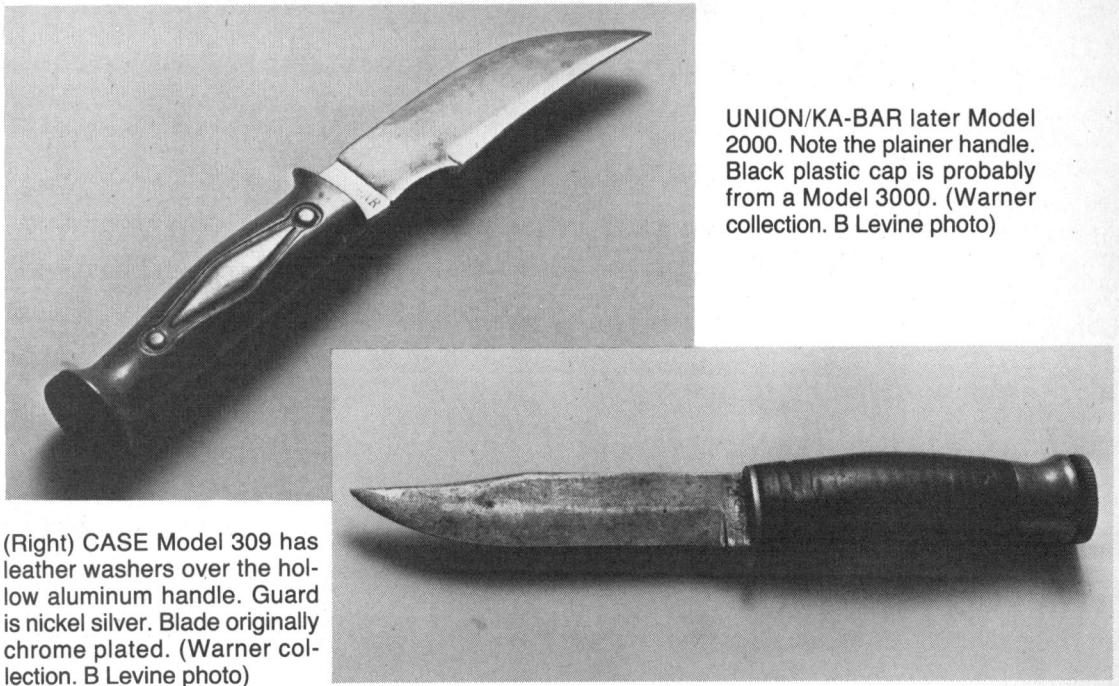

UNION/KA-BAR later Model 2000. Note the plainer handle. Black plastic cap is probably from a Model 3000. (Warner collection. B Levine photo)

(Right) CASE Model 309 has leather washers over the hollow aluminum handle. Guard is nickel silver. Blade originally chrome plated. (Warner collection. B Levine photo)

(and could not resist buying) was a Model 2000 with a 4½-inch blade. The front ricasso of the blade is marked in three lines: KA-BAR/ PAT. AUG. 31, 1926/ PAT. CAN. 1923. The reverse ricasso is marked UNION CUTLERY CO./ OLEAN, N.Y.

The patents turn out to have been design patents for the blade shape. Union described this as, "A new design which neatly combines the skinning blade with the general utility blade. Has corrugated thumb hollow in back of blade." The U.S. patent was valid until about 1933. My knife has a presentation crudely scratched in the end of the aluminum pommel: DR.A.W.A./12-25-34.

Ken Warner has a different looking and probably later Model 2000. The handle is plainer and ⅜-inch shorter. The guard is also shorter, and the patent designations were left out of the blade stamping. This knife has a black composition cap, but I believe this was a replacement cap that came from a Model 3000. The Model 3000 is identical to the Model 2000, except that the handle and cap are black composition rubber.

The remaining three models of Union hollow-handle knives had saber-ground, deeply swaged clip-point blades that were obviously inspired by the Marble's Ideal pattern. The 2701-5-inch and 2071-6-inch had aluminum handles and different blade lengths. The 3071-5-inch had a black rubber composition handle. All five Union models were sold with a flimsy brown leather sheath.

Unlike Union, which opted for light weight and easy to manufacture all-aluminum or all-plastic handles, W.R. Case opted for heavier but also sturdier and more comfortable leather washers-over-aluminum construction. Case's Model 309, like the illustrated example belonging to Ken Warner, has a 5-inch saber ground blade that was originally chrome-plated, though only a few tiny patches of the original chrome remain on this knife.

The heart of the Case handle is an aluminum tube with a 9/16-inch inside diameter—the Union is the same size inside. Its aluminum pommel with threaded cap was evidently attached to the tube after the 23 leather washers were driven down on to it. The small finger guard is nickel silver. The compass inside the cap is French, as on the Union Model 2000, but its card and its

State of the art now in the hollow handle knife is the one-piece knife- handle, guard and all machined from the solid. A leader at this neat trick is Chris Reeve of South Africa.

Several makers have figured out how to get stuff inside a knife handle in other ways, such as shown in this Kevin Hoffman lightweight survival kit.

(Below) This is the original drawing furnished Randall by Capt. Ingraham.

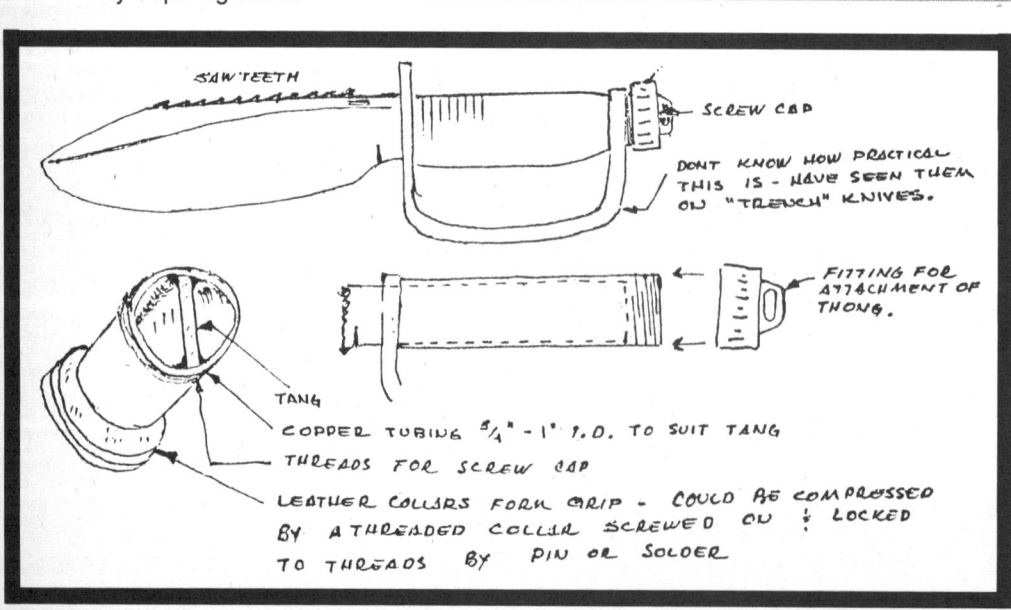

Circa 1940 Case catalog cut, D. & L. Ferguson.

HUNTING KNIVES

No. 309

No. 309 — Has 5-inch blade, saber ground, mirror finished and chromium plated. Nickel silver guard. Handle is leather over aluminum. Handle is hollow, making a water-proof match safe, with aluminum screw cap, which has a reliable compass fitted on the inside.

1934 Union/Ka-Bar catalog cuts, courtesy Roy Erhardt.

No. 3000

Threaded knob at end of handle, has reliable compass set into the under side of it. Knob opens water-proof match compartment in composition rubber handle. Thumb notch in blade is finely corrugated.
No. 3000—4½" blade with sheath $3.00

No. 2000

Same as No. 3000 except handle is aluminum.
No. 2000—4½" blade with sheath $3.00

No. 2071

Aluminum handle with match case and compass same as No. 2000—same blade as No. 571.
No. 2071—5" blade with sheath $3.25
No. 2071—6" blade with sheath 3.50

No. 3071

Same handle as No. 3000 with No. 571 blade.
No. 3071—5" $3.25

mounting are plainer. Both compasses have beveled glass covers.

It is interesting to note that Captain Ingraham's original proposal to Randall called for his hollow-handle knife to have leather washers over the tubular handle. For this reason I suspect that his design was probably inspired by a Case knife that he saw. It might have been a Model 309 made, according to Ferguson, from 1937 to 1949, or else it might have been its earlier predecessor, the Model 334. This had the same handle as the Model 309, but it had a 5-inch upswept saber-ground blade with serrated thumb rest.

The Model 334 seems to have been Case's answer to the Union Model 2000, only with the added attraction of the leather washer handle. At the same time Case also offered a Model 709. It had virtually the identical aluminum handle as the Union 2000 and 2071, but with a somewhat differently shaped 5-inch saber clip blade. Both the 334 and the 709 were introduced by Case in 1934. Case dropped the aluminum-handled 709 in 1942. The 334 may have been dropped as early as 1937, when the 309 came along.

Throughout the history of the American cutlery industry and in Sheffield and Solingen for even longer, knife firms have contracted manufacturing back and forth amongst themselves. This has permitted particular firms to concentrate on making certain specialty patterns such as rigging knives or utility knives, which are then sold in various styles with various markings by a number of different and competing firms. Considering how similar the Case and Union hollow-handle knives were, and how limited the demand for them must have been, it is possible that all these knives could have been made in one factory.

So now we have carried our hollow-handle history from the 1980s back to the 1930s. Is that the end, or rather the beginning? I don't believe so. As with so many of our good "modern" cutlery ideas, this one can be traced back to 18th century France. I have seen one hollow-handled 18th century French knife that had another smaller knife inside the handle. I saw a picture from 1771 of another knife that had a sharpening steel inside its handle. As to the match-safe handle of the 1930s, I have not seen an authentic earlier version of it—yet. I would not be greatly surprised if one were to turn up tomorrow.

Circa 1934 Case catalog pictures, courtesy D. & L. Ferguson.

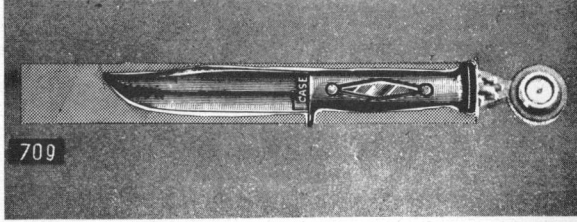

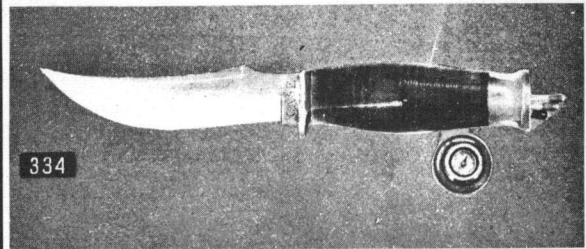

No. 709. HUNTER (With Compass)—Five inch sturdy saber blade; corrugated thumb grip on back. Chrome finished. Metal handle, with water-proof match container in handle and compass in cap. With leather sheath.

No. 334. HUNTER (With Compass)—Five inch heavy duty blade. Chrome finished. Leather washer handle over solid metal water-proof match container; screw top enclosing compass. The only leather handled compass and match container Hunting Knife on the American market. Adaptable for every purpose of the most discriminating Scout, Hunter or Sportsman. With leather sheath.

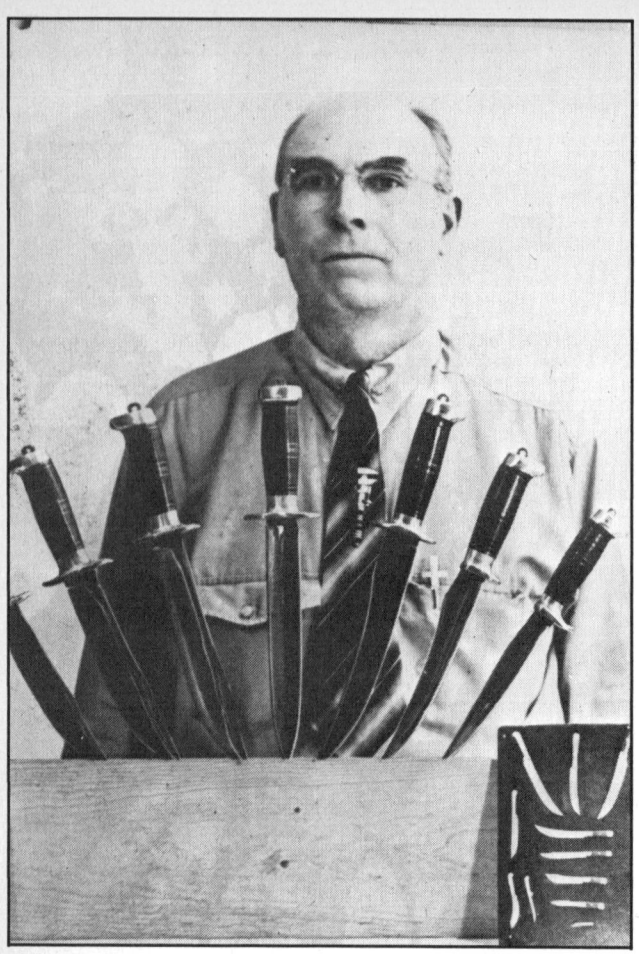

The man himself, Frank J. Richtig, with his leather-handled fighters and some miniatures.

MORE ABOUT RICHTIG KNIVES

by HARLAN SUEDMEIER

JAILBREAK! A word that brings visions to most minds, of men in striped clothing climbing prison walls, running and hiding. What about breaking *into* jail!

That's what Frank J. Richtig did with a knife in 1938. As Richtig was demonstrating and selling his handmade knives in Cedar Bluffs, Nebraska, the local marshal approached him with a problem. It seems the marshal had lost the key to a padlock securing one of the cell doors at the local jail. Selecting a knife from his display, Richtig asked to be shown to the lock. It turned out to be a monster padlock with a ⅝-inch loop. He placed his knife on the loop and, with a few well placed blows of a hammer, cut cleanly through the metal. The story spread around the area rapidly and Richtig for several years had the padlock on display in his shop. This type of demonstration was used many times by Richtig as he traveled around in Nebraska and surrounding states to sell his knives.

Setting up the display was not only the usual arranging of product in an eye-catching manner, but also the handling of heavy tools. In this case it was a large blacksmith anvil. It was this anvil and related items that were to become this young knifemaker's sales tools for many years to come.

Frank Richtig and his wife Mary traveled to Lincoln, Nebraska, from Clarkson in the early 1930s to the state fair, a trip of 85 miles. The products they hoped to market to the large crowd were knives; kitchen cutlery and hunting knives. Where does the anvil work into the picture? Is he going to forge blades? Hardly! This young blacksmith was of a new breed of knifemakers, a profession almost unheard of in those years. The blades he was marketing were made by the stock-removal system, a term probably not even used then. He "ground them out," then put them into proper working hardness and toughness by heat treating them to obtain the keen

> *EDITOR'S NOTE:*
> *We're happy to tell you that the author of this informative article first met Frank W. Richtig's knives in these very pages only several years ago. A Nebraskan himself, Suedmeier has since acquired an extensive collection of Richtig knives and memorabilia. Should you have information for him, address him at RFD 2, Nebraska City, NE 68410. K.W.*

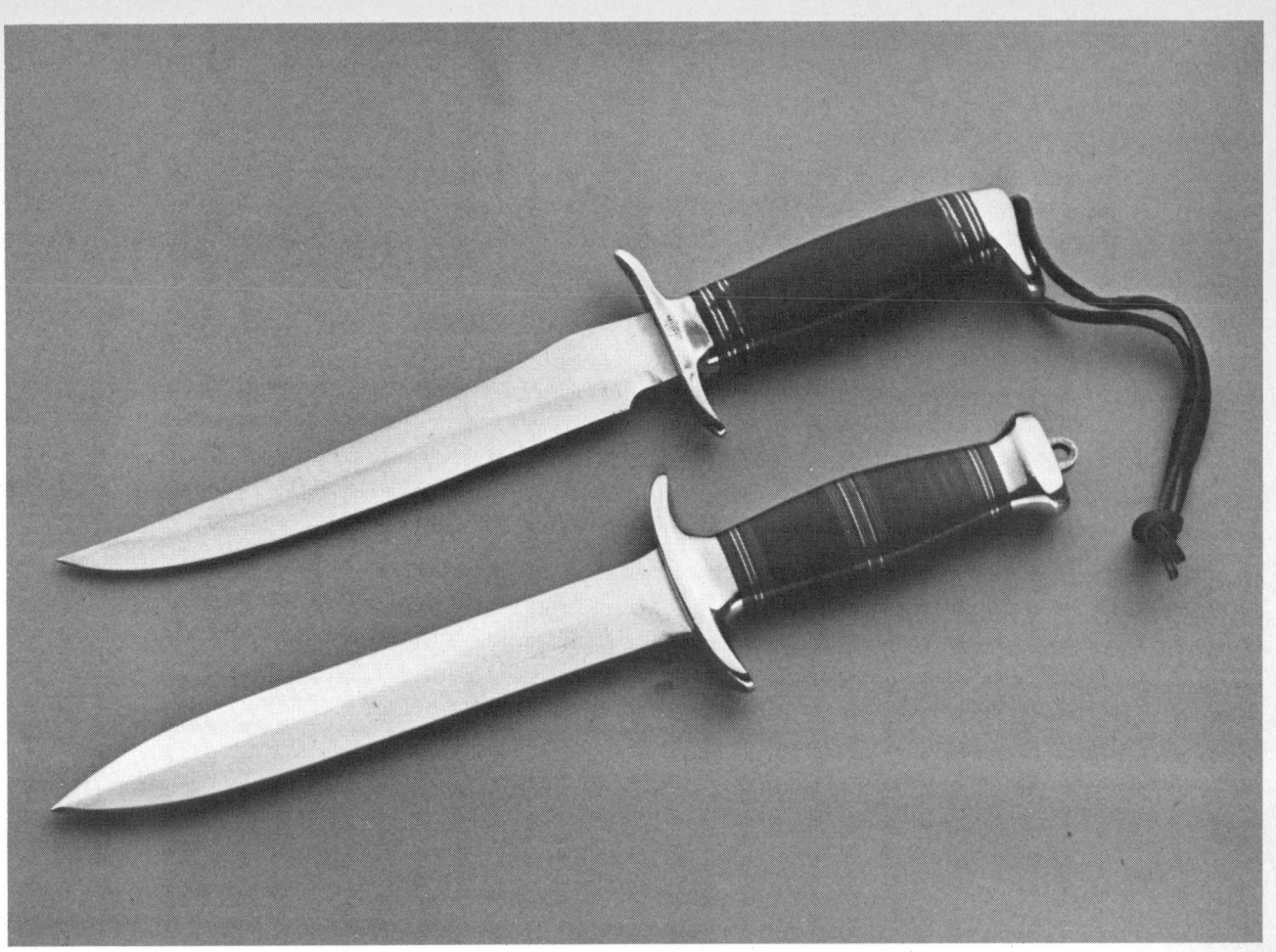

Classic Richtig fighters from the author's collection are right in the mainstream of American personal cutlery. (Weyer photo)

edges that he was to demonstrate.

How do you demonstrate a knife? This brings the anvil back into the picture. Richtig had developed, mainly by trial and error, his own tempering process. His demonstration was sensational to say the least. He would choose a railroad spike, old buggy axle, horseshoe or any other similar item and place it on the anvil. With a knife from his display, he would cut the selected item into two pieces by hammering it through. Then, with great showmanship, he would take the same knife and cleanly slice a sheet of newspaper to show that it was still sharp. Inevitably, the spectators were impressed enough to buy some of these wonderful knives. Throughout his career this was the method he used many times. Not just at this fair, but county fairs, picnics, and other celebrations. Sometimes he would just set up on a busy street to sell without the benefit of a crowd-drawing event. He was his own event. This demonstration and his good knives were the major factors that made Frank Richtig famous and put Clarkson on the map.

In 1936, Richtig and his iron-cutting knives were featured in the Ripley's "Believe It Or Not" column that appeared in many newspapers across the nation. This column gave Mr. Richtig publicity and fame from coast to coast and was probably the most important event of his career. Orders came in from all over the nation and some foreign countries.

The several tons of cut steel from his demonstration on display by now gave great testimony to his process and ability. In 1938 another event gave greater credit to Mr. Richtig's ability. At a gathering of more than 200 blacksmiths belonging to the National Blacksmith and Welders Association, he was asked to explain and demonstrate his system and techniques. Under the very watchful eye of these 200-plus critics, Mr. Richtig made his demonstration of steel cutting. The group was so impressed that they sent him a letter of commendation. This letter paid tribute to him as a Master Ironsmith for his tool and knifemaking abilities.

Frank Joseph Richtig, of Czech descent, was born December 28, 1887, on a Colfax County, Nebraska, farm. In 1906, at age 19, he went to work as an apprentice in a blacksmith shop. Two years later, he and a partner set up their own shop in Clarkson. They operated the blacksmith business and sold Dodge and Dort

IMPORTANT!

OUR GUARANTEE!

READ CAREFULLY!

Our knives are fully guaranteed as to workmanship and material under **ordinary use**. If knive proves to be defective in any way within six months after purchase, return same to us and we will gladly replace it. However, if the knife blade back shows it has been hammered upon or shows abuse in anyway, the guarantee is void and the knife will not be replaced. We recommend butcher steel or fine stone for sharpening our knives, and under ordinary use they will give you life-time service. This guarantee must be returned with the knife. Write for detailed catalogue.

FRANK J. RICHTIG
Manufacturer of Hand-Made High Grade
QUALITY CUTLERY

CLARKSON, NEBRASKA

DEAR SIR:—

It pleases me greatly that you are interested in my special **hand-made knives**. These knives are made of high-grade steel and are suitable for all ordinary uses in the home or place of business. They will do all we claim for them.

In reference to the cutting of cold chisels, axles and many other steel articles, I wish to say that in my steel and iron-cutting demonstrations, I use the same steel and temper you will find in my regular stock knives. The size and thickness of the blade is the same, the only difference you will find is in the grinding of the cutting edge. I do not sell my knives for the purpose of cutting steel and iron. The purpose of my steel-cutting demonstrations is to show the toughness and temper in in my knives.

Many thousands of people have seen my steel-cutting demonstrations and were greatly amused by them. Striking a knife with a heavy hammer in cutting steel requires special skill and experience, both of which I have learned and mastered during the thirty years I have been making and improving these knives.

My knives are made for general all-around use where good, substantial knives are required.

I recommend "butcher's steel", fine stone or oil stone for sharpening my knives. Thanking you for your kind inquiry, I remain, Yours truly,

(Write for Catalogue.)

F. J. Richtig.

Every knife is stamped with my name and address on the handle, reading as follows:

**HAND-MADE BY
F. J. RICHTIG
CLARKSON, NEBR.**

Richtig also showed full details on his handle construction in his catalog. Note that all corners are radiused, which is important.

(Opposite page) In his catalog, Frank J. Richtig told it fair and square—read his letter.

These spikes were cut as shown by the master knifemaker himself with knives like these.

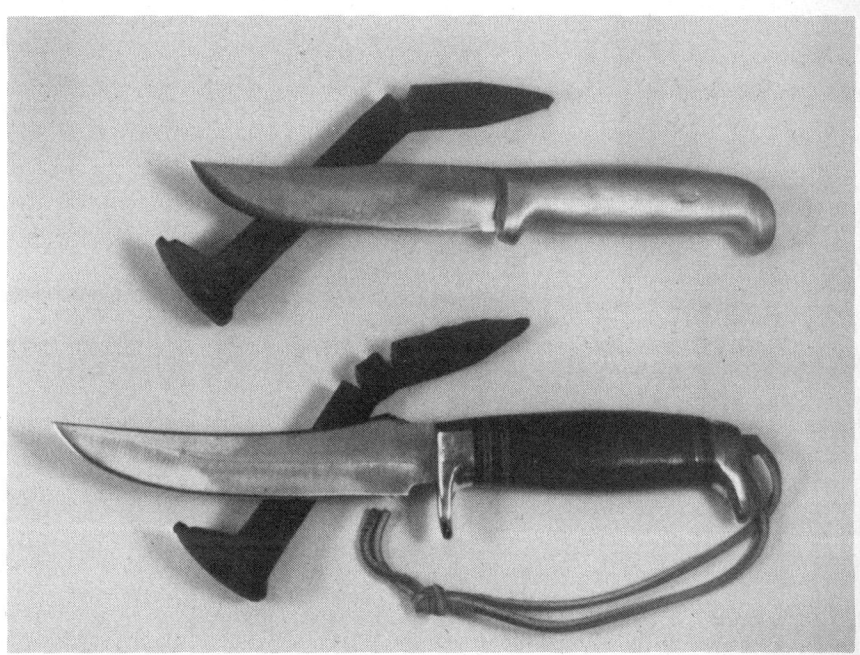

automobiles until 1923 when Richtig sold his share to pursue other interests.

This other interest had started developing in about 1916. He had been experimenting with a tempering process for knives. This experimenting would lead to the use of a Paragon electric oven for heating his blades. In July of 1925, Richtig leased a shop and began to produce his knives. He built several pieces of equipment to help in his production, including grinders, a double-wheeled buffer and casting equipment. The casting equipment was used to pour aluminum handles onto his blades. These handles were very durable and sanitary as no spaces developed for food or other debris to accumulate.

A complete line of kitchen and utility knives were produced and cataloged with aluminum handles and blades of $1/16$-inch tool steel. Orders for custom knives and special tools were also received and filled. This aluminum handled line was by far the bulk of Richtig's production. An old ledger for 1949-1953 shows an average of about 350 of those knives per year. Richtig's peak productive years continued through the '50s. His kitchen knives can be located still in use in many homes throughout the Midwest. I have some of his blades that have been sharpened to almost nothing.

He also made hunting knives with aluminum handles. They were constructed of $1/8$-inch blade material. Six styles and sizes were listed in his brochure, but I have found 15 to 18 different variations over the years. These are the second most desirable for collectors to obtain. I have talked with many hunters who still use Richtig hunting knives, and would not part with them for any amount of money or any knife in trade.

By far, the most sought after and valuable of Mr. Richtig's knives are the ones with brass guard and buttcap with leather and fiber washer handles. I have found only one brochure listing this style. It was printed very early in his career and has three styles of knives listed: 6-inch hunter, 6-inch dagger, and 6-inch hunter-fighter combination.

The blades of these knives were of $1/8$-inch material. Most of the early knives had a lanyard loop provided by extending the tang through the buttcap and drilling a hole in it. This feature was used extensively until the

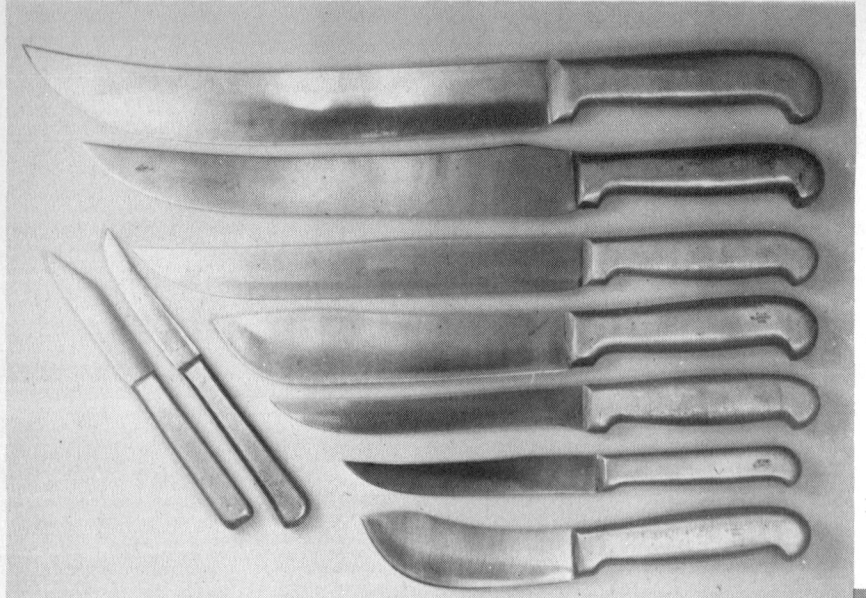

Richtig kitchen and utility knives were made in a wide range of sizes and shapes, but all had the "durable and sanitary" cast aluminum handles.

Very early hunter and fighter prototypes show the straightforward approach Richtig took to all his designs. The center knife looks like a later KABAR—more mainstream stuff.

late 1940s. At this time Richtig changed some features that help date his knives. He started using thicker leather washers for the handles, with fewer fiber and brass spacers. The shape of the buttcap was changed to more of a crown design. My personal opinion is that these later knives were not as attractive. The finish also started to suffer as well. Possibly age was starting to take its toll as he was well into his 60s. The late brass guards are not as finely sculptured as the early ones. The fit of the guard to blade still retained a high standard. The only soldering I have seen was on a very rare knuckle knife.

The blade material used by Richtig in all his knives was purchased from a large Midwest steel supplier. I have a purchase order book that lists the type of steel. It is listed by a company product name, not by the A.I.S.I. designation. I have been in touch with the company but have not been able to obtain the exact makeup of the steel to date. I do have a couple pieces of unused stock that came from his shop when the estate was auctioned.

The tempering process that gave this steel the iron-cutting ability was taken to his grave by Frank Richtig. In talking with several people who had worked with him, I have been able to piece together much of the process. I have not tried to cut steel yet. I would like to have more information on the steel first. In Rockwell testing several of his finished blades I have found they are not extremely hard as most people would believe. There seems to be a certain "toughness" in them that is hard to explain. You have to work with a blade to understand.

Once acquainted with Richtig knives, they are very easy to recognize. Most were marked with one of several stampings, but not all. Three obviously very early aluminum handle knives have been stamped "F.J.R." in a random pattern. The handles of these knives are also different from one another and unlike his normal production. I feel they are some of his very early efforts.

The most common stamping was "F.J.R." over "Clarkson, Neb." in a small oval pattern ¼-inch by ⅜-inch. This was used on the handles of the aluminum

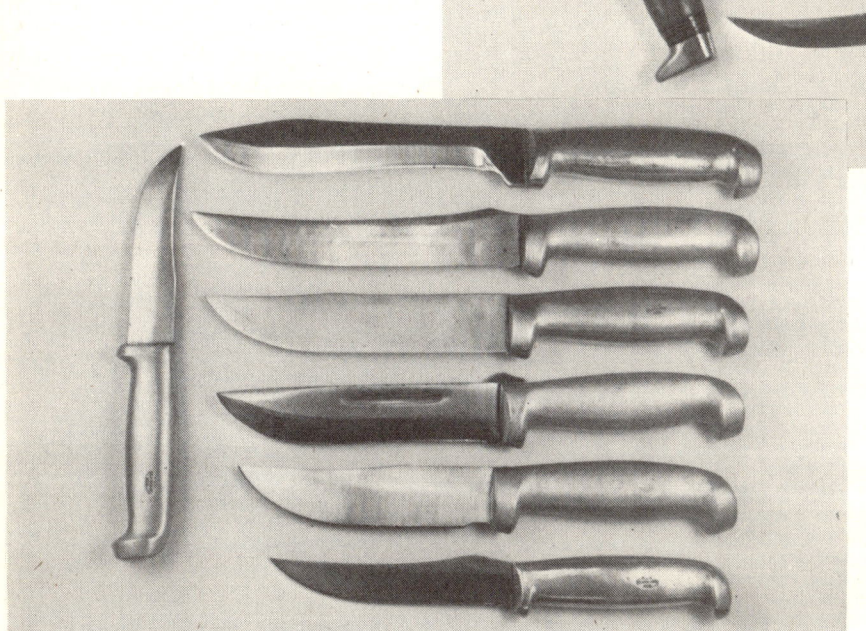

Leather-handled Richtigs were not all large knives, as this group of medium-sized knives shows. The knife at left has a bone handle.

Before he was finished, Frank Richtig made utility hunters—with stiffer blades than the kitchen knives, but with similar cast handles—in a wide range of shapes and sizes. The top knife looks like a Puma White Hunter model.

knives and the guard or buttcap of the leather handled knives.

Later, a rectangular stamping "Handmade By F.J. Richtig, Clarkson, Neb." was used on the aluminum handled knives. There was not room to use it on the leather handled ones as it was 5/8-inch by 1¼-inch. About this same time he started using a trademark stamp of a man standing over an anvil with upraised hammer. The design obviously came from the sketch used in the Ripley's column. This was stamped on the reverse side of the handle. About 20 percent of the knives marked with the larger stamp have the trademark stamping.

I just recently found an aluminum handled butcher knife with this trademark acid-etched on the blade. It is the only one that has been found marked in this manner.

Richtig knives also gained great acclaim during World War II. Being too old to enter the war directly, he performed his patriotic duty by producing fighting knives. Many of these were given, free of charge, to local residents entering the service. As his fame spread, orders came from all over the world.

Many letters attest to the quality of his knives being proven in combat. Three letters displayed in Mr. Richtig's shop complimenting and thanking him for gift knives bear the signatures of Dwight D. Eisenhower, Chester W. Nimitz and Douglas MacArthur. A photo autographed by Nimitz, showing the signing of the treaty ending World War II on the USS Missouri, accompanied the letter.

I personally had an interesting conversation with Frank Miller of Clarkson, a very close friend of Richtig, relating to an experience with one of his knives. During World War II, Miller had used a Richtig knife to actually dig a foxhole, under fire, having lost his entrenching tool. After digging a depression deep enough, in very rocky soil, to protect himself, the tip of the blade was blunted and dulled. Sometime later, after returning home, Miller showed his knife to Mr. Richtig and related the story. Richtig offered to reshape and sharpen it, but Miller declined, saying he wanted to keep it this way

EIGHTH ANNUAL EDITION 35

as a remembrance. He still has the knife today in the worn and blunted condition.

Miniatures were also a product of Richtig's skilled hands; not only miniature knives, but a variety of other items: actual working replicas of monkey wrenches, scissors, anvils, vises, hammers and whatever else took his fancy.

Richtig was active in knifemaking, though at reduced production rate, well into his 80s. Through most of these years he had operated the shop by himself, only occasionally hiring help. He had been offered the opportunity to expand into a factory-type operation by a large manufacturer, but made the decision to remain a small one-man shop.

In the search for Richtig knives, memorabilia and related facts, I have conceived a profile of an interesting man: He was energetic and could not sit still for any length of time. He loved to play pool and did so quite often, being very skilled at the game. He would stop work to play the game but did not linger, going right back to work. He loved to talk to people and always had time to do so. If you went to his shop to buy a knife, you would not be able to leave immediately, because he would relate the process used to create your knife and would be quite lengthy about it. In just the opposite vein, if you offended him in any way and "got on his bad side," you would be lucky to purchase a knife at any price.

The value of a Richtig is a very interesting subject in itself. According to his brochures, the aluminum handle knives sold from a low of 50¢ to the top listed price of $5. The leather-handled ones sold at $8. In later years, when brochures were no longer used, the prices were about double, still quite a bargain. Today's market on the aluminum kitchen models is from $15 to $150; the aluminum hunting models from $50 to $250; and the leather handled styles from $200 to $1200. Of course, all these prices depend on style and condition as with any knife.

Frank J. Richtig was a pioneer of handmade knives as we know them today. With a career spanning over 50 years, he truly made his mark in the trade.

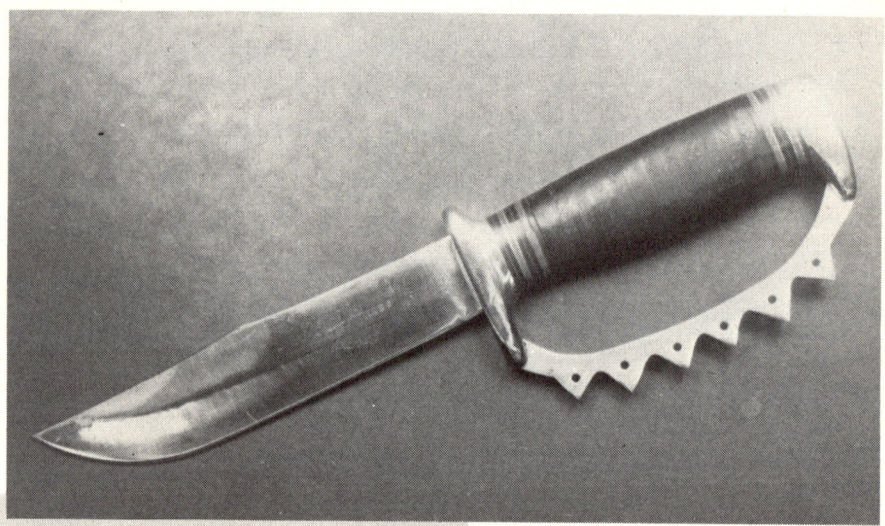

Knuckle-bowed Richtigs were not usual at all. On this one, the bow is soldered to the guard and pommel.

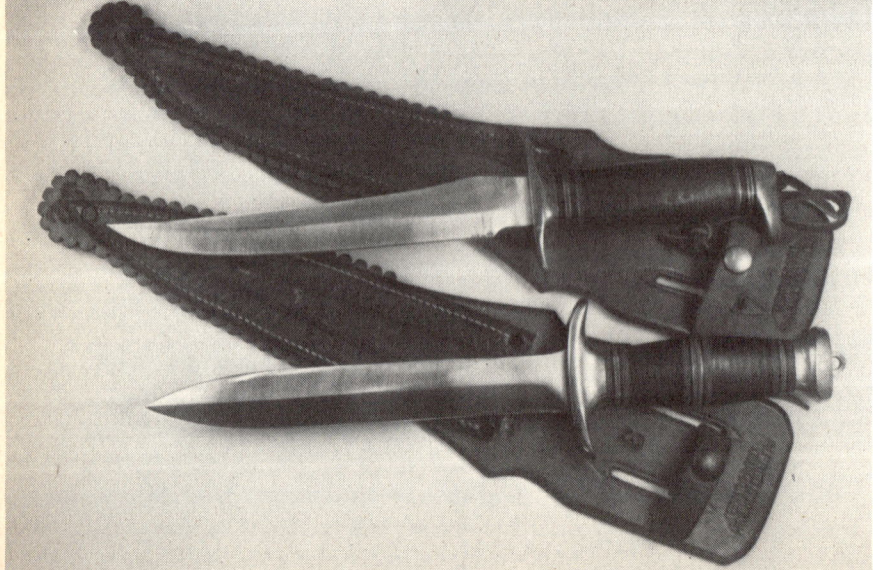

Many Richtig fighters went to war in distinctive Alfred Cornish sheaths. Cornish, of Omaha, was prominent in leatherwork in Nebraska.

Knives of the Gauchos

by
ABEL A. DOMENECH

BORN UNDER the immensity of pampa and sky, the origins of the *gauderios* (a primitive synonym for *gaucho*) remains hidden in the misty dawn of the Argentine history. First named as such, gauchos appeared in tales dated as far back as the 1600s or perhaps the early 1700s, in descriptions made mainly by foreign visitors traveling through our virgin plains, referring to those extraordinary riders whose veins mixed the bloods of Spaniards and Indians.

The figure of the gaucho has evolved from the original sense of a nomad class, a skillful horseman, hunter of wild cattle, through several meanings, probably reflecting the changes of political, cultural and economic factors; arriving today at the quasi-mythical and romantic representation of the Argentine native, riding on his brave *criollo* horse to the setting sun at the end of the pampa.

The end of the true gaucho, probably during the third part of the 19th century, was due to several factors: changes in life customs and field management, territori-

"... No other shelter than the sky, nor other friend than the facón"

from José Hernandez

A modern "gaucho" essays snatching a ring with a stick at full gallop in a *carrera de sortijas*.

al division and adoption of such "modernities" as barbed wire, the telegraph, the railroad and a marginal reach of culture, together with the end of our Indian and Civil wars. Such glamour contributed to the aura created around his figure, and to the meaning he acquired for the present Argentine citizen.

The gaucho, often compared with the American cowboy, shared with the latter his love and skill with horses, and his knowledge of the different tasks related to country and cattle, together with his high esteem of his own freedom. On the other hand, other efforts to make parallels about their ways of life and fate had different approaches, which in my opinion not always succeeded, as gauchos and cowboys, though sharing said points in common, lived their own different styles and historic events.

That includes the weapons used, considering that the quick adoption of firearms by Americans was not followed by southern counterparts. As a matter of fact, gaucho weapons consisted of a classic triplet: boleadoras, lazo (lariat) and cuchillo (knife).

It has been said several times that without his horse the gaucho wouldn't have existed. The horse, being such a critical and main point of his existence, seems to be the center of his universe.

Some authors, with whom I humbly join, maintain that his knife, "su cuchillo," was the center of his existence, to such a point that with his knife, he would have been able to survive, even without a horse, or at least, his knife would have helped him to get another horse. His knife was then everything: weapon, tool, companion of his loneliness. Domingo F. Sarmiento, politician, teacher, statesman, writer and President of Argentina between 1868 and 1874, wrote the following paragraphs in his famous book *Facundo:*

> The gaucho goes armed with the knife he has inherited from the Spaniards . . . The knife, more than a weapon, is an instrument which serves him in all his occupations: he can't live without it; it's like the elephant's trunk, his arm, his hand, his finger, his every-

Two ever-present subjects in the gaucho life: the horse and the knife. Note the way gauchos carried coins in the *tirador*, a wide leather belt with a special buckle called a *rastra*.

(Left, below, bottom right) Very fine and original puñal, silver mounted, of the classic *Libertad* brand. The spiral treatment is called *galloneado*.

thing.

The gaucho boasts of valor, and the knife shines at every moment, making circles in the air, at the least provocation . . . The ordinary man of other countries takes the knife to kill, and kills; the Argentine gaucho unsheaths it to fight, and he only wounds . . . his objective is only to "mark," to make a scar on the rival's face, to make an indelible mark . . .

. . . A wide circle gather round the fighters, the eyes follow passionately and lustily the sparkle of their "puñales," that don't cease to shake for a moment . . .

But, which were the origins of the gaucho knife, and the different types used by the native of the plains? Contrary to the popular image of the gaucho, holding a *facon,* it wasn't one but several types he used. Let's try to explain, at least in part, the dark origins of that legendary blade.

First of all, let me refer as "cuchillo criollo" (or "native knife"), to the group of knives we are going to study; that is a general term to encompass all the variants. The cuchillo criollo, or at least its ancestors, was no doubt brought to our lands by the Spanish conquistador. The knife was for sure part of the modest arsenal brought by Pedro de Mendoza in 1536, together with swords and spears. Later *facones* were made with broken sword blades. Those first knives were of different origins too, mainly those made in Flanders—a region that lies to the northeast of France today, part of Belgium and south of Holland. Also, Toledo and Segovia in Spain were proud and famous suppliers of legendary steels and blades. And, perhaps strangely enough, Germany exerted a great influence not only in knives, but also in other pieces of wear of the first settlers.

The first locally and crudely made knives "made after the pattern of those brought from Flanders" as it says in a story written in 1556, kept those influences, and used whichever material was at hand: old sword blades, iron bars, iron straps from barrels and chests, and files, much appreciated by the gauchos for knife blades. The forms and names taken by those first knives were different and diverse. The names are a problem particularly

El Duelo, drawn by Osvaldo Gasparini for this article, shows how valor was demonstrated by gauchos. The ultimate disgrace was to kill the other fellow.

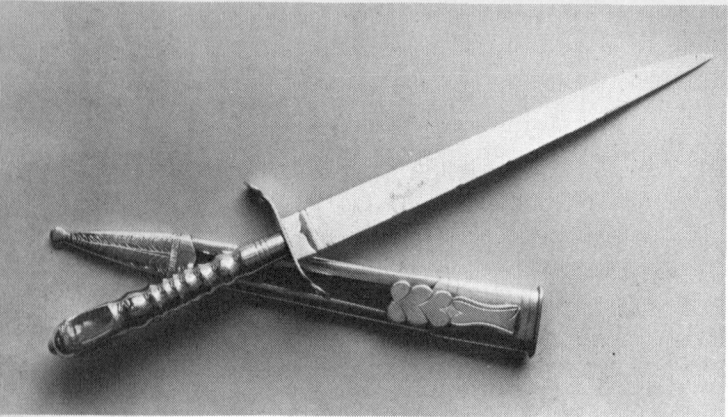

Facón with blade made in Germany by Mann & Federlein. This brand was rather popular here, and author has seen Bowie-type hunting knives made by the same firm.

Old "F. Herder Abr. Sohn" brand knife made and entirely mounted in white metal in Germany probably during the first third of this century. The blade has the typical 6-inch triangular punal shape, and the general treatment of the scabbard is both Germanic and gaucho.

Gaucho's tirador with coins, rastra and the long knife together provide belly support and protection.

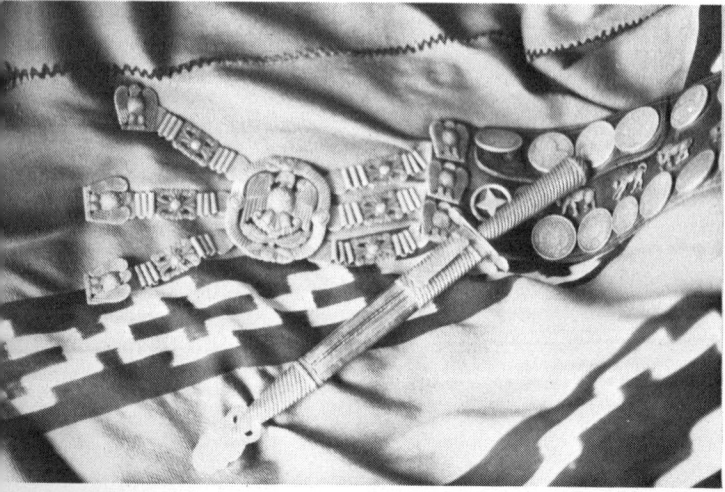

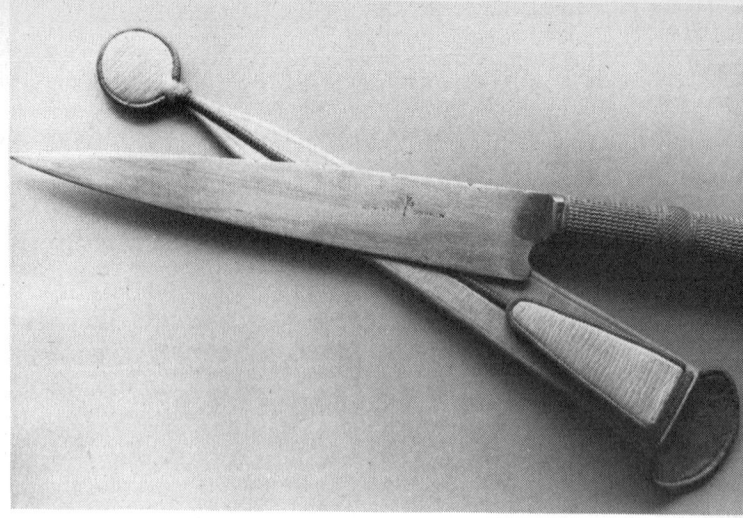

An unusual puñal: an Arbolito blade has been re-handled by master craftsman Ricardo Gonzalez of Pila Province near Buenos Aires. It shows a typical braiding work of *tientos*, very thin leather thread. This type of work is a very old gaucho craft.

A very fine set of "Herder" brand knives made in Germany (one with ivory handle) and patterned for the Argentine market. These knives were in the importer's showcase and probably date from the first third of this century.

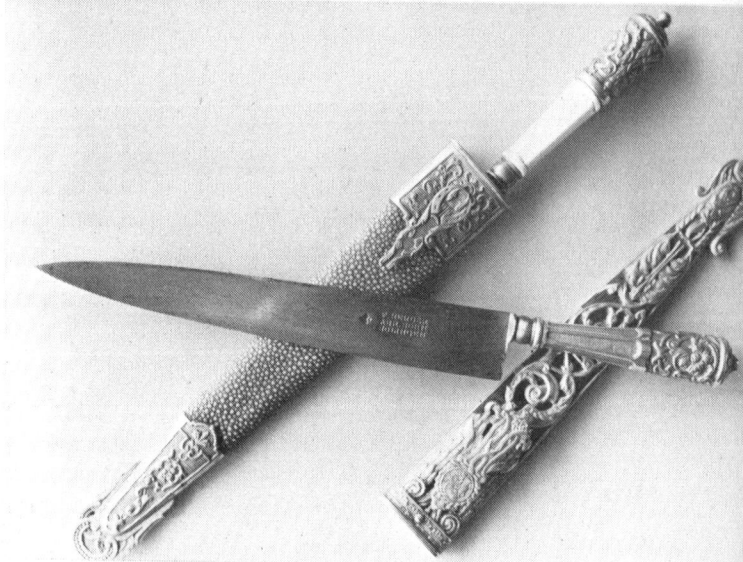

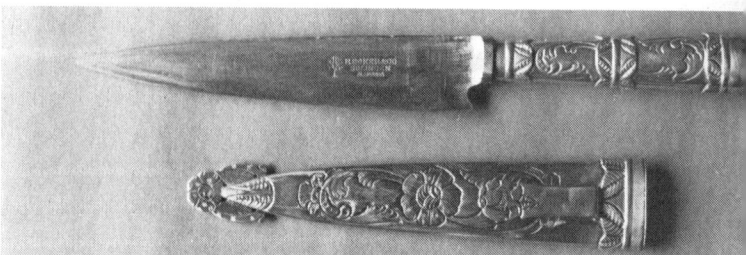

A silver-mounted old Boker Arbolito blade, marked *Solingen* and *Alemania*. Another 6-inch punal, it is a mainstream gaucho knife.

due to the fact that authors do not agree in the characteristics which make a particular knife.

That difficulty, I believe, starts in the nonexistence of bibliography or studies in this respect, the poor education of the natives who passed the names through generations, and the general confusion created by more cultivated classes, including writers and journalists, who used the different names of our knives focusing more on poetic or dramatic effect than on valid description or true name. I mean, for example, that certain writers sometimes preferred the term *daga* (dagger) or *puñal* (poniard), to "knife" or "cuchillo".

Anyway, and considering the writings of leading domestic authors, dealing with customs and folklore, and the general local acceptance, we will distinguish the following types of main interest:

Cuchillos Criollos { PUÑAL, CUCHILLA, FACON, DAGA }

It is interesting to note here, that contrary to foreign knife types, which always are displayed *out* of their sheaths, the Argentine knife is almost always shown sheathed, making a strong point in the decoration of its sheath and handle, and giving the wrong impression that the blade quality was secondary to our users.

Actually, the gaucho gave prime importance to the quality of his blade, which came (only the blade) from Germany, France and England, and was locally finished with handle and sheath, generally by silversmiths or craftmen, but sometimes by its users.

The name *el puñal* sounds curious to the historian, as this knife has several particular characteristics that wouldn't classify it as a European poniard. Perhaps its name comes from the Latin *pugna* (fight); or from *puno* (fist); that is, "knife that fits in a fist." The *puñal* is the most characteristic type of gaucho knife, and perhaps the more interesting. Present in all collections, and being used today, not only by countrymen, but by the city dweller in his Sunday *asado* (barbecue). It is, in my opinion, the most decorative type and artistic of all. It has a false edge and no guard, and its elegant spear-shaped blade of European manufacture is striking.

The *facon* is the typical, and perhaps more primitive, gaucho knife, commonly associated to the word "gaucho." It actually was a fighting knife, although the gaucho used it skillfully in his daily tasks. The name itself is usually related to the Portuguese idiom where *faca* means "knife," thus *facón* would be "big knife." Some authors refer to the Latin word *falx*, a "curved bladed knife" or to the French *fauchon*, an old short sword of wide and curved blade. The gaucho *facón* has a slim blade of 12 to 15 inches in length, and 1 to 1½ inches in width. It was made from old swords, sabers or bayonets in the beginning, at least. It had a single edge, and sometimes a short false edge. It *always* had a guard called *gavilan,* sometimes shaped as an "S" or like a half moon, or simply a straight bar, to protect the users' hand.

Similar to the facón, the main characteristic of the *daga* is its double-edged blade, straight, thin and well-pointed. There existed a particular and interesting type of daga, called *caronera* which had a very long blade of 30 to 35 inches, that due to its length was carried between the *caronas,* a leather part of the gaucho's saddle, thus its name. Caroneras didn't have guards, to make drawing from the saddle easier. Common dagas could have some type of guard or not.

All of the old *puñales* observed had blades made in France, Germany or England. The real story of the origin of its pattern or shape is a mystery, as is the correct date of its first appearance, probably at the beginning or the middle of the 19th century. The following comments can be made:

The most common references in old texts mention the "Flanders knife."

The blade of the puñal has a similarity with the Mediterranean dagger, which was used in the south of Spain and France, between the 17th and 18th centuries.

We might trace a common origin in the Mediterranean dagger for both our Argentine puñal and the American Bowie. To me it seems probable, if we consider the influence of Spaniards and French on our River Plate area, and similarly on the Mississippi/Texas frontier. The patterns of the blades of the Mediterranean dagger (actually not a dagger, but a single-edged weapon), the puñal and the Rezin Bowie type speak for themselves.

On the other hand, we cannot ignore the similar treatment of handles, sheaths and blades of some 19th century German knives to these gaucho knives. Also of Germanic origin are other parts of the riding apparel of the gaucho, as, for example, certain types of stirrups. Also, German origin blades have always been highly regarded in Argentina. The only "classic" brand presently available here is the famous *Arbolito* or Tree Brand (from Boker-Solingen) whose officials were very kind to supply interesting information about their blades. That brand, identified by a small tree, was often referred locally as *la del arbolito* (that with a tree). A famous Argentine writer, Jorge Luis Borges, himself names a knife this way in his short story "El Encuentro."

Interestingly enough, very few of the brands considered classical are known to the general public of today. As a matter of fact, I could trace around 30 different names during my research, all of them used presently by out-of-business importers. Some of those brands are: ARBOLITO—DEFENSA—DUFOUR—LIBERTAD—J.M. MALHAOS—BROQUIA & SCHOLBERG—W.R. KIRSCHBAUM—JOSEPH RODGERS—E. HERDER ARB. SOHN.

Some other facts about the puñal are worth mentioning:

First, the division between handle and blade is re-

The floral motifs and the round button enclosed by the sheath, denotes its "oriental" manufacture—this is an old Uruguayan puñal.

(Below) This large facón has a 15-inch blade, silver-mounted handle and sheath with gold applications of small flowers. Obviously, the original owner was of the monied class.

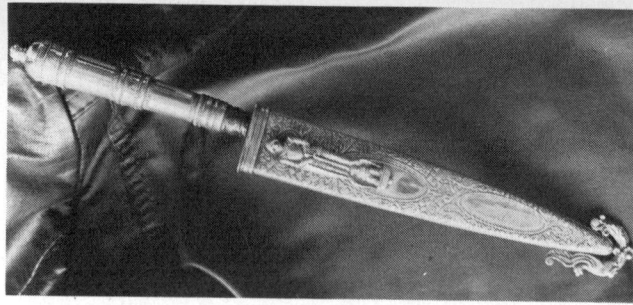

This is an 18th century German knife, which shows the influence of that country in our knives. Blade, although in very good condition, shows no brand name or maker's marks.

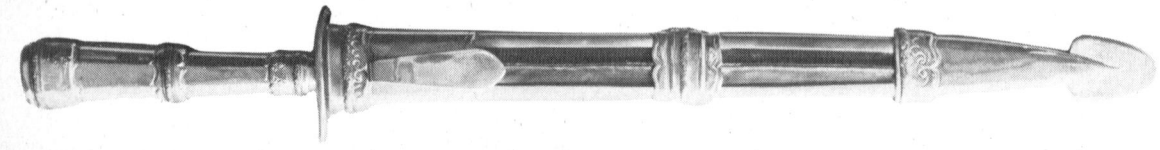

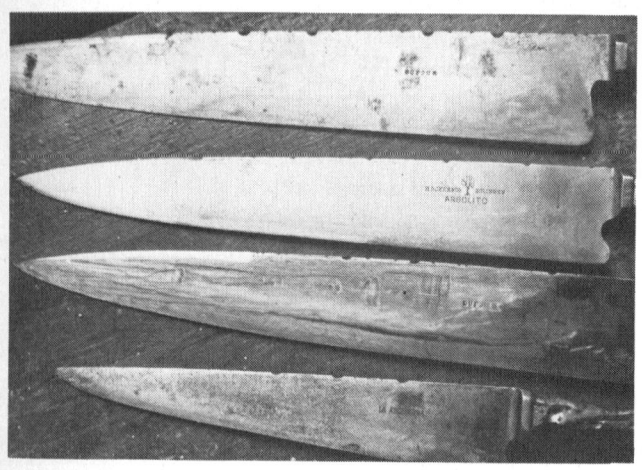

These very old but serviceable blades show the most looked-for brands. There are two Dufour, one old Arbolito and one rare La Argentina brand.

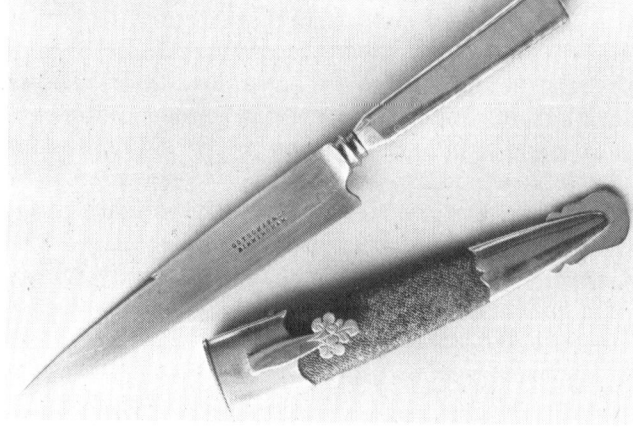

This is not a gaucho knife either, but a 5-inch English-made knife made at Birmingham by "Gotscher & Co." The sheath is elephant ear skin and metal.

ferred as the "button," actually a metal protusion, which in Argentine knives is of angular shape, and in Uruguayan and Brazilian knives is rounded and generally enclosed by an extension of its sheath.

Then, the thick back of gaucho knives was almost always decorated with cuts or file work. The use and origin of such "cuts," is subjected to different theories, as follows: They were used to break the edge or slow the knife of the opponent during a fight. Others suppose that they were intended to retain the knife in its sheath by means of an internal detent. Other "uses" include to cut fencing wires and to use them as an abacus to count heads of cattle.

Personally, I believe they were pure cosmetics which, no doubt, could have been used in any of the above mentioned tasks. The cattle counter theory suggests a connection between our knife and certain British-origin blades, especially from Scotland, and the English cattle breeding migration to South America during the 19th century.

Common using gaucho knives display metal or wooden handles, sometimes horn. Silver handles often with elaborate designs, are found in knives from the second half of 19th century to the present. Gold is also found later in that century in knives belonging to the upper classes, wealthy *estancieros* and certain military figures. Sheaths were made of leather or metal, usually matching the pattern of the handle. Sheaths combining leather with metal reinforcing (as in English Bowie knives, by the way) were not unusual.

Elaborate knives made of rich metals were, of course, not in the hands of gauchos, whose poverty didn't allow for any luxury, but were worn by their rich employers.

The traditional way of carrying the knife was on the gaucho's back, crossed in such a way that the top of the handle almost touched the right elbow. The edge of the knife was upwards so that, as the old gaucho saying has it, when drawn from its sheath "the knife goes out cutting." This particular use seems of Spanish origin, as it

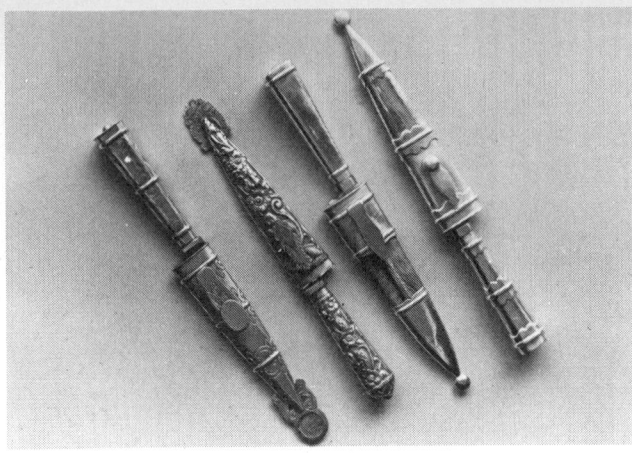

These are small puñales called *verijeros* (groiners). All have silver handles and sheaths, and are of modern manufacture. The blades use new Arbolitos about 5 inches long.

Nice puñales of the classic Defensa brand, make a very special matched pair said to have come from the display case of the importer. One of them has the initial "L.M." in gold on its handle.

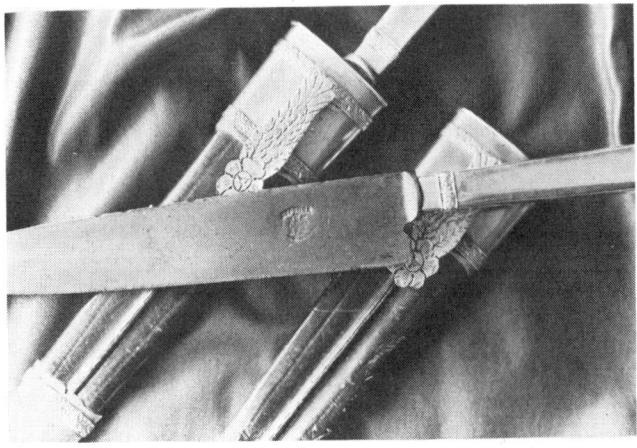

might go to prove the famous painting by Velazquez "The Triumph of Baco"—1628—in which one subject wears a dagger in a very "gaucho way" in his back. This position allowed carrying a fairly large knife without discomfort, especially when riding a horse.

Other ways of carrying, used even today with smaller knives, are: crossed in the front of the belt or on the right hip, with the handle pointing outside, and its edge downward. Other carries have included in the boot, under the armpit, and, with the caronera, between the saddle leathers.

The gaucho used his knife in his everyday life. It was, in fact, his main and sometimes only tool. He used it for eating, as a knife, fork and toothpick. He used it to kill cattle, and to skin and butcher them. Gauchos were very skillful in making their own apparel and in braiding leather: reins, parts of their "recado," lariats, mats. He used, in all his crafts, his faithful knife. He also cut wood, wire, prepared the gourd for his *mate*, the typical beverage. Knives were often used as ranging tools to take field references. And he used it, of course, as defensive weapon, as cutting tool, even to be the makeshift point of a spear.

There is a use given by the gaucho, which led to a legend about his own figure—his knife as a deadly fighting weapon. It is commonly referred through tales written in those far times, the quickness with which the *facon* was unsheathed under the smallest provocation and the skill of those men in handling it. The knife was how gauchos ended any sort of difference: be it a discussion about the talent of a rival as a "payador" (a popular singer often compared with the troubadour of the Middle Ages) or to deal with the reputation of a man as the "best knife of a region." Those fights rarely ended with the death of one of the rivals. The goal was just to mark the face of the opponent; to make the loser remember his defeat for the rest of his life.

The way the gaucho fought was very particular: he took off his spurs, to be free to jump or step back; and covered his left arm with several turns of his "poncho" by way of a shield, same as the Conquistadores rolled their cloaks when fencing. A rather long "tail" of the poncho was left unrolled, to be thrusted into the rival's face, to confuse or blind him.

All kind of tricks were used to win the fight by marking the opponent: throwing dust in his face, making him step on the poncho and throwing him off balance, and so on, were all ways to *madrugar* one's rival. All these facts have been recalled in lots of stories, books and paintings, leading to the myth around the gaucho.

The golden era of facones and puñales is gone. The windows of souvenir shops in Buenos Aires show lots of cheaply made puñales, sometimes of silver, with gold inlays of more or less good taste. It's better not to look at the quality of their blades. These are the knives for tourists and some week-end local traditionalists.

In spite of this deceptive landscape, the knife *aficionado* still has a couple of ways of getting a good *cuchillo criollo* even nowadays. There exists a small group of artisans and silversmiths who can assemble a good knife, more or less decorated or plain, according to the customer's taste and budget, and using a good blade. If the customer is fortunate (and wealthy enough) to find an old blade like Dufour, Defensa or Libertad, he can end with a very nice and important piece of collection.

The other approach, is to search in the several antique shops of Buenos Aires and find an old and authentic knife, sometimes with the mark of an old famous silversmith, or bladed with one of the major brands of old times. This is a costly but rewarding way of getting a good knife.

For sure, gauchos are gone forever, but they still live in the hearts of our countrymen. For a big group of traditionalists of this country, who keep their knives ready, together with all the pieces of memorabila belonging to those men which helped in some way to make our history, the gaucho and his knife live today.

Handmade Knives in Argentina Today

by ABEL A. DOMENECH

Alfredo Kehiayan at his workshop. He shows a camp knife which perhaps denotes his Armenian ancestry.

HANDMADE KNIVES are not as popular nor the field so sophisticated as in the U.S.A. Although there are several factors governing this, the continual economic problem Argentina has been suffering during the last years has been decisive. A "custom" knife made here sells from 200 to 400 dollars, the monthly salary of a typical employee, and very often twice that of a worker.

In spite of this, there exist a good number of knife collectors, and a few good artisans satisfying both them and other knife users. In this we are following the old tradition of Argentine love and good use of knives, set forth by our ancestors.

There are several ways of getting a nice knife here: gun shops and sport stores stock a good array of imported factory knives—those coming from Germany, like Arbolito or Puma are highly regarded—and sometimes an American handmade knife reaches our coasts. An old tradition still survives; that of making handles and sheaths, employing woods, metals and antlers for imported blades. That results in hunting knives or some sub-type of gaucho knife.

There has appeared during the last—say—10 years, a small crop of artisans making the complete knife. The quality level obtained is, for some of them, comparable to their American counterparts, but the sophistication level of U.S. models and decoration resources can't be reached, due to the economic barrier.

I feel sometimes, that the outward appearance of our handmade knives resembles those American products of around 1975/80; that is, pure "using" hunting knives, with perhaps some Bowie, fighter or survival types, but no art blades, fancy file work or "Star Wars" types. The dominant method is stock removal; I do not know of anybody making forged blades at present.

Technical literature in Spanish is almost nonexistent, and this author is presently working on one which is considered the first book in Spanish entirely devoted to knives, which hopefully will be edited by mid '87. DBI's KNIVES is awaited every year with impatience.

Again like the U.S.A. of 10 years ago, Argentina

A slim Perpina-brand knife—wood handle and brass fittings.

This version of the drop-point hunter by Kehiayan has full tang and handles of jacarandá of Bahia. It is flat-ground.

(Right) A Kehiayan hunting knife of traditional style with 6-inch blade (top); and a heavy multi-purpose knife with a 9-inch heavy blade. Pouch type sheaths are handmade by Keniayan.

seems to be acquiring knifemakers very quickly. One of ours who has been at it a while is Alfredo Kehiayan. I'd like to describe his knifemaking for you:

Alfredo's workshop wouldn't surprise an artisan of 100 or 200 years ago too much. He relies almost entirely on hand tools to make his knives—files, hammers, handsaws and emery cloth serve him well in his craft. When I asked him about his first knife, he told me that he made it, almost in play, when he was 15 or 16. Alfredo, whose Armenian ancestry is evidenced in some of his blades, explains that his present craftmanship was self-taught, taking advantage of his previous work as machinist, working with metals, dealing with heat treating and the forge. His skill with leatherwork has helped as well.

The design base of his knives is broad, and reflects his strong point of view about the knife. He employs the stock removal method, and his models are of the full tang type; some of these tangs are tapered. The union of blade and guard is silver soldered, and the fit of the different components of guard and handle—wood, brass and steel—is flawless.

A personal touch in Keyhiayan handles is the use of hollow rivets. He also prefers nicely figured local woods for handle material and mistol, retamo, jacarandá and curupay are some of his favorites.

The blade finish is a mirror polish he obtains entirely by hand, using emery cloth of different grades. And Alfredo makes his own leather sheaths of pouch type, wet molded to the knife with his own process, and retaining it without straps.

The Argentine artisan, starts with blade stock of different widths, preferring at present an SAE 6180 alloy of chromium and manganese content. He sends his blades to a local laboratory for heat treating according to his specifications, obtaining an RC reading of around 59 degrees, which he prefers.

Kehiayan himself doesn't recognize a definite trend in his work, but I would suggest three basic distinct types:

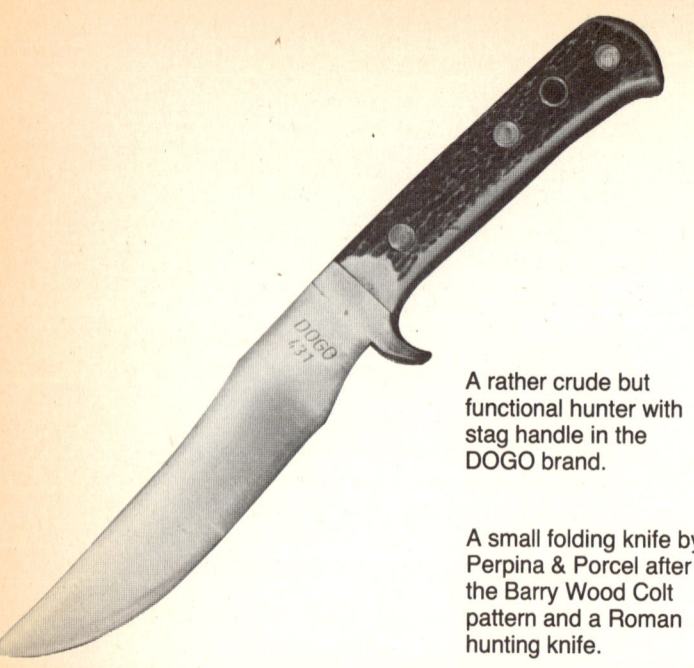

A rather crude but functional hunter with stag handle in the DOGO brand.

A small folding knife by Perpina & Porcel after the Barry Wood Colt pattern and a Roman hunting knife.

a) An all-purpose hunting knife of classic lines, a mixture of Bowie and *criollo* knife, of elegant lines, which I consider his most representative type.
b) A drop-point hunter with hollow ground blade, following current trends.
c) Classic recreations of Bowie types, fighters, Germanic hunters, etc.; all stylized and adapted to practical use.

Alfredo refuses to adopt fancy decorations for his knives, such as filework or engraving. He feels that his are using knives, although a good part of his production ends in collector hands.

He considers that his present output reflects the best knife he can make, but he says he is fortunate enough to learn something new every day. In his own words, handmaking knives is for him more a way of life than a way of earning his living. There are others and, I hope, more to come.

Acknowledgements

The author wishes to thank the people who made this article possible, specially the photographic production:

"La Cina Cina," a little place in San Antonio de Areco, where tourists can get an interesting view of gaucho attire, traditions and folklore, was the setting for the gaucho photographs, thanks to the courtesy of owners Guillermo and Marisa Ramirez.

Juan José Draghi, a master silversmith, allowed me to photograph his workshop and production. He also divulged some of his "secrets of the trade" and imparted his knowledge of our inherited customs.

Alfredo Kehiayan, one of our very few "custom" knifemakers, showed me how he made his knives and explained his feelings about what he calls "a way of life."

Mr. and Mrs. Setian, owners of "Alhambra," a very well-known antique shop, showed me and allowed me to photograph their very important collection.

A final word of thanks for suffering friend Raul Andres, who painstakingly checked my handwriting, correcting my "poor man" English.

Alhambra Antiguedades (Mr. and Mrs. Setian owners)
Humberto 1° 423
(CP 1103) Buenos Aires, ARGENTINA

La Cina Cina
Bartolome Mitre 9
(CP 2760) San Antonio de Areco — Pcia. de Bs Aires, ARGENTINA

Juan Jose Draghi
Calle General Alvear 145
(CP 2760) San Antonio de Areco
Provincia de Buenos Aires
ARGENTINA

If you ever drop by San Antonio de Areco, a "must" visit when touring in Argentina, you can visit Juan Jose at his workshop-showroom.

Not a Randall blade, but a tribute to the man made by Carlos R. Mosci of LaPlata.

TRENDS

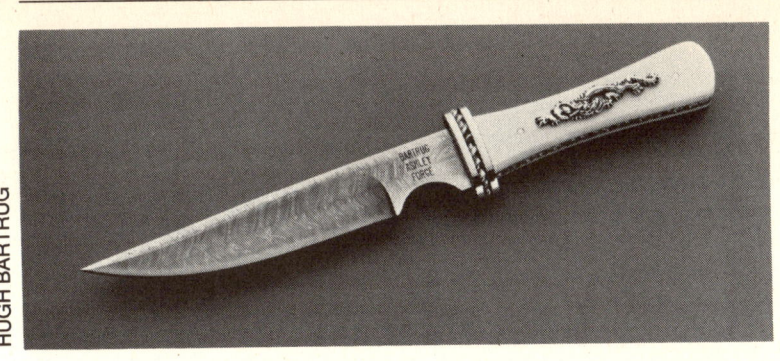

HUGH BARTRUG

There could be dozens of subdivisions of this view of knives. We're trying to provide both in-depth views of what is happening in the mainstream of knifemaking, and also look at the fringes. We think some of those will become mainstream soon.

We're showing mostly hand or benchmade knives here, made one at a time and usually hand-ground and hand-finished without jigs or fixtures. Some knives, folders particularly, benefit from machine work or other precision techniques and so there are some such here. Some commercial knives fall into our categories, as well, either for their functional design or particular good looks.

These are the trend-setting knives, as we see them.

Ken Warner

Bowies
Movie Knives
The Working Straight Edge
Straight Standards
Leather and Other Stuff
Knives in the Kitchen
The Folding Standards
Simple Knives
Carving Sets Anyone?
Single-Edged Fighters
Trout and Bird Knives
The Return of the Sabertooth
Swords and Other Fantasies
The Kopis, the Kukri and All That
Miniatures Keep Growing
Gents Table Cutlery
Miscellany
Knives of the Year

EIGHTH ANNUAL EDITION 47

TRENDS
THE SHAPES OF BOWIES

ONLY TWO kinds of people buy Bowie knives—the sophisticated and the unsophisticated. Semi-sophisticated knife buyers shy away, considering the Bowie an obvious solution . . . which it is. At that same level, four is the obvious solution when the question is, "How much is two and two?"

For a century and another half of a century the Bowie knife, by which then was meant almost any large knife carried as a sidearm and which now pretty well means, unless otherwise stated, a large clip-point knife with double guards, has been a sound solution to most problems approached with large knives. That is, the Bowie has a pretty fine point and the size gives it plenty of strength overall.

Indeed, the only reason not to carry a Bowie knife around for such problems is that, in general, a real Bowie is a pretty big package. The fact that the Bowie can be scaled down and can become an ordinary hunting knife—normally you take off one of the guards—is possibly the best evidence of the genuine utility of the shape. Those are only some of the reasons why we regularly see a lot of pictures of Bowie knives coming in to this publication, as you will note here.

The Bowie is a well-understood and attractive package to most knife buyers, and affords, as you will also see here, craftsmen a chance to work in the oldest of styles, in melds of the old styles and new lines, or to go all the way up to the minute and leave everything traditional but shape behind. The Bowie as modernly made can be as stark as a 2x4 or as fancy as a flower arrangement—it is all in the hand of the craftsman and the eye of the beholder. There are going to be Bowies for a long, long time, as there have been already.

Ken Warner

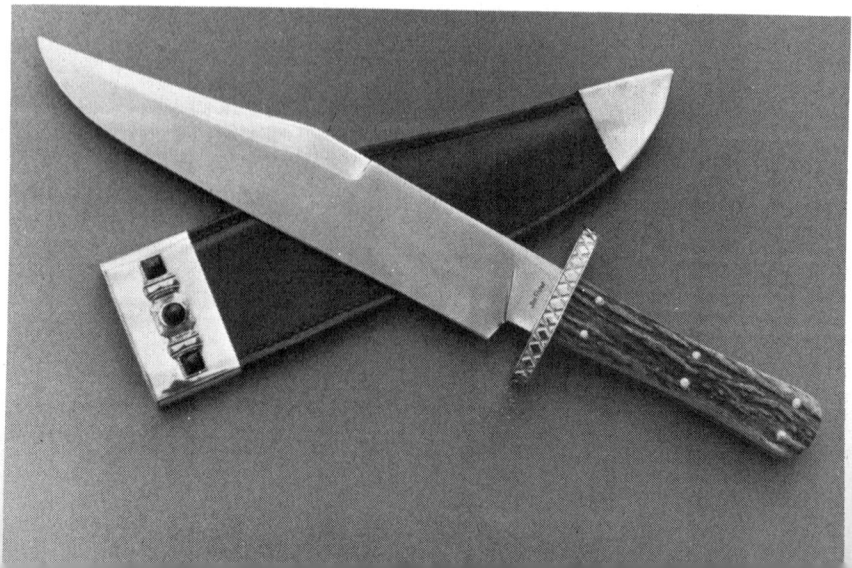

That's a 10-inch blade, so this Jim Fister knife not only looks massive, it is massive.

BOWIES
Classic Bowies

This is a 20th century Bowie with a solid riverboat look to it by Ron Frazier.

Fred Slee's crown stag Bowie is at the very centerline of classic styling for stag. (Weyer photo)

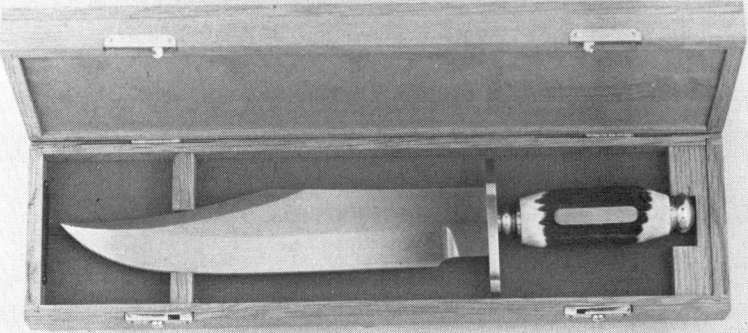

(Left) Jimmy Lile also knows how to make big-looking Bowies in the no-fooling Iron Mistress look.

This simple Sheffield style by Lanny Hartman is in ivory Micarta, nickel silver, at 12½ inches overall.

Dwight Towell does an elegant Mediterranean pre-Bowie in Damascus. (Weyer photo)

EIGHTH ANNUAL EDITION **49**

BOWIES
Modern Bowies

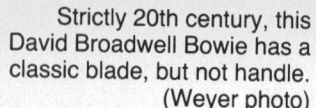

Strictly 20th century, this David Broadwell Bowie has a classic blade, but not handle. (Weyer photo)

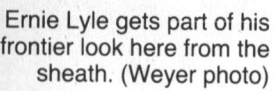

Ernie Lyle gets part of his frontier look here from the sheath. (Weyer photo)

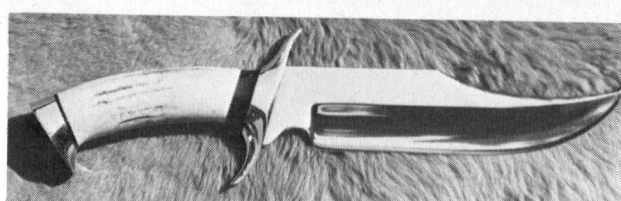

Racy 10-inch Bowie by Gordon Grebe is lots bigger than it looks here.

Raymond Cover's straightforward slim blade with crown stag and a touch or two brings the Bowie right up to now.

This nice big Joseph Keeslar Bowie has curly maple and silver wire and its very own shape. (Weyer photo)

Jim Crowell's simple clip-point shows how the Bowie can do what its designer wants. (Weyer photo)

Harold Pierce reinterpreted the idea of the backwoods blacksmith Bowie to come up with this biggie—it has a 14-inch blade. (Weyer photo)

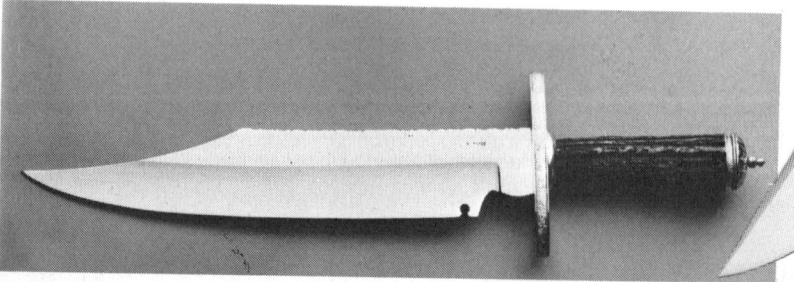

Don Fogg made this 8-inch Bowie type with modern shape, but a timeless look. (Weyer photo)

Gents' Bowies
BOWIES

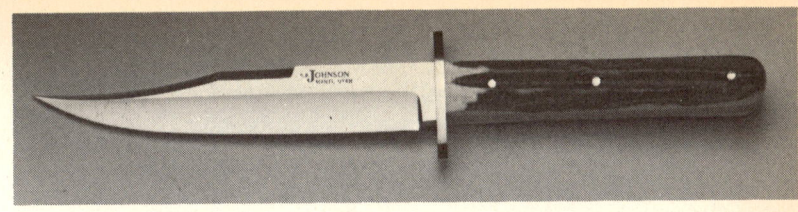

(Right) Severe IXL styling was followed for this Steve Johnson Bowie with 5-inch blade. (Weyer photo)

Charlie Weiss committed another small classic in this 7½-inch Bowie engraved by Franz Marktl. (Weyer photo)

Steve Brooks got a lot of maiden hair pattern into this 6-inch Bowie, handled it in ivory.

Team work put this Bowie together. Butch Beaver made the blade and after Jim Sornberger engraved it, Judy Beaver did the handle. (Weyer photo)

Lee Ferguson made this big Bowie hunter and engraved it himself. (Weyer photo)

(Right) Mike Leach likes this Bowie of his very well, borrowed from the San Francisco cutlers for his style. (Weyer photo)

This small classic by Ken Ward has ivory scales and a 6½-inch blade. (Weyer photo)

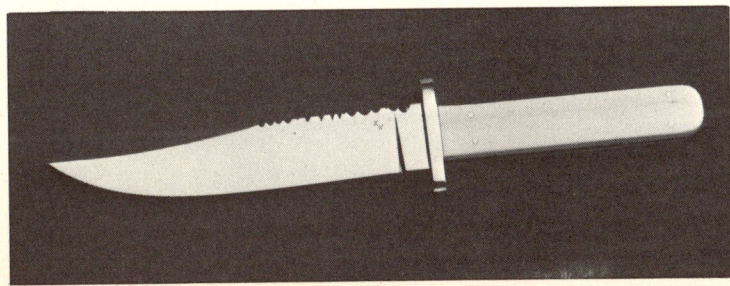

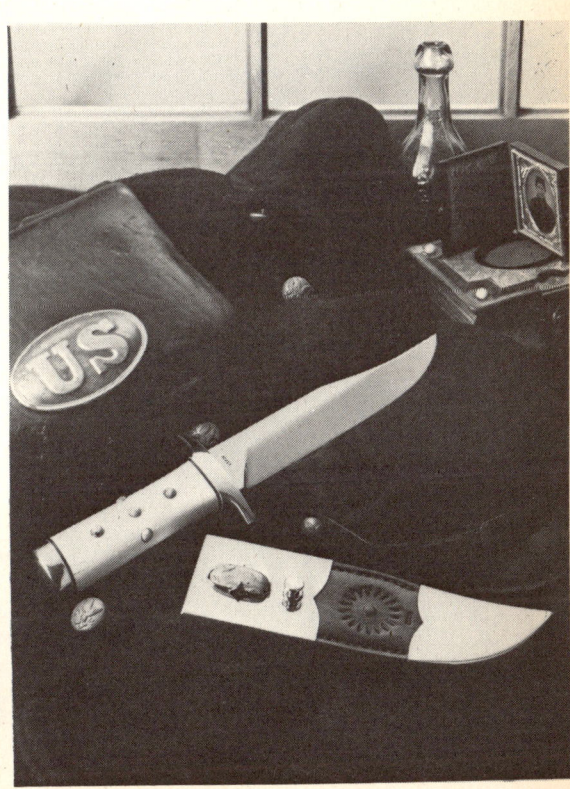

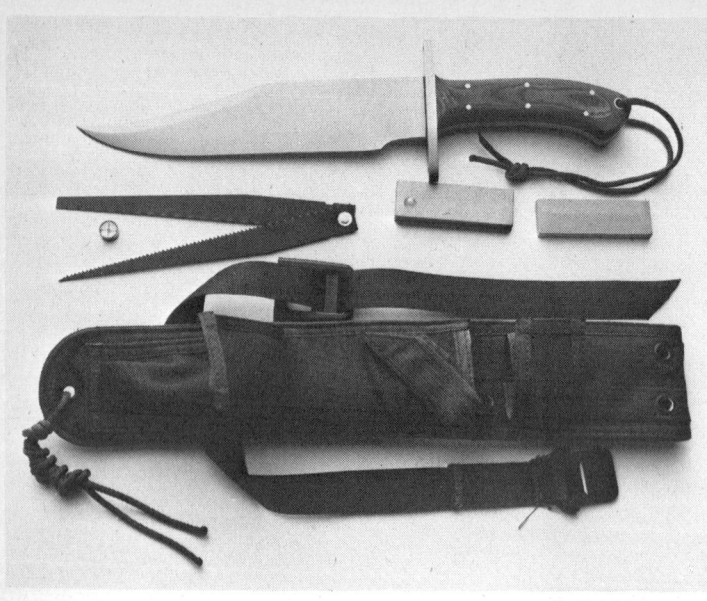

John Wagaman of North Carolina builds a subhilt into his broad-bladed Bowie.

Steve Allen does the survival Bowie like this, sensibly includes saws, compass, fire starters as sheath baggage. (Weyer photo)

(Below) Yes, there is a "survival" Bowie and this is Ralph Dewey Harris' version with 10½-inch stock.

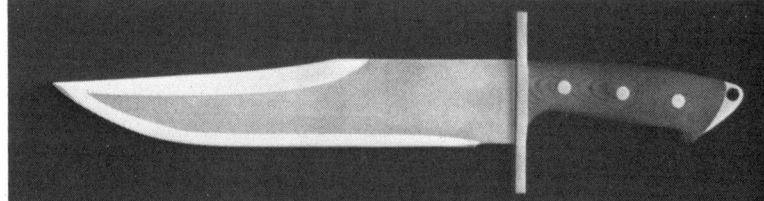

BOWIES
Today's Working Bowies

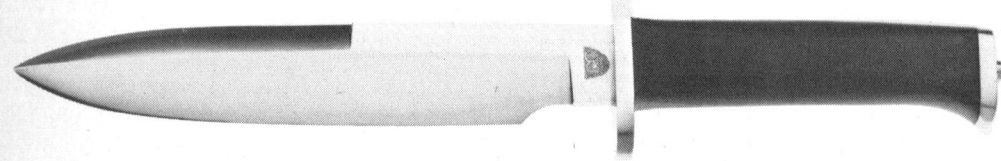

Dan Maragni calls this a "big spear point," builds it tough. (Weyer photo)

Walter Erickson's mildly wild Bowie offers fencer grip, blade-catcher guard and an inlaid Celtic cross. (Weyer photo)

Tarheel James Wade works the Iron Mistress shape with modern combat styling to get this Bowie. (Surles photo)

52 KNIVES '88

TRENDS
MOVIE KNIVES

KNIFEMAKERS hungry for publicity and film makers hungry for gimmicks have found each other over the past several years with that intensity normally reserved for relationships between boys and girls. While the fad lasts, there are going to be a lot of movie knives.

Normally, a movie knife is a collaboration between the requirements of the script, the possibilities of the knifemakers' talents and the perceptions of the movie director and, often enough, the principal star. Sometimes, however, a knife becomes a movie knife somewhat accidentally.

One knifemaker was startled in a movie theater to discover that the knife he had just seen thrown into a miscreant's chest was one of his—he had made it. He was mildly upset because it was a very nice folding knife and not really intended for such shenanigans, however nicely filmed. Also, he didn't get a credit.

Several fellows are making rather a specialty of getting credits, notable among them Jimmy Lile, Jack Crain, and Gil Hibben. Two fellows who specialize in knife-using protagonist roles are Sylvester Stallone and Arnold Schwarzenegger. Their movies have spawned more clones and away we have gone.

There have come to be, of all things, knives intended for movies yet unborn. Apparently, one interests a movie person and hopes. You will see here a set of knives with handles made especially large so they will fit Sylvester Stallone's hands.

Meanwhile, over on the tube, McGyver is doing wonders with his Swiss Army knife and it is possible sometimes to catch that particular James Bond movie where the redoubtable spy—played by one of several what's-his-names—slips a couple of little knives out of a briefcase and fends off a villain permanently during an epic struggle in a European train compartment. It may be that same movie which features a remarkably ugly lady from the local KGB office with poison-tipped blades in her shoes.

The most interesting thing about movie knives in this changing world is their effect on sales. No doubt the fellow who made the Iron Mistress that Alan Ladd flourished in the movie of the same name sold a few knives as a result. Now, in our new world which seizes new things exponentially in steeper and steeper and quicker and quicker curves, a single movie can found a knifemaking industry. Rambo knives are the chief latterday examples, but there have been and probably will be others.

How far will it all go? Well, possibly farther than hula hoops, but certainly not the distance of the Model 1911 Colt semi-automatic 45-caliber pistol. Indeed, they say out there that the hollow-handled knife has about run its course. Some fellows who own low-numbered Rambo knives have been seen hawking them at lower-than-expected prices.

With typical showbiz attention to historical and technical truth, we can expect movie knives to rise to the level of that famous snub-nosed revolver with its silencer which appears again and again in detective flicks, but we cannot hope movie knives will reach the pinnacle represented by the use of 1892 Winchester carbines in films about the Civil War. Regardless of all that, to the extent that they stimulate knife sales and create a market, knifemakers are all for movie knives. Why not?

Ken Warner

In these scenes from the movie *Predator*, we see the several designs of Jack Crain, prepared especially for the movie. Frost Cutlery has become the source for authorized replicas of these through an arrangement with Crain. (Photos courtesy of 20th Century Fox)

This hard-nosed fighter by Chuck Stapel was given to singer-actor-movie production executive Kenny Rogers at a concert—maybe yet another bid for movie knife stardom? (Fitzgerald photo)

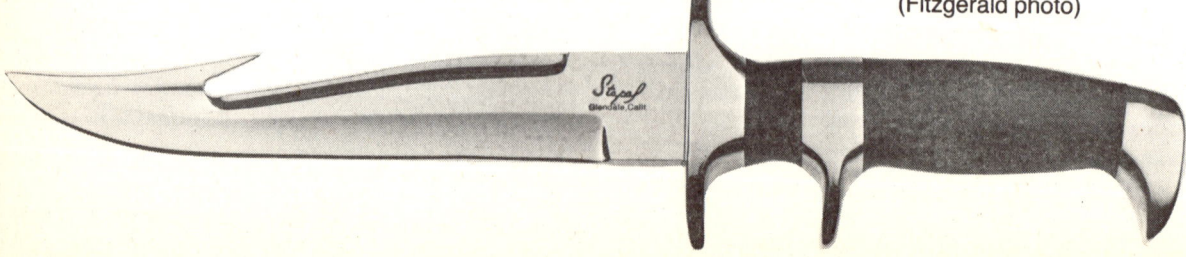

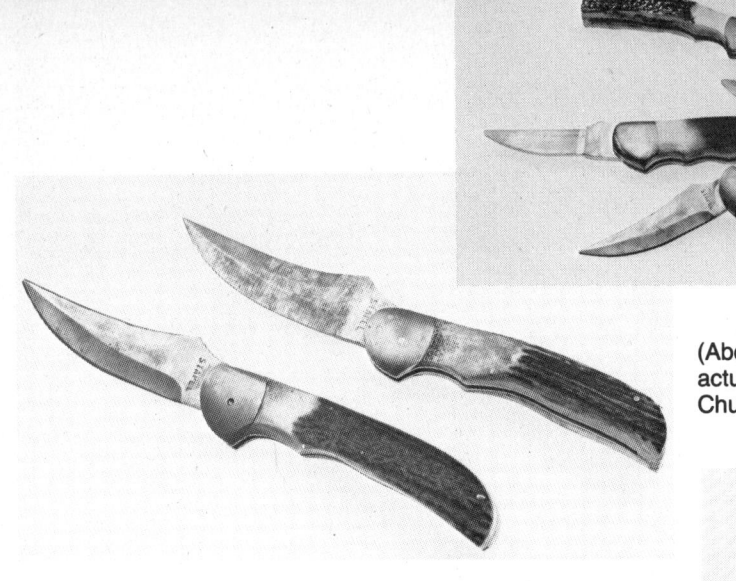

(Above, below and left) These are "real" movie knives, the actual implements filmed for *No Mercy* with Richard Gere. Chuck Stapel made them. (Fitzgerald photos)

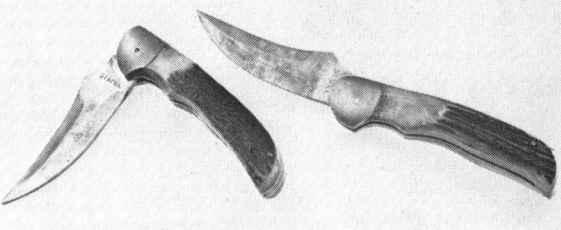

(Below right and below) These are knives made for a movie unscripted and undeveloped, except by knifemaker Doug Sontheimer, who presented them to Sylvester Stallone.

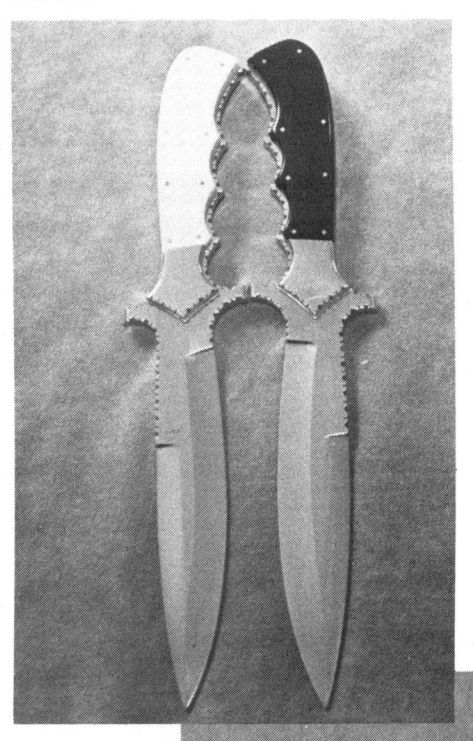

(Above and right) Joe Candrella made the gavel knife plotted into a *Hardcastle and McCormick* segment. Judge Hardcastle—Brian Keith—shows it off.

EIGHTH ANNUAL EDITION **55**

TRENDS
THE WORKING STRAIGHT EDGE

IT WOULD NOT be entirely correct to say that a vast tide of public apathy has arisen on behalf of the somewhat curious working straight edge pattern, but it would not be true to say it has shown anything like the early appeal of the ubiquitous tanto. It would seem the straight-edged knife with the fine point is to be an acquired taste if it is a taste at all to the American knife buying public.

That does not mean, in the opinion of your reporter, that the straight edge is not both interesting and useful as knife patterns go. Apart from the six or eight reported last year, a few more have been sent along here, and a great many more are noticed out on the tables at knife shows. This is particularly true of a form of a folding knife blade called the Wharncliffe. Further, knifemakers tell me the Wharncliffe sells very well *whenever* it is put into a handmade folder. That should not be surprising since it sold very well whenever it was put into a folder any time in the last 150 or 180 years.

So august a presence as Robert W. Loveless sent along his version, a very robust near-camp-sized straight-edge which is a very attractive belt tool for the outdoorsman. Like any straight edge, Loveless' can really get into a cut.

Semi-Viking D.E. Weiler sent along the smallest of scramasaxes or a nifty Northland boot knife. Regardless, it has the fine point and the straight edge and it works very well, so it's a working pattern.

Those, and the others that have come forth or have been seen, are most welcome, but it is quite obvious that this particular Rome is not going to be built in a day, or even a year. Your reporter has not yet come to believe the American working straight edge is an answer in search of a question, nor does he believe it a solution to a problem that doesn't exist. Still, the idea of 4 or 5 or 6 straight inches of edge is not usual, and so it may be a while before every catalog has to have one.

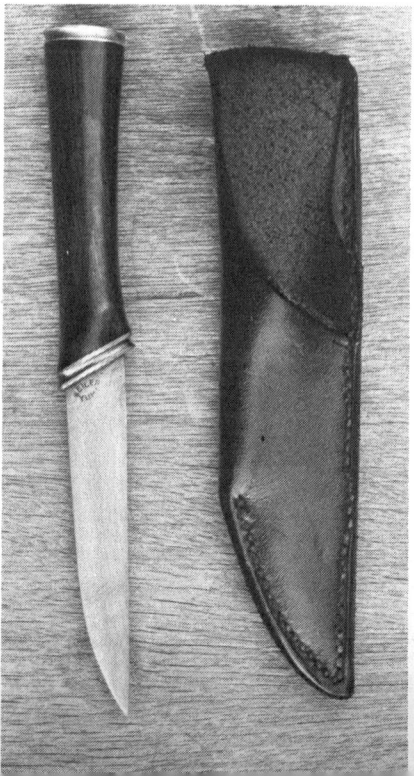

This Don Weiler small sax is a very comfortable knife. Sharp, too. (Warner photo)

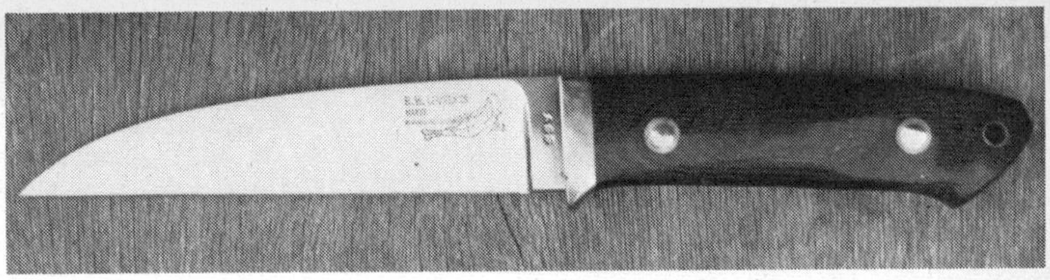

Bob Loveless provided the serial number here—ASS—to stand for "American Standard Straight," he said, and it goes with the rear view of the logo lady real well. (Warner photo)

James J. Barry's yachtsman's special is a broad working straight edge.

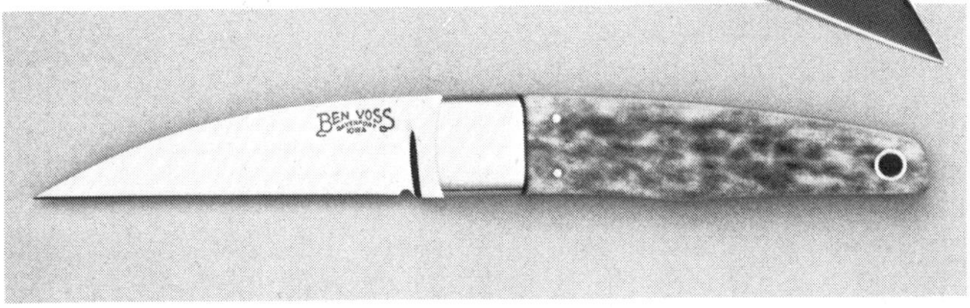

Ben Voss sees the working straight edge as a small utility knife and makes it that way.

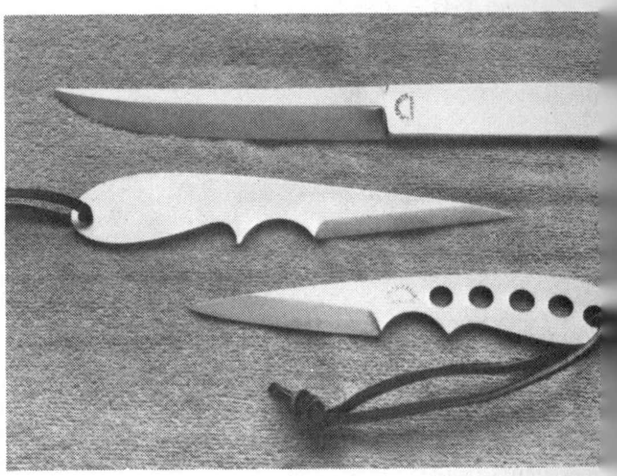

L.M. Erickson's backpackers include very useful straight-edged patterns.

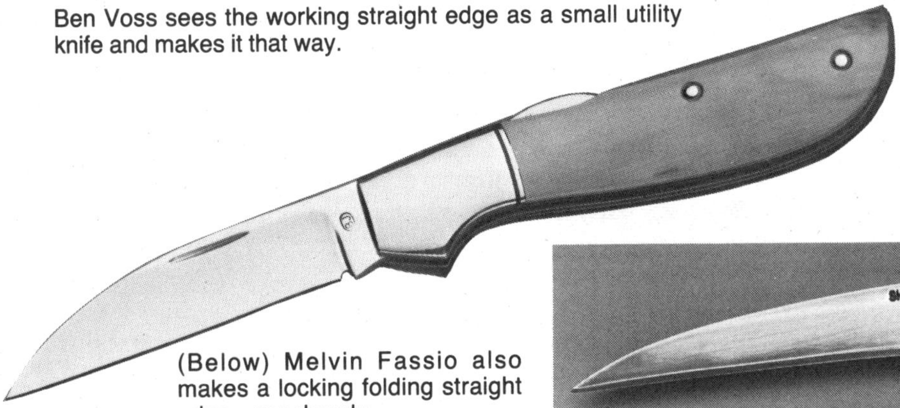

Bob Jones has made this sort of handsome Wharncliffe pattern for years. (Weyer photo)

(Below) Melvin Fassio also makes a locking folding straight edge—very handy.

Shiva Ki made this handsome knife last year, and finally this photo does it justice. (Weyer photo)

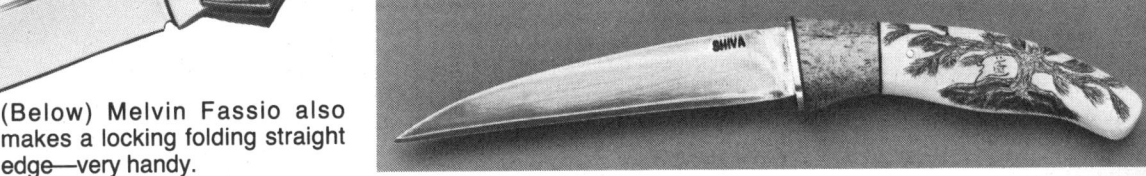

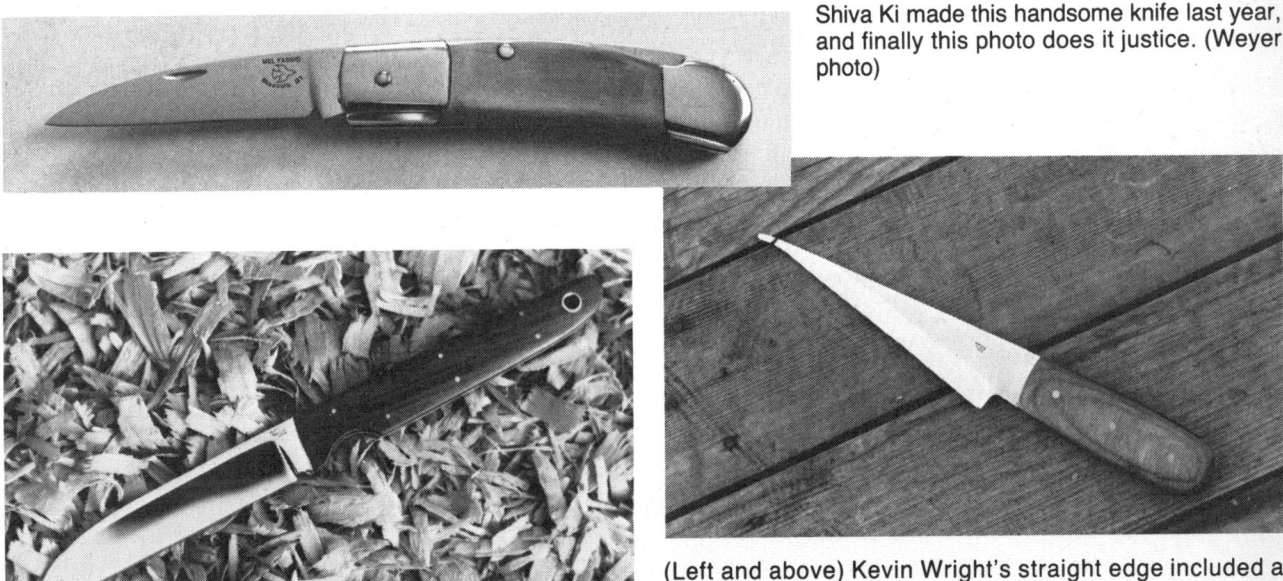

(Left and above) Kevin Wright's straight edge included a sheep's-foot utility knife and his personal butchering tool used on rabbits and deer equally well.

EIGHTH ANNUAL EDITION

TRENDS
STRAIGHT STANDARDS

IF THERE has been a change in straight knives since last reported on here last year, it has been in the direction of increased competence on the part of knifemakers both in constructing a knife and in presenting it in photos and personally. They are getting doggoned slick out there, people.

This year, we split off the Bowies because there are an awful lot of Bowies. The rest of the mainstays of the custom knife business—hunters, fighters and boots, daggers, camp knives and tantos—are here. Taken all together, this selection of straight knives may be the most handsome such selection ever presented.

The well-done hunters stay with us. They are not only neatly made, but they are more sophisticated than in the past. The plain truth seems to be that there have been general-purpose hunting knives of entirely useful design for hunters for years; it is, really, only in specially-adapted designs or highly-finished work that a knifemaker can twist out his own special mark or design style.

So, we have hunters with somewhat changed detailing again this time. You will see them in both regular steels and in pattern Damascus and such as that. With the advent of commercial Damascus bar stock in plentiful supply, it gets pointless to differentiate on the basis of the steel used. Bear in mind there will still be a price difference to go with the visual difference.

It does seem as if, in contrast to hunters, the tanto design is standardizing itself. First, there is the "real" or close-to-samurai tanto, which is simply the big knife of the Japanese gentry of years gone by. Second, there is the tanto specialized as a hard-duty knife, sort of a tanto pry bar. Third, there is the tanto as hunter. (There is at least one knowledgeable person in the business who claims that the typical tanto, with the angular point now seen, was actually a pattern used by the Japanese to skin eels. A knifemaking trapper of my acquaintance says there is nothing like a small tanto for skinning beaver. At any rate, a tanto as a hunter is definitely with us.) And fourth, there is the stylized and Americanized tanto as an expression of good looks in a knife, those good looks depending entirely on the knifemaker's own tastes.

There are, in short, tantos for just about everyone, but they are toning down the wildness, finally. It has been interesting, the past 5 or 6 years, watching the tanto as a knife design get wildly improvised to the point where this reporter would not have been surprised to see a tanto sickle. It has not, however, come to that path.

Fighters and boots have settled down as well. Each is separated into two categories—the tough-duty working-finish knife, and all the others, including some very fancy knives indeed. This reporter hesitates to admit that he thinks of them in terms of enlisted men's knives and officers' knives, but to an extent that is how it is. Since there are a lot more enlisted men than there are officers, the working-dress fighters are doing very well in the marketplace.

(cont'd. page 76)

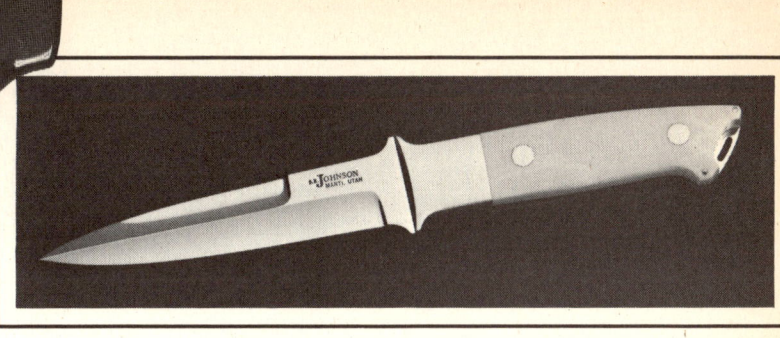

The minimized classic by Steve Johnson has just enough in all the right places. (Weyer photo)

The chute knife is supposed to look exactly like this new one by Jimmy Lile. It's a rule.

STRAIGHT STANDARDS
Classic Fighters

This big clean fighter by William Garner is not like the old classics, but it looks as if it ought to be. (Long photo)

This Stanley Fujisaka fighter belies its size—it's 15 inches overall—with its subtle lines. (Kojima photo)

David McDearmont's family of fighters are each different and each related. (Weyer photo)

G.W. Stone is back and here he is with the stout and clean fighters he always made, now with Jim Erickson.

This short Goltz fighter has a rosewood handle and clean lines. (Weyer photo)

Composite of interframe and full tang design seem to make sense in this big fighter by Frans Van Eldik of the Netherlands.

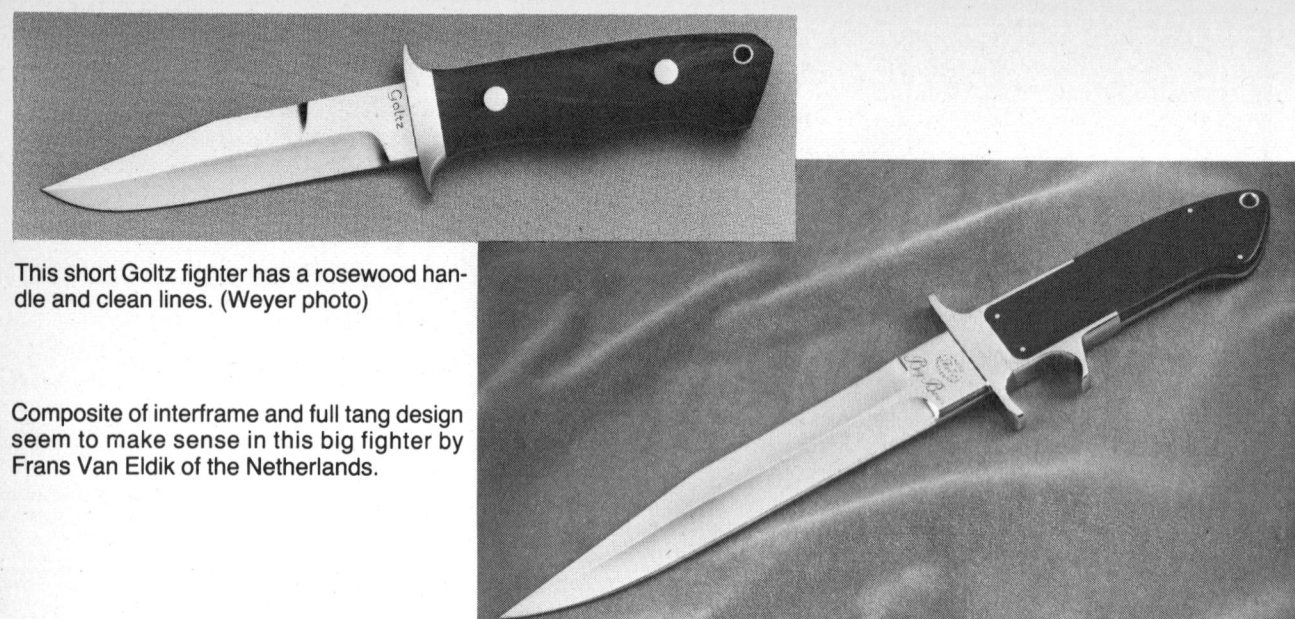

A big Al Faulkner knife has the right profile, careful quillons and black Micarta.

STRAIGHT STANDARDS
Classic Fighters

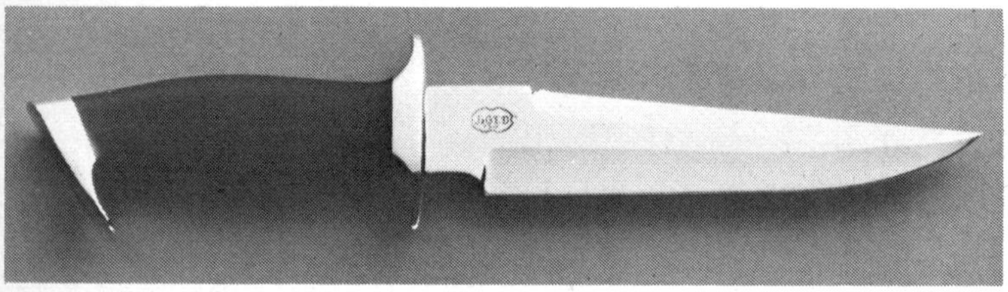

Eager Greg Smith blade shape defines a classic fighter, which Smith calls the "Colonel's Bowie." (Weyer photo)

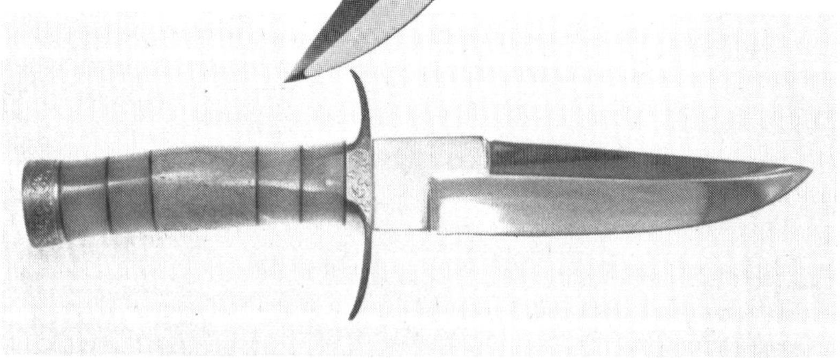

Somewhat dressy Bill Amoureux fighter is big—has a 7-inch blade. Engraving is by George Sherwood, the handle has oosic and amber.

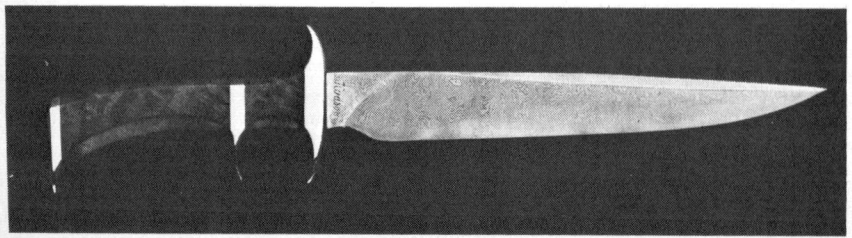

Damascus and a subhilt and burl walnut often mean Robbin Hudson and so it is here in this 8½-inch bladed fighter. (Weyer photo)

William Wood's Persian sort of fighter in 440C and burl walnut offers eagles and mountains by Bruce Shaw.

Chris Dahl's pair of full-tang dressy fighters show off lots of engraving. (Weyer photo)

R.D. Nolen here hits two licks on behalf of the genuinely fancy fighter, your choice of ivory or cocobolo. (Weyer photo)

STRAIGHT STANDARDS
Fancy Fighters

Dave Morton's engraving dresses up Bob Papp's handsome guardless fighter. (Weyer photo)

The classic shape, with continental touches, by D. F. Kressler is embellished with ivory and first class engraving. (Weyer photo)

Pat Tomes' slim and stylish fighter is engraved and boxed by Jon Robyn. (Weyer photo)

E.J. Hendrickson's forged duty knife is severely plain and practical. (Traynor photo)

This heavy-duty knife, dull-finished for business, is by William Harsey for Al Mar and is called "Shiva."

STRAIGHT STANDARDS
Utility Fighters

Colin Cox thinks a fighter should look tough and this Tefloned sample certainly does. (Weyer photo)

(Below) This is Edmond Davidson's heavy all-integral fighter of S-7 steel. (Scadlock photo)

Robert Parrish made this flat full-sized fighter for the fellow who needs minimum bulk to come out of a sheath quick.

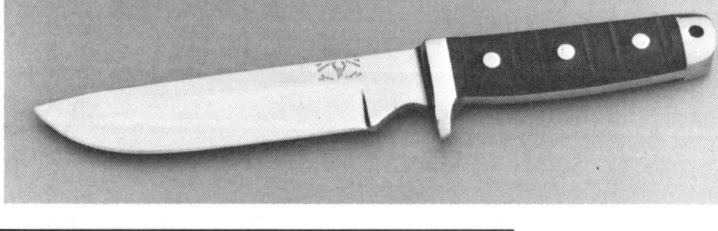

These are utility-class knives for Shiva Ki who intends them for serious use. (Scadlock photo)

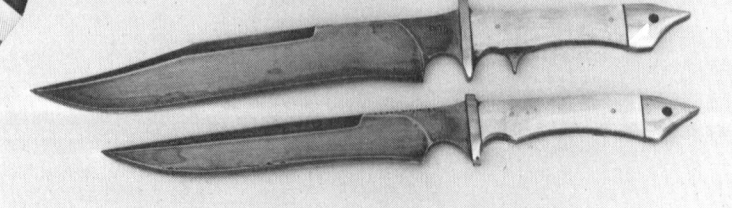

Jim Fuller now makes plain and simple fighters to go with his moderately priced hunters. (Weyer photo)

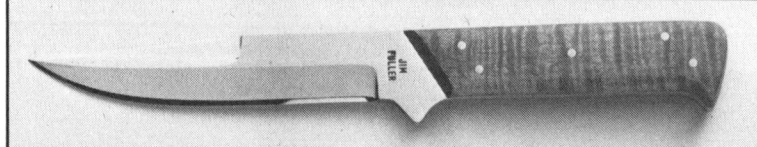

Ron Lake presents his clearly defined line in a classic double-edged fighter in stag. (Weyer photo)

Charles Ochs makes a standard fighter as a no-nonsense double-edge, forged in 5160 steel.

Steve Allen's one-piece double-edges are minimum bulk or concealment knives. (Weyer photo)

STRAIGHT STANDARDS
Double-Edged Fighters

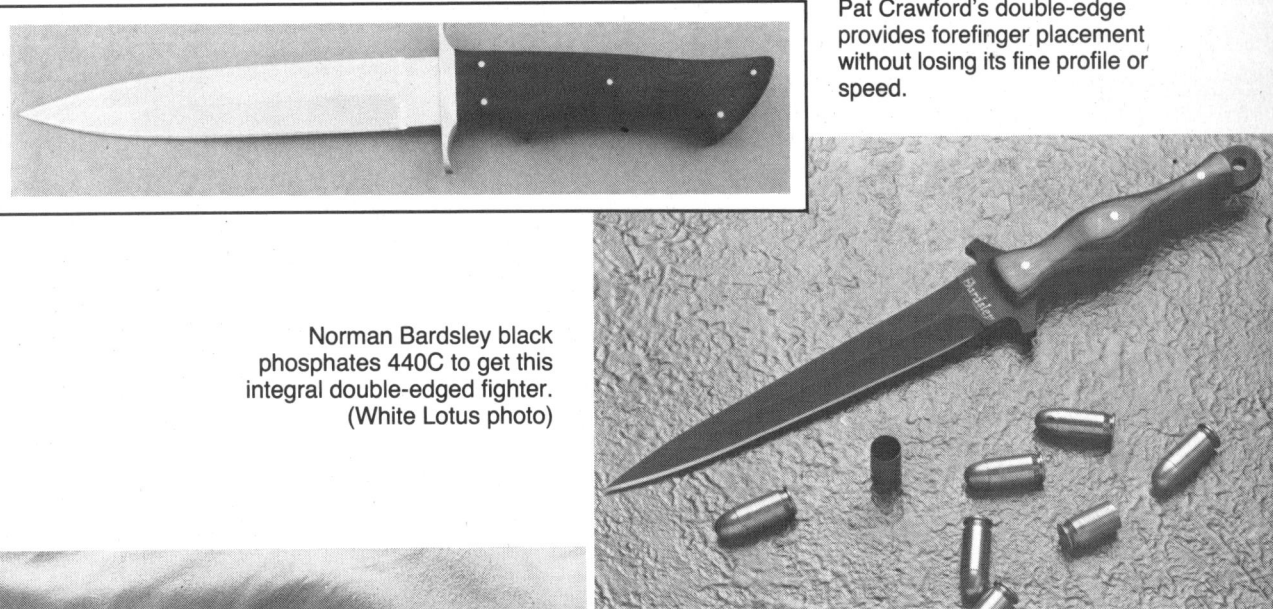

Pat Crawford's double-edge provides forefinger placement without losing its fine profile or speed.

Norman Bardsley black phosphates 440C to get this integral double-edged fighter. (White Lotus photo)

C.A. Jones grinds this double-convex fighter—note there is no spine—from 5/32-inch 01 steel.

STRAIGHT STANDARDS
Boot Knives

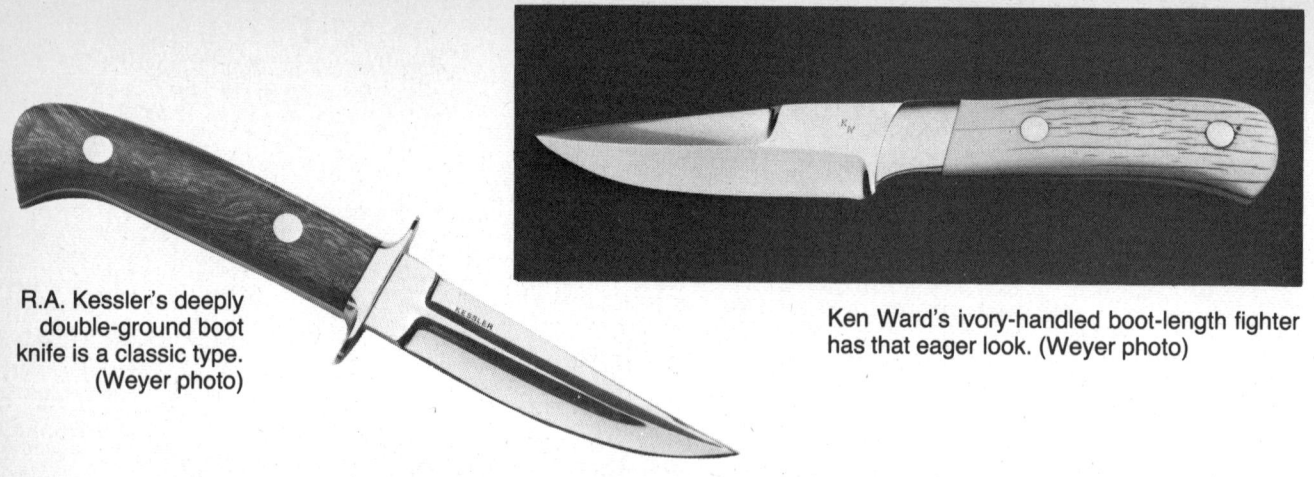

R.A. Kessler's deeply double-ground boot knife is a classic type. (Weyer photo)

Ken Ward's ivory-handled boot-length fighter has that eager look. (Weyer photo)

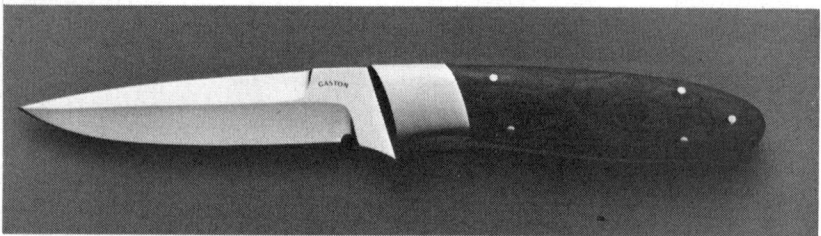

Ron Gaston gets a lot of thrust into his boot knife in ATS34 and ironwood. (Weyer photo)

Slim stag boot knife by Tommy Lee in Damascus has the look of gentry. (Scadlock photo)

William Keeton's short-bladed boot knife offers plenty of hand grip.

Ben Voss says this is a utility boot, or "sort of a sgian dubh," and so it is.

STRAIGHT STANDARDS
Utility Hunters

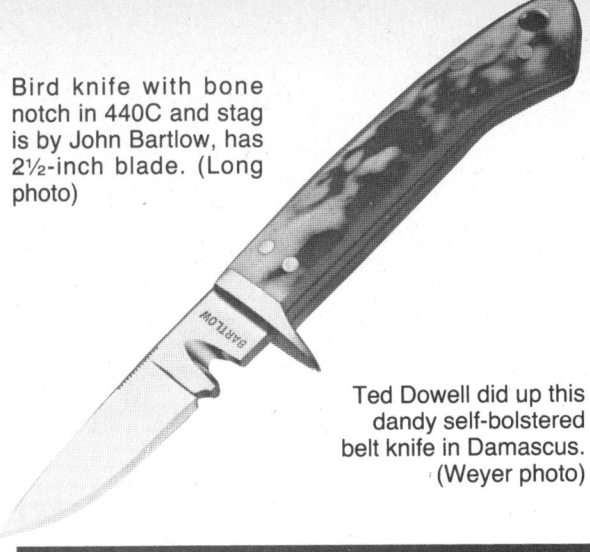

Bird knife with bone notch in 440C and stag is by John Bartlow, has 2½-inch blade. (Long photo)

Ted Dowell did up this dandy self-bolstered belt knife in Damascus. (Weyer photo)

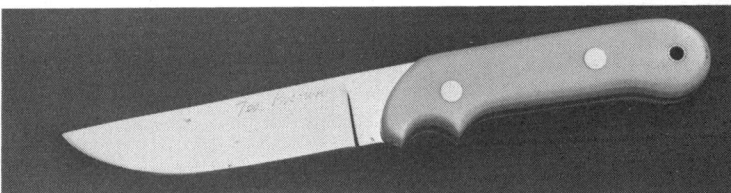

This is a very clean-lined, easy-to-sheath profile in 440C and Micarta by Ted Brown. (Weyer photo)

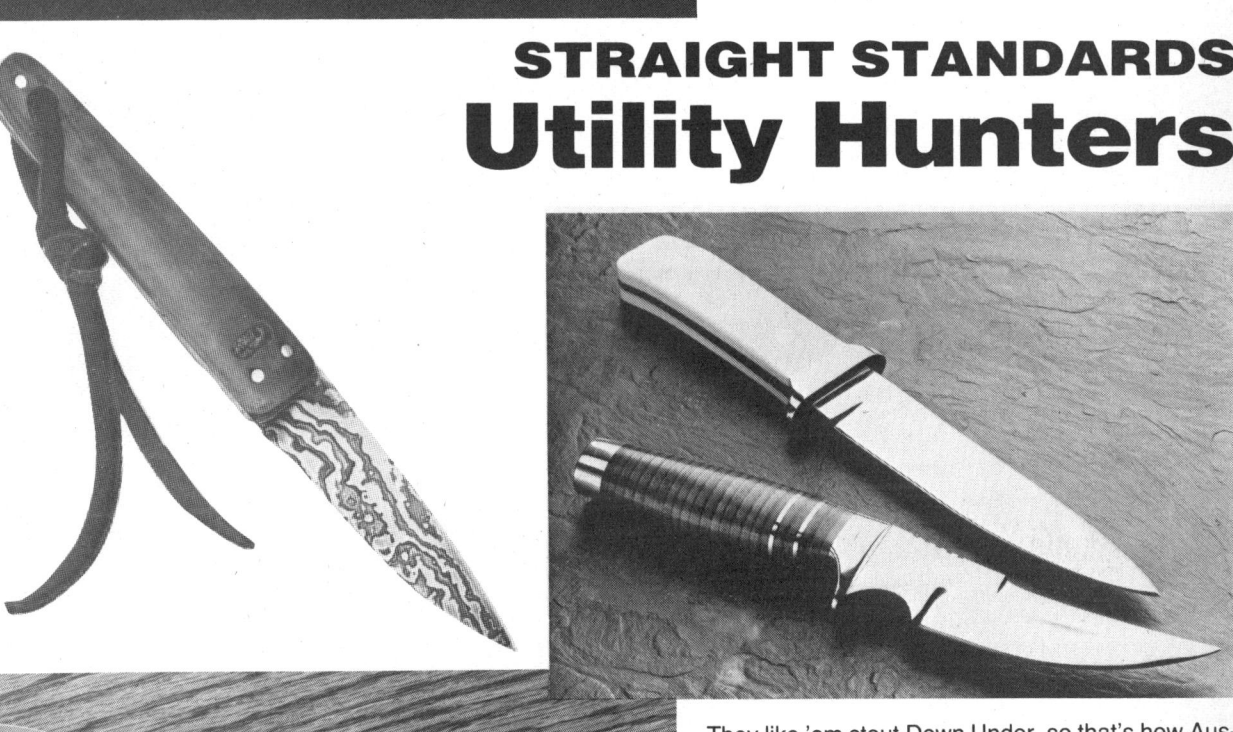

They like 'em stout Down Under, so that's how Aussie Peter Brown furnishes them.

(Above left) Plain-Jane caper by Shiva Ki in Damascus will ride in a pocket sheath around town, too. (Scadlock photo)

(Left) This straight spearpoint will do about all of it. It's by D.B. Brown.

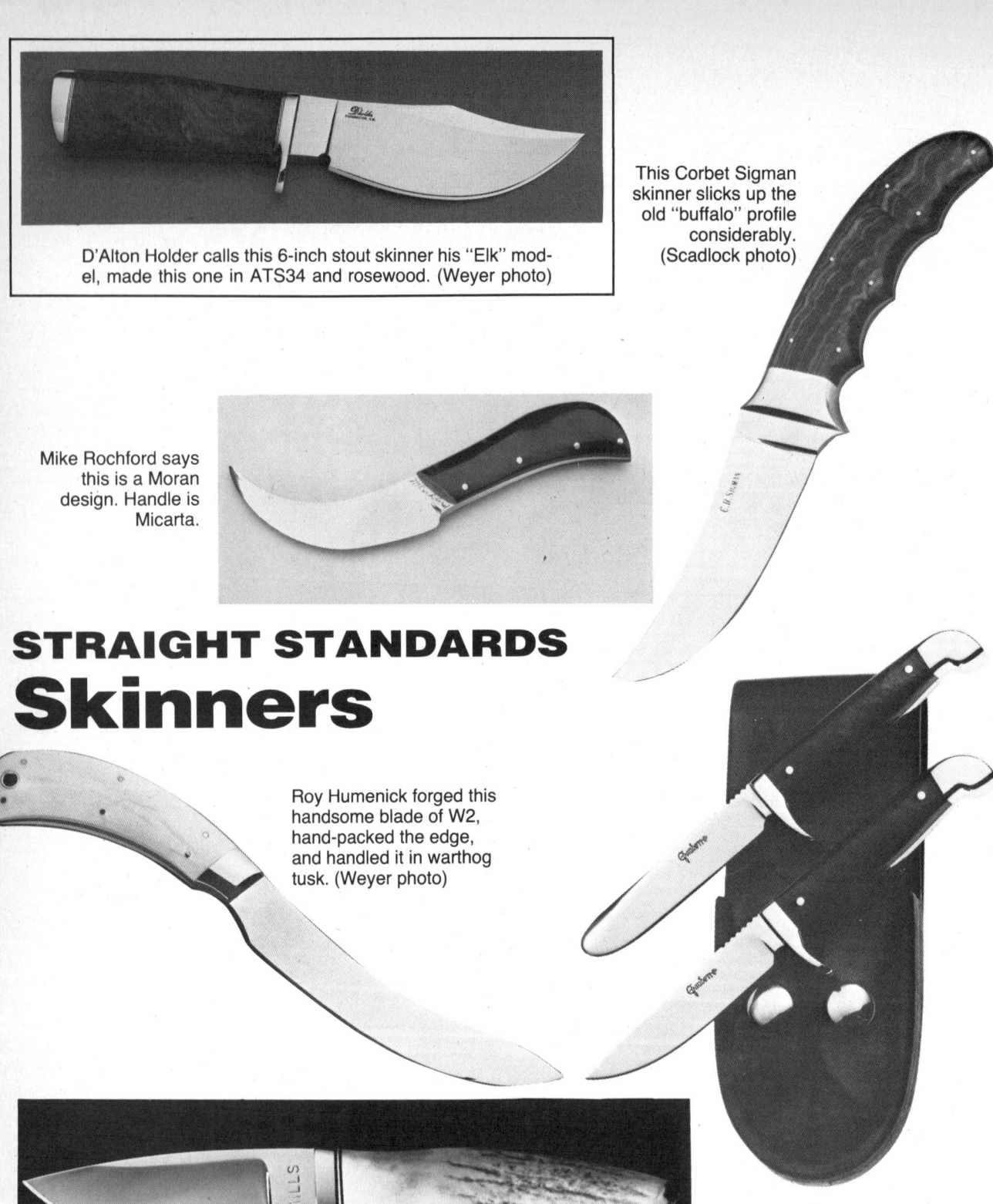

D'Alton Holder calls this 6-inch stout skinner his "Elk" model, made this one in ATS34 and rosewood. (Weyer photo)

This Corbet Sigman skinner slicks up the old "buffalo" profile considerably. (Scadlock photo)

Mike Rochford says this is a Moran design. Handle is Micarta.

STRAIGHT STANDARDS
Skinners

Roy Humenick forged this handsome blade of W2, hand-packed the edge, and handled it in warthog tusk. (Weyer photo)

Caper-skinner set is from Lin Gaudette in ATS34 and ironwood burl. (Weyer photo)

This heavy Andy Mills skinner is his Model M-4, has an Axis deer handle.

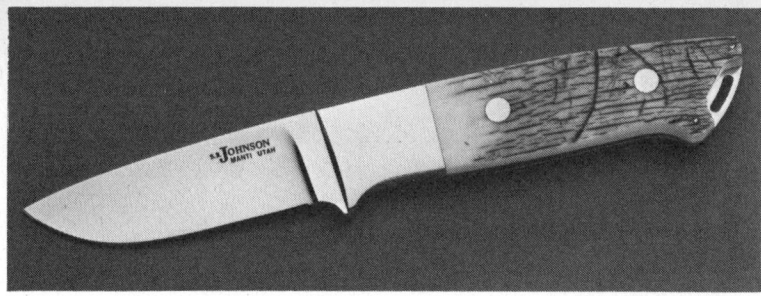

Bark ivory and stainless fittings and ATS34 are all it takes for Steve Johnson to make a classic. (Weyer photo)

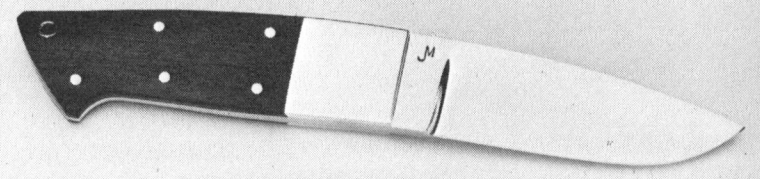

This Jeff C. Morgan bolstered drop-point has partridge wood scales. (Scadlock photo)

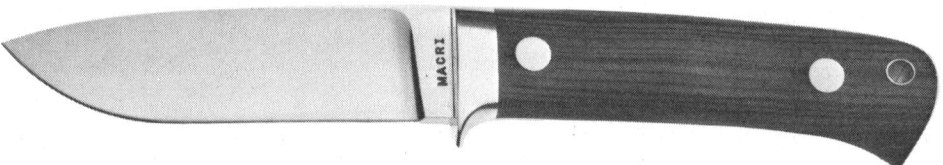

This is another classic (read "Loveless") drop-point profile by Mike Macri. (Weyer photo)

STRAIGHT STANDARDS
Drop-Point Hunters

Mike Yurco's working drop-point is nearly a knuckle knife.

A little more push on the drop-point theme can get you this profile in ATS34 by Charles B. Bolton. (Weyer photo)

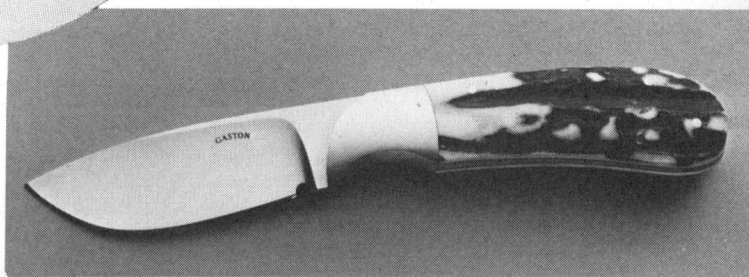

Broad drop-point or drop-point skinner? Either way, Ron Gaston made it with a 3-inch blade of ATS34. (Weyer photo)

STRAIGHT STANDARDS
Fancy Hunters

This integral nickel silver guard and pommel are all the fancy this Fielder skinner needs. (Grout photo)

This is Ralph Turnbull's birdhead grip in snakewood on a semi-skinner. (Long photo)

Steven Rapp made this hunter fancy with line and curve—and some *very* nice stag antler. (Weyer photo)

Jim Ence forged his own Damascus for this short skinner, had Rick Fields scrim the ivory. (Weyer photo)

Wire-wrapped handles are neat on his swords, so why not on a hunter by Tom Maringer? (Ver Hoeven photo)

Mick Koval went for fancy here with ivory and engraving and an initial plate. (Weyer photo)

STRAIGHT STANDARDS
Classic Daggers

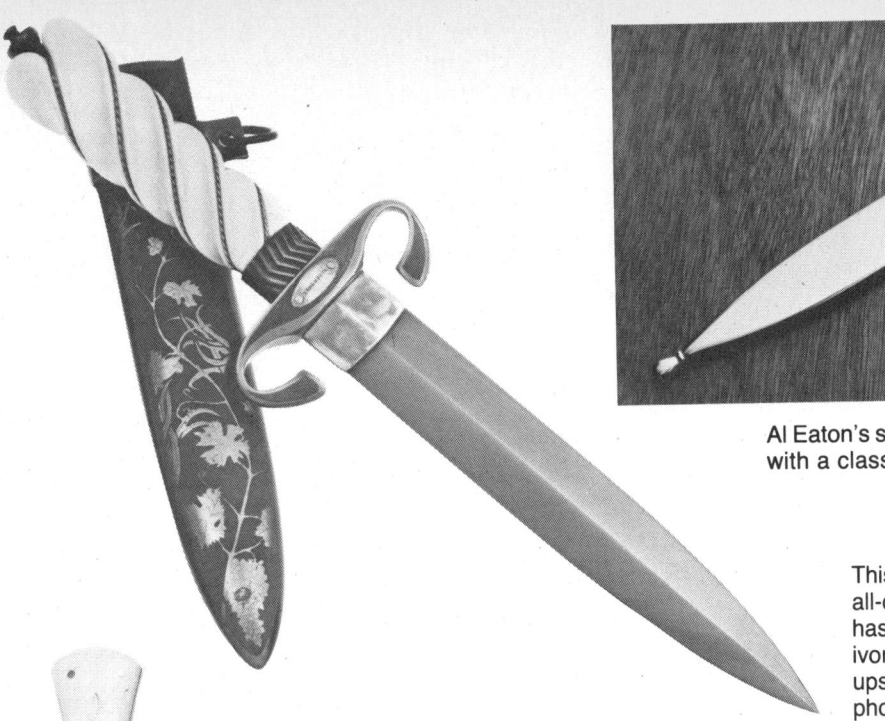

Al Eaton's small dagger is provided with a classy nickel-silver sheath.

This Dave Longworth all-out deluxe dagger has hot-blued steel, ivory, etching—very upscale. (Scadlock photo)

Tommy Lee has a classic straight Eastern dagger here in ivory, gold and Damascus. (Weyer photo)

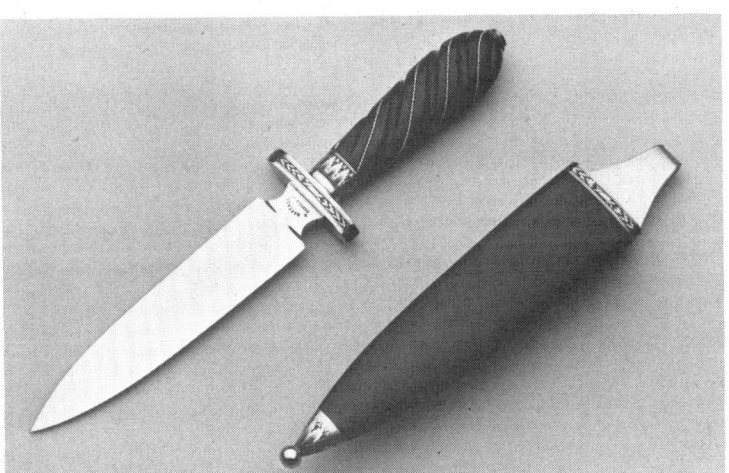

Buster Warenski does both handle and sheath very well indeed. He engraves his own. (Klinefelter photo)

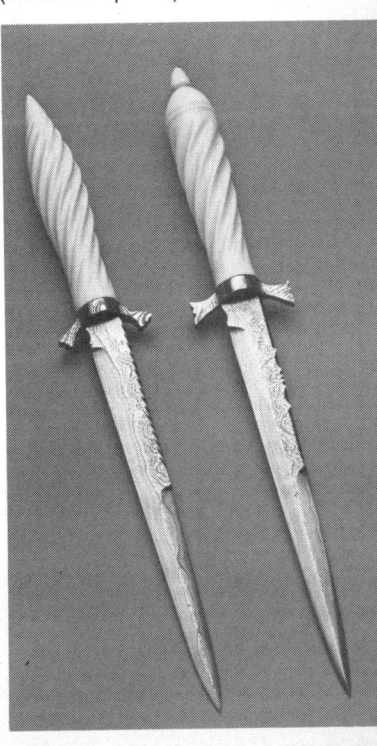

This pair of Sid Birt Damascus daggers are not twins. (Weyer photo)

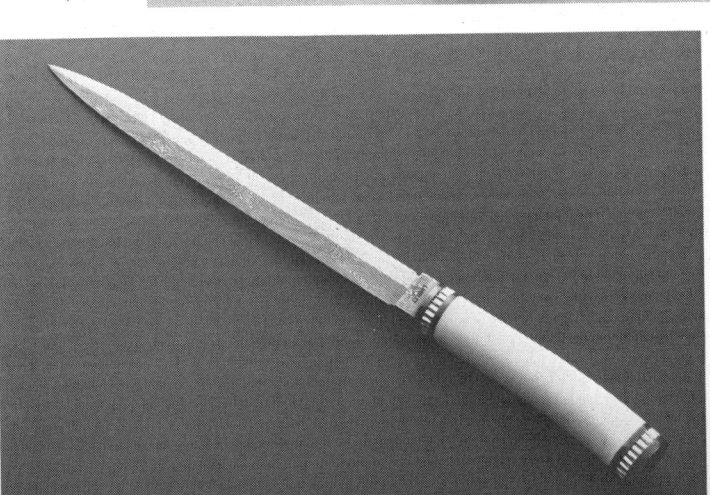

Mick Langley polished stag for the handle, added blue steel, nickel silver and a Damascus blade for a classic look. (Weyer photo)

STRAIGHT STANDARDS
Esthetic Daggers

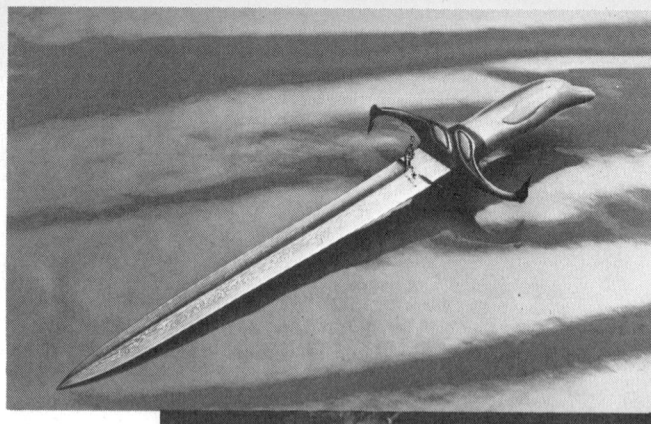

A creative Kemal dagger with a porpoise, this straightforward blade is no fluke, though its quillons are. (Weyer photo)

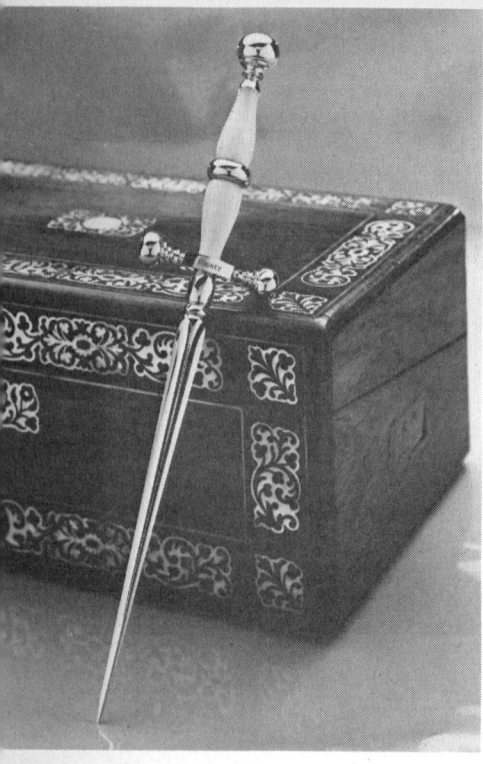

Extra-careful grinding of the fluted blade and plain and simple ivory make this Willie Rigney stiletto very artistic. (Weyer photo)

This out-of-the-ordinary dagger is by Doug Casteel in 440C. (Long photo)

This is an integral interframe stiletto by Billy Mace Imel, engraved by R.E. Skaggs. (Weyer photo)

Relative newcomer Wolf Loerchner demonstrates he has found the handles and a good engraver—Martin Butler. (Weyer photo)

This fanciful Damascus curved dagger by Sid Birt was scrimmed by Skaggs. (Weyer photo)

STRAIGHT STANDARDS
Esthetic Daggers

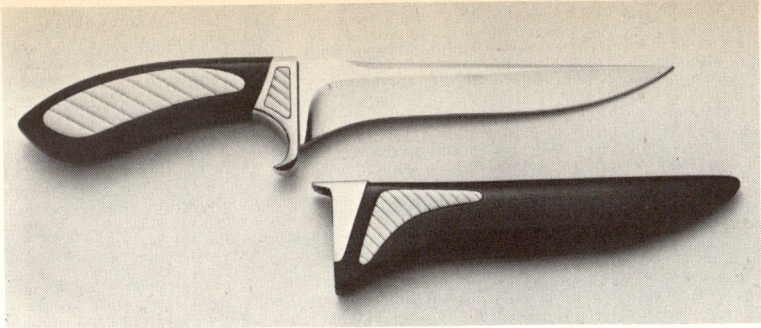

Butch Beaver says this is a Persian fighter. It's in blackwood with ivory inlay. (Weyer photo)

Steve Jernigan does his Persian fighter with a mosaic handle in Italian *smalti* tiles. (Weyer photo)

Scott Lankton's blade and Barbara Cricchio's handle make a right nice Viking knife. (Weyer photo)

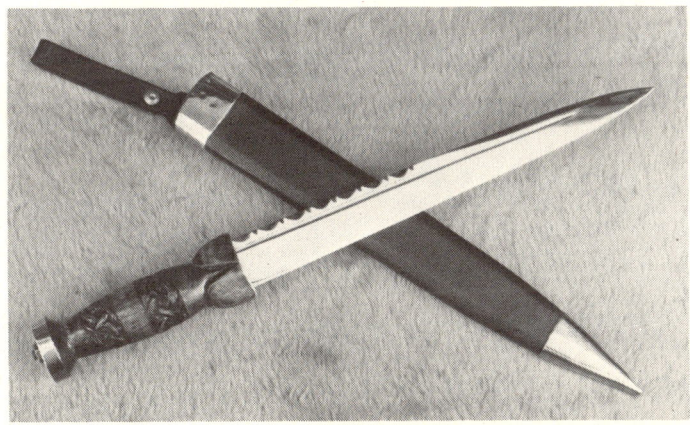

This Jacobite dirk by Vincent Evans is in 5160 steel trimmed in brass.

Water buffalo on one and impala on the other keep these Mid-Eastern profiles from being a matched pair by Ed Brandsey. (Weyer photo)

Chris Reeve took a break from military knives to make this kindjal—whale ivory, ebony, sterling silver, Damascus with selective copper plating and all. (Weyer photo)

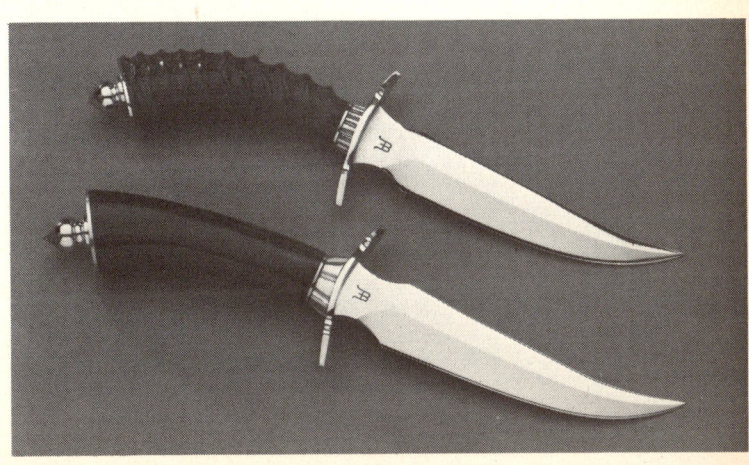

EIGHTH ANNUAL EDITION 71

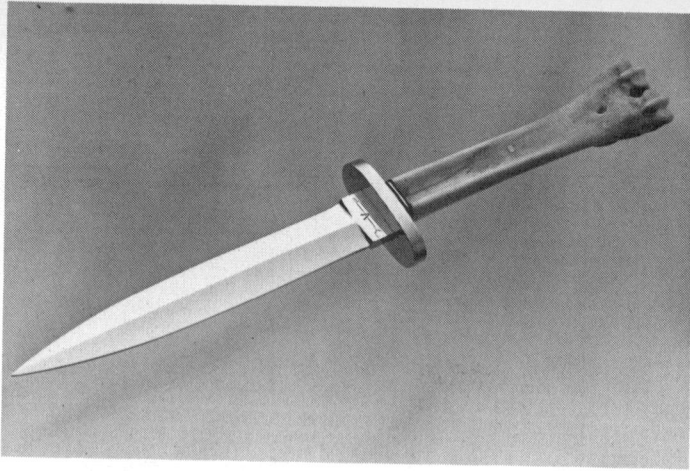

Walt Harless combines deer bone and style to get a clean-looking dagger. (Long photo)

This is E.J. Hendrickson working in the grand New American tradition with silver wire on this full-tang push dagger.

STRAIGHT STANDARDS
Working Daggers

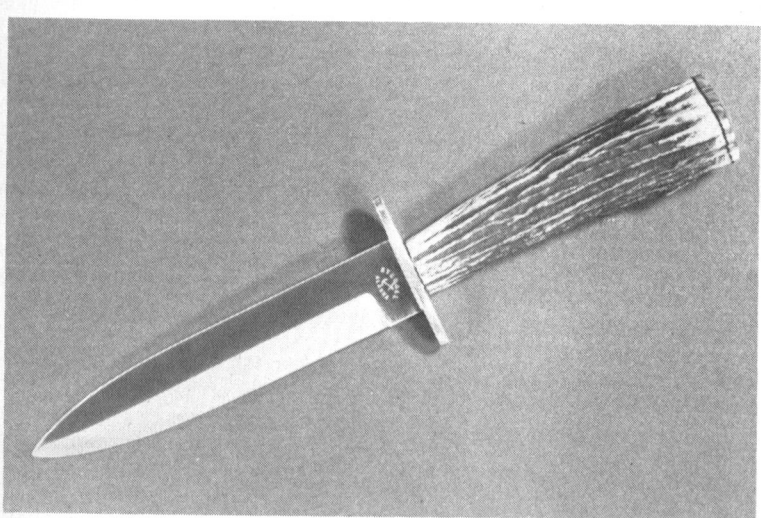

Keith Stegall filed the brass butt cap to match the stag handle of this straightforward dagger.

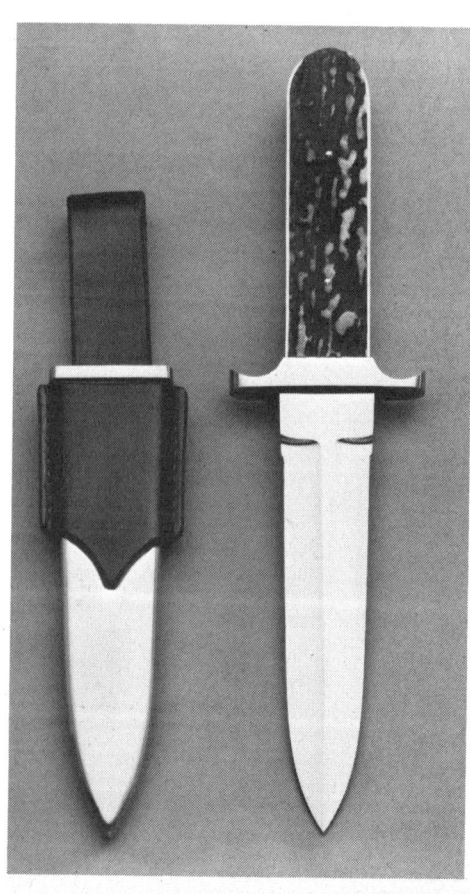

California wrapped-handle dagger by Lloyd Pendleton is all stainless, stag, leather and gold pins. (Weyer photo)

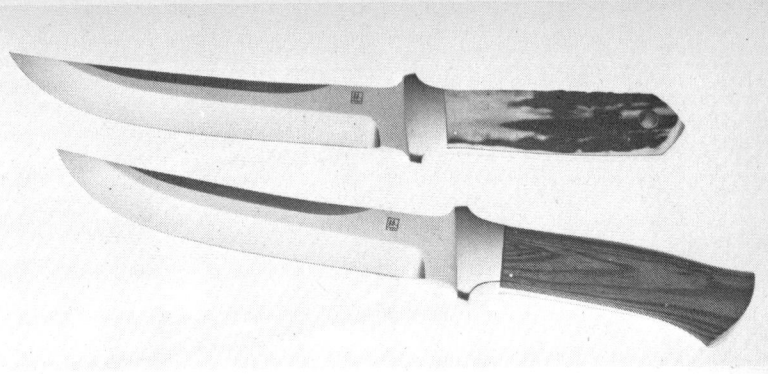

Bob Lum idealizes the tanto into the camp-survival role—your choice of stag or bocote.

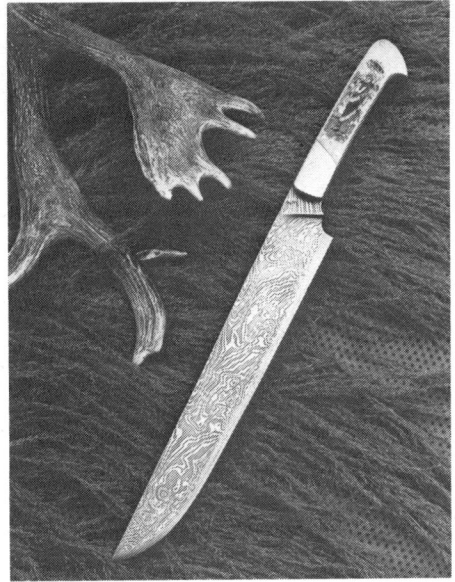

Tim Zowada's heavy Damascus camp knife has ivory and scrimschaw, too. (Weyer photo)

The Bill Moran Colorado camp knife at 10 inches has curly maple and silver wire inlay. (Holter photo)

STRAIGHT STANDARDS
Camp Knives

These are limited edition custom camper knives by Tai Goo in *san mai* steel.

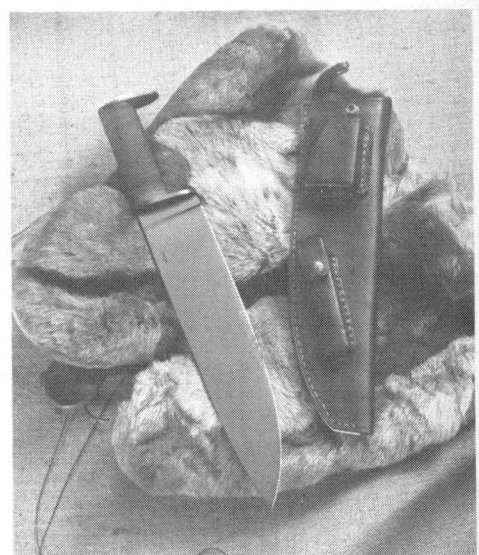

Robert Macri does this camp knife up for use in the Artic—oval handle, miscellaneous gear, long enough to cut snow, and big enough to handle gloved.

C.E. Haynes does an ivory and Damascus camp knife, too.

Norman Bardsley's heavyweight camp knife in bead blasted 440C is a very all-purpose design. (White Lotus photo)

This big Damascus camp knife by Larry Pogreba has a desert ironwood grip. (Weyer photo)

STRAIGHT STANDARDS
Camp Knives

Hugh Bartrug forged this 8-inch survival camp knife with hard edge and soft back. (Weyer photo)

This is a Louisiana camp knife in the Schively pattern according to Frank Vought who made it. (Weyer photo)

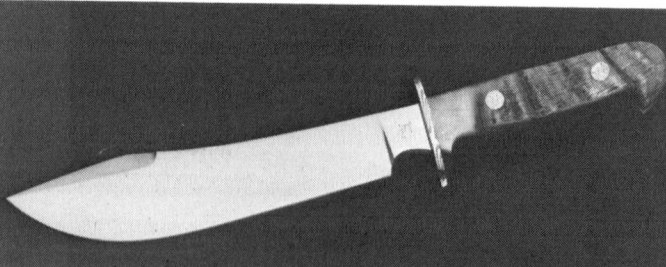

Joel Ellefson went to Will & Finck to get his camp knife design. (Weyer photo)

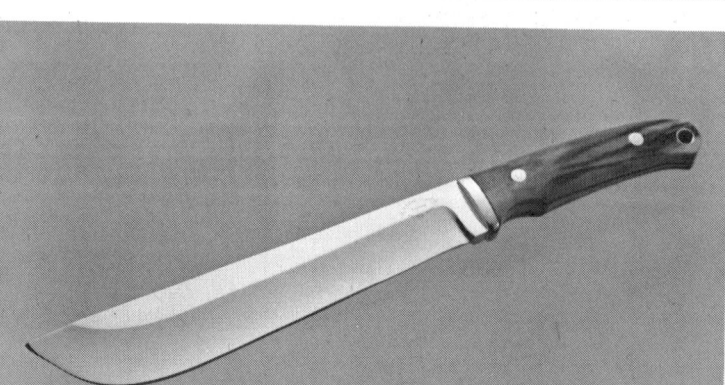

Really heavy customer-designed camp knife was nicely made by Wayne Clay in ATS34. (Long photo)

STRAIGHT STANDARDS
Tantos

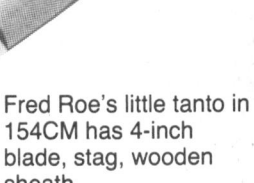

Clean-cut American lines distinguish this Stanley Fujisaka tanto in ATS34, brass and rosewood. (Kojima photo)

Ray Beers ground a Damascus bar for this tanto blade, trimmed it in nickel silver, ebony and abalone. (Weyer photo)

Fred Roe's little tanto in 154CM has 4-inch blade, stag, wooden sheath.

Shiva Ki's ivory handled tanto shows a mystic tree, two Buddhas, and a temper line. (Weyer photo)

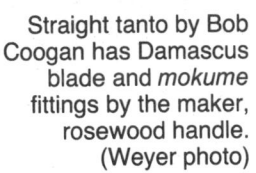

Straight tanto by Bob Coogan has Damascus blade and *mokume* fittings by the maker, rosewood handle. (Weyer photo)

The "armor-piercing" point makes this John Salley ivory-handled tanto tougher than it looks. Scrimmed by Engnath. (Weyer photo)

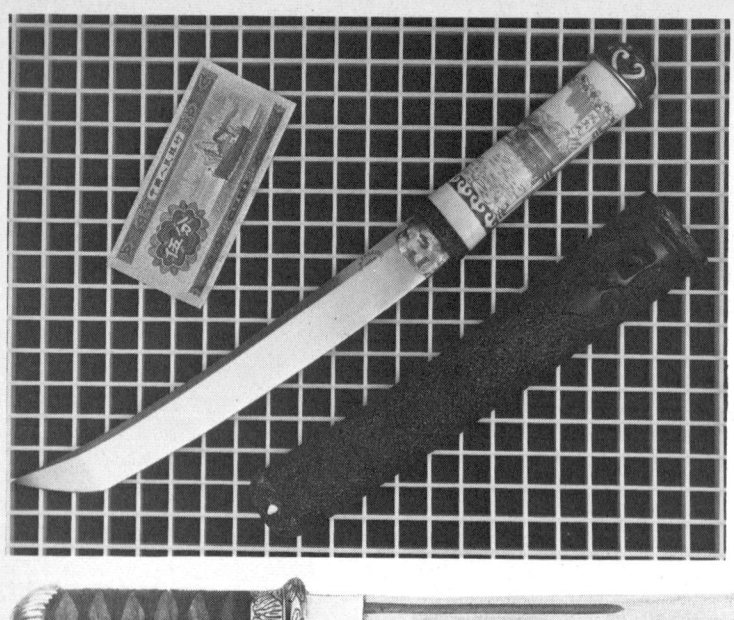

This Ron Frazier tanto may or may not be in a traditional style, but it looks that way.

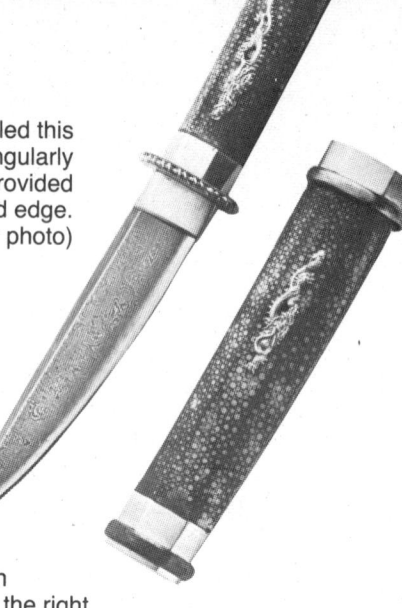

Hugh Bartrug styled this tanto more angularly than standard, provided a serious curved edge. (Weyer photo)

Short Butch Goodwin traditional tanto puts the right things in the right places with an 8-inch blade.

STRAIGHT STANDARDS
Tantos

Traditional styling with black lacquer, rayskin, wrapping, blade shape is nicely done in this Larry Green tanto. (Weyer photo)

Deluxe Jim Kelso-Louis Mills partnership tanto has pine and bat motifs, silver and gold, rayskin, artistic lacquer works.

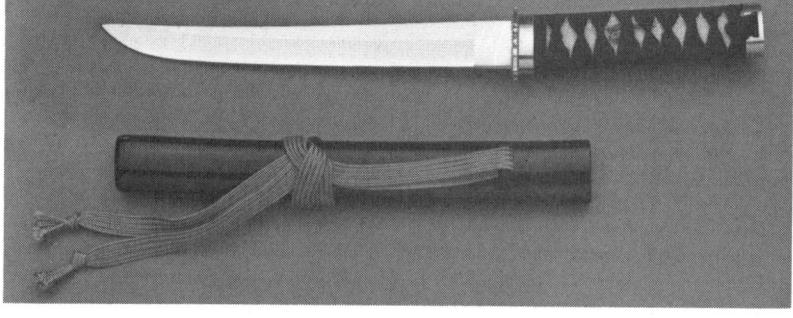

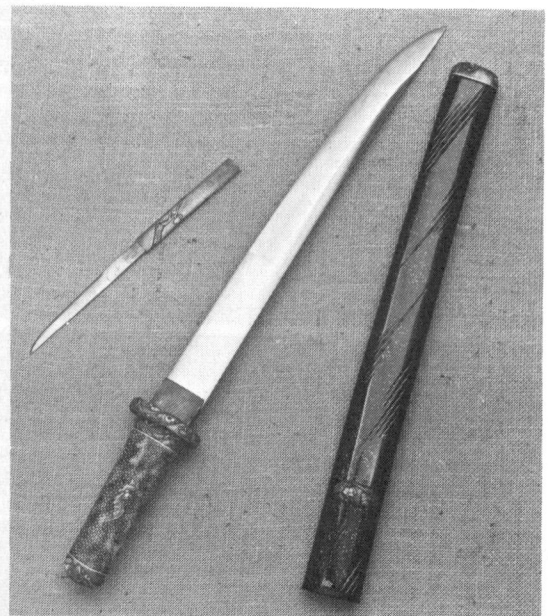

(cont'd. from page 58)

It does seem to be true that the specialization in duty knives toward so-called "survival" designs and heavy-duty knives in the camp knife persuasion has made it possible for makers to take some weight out of their pure fighters and that is a good thing indeed. Such a knife should be lively.

Finally, there are the daggers. There are always daggers. These generally two-edged, generally symmetrical pieces of serious cutlery just don't go away. Whether styled for an alien king on another planet or slicked-down to suit the most severe terrestrial taste, the dagger remains a prime expression of the knifemaker's talent. Actually, there are two principal reasons for the health of the dagger idea: knifemakers like to make them and people like to buy them.

Remember, these are all the standard stuff. We're in the mainstream of handmade knives here. The water is running faster and deeper, though, which is good.

Ken Warner

TRENDS
LEATHER AND OTHER STUFF

THERE ARE TWO things about leather that get clearer and clearer as time goes on. First, knife-carrying leather design gets more and more important to the user, and second, simpler is always better. Even so, there remain several ways to consider the matter.

When we speak of leather, we also mean canvas and Kydex and tropical wood and sheet metal and fiberglass—it's all "leather" once it is made into a sheath. And it wouldn't hurt to set up sensible ground rules to this discussion: The purpose of a sporting or working knife sheath is to keep its knife safely and conveniently and comfortably at hand during repeated use over long periods of time. For some classes of military or defense knives, that same set of parameters applies. For some emergency knives, the emphasis is different—safety is important, still, but convenience and comfort go on the list below quickness, certainly, and concealability often.

That leaves wide scope for any knifemaker or leather specialist, and many use it. There are some pretty complex holsters out there.

Somewhere near the top of this scale has to be the two-knife buscadero quick-draw set pictured here. Harold Crisp and his leather guy Roger Honer had a lot of fun with that. Somewhere near the bottom, I suppose, was the practice of a fellow I knew who sometimes had to travel the world unarmed when he'd rather not. He carried some cardboard and a manila folder and some tape in his attache case and with them constructed a sheath in each country for the first steak knife, cook's knife or hardware store purchase he got his hands on, usually somewhere along the way from the airport to the hotel.

This is not the place for a primer on leather. We are simply showing a collection of the sorts of sheaths knifemakers furnish these days. It does look as if they're paying attention.

Ken Warner

Harold Crisp in his Roger Honer's two-knife buscadero outfit and its Texas-style commemorative Bowies. (Weyer photo)

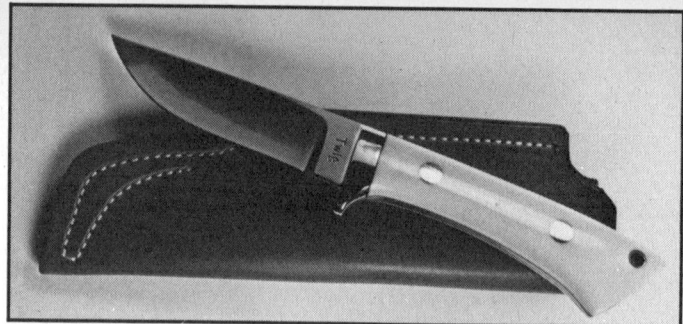

This K.M. Davis hunter is done up with a first-class stiff pouch, always a solid choice.

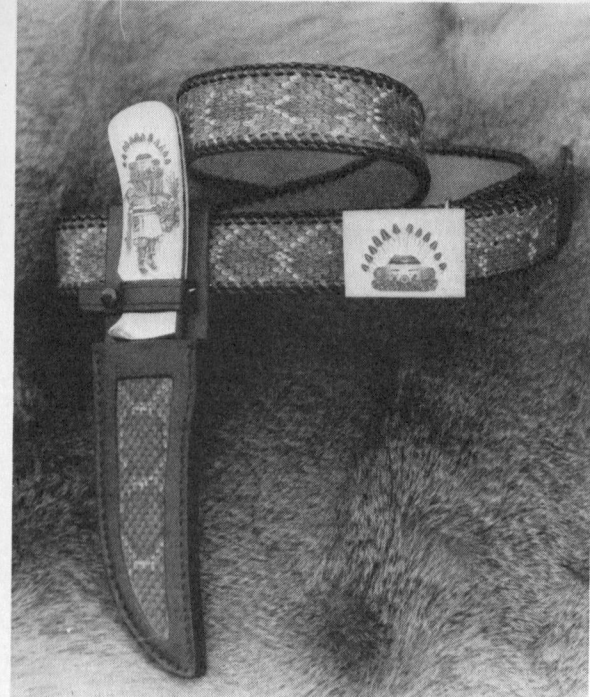

Newman Smith did this snakeskin outfit for a Lynn Sampson knife scrimmed by Peggy D. Smith.

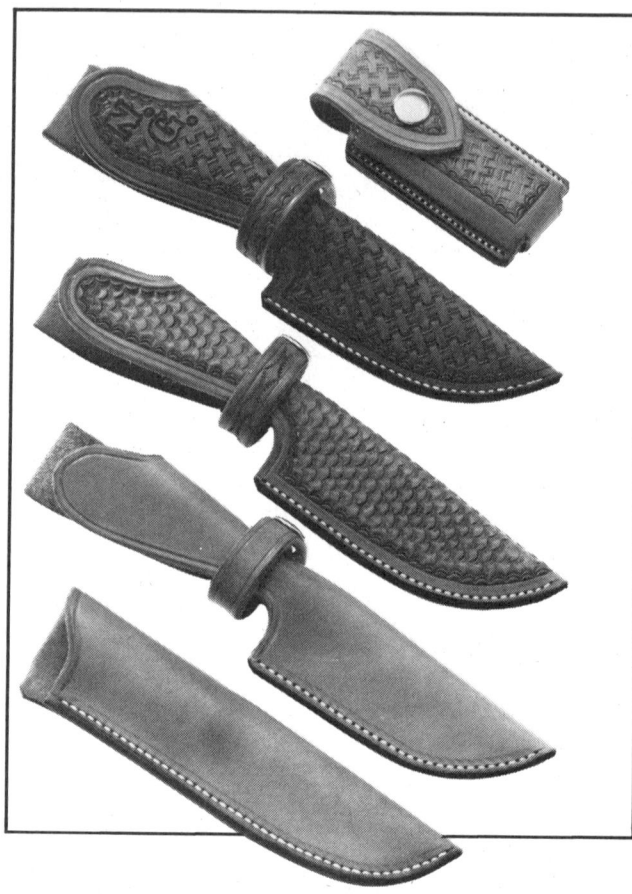

(Above) Kydex, heat-formed, is getting to be a common sheathing option, shown here as Kevin Hoffman furnishes it for a boot knife, held in by the heat-formed flap over the guard.

(Above right) A combination of the sheath styles Ruffin Johnson furnishes with his knives. (Weyer photo)

(Right) This is a Rob Simonich Wilderness in a very serviceable formed leather pouch. (Third Eye photo)

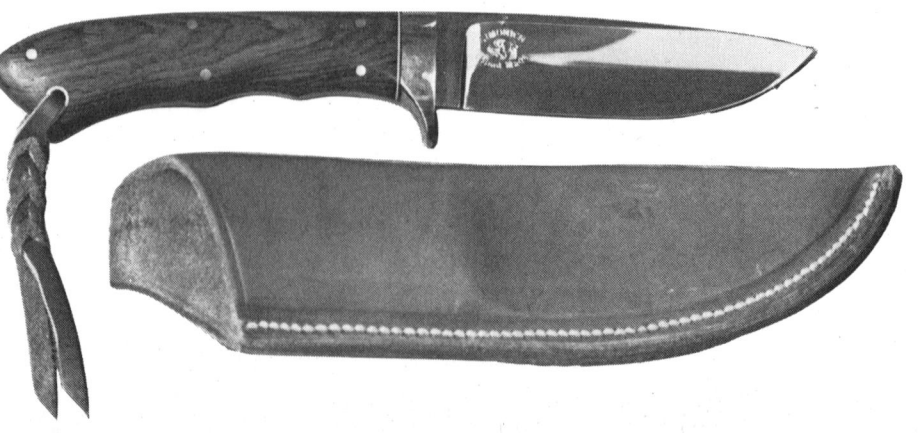

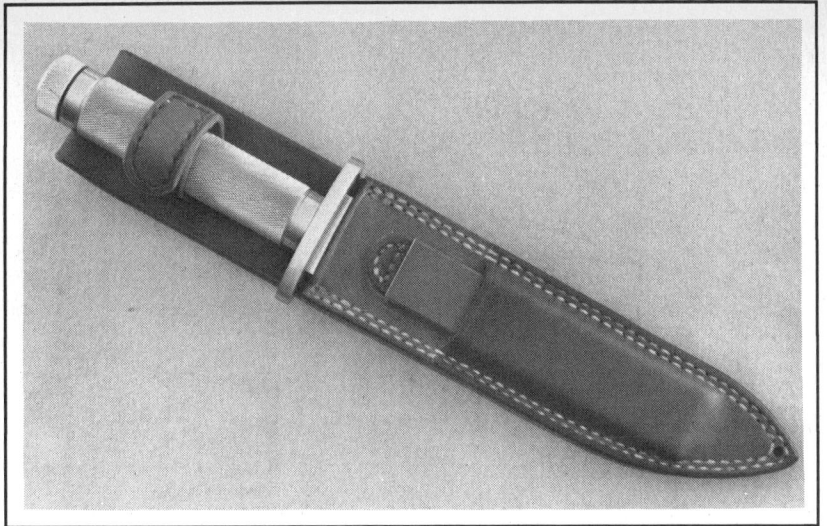

Packaging even a small axe with a knife is a challenge, here met neatly in an Andy Mills combination.

The trick with heavy-duty knives is keeping everything slim and solid as this sheath-with-stone does. Note the Velcro retainer—very nice.

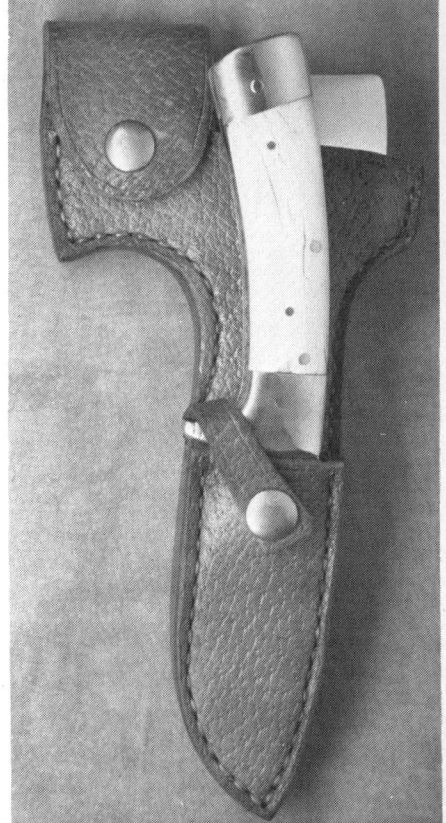

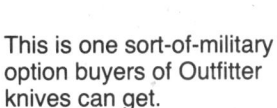

This is one sort-of-military option buyers of Outfitter knives can get.

This handsome Wayne Valachovic fighter is even more dressy when paired with its stag sheath. (Weyer photo)

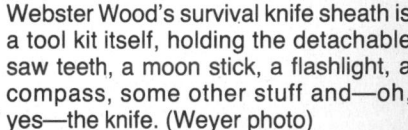

Webster Wood's survival knife sheath is a tool kit itself, holding the detachable saw teeth, a moon stick, a flashlight, a compass, some other stuff and—oh, yes—the knife. (Weyer photo)

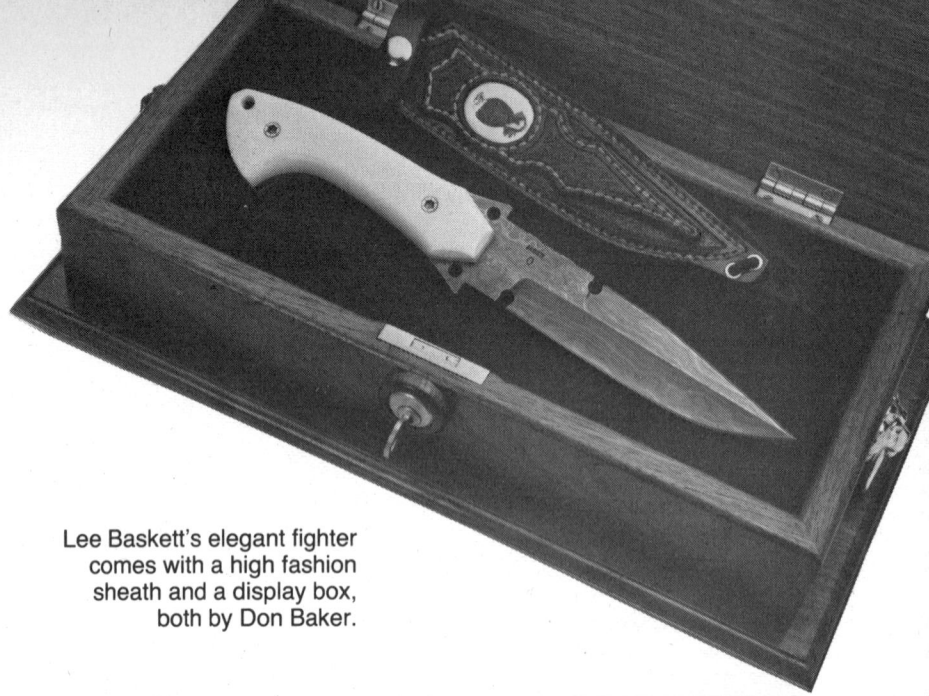

Lee Baskett's elegant fighter comes with a high fashion sheath and a display box, both by Don Baker.

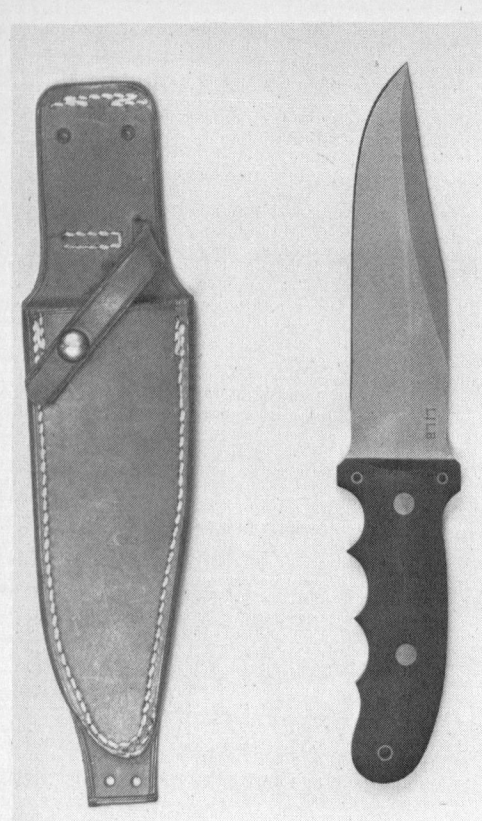

Here's another way to minimize the carried bulk of the big knife, designed by and made for Jimmy Lile. (Kiehl photo)

Norman Bardsley makes rather a specialty of high fashion leather with snakeskins and other exotic stuff. (White Lotus photo)

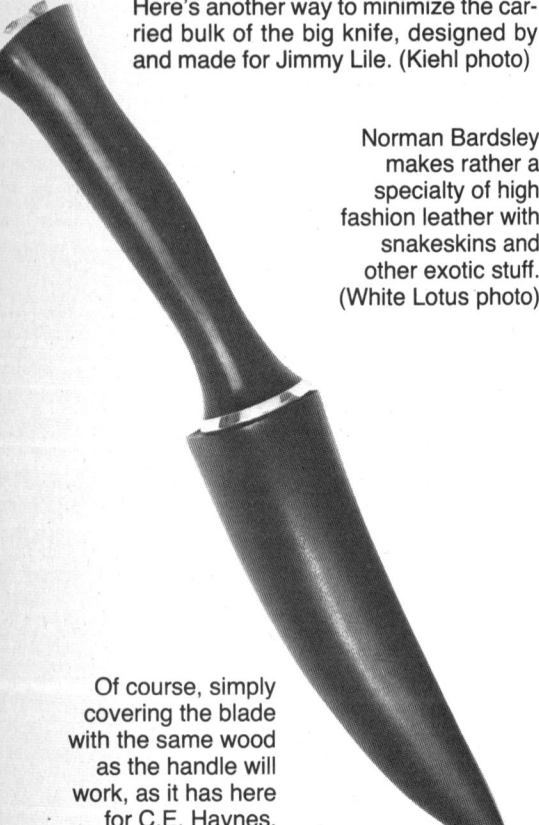

Of course, simply covering the blade with the same wood as the handle will work, as it has here for C.E. Haynes.

Velvet-lined walnut with leather caps sheaths this big knife Scott Shoemaker calls *Seishin*. (Pfahler photo)

TRENDS
KNIVES IN THE KITCHEN

KITCHEN KNIVES are made in a wide variety of blade shapes and sizes. I would guess we all have our favorites and we all have those that find their way to the back of the drawer and live there. I recently asked myself: "Which are my favorites?" to see if they followed any specific style, size, composition—could I learn anything about kitchen knives in my own kitchen?

I'll start by saying I couldn't nail down any pattern or type I preferred overall nor did I find any I will *never* use, but it was fun trying. I did reach some conclusions—some that didn't surprise me and a few that did surprise me.

I gathered roughly 35 knives and began to sort and group them according to size. I might say 35 is not a normal inventory for a normal kitchen, but groups of knives rotate through the Warner kitchen for obvious reasons. We aren't a normal household when it comes to knives.

Five of the 35 were paring-size knives, 10 were utility types at 3½ to 7 inches, 10 were butcher or chef knives. There were four assorted steak knives, three medium-size folders and three really specialized knives.

Of them all, 25 were various stainless steels and 10 were high carbon steel. A third were handmade.

In order to refresh my memory of these knives, I virtually emptied the refrigerator and gathered food and knives on the kitchen counter. I have a great deal of counter space and that is a blessing. My counter is made of laminated oak and I treat it as a big cutting board. The food included cabbage, carrots, celery, gherkins, tomatoes, Muenster cheese, a roll of pepperoni, a sirloin roast, mushrooms, apples, oranges and onions and there were a few non-edibles, as well.

The paring knives work real well with the fruit and quartering the gherkins. Most of my paring knives are carbon steel and they do stain, but they sharpen quickly and their blades are thin. Only two have sharp points, and I haven't missed the points. I know some use paring knives most often up in the air, cutting toward them—peeling or cutting with the knife coming to rest on their thumb pad, or palm. Cooks who do this are very practiced or their knives aren't very sharp. I'm not that practiced, so I use a peeler instead of a knife because I take off more than the fruit skin when I don't.

The utility knives work on the cheese, pepperoni, mushrooms and tomatoes. Cutting cheese from a block is easier when I lightly grease the knife with butter or dip it in hot water, then the cheese doesn't adhere to the knife. You can get more uniform cuts when the cheese is cold, of course. The roll of pepperoni does well when you draw the knife through in one stroke rather than chopping a slice and this is also easier. The mushrooms are those big kind for stuffing—I sometimes slice and saute them, and sometimes I remove the stems and dice and stuff all with the 6-inch utility knife that has a very thin blade. Mushrooms are fragile and thick blades tend to break them up.

Tomatoes, especially ripe ones, are the supreme test for sharp thin knives. The test comes when you attempt thin cuts or wedges without undue pressure which will

The Addison butcher knife slides through Warner-grown tomatoes. (Place photo)

A Coleman-Western lightweight often cuts cheese on picnics, short blade or no. (Place photo)

Martin Kruse makes this small chef's knife from 1095 steel and oak. (Buckman & Marsh photo)

This 3½-inch kitchen utility knife is made with A2 steel and Micarta by Roy Blaum.

send the juices and membranes squirting away from the skin of the tomato. With a sharp, thin utility knife you draw it through the tomato with no resistance and no "dismembranement."

The butcher or chef knives work on the sirloin roast, onions, cabbage, carrots and celery. I have an 8¼-inch butcher knife that really is a favorite of mine. It really takes the chore out of the big jobs. In this instance, I cut the sirloin roast into sirloin tips in a matter of seconds. The head of cabbage submitted quickly under the knife as well. This one is carbon steel with riveted oak handles. It's not up for an art award, but for function and execution, it's up high on the list. I have 6-, 8-, 10-, and a few 12-inch chef knives. I found the 6-inch and the 10-inch knives, with thin blades, to be most used. Onions can be so slippery, carrots can be obstinate, and celery non-uniform, but this shape can really make the work simple.

Steak knives, folders, and specialized knives don't get much preparation work, but they do their fair share in other directions. Our steak knives are often found on the table, but I know some of you use them for feats not to be believed. You really owe it to yourself to get some real knives that you can sharpen and maintain—no one should have to saw their food forever.

My folders are more emergency aids. They are so handy away from home, especially at a restaurant. You've been to one at least where they expect you to cut your food with flatware that finds butter a challenge. Folders are also useful in someone else's kitchen when you're helping out. These specialized knives are seldom used, but when they are needed nothing else does the job quite as well.

In review, I realize I could get by with just a few knives like the parers and the chef's, but I don't *have to*. One of the luxuries is personal option. I don't *have to* choose one all-purpose knife. I don't have to carry all my choices wherever I go. They are there in the kitchen where I use them, when and if I need them.

My only *have tos* for a kitchen knife are:
1. It has to be sharp.
2. It has to be clean and accessible.
3. It has to be fairly easy to sharpen.

And, of course, I want a good selection.

Now my kitchen knives are mainly for food preparation. My idea of testing knives does not include chopping trees, making slivers of dense metal objects, sawing or chopping either frozen foods or manila rope, defrosting refrigerators, or living in the dishwasher. Real testing takes time. It takes continued daily performance through a variety of chores normal to food preparation to be able to rely on a given knife functioning the way you expect it to every time, with minimal maintenance.

The following are some of my time-tested blades, listed purely according to my biased opinions:

The paring knife is Ed Addison's, a custom-maker who regrinds saw blades. It has a 2½-inch blade and has no sharp point at the end. The handle is oak held in place with two rivets.

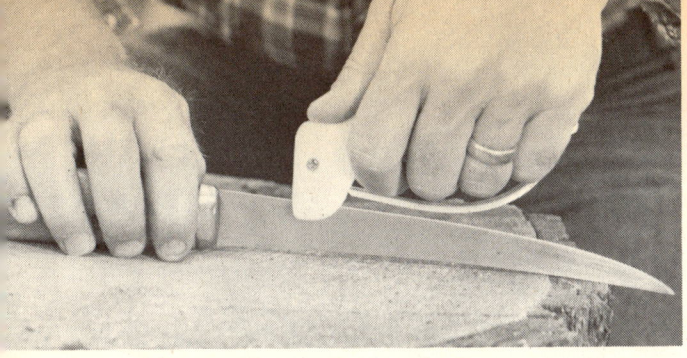

This is not the only way to get knives sharp, but it works better than you might think. Gadget is from Dale Fortenberry at Fortune Products.

Phil Baldwin put it all in this Chinese cook's knife—tiger-stripe Damascus, mokume ferrule, rosewood handle. (Weyer photo)

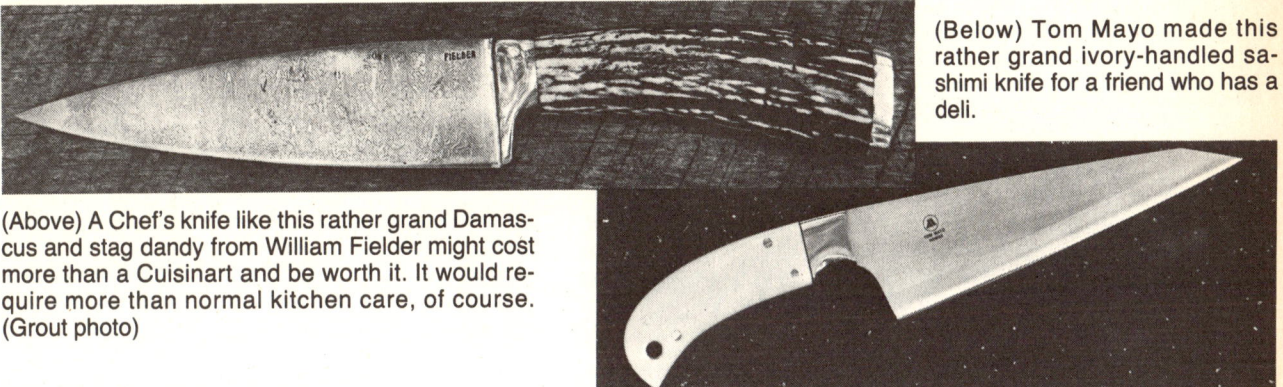

(Above) A Chef's knife like this rather grand Damascus and stag dandy from William Fielder might cost more than a Cuisinart and be worth it. It would require more than normal kitchen care, of course. (Grout photo)

(Below) Tom Mayo made this rather grand ivory-handled sashimi knife for a friend who has a deli.

There are two utility knives I enjoy using. One is A.G. Russell's Solingen-made knife with a 6-inch blade of stainless steel, and a wood handle that is riveted. This knife has good balance. The other is by Masahiro, made for Spyderco. This is my only serrated-edge favorite made of high carbon stainless steel. We got it from Atlanta Cutlery.

The butcher and chef knives are my most used knives. Again, Ed Addison makes a 6-inch chef and 8¼-inch butcher knife. The blades are reasonably thin and resharpen quickly. And A.G. Russell's 8¼-inch chef's knife of stainless steel which functions as well as it looks.

My favorite functional steak knife is by Pat Tomes, who made it after listening to some sage advice from his better half.

And my recent favorite lockback folder is from Gerber Knives. It has a sand-blast blade finish and a Zytel handle with checkering.

Maintaining a sharp edge on a knife in the kitchen is a common problem, not usually resolved until all the inventory on hand is so dull one cannot prepare the oncoming meal. There are many devices and stones on the market today to alleviate this but somehow it tends to get pushed down on the priority list of things to do. Professional chefs I have seen usually touch up a knife with a steel before each use. Unfortunately, we Warners are of neither the habit nor training to do this.

I won't elaborate on all the sharpeners one can get, but I will state if you have a knife with a good edge already a few downward strokes on a Crock Stick will generally maintain it.

Maybe this has got you wondering about your own kitchen knife inventory; maybe you want to re-evaluate your needs. Here are a few suggestions:

- Find the knives you have that feel comfortable in your hand, take note of the weight and size, and when and if you shop, go for the ones you are familiar with.
- If you like all kitchen utensils cleaned in the dishwasher, you'll have to pass over some knives that won't tolerate that kind of abuse.
- You may not need new knives at all. Just sharpening up the ones you have may do it. Almost anyone will freely give you advice on how to keep them sharp.
- It's been my experience that hunting knives don't function as well in my kitchen as they may in the field. Most of the big butchering is done before it gets in the kitchen in most homes, so thick and wedgy knives are not a must, nor do they guarantee a big job made easy.

I enjoy knives. I like trying out the new ones, the hand-made ones, some commercial standards, and the ones that evolved out of car springs. It's something of a pastime with me. You may not see knives the way I do, nor lend them the significance over the pots and pans. But if you have good sharp knives in the shapes and sizes that suit you, you may save time, money, and kitchen hassles. You have an array of choices, if you want them, in kitchen cutlery, so don't settle for non-functional knives or for getting by with dull or inadequate knives—treat yourself—and enjoy. Sharp knives are the only food processors I need.

Deborah Warner

TRENDS
THE FOLDING STANDARDS

ONE REASON that underlies the immense popularity of the large one-blade folder among collectors and users of handmade knives is the fact that big folders are the main game in the commercial hunting knife business these days. We all know that we can credit Buck for making this happen; the corollary is that straight knife sales among major companies are definitely taking a beating. And to look around you here will tell you why—big folders are nifty knives.

Except for a very few, custom makers eschew any attempt to make knives that look and work like, let's say, a Remington Stockman's knife. There is probably a legitimate concern as to whether or not such a knife at $150 or so or more would sell, and then there are also the annoying difficulties involved in putting three blades together and making them all walk and talk. Still, you will see pictures of a few knives here which work both sides of that particular street—that is, they use 440C or 154CM or D2 in multi-blade designs patterned after the great old knives and create really nice pocketknives.

Another thing about folding knives has to be the prices. There are a lot of fellows who do not even blush asking $300 for a plain large jackknife with a pearl handle. There are some other fellows who will, of course, hand you perfectly nice jackknives all day at $100 each. Still, the trend in prices seems to be up, to a point where embellished folding lockblade hunters might average $400 or more.

As you go through the categories, large lockblades, self-defense knives, working pocketknives, multi-blade designs and fancy folders in many types—you see a lot of other knives which are pricey. We don't deal directly with prices in this book because it is an annual and it is kept and they change so much, but it is fair to say that upper level folders aren't getting any cheaper, whatever the working class knives are doing.

Once more, it is happy to note, this selection of several dozen folding knives, handmade mostly in the United States, is about as good-looking such a collection as has ever been assembled. That is a nice trend to be continuing and perhaps it will.

Ken Warner

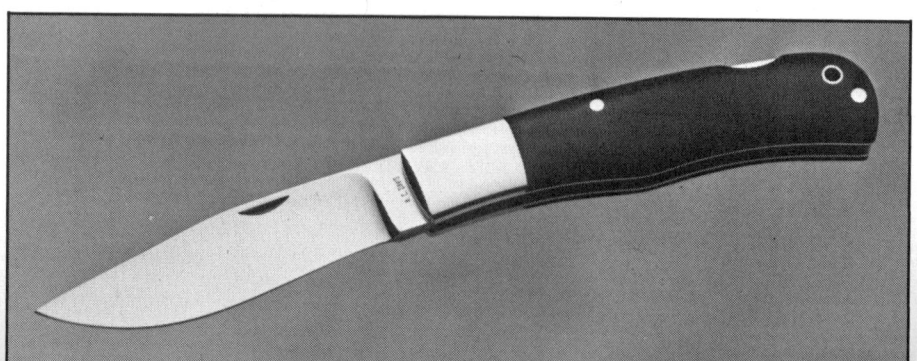

Classic W.C. Davis in black Micarta and ATS34. (Long photo)

Rob Simonich calls this short (2-inch) skinner his "Fat Boy" (Third Eye photo)

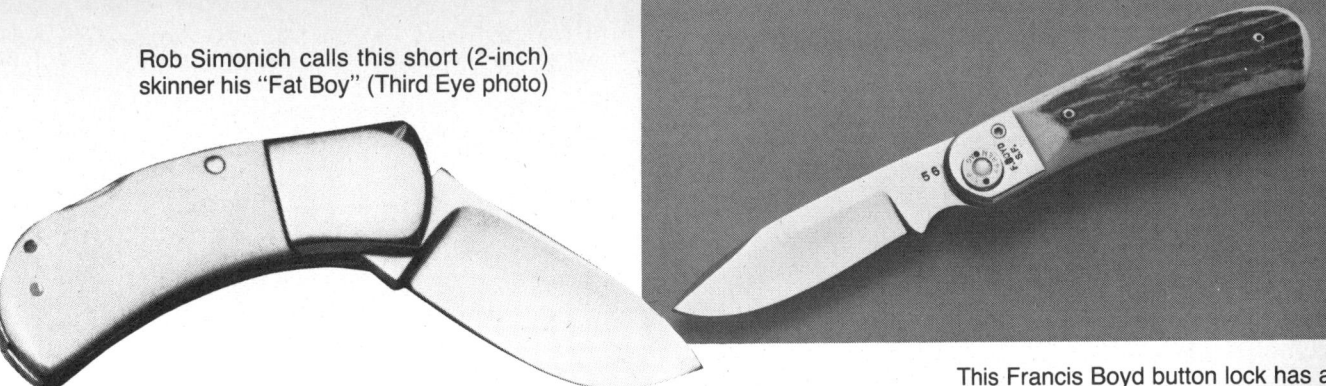

This Francis Boyd button lock has a 44 Magnum button. (Weyer photo)

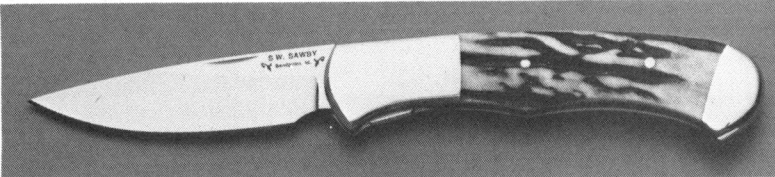

Scott Sawby says this one of his has a "self-lock release." (Weyer photo)

THE FOLDING STANDARDS
Lockback Hunters

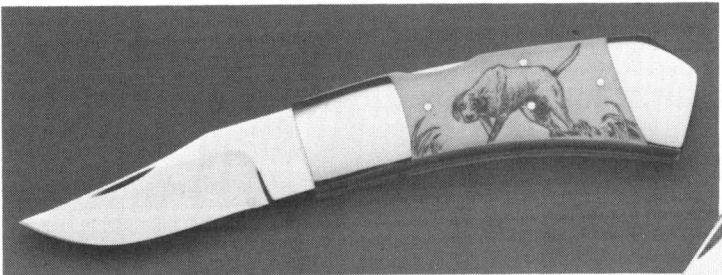

C.T. Conn makes this stout clip-point with a mid-release lock. (Weyer photo)

Jess Horn, who showed them how, is still showing them with his Remington bullet replica.

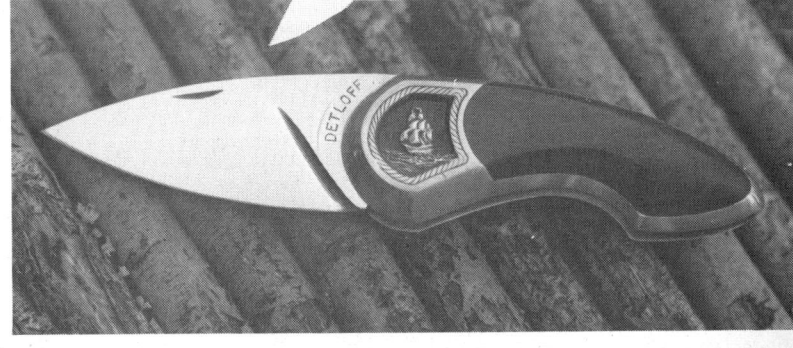

Larry Detloff doesn't see a reason to change his successful shortie hunter. That's Shaw engraving.

Robert Coogan's locking skinner is in 01 steel and rosewood.

EIGHTH ANNUAL EDITION **85**

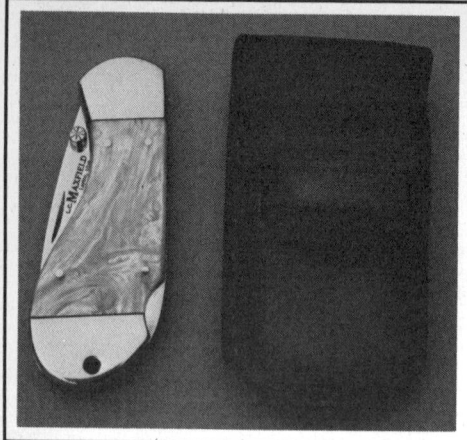
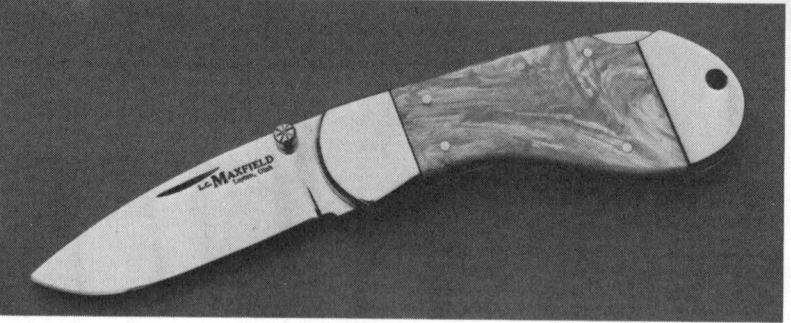

Lynn Maxfield calls this his Cat's Paw and makes a Kitty's Paw smaller.

William Harsey makes a very careful big folder. (Weyer photo)

THE FOLDING STANDARDS
Lockback Hunters

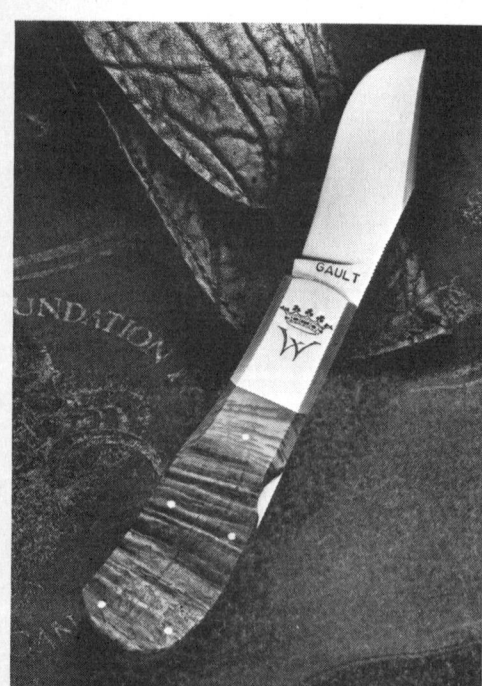

Clay Gault made this one for (no foolin') the present Duke of Wellington.

Steve Mullin's folder has everything and Steve did it all.

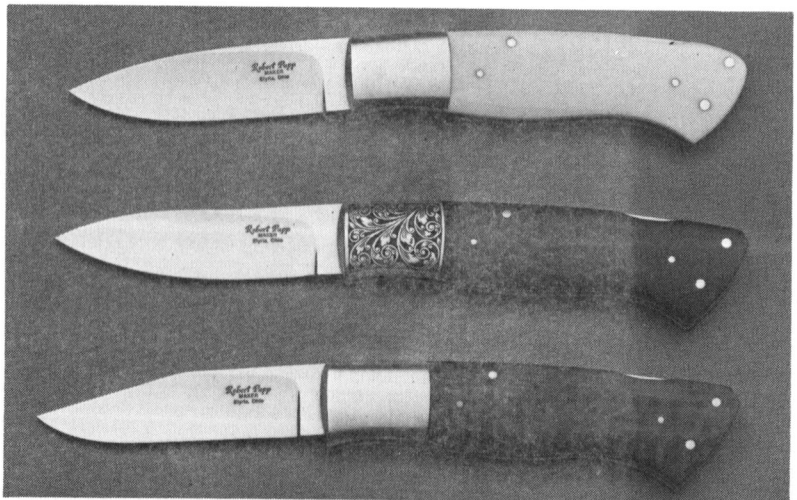

Robert Papp makes them look right, whether in ivory, blackwood or snakewood. (Weyer photo)

This lean and mean folder is a 4-inch fighter by Ralph Dewey.

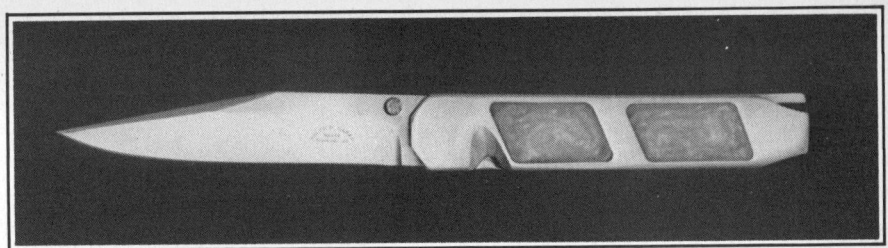

It's double-edged, but just sharpened on one side, this Price-style folding dagger by John Busfield.

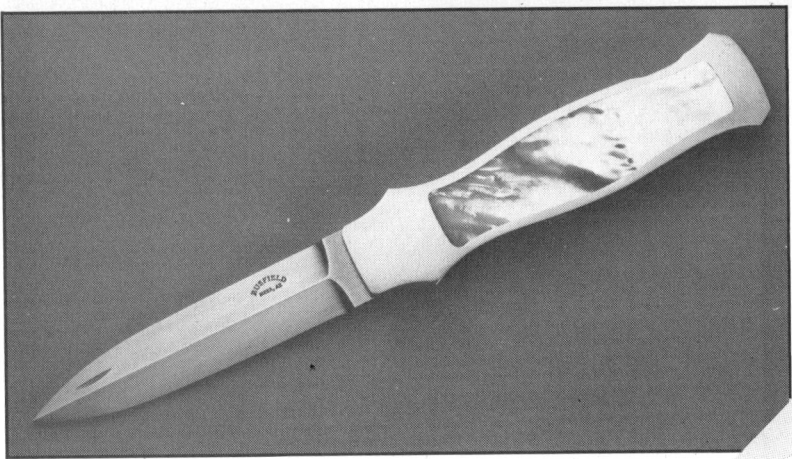

A serious one-hander, this Boguszewski folding boot is black linen Micarta and 440C. (Weyer photo)

THE FOLDING STANDARDS
Defense Folders

Classic shape of this Shiro Furukawa will never get out of fashion. (Weyer photo)

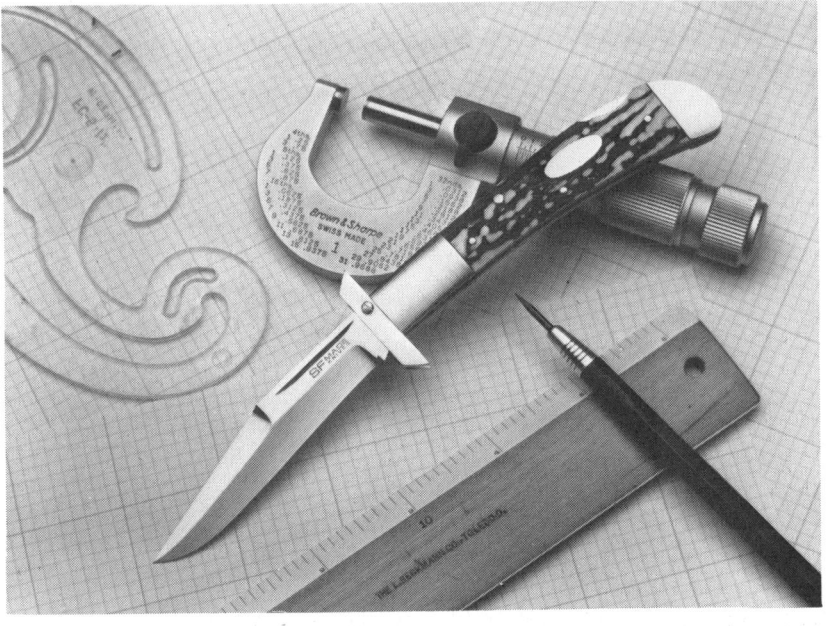

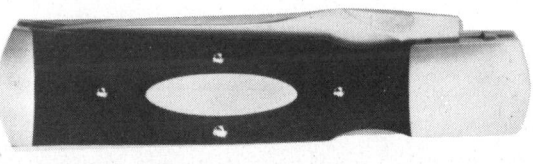

(Above and left) This folding fighter by Durvyn Howard has front lock and opens very easily.

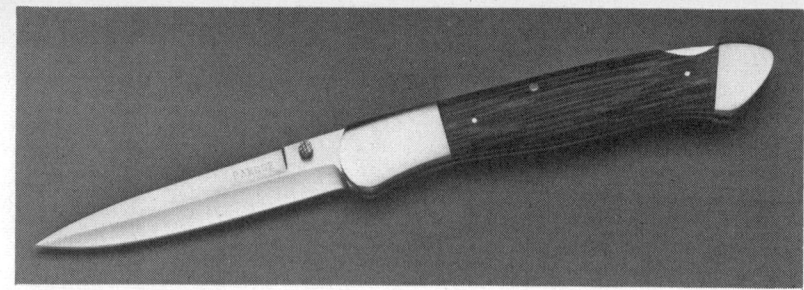

Mel Pardue's rear-locking boot is double hollow-ground. (Weyer photo)

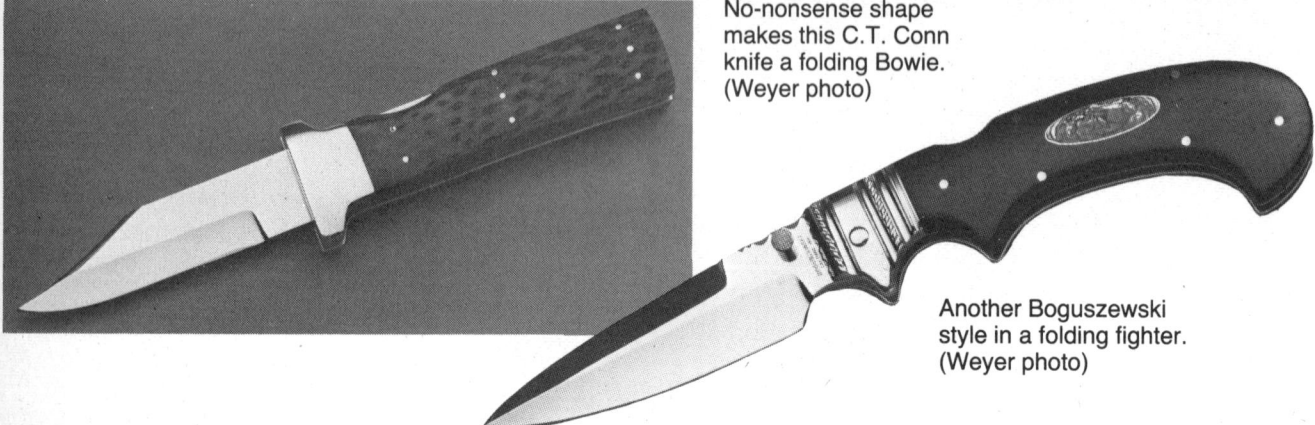

No-nonsense shape makes this C.T. Conn knife a folding Bowie. (Weyer photo)

Another Boguszewski style in a folding fighter. (Weyer photo)

THE FOLDING STANDARDS
Defense Folders

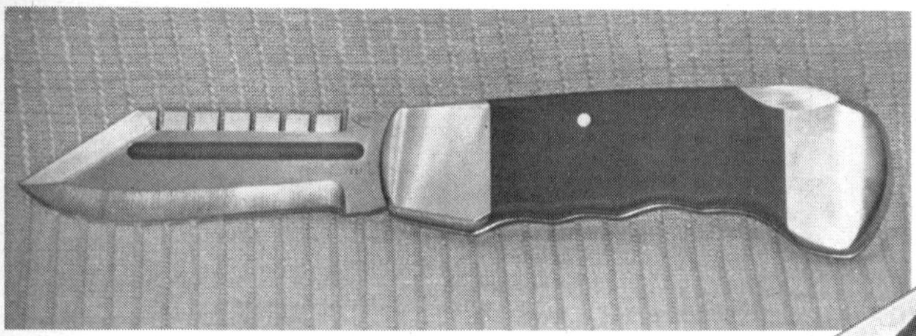

This Chuck Garlitis heavyweight is sharp all the way around—its sheath protects that upper edge.

The upscale fighter for the discriminating, this Centofante has ivory, scrimshaw, engraving and workmanship besides the design. (Weyer photo)

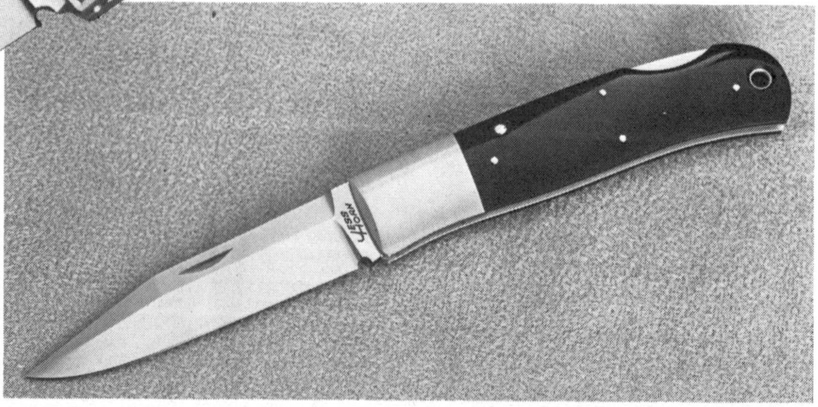

This is the Jess Horn vision of a folding fighter in black buffalo.

Big guy in red bone is by Rendon Griffin. (Weyer photo)

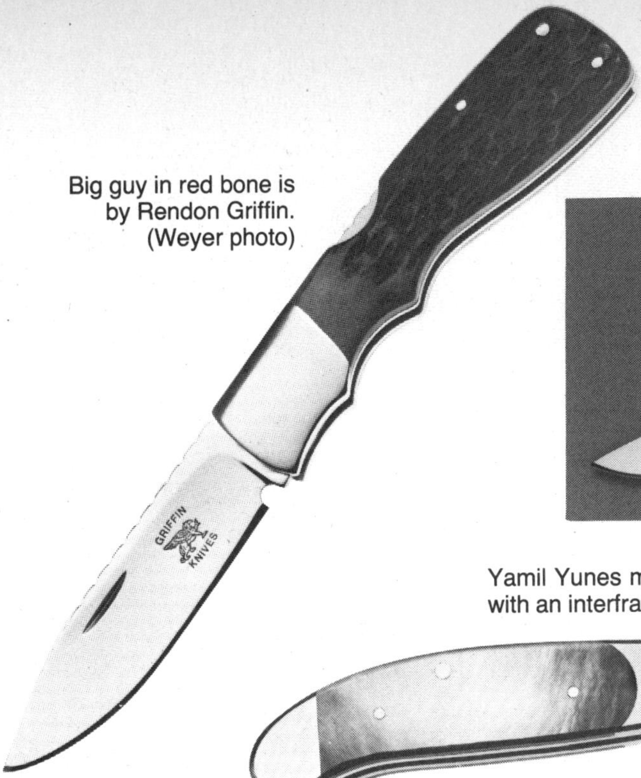

Jim Fuller calls this a Georgia Lock Back, so that's what it is. (Weyer photo)

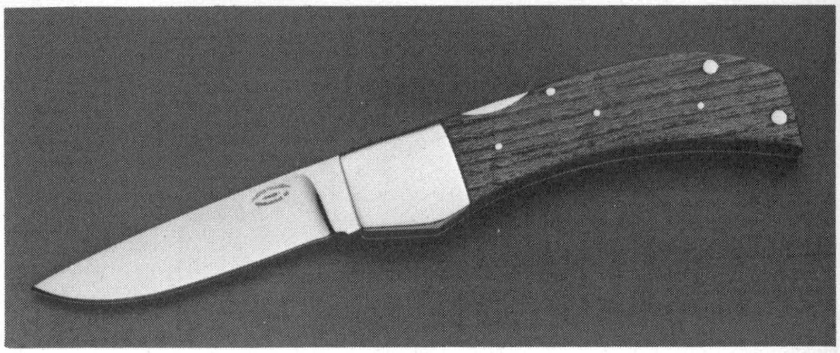

Yamil Yunes makes this 2½-inch slip-lock with an interframe look to it. (Weyer photo)

THE FOLDING STANDARDS
Working Folders

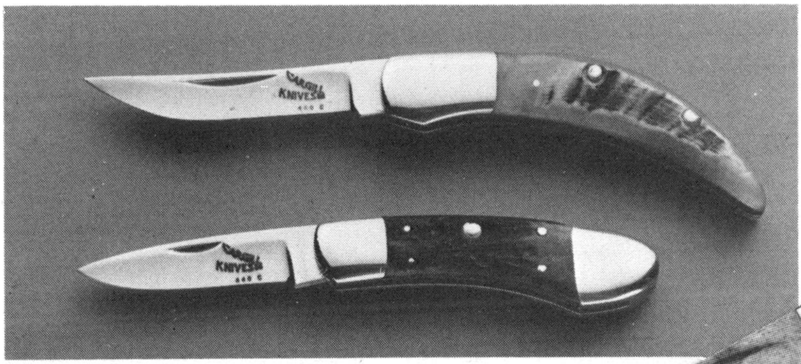

Bob Cargill does these in 440C, styles them himself. (Weyer photo)

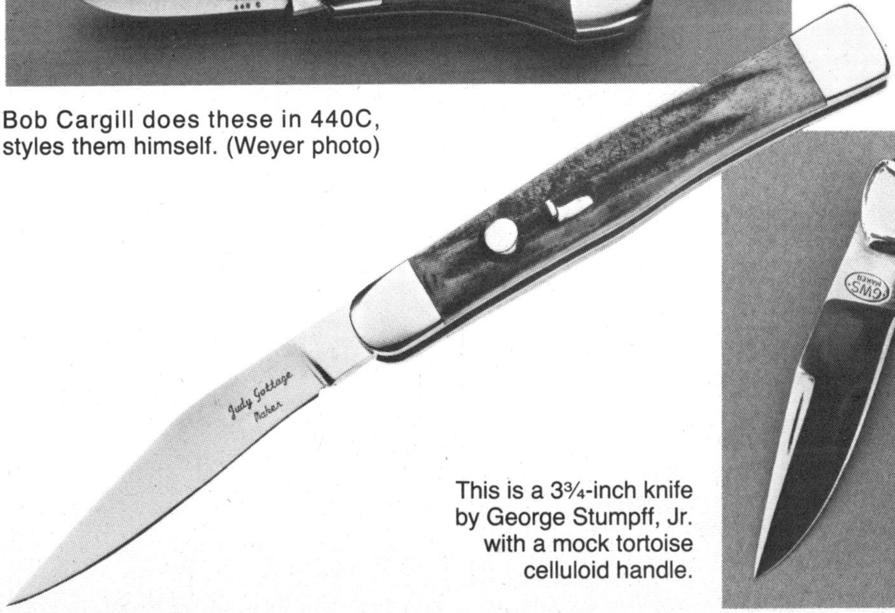

Judy Gottage made this stag folder so you could open it quick if you wanted to. (Weyer photo)

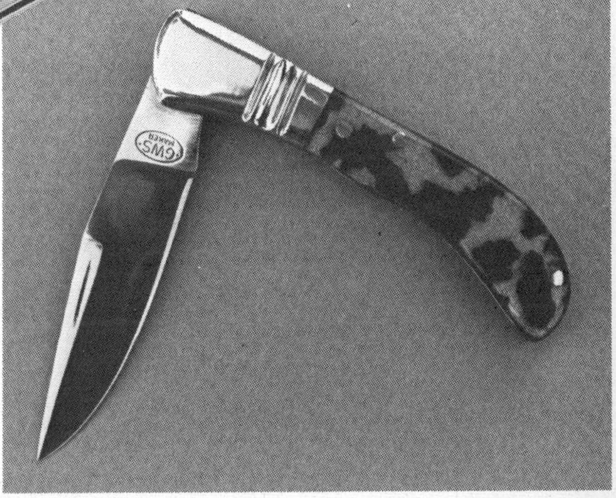

This is a 3¾-inch knife by George Stumpff, Jr. with a mock tortoise celluloid handle.

EIGHTH ANNUAL EDITION **89**

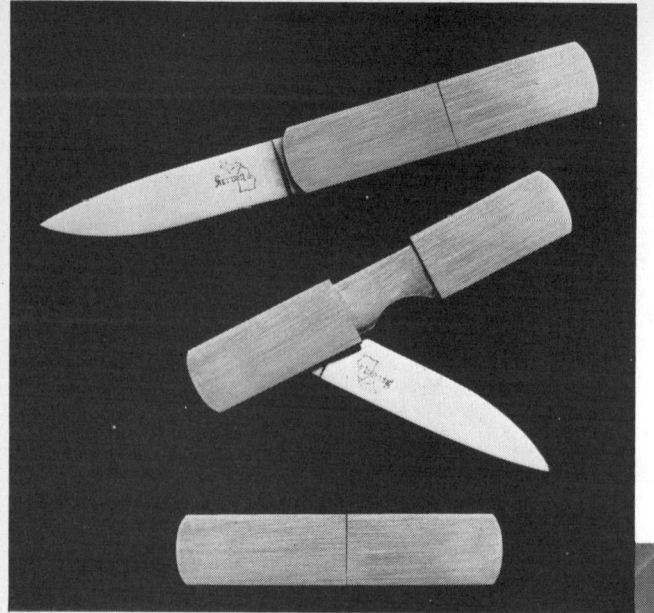

Jim Serven makes this sliding lock pocket piece all in stainless steel. (Weyer photo)

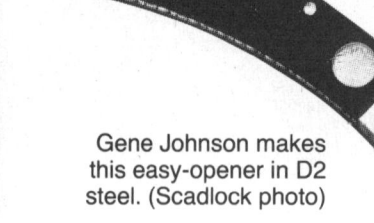

Gene Johnson makes this easy-opener in D2 steel. (Scadlock photo)

This is a working hunter by James H. Poag.

THE FOLDING STANDARDS
Working Folders

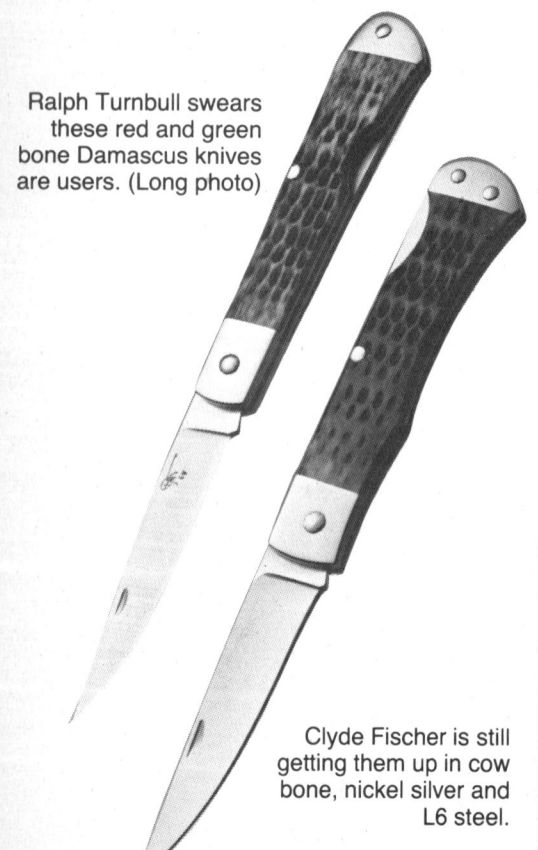

Ralph Turnbull swears these red and green bone Damascus knives are users. (Long photo)

Clyde Fischer is still getting them up in cow bone, nickel silver and L6 steel.

A.D. Rardon calls this pattern the Goose-Neck Folder, makes it in 440C. (Weyer photo)

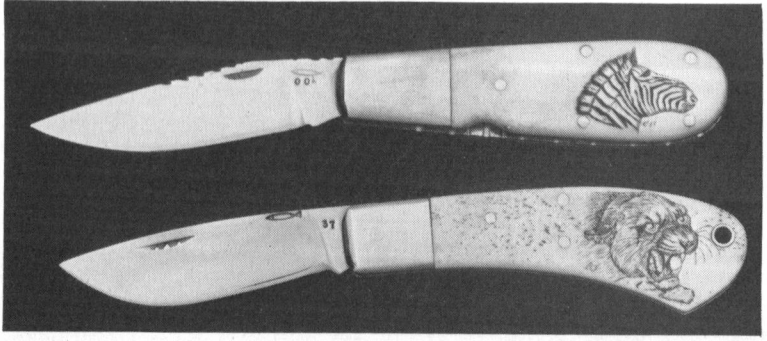

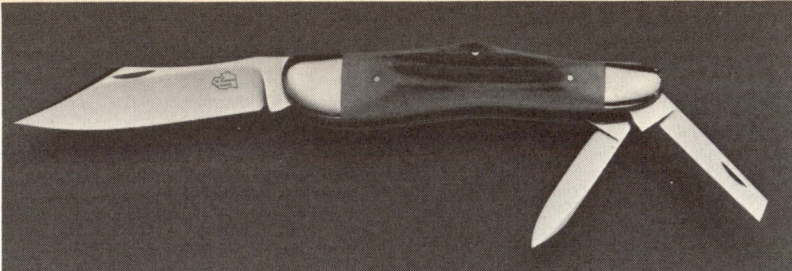

This Robert Enders Norfolk whittler is another Sheffield style recreated in 440C. (Weyer photo)

Mark Wahlster calls this a serpentine pen and so it is in 440C.

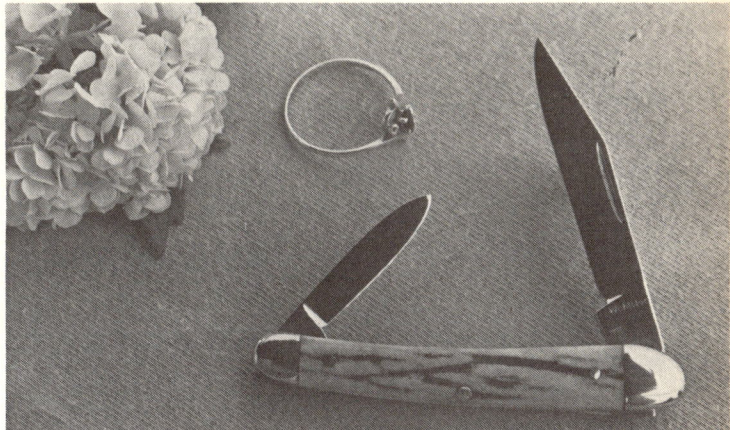

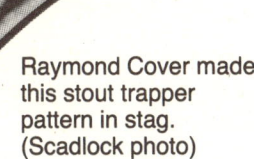

Raymond Cover made this stout trapper pattern in stag. (Scadlock photo)

THE FOLDING STANDARDS
Multi-Blade Knives

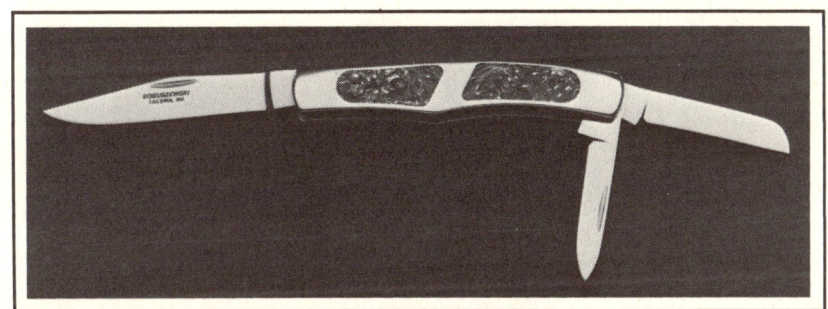

This interframe whittler is called a three-blade stock by Phil Boguszewski who made it. (Weyer photo)

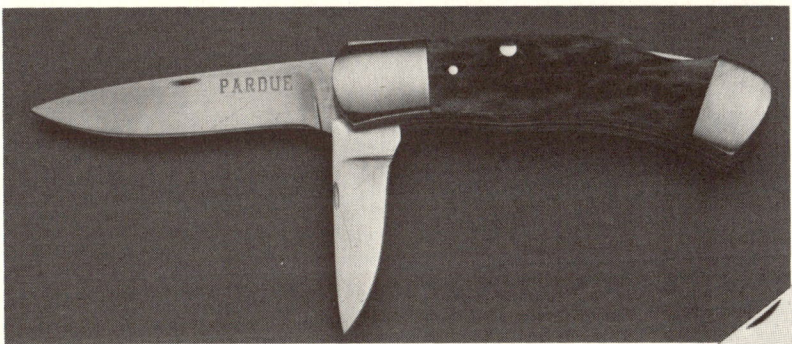

This Mel Pardue Red Pick Bone folder locks both blades. (Weyer photo)

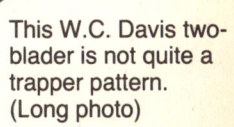

This W.C. Davis two-blader is not quite a trapper pattern. (Long photo)

EIGHTH ANNUAL EDITION **91**

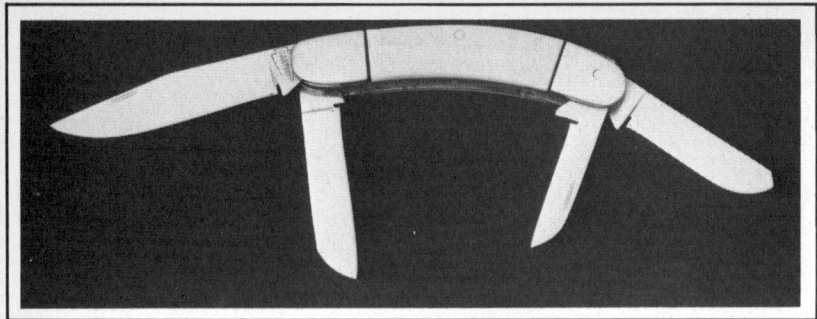

Four-blader by M.D. Gartman is in ATS34 and ivory.

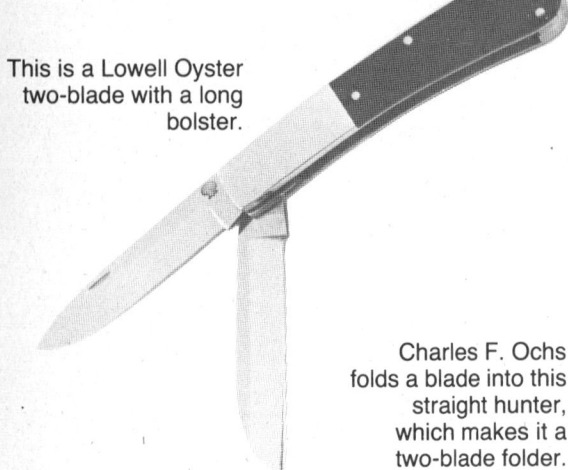

This is a Lowell Oyster two-blade with a long bolster.

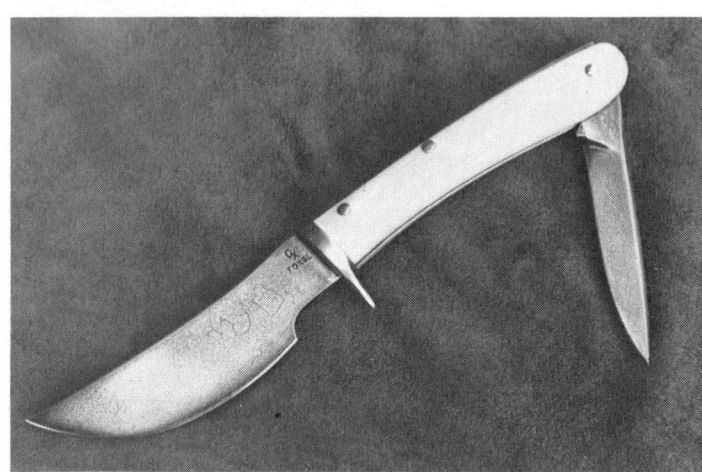

Charles F. Ochs folds a blade into this straight hunter, which makes it a two-blade folder.

THE FOLDING STANDARDS
Multi-Blade Knives

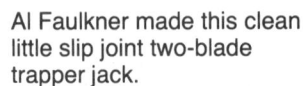

Al Faulkner made this clean little slip joint two-blade trapper jack.

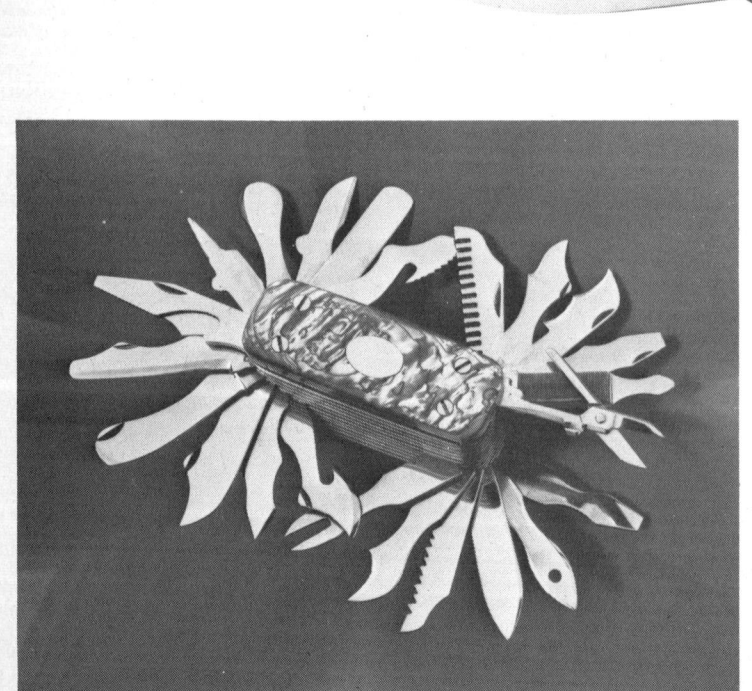

Yasuhiro Fujimoto takes multi-blading to an extreme, but it's fun. (Weyer photo)

THE FOLDING STANDARDS
Fancy Folders

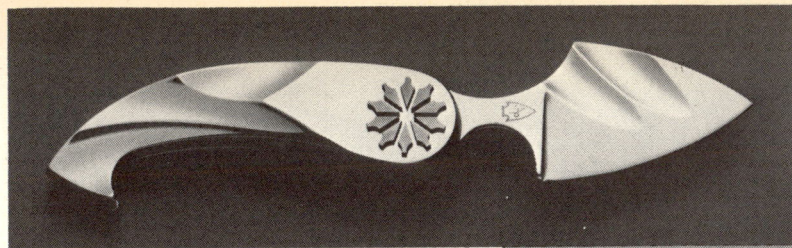

Ray Appleton's technocratic multilock named "Goldie" is his own very personal design. (Weyer photo)

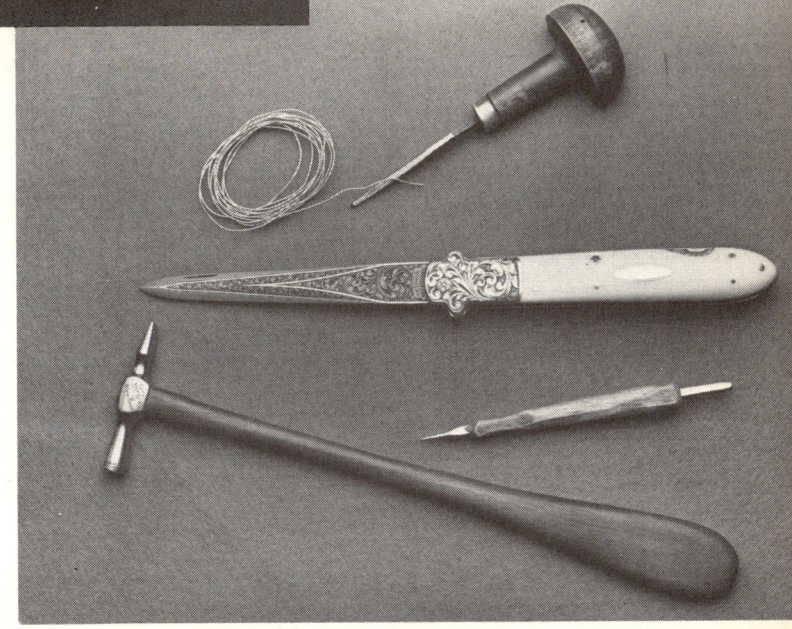

H.H. Frank has staked out the folding dirk territory long since, and does it just right.

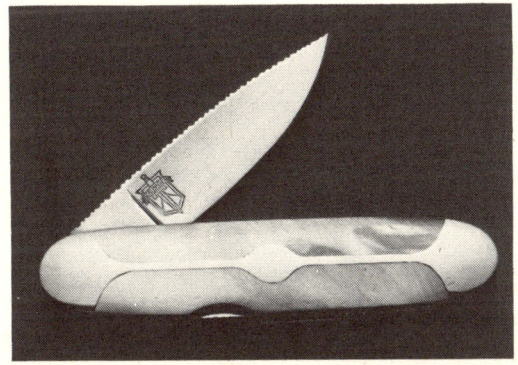

The gent's knife in the classic style is here done up by Richard Spinale.

Doc Hagen has an inner interframe here—very handsome. (Weyer photo)

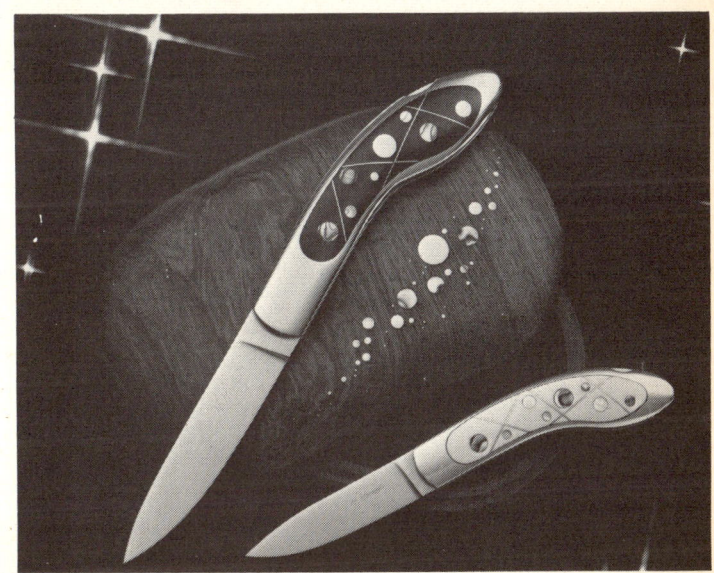

Harumi Hirayama's flights of fancy put stars in clear sight. (Weyer photo)

Paul Myers' slip-lock has a really different look, perhaps because of Mel Wood's engraving.

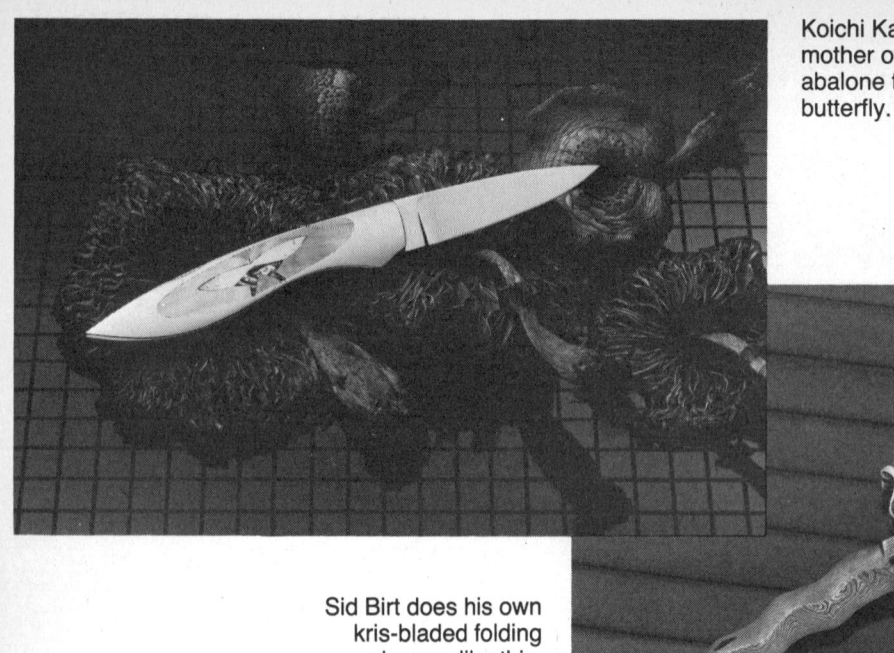

Koichi Kagawa inlays mother of pearl and abalone to find a butterfly. (Weyer photo)

Sid Birt does his own kris-bladed folding dagger, like this. (Weyer photo)

THE FOLDING STANDARDS
Fancy Folders

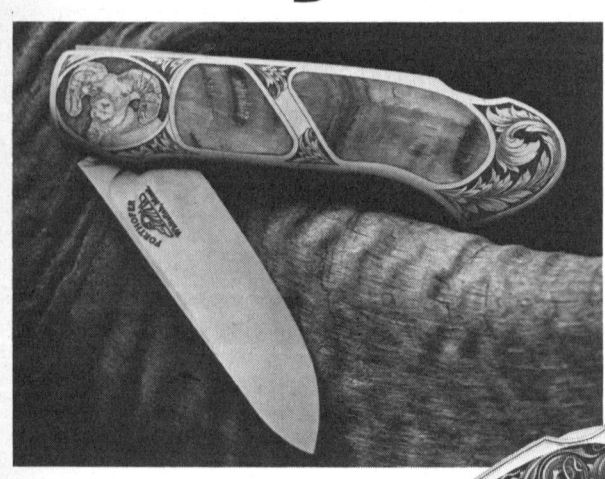

Steve Hoel put sheep horn and gold together with Steve Lindsay's help for this elegant folder.

All-out sheephunter special is by Pete Forthofer. (Rice photo)

This simple Ron Lake folder is in hard-rolled 18K gold and mother-of-pearl, which is fancy enough. (Weyer photo)

Finally, Steve Lindsay had to try it all, so here it is in 24K gold and steel. (Weyer photo)

94 KNIVES '88

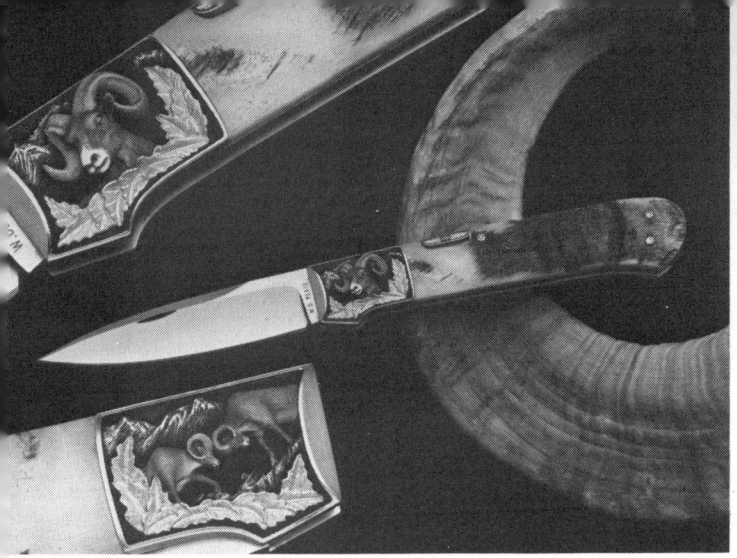

(Above left) W.D. Pease can go for the 100 percent sheep hunter business, too, and he does it like this. (Weyer photo)

(Above right) Bill Simons made this neat little gent's locking folder. (Long photo)

(Left) John Busfield fitted this folder up with gold and other stuff. (Weyer photo)

THE FOLDING STANDARDS
Fancy Folders

Steve Schwarzer fancied this remarkable crown antler with his usual grotesquerie. (Weyer photo)

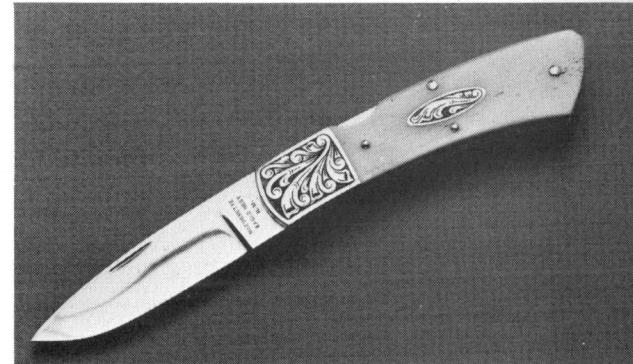

Harvey McBurnette did a D2 blade, polished stag, calls it Spirit River.

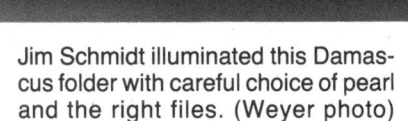

Jim Schmidt illuminated this Damascus folder with careful choice of pearl and the right files. (Weyer photo)

Worm (Leon Pittman) did this in Damascus and tortoiseshell. (Weyer photo)

EIGHTH ANNUAL EDITION **95**

TRENDS
SIMPLE KNIVES

IT IS not easy to write of the simple knife. It is—that simple knife—much easier identified than described, as you will see.

There are several forms of simplicity. There is the simple shape, the simple assembly, the simple surface, and the simple intent or function. Those do not get us anywhere near such less obvious matters as simple metallurgy, simple grinding, simple materials.

History and custom play a part here. A common three-bladed pocketknife pattern is thought of as a pretty simple and straightforward knife by anyone who never tried to make one by hand. A French chef's knife is bound to be a plain, flat, simple knife, but it is very easy to have one ground wrong. What could be simpler in the cutlery field than a bayonet? The answer is almost anything that doesn't have to be securely fastened, quickly and easily, to the end of a rifle.

We had better start approaching what is indeed a simple knife. And then let that build until it becomes no longer simple, having had one or another layer of complication laid upon it.

Leaving aside knives that fold, we can start with most of the common butcher pattern knives, those with plain steel flat blades, and handles of wooden slabs riveted through. Regardless of pattern, all such are simple knives. Chefs knives and cooking knives and kitchen knives made with forged bolsters are more complicated, but still simple—they have simple shapes, they are a simple assembly, and so on. Their manufacture is more complex, of course.

Over the past few years a great many custom knifemakers—and following them, a number of commercial sources—have made what we have chosen to call "naked steel" knives. These are knives made, handle and all, from one piece of steel. A lot of things could be simpler. Most are made by stock removal and given a rather complicated heat treatment. Except in their most rudimentary form, such one-piece steel knives often require very complicated equipment of the knifemaker in order to be made economically. So, in the main, the satisfactory one-piece knife is an un-simple knife.

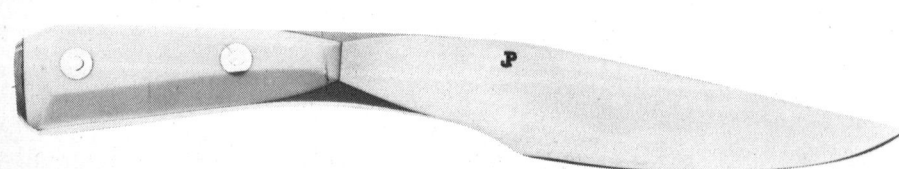

This James Porter deer hunter knife is only an 01 blade, two slabs of Micarta and two brass rivets, but it is made elegant by its surfaces and their relationships one to the next. (Weyer photo)

Then there is a wide array of very common patterns, made for generations, which we may think of as simple knives even though, compared to the butcher patterns, their manufacture and their shapes and their assembly are somewhat complicated. This covers most of the hunter patterns and belt knives, whether full tang, stick tang, half-tang in construction, whether forged or merely ground to shape, with or without guards and pommels, so long as we are talking of the simpler shapes and easy grinds.

It does not take long to un-simple such a simple knife. For example, you could put a D-guard on it, or brass knuckles; for another example, you could grind in a gut-hook; you could provide some saw-teeth; you could even give it simply a second edge—every one of those options turns a simple knife into a complex knife and clutters up the handling unbelievably.

There are knives which are simple in function. Perhaps the cleanest and clearest example of such a knife would be the Fairbairn-Sykes dagger. This is a single-function weapon built with the capacity for a clean, deep stab, and very little else. The typical skinning knife with a broad blade, curved edge and hardly any point at all is another functionally simple knife—it will slice and that is all.

There was, an issue or two ago, a knife by Charles Weiss on the cover of this publication. It was a very simple single-edged dagger shape, most uncomplicated in profile. However, its handle was a hollow silver casting and that simple-looking fellow was quite a complicated knife. On that same cover was a straight-forward locking folder by Lance Kelly with very strong and clean lines, but it wasn't simple because it was covered with very complex engraving and inlaying and it had, therefore, a complex surface. The application of a camouflaged Teflon finish to W.C. Davis' austere fighting knife on that cover did not make a complex knife of it, however.

Such technological advances as deep hollow-grinding, mixed bright and dull finishes, no-solder guard joints are not simple. No Damascus knife is simple, but many forged steel knives are.

Simplicity is a virtue. As I have heard some people in Pennsylvania say admiringly: "It's plain."

Here are some virtuous knives of the current crop.

Ken Warner

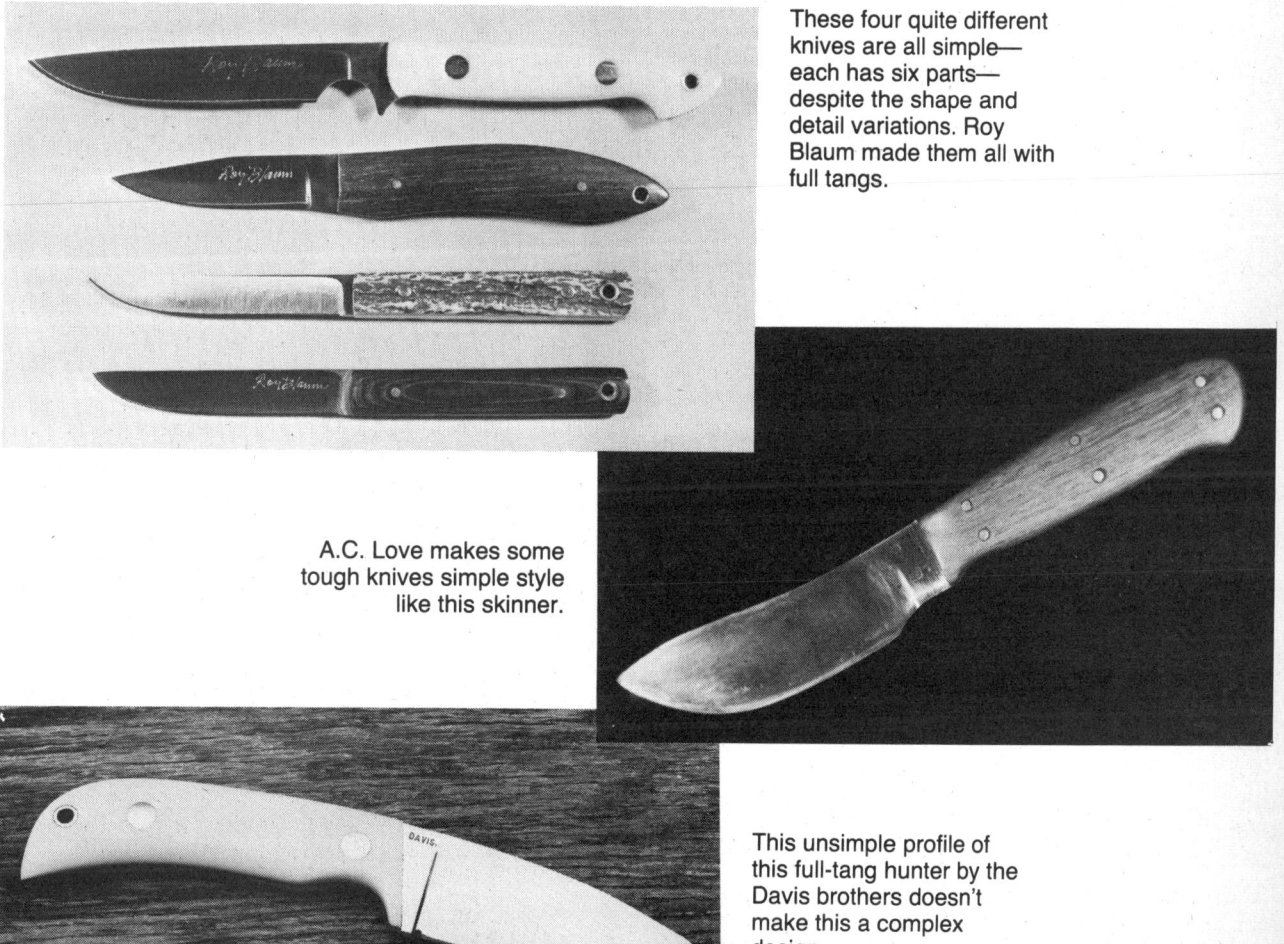

These four quite different knives are all simple—each has six parts—despite the shape and detail variations. Roy Blaum made them all with full tangs.

A.C. Love makes some tough knives simple style like this skinner.

This unsimple profile of this full-tang hunter by the Davis brothers doesn't make this a complex design.

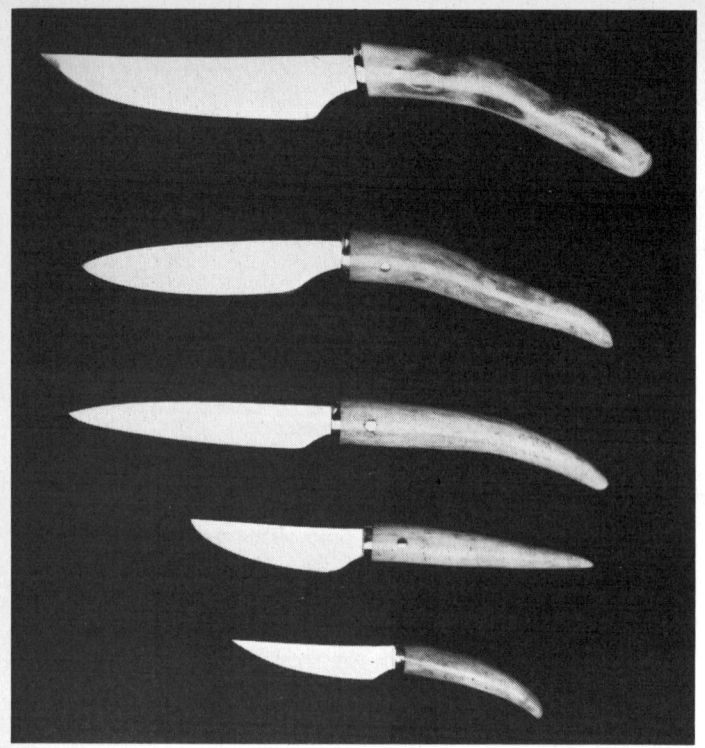

(Left) These C.E. Haynes knives all have pinned stick tangs and each has four parts. Shows that variety does not depend on complexity.

This tiny lady's purse knife by Jeff C. Morgan is getting down to real basics, even if it does have pearl scales. (Fitzgerald photo)

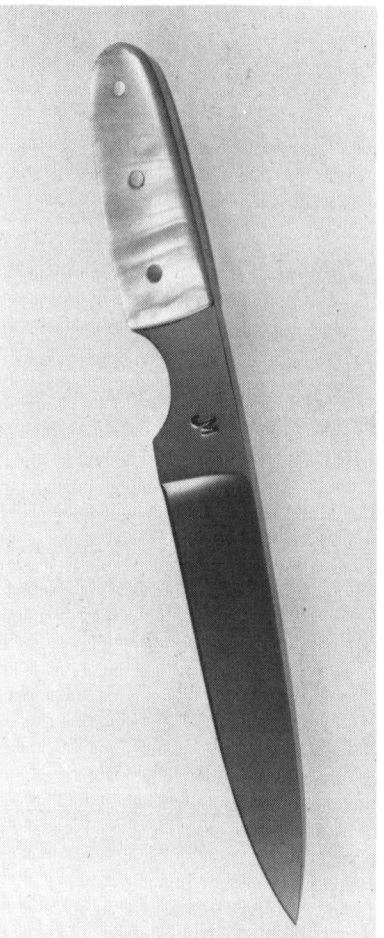

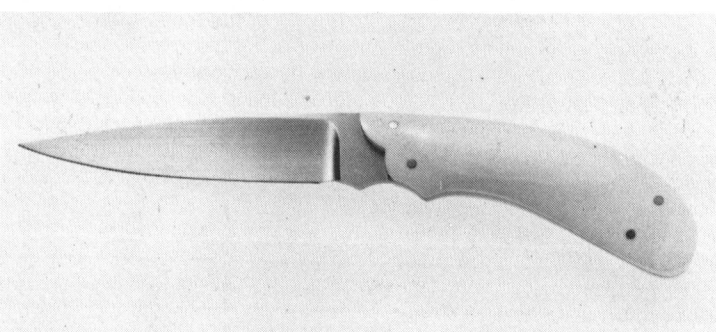

This is, and we quote maker Jim Sornberger, "a plain-Jane using knife." It's elephant ivory and 154CM so it's not a *cheap* using knife. (Fitzgerald photo)

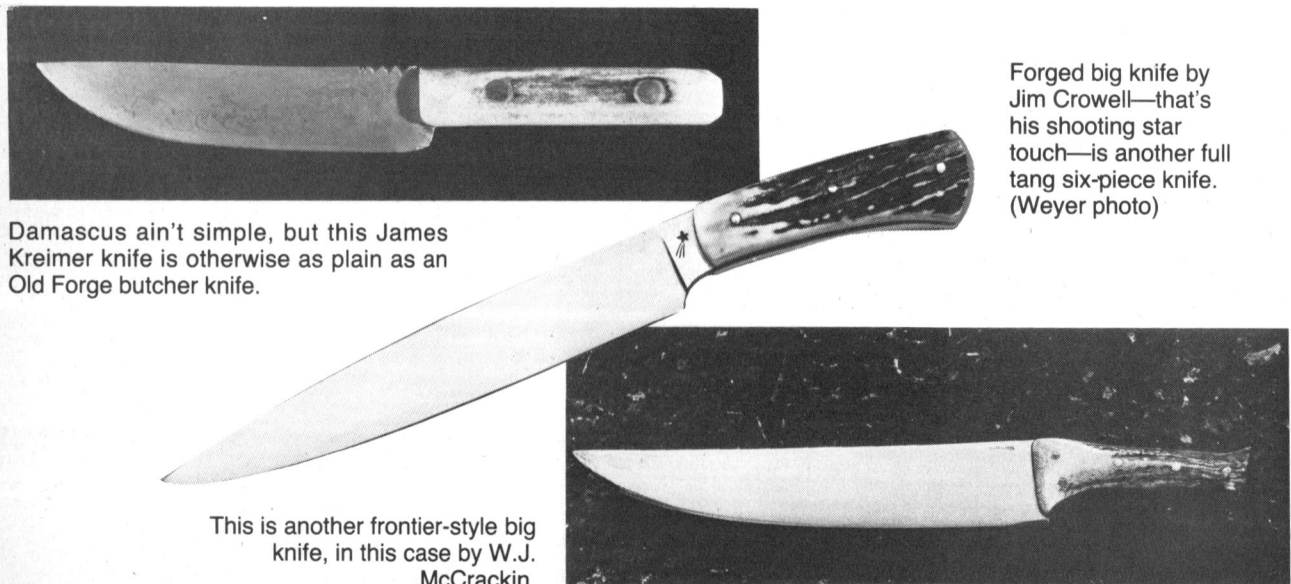

Damascus ain't simple, but this James Kreimer knife is otherwise as plain as an Old Forge butcher knife.

Forged big knife by Jim Crowell—that's his shooting star touch—is another full tang six-piece knife. (Weyer photo)

This is another frontier-style big knife, in this case by W.J. McCrackin.

98 KNIVES '88

TRENDS
CARVING SETS, ANYONE?

THERE ARE very few knifemakers who have not made *one* carving set, but there are not many who make many sets. First, I suppose, carving has somewhat left the scene, save the obligatory holiday fowl generally dismembered in the kitchen. And then, well, they can be a lot of trouble, carving sets can.

There are two general categories, I find. There are the knife and fork done in the maker's personal style and unmistakable, or as sets here by Pugh and Hudson and Schoenfeld. And those done up and styled more usually.

Mostly, the forks are two-tined in classic carving fork usage. Nearly all are handmade, but sometimes the craftsman will simply "borrow" fork parts from another set.

As for technique, it's the same old breakdown—some forge and some grind.

Ken Warner

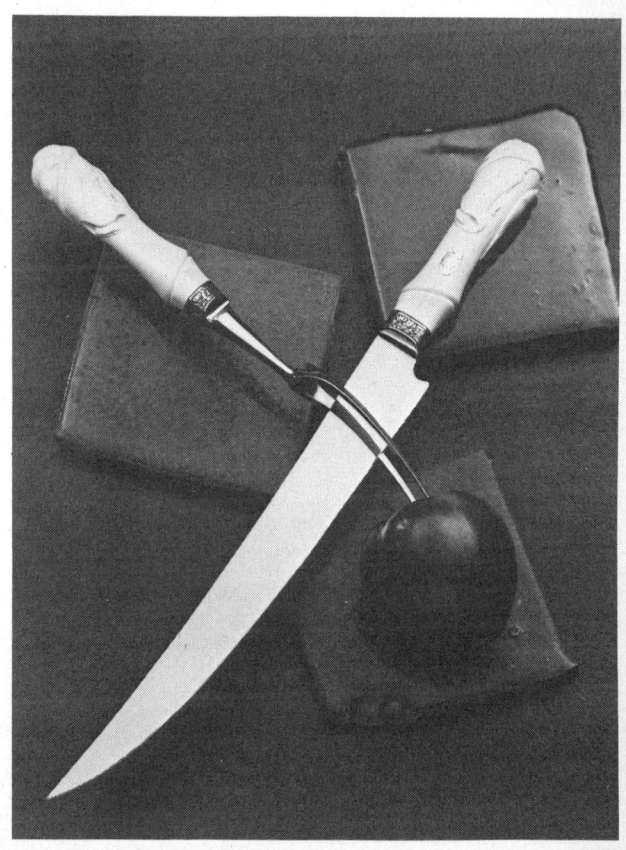

Deluxe carving set by T.M. Dowell is scaled beautifully and much bigger than it looks—the knife is nearly 19 inches long. Set is engraved by Ron Skaggs. (Weyer photo)

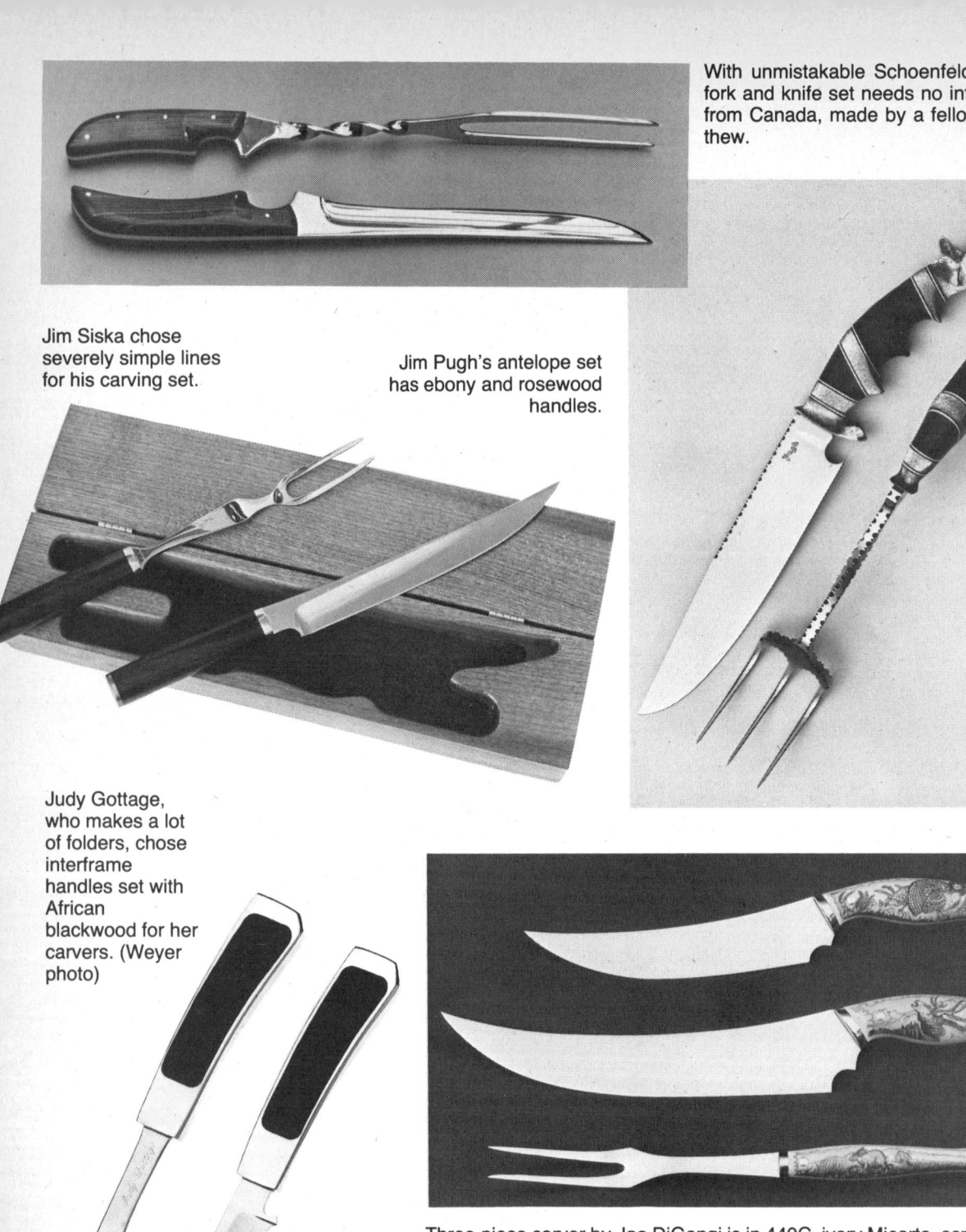

With unmistakable Schoenfeld handles, this fork and knife set needs no introduction—it's from Canada, made by a fellow named Matthew.

Jim Siska chose severely simple lines for his carving set.

Jim Pugh's antelope set has ebony and rosewood handles.

Judy Gottage, who makes a lot of folders, chose interframe handles set with African blackwood for her carvers. (Weyer photo)

Three-piece carver by Joe DiGangi is in 440C, ivory Micarta, scrimmed by Jake Bell in game scenes.

Forged carving tools by Robbin Hudson have his typical octagonal walnut and brass handles.

100 KNIVES '88

TRENDS
SINGLE-EDGED FIGHTERS

SOON OR LATE, some uncontrollable pendulum of taste and fashion is going to swing and one'll be seeing a lot of single-edge so-called fighting knife designs. They may be called utility knives or something similar (survival maybe?) and they may have what we think of as double-edged shapes, but there will be just that one edge.

There are more than one or two reasons this is easy to forecast:

- A single edge is easier to make, all else equal, and stronger or lighter—your choice, but you don't get both.
- A single edge is easier to deal with in everyday work, and I say that as a great double-edge fan. If you don't believe it, you never tried it. And you might ask a fellow who makes sheaths for views on the subject as well.
- A single-edged knife is legal—all else equal—in jurisdictions where the double edge can get you in bad trouble. It's a question of definition. Your lawyer could argue in many places that your single-edge is just a big knife; in a lot of those same places, two edges means "dagger" and a dagger is a bad no-no.

Those presumably well-meaning folks on power trips who draw up laws and regulations for us lesser beings have said dagger-carrying is a felony in a great many city and state codes. (No, they don't know what a dagger is or anything else on the subject, but compound ignorance has never given a legislator pause.)

Besides, you're not giving up much if you stick to one-edged knives, truth to tell. *Any* 4- to 6-inch knife of sturdy build with some point and a sharp edge will work out fine. Maybe it won't be optimal, but 90 percent is good.

Ken Warner

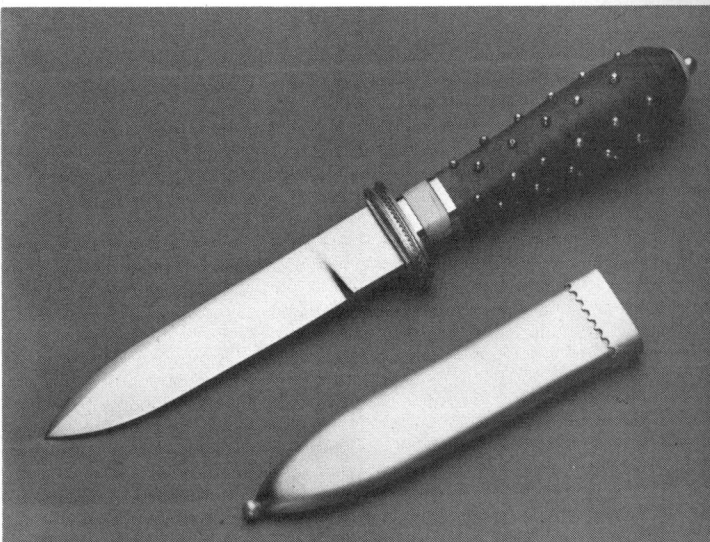

In old San Francisco, cutlers made belt knives like this modern one by Patrick Donovan for serious social purpose. (Johnson photo)

Classic Kuzan Oda meld of styles is a single-edge no-nonsense design in 154CM and black Micarta.

Phil Hartsfield calls this the Choora, and neither it nor the original Afghan knife needs a second edge.

Here's another traditional American large hunting knife, this one by Jimmy Fikes.

Mel Pardue sees no need for a second edge on a slim boot knife like this. (Weyer photo)

A fancy Scots-style utility knife by Pat Crawford.

There would be very little difference in use between Doc Hagen's stag-handled hunter and Gordon Dempsey's tiger-striped short Damascus fighter. (Hagen photo by Weyer)

Old-timey Bowie by Jim Crowell is just a long hunting knife, right? (Luther photo)

TRENDS
BIRD AND TROUT KNIVES

WE MAY BE reasonably certain that a fellow named Gary Powers considered the gear that went with him on his U2 flights over Russia very carefully. As it actually happened, it didn't make a hoot of difference what Powers packed, but he thought about it a lot.

For a knife, he chose a bird and trout pattern, a small game knife from Randall. It was a very sensible choice and you, too, can make such choices. And the spread of designs is a lot wider than Powers had to pick from.

The range now starts with Jack Crockford's finger length (handle and blade) minimum numbers a veteran guide (and state game commission boss, too) has found capable of cleaning trout, ruffed grouse and quail to suit him. It gets up to about the Randall design in size.

Some of these knives are as ruthless as barbed wire, others as refined as a sword cane. Meat hunter or gentry? Well, maybe.

They run slim, and they run short and stout. Probably more of them are a little fancy than straight hunters are. And they almost universally offer a pretty fine point.

We call them bird and trout knives, which means small game knives. What they are are pocketknives for fellows who don't like to fold their tools.

Ken Warner

Tiny Jack Crockford has everything for the grouse hunter who trouts, to include the blood scoop on the handle corner.

This Bill Herndon pearl-handled bird knife is just a little longer than a dollar bill.

Wayne Olson makes the point that a trout knife has to be comfortable edge up. (Semmer photo)

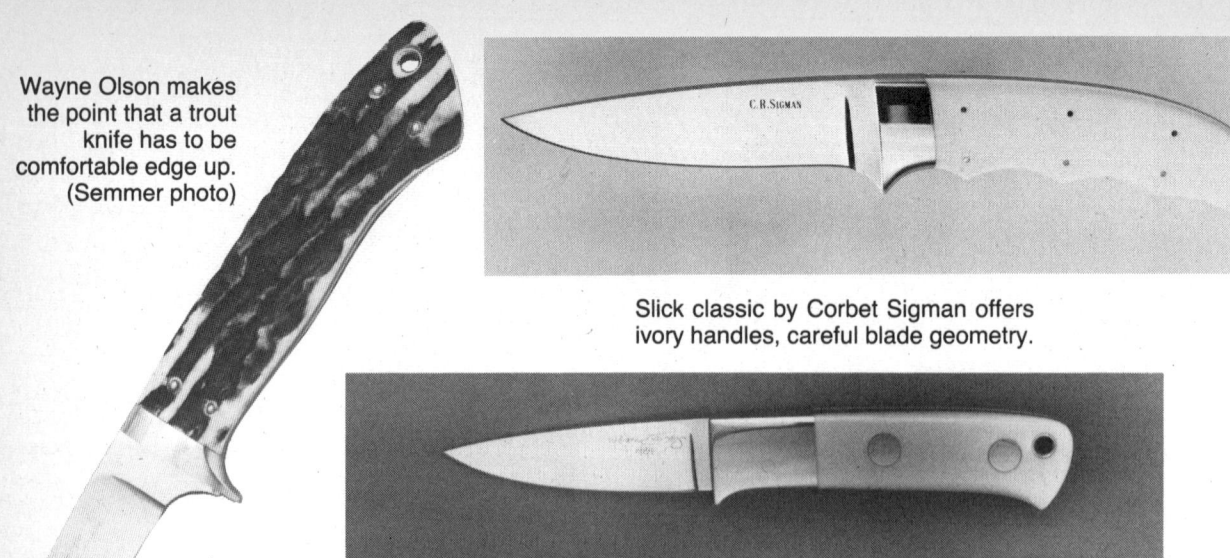

Slick classic by Corbet Sigman offers ivory handles, careful blade geometry.

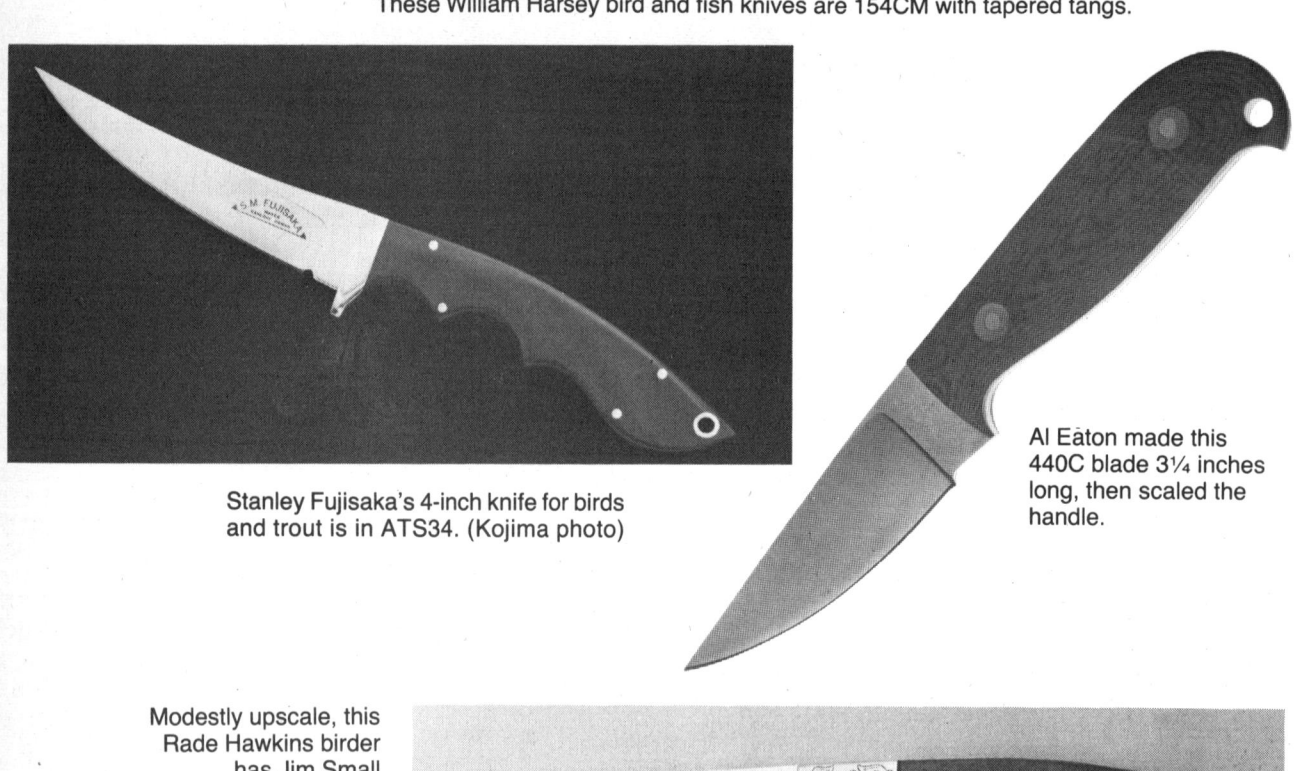

These William Harsey bird and fish knives are 154CM with tapered tangs.

Stanley Fujisaka's 4-inch knife for birds and trout is in ATS34. (Kojima photo)

Al Eaton made this 440C blade 3¼ inches long, then scaled the handle.

Modestly upscale, this Rade Hawkins birder has Jim Small engraving, pink ivory handle.

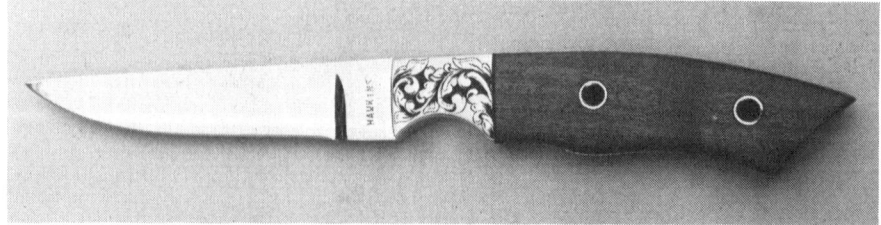

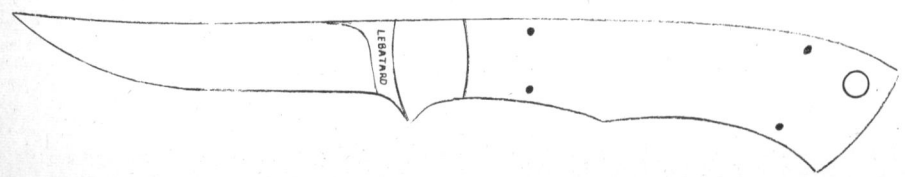

This Paul LeBatard outline practically defines the standard trout-and-bird shape.

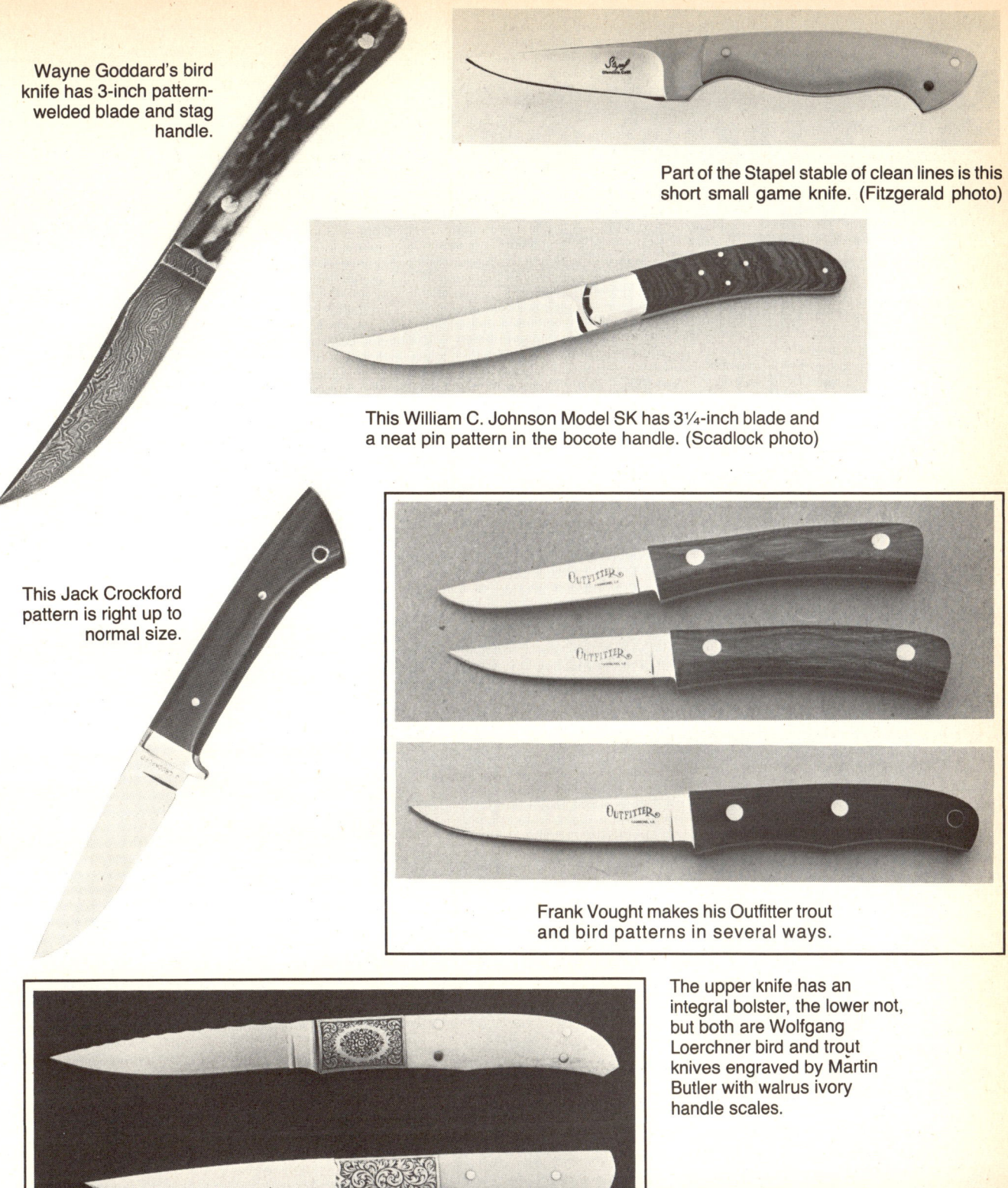

Wayne Goddard's bird knife has 3-inch pattern-welded blade and stag handle.

Part of the Stapel stable of clean lines is this short small game knife. (Fitzgerald photo)

This William C. Johnson Model SK has 3¼-inch blade and a neat pin pattern in the bocote handle. (Scadlock photo)

This Jack Crockford pattern is right up to normal size.

Frank Vought makes his Outfitter trout and bird patterns in several ways.

The upper knife has an integral bolster, the lower not, but both are Wolfgang Loerchner bird and trout knives engraved by Martin Butler with walrus ivory handle scales.

J.T. Downie makes nice smooth lines in his bird and trout knife.

TRENDS
RETURN OF THE SABERTOOTH

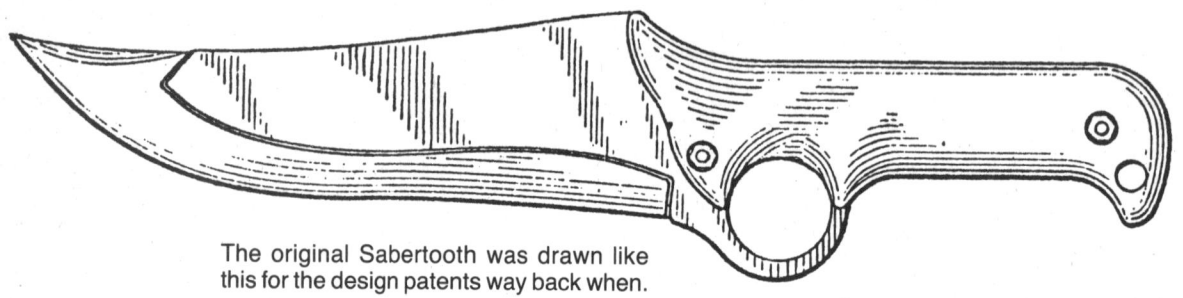

The original Sabertooth was drawn like this for the design patents way back when.

JEFFERSON Spivey has shown up again. Actually, he says he's been there all the time.

And who is Jefferson Spivey, you might well ask?

Jefferson Spivey invented and got a bunch of publicity for his Sabertooth, which he said was the ideal trail-riding horsebacker's knife way back in 1967 and again in 1977. That was in GUN WORLD, and very likely thanks to Jack Lewis who grooves on horses and on knives. And on the odd promoter.

Now Spivey is revved up with the new sawtoothed Sabertooth and champing at the bit to fill your $225 order. It's nice to think a fellow can invent knives one decade and his own saddle the next and ride a spell in between and then get back to us.

And here he is.

Ken Warner

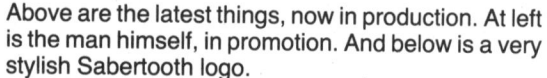

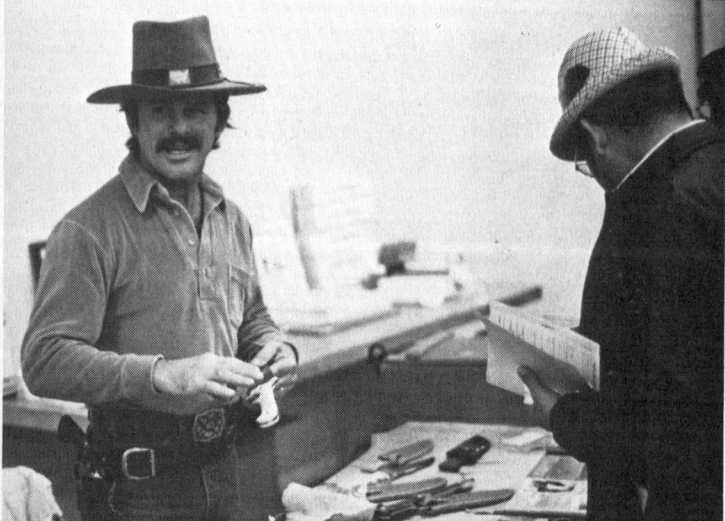

Above are the latest things, now in production. At left is the man himself, in promotion. And below is a very stylish Sabertooth logo.

TRENDS
SWORDS AND OTHER FANTASIES

ONE OF this writer's favorite bits of whimsy is the political slogan that goes: "Don't vote. It encourages them." I'm beginning to feel that way about the variety of fantasticalia amongst us.

Swords—swords made to exacting standards, if not original design, in the 1980s—are pretty fantastic. They make as much sense as fantasy fiction, one branch of which is called "sword and sorcery," but no more.

And the more outrageous creations we call fantasy knives are, if possible, just the least bit farther out in fourth field (the game they're in doesn't have the simple left, right and center fields). Some have gone beyond being difficult to make unto being almost impossible to hold.

And do you think talk like this is going to do anything to discourage fantasy? I don't. The genie is out of that bottle and we may as well put up the stopper. Our best hope is it stops short of a feeding frenzy.

In the meantime, here they are, all the somewhat weird pretties, and perhaps an ugly or two. Doesn't seem to matter, one way or the other.

There is no comfort in what I heard a swordmaker mutter: "Those fighting knives in camo sheaths—those are the fantasy knives." Or is there?

Ken Warner

Tom Maringer and a sword—a straight-bladed Arkansas katana, scabbarded for back carry and called "Ninja-To."

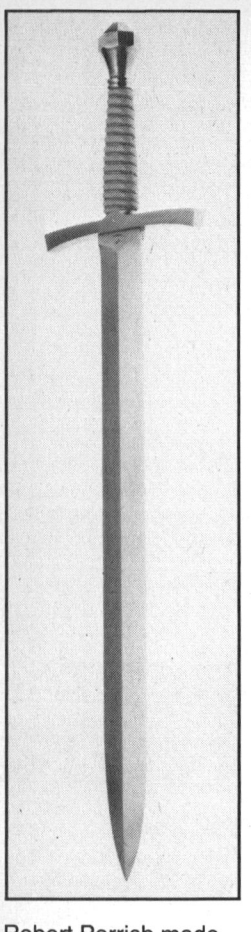

Robert Parrish made this knightly type sword.

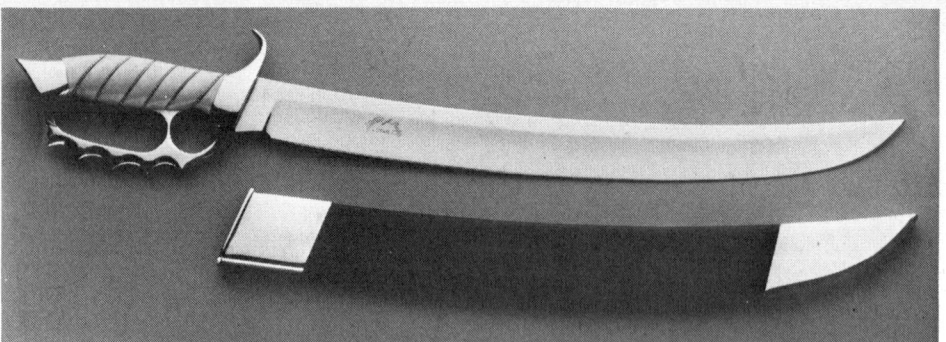

Steven Rapp forged this 16-inch cutlass blade, did the wrapped handle in ivory Micarta. (Weyer photo)

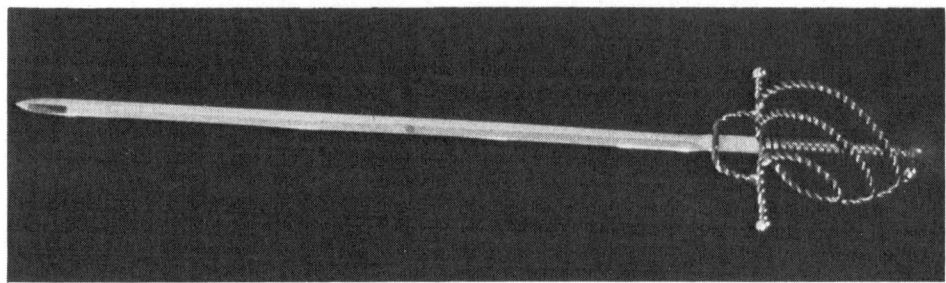

Rob Johns and John Damagala of Medieval Customs make this rapier and others.

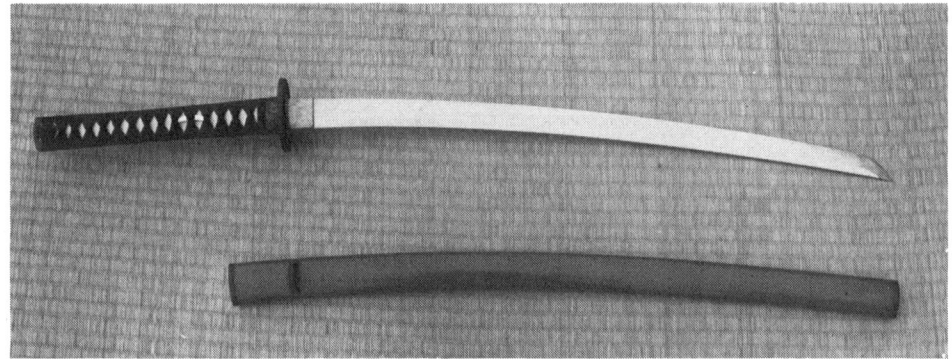

Michael Bell makes katanas from sponge iron in the old way.

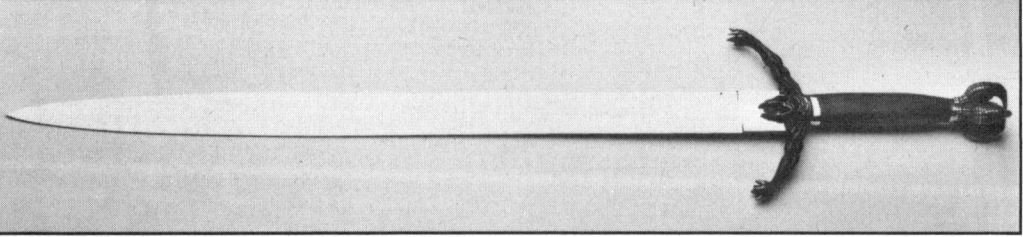

Jody Sampson made this gargoyle-hilted broadsword.

108 KNIVES '88

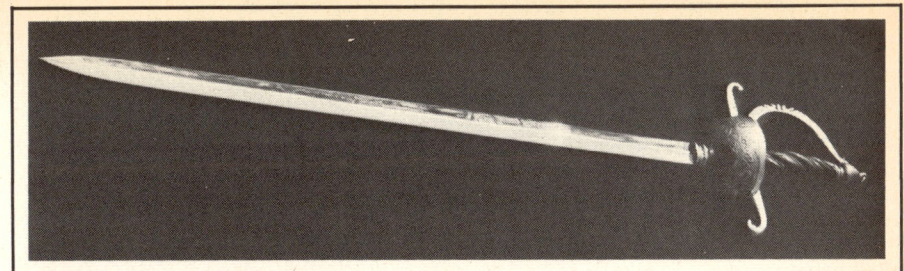

Daniel Watson of Angel Swords calls this forged 45-inch sword his "Cavalier Battlesword."

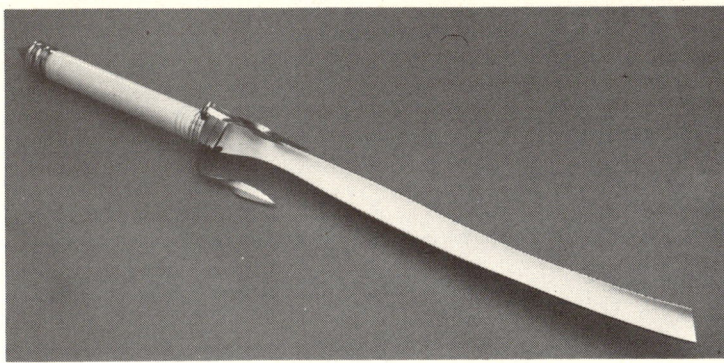

Mickey Tedder's imaginative trident-guarded slicing sword has a 24-inch blade. (Weyer photo)

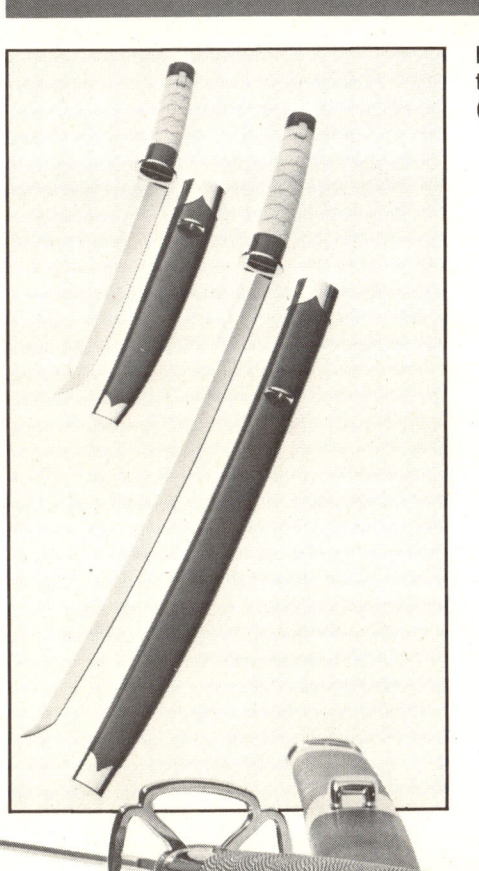

Matching katana and tanto are by Ray Beers. (Weyer photo)

Scott Lankton seems to make at least one nice Viking sword a year. This one has a 31-inch blade. (Weyer photo)

For probably visible reasons, Maringer calls this Katana 2001. (VerHoeven photo)

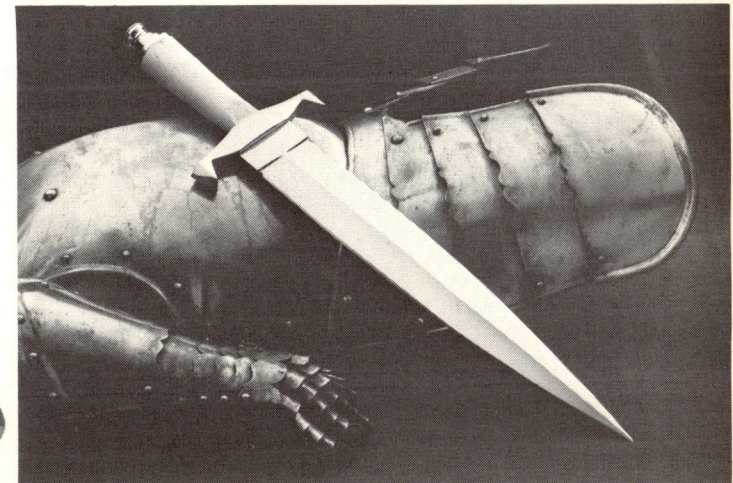

Judy Gottage and Chuck Stewart teamed up to make this 17-inch short sword. (Weyer photo)

EIGHTH ANNUAL EDITION 109

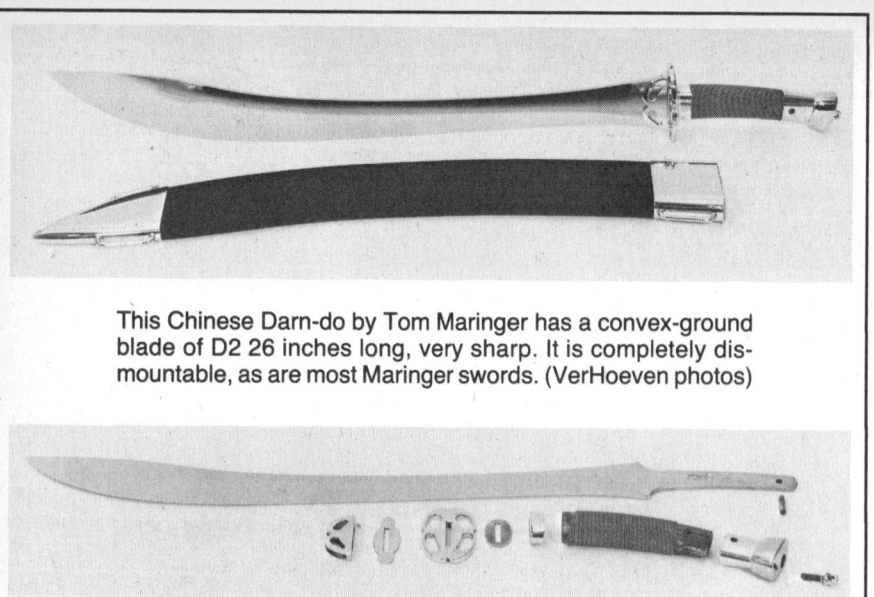

This Chinese Darn-do by Tom Maringer has a convex-ground blade of D2 26 inches long, very sharp. It is completely dismountable, as are most Maringer swords. (VerHoeven photos)

This 5-pound Norm Bardsley "Dragonslayer" offers arrowheads, an axe and a kris in just a foot of blade. (Weyer photo)

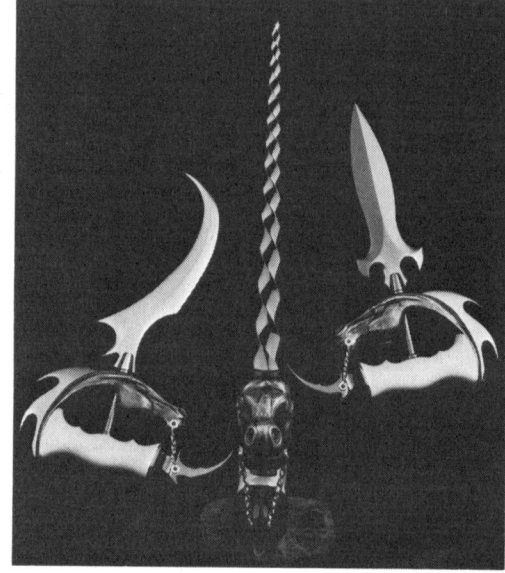

Paul Fox is running for the presidency of fantasy, calls this the Tricorn. (Weyer photo)

The other party's candidate is Gil Hibben who did this Black Widow from a Paul Ehlers design. (Weyer photo)

Fairly straightforward dagger for a ceremony a long way elsewhere, this Robert Lutes fantasia has an 11½-inch blade, ivory and amber grip. (Weyer photo)

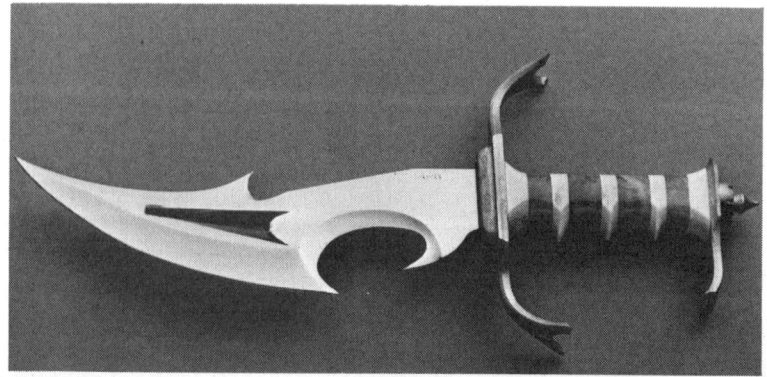

110 KNIVES '88

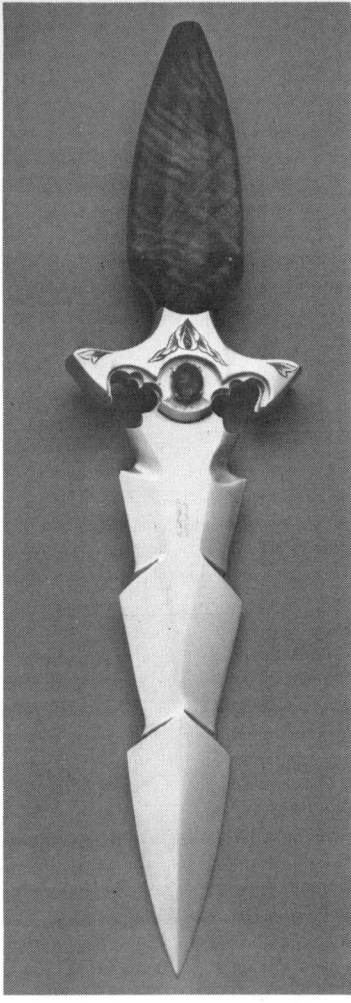

Frank Gamble handworked the blade of this 12-inch "Freedom Flame" dagger, says he doesn't want to make another. (Weyer photo)

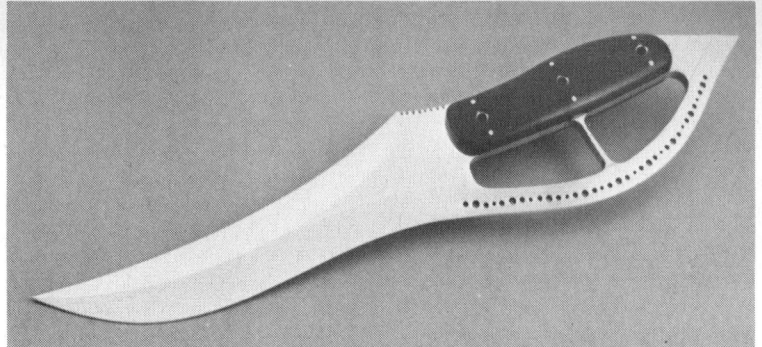

Plain Jane by Pat Crawford would not long ago have been a fantasy knife.

Once this simple Dave Longworth snake would have been a wild one, but no more. (Scadlock photo)

This Curt Erickson dagger is merely fancy by today's exotic standards. (Weyer photo)

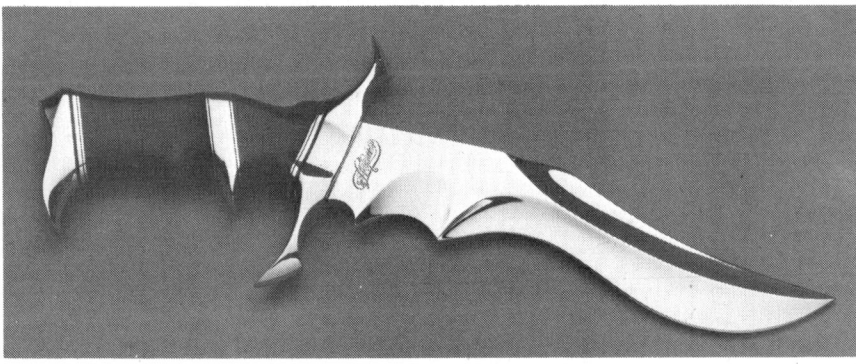

Grinding like this Bill Luckett work is itself fantastic. (Weyer photo)

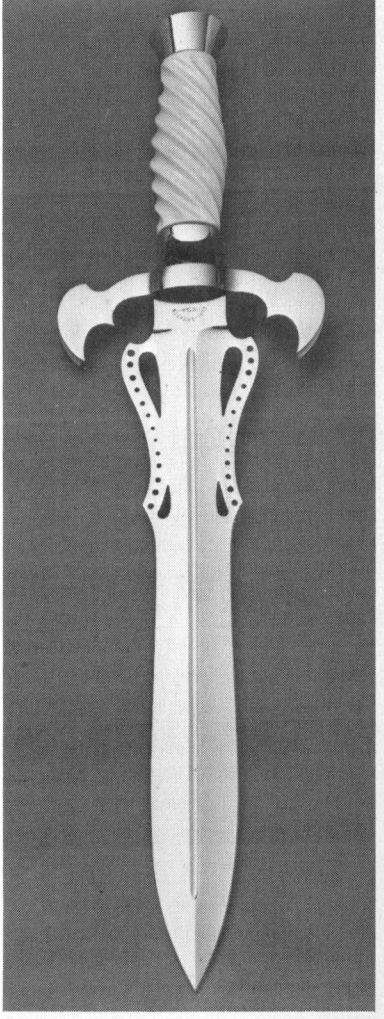

EIGHTH ANNUAL EDITION **111**

TRENDS
THE KOPIS, THE KUKRI AND ALL THAT

ALEXANDER the Great would have been proud. The basic fighting short sword his troops carried across the roof of the world into India is now conquering America. Crooked knives have not only established a beachhead, they are breaking out all over in sizes from as short as 5 inches to as long as 24 inches.

These Kukris—most people call them all the kukri, but the kukri is a rather obvious descendant of a knife the Greeks called the kopis—are available fresh—or perhaps a little rusty—from arsenals in India, from non-arsenals in Japan, from the hands of many American knifemakers, and even, it has come to pass, from American factories. It is unlikely, but not impossible, that the kukri shape will become the next year's tanto, nor is it likely the kukri will develop a selling explosion like the knives of Rambo, but there is distinctly a bunch of kukris out there.

This is no surprise attack. Atlanta Cutlery has been selling thousands of GI-type kukris every year for half a decade at least. Kukris are the national knives of Nepal, and therefore of Gurkhas, the much admired mercenary battalions of the British Army. Each and every kukri, therefore, carries the stuff of legend in its crooked shape.

We have seen them as short as 5 inches in a standard working-class fighter-style. We have seen them in parade versions. We know of one fellow, who's also known to you, who thinks the kukri is a great sidearm and has practiced diligently to become expert with it. You can look foward to manuals and treatises on the subject. After all, anyone who has seen a manual which seeks to instruct users in how to make a Woodsman's Pal perform in combat—yes, there really was one such in World War II—should not be suprised at anything when it comes to large knives.

And what of reality? Reality seems to be that for the expert user the kukri style has much in its favor. This writer has used one some, but has never learned *how* to use it. The result has been that at about every 20th or 30th stroke something unusual happens and a great deal of work gets done. However, it is this writer's opinion that learning to use the kukri is at least as difficult as learning to serve a tennis ball adequately.

It is not expected that that will make any difference at all. All those crooked knives are flooding onto the beaches and we are going to have to deal with them. You can see a sampling right here so you can begin to get ready.

Ken Warner

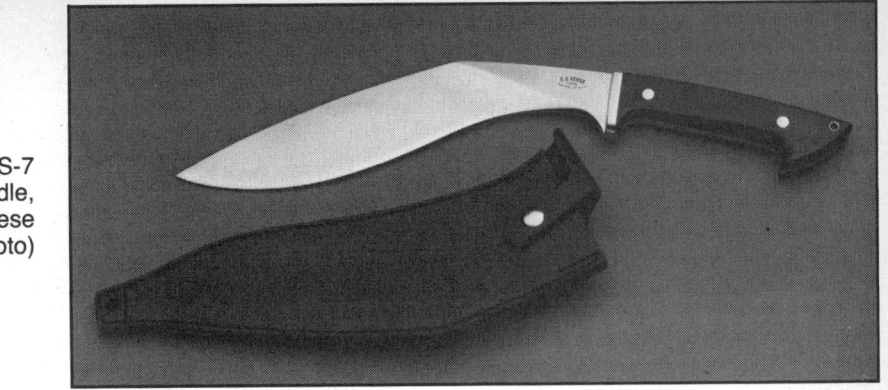

Roy Genge's kukri has an S-7 blade, black phenolic handle, and a distinctly un-Nepalese handle shape. (Weyer photo)

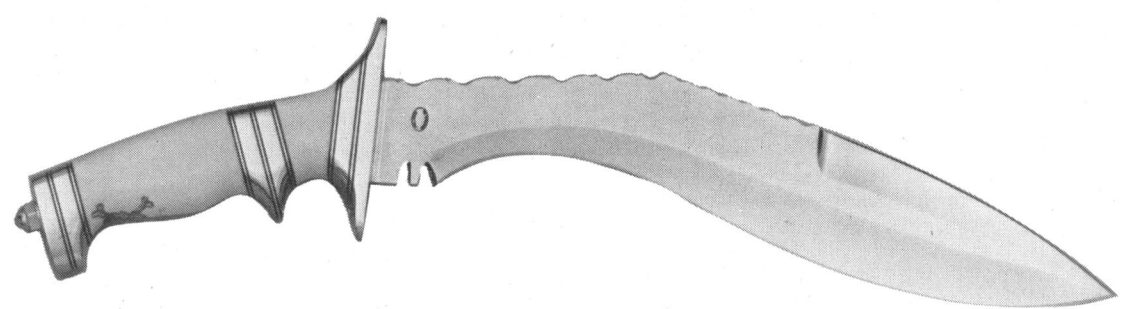

White Micarta and 440C and correct ricasso ornament distinguish this Paul Halloway kukri. (Scadlock photo)

This is Phill Hartsfield's kukri and companion, both in cord-wrapped tool steel. (Weyer photo)

W.C. Davis is finding good sales for this modified kukri shape in a military-finish fighter. (Long photo)

This Chuck Stapel crooked fighter is somewhat uptown in ivory and Bruce Shaw engraving. (Fitzgerald photo)

Frank Vought makes another blue-collar kukri in the survival series of his Outfitter label.

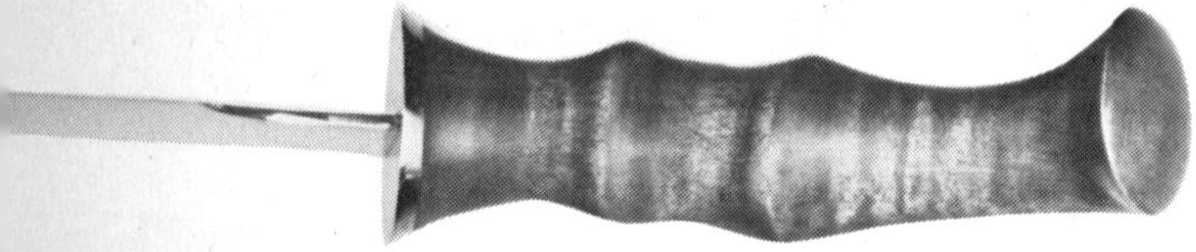

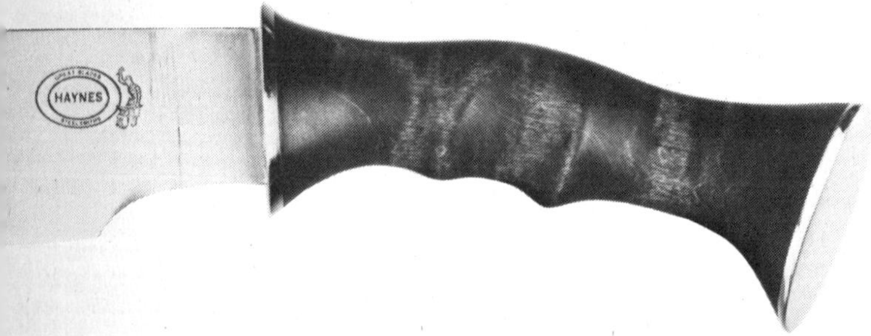

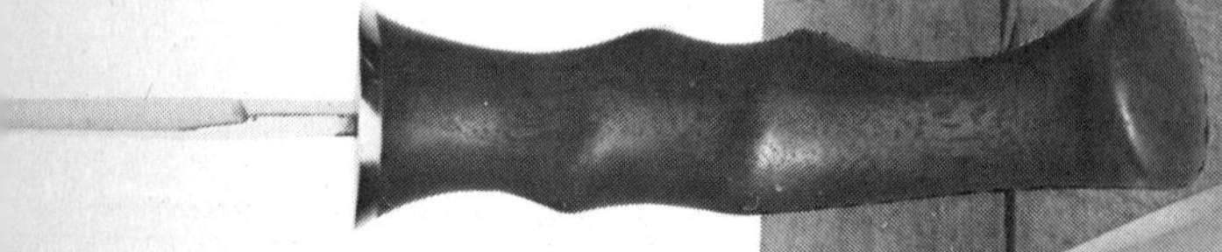

For a wide variety of knife shapes and sizes, C.E. Haynes has adapted the typical Nepalese kukri handle look.

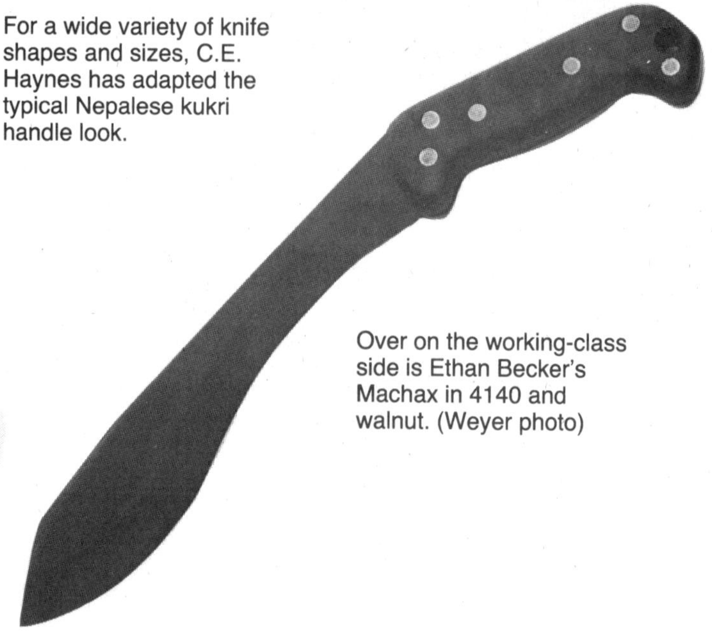

Over on the working-class side is Ethan Becker's Machax in 4140 and walnut. (Weyer photo)

(Right) This is an S-curve fighter from Scott Shoemaker in A-6 steel, brass and kingwood. (Pfahler photo)

TRENDS
MINIATURES KEEP GROWING

THOSE who specialize in making miniature knives have formed The Miniature Knifemakers' Society. The secretary is Gary Kelley and this is what he has to say:

"We formed our Society in April of 1987 with 14 Charter Members and at this writing number 22. Our goals and activities include:

1. Promoting miniature knife collecting.
2. Helping each other make better miniatures.
3. Increasing public awareness and rewarding collectors who show their collections.
4. Offering guarantees of our work.

"We begin to accomplish this with news releases and photos for writers and the media. We send our membership list to collectors of miniatures who ask for it. Our newsletter helps with Goal Two—we share tips and techniques, sometimes arrange material swaps. And at shows, we offer certificates to miniature collections on display.

"Goals Three and Four will be met if we faithfully follow up this course," Kelley believes. "Credibility will be our reward."

It is the intention of the Society to provide more than a promotional background. It has, for instance, asked KNIVES '88 to tell you that even hardened and tempered tool steel miniatures are frail objects when faced with real work. Do not defy the laws of physics by prying with them.

Deborah Warner

Minature Knifemaker's Society	
CHARTER MEMBERS	13. Gary Kelley
1. Earl Witsaman	14. Sid Birt
2. Jim Pugh	
3. Ken McFall	
4. Kevin Wright	ANNUAL MEMBERS
5. Tom Edwards	15. Chuck Stapel
6. Al Eaton	16. Mark David Wahlster
7. Ray Beers	17. Mike Wesolowski
8. Terry Kranning	18. Don Hedrick
9. Tom Hetmanski	19. Larry Harley
10. Paul Myers	20. Harry L. Stalter
11. Alex Rose	21. Gordon Chard
12. Wayne Goddard	22. Mike Tamboli

This Lee Baskett fighter is about the upper limits for a miniature. Sheath is by Baker. (Scadlock photo)

(Right) The Katana by Terry Kranning, is 5 inches long and handled in ivory; the dagger by Gary Kelley is Damascus, mokume and pearl; the single-edged Mark Wahster sword is flat-ground Damascus. (Kelley photo)

This is an Earl Witsaman dagger in a 6-inch bell jar. (Warner photo)

Jim Pugh has translated his entire line of art knives into miniatures, feature for feature, line for line.

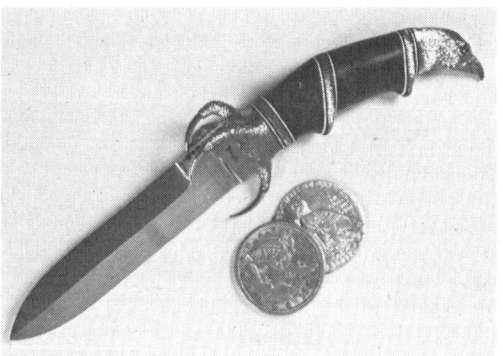

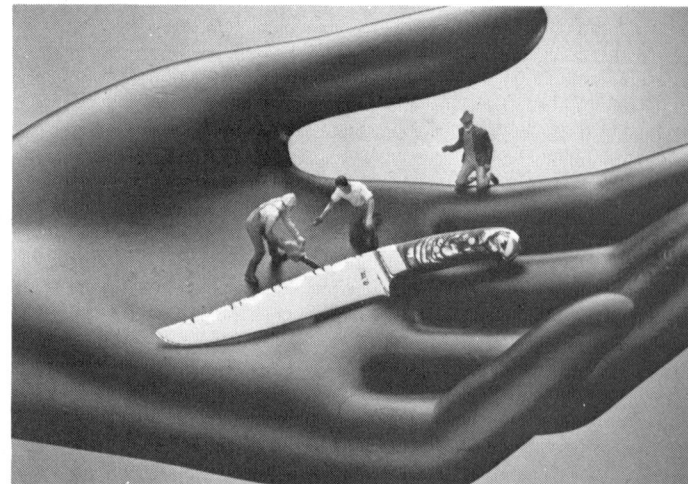

Confused? That's a normal-sized hand and those are very tiny figures and the knife is a miniature by Earl Witsaman. (Weyer photo)

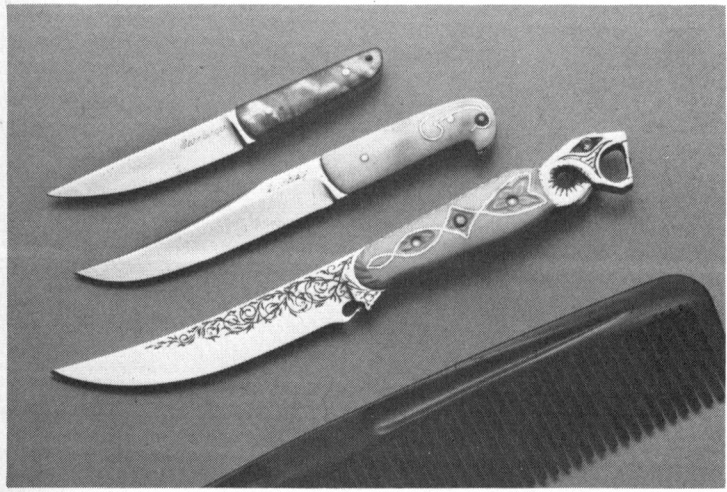

Traditional Katana comes apart traditionally. It's wire Damascus and curly maple by Scott Shoemaker. (Pfahler photo)

The long one is 3 inches; that apart, these knives have all the trim and technique normal to Jim Sornberger. (Weyer photo)

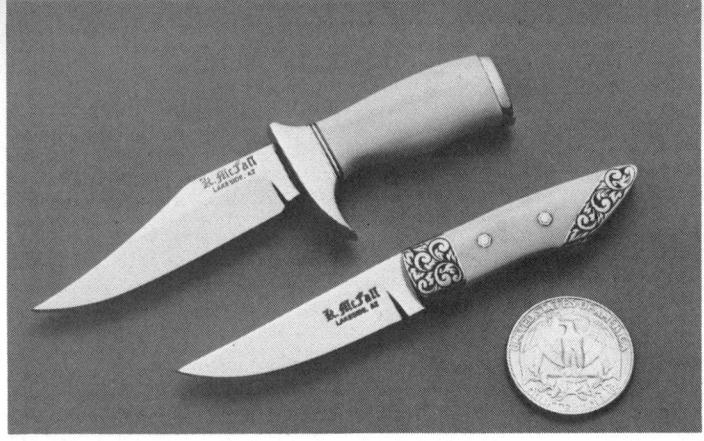

Ken McFall does these in ivory and ATS34, has the engraving nicely scaled. (Weyer photo)

Tom Hetmanski bayonets are close copies of the originals. (Scadlock photo)

The blade of this Michael Walker locker is 1 inch long. The knife is furnished with two sets of handle scales—black pearl and black Micarta.

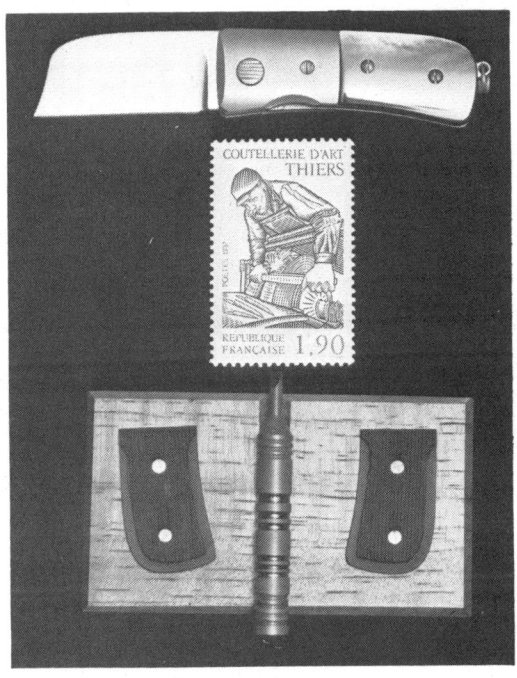

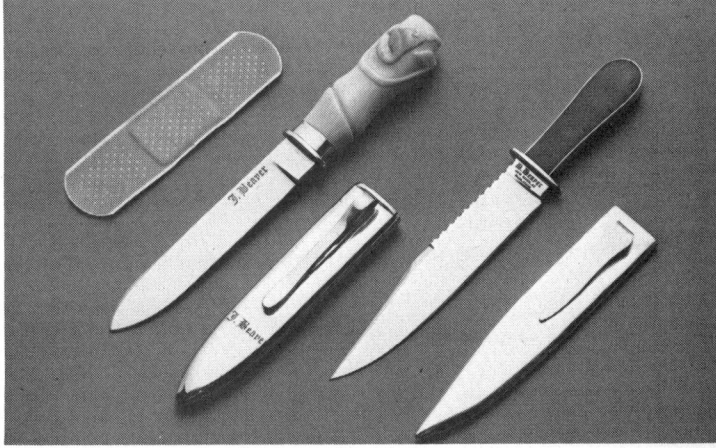

This pair of daggers by Butch and Judy Beaver, carved and bound and furnished with nickel silver sheaths pass the test—they look just right until you notice that's a Band-Aid in the picture. (Weyer photo)

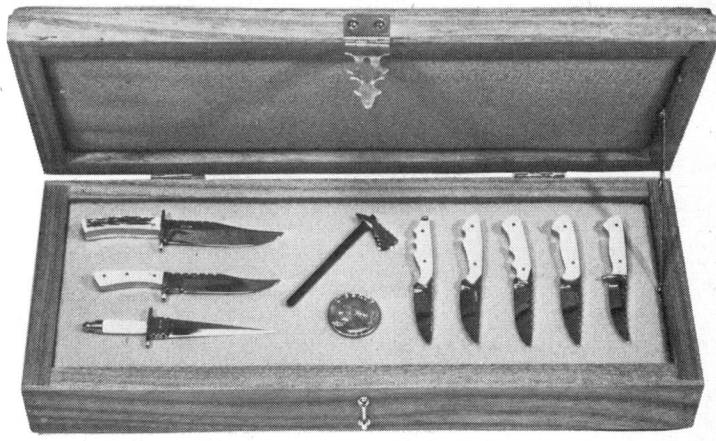

Harry Stalter's miniatures are under 3 inches, heat treated on demand in 440C.

Jerry Rados Persian styled miniature fighter is all Damascus but the handle scales. (Weyer photo)

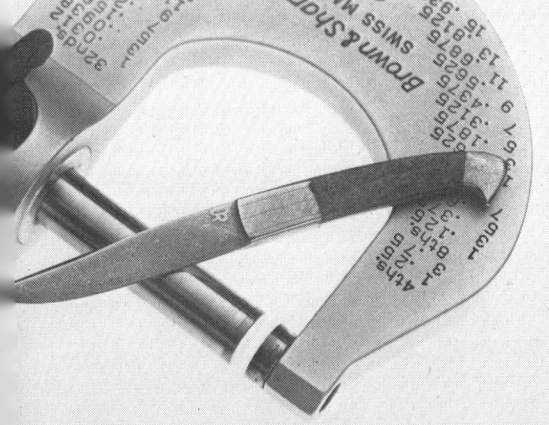

(Right) This Shiro Furukawa miniature Randall collection offers gold, ivory and silver as well as 440C. (Weyer photo)

Classic Damascus dagger by Robert White, Jr.

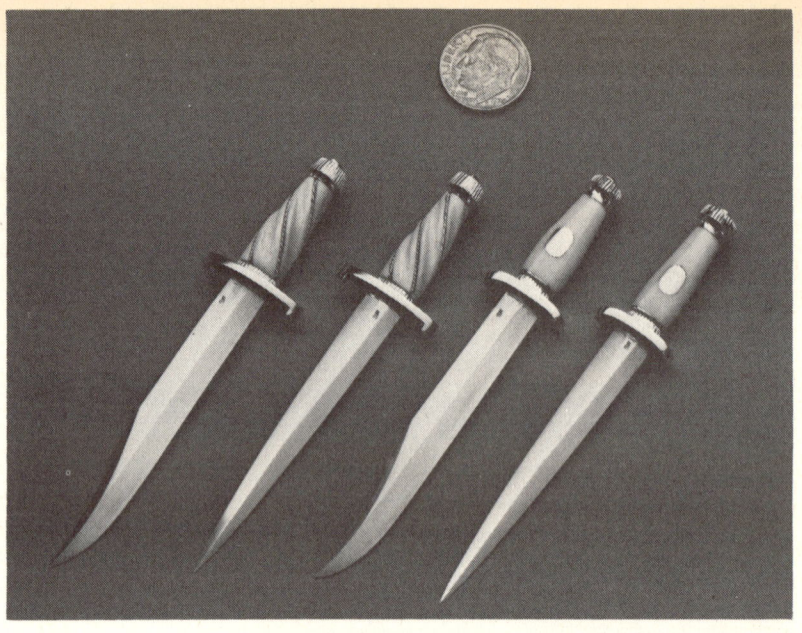

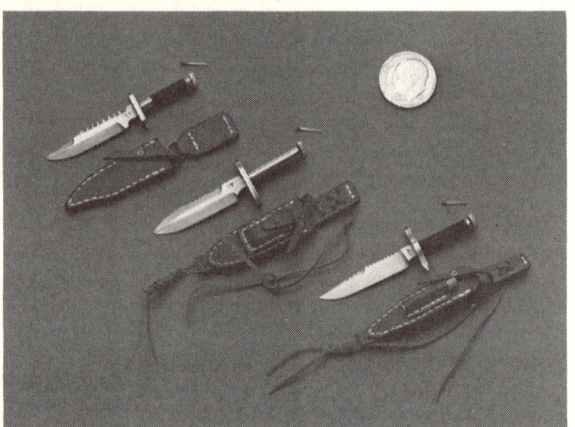

Those are fingers behind this Damascus and ivory Micarta miniature by Kevin Wright.

(Left) Tasaki Seichi miniature Rambo, Commando and Randall knives have miniature sheaths and the sheaths have miniature stones and there are also miniature matches, and smaller bugs that bite 'um. (Weyer photo)

This is the usual range of Terry Kranning miniatures, often furnished with full using instructions.

Gordon Chard's little 440C Bowie has a wooden sheath. (Raines photo)

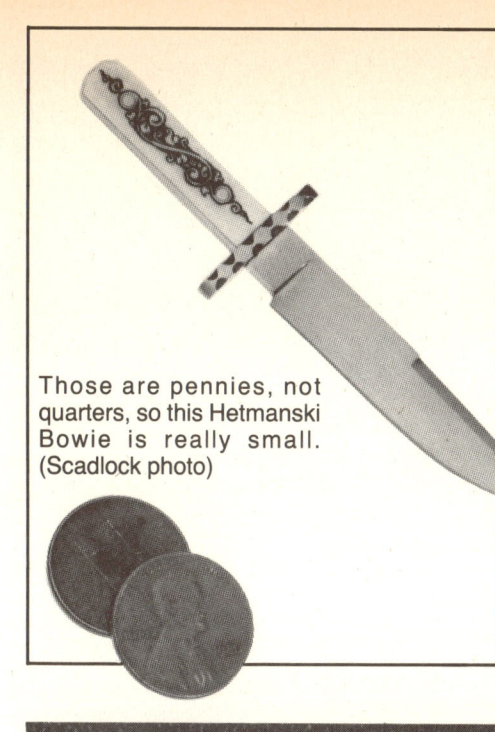

Those are pennies, not quarters, so this Hetmanski Bowie is really small. (Scadlock photo)

Tantos, a ghost-handled dagger, and a sub-hilt fighter by Butch and Judy Beaver are shown with special hand-made ebony chopsticks, also miniature. (Weyer photo)

Terry Kranning made this small Bowie to match the giant one.

Know how big a Canadian dime is? Not very, but these are Jack V. Peterson locking folders.

One miniature collector's goal is to get big-name knifemaker miniatures and here is one such from Bill Moran. (Holter photo)

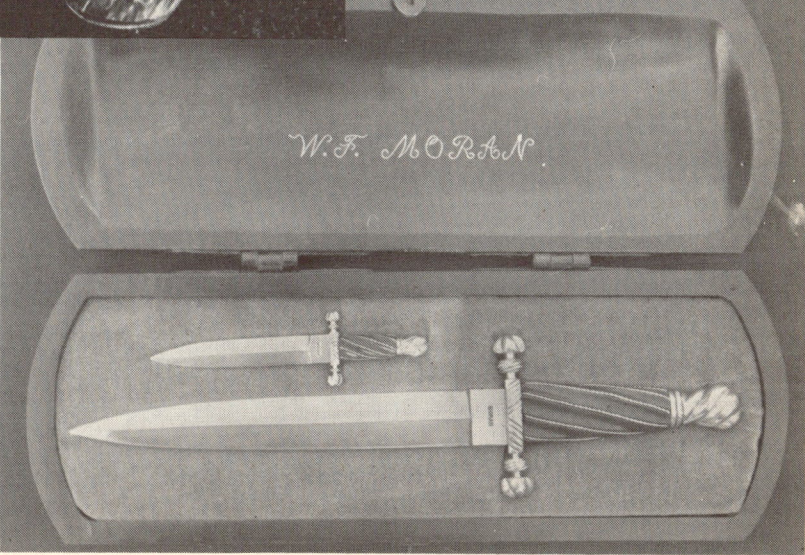

TRENDS
GENTS TABLE CUTLERY

IN THE chummier days of some years back, when the Guild Show was smaller, there was a group that met one evening during each show to dine out. Any knifemaker in the group had to fetch his own tools, and some of the sets were remarkable. Indeed, many were subsequently shown in these pages.

Ever since, one or another fellow has essayed the production of his (or someone's) personal cutlery and you see a collection of the relatively recent here. It might be when the hot patooties and high mucka mucks were going head-to-head in K.C., MO, the sets came out a little jazzier, but these all look OK to me.

Don't get the idea, by the way, that your reporter ever *saw* those roast beef dinners. For several years he carried his personal set of folding eating tools to the great ShowMe state—and modest technical marvels they are, by the way—but the opportunity never arose to test them in competition, as it were, at a Guild show. Doubtless an oversight.

Neither do we know why there has never been a set called a "lady's table set." Doubtless another oversight.

Ken Warner

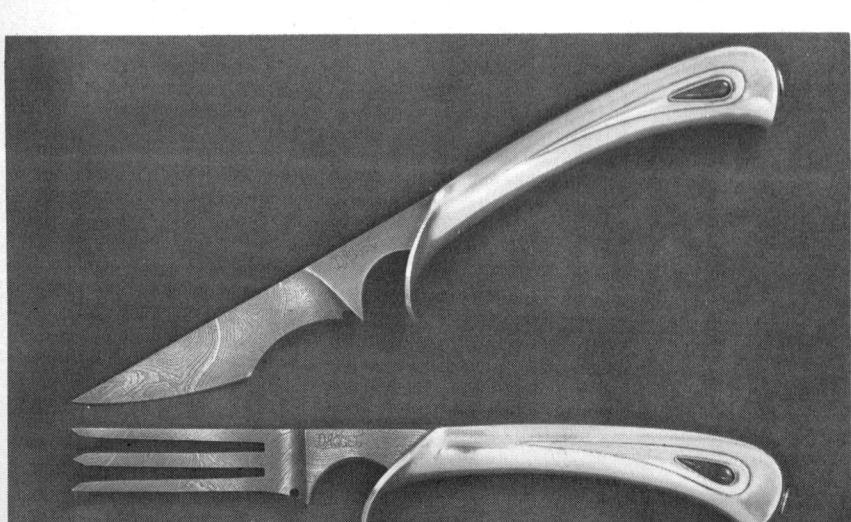

Definitely Dagget—Dan Dagget—is this sterling silver-lapis lazuli-Tom McLane Damascus personal table service. (Bloomer photo)

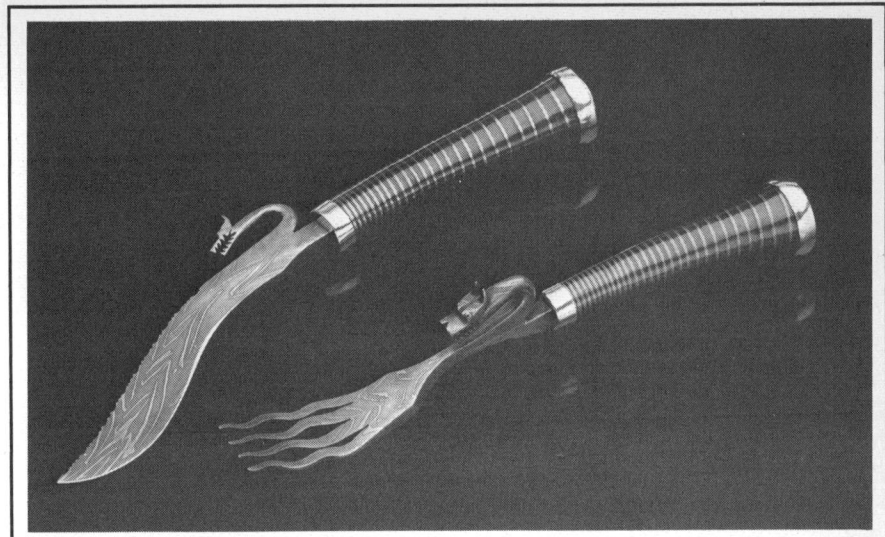

Definitely Lankton—Scott Lankton—in Damascus, enamel and sterling, and also idiosyncratic. (Weyer photo)

A full three-piece set by Paul Myers offers 440C, nickel silver, ivory and the embellishments of Gary Blanchard. (Weyer photo)

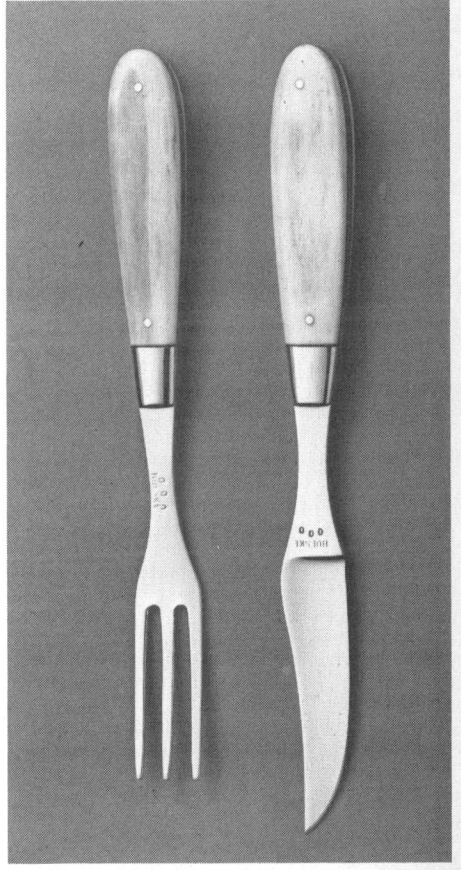

Straightforward Chubby Hueske made this straightforward dinner set, probably in D2, certainly with fossil walrus ivory. (Weyer photo)

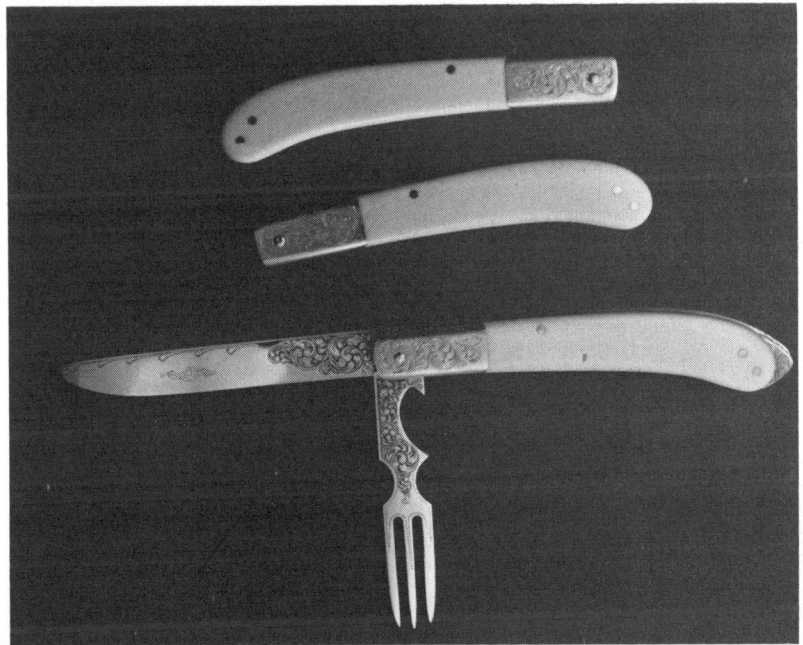

Aaron Pursley's folding "hobo" (from the old collector term for the design offered even today by Kabar) has an extra set of scales so each side can be complete in use. (R/R photo)

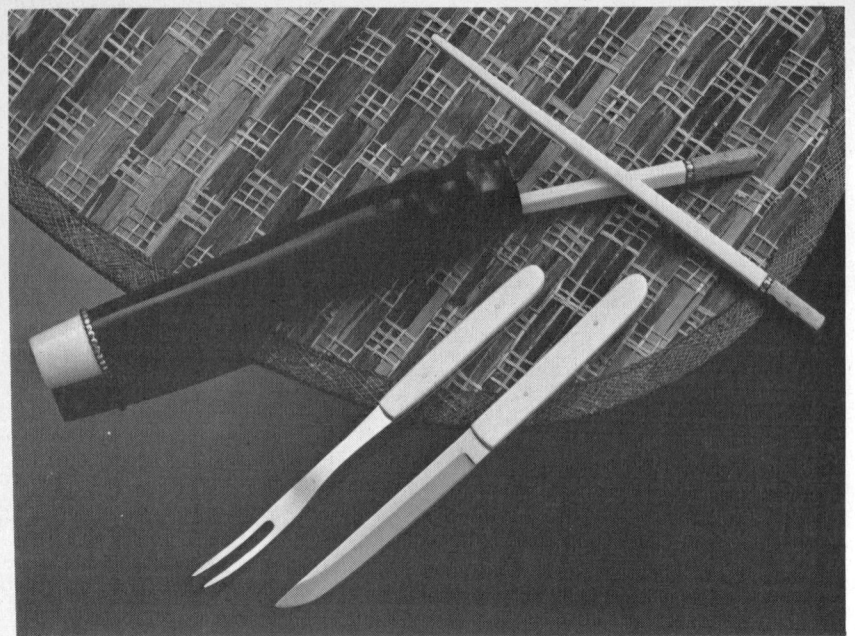

For a gent dining Chinese—or Vietnamese or Japanese—Gene Harrison furnishes his knife and fork with matching ivory chopsticks. (Weyer photo)

This three-piece set in 440C and black lip pearl by Paul Myers is for little people—the knife is 3⅝ inches overall.

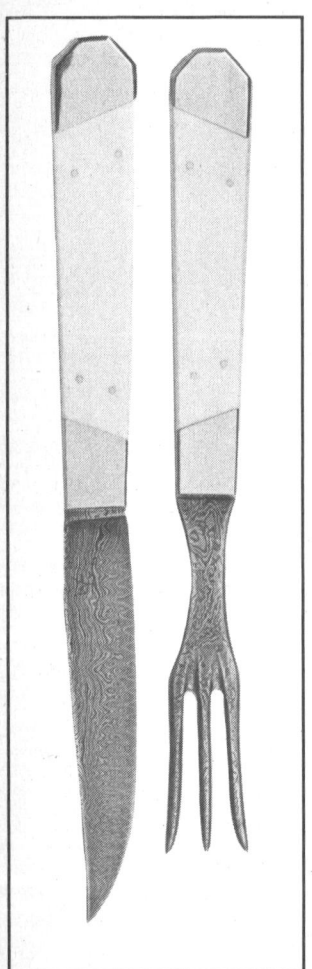

Wayne Goddard uses pattern-welded blades, stainless steel bolsters and ivory slabs in his gents set.

Al Eaton obviously knows at least two ways to style gents dinner sets because here *are* two.

Bob Enders deluxed "hobo" also offers the auxiliary scales. (Weyer photo)

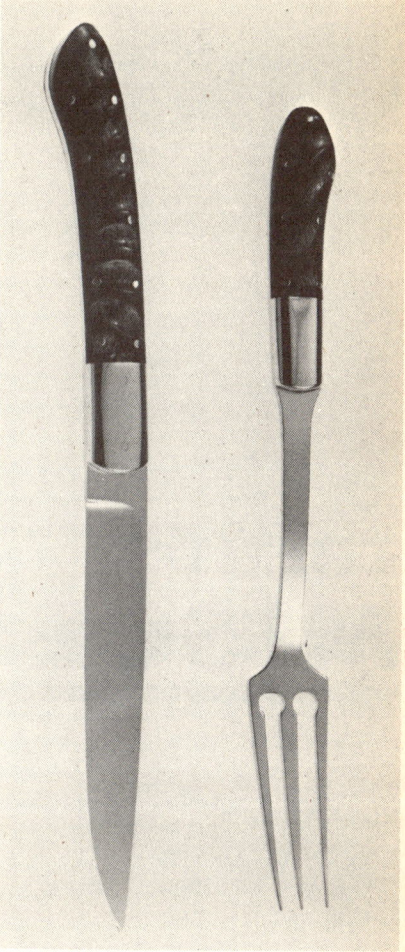

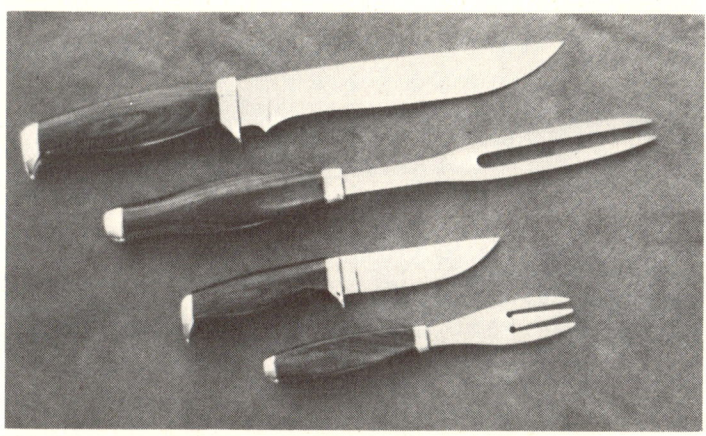

Keith Coleman did both a table set and carvers to match an ATS34, nickel silver and cocobolo.

Justin Morgan knife and fork are slickly new, except for those practical and somewhat old-timey fork tines. (Fitzgerald photo)

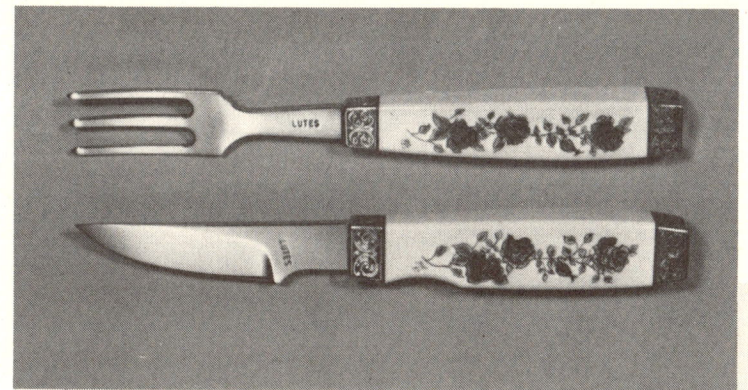

In 440C, ivory and nickel silver crafted by Robert Lutes we see scrim by Gayle McGrath and engraving by Earl Bertrand.

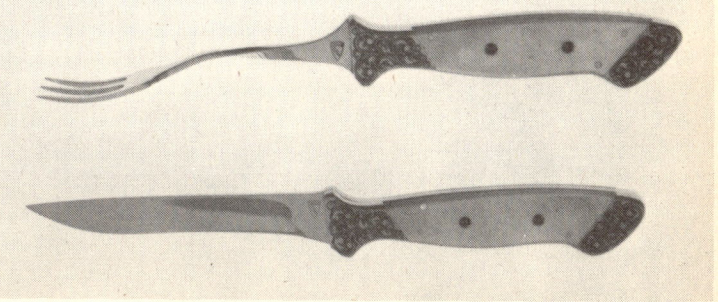

Norm Levine's personal knife and fork is in pearl, with emeralds set in gold, and engraved by Fred Harrington.

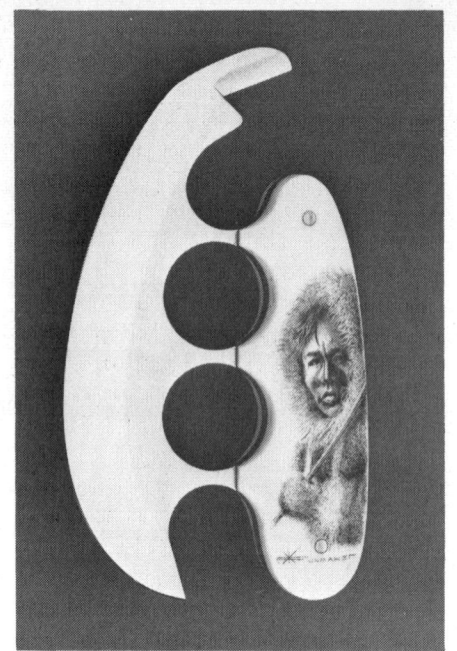

Bill Kennedy's ooloo skinner has a little ripper blade and he makes quite a few of them. (Jenkins photo)

TRENDS
MISCELLANY

NOW WE'RE into *groups* of miscellany, meaning stuff you ought to see soon, but not big enough stuff for its own pages. This time, the groups include several funny knives, some hunter axes with class, some knives as tools, and the annual straight razors.

Besides those, there's a toymaker's wooden letter opener, a very serious club-with-knife, and the ever-popular obsidian ceremonial dagger. It's once again a mixed bag.

Ken Warner

(Right and opposite page) Whimsical Mike Yurko brought both a switchblade and a pocketknife to the Knoxville show.

Don Andrews made—of course—a wrist rocket (slingshot) knife from—of course—impala horns mounted and trimmed in—of course—sterling silver. (Weyer photo)

124 KNIVES '88

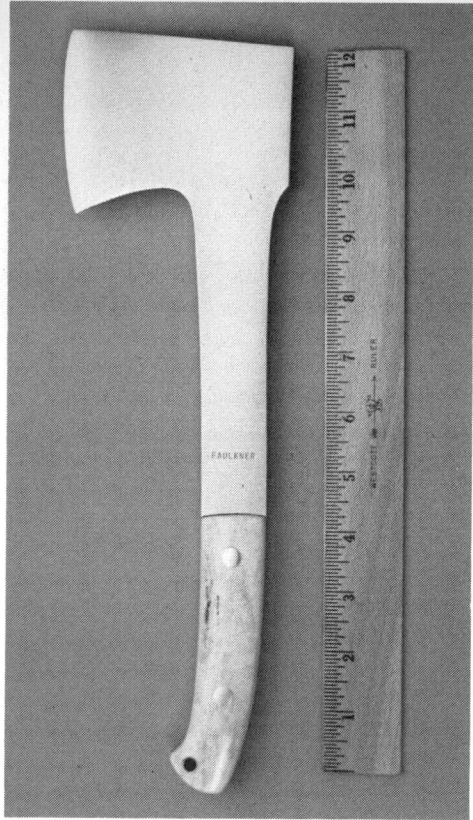

Al Faulkner's little axe has clean lines and polished stag grips.

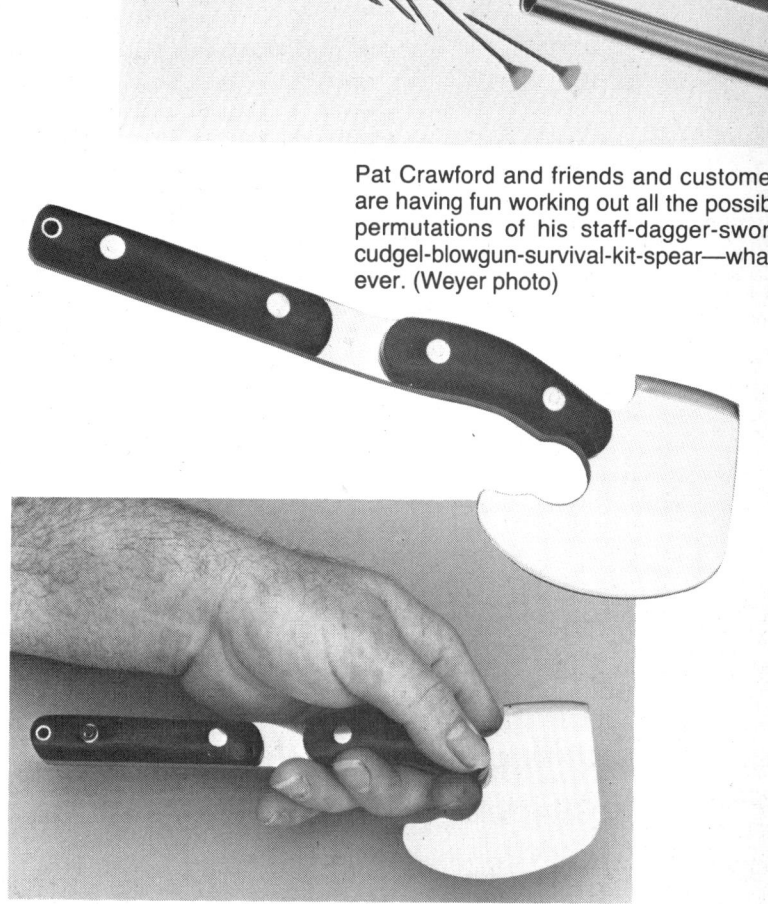

Pat Crawford and friends and customers are having fun working out all the possible permutations of his staff-dagger-sword-cudgel-blowgun-survival-kit-spear—whatever. (Weyer photo)

(Top and above) This big game axe by Mike Thourot has two hand grips so it can be used two ways. (Scadlock photos)

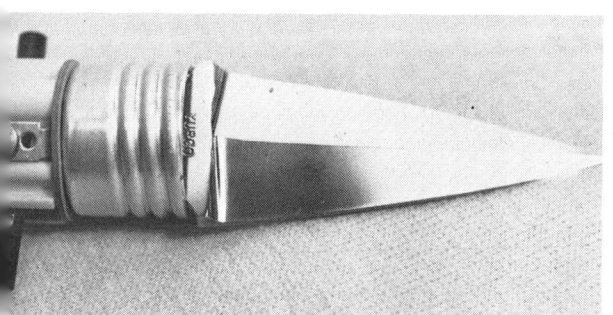

Pat Tomes is upscaling machetes and axes toward both style and efficiency. (Weyer photo)

EIGHTH ANNUAL EDITION **125**

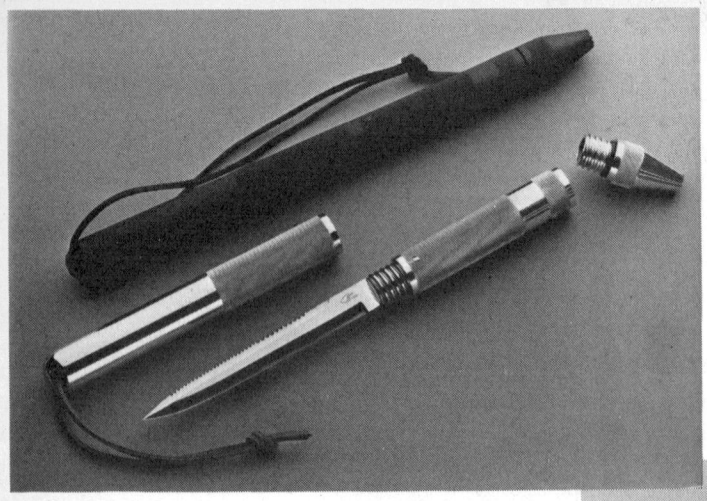

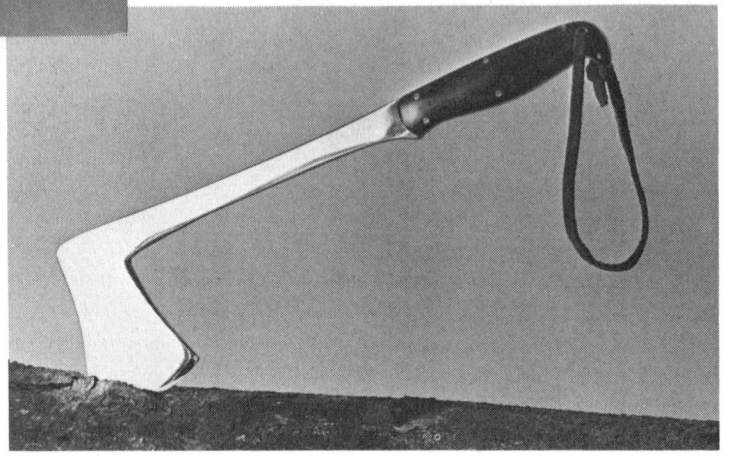

A matching Knapp saw and knife? See John R. Reynolds. (Vannoy-Rhoades photo)

Simply a stout thumper in Tefloned aluminum with a long blade and a small storage cavity sells well for Colin Cox as the "Secret Weapon." (Weyer photo)

Stylish handaxe in ¼-inch 440C is by Gary Mosser.

(Above, right, and below) Charles Ochs made the wedge-ground Damascus razor; Lowell Oyster made the razor-shape patch knife; and Butch Beaver has put many special touchers—for instance, three of the four blade tangs repeat the handle motif— into his outstanding razor group (Beaver photo by Weyer)

Melvin Nishiuchi made these wedding knives with curly koa matched handles.

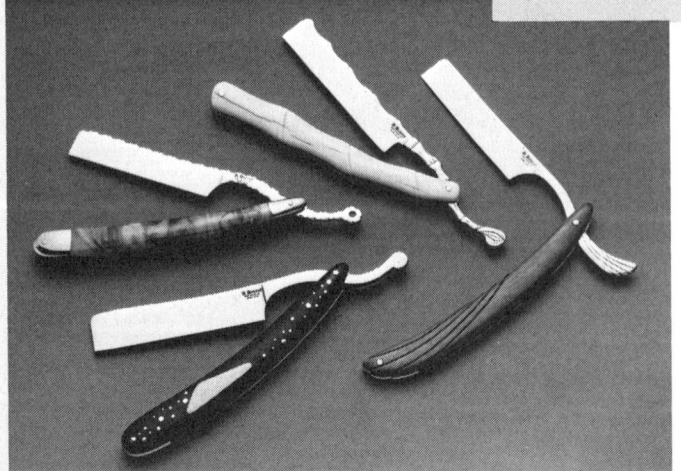

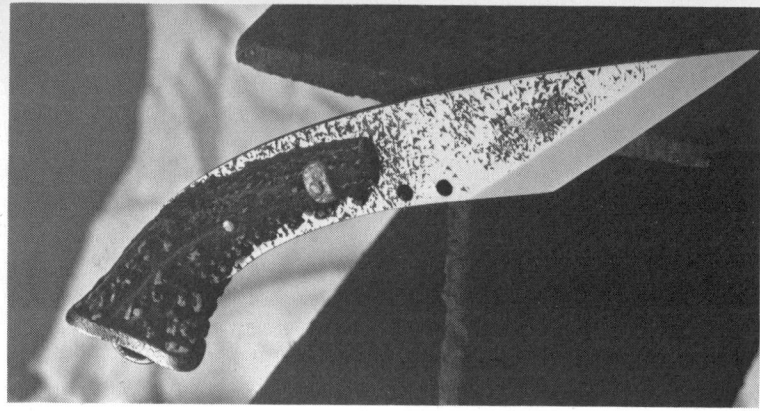

(Left) This very artistic Japanese-style carver is by N. Nomoto, offers unusual crown stag treatment. (Weyer photo)

(Below and right) Kevin Wright's taxidermist knife is in L6; his set of three curved-tip carvers are forged of L6, too.

(Left) Toymaker Harry Janke (1556 Chapel Ct., Northbrook, IL 60062/312-272-1061) makes this wooden folding letter opener.

(Right) This is Mike Yurco's rendition of a belt buckle knife. (Weyer photo)

(Left) Don Andrews made his handle from Armadillo tail. (Andrews photo by Weyer)

Ron Glover's snap-lock design permits wide variety in blade shapes. (Weyer photo)

The obsidian dagger has not left us. This prototype of his Jaguar was done in black obsidian by Errett Callahan.

TRENDS
KNIVES OF THE YEAR

WHILE some people were recognizing knifemakers and knifemaking, knifemakers have spent a great deal of time lately recognizing Texas. In fact, one fellow captioned a photo of his commemorative knife a "Sesqui-Bowie," and forever all knives in commemoration of Texas' 150th year shall be "Sesqui-Bowies" to this publication.

One knifemaker who got recognized was George Herron who wound up in a Hall of Fame, but didn't get photographed. Another was Larry Harley who got into an art gallery and did get photographed.

These and other notable things for the year may be seen nearby.

Ken Warner

For his first-ever complete knife, the always practical Jim Kelso chose a jade blade to go with an all-out ebony and silver handle.

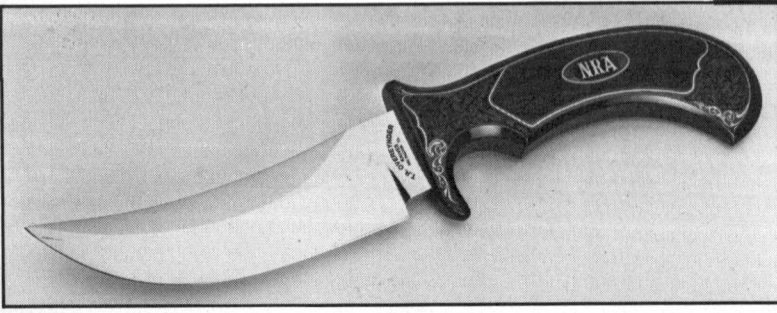

To accompany the first of an American Master Series of guns and accessories commissioned by the National Rifle Association, T.R. Overeynder made this handsome knife engraved by Ron Smith. (Chase photo)

David Taylor commemorated something or other by joining the Marines. He'll be back. (Weyer photo)

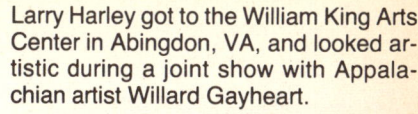

Larry Harley got to the William King Arts Center in Abingdon, VA, and looked artistic during a joint show with Appalachian artist Willard Gayheart.

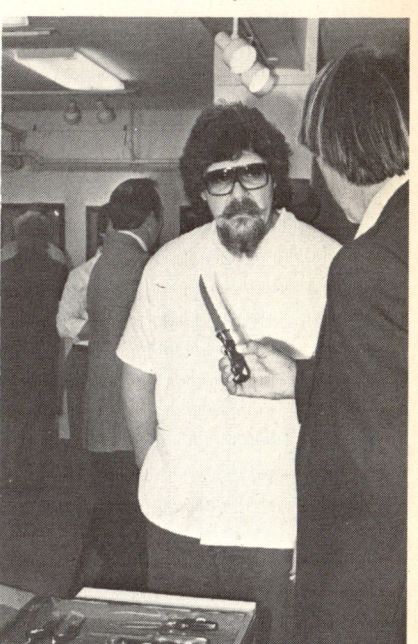

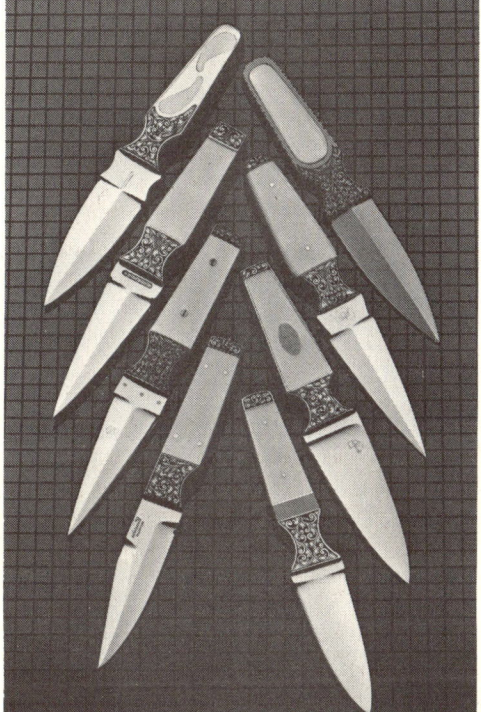

(Left and below) Members of the Great Lakes group of knifemakers did a series of interpretations of the same boot knife as a project; the seven Tennessee Knifemakers Association members figured they did well to get one knife by each in the same photo. (Weyer photo; Long photo)

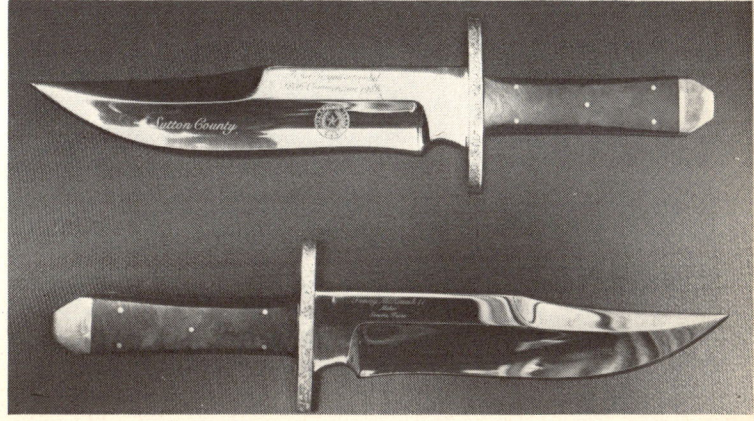

This is Sutton County, Texas' Sesqui-Bowie by Tommy McKissack.

Bill Moran did this one-of-a-kind cattle-brand knife as a Sesqui-Bowie. (Holter photo)

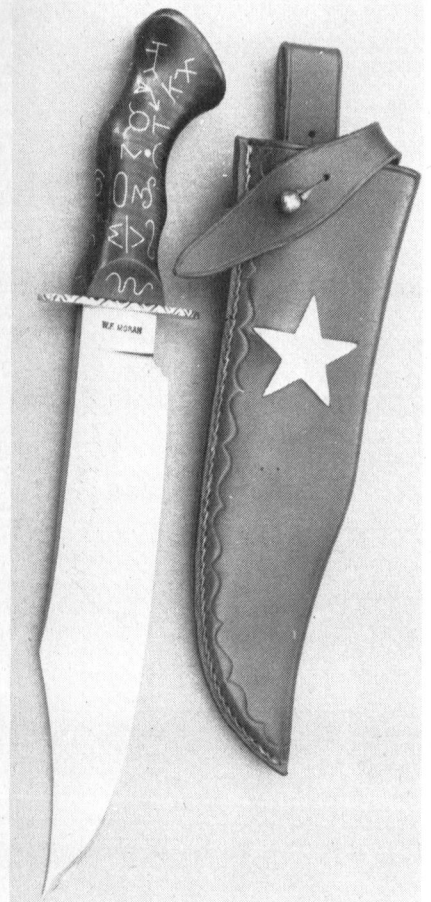

Aaron Pursley's Sesqui-Bowie is kind of small, and it folds, but he got Texas on there OK. (Weyer photos)

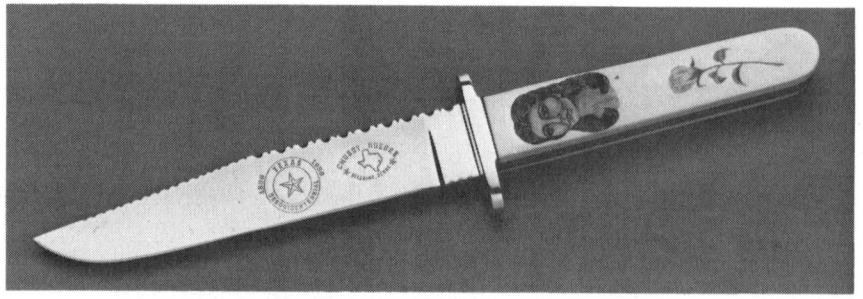

Chubby Hueske chose the legendary Yellow Rose of Texas for the theme of his Sesqui-Bowie. (Weyer photo)

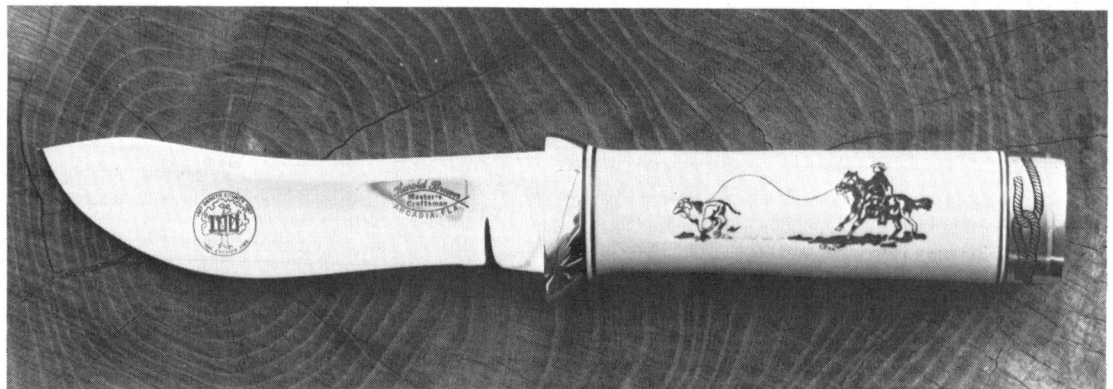

This is not a Sesqui-Bowie. This is Harold Brown's Peace River skinner, one of 20 done for the centennial celebration of Arcadia, Florida, which is in fact a cattle country town. (Action photo)

RON FRAZIER

We hope in this part of the book to provide some factual background for the decisions we think the readers will be making about their own knives, knives they own and knives they hope to own. The subject has become vast in the past 10 years. More people now know more things about knives than ever before and that has the inevitable result that more people will continue to find more new things as time goes on. This is how this part of the state of the art looks now.

Ken Warner

**Knives from Rasps
Hurrah for Titanium, We Think
The Study of Steel and Sharp
Engravers
Scrimshaw
Etching and Carving
Scriptural Wood**

STATE OF THE ART

STATE OF THE ART
KNIVES FROM RASPS

A KNIFE made from a good rasp, properly tempered, will cut a 1-inch rope 150 to 200 times and still hold a good enough edge to shave your arm, according to Al Pendray. It will also have a distinctive look.

Making knives from old rasps is not new. Our own pioneers did it all the time and large numbers of such knives have been found among collections of American Indian artifacts.

"For years when I was a kid I made everything out of rasps," says Al Pendray. "They had good carbon steel. I made knives and hatchets and we made a lot of our tools for shoeing horses from rasps."

Al is a farrier by trade and he and his family are known to be among the best thoroughbred shoers in the country. Pendray is also a bladesmith who has become somewhat of a legend among knifemakers.

Naturally, the Pendray clan has plenty of used rasps available—what could be better than to recycle them into extremely high quality using or hunting knives at $75 to $300 each? Unfortunately, modern American rasps are made of mild steel and case-hardened. They are useless for forging into knives and not very efficient for the professional farrier, either.

"These rasps I use are made in Bellota, Spain," explains Al, working with one he is forging into two knives. "The bullfighting swords are made in Bellota, too."

So, the first ingedient is a good carbon steel rasp. And Pendray first rough forges the rasp into the rough shape of the shape of the knife.

"I'm a hammer man, not a grinder," he grins. "So I forge them as close to finish as possible. Then I just rough grind to finish the profile and then grind the bevel."

He grinds the steel while it is hot to take the rasp's teeth off near the cutting edge. He leaves traces of the teeth on the sides and you can see them on his finished knives.

Pendray normally gets two knives out of a big rasp unless he's making a big Bowie or something like that. He'll usually get a clip-point and a small skinning knife out of one rasp. He prefers to make them with a solid tang and no guards to keep the prices down. He also makes them with a stub tang and guard, but those are more complicated and he really likes to keep his rasp knives simple, functional and cheap.

Once the rough forging and rough grinding is finished, the smith stress-relieves the blades by slow cooling, heating them to just above critical temperature and then puts them in a barrel of lime or lets them cool slowly in the gas forge. Critical is about 1450 degrees depending on the alloy and the carbon content. You can use a magnet to detect critical because the steel goes non-magnetic at that temperature.

"After doing it a while with a magnet you'll be able to tell at what color you want to quench it," Pendray explains, and he never uses a magnet any more.

The next step is to grind the blades down to 120 grit. He likes them to be as close to finish as possible before heat-treating. Pendray's method of heat-treating is es-

(PHOTOS BY DAVID PHILLIPS)

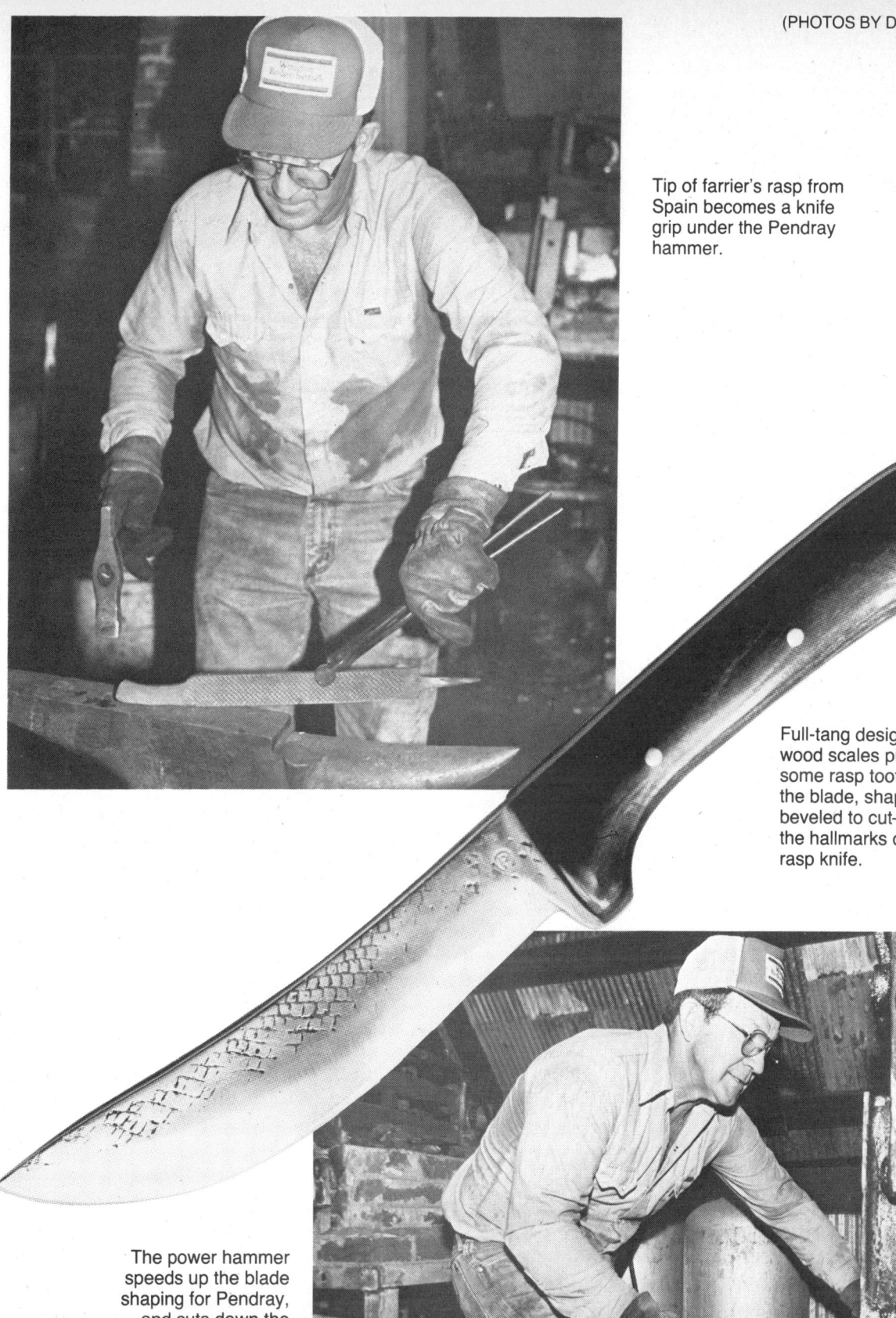

Tip of farrier's rasp from Spain becomes a knife grip under the Pendray hammer.

Full-tang design, simple wood scales pinned on, some rasp tooth pattern in the blade, shaped and beveled to cut—those are the hallmarks of a Pendray rasp knife.

The power hammer speeds up the blade shaping for Pendray, and cuts down the number of heats the blade takes.

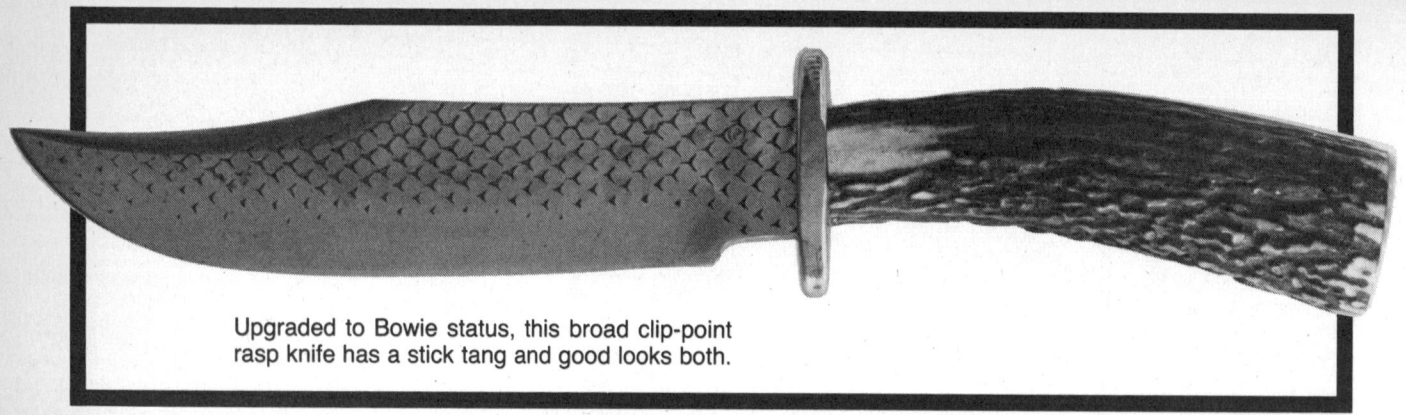

Upgraded to Bowie status, this broad clip-point rasp knife has a stick tang and good looks both.

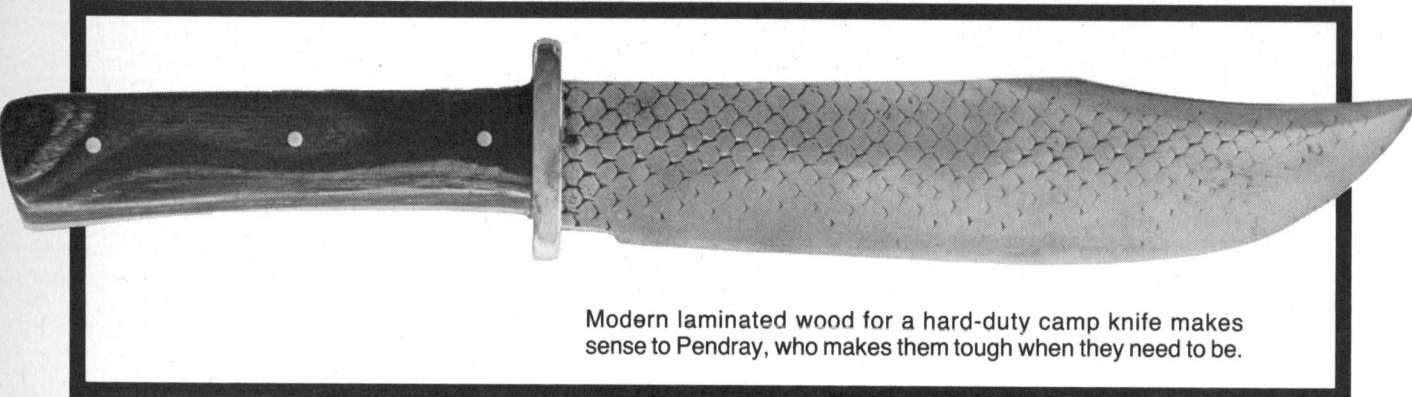

Modern laminated wood for a hard-duty camp knife makes sense to Pendray, who makes them tough when they need to be.

sential to get the performance he demands. It may seem unnecessarily long or complex, but the smith is after a product, not an easy life.

The first step of the heat-treating is to bring the knives up to just above critical temperature. The grain structure of the steel enlarges in proportion to the amount you heat the blade above critical and the length of time you keep it at that temperature, so it's important to stay as close to the line as possible.

"You want to keep it above that temperature for a couple of minutes and then quench it," says Pendray. "I quench it in oil. It has to drop down to nearly room temperature—they say don't go below 70-80 degrees. I immediately go into a pot of hot oil at the temperature I want. I keep a thermometer in it so I've got an accurate control."

The steel can be hardened to different degrees depending on the intended use of the knife. A survival knife is going to be used for a lot of chopping and prying and bending so it's wise to make it a little softer so it's tougher and won't shatter. If the edge is all-important, then you need a harder steel after tempering. Although he does not hold a degree in metallurgy, Pendray understands completely all practical and theoretical aspects of the steels and alloys that he works with and he puts his knowledge into continual practice to achieve the desired result.

Pendray draws the blades at about 475 degrees. He does that three times to ensure that the whole piece is brought up to that temperature. Then it cools almost to room temperature and then back into the oil. The second draw lasts 5 minutes and the third goes in for 30-40 minutes or he just lets it cool down in the oil.

When the steel has been properly hardened by this method, Pendray grinds the surface to bring it up to a finished edge and polish. "You can buff it if you like," he says, "but normally on these rasp knives I don't go to a mirror finish because they're used as tools and the rasp teeth are already showing a pattern on there so it's not going to have a polished blade above the edge anyway."

Pendray uses a variety of materials for the handles, usually Micarta or wood and sometimes stag. He doesn't usually go for more exotic materials for the rasp knives since, he says, people don't really want to pay that price for a using knife.

"It's the top of the line carbon steel," says Pendray of the rasp steel. "It makes as good a cutting blade as just about anything you can get."

He compares it with the best pattern-welded blades and with the Japanese type of steel, but those take a lot more work. With the rasps he can get the same kind of quality edge over and over. For Pendray, making knives from rasps is a form of relaxation which gives him a break from some of his more demanding work. And, above all else, it certainly beats throwing the old rasps away.

David Phillips

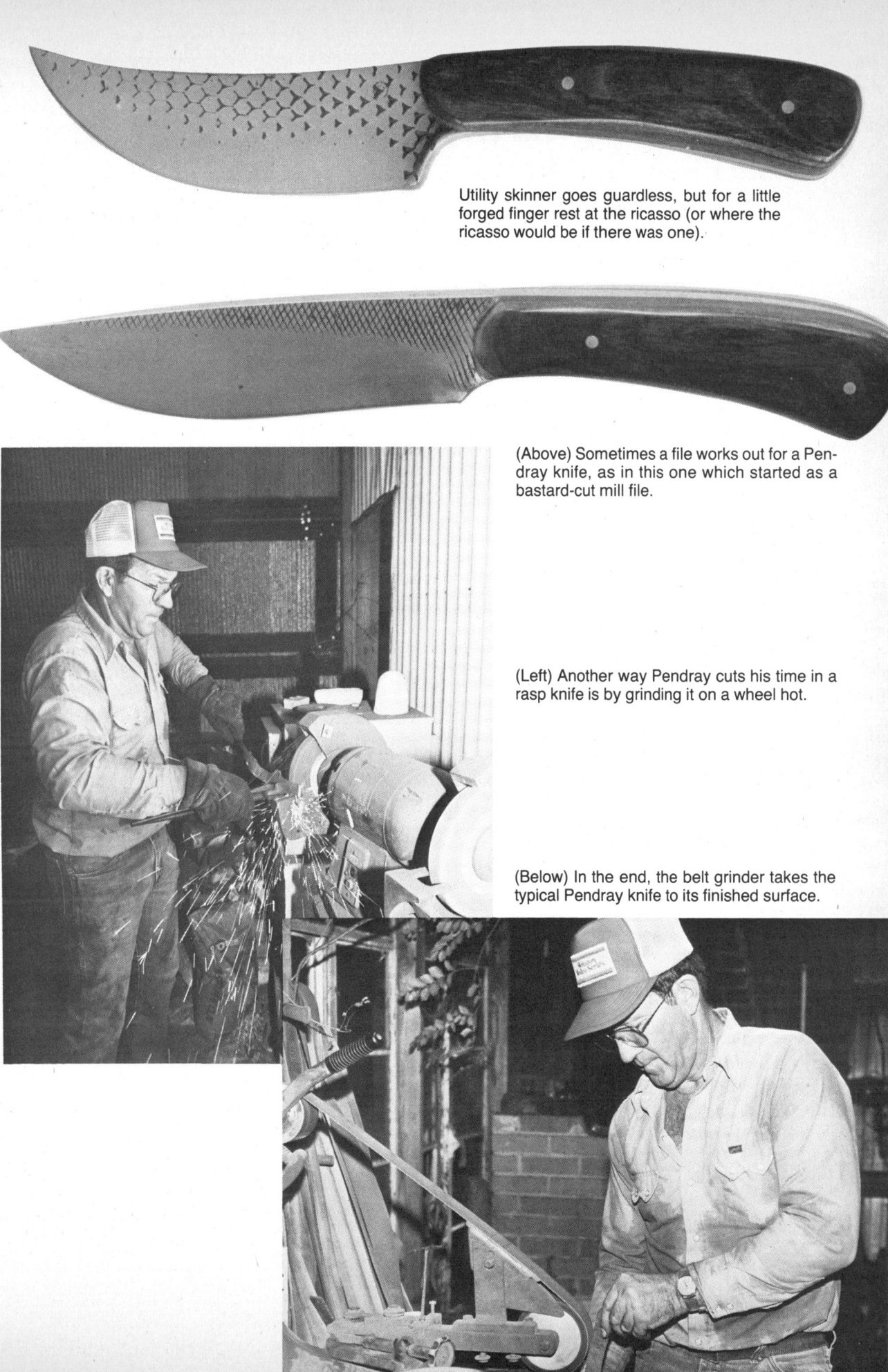

Utility skinner goes guardless, but for a little forged finger rest at the ricasso (or where the ricasso would be if there was one).

(Above) Sometimes a file works out for a Pendray knife, as in this one which started as a bastard-cut mill file.

(Left) Another way Pendray cuts his time in a rasp knife is by grinding it on a wheel hot.

(Below) In the end, the belt grinder takes the typical Pendray knife to its finished surface.

STATE OF THE ART
HURRAH FOR TITANIUM, WE THINK

EXCEPT FOR a very few, the titanium knife has been more thought of and talked about than accomplished. We have been privileged recently to examine Michael Walker's second all-titanium knife and it is some kind of impressive. That is, the knife is impressive as a decorative tour de force, as a profile of enormous appeal, as a little machine for locking and unlocking about as simple as you can get it, and not very likely as a using knife. Apart from the damage one might do to one's pocketbook should he attempt to sharpen a pencil with such a creation as a titanium blade, there remains a question of how good it can be—even hard titanium is pretty soft. Certainly this reporter never even considered testing that Walker knife.

Titanium has marvelous properties, we are told from all quarters. Timothy Wright, for instance, thinks of it as the supreme material for a folding knife, excepting for the blade and the handle scales. As long ago as the '70s, Barry Wood was making a fair part of his special designs with titanium. And those are only the makers whose names come quickly to mind on this subject. Buck Knives, of course, has a titanium-framed big folder in the stores.

Titanium itself is a rather peculiar metal. It is used industrially for very high-stress applications—places where resistance to heat is important, for instance. It has one especially interesting property—it anodizes with heat to a wide variety of colors, most of which have been mastered by the team of Michael and Patricia Walker. And, of course, it is very light in weight and very strong. It just doesn't get very hard from the knife edge point of view.

There is now perhaps another solution to the titanium knife. It is possible—and people are doing it commercially—to put titanium nitrides on the surface of tool steel, getting a molecular bond and creating a very hard knife surface. This is done in industrial service to such things as drill bits. In one test conducted by the maker of the equipment for doing the job, a plain drill bit and its nitrided twin were set to the same number of holes. The plain bit made 27 holes and gave up; the golden titanium-coated bit had drilled 300 holes when the people doing the test got tired of fooling with it.

So what? Well, so Norman Bardsley found out about this first and started having knives done and you see some of them here. Indeed, in a spirit of adventure, your reporter sent a most inexpensive ready-made blade and a check along to Bardsley to have it run through the same process, but Bardsley sent one of his own through instead and sent it along.

It may very well be that this is the knife making technique that answers almost all the questions. The Rockwell "C" number associated with the coating on these knives is somewhere in the 80s. Bardsley has used it on knives made of 154CM; your reporter's knife was one such.

Sad to relate, this was not the year for a great deal of editorial testing. We did crunch up some Manila rope and whittle a bit and so far, so good. It's perfectly obvious the titanium nitride didn't hurt the blades and it is very pretty, and normal use isn't going to have it off there.

Of course, it's not a simple world, so there are problems. The first one is that the nitriding process requires the blade be held at 800 degrees Fahrenheit for some hours. Right off that means it would draw a lot of steels too far down. Bardsley handles it by letting the nitriding be his final draw.

"One thing I like about the potential for the nitriding process," says Michael Walker, "is that you could then put 154CM into service at 55 or 56 RC and get a really tough knife with a very hard surface."

Another problem is that if the knife is used enough to dull it or nick it, sharpening it will scrub the titanium nitride off the edge. For a genuine emergency knife, one to be stored for 10 or 20 years, that's not a problem. For a using knife, it would be possible to go through the process again, provided the handle and other parts were demountable.

The material is a nice golden color; it is acid proof and stainless; it is very hard; it is not all that expensive—$45 does a 7-inch or 8-inch (overall) knife. That is down there in a class with Teflon coating and such.

A lot of people are no doubt going to try it, and we will undoubtedly know more next year. The titanium nitride coating seems to be one new way to go, one new step in that search for the perfect knife, the one that never gets dull and never gets rusty.
Ken Warner

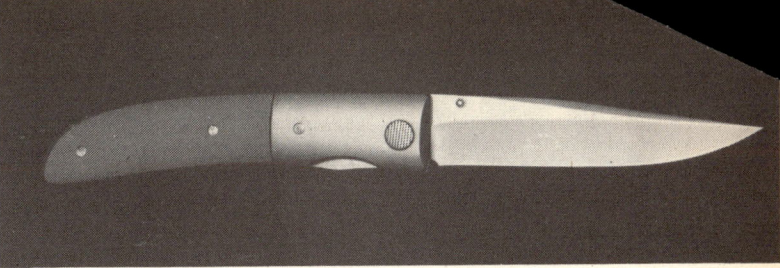

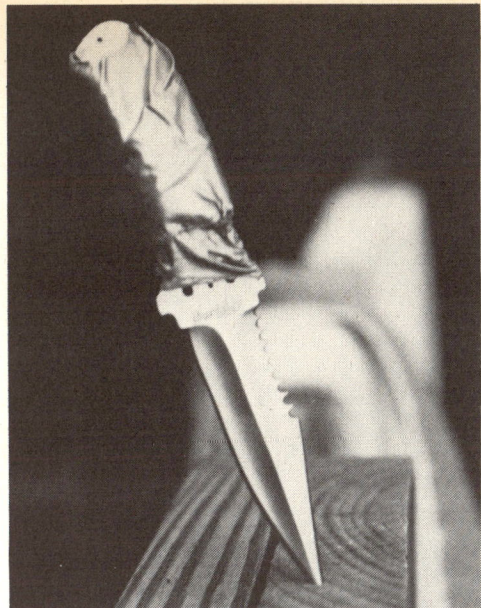

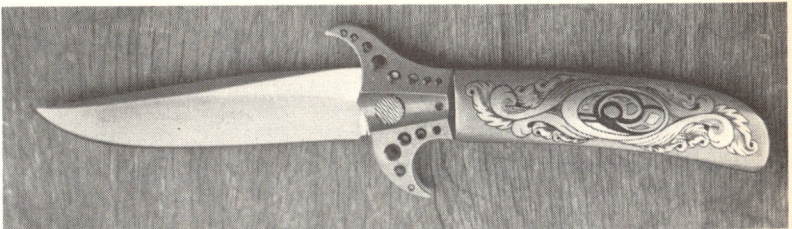

(Above and below) The plainer of these Michael Walker knives has a hot pink and green blade, so it is called Miami Vice. It is all-titanium knife number one. The other has a hot pink and gold blade and all those curlicues are blues and grays and such and so all-titanium knife number two is called Fire and Ice.

Norman Bardsley skeleton utility boot is coated with titanium nitrides, has a very hard golden surface. The tape? Why, it protected the tender editorial fingers. (Warner photo)

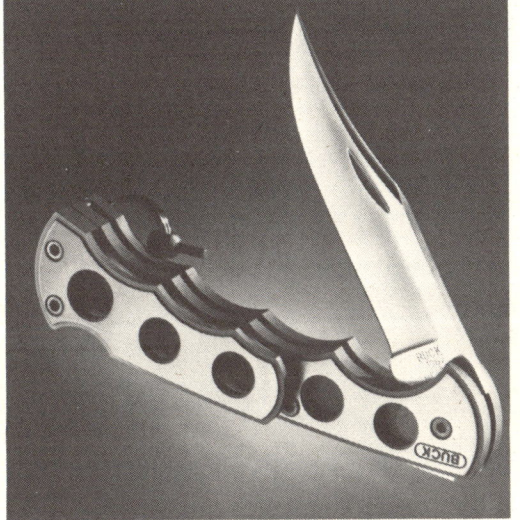

The Buck entry in the titanium sweepstakes has a steel blade, too, but is notably lightweight.

(Above) These are typical Bardsley candidates for nitriding. He can offer the service and the gorgeous color without much change in method. (White Lotus photo)

The Walkers—Michael and Patricia—have done a galaxy of bright-handled folders, most with steel blades. Miami Vice is at center here.

STATE OF THE ART
THE STUDY OF STEEL AND SHARP

THE KETTLE IS boiling on all technical fronts so hard it is time to take a breather and just hit the high spots:

• Blades of cable steels are still big news, but those grand blades reported are not *easy* blades. Properly assembling a blade from wire cables is more, not less, complicated than pattern-welding from the bar. More next year.

• Testing blades is getting on everyone's mind and some folks' nerves. There will be a lot about that next time.

• Titanium is big news, but is reported separately in this issue.

• One well-known commercial firm says its rolled-to-order blade steel will rival hand-forged metal, but that's reported separately, too.

• *Mokume-gane* which may coarsely be described as pattern-welding non-ferrous metals will be the next big decorative thing.

• Authentic old-timey knives made from files and rasps and such by smiths are springing up. Apart from Pendray's reported separately, we show a couple here.

• A lot of makers are buying Damascus bars, some to grind, some to reforge. And others buy forged-to-shape blades, and there are going to be more arguments, not fewer, since some smiths resent the commercial Damascus. Meanwhile, Rob Charlton throws fuel (charcoal, one hopes) on the fire by seriously promoting the virtues of forging for Damascus blades. Interesting.

• People are coming up with whole new ways to make folders fold, straight knives cut, swords assemble—it's all on a boil. In pictures, here are a few of those high spots.

Ken Warner

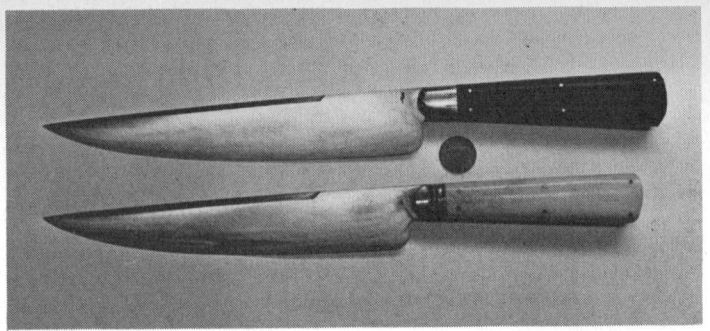

(Left) Jim Rubley calls these working knives, smiths them from files, leaving somewhere a trace of the tooth pattern.

Even the experimentalist, Bill Buchner, did so with this one of a kind kitchen knife. Forged, of course.

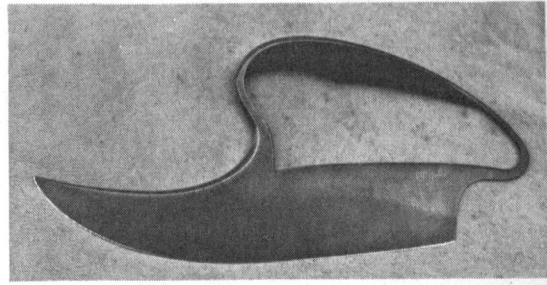

Three new forged-to-shape patterns from Rob Charlton's Damascus-USA. (Weyer photo)

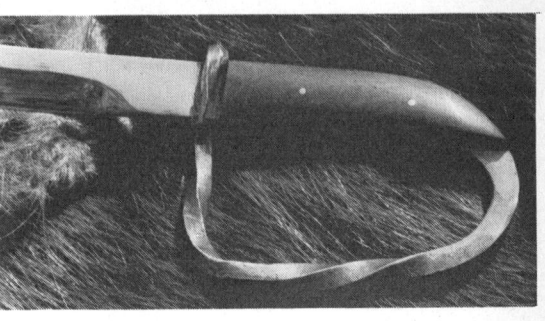

(Above) Martin Kruse took the tang right on around to make this D-guard.

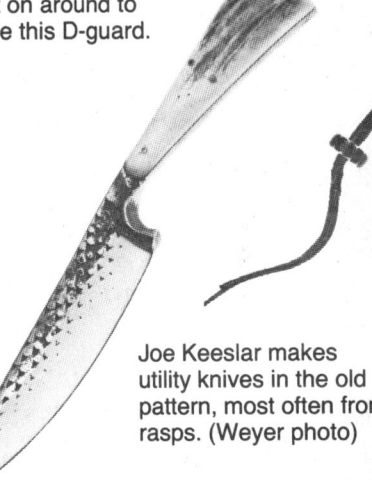

Joe Keeslar makes utility knives in the old pattern, most often from rasps. (Weyer photo)

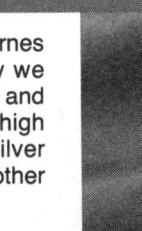

(Opposite page, above and right) Gary Barnes is well-known as a smith and so nearby we show two of his newest efforts — a titanium and 440C personal knife, quite elegant, with high tech Kydex sheath, and Barnes' nickel-silver roll-engraved scales on a Beretta knife, another different thing for knifemakers to do. (Klinefelter photos)

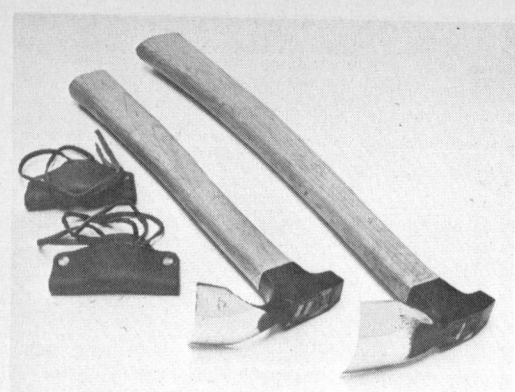

Hugh Bartrug makes his already lively Damascus blade dance with etching—this is the "Gladiator." (Weyer photo)

Out in the northwest, handmade sculptor's tools come from Kestrel Tool.

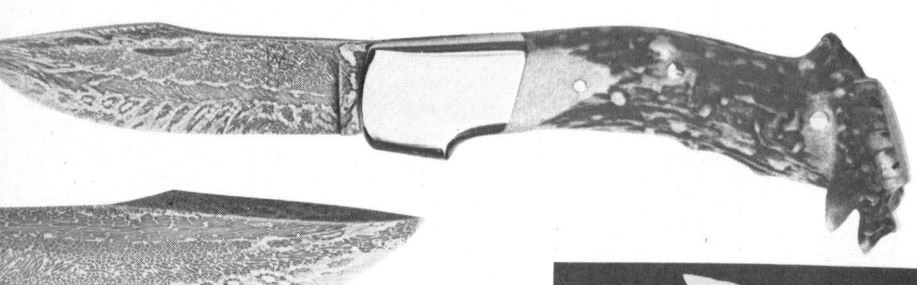

Wire Damascus folder shows (both sides) Wayne Goddard's daisy pattern.

(Below) Larry Fuegen makes a lot of these springless folders and makes them nicely indeed. (Weyer photo)

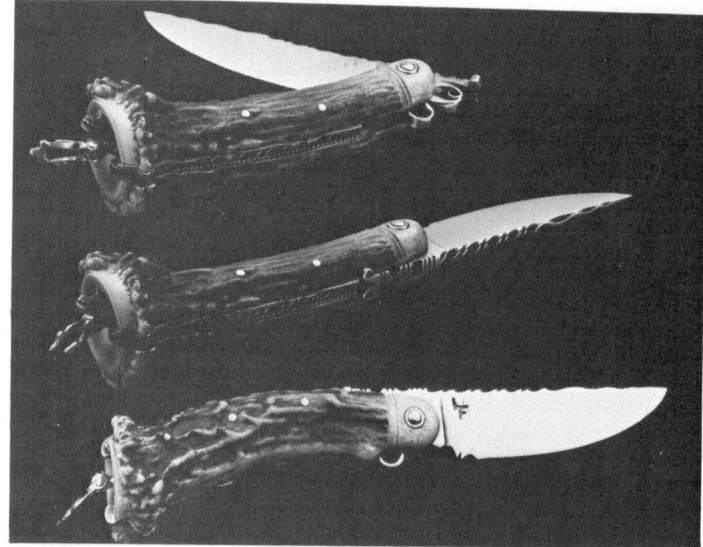

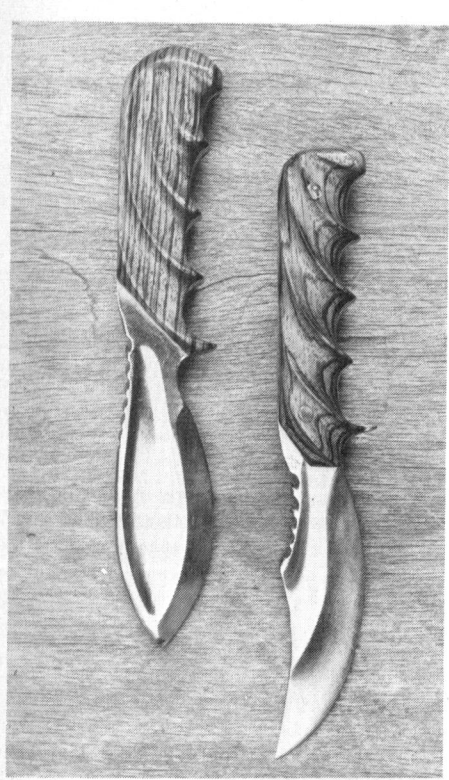

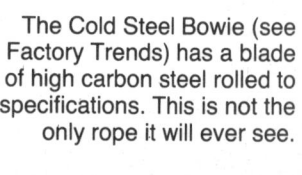

George Walker hammers out an occasional Damascus blade in all tool steel, says it ain't easy, but it's good.

With hand-held grinding tools, Larry Di-Tommaso does wild stuff like this.

The Cold Steel Bowie (see Factory Trends) has a blade of high carbon steel rolled to specifications. This is not the only rope it will ever see.

STATE OF THE ART
ENGRAVERS

ANOTHER year has simply meant more work for engravers. It hasn't been that everyone is flush, but that customers are another year more familiar with the *idea* of engraving.

It hasn't been so long, you know, since silver mounts and some file cuts made about as fancy a knife as you could get. Engraving—read hammer and chisel cut designs—was what you did for a favorite gun, not a knife.

Now, just a couple decades later, it's easy to find $2,000 engraving on $500 knives, and, even worse, $800 engraving on $50 knives. However, it really isn't polite to speculate how much a given fellow ought to spend on his haircuts, his neckties, or his engraving.

Anyway, here's quite a bit of the latest good stuff.

Ken Warner

(Above) This is a Powell & Brown gun knife with full coverage by Mel Wood.

California dagger by Steve Price with Belgian engraver Raymond Baptiste's full coverage. (Fedorak photo)

EIGHTH ANNUAL EDITION 141

Old Dominion Hand Engravers, a new studio group, did these knives by Hedrick and Osborne. (Long photo)

Willie Rigney dagger embellished with the full-court press by Gary Blanchard—gold wire, blued steel, turquoise and more. (Weyer photo)

Billy Bates touched up this clean Reeves hunter.

(Above) Frans Van Eldik, a Hollander, got Eduard Vos, a Belgian, to engrave these hunters.

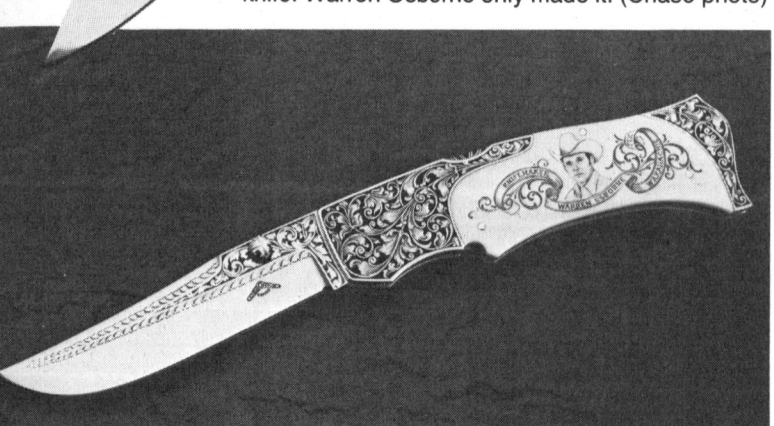
Ron Smith designed, engraved and scrimmed this knife. Warren Osborne only made it. (Chase photo)

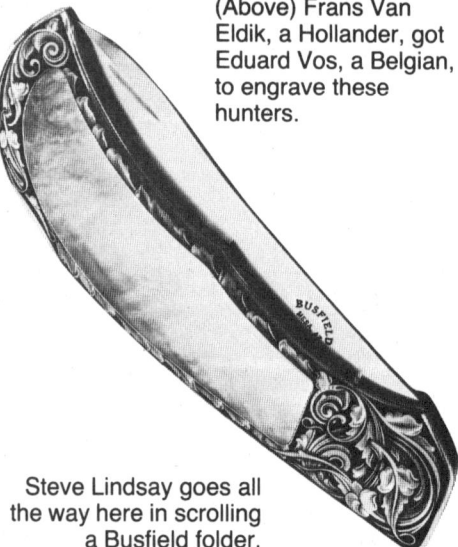
Steve Lindsay goes all the way here in scrolling a Busfield folder.

This nearly secret engraving by Fred Harrington adorns a Michael Zscherny knife. (Weyer photo)

Stylized and handsome Rolf Peter thistle motif on a D.F. Kressler knife.

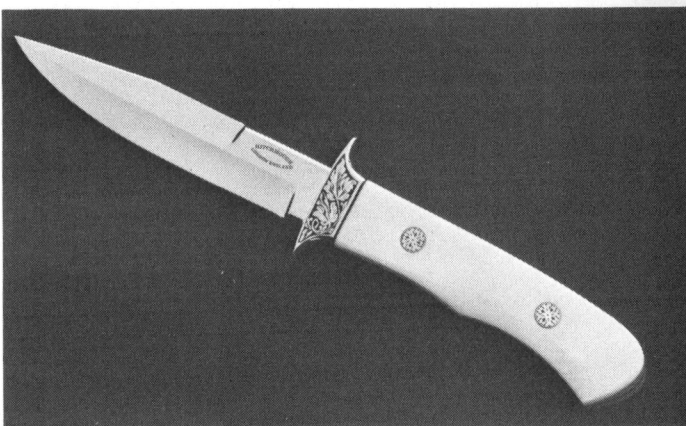
W.P. Sinclair has elaborated this clean Hitchmough fighter.

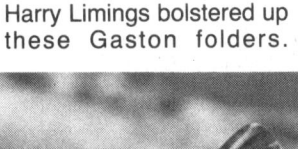
Floral motif by Andrew Raftis is nice on a Turnbull knife.

Harry Limings bolstered up these Gaston folders.

This is Ben Shostle work on a Minnick knife.

This is Bruce Shaw scroll and relief on a Chuck Stapel knife. (Fitzgerald photo)

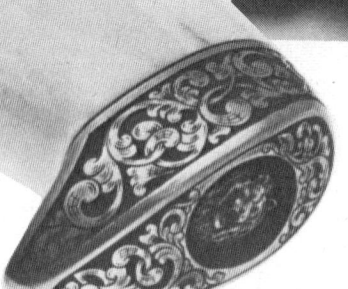

A Rick Eaton bolster treatment.

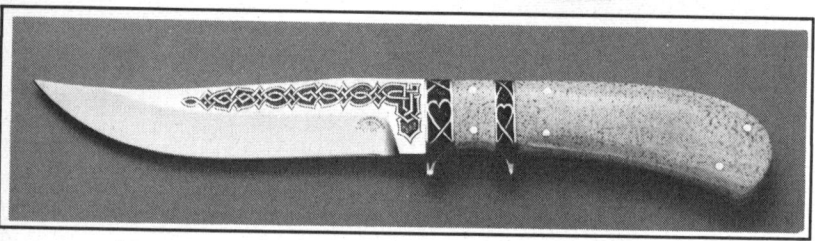

Persianate embellishment for a subhilted Sornberger knife, all work by maker. (Weyer photo)

Harry Mendenhall made this fighter and engraved it. (Boyer photo)

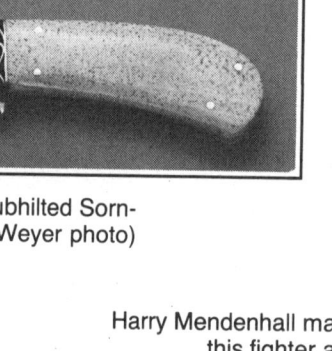

Scorpion crouches among leaf scroll by Fritz Oberdorfer on a Richard Hehn knife.

Blades engraved by Ed Delorge.

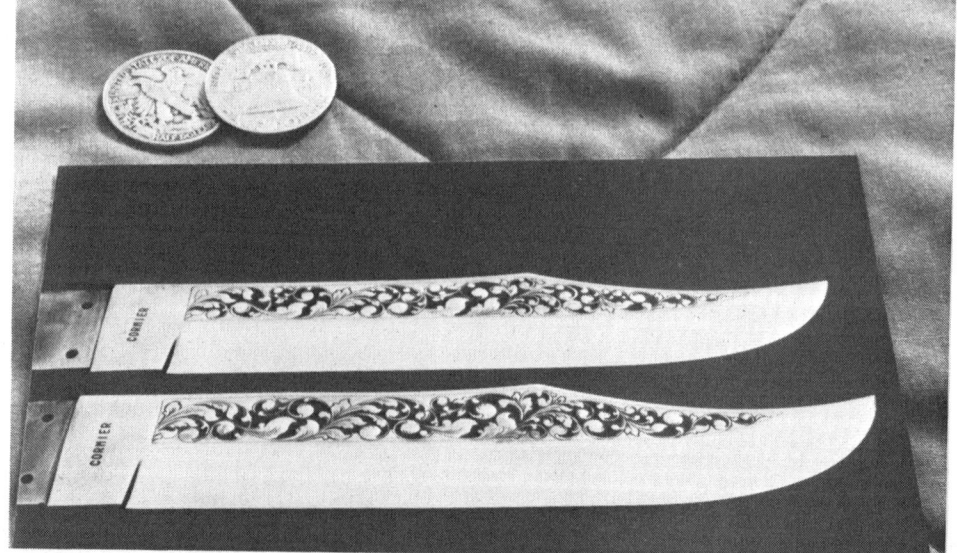

144 KNIVES '88

Full coverage on this Colin Cox fighter is by Lewis Sanchez. (Weyer photo)

John Kudlas engraved this gift folder.

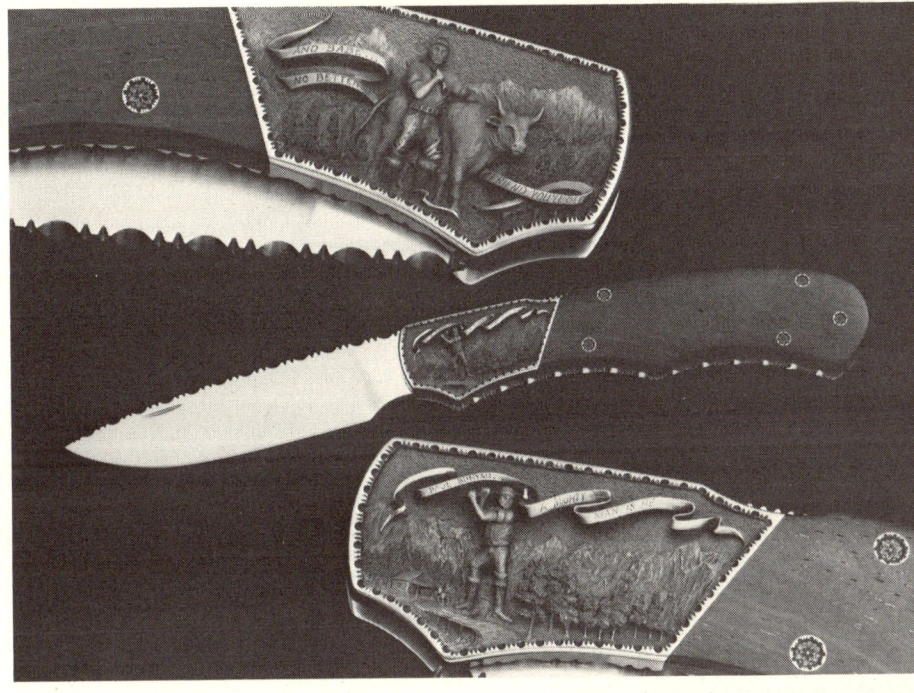
Gary Blanchard did Paul Bunyan, and even Babe, on this Boguszewski folder. (Weyer photo)

Martin Rabeno's wolf stares out of Jess Horn's folder.

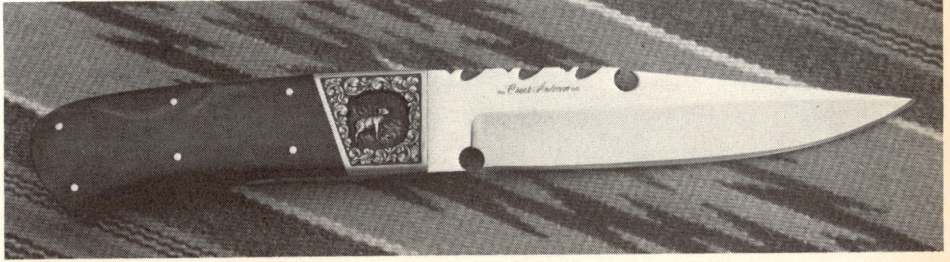
Chuck Anderson knife has Bruce Shaw scroll and relief engraving.

STATE OF THE ART
SCRIMSHAW

WE'VE hit another trough in the world of scrim. We have furry animals, birds, naked women, Indians and a couple of miscellaneous scenes. That's it—no Martians, no landscapes, no street scenes, no astronomy, no views of a technological society, no battles, and neither cowboys nor their horses.

Variety is not the scrimshander's spice, it seems. Excellence suits them, and they have it, as you can see here, but very few scrimmers stray very far off the clearly beaten path.

There are a couple of sets of ships or boat scenes on view, and a quizzical view of the world of laws. These apart, it's—you guessed it—animals, birds and the rest. But nice, mind you.

Ken Warner

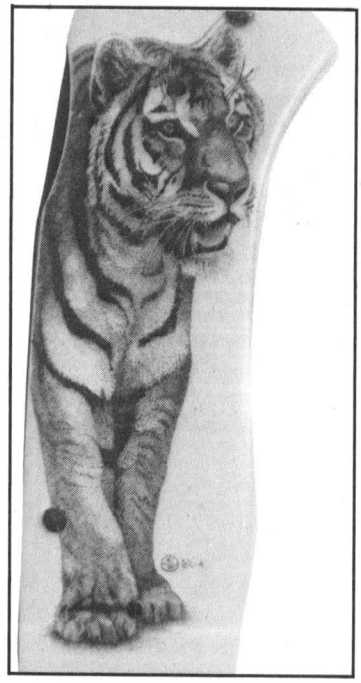

Expectant tiger is by Charles W. Hargraves.

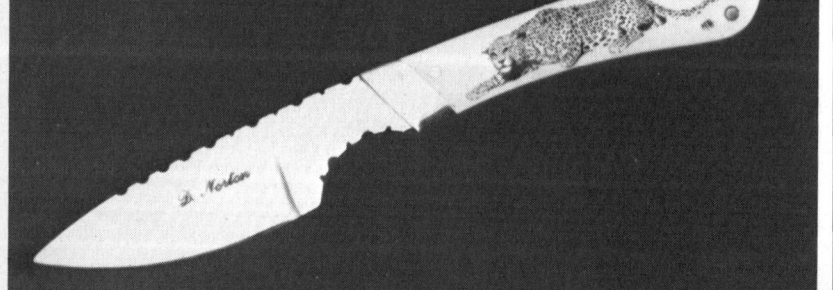

Resting leopard on a Don Norton knife was scrimmed in ivory by Dennis Holland. (Terry photo)

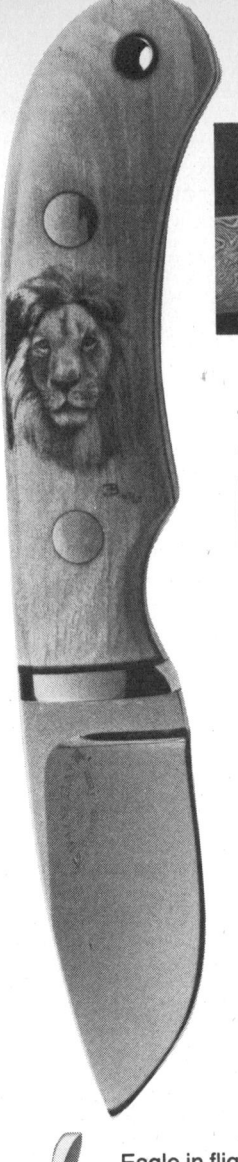

Maned lion by Bob Engnath gazes on us from a Wayne Clay knife. (Fitzgerald photo)

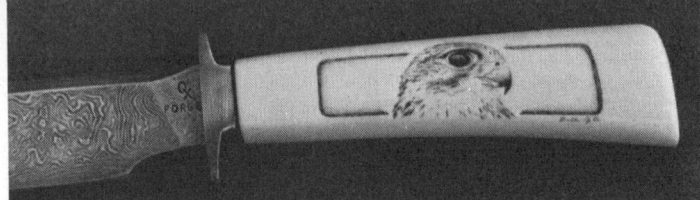

Highly styled raptor by Belle Ochs stares balefully from, naturally, an Ox Forge knife. (Below) Eagle head scrimmed in a carrier pose is by Carole McWilliams on a McWilliams Bowie.

Trophy deer by Guy Dahl appears on a Dahl knife.

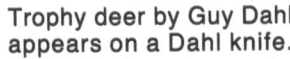

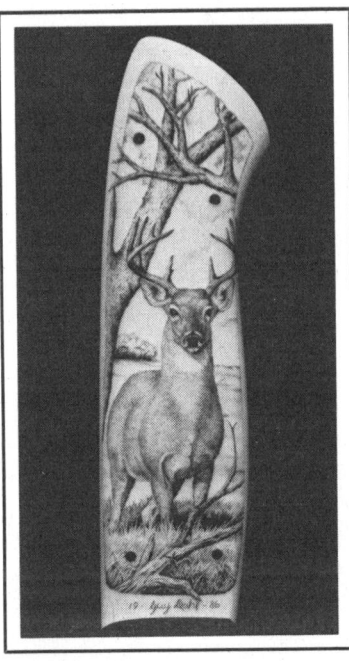

Panda scrimmed in color by Richard DiMarzo covers an ivory sheath and handle with a Ray Beers blade. (Weyer photo)

Eagle in flight along a Gwozdz fighter handle in ivory is by John Stahl. (Weyer photo)

George Walker makes knives and Karen scrims them.

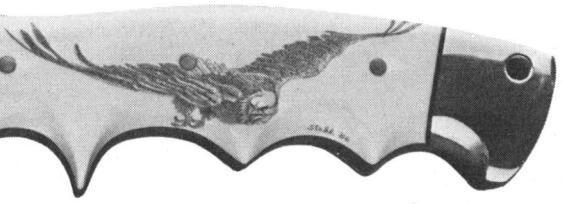

Sleeping lady by Dennis Holland rests on the fossil walrus ivory of a Don Norton knife handle. (Weyer photo)

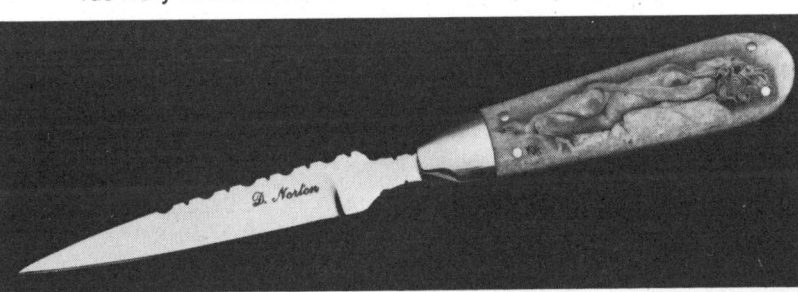

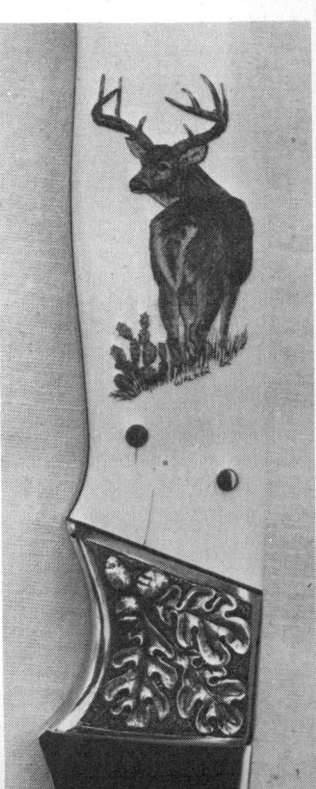

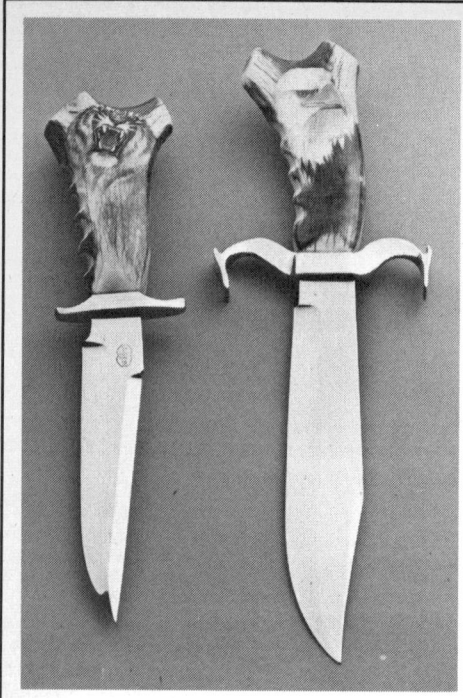

Alice Semrich provided the set of images for this set of knives by Greg Smith and Peter Semich. (Weyer photo)

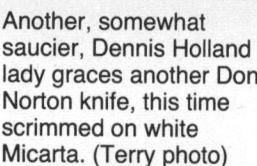

Another, somewhat saucier, Dennis Holland lady graces another Don Norton knife, this time scrimmed on white Micarta. (Terry photo)

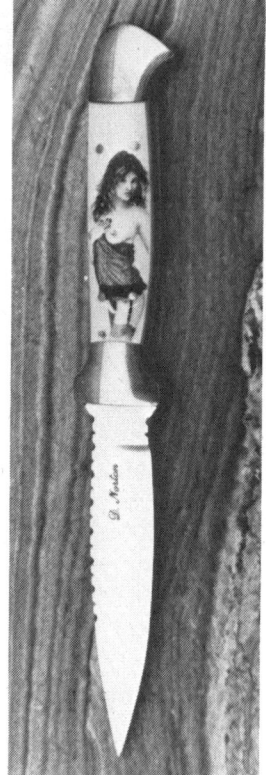

Surf rescue boat gets off the beach in a scene by Charles Hargraves on a Bob Papp knife.

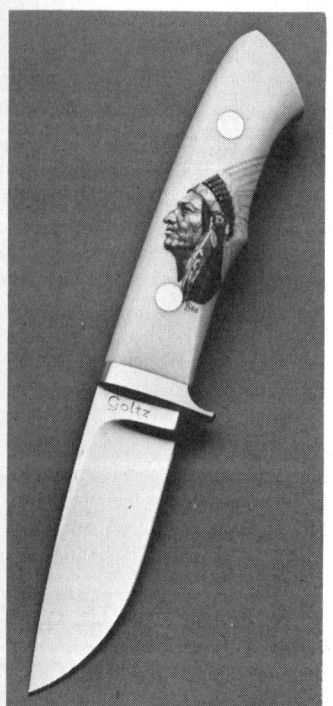

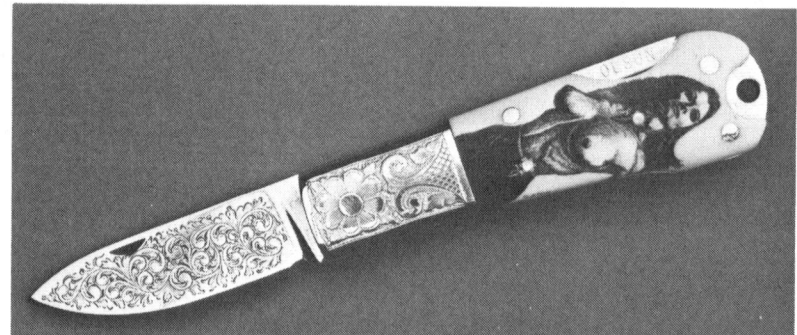

Robert Satre scrimmed his Canadian wild one on a Rod Olson folder.

Raymond Cover put this chief on the Micarta handle of a Warren Goltz knife. (Weyer photo)

Feathery dragon by Sandra Brady suits this Tommy Lee handle.

Rick Fields scrimmed this warrior on the ivory handle of a Jerry Rados knife. (Weyer photo)

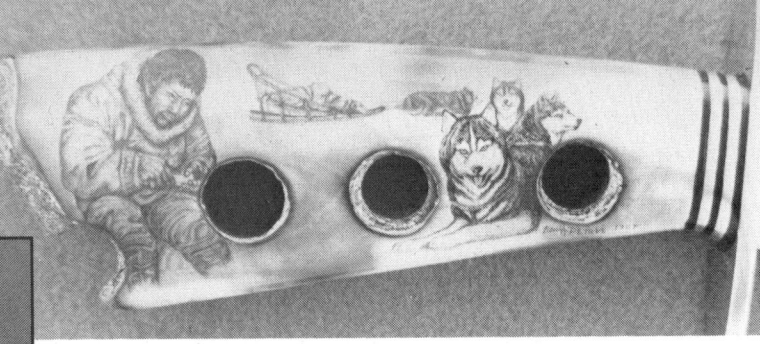

Al Warren uses genuine artifacts—this may be an arrow straightener—as knife handles scrimmed with Eskimo scenes.

(Below) Charles W. Hargraves found another sort of woman entirely on this knife.

A set of four riverboats on a set of four push daggers. The knives by Tomlinson; the boats by Charles Hargraves.

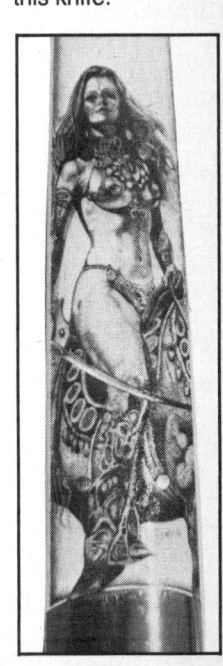

The difference between Law and Justice is scrimmed onto a Dennehy knife by Gigi. (Tocci photo)

Alan Jiranek scrims this singer on Errett Callahan obsidian knives.

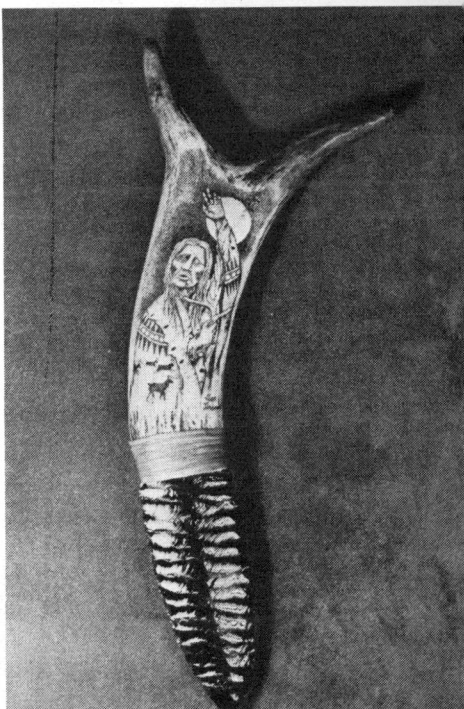

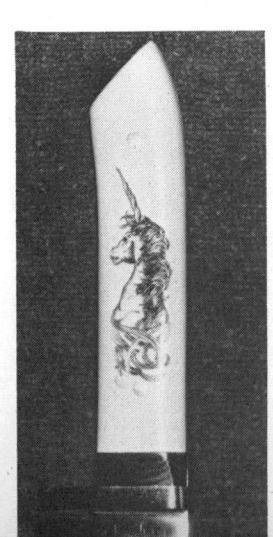

Pert unicorn by Michelle Ochonicky on a Micarta handle.

EIGHTH ANNUAL EDITION 149

Gary Van Ausdle pulled another tour-de-force with this short sword. (Weyer photo)

STATE OF THE ART
ETCHING AND CARVING

WELL, the etchers of the world have not risen, formed ranks and marched. Exactly one etcher submitted photos. Why? Maybe etching suffers because of its repeatability. Maybe folks just naturally believe that there's no such thing as a one-copy etch job. They're wrong when it comes to knives, of course.

Carvers and others of that ilk are very busy. We have a little run on eagles and folks in hoods, but it does seem that knife buyers recognize value in carving.

With carving and the allied skills of silversmithing and casting, the opportunity is there for some all-out attacks on the collector pocketbook. The results are most handsome.

It's not all heavyweight. There are a bunch of knives here with nice *little* carved touches.

Ken Warner

Kemal's dragon sports a marvelous set of carved scales. (Weyer photo)

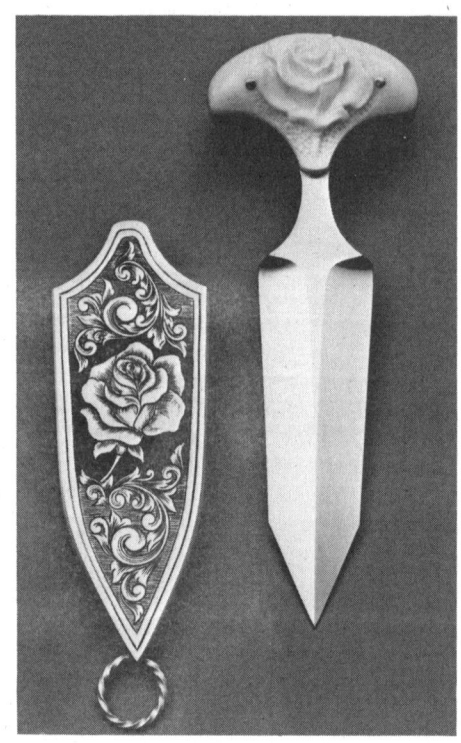

Jim Sornberger did all the work on this push dagger.

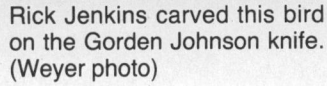
Rick Jenkins carved this bird on the Gorden Johnson knife. (Weyer photo)

Ray Beers Novy eagle was carved by John Alward. (Weyer photo)

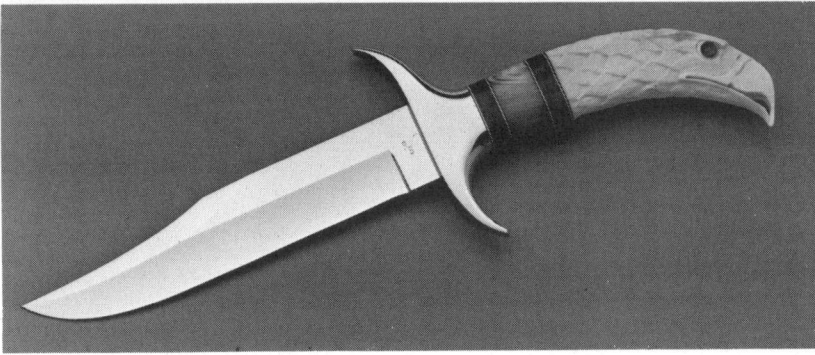

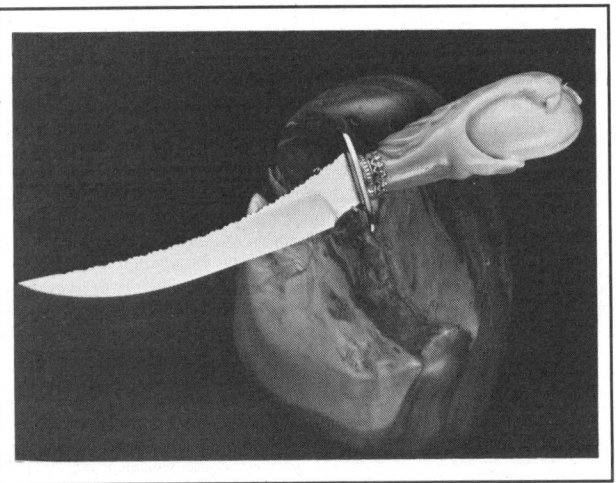

Richard DiMarzo fitted a Norm Levine blade with a claw-and-egg handle. (Long photo)

Jim Serven calls these grotesqueries "defense spikes."

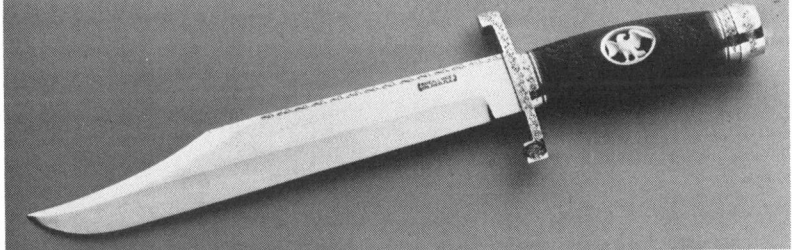

(Below) Rothenburger Waffeneck carved and engraved this Richard Hehn skinner.

This Randall knife was embellished by Tom Leschorn (Weyer photo)

Larry DiTommaso sculpts production knives like this LB-7 with hand-held grinders.

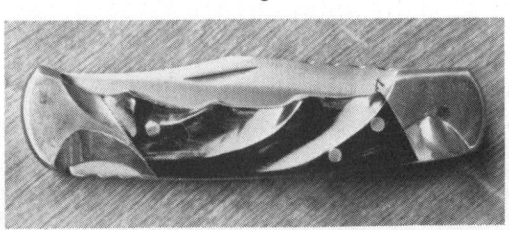

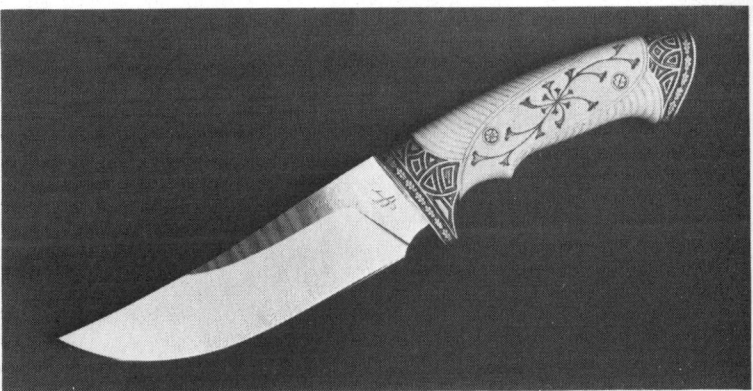

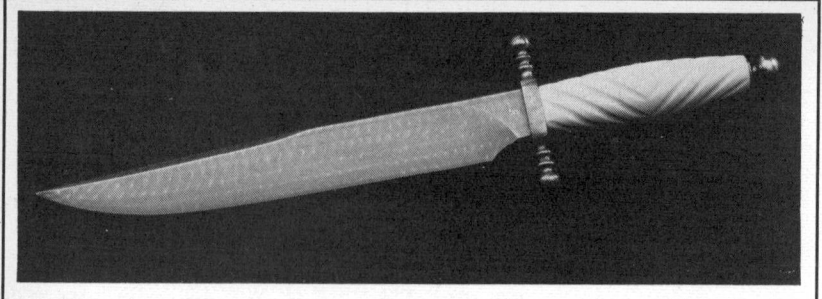

Herringbone pattern handle was carved by the maker, Jerry Rados. (Weyer photo)

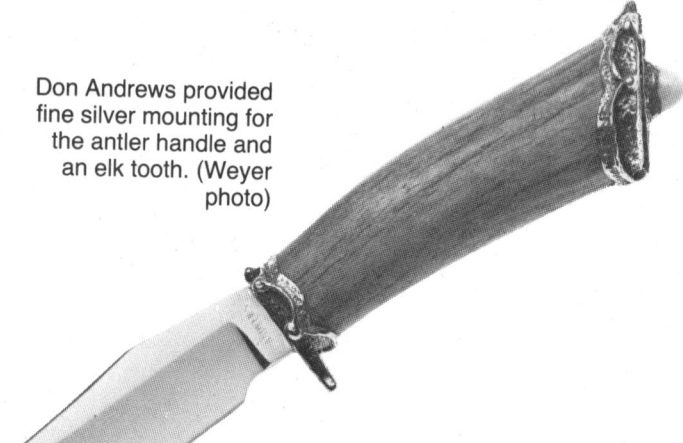

Don Andrews provided fine silver mounting for the antler handle and an elk tooth. (Weyer photo)

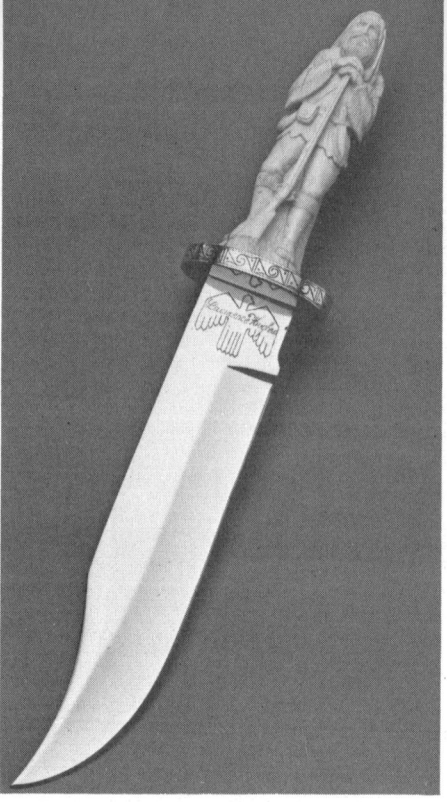

Dennis Holland carved this Lawrence Hughes knife engraved by Frank Clark. (Weyer photo)

Simple bird handle was carved by the knifemaker J.R. Weiland, Jr.

Steven Rapp did all the work on his Will & Fink copy. (Weyer photo)

Dan Peterson carved this nice walnut eagle on his own knife.

Spiraled handle in ivory is by the maker Dwight Towell.

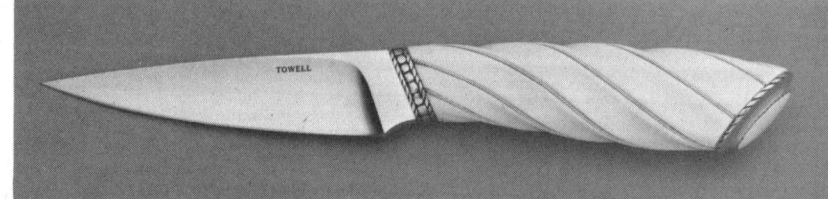

152 KNIVES '88

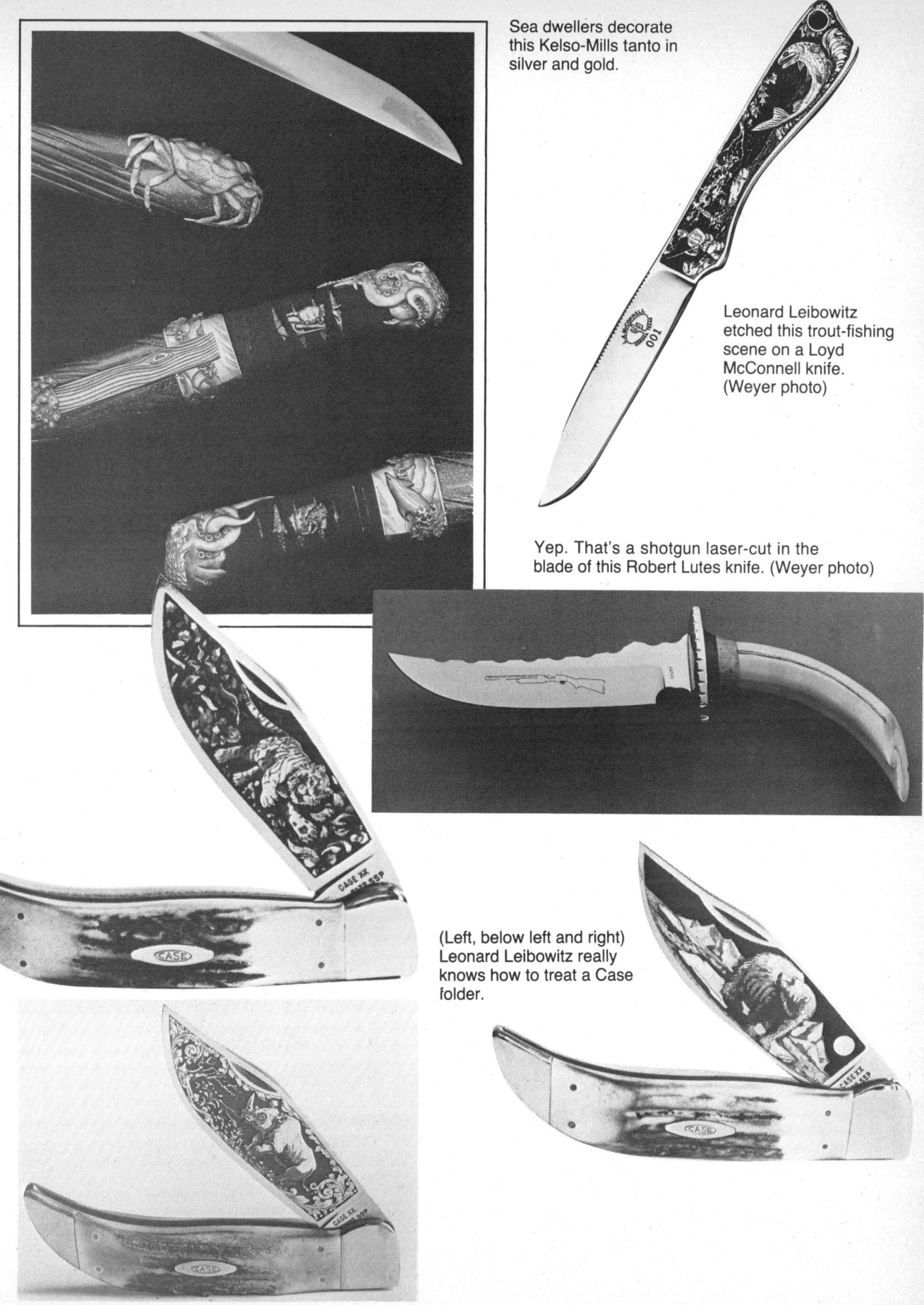

Sea dwellers decorate this Kelso-Mills tanto in silver and gold.

Leonard Leibowitz etched this trout-fishing scene on a Loyd McConnell knife. (Weyer photo)

Yep. That's a shotgun laser-cut in the blade of this Robert Lutes knife. (Weyer photo)

(Left, below left and right) Leonard Leibowitz really knows how to treat a Case folder.

STATE OF THE ART
SCRIPTURAL WOOD

REFERRING to the Bible, we learn from Exodus, Chapters 25-38, that when the Israelites came to the Promised land and Moses came down from Mt. Sinai, he told the children of Israel to bring free-will offerings of gold, silver, gems, linens, furs, dyed skins, and shittim wood, to be used in the building and furnishing of the sanctuary of God, or place of worship, the Jewish Tabernacle. They were told to use shittim wood in the building of the walls, pillars, tables, and altars.

Frank Bell enjoys, you might imagine, incorporating shittim wood. This one was engraved by Ron Smith.

They were told to make the Ark of the Convenant of shittim wood and overlay it with pure gold inside and outside and to cast four rings of solid gold, one for each corner of the ark, or two for each side, and make staves of shittim wood, overlayed with gold, the staves to be put in the rings, one on each side for bearing the Ark.

Shittim wood was considered very precious and sacred. The only specific wood mentioned as used in the Tabernacle. (Some versions of the Bible, for example the King James version, specify acacia wood. This is a family of trees of which the shittim tree is a member. Perhaps the name of the specific wood was considered objectionable to the British translator.) (*Ed. Note:* The New American Standard Bible says acacia, too, according to the Associate Editor.)

Shittim wood is close-grained and hard, of a fine orange-brown color. It was very common in the peninsula of Sinai, and it is not known to grow in any other country except on the mountains of northern Alabama where the roots of the trees are used in making furniture, canes, and other ornamental novelties.

D.C. Sawyer, government landscape architect in connection with park development of Monte Sano State Park, overlooking Huntsville, AL, has this to say:

"Shittim, the rare tree which has brought so much attention to Monte Sano State Park, is a small irregular tree, usually 6 or 8 inches in diameter and 20 feet or more tall. It has brownish, scaly bark and a simple leaf. Its flowers are small in feathery clusters, and appear in spring about the time the leaves are full grown.

"The shittim tree is not particularly handsome, yet it often is cultivated for ornamental purposes, more as a curiosity, however, than for anything else, as it is one of the rarest of trees. The heartwood is dark and durable. The fact that an orange dye can be extracted from it is said to have caused the destruction of the most accessible trees during the Civil War."
Frank Bell

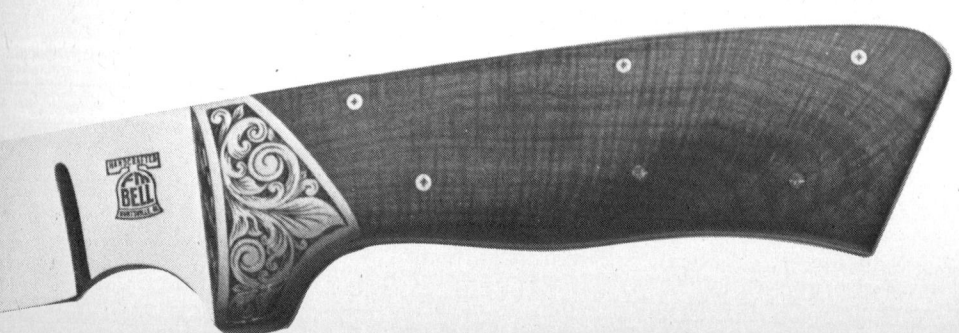

On this Billy Bates-engraved knife we can see the nice marbling of well-chosen shittim wood but not its handsome orange-brown-black coloring.

FACTORY TRENDS

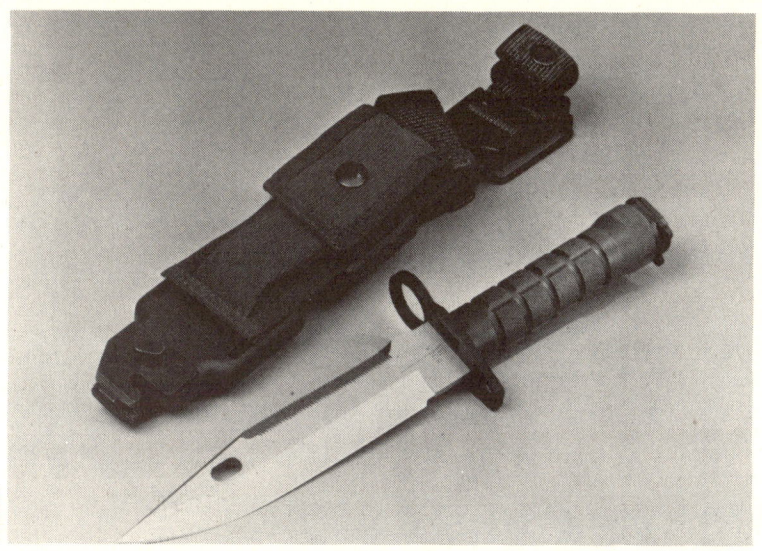

Here is background, both technical and historical, against which the reader can judge and consider commercial cutlery for his own use. Despite a natural tendency to market the tried and true, the factories try to meet new needs every year.

We'll look at the old standard patterns, too. They are all knives, and these are the knives that sell in millions every year.

Ken Warner

Lynn Thompson Goes Bowie
The New Fancies
New Knives in Production

FACTORY TRENDS
LYNN THOMPSON GOES BOWIE

MODERATELY victorious in the great tanto war, Cold Steel's impresario Lynn Thompson has looked for new objectives, new campaigns. He has found the Bowie, a 150-year old hassle with the potential for a niche in which to fit Cold Steel, Inc.

Not since George Leonard Herter and his Model Perfect everything (including, by the way, knives) has the sporting durable goods consumer been treated to such an unabashed pitchman. Lynn Thompson takes a back seat to nobody and he takes a fellow who looks and acts like a bodyguard to national trade shows, too.

Here is Lynn in full flow on his company's newest knife, to be called the Trailmaster:

"When I started work on the Trailmaster project 2 years ago, my primary objective was to build a Bowie-style blade that would exhibit the same qualities as the very best of the forged blades and thereby totally outperform *all* commercial knives and the vast majority of

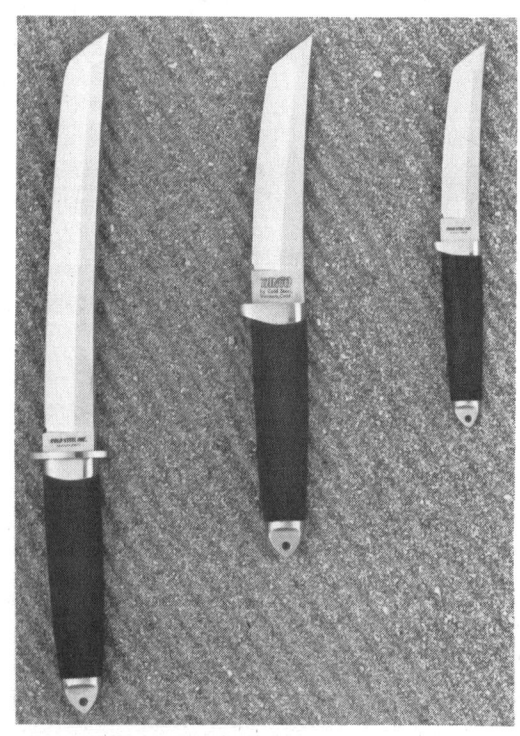

Lynn Thompson's working tanto put Cold Steel on the big-time map. These are standard, small, and magnum versions.

This is the Trailmaster—nice and simple and big. Tough, too, says Lynn Thompson.

custom made knives. I enlisted the services of Dan Maragni to help."

So much for objectives. In essense, Thompson sought a knife that will perform well at such everyday chores as cutting ropes, either free-hanging or otherwise, poking through the walls of 55-gallon drums and getting flexed in a vise. With these as his ideals, Thompson found, in forged blades, four key factors:

1. Steel Selection
2. Grain Alignment
3. Grain Refinement
4. Individualized Heat Treatment

In other words, Thompson says the bladesmith *does not add* anything to the steel by forging it, but does have the facilities to fully exploit the material. Having identified the key elements, Thompson and Maragni set out to try and incorporate them into a production knife.

So Thompson then got into steel, of course:

"Dan and I spent a lot of time testing different types commonly used by bladesmiths like 5160, W1, W2, 01, 1095 and 1045. While some of these steels came very close to what we felt would be optimum, none were quite right. After further research with our manufacturer, we decided on a very high carbon low alloy steel.

"The increased strength achieved by forging a blade to its final shape and profile is obtained by manipulating its original 'grain flow' along the length of the blade regardless of shape. Cold Steel duplicates this process by ordering steel directly from the manufacturer and then specifying how the final directional stages of rolling take place and by cutting the blade profiles from the finished sheet parallel to the rolling direction to use the 'grain flow' to greatest advantage."

It goes without saying that Lynn Thompson and Dan Maragni further specified the best of heat treatment on the best of equipment for this superior steel, called "Carbon V" by Thompson. And the quality control procedures are to be pretty good, too.

The result is a nice-looking Bowie, if photos are any guide. It has a checkered plastic handle and a beautiful satin finish. The guard is brass. The knife has a 9½-inch blade of $5/16$-inch stock and a 5-inch handle. It weighs 18 ounces. It is flat ground and may even have a "rolled edge." ("Rolled edge" is what folks say when they don't want to say "Moran edge.") It comes with a "super rugged" leather sheath.

We'd no doubt say more, but by press time Thompson hadn't sent a knife. He didn't bother us with any dumb detail like Rockwell hardness tests or steel analyses either.

Ken Warner

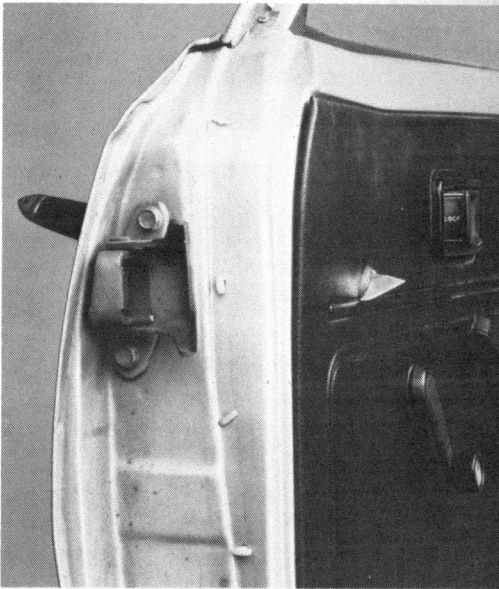

This "test" of a Cold Steel tanto received a lot of attention, in and out of print, as do many things Thompson thinks up.

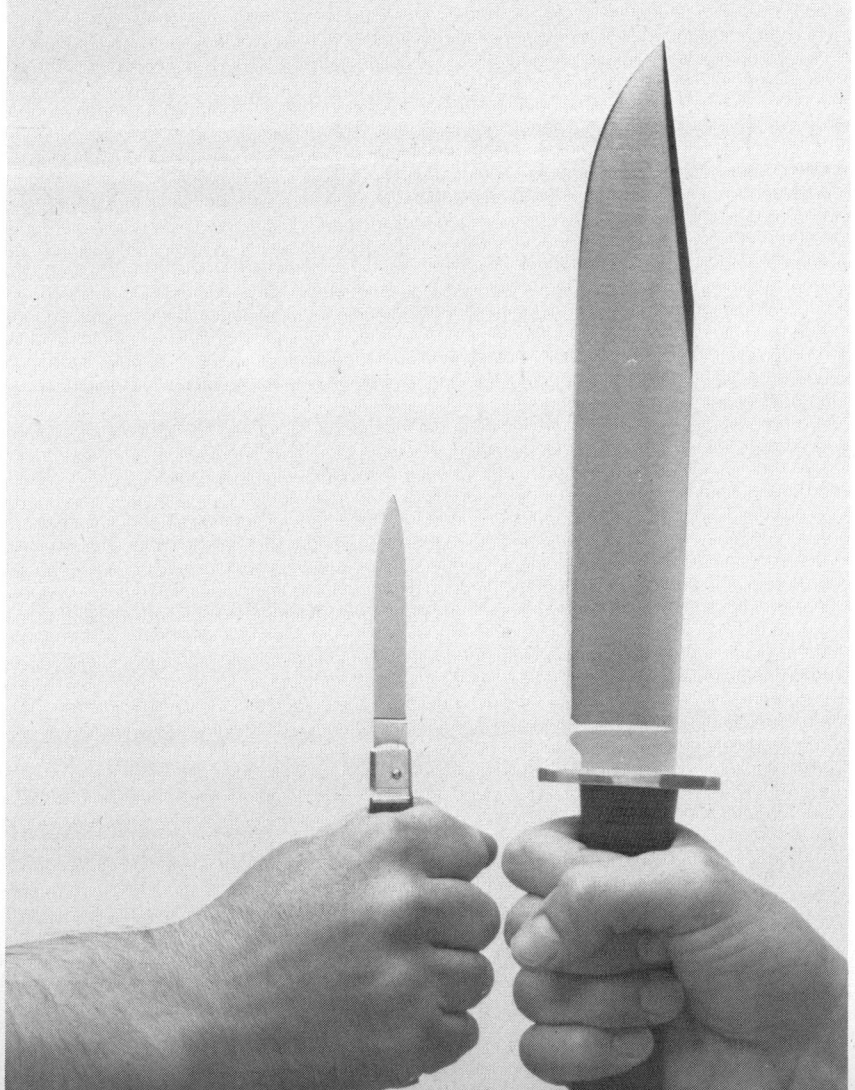

(Left) In the Crocodile Dundee comparison, the Trailmaster looks good. The one on the right is a knife in the sense of the movie.

FACTORY TRENDS
THE NEW FANCIES

IT USED TO be that a fancy knife had pearl handles and a little filework if it was made in Sheffield. To get something genuinely embellished, a fellow could go to a jewelry store; even today most jewelry stores will have a couple of silver and gold pen or watch chain knives around.

But fancy as a general rule, available down at the hardware or over at the sporting goods, right over the counter—that's *now*. They are marketing U.S.-made and imported folders these days in a host of patterns, right up to the big folding hunters, with one or several of all these embellishments factory-applied:

- Special materials and surfaces, such as ivory, pearl, gold and silver plate, abalone, India stag, turquoise.
- Engraving—real cut engraving.
- Engraving—real roll engraving.
- Etching—imitating engraving.
- Etching—presenting scenes and legends.
- Inlays—of a variety of special effects, including miniatures of game animals and birds, cast in pewter or scrimmed on ivory.
- Scrimshaw—hand scratched, hand-colored.
- Scrimshaw—photo etched.
- Scrimshaw—rolled or impressed with a die.
- Filework on all metal.
- Carving, including laser-carving, of wood and synthetic handle materials.

In fact, some smaller factories don't offer many plain knives. Wyoming's Powder River folders are almost all embellished, as one example. In this respect, we're about at the level of the rolled-in patterns on the sides of pump shotguns, but there it is.

Maybe Kershaw didn't invent the term "pocket jewelry," but they sold a lot of small and jazzy pocketknives with it over the years. Now your can get at least five kinds of embellishment from the signed work of scrimmer Gary Harbour through four types of etching, all on Kershaw knives.

Gutmann has signed scrimshaw by Bonnie Schulte, gets engraving cut in Ferlach in Austria, and electroplates and cuts brass surfaces in high relief. Jet-Aer has made it possible to buy an all-stainless knife with a cut game scene filled with gold for way under $20.

Gerber's another one with signed scrim, theirs by Jim Blair. They do it with inlays. Besides that they'll engrave, etch or imprint to personalize a knife. Matthews Cutlery in Decatur, GA, specializes in Solingen cutlery—some gold worked, some engine-turned, some with horn, pearl, ivory, heavy etching. Even Western Cutlery is putting turquoise in knife handles.

Schrade, with a lot of success in their Scrimshaw Line behind them, takes it further. Their American Indian series presents a scrim-style design on a white handle, the whole encased in a beaded leather belt sheath, and their big lockbacks can be had with engraved bolsters and tooled leather holsters.

So that's all a start. It's going to get fancier and fancier. We have come to the time that fancy sells.

Ken Warner

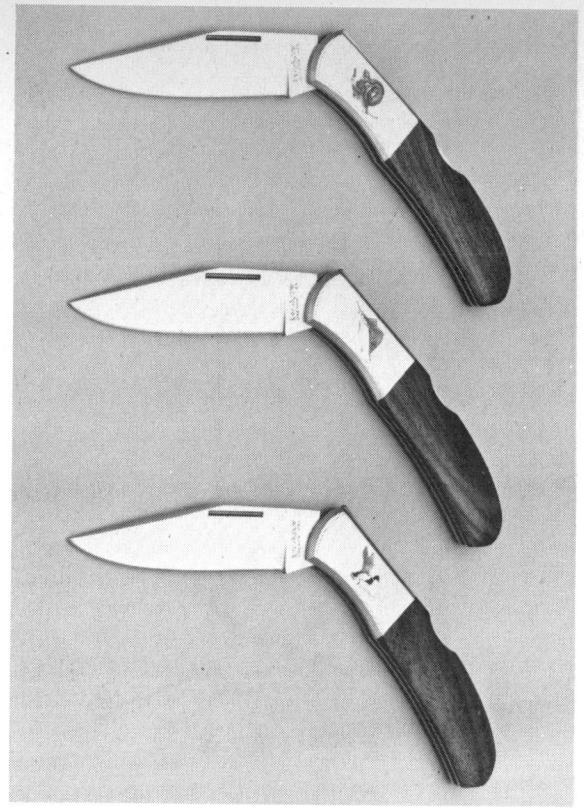

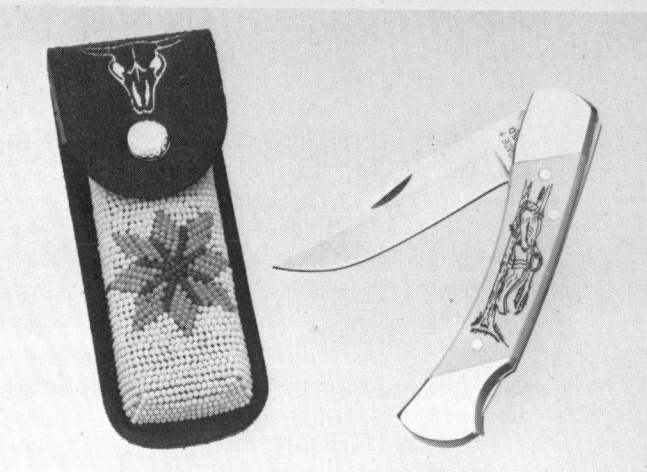

Schrade's American Indians series continues. This is the Sun Dance, scrimmed and beaded in a limited serial numbered edition.

Kershaw color photo-etches some knives. One series shows wildlife in choices from rainbow trout to bighorn sheep.

Precise International calls these the Forte Specials. They're nickel silver and etched. Center knife combines Micarta and nickel silver.

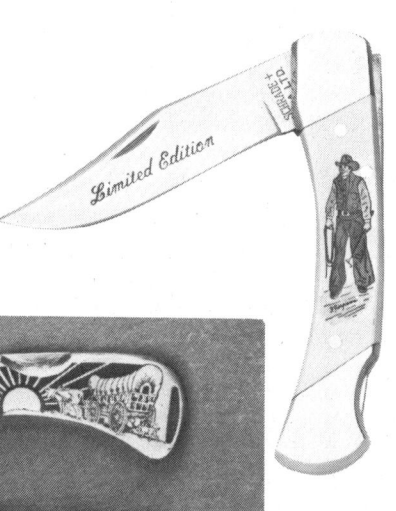

Besides the Indians, Schrade also does cowboys and did just 10,000 of this knife.

Those are "minted honkers" on a nice Kershaw folding hunter.

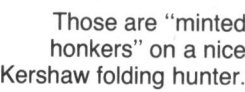

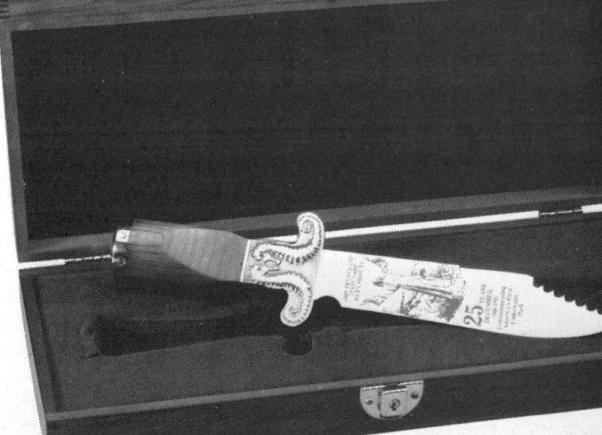

Wenoka commemorated the undersea park at Key Largo, FL, with this fancy divers knife.

EIGHTH ANNUAL EDITION **159**

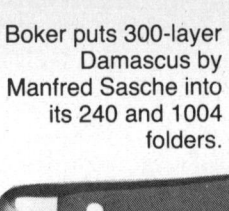

Boker puts 300-layer Damascus by Manfred Sasche into its 240 and 1004 folders.

Santa Fe Stonework did some of this stuff for knife companies, now does some on their own label.

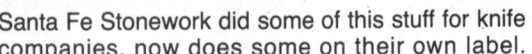

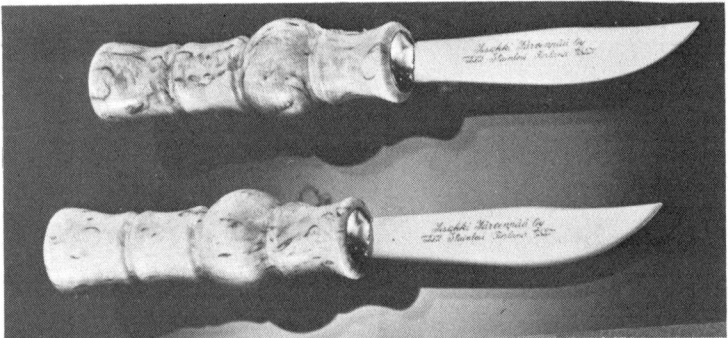

Just a little different are these Finnish fruit knives from Suomi Shop with turned burl wood handles.

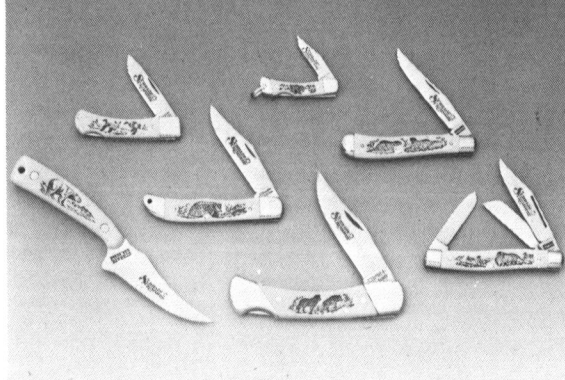

This is the regular Schrade Scrimshaw line—just a little special.

David Yellowhorse, a Navajo, did this special series in turquoise, brass and wood for Buck's Custom Shop.

The Precise Deerfield Damascus folder has pattern-welded blade, cast nickel-silver bolster, and plenty of filework at about $100.

FACTORY TRENDS
NEW KNIVES IN PRODUCTION

IT WAS a big year in factory knives, so this reporter is going to get right to those knives, company by company, mark by mark:

Alcas—Yes, there is another Solution. It's a smaller version called Solution's Spirit. **Beretta**—The Beretta line continues, and is to be augmented with custom knifemaker designs. One such is a Gary Barnes/Beretta folder with rolled engraving. **Boker USA**—The name has changed slightly to suit new ownership, but quality products still continue. Boker has had a titanium folder for years and this year it will get the spotlight. Manfred Sacsche of Dresseldorf, Germany, has provided 300-layer Damascus for a host of Boker knives. The lockbacks include the models: 240, 1004, and the Boker Damascus III.

Buck makes the M9 Bayonet, the new official U.S. Army bayonet. It weighs 1.8 lbs. and its overall length is 12¼ inches. The handle is of Zytel and the blade is forged steel. A new saw has both coarse and fine-toothed sides, with Kraton handle and leather sheath. Buck is celebrating its 25th anniversary with their famous folding hunter marked "Buck's Famous Folding Hunter/Ranger 1963-1988 25th Anniversary." **Calmont Cutlery** continues their Retractable Point Protector knife system with additional sizes and a fluorescent orange handle option.

Camillus got Santa Fe Stoneworks to help with their "Stonecraft" series. Their other series is "Woodcraft"—eight models, all American made. **Case** has new fillet knives and is going strong with the XX-Changer—a lockblade with three interchangeable blades. **Catoctin Cutlery** is into some major importing such as the German Air Force issue combat knife; the British issue "MOD-4" J/S used also a rescue knife in British commercial airlines; the German Special Police knife issue from SEK; and Lynx Kitchen Cutlery made in Mexico.

Cattle Baron Leather Co. has a "Manchu" Chinese warlord knife. It features some unusual grind lines and unique serrations. **Cold Steel** has a Bowie, and the full story is on page 156. **Coleman-Western** likes its Rough Cut series. The 952 and 954 folders have two blades, one that locks, the other serrated. Their sheath knives include the R14 skinner and R16 hunter.

Colonial, along with a new logo and a new national sales manager, has four new knives, all folders at prices from $12 to $21. **Damascus USA** has worked hard on forged-to-shape blades in Damascus. There are also carving sets by Ken Largin, Gil Hibben's "Manhattan Boot," Gene Baskett's 8-inch hunter. **Frost** has a full line as always, and this year has an exclusive with Jack Crain to reproduce 500 "Predator" models, complete with wood cases.

Gerber was sold to Fiskars, but you couldn't tell it. They have a variation of their BMF which they call the Predator CS. **Gutmann** has mini lockbacks in various styles, and some new tantos and survival knives. **Hoffman** has "Condors" in a mid-price range, and has changed the 911 emergency lockback tool, too.

Imperial/Schrade's new list includes lightweight lockbacks—the Firebird and Nighthawk; two Old Timer lockbacks; Bruin and Bearhead; and two gent's utility knives. **Kershaw** has added to the pocket jewelry line and also has a 12-Meter Rigger's knife with sheepsfoot blade, shackle tool, marlin spike and screwdriver. They carry six different Officer Ranch folders, now. **Leatherman's** all-in-one tool has a smaller brother now. Size is 2⅝ x 1 x ½-inch and retails for about $36.

Lifeknife has been selling their Life Axe to many emergency rescue squads with favorable reports. The Life Staff, and their standard line continues on. **Loray** has two different motorized belt sharpeners. The M-190 is for your workshop and the M30-A boasts it can be used commercially. They also have five custom made knives. **Al Mar** is selling the Tanken series—four Occidental tantos called Shugoto I and II, Scout, and Phantom. The airweight locking folders all have ATS34 steel, Zytel handles and nylon pouch. The SERE fixed and folding knives include two of each.

Museum Replicas: To quote their catalog: "Hand forged edged weapons for collectors, re-enactment groups, and military history buffs." They carry an extensive line of functional replicas of medieval weapons, priced from $25 to $340. **Pacific Cutlery** is out of business. **Parker Cutlery** has all-American made knives in Damascus steel, and custom knifemaker Randall Gilbreath has created a whole benchmade line in collaboration with Parker.

Precise has 8 new models in pocket and sheath knives done in Damascus steel and retailing for $50 to $200, and William C. Johnson, custom knifemaker, is making a limited edition sheath knife for Precise. **Cecil Quirino,** importers of Philippino cutlery is now **Kris Cutlery.** This year they offer a kris balisong. **Dale C. Rau** of B&D Trading Co. handling the Executive Edge series, now is importing the Brazilian Zakharov line.

Remington has the R1613 "Fisherman," the 1987 Replica Bullet Knife. **A.G. Russell** continues to sell collectors knives through the mail, as well as design new models for his Knife Collectors Club. **Santa Fe Stoneworks** likes to be known for their supplies of precious stones, gems, and minerals as well as custom handle artisans.

Smith's, possibly the oldest firm that produces the Arkansas stone as well as a variety of other sharpeners, just celebrated their 100th anniversary. **Spyderco** has a straight-edged paring knife with ribbed polymer handle to compliment their bigger utility serrated edge knife. **Taylor** has a new survival angle—a bow and arrow and, yes, a knife, too—all boxed to sell in the upper $60 range. Larry Harley designed for Taylor/Seto the Harley Skinner 7-inch OAL with 3-inch blade which sells for $32.

United Cutlery Corporation and Boker Tree Brand has jointly put out a 3¾-inch Copperhead Pattern folding pocketknife in the mid-$30 range. **Utica** has medallion lockbacks in your choice of brass, copper, or nickel silver construction. The medallions can be gold, silver, or multicolored cloisonne. **Rudolph Weber, Jr.** has a new 18-page catalog in full color of his Solingen-made line. **Wenger's** plant had a fire which wiped out 25% of their warehouse, but they are up and running and filling all the orders to include their new Dynasty models.

Deborah Warner

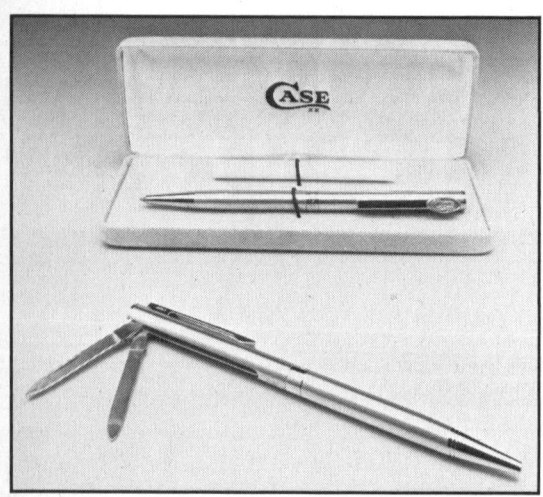

The ultimate commentary on civilization may be Case's pen/knife, a ball-point pen equipped with a blade to trim goose quills.

High style and heavy construction are in the same sailor's package from Kershaw.

High style again in a deluxe Damascus skinner-caper set from Damascus USA. (Weyer photo)

Photographed American-style, Muela knives from Spain look very good. (Weyer photo)

(Above and below) Beretta is in the planning stages with a Beretta-Loveless series, for which you see a prototype in stag here. And Ron Lake's LakeR side is in pre-production for his Hip mate, a mortise-handled hunter with a no-fooling tweezer in it. (Klinefelter and Weyer photos)

Another high-tech Buck number is their new and quite small Mini-Buck—three color choices and under an ounce.

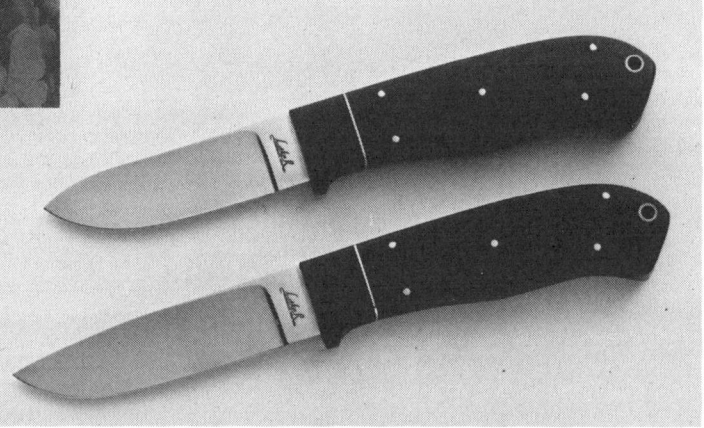

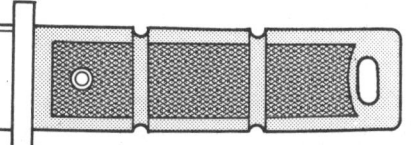

Al Mar's Tanken comes in this and three other blade shapes, all practical adaptations of Japanese ideas in stainless steel, brass and Zytel.

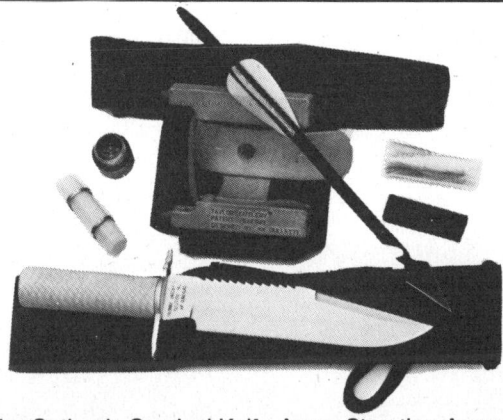

Taylor Cutlery's Survival Knife Arrow Shooting Accessory (SKASA) incorporates a broadhead shooter as well as a knife. (Scadlock photos)

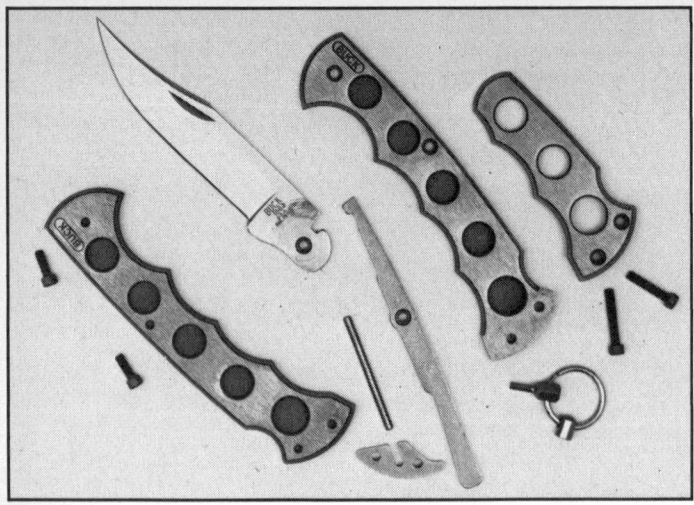

This is what any owner can do to Buck's titanium-handled #1862 folder, and Buck provides the tool. (Levine photo)

Tekna practically *means* high-tech, none more so than their see-through folder.

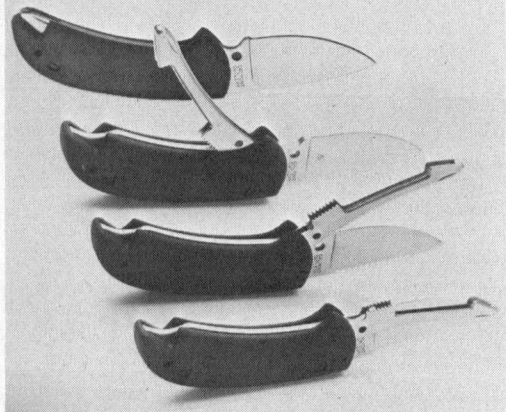

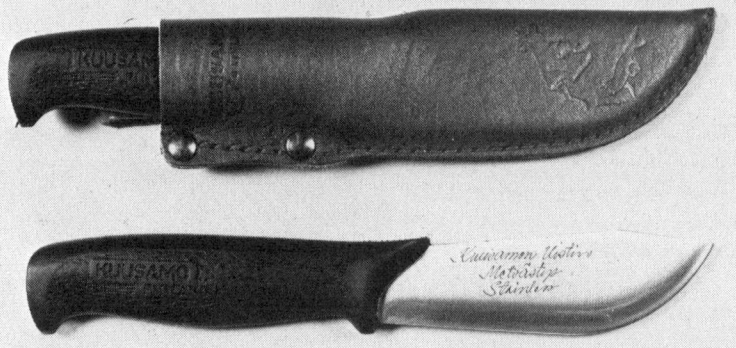

(Above left) Calmont is refining their basic hunter—new sizes, new blade-guard features, new colors.

(Above right) Efficient Finnish skinner in a very safe and sensible sheath is from Ken's Finn Knives.

(Below and right) The enormous two-hand sword from Museum Replicas (Div. of Atlanta Cutlery) was inevitable and, in the event, has turned out nicely.

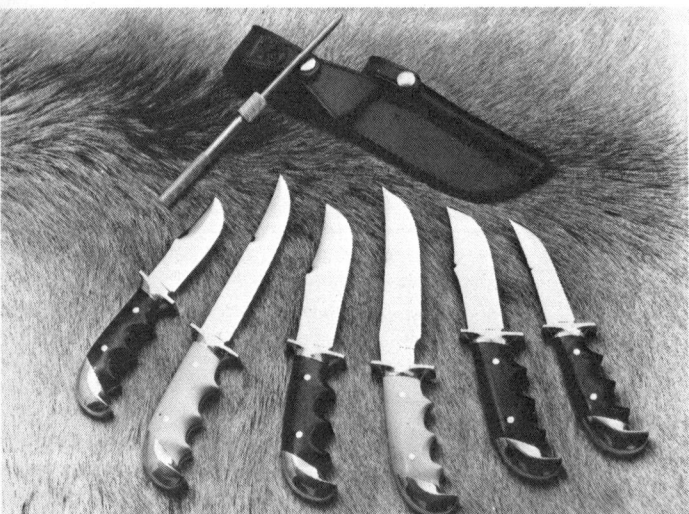

Bauska knives—the whole line shown here—are to be handmade, marketed by the well-known firearms firm.

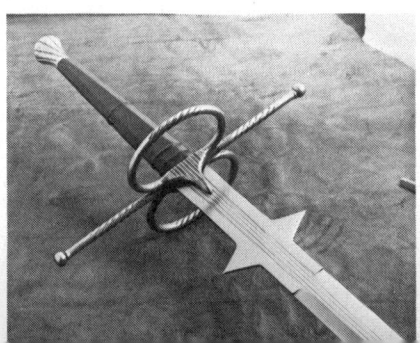

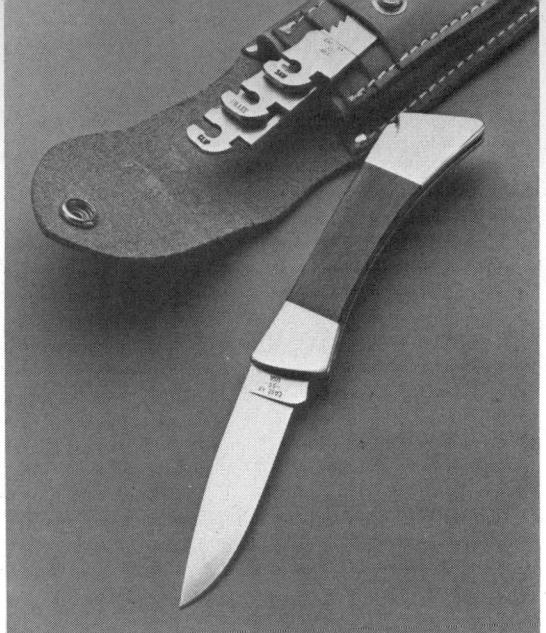

Case XX-Changer actually comes with all four blades—clip, drop point, fillet and saw-with-screwdriver.

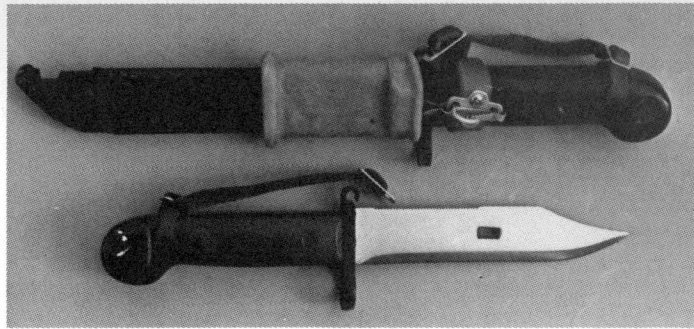

Catoctin Cutlery brings in this Hungarian AKM bayonet with all the modern bayonet conveniences.

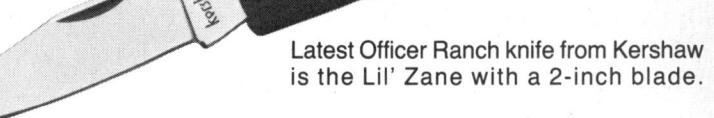

Latest Officer Ranch knife from Kershaw is the Lil' Zane with a 2-inch blade.

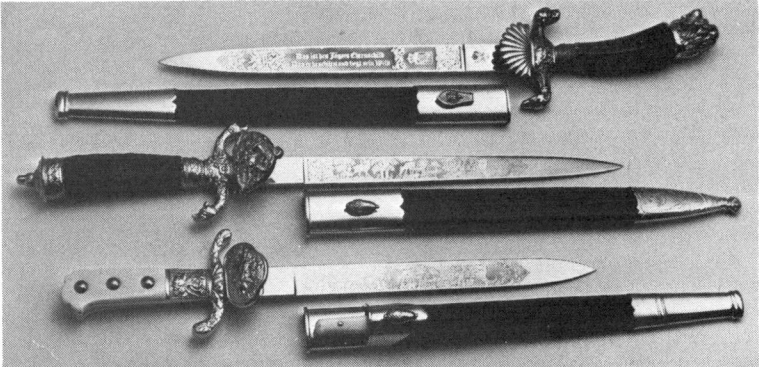

German hunting daggers from Rudolph Weber, Jr. have the old-time look and detailing.

Colonial's new LK95 has its own look and a nice size and weight.

Coleman/Western offers Roughcuts—one blade smooth, the other serrated—in two folder sizes.

EIGHTH ANNUAL EDITION **165**

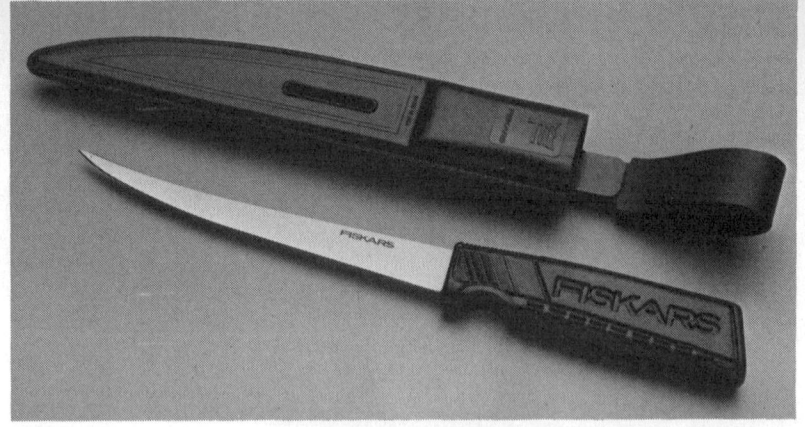

Fiskars says this fillet knife handle is a "power grip," and with it the work goes faster and safer.

The Spirit of the Solution—the distilled essence of Alcas' knife-axe tool—is smaller, presumably for detail work.

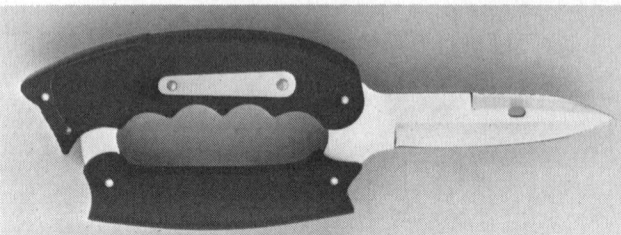

Another Kershaw bladed tool—the all-out high-tech shears.

The diverse divers knives of Wenoka come in blade profiles and colors that change, but they all go in the same sheath.

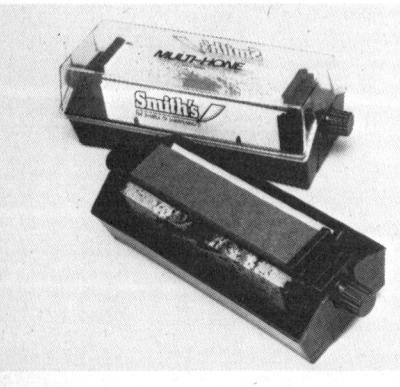

(Left and above) This Dan's Whetstone set-up offers two surfaces; the more complex Smith's outfit offers four.

166 KNIVES '88

(Left) Wenger's biggest Swiss Army Knife has been demagnetized so that a new combination compass/map rule will work. The new gadget comes with 15 other blades, is also available in a couple of smaller models.

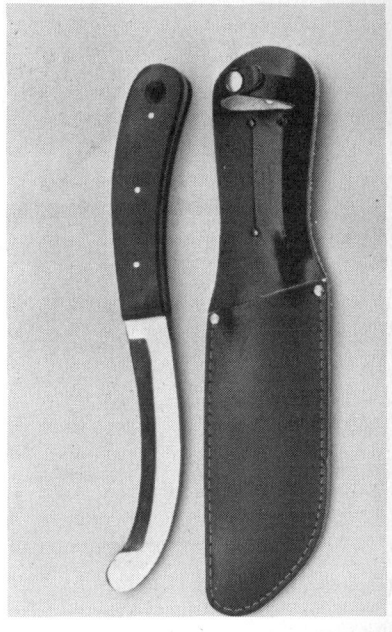

Rudolf Weber, Jr. is the source for this German-style bush-cum-survival knife in the White Hunter tradition.

Catoctin Cutlery sells this British-made rescue knife, a safe design for cutting belts, clothing and webbing.

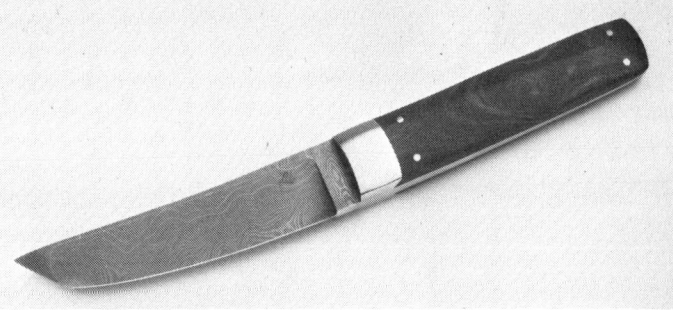

Lee Bench Made Knives are still with the tanto shape in American made Damascus. (Weyer photo)

Buck's new field saw is, of course, the "SawBuck"— fine-toothed one side; coarse the other.

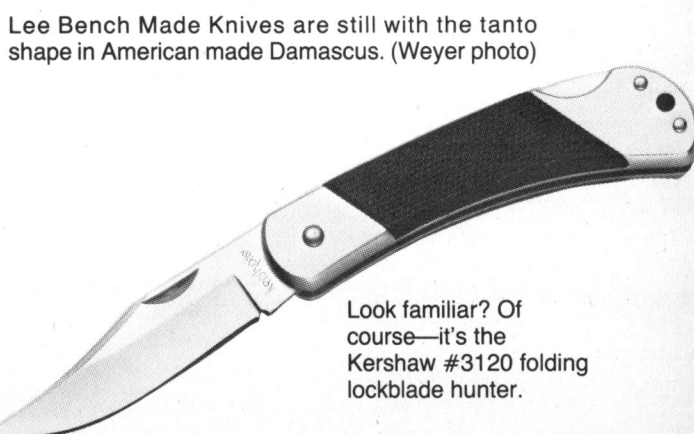

Look familiar? Of course—it's the Kershaw #3120 folding lockblade hunter.

EIGHTH ANNUAL EDITION **167**

(Left) Just a little upscale is this Damascus carver set from Damascus-USA. (Weyer photo)

Rough-and-ready British approach to the stout survival knife is this issue knife from Catoctin Cutlery.

Tekna tucks a little something for almost any unexpected occasion into its high-tech survival outfit.

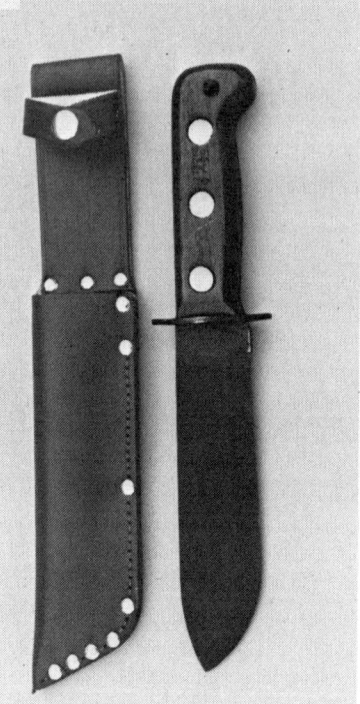

In commemoration of their having perfected the folding lockblade knife a quarter-century ago, Buck offers these special etched Hunters and Rangers.

New handle scales and a Roughcut blade don't change a grand old idea much. This is the Coleman/Western 955.

Now there are five Kraton-handled Bucks, three more than last year.

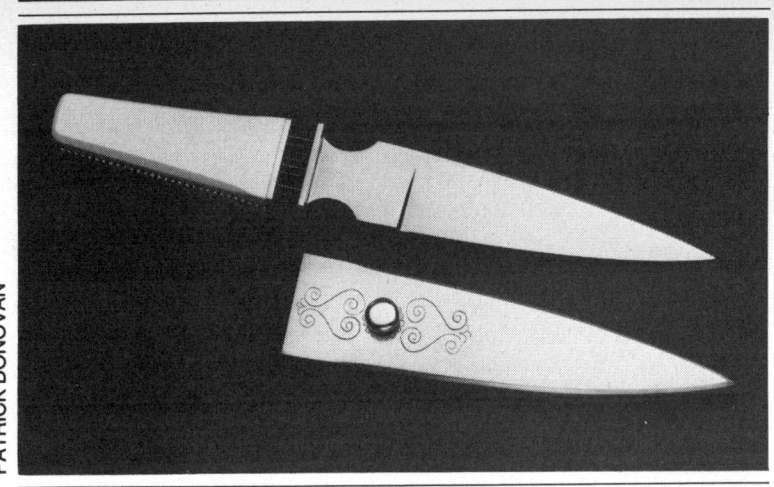
PATRICK DONOVAN

DIRECTORY

The only reason a maker or a source in the United States is not listed somewhere in this section is that we didn't hear of him or it, or something went wrong. This is intended to be a complete directory for knive owners. If you know of someone who should be in this Directory and isn't, please write and tell us. If you are that someone, please write. We'll appreciate it.

It is not a catalog, so there will be incomplete entries, though not many. And with probably 1,000 or more entries, it will have omissions. Very often, that will be the result of error on the part of the omitted. We tried to give everyone a chance.

The Directory is divided into different lists. The biggest is a compilation of short profiles of custom knifemakers, followed by a state-by-state list of those same knifemakers, membership lists of professional knifemaker associations and then a photo index to previous editions. Then we list specialty cutlers; general cutlers, importers and foreign cutlers; sources for knifemaking supplies; mail-order houses that specialize in knives; knife services, which include scrimshanders, engravers, leatherworkers and several other categories; and finally, we list major organizations and publications. Those seem the most useful categories. We hope they work for you.

Ken Warner

Custom Knifemakers
Knifemakers State-by-State
Official Membership Lists
Photo Index
Specialty Cutlers
General Cutlers
Importers & Foreign Cutlers
Knifemaking Supplies
Mail-Order Sales
Knife Services
Organizations & Publications

Custom Knifemakers

This is probably the biggest list of currently working knifemakers in print. If someone is listed here, he or she makes knives.

Over the years we have published this list, some of those listed have stopped answering mail from us and we have begun to drop those listings. There is a list of those dropped at the end of this section.

There are other lists worth consulting following this part of the Directory. Each knifemaker organization was asked, immediately before press-time for its current membership list. All names given are shown. And there's a new state-by-state list.

A great many of the knifemakers in this Directory charge a fee to send catalogs. At a minimum, inquire with a self-addressed and stamped envelope, or send $1. Some charge $2 or $3 or more, but deduct that charge from a knife order.

A CUT ABOVE (See Phill Hartsfield)

ED ADDISON, 325 E. Pritchard St., Asheboro, NC 27203/919-625-1769
Specialties: Working straight knives in standard factory butcher patterns. **Patterns:** Kitchen, fish, and hunting knives; variety of woods offered. **Technical:** Grinds 01 steel, 440C; uses saw blades. **Prices:** $16 to $100. **Remarks:** Full-time maker; his first knife sold in 1961. **Mark:** Name, city, state

YOSHIHITO AIDA, 26-7, Narimasu 2-chome, Itabashi-ku, Tokyo 175, JAPAN/(03)-939-0052
Specialties: High-tech working straight and folding knives in own designs. **Patterns:** Tantos, Bowies, lockbacks, miniatures. **Technical:** Grinds 440C, ATS34; works in traditional Japanese fashion for some handles and sheaths. **Prices:** $170 to $500; some higher. **Remarks:** Full-time maker; sold first knife in 1978. **Mark:** Y. AIDA

ALASKA KNIFE & SERVICE CO. (See Thomas A. Trujillo)

DARREL ALEXANDER, Box 745, Big Piney, WY 83113/307-276-3734
Specialties: Straight working knives in traditional styles. **Patterns:** Hunters, boots, and fish knives. **Technical:** Grinds D2, 440C, and 154CM. **Prices:** $55 to $95; some $240. **Remarks:** Full-time maker; first knife sold in 1983. **Mark:** Name, city, and state

MIKE "WHISKERS" ALLEN, Rt. 1 Box 1080, Malakoff, TX 75148/214-489-1026
Specialties: Folding and straight working knives. **Patterns:** Hunters, tantos, Bowies, swords, and miniatures. **Technical:** Forges to shape Damascus, and grinds 440C, and ATS34. **Prices:** $85 to $185; some $2,000. **Remarks:** Full-time maker; first knife sold in 1984. **Mark:** Whiskers and serial number

STEVE ALLEN, 200 Forbes St., Riverside, RI 02915/401-433-0235
Specialties: Working straight knives. **Patterns:** Hollow-handle survival knives, Bowies, camp and fish knives. **Technical:** Grinds 1095, 440C, and 154CM. **Prices:** $100 to $350; some $1,000. **Remarks:** Full-time maker; first knife sold in 1982. **Mark:** Running River

TIM (R.V.) ALVERSON, Box 92, Keno, OR 97627/503-884-9119
Specialties: Fancy working knives in custom designs. **Patterns:** Folding lockers, miniatures, boots, fighters, and hunters. **Technical:** Grinds 440C, 154CM; buys some Damascus. **Prices:** $80 to $150; some $400 and up. **Remarks:** Part-time maker; first knife sold in 1981. **Mark:** Rosebud or R.V.A.

A.W. AMOUREUX, 3210 Woodland Pk. Dr., Anchorage, AK 99517/907-248-4442
Specialties: Straight working knives for heavy duty. **Patterns:** Bowies, fighters, camp knives and hunters for Alaska use. **Technical:** Grinds 440C, ATS34, and 154CM. **Prices:** $80 to $2,000. **Remarks:** Part-time maker; first knife sold in 1974. **Mark:** ALSTAR

CHARLES B. ANDERSON, West Shore, Polson, MT 59860/406-883-6165
Specialties: Straight high-tech working knives in own designs. **Patterns:** Hunting, kitchen, and fish knives. **Technical:** Grinds 01, D2, 154CM and 440C. **Prices:** $95 to $500; exceptional knives to $1,000. **Remarks:** Part-time maker; first knife sold in 1980. **Mark:** Full name.

EDWIN ANDERSON, 2050 Hillside Ave., New Hyde Park, NY 11040/516-488-7880
Specialties: Large hunters, fighters, and boot knives. **Patterns:** Standard classics. **Technical:** Grinds Stellite 6K, 01, and 125CM. **Prices:** $125 to $275; some to $750. **Remarks:** Part-time maker; first knife sold in 1977. **Mark:** Name over state.

VIRGIL W. ANDERSON, 16318 S.E. Taggart, Portland, OR 97236/503-761-4053
Specialties: Straight working knives and fancy pieces of his own design. **Patterns:** Bowies, boots, hunters, and push knives; some with bottle opener in blade. **Technical:** Grinds D2, 154CM, and F8 Silvanite. **Prices:** $100 to $250; some $500. **Remarks:** Part-time maker; first knife sold in 1984. **Mark:** Anderson.

DON ANDREWS, N. 5155 EZY St., Coeur D'Alene, ID 83814/208-765-8844
Specialties: Plain and fancy folders and straight knives. **Patterns:** Hunter with two butt caps; folder in a wrist pocket. **Technical:** Grinds D2, 440C, ATS34; does lost wax casting for guards and pommels. **Prices:** $50 to $100; some much higher. **Remarks:** Part-time maker; first knife sold in 1983. **Mark:** Name

ANGEL SWORD (See D. Watson)

W.E. ANKROM, 14 Marquette Dr., Cody, WY 82414/307-587-3017
Specialties: Folding and straight knives in own designs; also period pieces and working knives. **Patterns:** Hunters, fighters, and boots. In folders: lockers, slip joints, two-blades. **Technical:** Grinds A2, 440C, and ATS 34. **Prices:** From $125 to $350. **Remarks:** Full-time maker; first knife sold in 1975. Offers some engraving. **Mark:** Name

WILLIAM J. ANTONIO, JR., P.O. Box 186, Rt. 299, Warwick, MD 21912/301-755-6789
Specialties: Fancy working straight knives in his own designs. **Patterns:** Hunting, survival, and fish knives. **Technical:** Grinds D2, 440C, and 154CM. **Prices:** $125 to $395; some to $900. **Remarks:** Part-time maker; first knife sold in 1978. **Mark:** Name, city, state

RAY APPLETON, Box 321, Byers, CO 80103/303-822-5866
Specialties: One-of-a-kind folding knives. **Patterns:** Uniquely personal—multi-locks and high tech. **Technical:** All parts machined or ground; likes D2. **Prices:** $500 up. **Remarks:** Spare-time maker; made first knife to sell in 1986. **Mark:** AP connected in arrowhead; dated

ARMAGEDDON FORGE (See Scott Lankton)

ASHLEY FORGE (See Hugh E. Bartrug)

DICK ATKINSON, 2524 S. 34th St., Decatur, IL 62521/217-429-6746
Specialties: Makes working folders and straight knives. Uses own designs; some are fancy. **Patterns:** Hunters, fighters, and boots; in folders: lockers in interframes. **Technical:** Grinds, A2, 440C, and 154CM. **Prices:** $85 to $300; some exceptional knives. **Remarks:** Part-time maker; first knife sold in 1977. Likes filework. **Mark:** Name, city, state

RAY BAKER, P.O. Box 303, Sapulpa, OK 74067/918-224-8013
Specialties: Working high-tech straight knives. **Patterns:** Hunters, fighters, and boots, mostly own designs, but will make customer designs also. **Technical:** Grinds D2, 440C and 154CM. **Prices:** $40 to $135, some to $300. **Remarks:** Full-time maker; sold first knife in 1981. He scrimshaws some knives. **Mark:** R. BAKER

PHILLIP BALDWIN, P.O. Box 563, Snohomish, WA 98290/206-334-5569
Specialties: Elegant table cutlery; other exotics. **Patterns:** Contemporary and eclectic. Likes the challenge of axes and such. **Technical:** Forges W2, W1 and his own Damascus. **Prices:** From $300 to $950, some to $2,000. **Remarks:** Full-time maker; first knife sold in 1973. **Mark:** Angular "B" marked with chisel

JIM BARBEE, Box 1173, Ft. Stockton, TX 79753/915-336-2882
Specialties: Texas-type hunter's knives. **Patterns:** Solid using patterns. **Technical:** Grinds 440C; likes stag and Micarta and ivory. **Prices:** $125 to $200; some to $500. **Remarks:** Full-time maker and heat-treater. Sold first knife in the '60s. **Mark:** Name and town

ROBERT E. BARBER, 232 Peachwood Lane, Virginia Beach, VA 23452/804-463-0630
Specialties: Working straight knives, some fancy. **Patterns:** Hunters, skinners, fighters are his specialty. **Technical:** Grinds 440C and 154CM. **Prices:** $50 to $150. **Remarks:** Part-time maker; first knife sold in 1984. **Mark:** R.E.B. within rebel hat logo

NORMAN P. BARDSLEY, 197 Cottage St., Pawtucket, RI 02860/401-725-9132
Specialties: Straight working knives, some fancy. **Patterns:** Fighters, tantos, and boots. He does claws, minis, buckle, and push knives. **Technical:** Grinds D2 and 440C, and buys Damascus; offers Titanium nitriding coating process on blades. **Prices:** $150 to $350; some $1,500. **Remarks:** Full-time maker; offers scrimshaw and engraving; emphasizes carrying systems, plain or fancy. **Mark:** Name in script with logo

JOE W. BAREFOOT, P.O. Box 1248, Easley, SC 29641/803-843-2337
Specialties: Straight working knives in mirror finish and own designs. **Patterns:** Hunters, fighters and boots are standard; makes tantos and survival knives. **Technical:** Grinds D2, 440C and ATS34. **Prices:** $50 to $160; some to $500. **Remarks:** Part-time maker; first knife sold in 1980. Uses ivory and stag on customer request only. **Mark:** Barefoot print

TOM and WILLIAM BARMINSKI, 809 S. Del Norte Ave., Loveland, CO 80537/303-669-6783
Specialties: Straight high-tech working knives in own designs. Does etch or scrim some knives. **Patterns:** Hunters, fighters, and survival knives. **Technical:** Grinds D2, 440C and 154CM. **Prices:** $40 to $80 wholesale. **Remarks:** Brothers, Tom and William are full-time makers. Tom's first knife sold in 1981. Sells only to dealers. **Mark:** Signature

GARY L. BARNES, 305 Church St., Box 138, New Windsor, MD 21776/301-635-6243
Specialties: High art and working knives in his own designs. **Patterns:** Hunters, Bowies, and daggers; in folders: lockers, slip joints, multi-blades, and one-of-a-kind creations. **Technical:** Forges mostly; makes his own Damascus; uses exotic handle materials, and creates unique locking mechanisms. **Prices:** $300 to $1,500; some to $8,000. **Remarks:** Full-time maker, an A.B.S. Master. First knife sold in 1976. Most knives are embellished. Believes strongly in sole authorship. **Mark:** Name or an ornate B with a dagger through it.

BARR CUSTOM KNIVES (See Barr Quarton)

A.T. BARR, 54 Fox Circle, Denton, TX 76205/817-565-1580
Specialties: Full tang working knives. **Patterns:** Straight and folding knives in wide variety. **Technical:** Grinds A2, D2 and 440C. **Prices:** $75 to $325; some $1,000. **Remarks:** Part-time maker; first knife sold in 1979. **Mark:** Signature

E. ANDERSON

"WHISKERS" ALLEN

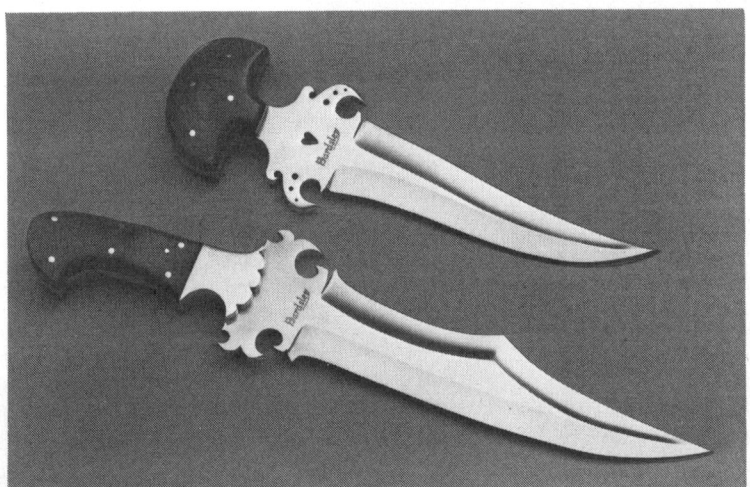

BARDSLEY

directory/custom knifemakers

JAMES J. BARRY, P.O. Box 1571, West Palm Beach, FL 33406/305-968-9305
Specialties: Straight high art and working knives in often unique personal designs of his own. **Patterns:** Hunters, daggers and fish knives predominate. **Technical:** Grinds 440C only. Prefers exotic materials for handles. **Prices:** $100 to $500; some to $4,000. **Remarks:** Full-time maker; first knife sold in 1975. Most knives embellished with filework or carving. Believes in sole authorship. **Mark:** JB as a brand

JOHN BARTLOW, 111 Orchard Rd., Box 568, Norris, TN 37828/615-494-9421
Specialties: Straight working knives, some fancy. **Patterns:** Makes hunters, fighters and survival knives; does some embellishing. **Technical:** Grinds and forges 01, 440C and ATS34; makes his own Damascus. **Prices:** $45 to $200; some $500. **Remarks:** Full-time maker, sold first knife in 1979. Field-tested knives as a guide and makes his knives for work. **Mark:** Last name

HUGH E. BARTRUG, 505 Rhodes St., Elizabeth, PA 15037/412-384-3476
Specialties: Offers straight and folding knives; prefers high art and period pieces. **Patterns:** Hunters, Bowies and daggers; in folders—hunters and traditional patterns. **Technical:** Forges laminated nickel and wrought iron; does some grinding. Uses 01 steel. **Prices:** $210 to $2,500; some to $5,000. **Remarks:** Full-time maker; sold first knife in 1980. **Mark:** Ashley Forge or name

LEE GENE BASKETT, 240 Oakwood Dr., Elizabethtown, KY 42701/502-769-5816
Specialties: Fancy working knives and fantasy pieces, often set up in desk stands. **Patterns:** Fighters, Bowies, and survival knives, as well as folding lockers, butterflies, and traditional styles. **Technical:** Grinds 01, 440C, buys Damascus. **Prices:** $95 to $300; some $1,500. **Remarks:** Part-time maker; first knife sold 1980. File work provided on most knives; unique packaging of knives. **Mark:** BASKETT

PETER BAUCHOP, P.O. Box 68, Hunt Valley, MD 21030
Specialties: Straight working knives and period pieces. **Patterns:** Fighters, swords, and survival knives; some scrimshawed. **Technical:** Grinds 01, D2 and 440C. **Prices:** $100 to $350; some to $550. **Remarks:** Full-time maker; first knife sold in 1980. **Mark:** Bow and axe (BOW-CHOP)

BEAR CLAW (See B.R. Bryner)

BEAR PAW (See Pitt)

BEAR'S CUTLERY (See Carl Jensen)

CHARLES BEAR, 4042 Bones Rd., Sebastopol, CA 95472/707-829-9110
Specialties: High-tech fantasy working knives. **Patterns:** Swords, period belt knives. **Technical:** Forges stainless tool steels; makes stainless Damascus. **Prices:** $200 to $500; some to $1,500. **Remarks:** Part-time maker; sold first knife in 1980. **Mark:** Stylized CB

GORDON H. BEATTY, Rt. 1, Box 79, Seneca, SC 29678/803-882-6278
Specialties: Working straight knives; some fancy. **Patterns:** Traditional patterns; hunters include a mini-skinner; letter openers. **Technical:** Grinds 440C, D2 and ATS34; makes knives one at a time. **Prices:** $45 to $200; some to $450. **Remarks:** Part-time maker; sold first knife in 1982. **Mark:** Name

DEVON BEAVER, Box 3067 New River Stage I, Phoenix, AZ 85029/602-465-7831
Specialties: Creates his own high art straight knives; does some working knives. Most knives are embellished. **Patterns:** Hunters, tantos and daggers are most usual work. **Technical:** Grinds 440C, 154CM and ATS34. **Prices:** $135 to $800; some very high. **Remarks:** Full-time maker. Judy Beaver helps with embellishment and is now making some straight art knives herself. First D. Beaver knife sold in 1979; first J. Beaver in 1984. **Mark:** Name, city, state in Old English type

P. F. BECK, 1504 Hagood Ave., Barnwell, SC 29812/803-259-5959
Specialties: Small working straight knives, especially for deer hunters. **Patterns:** Standard hunter and boot shapes; some experimental work. **Technical:** Flat grinds; mirror finishes. **Prices:** Low to medium. **Mark:** Name

MICHAEL R. BECKWITH, 48282 Donahue Dr., New Baltimore, MI 48047/313-949-2506
Specialties: Straight working knives; likes customer designs. **Patterns:** Hunters, fighters, and boots, but can provide axes, buckskinner and push knives. **Technical:** Grinds D2, 440C and 154CM. **Prices:** $80 to $200; some to $300. **Remarks:** Part-time maker; first knife sold in 1980. **Mark:** Last name

RAY BEERS, 9 Manorbrook Rd., Monkton, MD 21111/301-472-2229
Specialties: Straight working knives and a lot of fancy ones. **Patterns:** Fighters and tantos are his popular styles, but he makes everything. **Technical:** Grinds D2, 440C and 154CM. **Prices:** $65 to $300; some to $2,000. **Remarks:** Full-time maker; many patterns have a palm hunter handle. First knife sold in 1979. **Mark:** RB connected

JACK BELK, 5321 County Rd. 3, Marble, CO 81623/303-963-1900
Specialties: Does one-of-a-kind knives of his own designs. **Patterns:** Hunters, boots, and folders. **Technical:** Stock removal, hollow grinds. **Prices:** NA. **Remarks:** Does his own engraving. **Mark:** BELK

FRANK BELL, 409 Town & Country Drive, Huntsville, AL 35806/205-837-2016
Specialties: Both folding and straight knives in period pieces and working knives. **Patterns:** Hunters, Bowies, and daggers; in folders, he makes lockers, slip joints in gents and hunter styles. **Technical:** Grinds 440C, 154CM and ATS34. Makes sheaths of ostrich leather. **Prices:** $100 to $175; some to $800. **Remarks:** Part-time maker; first knife sold in 1977. **Mark:** Bell shaped logo or last name

MICHAEL BELL, Rt. 1, Box 1217, Coquille, OR 97423
Specialties: Straight knives in standard patterns in period pieces and high art knives. **Patterns:** Tantos, daggers, and swords; some knives are engraved. **Technical:** Forges W2, 1095, and makes his own Damascus. Bell served an apprenticeship to a Japanese swordmaker. **Prices:** $1,000 to $6,000; some to $10,000. **Remarks:** Full-time maker; his first sold in 1972. His steel and handles are made in traditional Japanese style. **Mark:** KUNIMITSU or DRAGONFLY

DON BENSON, 2505 Jackson St. #112, Escalon, CA 95320/209-838-7921
Specialties: Straight working knives in his own designs. **Patterns:** Axes, Bowies, tantos, and hunters. **Technical:** Grinds 440C. **Prices:** $100 to $150; some $250. **Remarks:** Spare-time maker; first knife sold in 1980. **Mark:** BENSON

DAVE BER, P.O. Box 203, Nooksack, WA 98276/206-966-4243
Specialties: Working straight knives for the sportsman; camp knives. Welcomes customer designs. **Patterns:** Hunters, Bowies, kitchen and fish knives. **Technical:** Forges and grinds saw blade steel, welded wire Damascus, 01, L6, and 440C. **Prices:** $75 to $125; some to $300. **Remarks:** Full-time maker; first knife sold in 1985. **Mark:** Ber

LARRY BERZAS, 208 W. 26th St., Cut Off, LA 70345/504-693-3335
Specialties: Straight working knives in customer designs. **Patterns:** Gator skinners, Bowies, swords and tomahawks. **Technical:** Grinds L6; bolsters are gas-welded to blades. **Prices:** $85 to $175; some $500. **Remarks:** Part-time maker; first knife sold in 1979. **Mark:** Bear's behind logo; double red dots on handle

LEROY BESIC, 40640 Campus Way, Hemet, CA 92344/714-652-3384
Specialties: Straight working and high art knives. **Patterns:** Hunters, tantos, and daggers. Does one-of-a-kind pieces, too. **Technical:** Grinds 440C. All knives hand finished with solderless joints. **Prices:** $165 to $225; some $1,200. **Remarks:** Full-timer maker; his first knife sold in 1979. Offers embellishment. **Mark:** Name, city, and state.

BEST FRIEND KNIVES (See John Phillips)

ROBERT F. BIRCH, P.O. Box 1901, Huntsville, TX 77340/409-291-1609
Specialties: Straight working knives. **Patterns:** Hunters, fighters and camp knives. **Technical:** Grinds 440C. Likes polished antler handles and pigskin sheaths. **Prices:** $90 to $300 and up. **Remarks:** Part-time maker; first knife sold in 1985. **Mark:** BIRCH

SID BIRT, RR3, Box 269A, Nashville, IN 47448/812-988-6502
Specialties: Grand straight and folding period pieces designed with a sure eye. **Patterns:** One-of-a-kind in all sizes, shapes and functions. **Technical:** Forges mostly; does some grinding, using W2, 1095 and his own Damascus. **Prices:** $600 to $2,500; some to $6,500. **Remarks:** Full-time maker; first knife sold in 1970. Son Dillon is a co-worker. **Mark:** BIRT

EARL BLACK, 3466 South 700 East, Salt Lake City, UT 84106/801-466-8395
Specialties: Straight and folding high art knives and period pieces. **Patterns:** Boots, Bowies, and daggers, in folders: lockers and gents. **Technical:** Grinds 440C and 154CM. Buys some Damascus. **Prices:** $200 to $1,800; some to $2,500 and up. **Remarks:** Full-time maker; first knife sold in 1980. Some knives are scrimmed or engraved. **Mark:** Name, city, and state

BLACK OAK (See Sayen)

ANDREW E. BLACKTON, 12521 Fifth Isle, Bayonet Point, FL 33667/813-869-1406
Specialties: Straight and folding knives; some fancy knives. **Patterns:** Hunters, Bowies and daggers head the list. **Technical:** Grinds D2, 440C and 154 CM. **Prices:** $125 to $450; some to $2,000. **Remarks:** Full-time maker. Offers some knives with embellishment. **Mark:** State of Michigan outline with knife across it and "Blackton the Great Lakes Knifemaker."

WILLIAM E. BLAKLEY, II, Rt. 4, Box 103, Fredericksburg, VA 22405/703-775-3773
Specialties: Simple working knives. **Patterns:** Hunters and skinners; some Bowies and daggers. **Technical:** Grinds 440C; offers D2 and 01 on request. **Prices:** $75 to $300. **Remarks:** First knife sold in 1984. **Mark:** WEB II

ROY BLAUM, 319 N. Columbia St., Covington, LA 70433/504-893-1060
Specialties: Straight and folding working knives in his own designs; makes lightweight easy-open folders a lot. **Patterns:** Hunters, boots and fish knives. **Technical:** Grinds A2, D2 and 154CM. **Prices:** $75 to $200; some to $500. **Remarks:** Full-time maker; sold first knife in 1976. **Mark:** Signature engraved

GREGG BLOMBERG, Rt. 1, Box 1762, Lopez, WA 98261/206-468-2103
Specialties: Working straight carving knives of traditional design. **Patterns:** Crooked knife; straight utilities; adzes. **Technical:** Forges and grinds W2, D2, 1095, and 440C. **Prices:** $40 to $125; some $300. **Remarks:** Full-time maker; first knife sold in 1978. Business name: Kestrel Tool. **Mark:** KESTREL with flying falcon logo

BLACKTON

BARTLOW

BARTRUG

BLACK

BER

BENSON

directory/custom knifemakers

L.H. BLOOMFIELD, P.O. Box 3588, Kingman, AZ 86402/602-757-8007
Specialties: Working straight knives, some fantasy pieces. Works largely with customer designs. **Patterns:** Hunters, boots, swords, survival and push knives. **Technical:** Grinds A2, 01, and 440A. **Prices:** $100 to $250; some $400. **Remarks:** Part-time maker; first knife sold in 1981. **Mark:** COYOTE KNIVES, city, state and date.

CHUCK BLUM, 743 S. Brea Blvd. #10, Brea, CA 92621/714-529-0484
Specialties: Bowies, combat knives and fancy pieces. **Technical:** Mostly flat grinds 440C; all fittings stainless. **Prices:** $125 to $1,200. **Remarks:** Part-time maker; first knife sold in 1985. **Mark:** Blum with sailboat logo

E.B. BOATNER (See Jimmy L. Fikes)

BOB-SKY (See Hajovsky)

BRUCE BOCHMAN, Box 693, El Granada, CA 94018/415-728-5302
Specialties: Straight working knives in traditional patterns. **Patterns:** Bowies, fish and bird knives. **Technical:** Grinds 154CM, and ATS34; all knives hollow ground, and mirror finished. **Prices:** $140 to $250; some $500. **Remarks:** Part-time maker; first knife sold in 1977. **Mark:** BB

PHIL BOGUSZEWSKI, 2102 North Anderson, Tacoma, WA 98406/206-756-9571
Specialties: Folding working knives; some are fancy. Most are his design. **Patterns:** He makes folding lockers and slip joints and some mini and miniature knives. **Technical:** Grinds D2, 440C and 154CM; does filework. **Prices:** $125 to $400; exceptional knives $800. **Remarks:** Full-time maker; first knife sold in 1979. **Mark:** Name, city and state

BRUCE BOHRMANN, 29 Portland St., Yarmouth, ME 04096/207-846-3385
Specialties: Straight sports knives, designed for use. **Patterns:** Hunters, fish and camp knives. **Technical:** Grinds 154CM; likes wood handles. **Prices:** All knives are $175. **Remarks:** Full-timer; sold first knife in 1976. **Mark:** Name, town and state.

CHARLES B. BOLTON, P.O. Box 6, Jonesburg, MO 63351/314-488-5785
Specialties: Straight working knives in traditional patterns. **Patterns:** Hunters, skinners, tantos, and miniatures. **Technical:** Grinds 440C, 154CM, and ATS34. **Prices:** $75 to $150; some $300. **Remarks:** Part-time maker; first knife sold in 1973. **Mark:** Bolton

BONE KNIFE CO., INC. (Owner: Charles Hipp), 4009 Ave. A, Lubbock, TX 79404/806-765-6812
Specialties: Working folding and straight knives in solid time-tested patterns. **Patterns:** Hunters to axes; fighters to miniatures; push knives to folding lockers. **Technical:** Grinds D2 and 440C. **Prices:** $125 to $500. **Remarks:** Owned and operated by Charles Hipp part-time. Old name. **Mark:** Bone

JEREMY BONNER, 85 Phoenix Cove Road, Weaverville, NC 28787/704-645-4565
Specialties: Folding knives of his own design; some are working knives and some of those are fancy. **Patterns:** Unique style; done one-of-a-kind, but in series—pierced blades, carved handles, castings—as an artist. **Technical:** Forges and grinds 01 and Damascus. **Prices:** $200 to $500. **Remarks:** Part-timer; first knife sold in 1978. **Mark:** BONNER

TILTON and JAMES BOWEN, Rt. 1, Box 225A, Baker, WV 26801/304-897-6159
Specialties: Straight stout working knives. **Patterns:** Hunters, fighters and boots; also offers buckskinner and throwing knives. **Technical:** Grinds D2 and 4140. **Prices:** $65 to $150; some $275. **Remarks:** Full-time makers; first knives sold in 1982-1983. **Mark:** Initials of both and BOWEN BLADES, WV

FRANCIS BOYD, 2128 Market St., San Francisco, CA 94114/415-431-0520
Specialties: Folders and kitchen knives. **Patterns:** Push button locked sturdy folders; San Francisco style chefs knives. **Technical:** Forges and grinds; mostly uses high carbon steels. **Prices:** Moderate to heavy. **Remarks:** Designer. **Mark:** Name

DENNIS BRADLEY, Rt. 3, Box 3815, Blairsville, GA 30512/404-745-4364
Specialties: Folding and straight working knives, some in high art style. **Patterns:** Hunters, boots and daggers; in folders: slip joints and two-blades. **Technical:** Grinds D2, 440C and bought Damascus. **Prices:** $75 to $200; some $750. **Remarks:** Part-time maker; first knife sold in 1973. **Mark:** BRADLEY KNIVES in double heart logo

EDWARD P. BRANDSEY, 406 St. Joseph Circle, Edgerton, WI 53534/608-884-4634
Specialties: Straight working knives and period pieces. **Patterns:** Hunters, fighters, Bowies; some buckskinner styles. **Technical:** Grinds 154CM, 440C and 01. **Prices:** $125 to $250; some $750. **Remarks:** Part-time maker; first sold knives in 1973. **Mark:** EB connected

LARRY BRANDSTETTER, 827 N. 25th, Paducah, KY 42001
Specialties: Bowie-era knives; some as working knives. **Patterns:** Old Sheffield Bowies and folders. **Technical:** Grinds 440. Likes ivory, stag, pearl. Casts handle parts when needed. **Prices:** $250 to $500; some to $950. **Remarks:** Spare-time maker; first knives sold in 1977. Not taking orders. **Mark:** L.D.B.

JIM BRAYTON, 713 Park St., Burkburnett, TX 76354/817-569-4726
Specialties: Working knives and period pieces, some fancy. **Patterns:** Bowies, hunters, fighters. **Technical:** Grinds ATS34, delivers it at 60 RC. **Prices:** $55 to $500. **Remarks:** Full-time maker; sold first knife in 1970. **Mark:** J.E.B, or name

DAN E. BRDLIK, 166 Campbell St. So., Prescott, WI 54021/715-262-5296
Specialties: Straight working knives; some fantasy pieces. **Patterns:** Fighters, boots and Bowies, especially utilitarian fighter designs. **Technical:** Grinds D2, 440C and 154CM. **Prices:** $65 to $250; some $500. **Remarks:** Full-time maker; first knife sold in 1983. **Mark:** DAN E. over stylized toothpick

WALTER J. BREND, 351 Pine Ave., Walterboro, SC 29488/803-538-8256
Specialties: Straight working knives; some fantasy types. **Patterns:** Fighters, Bowies and survival knives. Likes big knives, knives for military people. **Technical:** Grinds A2, D2 and ATS34. **Prices:** $150 to $500; some exceptional knives $3,500. **Remarks:** Full-time maker; first knife sold in 1980. **Mark:** Confederate flag

CLINT BRESHEARS, 2219 Belmont Lane, Redondo Beach, CA 90278/213-372-0739
Specialties: Straight and folding working knives. **Patterns:** Hunters, Bowies and survival knives. Folders are mostly hunters. **Technical:** Grinds 440C, 154CM and ATS34; prefers mirror finish. **Prices:** $125 to $175; some $300. **Remarks:** Part-time maker; first knife sold in 1978. **Mark:** CLINT KNIVES, city, state

WAYNE BREUER, 400 East Glenwood, Wasilla, AK 99687/907-373-2191
Specialties: Working straight knives, all fancy. **Patterns:** Hunters and camp and Bowie knives. Makes camp axes. **Technical:** Grinds L6, 440C, AEB-L and 154CM; likes wire inlay, scrimshaw, decorative filing. **Prices:** $60 to $150; some to $300. **Remarks:** Part-time maker; sold first knife in 1977. **Mark:** Signature

JACK BREWER, 2415 Brady Lane, Lafayette, IN 47905/317-474-1738
Specialties: Folding and straight period pieces and working knives. **Patterns:** Boots, Bowies and daggers; lockers and slip joints. Likes traditional types. **Technical:** Grinds A2, 01, L6; forges files. **Prices:** $18 to $125; some to $400. **Remarks:** Part-time maker; first knife sold in 1979. **Mark:** BREWER or JB connected

RICHARD A. BRIDWELL, Rt. 2, Milford Ch. Rd., Taylors, SC 29687/803-895-1715
Specialties: Working folding and straight knives. **Patterns:** Boot and fish knives, fighters and hunters; some folders. **Technical:** Grinds stainless steels and D2. **Prices:** $85 to $165; some $600. **Remarks:** Part-time maker; first knife sold in 1974. **Mark:** BRIDWELL logo

E.D. BRIGNARDELLO, Rt. 2, Box 152A, Beecher, IL 60401/312-946-6609
Specialties: Straight working knives; some display pieces. **Patterns:** Hunt-

ers, fighters, boots and Bowies. Also does some push knives. **Technical:** Grinds 440C, 154CM and ATS34; likes mirror finishes. **Prices:** $130 to $250; some to $500. **Remarks:** Part-time maker; first knife sold in 1978. **Mark:** Name and town

DAVID BROADWELL, P.O. Box 4314, Wichita Falls, TX 76308/817-692-1727
Specialties: Straight working knives, some fancy. **Patterns:** Hunters, fighters, tantos. **Technical:** Grinds 440C only; hand-finishes most. **Prices:** $150 to $600; some $2,200. **Remarks:** Part-time maker; first knife sold in 1982. Offers some embellished knives. **Mark:** BROADWELL-MADE, city and state

KENNETH L. BROCK, P.O. Box 375/207 N. Skinner Rd., Allinspark, CO 80510/303-747-2547
Specialties: Working full tang straight knives and some folders. **Patterns:** Hunters, survival knives, miniatures, and minis. **Technical:** Flat grinds D2; makes own sheaths. **Prices:** $50 to $250. **Remarks:** Part-time maker; sold first knife in 1978. **Mark:** BROCK with city, state and serial

MICHAEL BROOKS, 1108 W. 6th, Littlefield, TX 79339/806-385-6282
Specialties: Straight working knives to customer designs. **Patterns:** Tantos, Bowies, hunters, on up to swords. **Technical:** Grinds 440C, D2, and ATS34. **Prices:** $40 to $200. **Remarks:** Part-time maker; first knife sold in 1985. **Mark:** MB

STEVE R. BROOKS, Box 105, Big Timber, MT 59011/406-932-5114
Specialties: Straight and folding knives, some period pieces, some working knives. **Patterns:** Hunters, Bowies and camp knives; folding lockers. Offers axes, tomahawks and buckskinner knives. **Technical:** Forges 01 and his own Damascus. Uses 440C, too. **Prices:** $100 to $350; some $1,000. **Remarks:** Full-time maker; first knife sold in 1982. Some knives come embellished. **Mark:** Lazy SB

THOMAS A. BROOME, P.O. Box 4294, Kenai, AK 99611/907-262-7812
Specialties: Traditional working knives; straight and folding. **Patterns:** Full range of folders and a large variety of straight knives. **Technical:** Grinds D2, 440C, and ATS34. **Prices:** $75 to $175; some to $2,000. **Remarks:** Full-time maker; first knife sold in 1979. Business name Thom's Custom Knives. **Mark:** Full name, city, state in logo

MAX BROWER, 1721 Marshall St., Boone, IA 50036/515-432-2938
Patterns: Bowies, hunters, and boots. **Technical:** Grinds 440C, and 154CM. **Prices:** $60 to $150. **Remarks:** Spare-time maker; first knife sold in 1981. **Mark:** BROWER

BRAYTON

BOCHMAN

BOLTON

BRANDSEY

S. BROOKS

BOYD

directory/custom knifemakers

DAVID B. BROWN, Box 112, Doniphan, NE 68832/402-845-6831 **Specialties:** Folding and straight working knives; some are fancy. **Patterns:** Hunters, tantos and Bowies. In folding knives, makes lockers and butterflies. **Technical:** Grinds and forges W2, 440C and his own Damascus. Etches some. **Prices:** $85 to $750; some to $2,000. **Remarks:** Spare-time maker; first knife sold in 1979. **Mark:** D. B. Brown

E.H. BROWN, P.O. Box 1906, Eustis, FL 32727/904-669-1224 **Specialties:** Straight knives in standard patterns, generally period pieces and working styles. **Patterns:** Hunters, Bowies, survival and fish knives. **Technical:** Grinds D2 and 154CM. **Prices:** $250 to $350; some to $2,600. **Remarks:** Full-time maker; first knife sold in 1983. All knives are scrimmed. **Mark:** Name, city, state, and handmade.

HAROLD E. BROWN, Rt. 7, Box 335, Arcadia, FL 33821/813-494-7514 **Specialties:** Straight working knives. **Patterns:** Hunters, boots, Bowies; knife and hatchet sets. **Technical:** Grinds D2, 440C and 154CM. **Prices:** $100 to $350; some to $1,000. **Remarks:** Part-time maker; first knife sold in 1976. Embellishment available. **Mark:** Name and town with logo

L.E. "RED" BROWN, 3203 Del Amo Blvd., Lakewood, CA 90712/213-531-3994 **Specialties:** Working straight knives. **Patterns:** Hunters, Bowies and survival knives made for heavy-duty use. **Technical:** Grinds 01 only. **Prices:** $95 to $265; some $4,000. **Remarks:** Full-time maker; started selling knives in 1941. Some knives are embellished. **Mark:** Diamond B., autographed

PETER BROWN, 8 Myra Ave., Ryde NSW 2112, AUSTRALIA/02-807-3196 **Specialties:** Heavy-duty working knives. **Patterns:** Swords, fighters, tantos, hunting and fishing knives. **Technical:** Grinds 440C, 420 and ATS34; does own heat treating. Offers scrimshaw and engraving. **Prices:** $135 to $500; some to $800. **Remarks:** Spare-time maker; first knife sold in 1978. **Mark:** Interlacing PB

TED BROWN, 8609 Cavel, Downey, CA 90242/213-869-9945 **Specialties:** Working straight knives in traditional patterns. **Patterns:** Hunters, Bowies, fish knives. **Technical:** Grinds stainless steel; some integral work. **Prices:** $100 to $350; some to $500. **Remarks:** Part-time maker; first knife sold in 1982. **Mark:** Name, address in snake logo

RICK BROWNE, 1464 Gertrudita Ct., Upland, CA 91786/714-985-1728 **Specialties:** No heavy-duty knives. High-tech working straight knives in his own designs. **Patterns:** Hunters, fighters and daggers. **Technical:** Grinds D2, 440C and ATS34. **Prices:** $80 to $500; some $1,500. **Remarks:** Part-time maker; first knife sold in 1975. **Mark:** Name, city, state

C. LYLE BRUNCKHORST, 4106½ Highway 68 GVSR, Kingman, AZ 86401/602-565-3255/565-4467 **Specialties:** Working straight and folding knives, some fancy. **Patterns:** Functional hunters, backpacker knives. **Technical:** Grinds stainless steels; works for precision look. **Prices:** $100 to $300; some to $700. **Remarks:** Full-time maker; sold first knife in 1976. **Mark:** Name and serial

JACK and MORGAN BRYAN, 724 Highland Ave., Gardendale, AL 35071/205-631-3322 **Specialties:** Folding and straight working knives; some high-tech. **Patterns:** Hunters, survival and fish knives. In folders it's lockers—hunters and traditional patterns. **Technical:** Chip removal 01, D2 and 440C; use shop-made jigs and fixtures for some patterns. **Prices:** $50 to $150; exceptional knives $300. **Remarks:** Part-time maker; first knife sold in 1940. **Mark:** B in circle

BARRY R. BRYNER, 448 N. 1st Ave., Price, UT 84501/801-637-1343 **Specialties:** Folding and straight knives, most working knives. **Patterns:** Hunters, boots and kitchen knives. Folders include fighters and hunters. **Technical:** Grinds 440C. **Prices:** $90 to $150; some to $250. **Remarks:** Full-time maker; first knife sold in 1978. **Mark:** Name and town in logo

BILL BUCHMAN, 63312 South Rd., Bend, OR 97701/503-382-8851 **Specialties:** Straight working knives; some are high-tech. **Patterns:** Hunters, fighters and boots. Makes some saddle maker knives. **Technical:** Forges D2, 440C and Sandvik 15N20. Prefers 440C for saltwater; making his own Damascus. **Prices:** $75 to $150; some $225. **Remarks:** Part-time maker; first knife sold in 1982. **Mark:** BB or BUCHMAN

BILL BUCHNER, HC60, Box 35 B, Idleyld Park, OR 97447/503-498-2247 **Specialties:** Folding and straight working knives, many high art. **Patterns:** Folding lockers; slip-joints; forges his own patterns in whatever function required. **Technical:** Uses W1, L6 and his own Damascus. **Prices:** $100 to $600; some $2,000. **Remarks:** Full-time maker; started selling knives in 1978. Likes sculpturing and carving in Damascus. **Mark:** Signature

MARK A. BUCHOLZ, P.O. Box 670984, Chugiak, AK 99567/907-688-3660 **Specialties:** Straight working knives in standard patterns, some fancy. **Patterns:** Hunters, fighters, buckskinners and survival knives. **Technical:** Grinds 440C, 154CM, ATS34. **Prices:** $150 to $225; exceptional knives $1,250. **Remarks:** Full-time maker. **Mark:** Name, town and state in buffalo skull logo

DONALD M. BUCKBEE, 8704 Forest Ct., Warren, MI 48093/313-939-9676 **Specialties:** Straight working knives, some fancy. **Patterns:** The standards, folders, Bowies and tantos. **Technical:** Grinds D2, 440C, ATS34. Makes ultra-lights in hunter patterns. **Prices:** $100 to $250; some to $350. **Remarks:** Part-timer; sold first knife in 1984. **Mark:** Antlered bee—a buck bee.

JIMMIE H. BUCKNER, P.O. Box 162, Putney, GA 31782/912-436-4182 **Specialties:** Straight high-tech working knives, locking folders, primarily his own design. Accepts customer designs, too. **Patterns:** Hunters, fighters and camp knives. **Technical:** Forges 01 and 1095; his own Damascus; heat-treats his own. **Prices:** $100 to $300; some $900. **Remarks:** Full-time maker; first knife sold in 1980. **Mark:** J spade B; also JS, a journeyman smith with ABS.

JOHN BUGDEN, 106 So. 13th St., Murray, KY 42071/502-753-0305 **Specialties:** Straight working knives and period pieces. **Patterns:** Hunters, boots and survival knives. **Technical:** Grinds 01, 440C; buys Damascus. Likes filework. **Prices:** $55 to $85; some $200. **Remarks:** Full-time maker; sold first knife in 1975. **Mark:** J.W.B.

PON BURGER, 12 Glenwood Ave., Woodlands, Bulawayo, ZIMBABWE (Africa)/48628 **Specialties:** Folding and straight working knives; high art with his own designs. **Patterns:** Fighters, locking folders of traditional styles, and buckles. **Technical:** Grinds D2; embellishes all knives made. **Prices:** $175 to $350; some $600. **Remarks:** Full-time maker; first knife sold in 1973. **Mark:** BURGER

SKIP BURNETTE, 14 Wildwood Ct., Spartanburg, SC 29301/803-574-6768 **Specialties:** Straight high-tech working knives. **Patterns:** Hunters, fighters and camp knives. **Technical:** Grinds D2, 440C and ATS34. **Prices:** $65 to $125; some higher. **Remarks:** Spare-time maker; first knife sold in 1983. **Mark:** Name and town with pine trees

DAVE BURNS, 101 S.E. 27 Ave., Boynton Beach, FL 33435/305-734-8806 **Specialties:** Working straight knives in his design or yours. **Patterns:** Hunters, boots, Bowies, and survival knives. **Technical:** Forges and grinds 01, L6, and 1095. **Prices:** $45 to $135; some $250. **Remarks:** Full-time maker; first knife sold in 1980. **Mark:** Burns and serial number

JOHN BUSFIELD, 153 Devonshire Circle, Roanoke Rapids, NC 27870/919-537-3949 **Specialties:** Investor grade folders; high-grade working straight knives. **Patterns:** Price-style interframe folders; one-of-a-kinds; drop-point hunters, skinners. **Technical:** Grinds 440C, 154CM and ATS34 very well. Does interframes and inlays; uses jade, agate, jasper. **Prices:** $400 to $550; exceptional knives to $1,000. (Prices for plain knives, before embellishment.) **Remarks:** Full-time maker; first knife sold 1979. **Mark:** Last name, & address.

JERRY BUSSE, 11651 Co. Rd. 12, Wauseon, OH 43567/419-923-6471 **Specialties:** Working straight knives. **Patterns:** Heavy combat knives, Bowies, push knives, and camp knives. **Technical:** Grinds D2, 01, and 440C; hollow grinds most blades. **Prices:** $225 to $850; some $3,000. **Remarks:** Full-time maker; first knife sold in 1983. **Mark:** BUSSE in logo

GARY BUTLER, Unit 3/110 Harris St., Welshpool, Perth W.A. 6106, AUSTRALIA/Perth 361-2979
Specialties: Working straight and folding knives, some high-tech, in built-for-Australia design. **Patterns:** Translated standard U.S. patterns in mostly heavy knives. **Technical:** Grinds 440C. Likes bright finishes and hollow grinds. Uses titanium in some folders. **Prices:** $150 to $250 Australian. **Remarks:** Starting a Down Under Guild. **Mark:** Name, town, country

BUZZARD'S KNOB FORGE (See Jeff Hurst)

"BY GEORGE" (See George Englebretson)

CADILLAC BLACKSMITHING (See Larry Pogreba)

BILL CALDWELL, Rt. 9, Box 170-S, West Monroe, LA 71291/318-323-3025
Specialties: Straight period pieces. **Patterns:** Fighters, Bowies and survival knives; tomahawks, razors and push knives. **Technical:** Forges with sledgehammer, uses no power hammer. **Prices:** $400 to $3,500; some to $10,000. **Remarks:** Full-time maker and self-styled blacksmith extraordinaire; first knife sold 1962. **Mark:** Wild Bill & Sons

ERRETT CALLAHAN, 2 Fredonia, Lynchburg, VA 24503/804-528-3444
Specialties: Obsidian knives. **Patterns:** Modern conceptions, as well as Stone Age replicas. **Technical:** Flakes and knaps to order. **Prices:** $90 and up. **Remarks:** Full-time maker; sold first flint blades in 1974. **Mark:** Unmarked

DICK CAMPBELL, 20000 Silver Ranch Rd., Conifer, CO 80433/303-697-0150
Specialties: Straight and folding fancy working knives; some period pieces. **Patterns:** Bowies and fighters, guts and miniatures. **Technical:** Grinds 440C. **Prices:** $130 to $750; some to $1,200. **Remarks:** Part-time maker; first knives sold in 1975. Prefers natural materials. **Mark:** Name

JOE CANDRELLA, 1219 Barness Dr., Warminster, PA 18974/215-675-0143
Specialties: Folding and straight working knives; some fancy. **Patterns:** Daggers, boots, Bowies, and locking folders. **Technical:** Grinds 440C and 154CM. **Prices:** $100 to $200; some to $1,000. **Remarks:** Part-time maker; first knife sold in 1985. Business name is Franjo. **Mark:** FRANJO with knife as J

DANIEL L. CANNADY, Box 301, Allendale, SC 29810/803-584-2813
Specialties: Straight working knives in traditional patterns. **Patterns:** Drop point hunters, Bowies, skinners. Fish knives with concave grind. **Technical:** Grinds D2, 440C, and ATS34. **Prices:** $65 to $100; some $150. **Remarks:** Part-time maker; first knife sold in 1980. **Mark:** CANNADY

RONALD E. CANTER, 96 Bon Air Cir., Jackson, TN 38305/901-668-1780
Specialties: Traditional working knives in customer designs. **Patterns:** Beavertail skinners, Bowies, hand axes, and folding lockers. **Technical:** Grinds A1, 440C, and 154CM. **Prices:** $65 to $250; some $500 and up. **Remarks:** Spare-time maker; first knife sold in 1973. **Mark:** CCC intertwined

CANNADY

D. BROWN

BUCHNER

P. BROWN

CANTER

CALDWELL

directory/custom knifemakers

DON CANTINI, 3933 Claremont Pl., Weirton, WV 26062/304-748-4890
Specialties: Straight working and fancy knives. **Patterns:** Hunters, boots, daggers, minis and push knives. **Technical:** Grinds 440C and Damascus bars. **Prices:** $65 to $200; some to $800. **Remarks:** Part-time maker; first knife sold in 1976. **Mark:** Name, city, state in logo

BOB CARGILL, Route 1, Box 501-B, Oldfort, TN 37362/615-338-8418
Specialties: Largely folding working knives in his own designs. **Patterns:** Adaptations of traditional pocketknives in many styles. **Technical:** Grinds 1095, 440C, 440A and Damascus bars. **Prices:** $50 to $350; some $2,500. **Remarks:** Full-time maker; first knife sold in 1974. **Mark:** Cargill Knives or Cripple Creek

HAROLD J. "KIT" CARSON, 559 Congress Drive, Radcliff, KY 40160/502-351-9542
Specialties: Hard-working knives for military users; will make customer designs. **Patterns:** Fighters, tantos, survival types. **Technical:** Grinds stainless steels; likes ¼-inch stock, integral guards, socket head bolts. **Prices:** $75 to $175; some to $400. **Remarks:** Part-time maker; sold first knife in 1973. **Mark:** Name

FRED CARTER, 5219 Deer Creek Rd., Wichita Falls, TX 76302/817-723-4020
Specialties: High art investor-class straight knives; some working hunters and fighters. **Patterns:** Classical daggers, Bowies. **Technical:** Grinds a variety of steels. Uses no glue or solder. **Prices:** Generally upscale. **Remarks:** Full-time maker. Does his own engraving and inlay. Makes no folders. **Mark:** Signature in oval logo

DENNIS E. CASEY, 2758 Devonshire, Redwood City, CA 94063/415-365-2665
Specialties: Miniature straight knives in customer designs. **Patterns:** Various straight knives in miniature sizes. **Technical:** Grinds 440C, 154CM, and ATS34. **Prices:** $95 to $200; some $275. **Remarks:** Full-time maker; first knife sold in 1982. **Mark:** D.E. CASEY

DOUGLAS CASTEEL, Rt. 2, Box 237, Hillsboro, TN 37342/615-596-3142
Specialties: Fancy working knives in his own designs. **Patterns:** Boots, fighters, daggers, swords, and locking folders. **Technical:** Grinds 440C, 154CM, ATS34. All knives file-worked. **Prices:** $200 to $500; some $1,000. Swords $3,000. **Remarks:** Full-time maker; first knife sold in 1982. **Mark:** D. CASTEEL and year

CATTLE BARON LEATHER (See Tommy McKissack II)

TOM S. CELLUM, 23023 Birnam Wood Blvd., Spring, TX 77373/713-353-1223
Specialties: Working straight knives in traditional styles. **Patterns:** Bowies, camp knives, hunters. **Technical:** Forges W2, 01, 5165; makes own Damascus; prefers natural handle materials. **Prices:** $85 to $150; some to $300. **Remarks:** Full-time maker; sold first knife in 1982. **Mark:** Name

FRANK and MARK CENTOFANTE, P.O. Box 17587, Tampa, FL 33682-7587/813-961-0637
Specialties: Fancy folding working knives. **Patterns:** Locking folders and slip joints. **Technical:** Grinds 154CM and ATS34; high finishes. **Prices:** $200 to $425. **Remarks:** Full-time maker; first knife sold in 1968. Son Mark is co-worker. **Mark:** Name, city, state

JOHN A. CHAMBERLIN, 11535 Our Rd., Anchorage, AK 99516/907-346-1524
Specialties: Working knives in traditional style. **Patterns:** Hunters, tantos, large belt knives; some locking folders. **Technical:** Grinds ATS34, 440C, 154CM; uses some deluxe Alaskan materials, oosic and the like. **Prices:** $65 to $300; some higher. **Remarks:** Full-time maker; first knife sold in 1984. **Mark:** Name in shield and dagger logo

ROBERT CHAMPION, 3710 Harmony, Amarillo, TX 79109/806-359-0450
Specialties: Traditional working knives, both straight and folding. **Patterns:** Hunters, locking and slip joint folders; some sub-hilt fighters. **Technical:** Grinds A2 and 440C, also D2. **Prices:** $200 to $600; some $3,000. **Remarks:** Part-time maker; first knife sold in 1979. **Mark:** CHAMPION

GORDON R. CHARD, 104 S. Holiday Lane, Iola, KS 66749/316-365-2311
Specialties: High-tech working straight knives. **Patterns:** Fighters, boots, daggers and mini knives. **Technical:** Grinds D2, 440C and 154CM; Vascowear. **Prices:** $75 to $800; some $1,500. **Remarks:** Part-time maker; first knife sold in 1983. **Mark:** Name, town and state in wheat logo

JOHN E. CHASE, 217 Walnut; P.O. Drawer H, Aledo, TX 76008/817-441-8331
Specialties: Straight high-tech working knives in standard designs. welcomes customer designs. **Patterns:** Hunters, fighters, daggers and push knives. **Technical:** Grinds D2, 440C and 154CM; does mirror finishes, mostly. **Prices:** $125 to $450; some $1,100. **Remarks:** Part-time maker; first knife sold in 1974. **Mark:** Last name in logo

BILL CHEATHAM, 2930 W. Marlette, Phoenix, AZ 85017/602-242-1497
Specialties: Straight working knives. **Patterns:** Hunters, fighters, boots and axes; also offers locking folders. **Technical:** Grinds 440C. **Prices:** $150 to $350; exceptional knives to $600. **Remarks:** Part-time maker; first knife sold in 1976. Still working after police work-related injury. **Mark:** Name, city state

DON E. CHEATHAM, 22 East 61st, Savannah, GA 31405/912-352-0075
Specialties: Working straight knives, some fancy. **Patterns:** Hunters, fighters and boots. **Technical:** Grinds D2, 440C and 154CM. **Prices:** $100 to $500; some to $1,000. **Remarks:** Full-time maker; first knife sold in 1983. **Mark:** D. CHEATHAM

CLIFF CHELQUIST, P.O. Box 91, Arroyo Grande, CA 93420/805-489-8095
Specialties: Skinners to Bowies, also locking folders and slip joints. **Patterns:** Customer designs; semi-skinners and other hunters. **Technical:** Grinds D2 and 440C. **Prices:** $75 to $150; some $300. **Remarks:** Spare-time maker; first knife sold in 1983. **Mark:** C or C.R.C.

CISCO (See Chuck Syslo)

D.E. (LUCKY) CLARK, Box 314 Woodlawn St. RD #1, Mineral Point, PA 15942/814-322-4725
Specialties: Straight and folding working knives. **Patterns:** Making customer designs now, working from drawing. **Technical:** Grinds D2, 440C, 154CM. **Prices:** $100 to $200 and up. **Remarks:** Part-time maker; only making knives to customer's designs; sold first knife in 1975. **Mark:** Name on one side; "Lucky" on other

J.D. CLAY, R.R. #1, Box 1655, Greenup, KY 41144/606-473-6769
Specialties: Straight and folding fancy working knives. **Patterns:** Hunters, boots, fish knives, and interchangeable blades. He also offers folding lockers and slip joints. **Technical:** Grinds 01, 440C. **Prices:** $90 to $175; some to $300. **Remarks:** Full-time maker; first knife sold in 1972. **Mark:** Name in small medallion in handle

WAYNE CLAY, Box 474B, Pelham, TN 37366/615-467-3472
Specialties: Both straight and folding working knives in standard patterns. **Patterns:** Hunters, fighters and kitchen knives. His folders include gents and hunter patterns. **Technical:** Grinds 154CM and ATS34. **Prices:** $125 to $250; some to $1,000. **Remarks:** Full-time maker; first knife sold in 1978. Highly finished functional working designs, made to complement fine firearms. **Mark:** Name

CLOUDY MT. IRON WORKS (See David Ber)

TERRY A. COHEN, 114 Barson St., Santa Cruz, CA 95060/408-429-9620
Specialties: Working straight and folding knives. **Patterns:** Bowies to boot knives and locking folders. Makes a mini-boot knife. **Technical:** Grinds stainless; hand rubs; tries for good balance. **Prices:** $85 to $150; some to $325. **Remarks:** Part-time maker; first knife sold in 1983. **Mark:** TERRY KNIVES, city and state etched

KEITH E. COLEMAN, 07 Jardin Rd., Los Lunas, NM 87031/505-864-0024
Specialties: Straight and folding working knives, some fantasy types. **Patterns:** Fighters, tantos and survival straight knives; swords; gents, fighters and hunters in folders. **Technical:** Grinds 440C, 154CM and ATS34. Prefers specialty woods; does file work. **Prices:** $75 to $350; some to $1,200. **Remarks:** Full-time maker; first knife sold in 1980. **Mark:** Name, city and state

KEN COLEMAN, 45 Grand St., Brooklyn, NY 11211/718-963-0773
Specialties: One-of-a-kind knives of unorthodox nature—functional sculpture or creative tooling. **Patterns:** None. **Technical:** Grinds 01, 440C and ATS34. **Prices:** $160 to $340; some $480. **Remarks:** Spare-time maker; first knife sold in 1982. **Mark:** Signature

A.J. COLLINS, 1834 W. Burbank Blvd., Burbank, CA 91506/213-848-4905 (Home: 213-767-3467)
Specialties: Working dress knives. **Patterns:** Street survival knives; swords; axes—definitely personal patterns. **Technical:** Grinds 01, 440C, 154CM. **Prices:** $100 up. **Remarks:** Sold first knife 1972; does business as Kustom Krafted Knives—KKK; full-time maker. **Mark:** Name

LYNN M. COLLINS, 138 Berkley Dr., Elyria, OH 44035/216-366-7101
Specialties: Working straight knives. **Patterns:** Field knives, boots and fighters. **Technical:** Grinds D2, 154CM and 440C. **Prices:** $85 to $135; some more. **Remarks:** Spare-time maker; first knife sold in 1980. **Mark:** Initials, asterisks

CONKLIN MEADOWS FORGE (See Gary M. Little)

BOB CONLEY, Rt. #14, Box 467, Jonesboro, TN 37659/615-753-3302
Specialties: Folding and straight working knives. **Patterns:** Folding knives include lockers, two-blades, gents, hunters and traditional types. Straight knives are hunters, Bowies, daggers and miniatures. **Technical:** Grinds 440C, 154CM and ATS34. **Prices:** $150 to $350; some $600. **Remarks:** Full-time maker; first knife sold in 1979. **Mark:** Full name, city, state

C.T. CONN, JR., 203 Highland Ave., Attalla, AL 35954/205-538-7688
Specialties: Folding working knives, some fancy. **Patterns:** A full range of folding knives. **Technical:** Grinds 02, 440C and 154CM. **Prices:** $125 to $300; some to $600. **Remarks:** Part-time maker; first knife sold in 1982. **Mark:** Name

MICHAEL CONNOR, Box 502, Winters, TX 79567/915-754-5602
Specialties: Straight and folding high art knives. **Patterns:** From hunters to camp knives to folding lockers of the traditional types. **Technical:** Forges 01 and his own Damascus. **Prices:** $150 to $600; some to $2,500. **Remarks:** Spare-time maker; first knife sold in 1974. ABS Master smith. **Mark:** CONNOR M.S.

JEFFREY D. CONTI, 3410 6th, Bremerton, WA 98310/206-377-4715
Specialties: Straight working knives in his design or yours. **Patterns:** Fighters and survival knives; hunters, camp knives and fish knives. **Technical:** Forges 01; grinds 154CM, ATS34 and D2. **Prices:** $60 to $170; some to $400. **Remarks:** Part-time maker; first knife sold in 1980. **Mark:** JC

CELLUM

W. CLAY

CHEATHAM

CARTER

KEITH COLEMAN

directory/custom knifemakers

ROBERT COOGAN, Rt. 3, Box 347-A1, Smithville, TN 37166/615-597-6801
Specialties: Working knives. **Patterns:** Unique items like ooloo-style Appalachian herb knife. **Technical:** Forges 01 and 3 percent nickel mild steel. Makes his own Damascus. All knives hand-finished. **Prices:** $65 to $500; some over $1,000. **Remarks:** Part-time maker; first knife sold in 1979. **Mark:** RC

GEORGE S. "STEVE" COPELAND, Star Route Box #36, Alpine, TN 38543/615-823-5214.
Specialties: Working straight and folding knives in traditional and fancy designs. **Patterns:** Wide range includes tomahawks, butterfly folders, camp knives, slip-joint folders. **Technical:** Grinds variety of steels. **Prices:** $60 to $350; can go over $1,000. **Remarks:** Part-time maker; first knife sold in 1979. **Mark:** Four-leaf clover, initials

CORBIN KNIVES (See Corbin Newcomb)

HAROLD CORBY, 1714 Brandonwood Dr., Johnson City, TN 37604/615-926-9781
Specialties: Straight and folding fancy working knives. **Patterns:** Hunters, fighters, Bowies and push knives, and traditional-type folders. **Technical:** Grinds 154CM, ATS34. Prefers natural materials. **Prices:** $100 to $600; some to $1,200. **Remarks:** Full-time maker; first knife sold in 1979. **Mark:** CORBY

JOSEPH G. CORDOVA, 1450 Lillie Drive, Bosque Farms, NM 87068/505-869-3912
Specialties: One of a kind designs; does some customer designs. **Patterns:** His fighter called the "Gladiator," hunters, boots, and cutlery. **Technical:** Forges 1095, 5160, and grinds ATS34, 440C, and 154CM. **Prices:** Moderate to upscale. **Remarks:** Full-time maker; first knife sold in 1955. **Mark:** Cordova made

JIM CORRADO, 2915 Cavitt Creek Rd., Glide, OR 97443/503-496-3951
Specialties: High-tech, high art folding knives. **Patterns:** Makes unusual and difficult pieces, following British and Continental historical design. **Technical:** Forges mostly L6, 154CM and his own Damascus. **Prices:** $200 to $500; some $3,000. **Remarks:** Full-time maker; first knife sold in 1974. **Mark:** Name, date and state with shield logo

SCOTT COSTA, Rt. 2, Box 503, Spicewood, TX 78669/512-693-3431
Specialties: Straight working knives. **Patterns:** Hunters, survival, fishing and divers' knives. **Technical:** Grinds only D2. **Prices:** $65 to $350; some to $650. **Remarks:** Full-time maker; first knife sold in 1985. **Mark:** SC connected

ELDON COURTNEY, 2718 Bullinger, Wichita, KS 67204/316-838-4053
Specialties: Straight working knives in his own designs. **Patterns:** Hunters and fighters, and one-of-a-kinds. **Technical:** Grinds and tempers L6, 440C and spring steel. **Prices:** $100 to $200; some to $1,500. **Remarks:** Full-time maker; first knife sold in 1977. **Mark:** Full name, city and state

GEORGE COUSINO, 22386 Beechwood Ct., Woodhaven, MI 48183/313-675-3284
Specialties: Straight working knives. **Patterns:** Hunters, Bowies, buckskinners and daggers. **Technical:** Grinds D2, 440C and 154CM. **Prices:** $85 to $125; some to $600. **Remarks:** Part-time maker; first knife sold in 1981. **Mark:** COUSINO

RAYMOND A. COVER, Rt. 1, Box 194, Mineral Point, MO 63660/314-749-3783
Specialties: Folding and straight knives in standard patterns, mainly working knives with high-tech materials. **Patterns:** Bowies and boots; two-bladed folders. **Technical:** Grinds D2, 440C and 154CM. **Prices:** $135 to $250; some to $400. **Remarks:** Part-time maker; first knife sold in 1974. **Mark:** Name

COLIN J. COX, 1609 Votaw Rd., Apopka, FL 32703/305-889-7887; 1-800-433-4188
Specialties: Folding and straight working knives and period pieces of his own design. **Patterns:** Hunters, fighters and survival shapes. Folding, two-blades, gents and hunters. **Technical:** Grinds D2, 440C and 154CM. **Prices:** $125 to $750; some to $1,500. **Remarks:** Full-time maker; first knife sold in 1981. **Mark:** Full name, city and state

COYOTE KNIVES (See L.H. Bloomfield)

JAMES H. CRAIG, 334 Novara, Manchester, MO 63021/314-391-8235
Specialties: Fancy straight working knives. **Patterns:** From hunters to swords to miniatures; some embellished. **Technical:** Grinds A2, D2 and 440C. **Prices:** $50 to $125; exceptional knives to $500. **Remarks:** Part-time maker; first knife sold in 1972. **Mark:** CRAIG

JACK W. CRAIN, Rt. 2 Box 221 F, Weatherford, TX 76086/817-599-6414
Specialties: Fancy period pieces of his own design in straight knives. **Patterns:** Bowies, daggers and survival knives; also limited edition commemorative Bowies. **Technical:** Forges and grinds D2, 440C and his own Damascus. **Prices:** $325 to $1,200; some to $4,000. **Remarks:** Full-time maker; first knife sold in 1969. **Mark:** Name with stylized crane

LARRY CRAWFORD, 1602 Brooks St., Rosenberg, TX 77471/713-341-5234
Specialties: Fancy straight and folding knives in traditional patterns. **Patterns:** Bowies, tantos, folders, interframes, and push knives. **Technical:** Forges 1095 and his own Damascus. **Prices:** $300 to $500; some to $800. **Remarks:** Part-time maker; sold first knife in 1983. **Mark:** CRAWFORD

PAT CRAWFORD, 205 N. Center, West Memphis, AR 72301/501-735-4632
Specialties: High-tech working folding and straight knives—self-defense and combat types. **Patterns:** Folding patent locks; interframes; fighters and boots. **Technical:** Grinds 01, 440C and 154CM. **Prices:** $35 to $500; some to $800. **Remarks:** Full-time maker; first knife sold in 1973. **Mark:** CRAWFORD

CRIPPLE CREEK (See Bob Cargill)

HAROLD CRISP, 3885 Bow St. N.E., Cleveland, TN 37312/615-476-8240
Specialties: Straight and folding fancy working knives. **Patterns:** Hunters to Bowies, tomahawks to miniatures. Folding lockers, both interframes and traditional styles. **Technical:** Grinds 01, D2 and 440C; also forges. **Prices:** $85 to $250; some $800. **Remarks:** Part-time maker; first knife sold in 1972. **Mark:** Initials or name

JACK CROCKFORD, 1859 Harts Mill Rd., Chamblee, GA 30341/404-457-4680
Specialties: Clean-lined working straight and folding knives, some period pieces. Works with customer design also. **Patterns:** Hunters and fish and camp knives; folders in traditional styles. **Technical:** Grinds A2, D2 and 440C. **Prices:** $150 to $250; some to $300. **Remarks:** Part-time maker; first knife sold in 1975. **Mark:** Name

ROBERT CROWDER, Box 1374, Thompson Falls, MT 59873/406-827-4754
Specialties: Straight working knives in traditional patterns. **Patterns:** Hunters, kitchen cutlery, Bowies, and fish knives. **Technical:** Grinds D2, 440C, and commercial Damascus. Filework on most knives. **Prices:** $55 to $150; some $400. **Remarks:** Full-time maker; first knife sold in 1985. **Mark:** Name, city and state in logo

JAMES L. CROWELL, Rt. 74, Box 368, Mtn. View, AR 72560/501-269-4215
Specialties: Fancy period pieces and working knives. Welcomes customer designs. **Patterns:** Straight knives from hunters to daggers, war hammers to tantos. Folding lockers and slip joints. **Technical:** Forges W2, 01 and his own Damascus. **Prices:** $400 to $1,000; some to $3,500. **Remarks:** Full-time maker; first knife sold in 1980. **Mark:** A shooting star. ABS Master Smith.

JOHN CULPEPPER, 2102 Spencer Ave., Monroe, LA 71201/318-323-3636
Specialties: Working straight knives. **Patterns:** Hunters, Bowies and camp knives in heavy-duty patterns. **Technical:** Grinds 01, D2 and 440C; hollow grinds. **Prices:** $75 to $200; some $300. **Remarks:** Part-time maker; first knife sold in 1970. **Mark:** Pepper

R.J. CUMMING, American Embassy Manama, FPO New York, NY 09526
Specialties: Custom designs, especially for military personnel. **Patterns:** Hunters, fighters, Bowies and one-of-a-kind straight knives. Diver's tool knife. **Technical:** Grinds D2, 440C and 154CM. **Prices:** $100 to $450; some to $1,700. **Remarks:** Part-time maker presently in Foreign Service; first knife sold in 1978. **Mark:** CUMMING

THOMAS CUTE, RD 4, Rt. 90, Cortland, NY 13045/607-749-4055
Specialties: Straight working knives; will work to customer designs. **Patterns:** Bowies, skinners, camp knives, rifle sling knives. Does miniatures. **Technical:** Grinds 01, 440C, and 154CM. **Prices:** $100 to $300; some $500. **Remarks:** Full-time maker; first knife sold in 1974. **Mark:** Full name

CYPRESS BEND CUSTOM KNIVES (See W.B. Ellerbe)

DAN DAGGET, 1961 Meteor, Flagstaff, AZ 86001/602-774-7537
Specialties: High art straight knives; many embellished with inlays or gems. **Patterns:** Hunters, fighters, daggers. **Technical:** Grinds 440C and buys Damascus. **Prices:** $550 to $2,000; some to $4,000. **Remarks:** Part-time maker; first knife sold in 1973. **Mark:** Name

CRIS W. DAHL, Rt. 4, Box 558, Lake Geneva, WI 53147/414-248-2464
Specialties: Straight high-art working knives. **Patterns:** Hunters, fighters and push knives. **Technical:** Grinds 440C and imported stainless steel Damascus. **Prices:** $180 and $600; some to $3,000. **Remarks:** Full-time maker. **Mark:** Cris W. Dahl maker

G. E. DAILEY, 577 Lincoln St., Seekonk, MA 02771/617-336-5088
Specialties: Big working knives and period pieces. **Patterns:** Bowies and swords. **Technical:** Grinds 01 and 440C. Does leather wrapping. **Prices:** $150 to $1,500. **Remarks:** Part-time maker. Sold first knife in 1982. Likes broadswords. **Mark:** Signature

DAN D. (See D. Dennehy)

DAN E. (See D.E. Brdlik)

ALEX DANIELS, 1410 Colorado Ave., Lynn Haven, FL 32444/904-265-8449
Specialties: Working straight and folding knives; some period pieces; makes using knives. **Patterns:** Hunters, Bowies and fish knives. Folding lockers, slip joints in traditional types. **Technical:** Grinds D2, 440C and 154CM. **Prices:** $95 to $175; some to $500. **Remarks:** Full-time maker; first knife sold in 1963. **Mark:** Daniels

CROWELL

COUSINO

P. CRAWFORD

COX

COVER

DANIELS

EIGHTH ANNUAL EDITION 181

directory/custom knifemakers

RICK DARBY, 4026 Shelbourne, Youngstown, OH 44511/216-793-3805
Specialties: Straight working knives. **Patterns:** Boots, fighters and hunters with mirror finish. **Technical:** Grinds 440C, 154CM and Stellite 6K. **Prices:** $85 to $125; some $160. **Remarks:** Part-time maker; first knife sold in 1974. **Mark:** R.J. DARBY

EDMUND DAVIDSON, Rt. 1 Box 319, Goshen, VA 24439/703-997-5651
Specialties: Working straight knives; some period style. **Patterns:** Heavy duty skinners and camp knives. **Technical:** Grinds D2, ATS34, S-7; likes integral patterns. **Prices:** $75 to $150; some to $650. **Remarks:** Full-time maker; first knife sold in 1986. **Mark:** Name in deerhead or truck logo

ROB DAVIDSON, 2419—25th St., Lubbock, TX 79411/806-762-1901
Specialties: Working folders and straight knives; some period pieces. **Patterns:** Battle axes to miniatures; daggers to swords; various types of folders. **Technical:** Grinds D2, 440C, and buys Damascus; keeps no patterns. **Prices:** $75 to $300; some to $1,000. **Remarks:** Full-time maker; first knife sold in 1982. **Mark:** Rocket logo

DAVIS BROTHERS KNIVES, 1209 Woodlawn Dr., Camden, SC 29020/803-432-3024
Specialties: Straight working knives. **Patterns:** Traditional; drop points; hunters and fish knives. **Technical:** Grind 440C, 154CM, ATS34; prefer full tang. **Prices:** $60 to $130; some to $200. **Remarks:** Part-timers; sold first knife in 1970. **Mark:** DAVIS

BARRY L. DAVIS, 1871 Pittsfield Rd., Castleton, NY 12033/518-477-5036
Specialties: Forged traditional and fancy straight knives and folders. **Patterns:** Daggers and Bowies; slip joints and folders. **Technical:** Makes Damascus; uses only natural handle materials. **Prices:** $400 to $1,200; some to $2,500. **Remarks:** Full-time maker; sold first knife in 1980. **Mark:** B in a D

DIXIE DAVIS, Rt. 3, Clinton, SC 29325/803-833-4964
Specialties: Straight working knives; some fantasies. **Patterns:** Hunters, fighters and boots. **Technical:** Grinds 440C, 154CM and ATS34 with mirror finish. **Prices:** $85 to $140; some to $200. **Remarks:** Part-time maker; first knife sold in 1981. **Mark:** DIXIE

DON DAVIS, 3918 Ash Ave., Loveland, CO 80538/303-669-9016
Specialties: Straight working knives in traditional patterns. Welcomes customer designs. **Patterns:** Hunters, utility knives, skinners, and survival knives. **Technical:** Grinds 440C, ATS34. **Prices:** $75 to $250. **Remarks:** Full-time maker; first knife sold in 1985. **Mark:** Signature, city and state

JESSE W. DAVIS, 5810 Hwy. 301, Walls, MS 38680/601-781-0036
Specialties: Straight and folding working knives in traditional and customer designs. **Patterns:** Tantos, Bowies, locking folders, and hunters. **Technical:** Grinds D2, 440C, and bought Damascus. **Prices:** $100 to $200; some to $450. **Remarks:** Part-time maker; first knife sold in 1977. **Mark:** Name or initials

K.M. "TWIG" DAVIS, P.O. Box 267, Monroe, WA 98272/206-794-7274
Specialties: Fancy working straight knives. **Patterns:** Hunters, boots, fish knives, does some Bowies and daggers. **Technical:** Grinds D2, 440C and 154CM. **Prices:** $95 to $150; some to $400. **Remarks:** Part-time maker; first knife sold in 1979. **Mark:** Twig

SYD DAVIS, 1220 Courtney Dr., Richmond, TX 77469/713-342-2597
Specialties: Folding and straight working knives. **Patterns:** Folding lockers and slip joints; some straight hunters and camp knives. **Technical:** Grinds D2 and 440C; forges his own Damascus. **Prices:** $100 to $250; some to $400. **Remarks:** Part-time maker; first knife sold in 1981. **Mark:** Name in script

TERRY DAVIS, Box 111, Sumpter, OR 97877/503-894-2307
Specialties: Folding working knives in traditional styles. **Patterns:** Lockers and slip-joints; some straight knives. Makes an all-ATS34 folding lock-blade survival hunter. **Technical:** Grinds 01, L6, ATS34; likes flat grinds. **Prices:** $125 to $400; some to $1,000. **Remarks:** Full-time maker; sold first knife in 1985. **Mark:** Name in logo

W.C. DAVIS, 2010 S. Madison, Raymore, MO 64083/816-331-4491
Specialties: Fancy working folding and straight knives. **Patterns:** Folding lockers and slip joints; straight hunters, fighters and Bowies. **Technical:** Grinds 440C, A2, ATS34; **Prices:** $80 to $200; some to $1,000. **Remarks:** Full-time maker; first knife sold in 1972. **Mark:** W.C. DAVIS

DANE and BARRY DAWSON, Box 10, Marvel, CO 81329/303-588-2266
Specialties: Fancy working knives, both straight and folding. **Patterns:** Offers over 100 different models. **Technical:** Grinds L6, 440C, ATS34; buys Damascus; does own heat treat. **Prices:** $100 to $300; some to $1,000. **Remarks:** Full-time maker; first knife sold in 1975. **Mark:** DAWSON

RICHARD DEARHART, Rt. 1, Lula, GA 30554/404-869-3816
Specialties: Working straight knives, his designs and customer designs; some period styles. **Patterns:** Hunters, fighters, Bowies and buckskinner knives. **Technical:** Forges and grinds; uses A2, 01 and D2, some 440C. **Prices:** $75 to $200; some to $350. **Remarks:** Full-time maker; first knife sold in 1967. **Mark:** Dearhart

DEER (See D. Laughlin)

DEER CREEK FORGE (See Quarton)

ROBERT A. DEFEO, 12 Morningside Dr., Mays Landing, NJ 08330/609-625-3744
Specialties: Straight working knives and period pieces. **Patterns:** Hunters, fighters and Bowies. **Technical:** Grinds D2, 440C and ATS34. **Prices:** $100 to $300. **Remarks:** Part-time maker; first knife sold in 1982. **Mark:** DEFEO

WILLIAM G. DEFREEST, P.O. BOX 573, Barnwell, SC 29812/803-259-7883
Specialties: Straight and folding working knives. **Patterns:** Fighters, hunters and boots; makes some folding lockers and slip joints. **Technical:** Grinds 440C,, 154CM and ATS34; clean lines and mirror finishes. **Prices:** $100 to $700. **Remarks:** Full-time maker; first knife sold in 1974. **Mark:** GORDON

GORDON S. DEMPSEY, P.O. Box 7497, N. Kenai, AK 99635/907-776-8425
Specialties: Working straight and folding knives; some period pieces. **Patterns:** Hunters, Bowies and ooloos; harpoons. **Technical:** Forges 01 and 5160; makes Damascus. **Prices:** $80 to $250. **Remarks:** Full-time maker; first knife sold in 1974. **Mark:** Name, city, and state

DAN DENNEHY, 13321 Hwy. 160, Del Norte, CO 81132/303-657-2545
Specialties: Working fighting and military knives. **Patterns:** Full range of straight knives, tomahawks, buckle knives. **Technical:** Forges and grinds; uses A2, 01 and D2. **Prices:** $135 to $250; exceptional knives to $3,500. **Remarks:** Full-time maker; started selling knives in 1942. **Mark:** DAN-D, city, state and shamrock

DOUGLAS M. DENT, 1208 Chestnut St., So. Charleston, WV 25309/304-768-3308
Specialties: Sportsman's knives; working straight and folding models. **Patterns:** Hunters, boots and Bowies, interframe folders. **Technical:** Forges and grinds; uses D2, 440C, 154CM and plain tool steels. **Prices:** $70 to $300; exceptional knives to $800. **Remarks:** Full-time maker; started selling in 1969. **Mark:** DENT

LARRY DETLOFF, 130 Oxford Way, Santa Cruz, CA 95060/408-427-1554
Specialties: Fancy working folders. **Patterns:** Gents, hunters and minis; some miniatures. **Technical:** Grinds 440C, 154CM and ATS34. **Prices:** $150 to $300; some to $450. **Remarks:** Part-time maker; first knife sold 1970. **Mark:** DETLOFF

PHILLIP DETMER, Rt. 1 Box 149A, Breese, IL 62230/618-526-4834
Specialties: Working straight knives, some to customer design, some fancy. **Patterns:** Bowies and daggers, hunters. **Technical:** Grinds high carbon and high carbon stainless steels. **Prices:** $60 to $300. **Remarks:** Spare-time maker; sold first knife in 1977. **Mark:** Name

CLARENCE DeYONG, 5211 Maryland Ave., Racine, WI 53406/414-554-1760
Specialties: Straight working knives in traditional styles. **Patterns:** Bowies, fighters, hunters, and tantos, and steak knives. **Technical:** Grinds 440C, 01,

and ATS34; does own scrimshaw. **Prices:** $65 to $110; some to $350. **Remarks:** Part-time maker; first knife sold in 1984; numbers knives. **Mark:** DeYong

D'HOLDER (See Holder)

DIAMOND "B" KNIFE CO. (See L.E. "Red" Brown)

JACK DIAS, P.O. Box 223, Palermo, CA 95968/916-533-9043
Specialties: Display knives; makes customer designs to order. **Patterns:** Wide variety of straight knives. **Technical:** Satin finishes standard; prefers natural materials. **Mark:** Name

JOSEPH M. DIGANGI, Box 225, Santa Cruz, NM 87567/505-753-6414
Specialties: Kitchen and table cutlery. **Patterns:** French chef knives; carving sets, steak knife sets; makes some camp knives and hunters. **Technical:** Grinds 440C; buys Damascus. **Prices:** $150 to $450; some to $1,000. **Remarks:** Full-time maker; first knife sold in 1983. **Mark:** J.D.

EARL E. DILLON, 8908 Stanwin Ave., Arleta, CA 91331
Specialties: Fancy folders and straight knives. **Patterns:** Contemporary interpretation of contemporary needs. **Technical:** Grinds 440C and AEB. **Prices:** $250 to $350; some over $500. **Remarks:** Part-time maker; sold first knife in 1984; collaboration with Chuck Stapel. **Mark:** STAPEL-DILLON

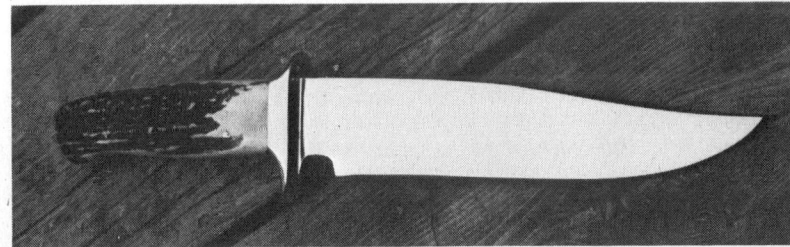

DETMER

E. DAVIDSON

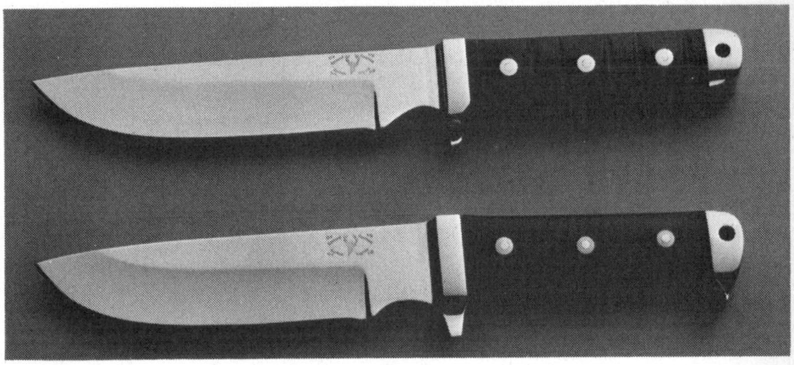

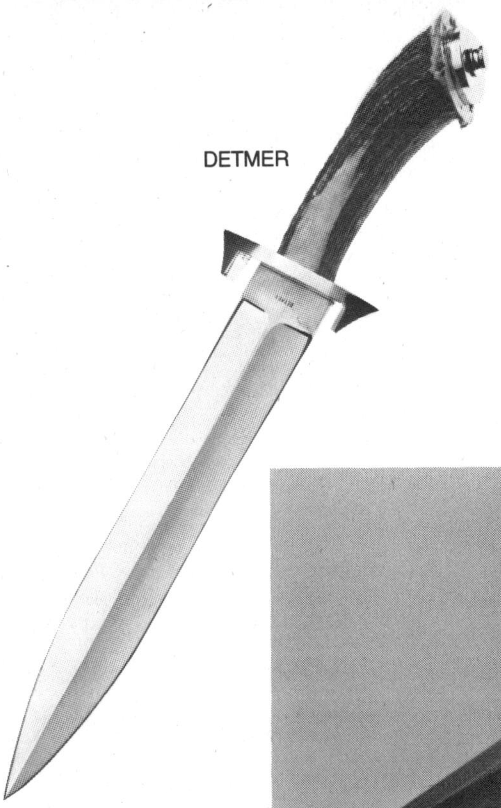

R. DAVIDSON

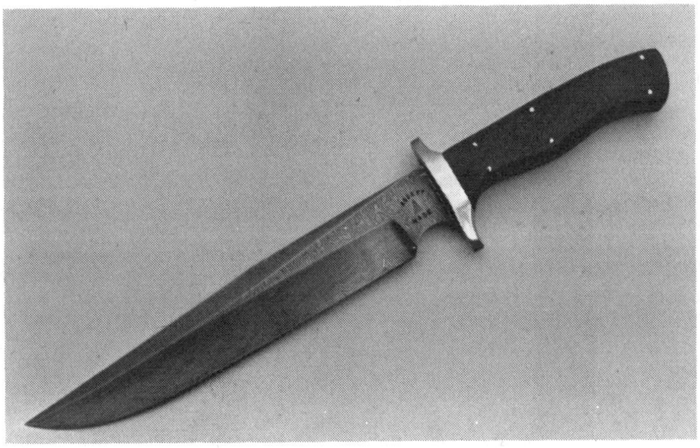

B. DAVIS

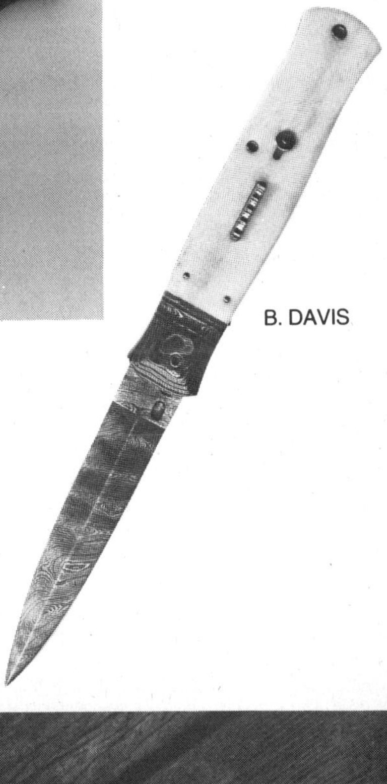

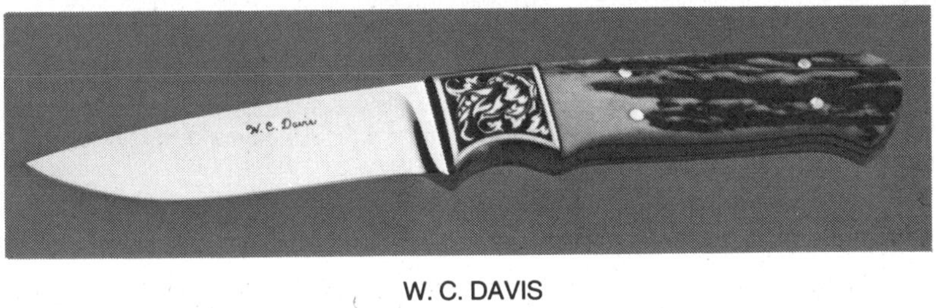

W. C. DAVIS

DEFEO

directory/custom knifemakers

FRANK J. DILLUVIO, 13611 Joyce, Warren, MI 48093/313-775-1216 **Specialties:** Traditional working straight knives; some high-tech approaches. **Patterns:** Hunters, Bowies, fish knives. **Technical:** Grinds D2, 440 C, CPM; works for precision fits—no solder. **Prices:** $75 to $350; some to $500. **Remarks:** Part-time maker; sold first knife in 1984. **Mark:** Circle FJD

GREG DION, 3032 S. Jackson St., Oxnard, CA 93033/805-483-1781 (evenings) **Specialties:** Working straight knives, some fancy. **Patterns:** Some hunter specials, such as a boar knife; camp and tanto styles. **Technical:** Grinds stainless steels; can CNC mill handle shapes. **Prices:** $85 to $160; some to $400. **Remarks:** Part-time maker; first knife sold in 1985. **Mark:** Name

MALCOLM C. DION, 820 N. Fairview Ave., Goleta, CA 93117/805-967-6714 **Specialties:** Fancy working straight knives. Welcomes customer ideas. **Patterns:** Hunters, tantos, camp knives; some buckskinner models. **Technical:** Grinds 440C, 154CM and ATS34. **Prices:** $150 to $300; some to $800. **Remarks:** Full-time maker; first knife sold in 1984. **Mark:** MAL DION with cougar head.

LARRY DiTOMMASO, P.O. Box 12233, Longview, TX 75602/214-236-4285 **Specialties:** Sculptured working knives. **Patterns:** Uniquely personal grinding and shaping of straight knives; also customizes commercial and other makers knives. **Technical:** Works in stainless steel with hand-held grinder and a minimum of other equipment. **Prices:** $50 and up. **Remarks:** Full-time maker; sold first knife in 1986. **Mark:** LAD

DIXIE (See Dixie Davis)

DOG KNIVES (See Dave Dugger)

JOHN DONAGHEY, P.O. Box 402021, Garland, TX 75046/214-272-7607 **Specialties:** Small working straight knives in personal designs; some camp knives. **Patterns:** Small Bowies and skinners; boots and fighters. **Technical:** Grinds 01, 440C and 154CM; likes exotic wood. **Prices:** $85 to $150; some to $300. **Remarks:** Spare-time maker; sold first knife 1981. **Mark:** JED

PATRICK DONOVAN, 1770 Hudson Dr., San Jose, CA 95124/408-267-9825 **Specialties:** Straight and folding working knives; period pieces. **Patterns:** Hunters, boots and daggers; lockers and slip joints in folders. **Technical:** Grinds 440C. Does own embellishments. **Prices:** $75 to $475; some to $1,200. **Remarks:** Full-time maker; sold first knife 1980. **Mark:** PATRICK

MIKE DOOLITTLE, 13 Denise Ct., Novato, CA 94947/415-897-3246 **Specialties:** Working straight knives in standard patterns. **Patterns:** Hunters, and fish knives. **Technical:** Grinds 440C, 154CM, and ATS34. **Prices:** $90 to $200; some $300. **Remarks:** Part-time maker; first knife sold in 1981. **Mark:** Name, city, and state

DICK DOROUGH, Rt. 1, Box 210, Gadsden, AL 35901/205-442-5497 **Specialties:** Working knives—folders to Bowies. **Patterns:** Fancy interframe folders, some two-bladed. **Technical:** Grinds 440C, D2, Uddeholm steel. **Prices:** $150 to $375; some to $625. **Remarks:** Part-time maker. Sold first knife in 1968. **Mark:** Name

DALE DOUGLAS, 361 Mike Cooper Rd., Ponchatoula, LA 70454/504-345-6169 **Specialties:** Folding and straight working knives. **Patterns:** Folding lockers and slip joints; hunters, boots and camp knives. **Technical:** Grinds D2, 440C and 154CM; heat-treats his own work. **Prices:** $75 to $150; some to $350. **Remarks:** Spare-time maker; first knife sold in 1980. **Mark:** Name

DOVE KNIVES (See Steve Rollert)

T.M. DOWELL, 139 N.W. St. Helen's Pl., Bend, OR 97701/503-382-8924 **Specialties:** Integral construction in working straight knives, and period pieces. Famous "Funny" folders. **Patterns:** Hunters to sword canes; Price-style daggers to tomahawks. **Technical:** Forges and grinds; uses D2, 440C and 154CM. Makes his own bright Damascus. **Prices:** $175 to $750; exceptional knives to $4,500. **Remarks:** Full-time maker; first knife sold in 1967. **Mark:** TMD logo

JAMES T. DOWNIE, R.R. #1, Thedford, Ont. NOM 2NO, CANADA/519-243-2290 **Specialties:** Serviceable straight knives; some period pieces; some folders. **Patterns:** Hunters, Bowies, camp knives and miniatures. **Technical:** Grinds D2, 440C and 154CM. **Prices:** $75 to $150; some $300. **Remarks:** Part-time maker; first knife sold in 1978. **Mark:** J.T. DOWNIE

LARRY DOWNING, Route 1, Bremen, KY 42325/502-525-3523 **Specialties:** Working straight and folding knives. **Patterns:** From mini-knives to daggers; folding lockers to interframes. **Technical:** Grinds D2, 440C and 154CM. **Prices:** $90 to $350. **Remarks:** Part-time maker; first knife sold in 1979. **Mark:** Name in arrowhead

TOM DOWNING, 129 So. Bank St., Cortland, OH 44410/216-637-0623 **Specialties:** Straight working knives, period pieces. **Patterns:** Hunters, fighters and tantos. **Technical:** Grinds D2, 154CM and ATS34; prefers natural handle materials. **Prices:** $100 to $225; some to $700. **Remarks:** Part-time maker; first knife sold in 1979. **Mark:** Name

DRAGON KNIVES (See Norman Levine)

BERYL DRISKILL, P.O. Box 187, Braggadocio, MO 63826/314-757-6262 **Specialties:** Fancy working knives. **Patterns:** Fighters, Bowies, hunters, and skinners; folding lockers. **Technical:** Grinds 440C and D2. **Prices:** $150 to $350; some to $4,000. **Remarks:** Part-time maker; first knife sold in 1984. **Mark:** Name

DUBBA (See Schulenberg)

DENNIS DUBLIN, St.11, Comp.23, RR2, Enderby BC VOE 1V0, CANADA/604-838-6753 **Specialties:** Working straight and folding knives, plain or fancy. **Patterns:** Hunters and Bowies; locking hunter; combination knife/axe. **Technical:** Grinds and forges high carbon steels. **Prices:** $100 to $400, and up. **Remarks:** Full-time maker; first knife sold in 1970. **Mark:** Name

BILL DUFF, P.O. Box 694, Virginia City, NV 89440/702-847-0566 **Specialties:** Straight and folding working knives. **Patterns:** Hunters and Bowies; folding lockers and interframes. **Technical:** Grinds D2, 440C and 154CM. **Prices:** $175 to $450; exceptional knives to $1,200. **Remarks:** Part-time maker; first knife sold in 1976. **Mark:** Name, city, state and date

ARTHUR J. DUFOUR, 8120 Dearmoun Rd., Anchorage, AK 99516/907-345-1701 **Specialties:** Working straight knives of traditional type. **Patterns:** Hunters, Bowies, camp and fish knives—grinds them very thin and pointed. **Technical:** Grinds 440C, ATS34, AEB-L. **Prices:** $140 to $165; some to $250. **Remarks:** Part-time maker; first knife sold in 1970. **Mark:** NA

DAVE DUGGER, 2504 West 51, Westwood, KS 66205/913-831-2382 **Specialties:** Working straight knives and fantasy pieces. **Patterns:** Hunters, boots and daggers in one-of-a-kind styles. **Technical:** Grinds D2, 440C and 154CM. **Prices:** $75 to $350; some to $1,200. **Remarks:** Part-time maker; first knife sold in 1979; not accepting orders. **Mark:** DOG

RICK DUNKERLEY, General Delivery, Cameron, MT 59720/406-682-4508 **Specialties:** Working straight and folding knives. **Patterns:** Mainly hunters, some hatchets, fish knives, skinners, and miniatures. **Technical:** Grinds D2, 440C, and 154CM. **Prices:** $65 to $130; some to $200. **Remarks:** Part-time maker; first knife sold in 1985. **Mark:** Full name, city, and state

MELVIN T. DUNN, 5830 N.W. Carlson Rd., Rossville, KS 66533/913-584-6856 **Specialties:** Folding and straight working knives. **Patterns:** Folding lockers and traditional styles along with straight hunters; fish and kitchen knives. **Technical:** Grinds A2, D2 and 440C; likes latest materials; does own heat treating. **Prices:** $60 to $100; some to $300. **Remarks:** Full-time maker; first knife sold in 1972. **Mark:** DUNN in oval

FRED DUVALL, Rt.8, Box 677, Benton, AR 72015/501-778-8368 **Specialties:** Folding and straight working knives. **Patterns:** Locking folders and slip joints in traditional styles. Straight hunters, fighters and Bowies.

Technical: Grinds A2, D2 and 440C. **Prices:** $75 to $150; some to $200. **Remarks:** Spare-time maker; first knife sold in 1981. **Mark:** DuVall

LARRY E. DUVALL, Rt. 3, Gallatin, MO 64640/816-663-2742
Specialties: Folding and straight fancy working knives. **Patterns:** Hunters to swords, minis to Bowies; makes lockers and butterflies. **Technical:** Grinds D2, 440C and 154CM. **Prices:** $150 to $350; exceptional knives to $2,000. **Remarks:** Part-time maker; first knife sold in 1980. **Mark:** Name and address in logo

EAGLE MOUNTAIN (See Al Krouse)

RUSSELL O. EASLER, JR., P.O. Box 301, Woodruff, SC 29388/803-476-7830
Specialties: Folding and straight working knives. **Patterns:** Hunters, tantos and boots. Locking folders and interframes. Some minis and miniatures. **Technical:** Grinds 440C, 154CM and ATS34. **Prices:** $85 to $250; some to $600. **Remarks:** Part-time maker; sold first knife in 1973. **Mark:** Name or name with bear logo

AL EATON, P.O. Box 43, Clayton, CA 94517/415-672-5351
Specialties: Fancy working straight and folding knives. **Patterns:** Hunters, fighters and buckskinners with gents and traditional folders; miniatures. **Technical:** Grinds 440C, 154CM and ATS34; does ivory and metal carving. **Prices:** $125 to $450; some to $2,000. **Remarks:** Part-time maker; first knife sold in 1981. **Mark:** Various forms of name

RICK EATON, 448 Winslow St, Crockett, CA 94525/415-787-2539
Specialties: His design or yours in fancy utility knives, folding and straight. **Patterns:** Hunters, fighters, boots; folding lockers. **Technical:** Grinds D2, 440C, 154CM, and ATS34; does his own embellishments. **Prices:** $150 to $500; exceptional knives to $1,500. **Remarks:** Part-time maker; first knife sold in 1982. **Mark:** R. EATON

THOMAS W. EDWARDS, 3232 N. 79th Ave., Phoenix, AZ 85033/602-849-1328
Specialties: One-of-a-kind miniatures only. Likes period pieces and fantasy types. **Patterns:** Anything goes. **Technical:** Grinds and forges; uses 01, 440C and purchased Damascus. **Prices:** $40 to $60; exceptional miniatures to $100. **Remarks:** Part-time maker; first piece sold in 1982. **Mark:** Name, city, state with scorpion

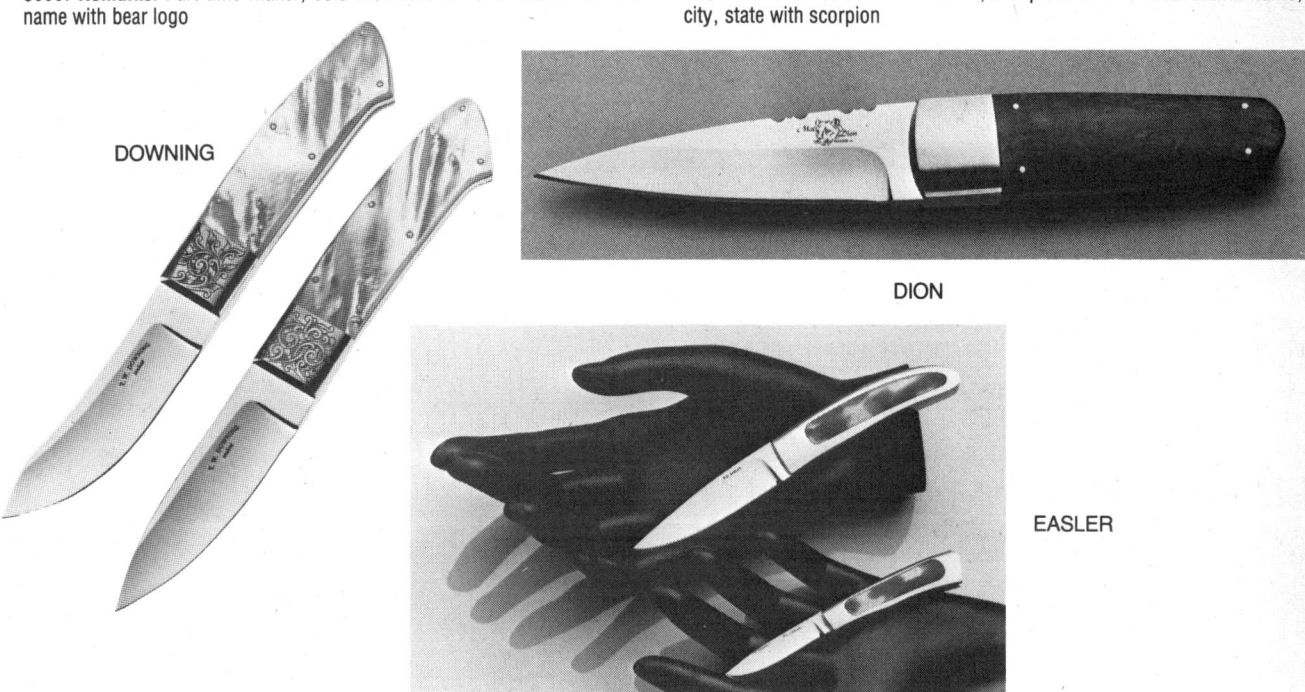

DOWNING

DION

EASLER

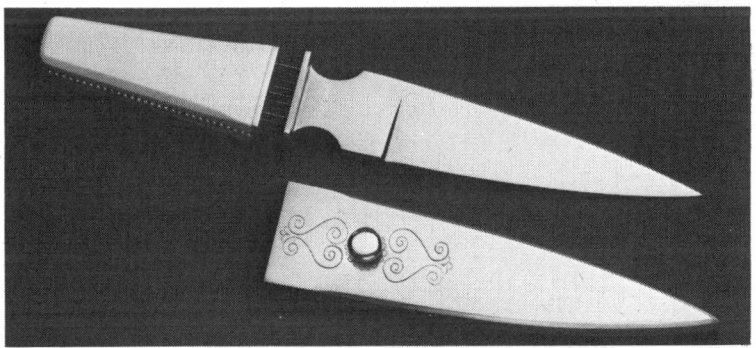

DONOVAN

DILLUVIO

directory/custom knifemakers

FAIN E. EDWARDS, 209 E. Mountain Ave., Jacksonville, AL 36265/205-435-4994
Specialties: Blacksmith-styled fancy working knives. **Patterns:** Bowies, patch and rifle knives; camp knives. **Technical:** Forges own Damascus; grinds D2. **Prices:** Full range. **Remarks:** Developed "Amensteel", but has reportedly sold it. **Mark:** Name with bleeding heart.

JOEL ELLEFSON, 1233 Storymill Rd., Bozeman, MT 59715/406-587-5905
Specialties: Fancy working straight and folding knives. Customer designs. **Patterns:** Hunters, daggers and fish knives. Does some buckskinners. **Technical:** Grinds D2, 440C and 154CM. **Prices:** $80 to $175; some to $300. **Remarks:** Part-time maker; first knife sold in 1978. **Mark:** Stylized E

W.B. ELLERBE, P.O. Box 712, Geneva, FL 32732/305-349-5818
Specialties: Fancy working straight knives. **Patterns:** Bowies to miniatures, tomahawks and buckskinners. **Technical:** Grinds 440C and ATS 34. **Prices:** $125 to $175; some to $800. **Remarks:** Part-time maker; first knife sold in 1971. **Mark:** Last name or initials

MARCUS ELLIOTT, 3 Bryn Maelgwyn, Llanrhos, Llandudno, Gwynedd, North Wales, Great Britain//0492-84352
Specialties: Fancy working knives; some period pieces. **Patterns:** Hunters, fighters and daggers. **Technical:** Grinds 01, 440C, and tool steel or SF67. **Prices:** $160 to $240; some $450. **Remarks:** Spare-time maker; first knife sold in 1981. **Mark:** Last name

JIM ENCE, 145 So. 200 East, Richfield, UT 84701/801-896-6206
Specialties: High art period pieces. Always looking to do something new and different. **Patterns:** Mirror finished, crisp lined art knives in daggers and fighters. **Technical:** Grinds 440C, 154CM; buys Damascus. **Prices:** $300 to $900; exceptional knives to $4,000. **Remarks:** Full-time maker; first knife sold in 1977. **Mark:** Name, city, state

ROBERT ENDERS, 3028 White Rd., Cement City, MI 49233/517-529-9667
Specialties: Pocket knives and working straight knives. **Patterns:** Old traditional folders with natural materials. **Technical:** Grinds D2, 01 and 440C. **Prices:** $125 to $300; some to $1,200. **Remarks:** Full-time maker; first knife sold in 1981. **Mark:** Name in state map logo

GEORGE ENGLEBRETSON, 1209 N.W. 49th St., Oklahoma City, OK 73118/405-840-4784
Specialties: Working straight knives and period pieces. **Patterns:** Hunters, Bowies, fish knives and axes—heavy-duty designs. **Technical:** Grinds. D2, 440C and 154CM. **Prices:** $75 to $100; some to $150. **Remarks:** Full-time maker; first knife sold in 1967. **Mark:** "By George," name and city

BOB ENGNATH, 1217 B. Crescent Dr., Glendale, CA 91205/818-241-3629
Specialties: Replica antique tanto blades and complete knives and swords. **Patterns:** Traditional Japanese; makes some miniatures. **Technical:** Makes soft back-hard edge blades with temper line. **Prices:** $125 to $350; some to $600. **Remarks:** Full-time maker/grinder; first knife sold in 1972. **Mark:** KO-DAN in Japanese script

THOMAS M. ENOS, III, 12302 State Rt. 535, Orlando, FL. 32819/305-239-6205
Specialties: Heavy-duty working knives; unusual knife designs. **Patterns:** Machetes, salt water sport knives, carvers and a variety of straight knives. **Technical:** Grinds. **Remarks:** No longer taking orders. **Mark:** Name in knife logo and date

CURT ERICKSON, 449 Washington Blvd., Ogden, UT 84404/801-621-4437
Specialties: Daggers and large knives, integral construction. **Patterns:** Period pieces; some Bowies. **Technical:** Sculpts and carves components; grinds 440C and commercial Damascus steel. **Prices:** $240 to $1,500; some to $3,000. **Remarks:** Full-time maker; first knife sold in 1982. **Mark:** Name, state

L.M. ERICKSON, P.O. Box 132, Liberty, UT 84310/801-745-2026
Specialties: Period pieces and straight knives. **Patterns:** Bowies, fighters, boots and hunters. **Technical:** Grinds 440C, 154CM and purchased Damascus. **Prices:** $200 to $900; some to $1,900. **Remarks:** Full-time maker; first knife sold in 1981. **Mark:** Name, city, state

WALTER E. ERICKSON, 23883 Ada St., Warren, MI 48091/313-759-1105
Specialties: Unusual survival knives and high-tech working knives. **Patterns:** Butterflies, hunters, tantos and survival knives. **Technical:** Grinds 01, D2 and 440C. **Prices:** $90 to $200; some to $600. **Remarks:** Spare-time maker; first knife sold in 1981. **Mark:** ERIC or ERICKSON

VINCENT K. EVANS, 556-B Kamani St., Honolulu, HI 96813/808-538-7288
Specialties: Period pieces and straight working knives. **Patterns:** Scottish patterns; clip point using knives. **Technical:** Forges and grinds 01, 440C, and 5160; his own Damascus. **Prices:** $50 to $300; some to $500. **Remarks:** Full-time maker; first knife sold in 1983. **Mark:** Bronze filled double E with fish logo

THE FARM FORGE (See Larry B. Wood)

MELVIN G. FASSIO, 2012 Rattlesnake Dr., Missoula, MT 59802/406-543-6160
Specialties: Working folders. **Patterns:** Folding lockers, hunters and traditional styles; in customer designs. **Technical:** Grinds 440C. **Prices:** $60 to $100, up to $200. **Remarks:** Part-time maker; first knife sold in 1975. **Mark:** Name and town, dove logo

HOWARD J. FAUCHEAUX, P.O. Box 206, Loreauville, LA 70552/318-229-6467
Specialties: Working straight and folding knives; some period pieces. **Patterns:** Locking folders in traditional styles; hunters, fighters and Bowies in straight knives with personal touches. **Technical:** Forges W2, 1095 and his own Damascus. **Prices:** $165 to $500; some to $1,500. **Remarks:** Spare-time maker; first knife sold in 1969. **Mark:** Last name

ALLAN FAULKNER, 6103 Park Ave., Marysville, CA 95901/916-743-1309
Specialties: Fancy straight and folding working knives. **Patterns:** Folding lockers of standard designs; also hunters, fighters and Bowies. **Technical:** Grinds D2, 440C and 154CM; prefers natural handle materials. **Prices:** $150 to $350; some to $1,500. **Remarks:** Part-time maker, first knife sold in 1978. **Mark:** Last name

STEPHEN J. FECAS, 117 Allee St., Clemson, SC 29631/803-654-6068
Specialties: Working straight and folding knives in standard patterns; some period pieces. **Patterns:** Hunters to claws, folding slip joints to buckskinners. **Technical:** Grinds D2, 440C and 154CM; most knives hand-finished to 600 grit. **Prices:** $140 to $400; some to $750. **Remarks:** Full-time maker; first knife sold in 1977. **Mark:** FECAS

DON FERDINAND, P.O. Box 2790, San Rafael, CA 94941/415-383-2479
Specialties: Working knives and period pieces. **Patterns:** Bowies and push knives; fish knives. **Technical:** Forges high carbon alloy steels—L6, D2; makes his own Damascus. **Prices:** $100 to $500. **Remarks:** Part-time maker since 1980; business name is Wyvern. **Mark:** df connected

LEE FERGUSON, Rt. 2, Box 109, Hindsville, AR 72738/501-789-5748
Specialties: Straight and folding working knives, some are fancy pieces. **Patterns:** Hunters, daggers and swords; folding lockers and slip joints. **Technical:** Grinds D2, 440C and ATS34; heat-treats his own work. **Prices:** $50 to $600; some to $4,000. **Remarks:** Part-time maker; first knife sold in 1977. **Mark:** Last name

WILLIAM V. FIELDER, 2715 Salem Bottom Rd., Westminster, MD 21157/301-848-1567
Specialties: Original designs in fancy working knives, both straight and folding. **Patterns:** Hunters, boots and daggers; folding lockers, both interframes and traditional. **Technical:** Forges W2, 01 and his own Damascus; likes wire inlay. **Prices:** $25 to $500; some to $1,000. **Remarks:** Full-time maker; first knife sold in 1982. **Mark:** FIELDER

JIMMY L. FIKES, P.O. Box 389, Orange, MA 01364/617-544-3049
Specialties: High art working knives; he calls some artifact knives. **Patterns:** From axes to buckskinners, camp knives to miniatures and tantos to tomahawks, but no folders. **Technical:** Forges W2, 01 and his own Damascus. **Prices:** $135 to $3,000; exceptional knives to $7,000. **Remarks:** Full-time maker. **Mark:** Clawed F

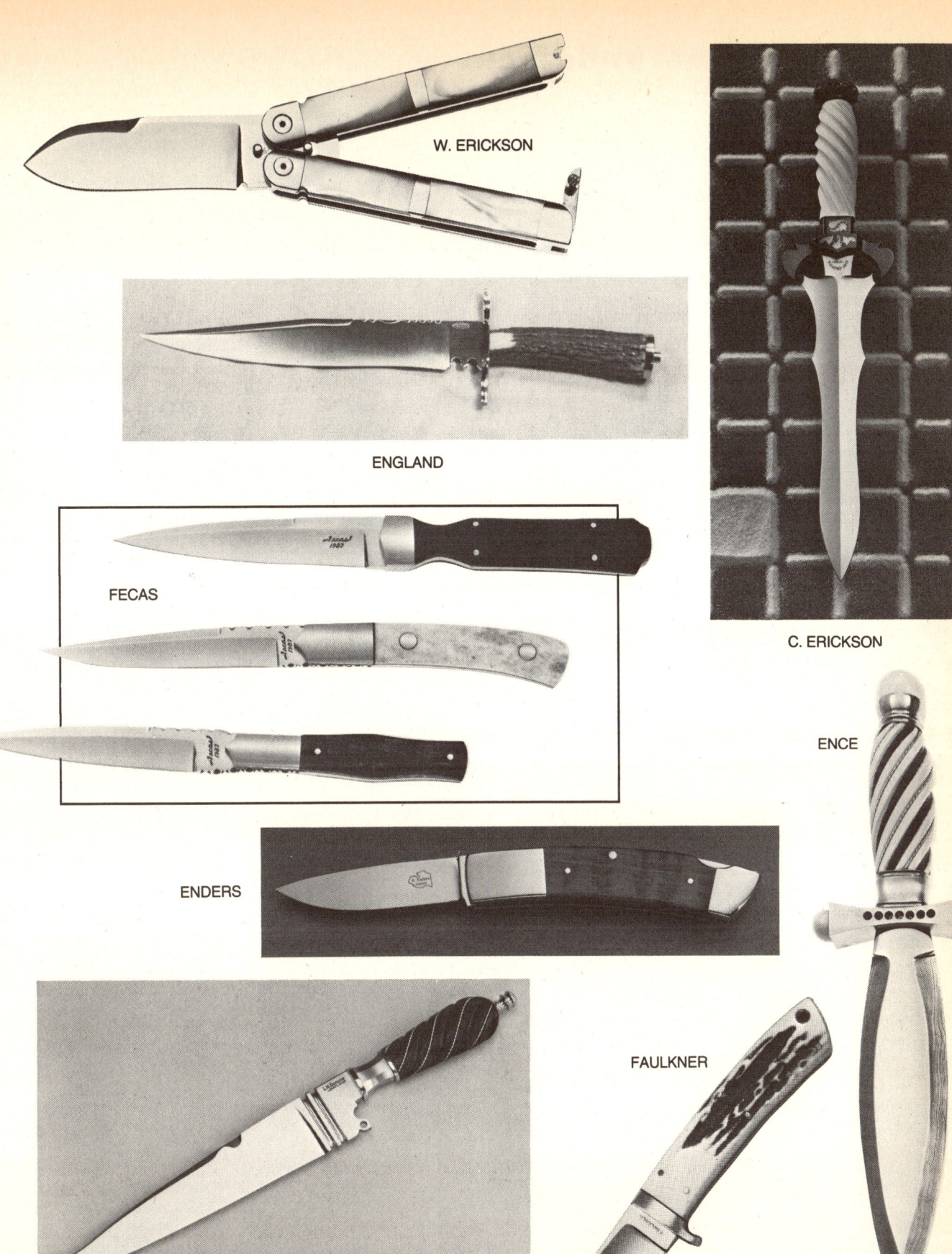

directory/custom knifemakers

L.C. FINGER, 1001-113 N, Weatherford, TX 76086/817-682-4901
Specialties: Working straight knives. **Patterns:** Hunters, boots, fish knives and axes. **Technical:** Grinds D2 and 440C. **Prices:** $55 to $175; some to $600. **Remarks:** Full-time maker. Not now taking orders for health reasons. **Mark:** Name in finger logo

CLYDE E. FISCHER, P.O. Box 310, Nixon, TX 78140/512-582-1353
Specialties: Working knives for serious and professional hunters. **Patterns:** Heavy-duty hunters and survival blades; camp knives and buckskinner knives, too. **Technical:** Grinds and forges L6, O1 and his own Damascus. **Prices:** $100 to $250; some to $800. **Remarks:** Full-time maker; first started selling in 1957. **Mark:** Fish

THEO. (TED) FISHER, 8115 Modoc Lane, Montague, CA 96064/916-459-3804
Specialties: Moderate-priced working knives in carbon steel. **Patterns:** Hunters, fighters, kitchen and buckskinner knives. **Technical:** Grinds O1, L6 and 440C. **Prices:** $65 to $90; exceptional knives to $300. **Remarks:** Full-time maker; first knife sold in 1981. **Mark:** Name in banner logo

JERRY FISK, Rt. 1, Box 41, Lockesburg, AR 71846/501-289-3240
Specialties: Working straight knives in traditional styles. **Patterns:** Bowies, fancy using hunters, camp knives. **Technical:** Forges 5160 and his own Damascus; does file work. **Prices:** $90 to $300; some to $800. **Remarks:** Full-time maker; first knife sold in 1980. **Mark:** Name

JIM FISTER, R. #1, Finchville, KY 40022/502-834-7841
Specialties: Straight and folding working knives. **Patterns:** Hunters, boots and buckskinners; patent lockers in folders. **Technical:** Grinds and forges O1 and 440C, and his own cable Damascus. **Prices:** $100 to $250; some $700. **Remarks:** Part-time maker; first knife sold in 1982. **Mark:** Full name

DENNIS FITZGERALD, P.O. Box 12847, Fort Wayne, IN 46866-2847/219-447-1081
Specialties: Straight working knives. **Patterns:** Skinners, fighters, camp and utility knives. **Technical:** Forges and grinds W2, O1, and his own Damascus. **Prices:** $150 to $500. **Remarks:** Part-time maker; first knife sold in 1985. **Mark:** Name and circle logo

JOE FLOURNOY, Rt. 6, Box 233, El Dorado, AR 71730/501-863-7208
Specialties: Working straight and folding knives; some period pieces. **Patterns:** Hunters, fighters and buckskinners; straight knives. **Technical:** Grinds and forges; uses D2, 440C and high carbon steels. **Prices:** $90 to $185; some to $350. **Remarks:** Part-time maker; first knife sold in 1977. **Mark:** Name, city, state

DON FOGG (See Kemal)

ALLEN FORD, 846 Thomas St., Roswell, GA 30075/404-992-3812
Specialties: Art knives in his own designs. **Patterns:** Bowies, daggers and hunters. **Technical:** Hand finishes every knife. **Mark:** A. FORD in script

PETE FORTHOFER, 711 Spokane Ave., Whitefish, MT 59937/406-862-2674
Specialties: Interframes with checkered wood inlays; working straight knives. **Patterns:** Both interframes and traditional patterns in folders; hunters, fighters and Bowies. **Technical:** Grinds D2, 440C, 154CM and ATS34. **Prices:** $165 to $500; some to $1,200. **Remarks:** Part-time maker; full-time gunsmith. First knife sold in 1979. **Mark:** Name and logo

AL FOSTER, St. Rt. 1, Box 117, Dogpatch, AR 72648/501-446-5137
Specialties: Working straight knives in traditional styles. **Patterns:** Bowies, and fish knives; likes trailing points and impala horn handles. **Technical:** Grinds A2, D2, 440C. **Prices:** $50 to $150; some to $350. **Remarks:** Full-time maker; sold first knife in 1981. **Mark:** Name in scorpion logo

ROGER FOUST, 1925 Vernon Ave., Modesto, CA 95351/209-522-2570
Specialties: Period pieces and fantasy styles. **Patterns:** Shifting to one-of-a-kinds. **Technical:** Grinds L6, 1095 and D2. **Prices:** $50 to $1,000. **Remarks:** Full-time maker; first knife sold in 1980. Not taking orders; starting a knife-making school. **Mark:** RM connected

ED A. FOWLER, Willow Bow Ranch, P.O. Box 1519, Riverton, WY 82501/307-856-9815
Specialties: Straight heavy-duty working knives. Makes knives to be used. **Patterns:** Hunters, Bowies, camp knives, skinners. **Technical:** Forges 5160 and his own Damascus; engraves all his knives; all handles are domestic sheep horn. **Prices:** $185 to $400; some to $700. **Remarks:** Spare-time maker; first knife sold in 1962. **Mark:** EAF connected

FOX VALLEY FORGE (See George W. Werth)

PAUL FOX, 80 Mineral Springs Mountain, Valdese, NC 28690/704-874-3400
Specialties: All-bolted construction, unusual one-of-a-kinds, but mostly folding knives. **Patterns:** High-tech folding fighters. Also makes straight daggers and fighters. **Technical:** Grinds O1, 154CM and purchased Damascus. **Prices:** $200 up to $6,000. **Remarks:** Full-time maker; first knife sold in 1977. **Mark:** Signature

HEINRICH H. FRANK, Box 984, Whitefish, MT 59937/406-862-2681
Specialties: High art investor-class folders; handmade and engraved personally. **Patterns:** Careful personal design in folding daggers, in hunter-size folders and gents knives. **Technical:** Grinds 07 and 01. **Prices:** $1,500 to $3,600; some to $12,000. **Remarks:** Full-time maker; first knife sold in 1965. Not now taking orders. **Mark:** Name, address and date

MIKE FRANKLIN, Rte. 41, Box M, Aberdeen, OH 45101/513-795-2571
Specialties: Small, lightweight hunters and boots. **Patterns:** Straight and folding knives, some period pieces. Does a variety of both, from his own designs. **Technical:** Grinds A2, 440C and ATS34; strives for fine design and execution in small working knives. **Prices:** $100 to $275; some to $750. **Remarks:** Full-time maker; first knife sold in 1973. **Mark:** Name

RON FRAZIER, 2107 Urbine Rd., Powhatan, VA 23139/804-794-8561
Specialties: Classy working knives in his own designs: some high-art straight knives. **Patterns:** Wide assortment of straight knives, including miniatures and push knives—does, he says, whatever he wants. **Technical:** Grinds 440C; offers satin, mirror or sand finishes. **Prices:** $85 to $700; some to $3,000. **Remarks:** Full-time maker; fist knife sold in 1976. **Mark:** Name in arch logo

ART F. FREEMAN, P.O Box 2545, Citrus Heights, CA 95611/916-725-5323
Specialties: Customer designs in working and some high art knives. **Patterns:** Hunters to Bowies; folding lockers to slip joints. **Technical:** Customers requests; doesn't copy any design under 50 years old. **Prices:** $100 to $750; some to $10,000. **Remarks:** Full-time maker; first knife sold in 1979. **Mark:** A Freeman in script

ALBERT J. FREILING, 3700 Niner Rd., Finksburg, MD 21048/301-795-2880
Specialties: Working straight and folding knives; some period pieces. **Patterns:** Boots, Bowies, survival knives, and tomahawks in 4130 and 440C; some locking folders and interframes; ball-bearing folders. **Technical:** Grinds O1, 440C and 154CM. **Prices:** $100 to $300; some to $500. **Remarks:** Part-time maker; first knife sold in 1966. **Mark:** AJF connected

W. FREDERICK FREY, JR., 305 Walnut St., Milton, PA 17847/717-742-9576
Specialties: Working straight and folding knives, some fancy. **Patterns:** Wide range—boot knives to tomahawks. **Technical:** Grinds A2, O1 and D2; hand finishes only. **Prices:** $55 to $90; some to $600. **Remarks:** Spare-time maker; first knife sold in 1983. **Mark:** FREY in script

DENNIS E. FRIEDLY, 12 Cottontail Ln., Apt. E, Cody, WY 82414/307-527-6811
Specialties: Fancy working straight knives. **Patterns:** Hunters, fighters, boots, ooloos, axes, minis and miniatures. **Technical:** Grinds 440C, ATS34 and purchased Damascus; prefers hidden tang. **Prices:** $135 to $900; some to $1,500. **Remarks:** Full-time maker; first knife sold in 1972. **Mark:** Name, city and state

LARRY FUEGEN, RR 1, Box 279, Wiscasset, ME 04578/207-882-6391
Specialties: Folding and straight working knives; some fancy, even unusual. **Patterns:** 18th and 19th century American primitive folders in crown stag.

Technical: Forges W1, 5160, his own Damascus. Works in exotic leather; shoots for individuality. **Prices:** $120 to $260; some to $500. **Remarks:** Full-time maker; first knife sold in 1975. **Mark:** LF connected

YASUHIRO FUJIMOTO, 2-3-2 Shibyuya, Shibuya-ku, Tokyo 150, JAPAN/03-400-4573
Specialties: High art working folders of his own design. **Patterns:** Folding locker, slip joints, patent locks; interframes and multi-blades. Also miniatures. **Technical:** Forges and grinds 440C, ATS34 and purchased Damascus. **Prices:** $100 to $700; some $10,000. **Remarks:** Full-time maker; first knife sold in 1949. **Mark:** Y. FUJIMOTO

STANLEY FUJISAKA, 45-004 Holowai St., Kaneohe, HI 96744/808-247-0017
Specialties: Fancy working straight knives. **Patterns:** Hunters and boots and personal knives, and folding knives. **Technical:** Grinds 440C, 154CM, and ATS34; clean lines, inlays. **Prices:** $150 to $250; some to $600. **Remarks:** Full-time maker; first knife sold in 1984. **Mark:** Name, city and state

JIM FULLER, P.O. Box 51, Burnwell, AL 35038/205-648-2083
Specialties: Working straight knives—lightweight and low cost. **Patterns:** Hunters, fighters and Bowies; straight and folding knives; utility knives. **Technical:** Grinds A2, 01, but mostly 440C. **Prices:** $60 to $150; some to $1,000. **Remarks:** Full-time maker; first knife sold in 1983. **Mark:** Jim Fuller

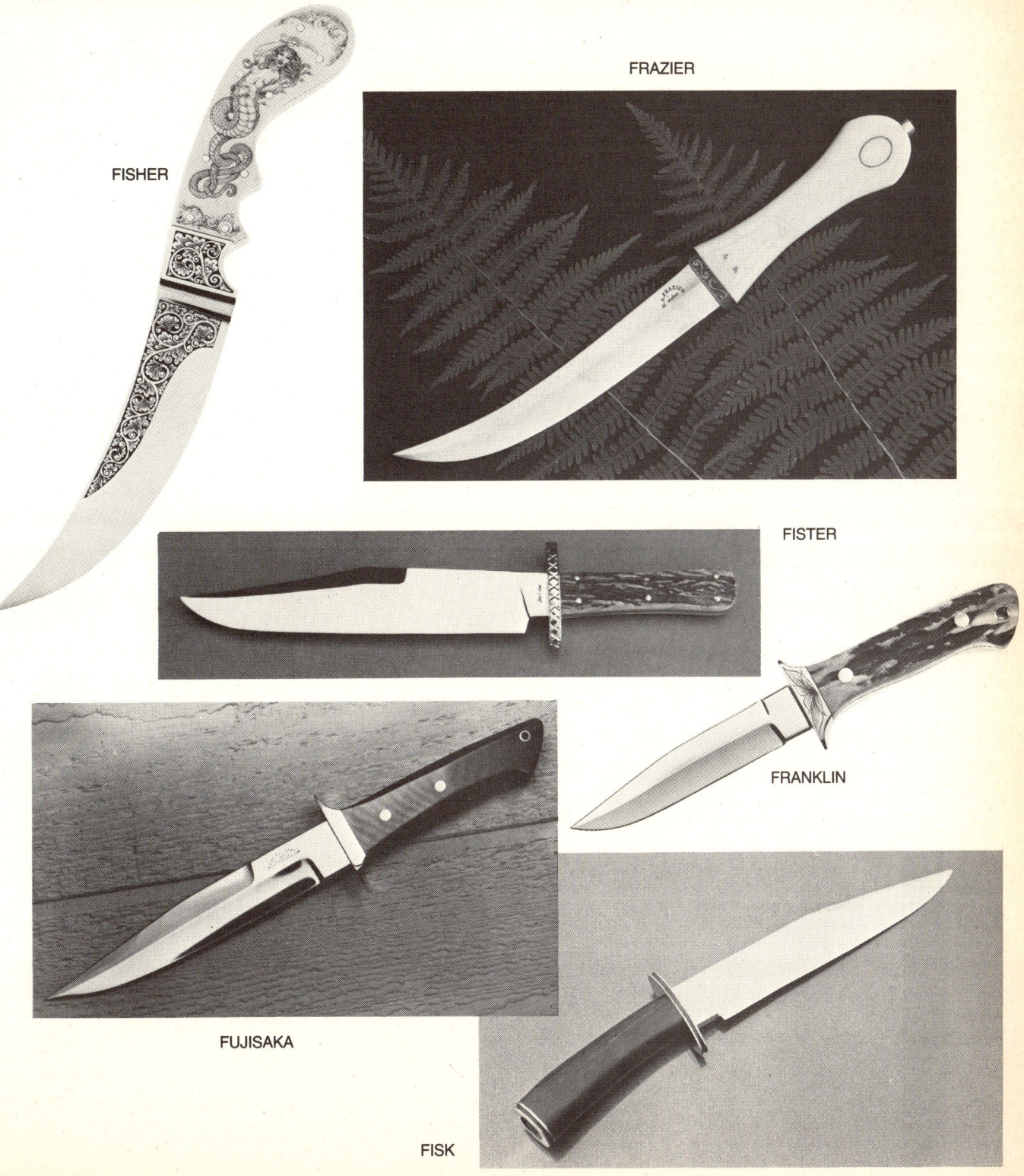

FISHER

FRAZIER

FISTER

FRANKLIN

FUJISAKA

FISK

EIGHTH ANNUAL EDITION

directory/custom knifemakers

JOHN W. FULLER, 6156 Ridge Way, Douglasville, GA 30135/404-942-1155
Specialties: Fancy working straight and folding knives in standard patterns. **Patterns:** Folding gents and hunting knives; straight hunters and fighters. **Technical:** Grinds D2, 440C and purchased Damascus. **Prices:** $75 to $300. **Remarks:** Part-time maker; first knife sold in 1978. **Mark:** Name, city, state

W.T. FULLER, JR., 400 S. 8th St., East Gadsden, AL 35903/205-546-8114
Specialties: Working folding knives. **Patterns:** Folding lockers, two-blades, fighters, hunters and traditional knives. **Technical:** Grinds D2 and 440C; does it all with one hand. **Prices:** $175 to $250; some to $600. **Remarks:** Part-time maker; first knife sold in 1975. **Mark:** One-Hander and name in hand logo

JOE FUNDERBURG, 1255 Bay Oaks Dr., Los Osos, CA 93402/805-528-2317
Specialties: Working straight knives; some period pieces. **Patterns:** Fighters, boots, daggers and push knives. **Technical:** Grinds D5, 440C and 154CM. **Prices:** $90 to $150; some to $1,000. **Remarks:** Spare-time maker; first knife sold in 1965. **Mark:** JF connected

SHIRO FURUKAWA, 4-7-7 Sakuragaoka, Tama-shi, Tokyo 206, JAPAN/ 0423-71-8263
Specialties: Both straight and folding working knives; some are high art. **Patterns:** His own designs especially for the outdoor life. **Technical:** Grinds D2, 440C and 154CM. **Prices:** $200 to $2,300; some to $5,000. **Remarks:** Full-time maker; first knife sold in 1977. **Mark:** SF MADE KNIVES

FRANK GAMBLE, P.O. Box 2243, Gilroy, CA 95021-2243/408-847-5067
Specialties: Scagel replicas; fancy working knives; some fantasy pieces. **Patterns:** Wide range of straight and folding knives; razors and miniatures. **Technical:** Grinds and forges; uses 440C; 154CM and ATS34 and buys Damascus; all knives hand-finished. **Prices:** $150 to $750; some to $2,000. **Remarks:** Full-time maker; first knife sold in 1978. **Mark:** Name

CHUCK K. GARLITS, P.O. Box 577, Rosman, NC 28772/704-884-2823
Specialties: Straight working knives, some fantasy pieces. **Patterns:** Hunters, Bowies; some swords and miniatures; locking folders and interframes. **Technical:** Grinds 01, 1095, and 440C. **Prices:** $65 to $125; some $800. **Remarks:** Full-time maker; first knife sold in 1983. **Mark:** Garlits inside fish logo

WILLIAM O. GARNER, JR., 2803 East DeSoto St., Pensacola, FL 32503/904-438-2009
Specialties: Working straight knives; some fancy pieces. **Patterns:** Hunters, kitchen and fish knives. **Technical:** Grinds 440C, 154CM and ATS34; all knives have heavy spines and sharp lines. **Prices:** $100 to $125; some to $200. **Remarks:** Full-time maker; first knife sold in 1985. **Mark:** GARNER

M. D. GARTMAN, Rt. 3, Box 13, Gatesville, TX 76528/817-865-6090
Specialties: Folding and straight working knives in standard patterns. **Patterns:** A large variety of folders, up to 5-bladed styles; some Bowies and miniatures. **Technical:** Grinds D2, 01, and 440C; likes unusual natural handles, swordfish bill for one. **Prices:** $85 to $135. **Remarks:** Part-time maker; first knife sold in 1982. **Mark:** GARTMAN inside arrowhead logo

RON GASTON, 330 Gaston Dr., Woodruff, SC 29388/803-439-4766
Specialties: Working period pieces; welcomes customer designs. **Patterns:** Hunters, fighters, tantos, boots and a variety of other straight knives. **Technical:** Grinds 440C, 154CM and ATS34. Hand-rubbed satin finish is standard. **Prices:** $100 to $350; some to $1,000. **Remarks:** Full-time maker; first knife sold in 1980. **Mark:** Name

LINDEN L. GAUDETTE, 5 Hitchcock Rd., Wilbraham, MA 01095/413-596-4896
Specialties: Traditional working knives in standard patterns. **Patterns:** Broad-bladed hunters, Bowies, and camp knives, some locking folders. **Technical:** Grinds ATS34, 440C, and 154CM. **Prices:** $125 to $275. **Remarks:** Full-time maker; first knife sold in 1975. **Mark:** Last name in Gothic logo

CLAY GAULT, Rt. 1, Box 287, Lexington, TX 78947/512-273-2873
Specialties: Straight and folding hunting knives. **Patterns:** Classic drop-points, other traditional styles in folders. **Technical:** Grinds Vascowear only; natural materials carefully chosen and hand-finished. **Prices:** $225 to $325; some to $500. **Remarks:** Full-time maker; first knives sold in 1970. **Mark:** Name or name with cattle brand

ROY E. GENGE, P.O. Box 57, Eastlake, CO 80614/303-451-7991
Specialties: High-tech working knives. **Patterns:** Bowies, axes, hunters, survival knives and buckskinners. Has made customer-designed kukris. **Technical:** Forges L6, 154CM and ATS34. **Prices:** $85 to $175; some $200 and up. **Remarks:** Part-time maker; first knife sold in 1968. **Mark:** Name, city, state

TOM GEORGE, P.O. Box 1298, Magalia, CA 95954/916-873-3306
Specialties: Fancy working knives. **Patterns:** Hunters, Bowies, daggers and buckskinners. **Technical:** Uses D2, 440C and 154CM; all knives hand-filed—uses no belt grinder. **Prices:** $175 to $1,200; some to $3,000. **Remarks:** Full-time maker; first knife sold in 1981. **Mark:** Name

RANDALL GILBREATH, P.O. Box 195, Dora, AL 35062/205-648-3902
Specialties: Fancy working knives; some one-of-a-kind knives. **Patterns:** Fighters, hunters, Bowies and miniatures. Locking folders in fighter and hunter patterns. **Technical:** Grinds A2, 01 and 440C; satin finishes. **Prices:** $100 to $150; some to $1,300. **Remarks:** Part-time maker; first knife sold in 1979. **Mark:** Name in a ribbon

E.E. "DICK" GILLENWATER, 921 Dougherty Rd., Aiken, SC 29801/803-649-6787
Specialties: Working straight sportsmen's knives. **Patterns:** Boot knives, hunters, fillet and steak knives. **Technical:** Grinds 154CM and ATS34. **Prices:** $75 to $400; some to $600. **Remarks:** Part-time maker; first knife sold in 1979. **Mark:** Signature

JON GILMORE, 849 University Place, St. Louis, MO 63132
Specialties: Simple straight knife designs, using natural materials. **Patterns:** Working knives and period pieces, including tomahawks, hunters, fighters and camp knives. **Technical:** Forges W1, 1095 and his own Damascus. **Prices:** $85 to $150; some to $250. **Remarks:** Spare-time maker. Currently only making the smaller-range knives. First knife sold in 1983. **Mark:** Initials form a logo

KEN GLASER, Rt. #1, Box 148, Purdy, MO 65734/417-442-3371
Specialties: Straight working knives in standard patterns. **Patterns:** Hunters, including buckles and mini knives. **Technical:** Grinds 01, D2 and 440C; prefers hollow grinds; likes file work. **Prices:** $75 to $125; some $250. **Remarks:** Full-time maker; first knife sold in 1983. **Mark:** Initials, KAG

RON GLOVER, P.O. Box 44132, Cincinnati, OH 45244/513-398-7857
Specialties: High-tech working knives, folding and straight. **Patterns:** Hunters to Bowies; has some interchangeable blade models; unique looking mechanisms. **Technical:** Grinds 440C, 154CM; buys Damascus. **Prices:** $70 to $500; some to $800. **Remarks:** Part-time maker; first knife sold in 1981. **Mark:** Name in script

WAYNE GODDARD, 473 Durham Ave., Eugene, OR 97404/503-689-8098
Specialties: Working knives and period pieces, straight and folding. **Patterns:** Camp knives to miniatures; makes heavy-duty traditional types; large display folders. **Technical:** Forges and grinds; uses D2, 154CM and his own Damascus, both pattern-welded and welded cable. **Prices:** $75 to $400; some to $900. **Remarks:** Full-time maker; first knife sold in 1963. **Mark:** Forged blades have WG connected and Journeyman Smith stamp; stock removal has initials.

PAUL S. GOERTZ, 201 Union Ave. S.E., #207, Renton, WA 98056/206-228-9501
Specialties: Straight working knives for outdoorsmen. **Patterns:** Kitchen cutlery; camp, bird and fish knives, and hunters. **Technical:** Grinds 440C, ATS34, and 154CM. **Prices:** $50 to $175; some $450. **Remarks:** Full-time maker; first knife sold in 1985. **Mark:** Signature

directory/custom knifemakers

JIM GOFOURTH, 3776 Aliso Cyn. Rd., Santa Paula, CA 93060/805-659-3814
Specialties: Period pieces and working knives. **Patterns:** Bowies, folding lockers, patent lockers and others. **Technical:** Grinds A2 and 154CM. **Prices:** Moderate. **Remarks:** Spare-time maker. **Mark:** JG interconnected

T.S. GOLDENBERG, P.O. Box 963, Herndon, VA 22070
Specialties: Working straight knives and period pieces to customer order. **Patterns:** Hunters, boots, Bowies and tomahawks, axes. **Technical:** Grinds A2, 01 and 440C. **Prices:** $90 to $175; some to $350. **Remarks:** Part-time maker; first knife sold in 1975. **Mark:** Surname in mountain; some with TEDDYHAWK

WARREN L. GOLTZ, 802 E. 4th Ave., Ada, MN 56510/218-784-7721
Specialties: Fancy working knives in standard patterns. **Patterns:** Hunters, fighters and Bowies; camp knives. **Technical:** Grinds D2, 440C and ATS34. **Prices:** $95 to $450; some to $850. **Remarks:** Full-time maker; first knife sold in 1984. **Mark:** Goltz

TAI GOO, 506 W. First St., Tempe, AZ 85281/602-894-2763
Specialties: High art and fantasy knives; some working knives. **Patterns:** Fighters, daggers, buckskinners and miniatures. **Technical:** Forges and grinds; uses 01, 440C and his own Damascus. **Prices:** $350 to $1,800; some $10,000. **Remarks:** Full-time maker; first knife sold in 1978. **Mark:** Chiseled signature; mark in spacer and tang

BUTCH GOODWIN, 1345 Foothill Dr., Vista, CA 92084/619-758-4237
Specialties: Period pieces and working knives. **Patterns:** Integral Damascus fighters, Bowies; makes swords, miniatures, and large display folders. **Technical:** Forges L6, 1095, welded wire Damascus, pattern-welded Damascus. **Prices:** $100 to $350; some to $1,000. **Remarks:** Spare-time maker; first knife sold in 1983. **Mark:** Anvil G

GORDON (See De Freest)

DANTE GOTTAGE, 21700 Evergreen, St. Clair Shores, MI 48082/313-293-6615
Specialties: Straight working knives in traditional patterns. **Patterns:** Fighters, tantos, large camp knives and miniatures. **Technical:** Grinds 01, 440C and 154CM. **Prices:** $100 to $400; some to $500. **Remarks:** Part-time maker; first knife sold in 1975. **Mark:** Gottage Custom Knives

JUDY GOTTAGE, 21700 Evergreen, St. Clair Shores, MI 48082/313-293-6615
Specialties: Folding and straight knives in her own design and traditional patterns. **Patterns:** Integral and interframe folders in many styles; some fish knives. **Technical:** Grinds 440C, 154CM and commercial Damascus. **Prices:** $175 to $600; some to $2,500. **Remarks:** Full-time maker; first knife sold in 1980. **Mark:** Judy Gottage

GREGORY J. GOTTSCHALK, 12 First St. (Ft. Pitt), Carnegie, PA 15106/412-279-6692
Specialties: Fancy working straight and folding knives in customer designs. **Patterns:** Hunters to tantos, folding lockers to mini knives; most are mirror finished. **Technical:** Grinds 440C, 154CM and purchased Damascus. **Prices:** $60 to $400; some to $2,000. **Remarks:** Part-time maker; first knife sold in 1977. **Mark:** Full name in crescent

WILLIAM R. GRANQUIST, 5 Paul St., Bristol, CT 06010/203-582-4012
Specialties: Working straight knives and period pieces. **Patterns:** Hunters, fighters, boots and Bowies. **Technical:** Grinds A2, D2 and 440C. **Prices:** $75 to $125; some to $300. **Remarks:** Part-time maker; first knife sold in 1978. **Mark:** GRANQUIST

GORDON S. GREBE, 3605 Arctic #1109, Anchorage, AK 99503/907-243-2525
Specialties: Working straight knives and folders; some fancy. **Patterns:** Does tantos, Bowies, boot knife-fighter sets, locking folders. **Technical:** Grinds stainless steels; likes ¼-inch stock and glass-bead finishes. **Prices:** $75 to $250; some to $2,000. **Remarks:** Full-time producer; sold first knife in 1968. **Mark:** GSG in lightning logo

L.G. GREEN, 4301 W. 63rd, Prairie Village, KS 66208/913-432-6950
Specialties: Working straight and folding knives; some period pieces. **Patterns:** Folding lockers and interframes; makes hunters, tantos and daggers in straight knives; and mini knives. **Technical:** Grinds D2, 154CM and ATS34; has special sheaths. **Prices:** $140 to $275; some to $700. **Remarks:** Part-time maker; first knife sold in 1979. **Mark:** L.G.

ROGER M. GREEN, 3412 Co. Rd. 1022, Joshua, TX 76058/817-641-5057
Specialties: Straight working and some fancy knives in traditional designs. **Patterns:** Hunters, boots, Bowies and daggers. **Technical:** Grinds 440C and D2; prefers flat grinds; does his own scrimshaw. **Prices:** $85 to $150; some to $500. **Remarks:** Spare-time maker; first knife sold in 1984. **Mark:** R.M. GREEN

MICHAEL GREGORY, 211 Calhoun Rd., Belton, SC 29627/803-338-8898
Specialties: Working folding and straight knives. **Patterns:** Hunters, tantos, folding locker and slip joints, boots and fighters. **Technical:** Grinds 440C, 154CM and ATS34; mirror finishes. **Prices:** $85 to $140; some to $500. **Remarks:** Full-time maker; first knife sold in 1980. **Mark:** Name, town in logo

ROGER GRENIER, 4595 Montee Saint Hubert, Saint Hubert, P. Que. J3Y1V3, CANADA/514-676-7128
Specialties: Working straight knives. **Patterns:** Heavy-duty Bowies, fighters, hunters; swords and miniatures. **Technical:** Grinds 01, D2 and 440C. **Prices:** $70 to $225; some to $800. **Remarks:** Full-time maker; first knife sold in 1981. **Mark:** GRENIER in logo

HOWARD A. GRIFFIN, JR., 14299 S.W. 31st Ct., Davie, FL 33330/305-474-5406
Specialties: Straight and folding working knives. **Patterns:** Hunters, Bowies, locking folders; especially likes his own pushbutton lock design. **Technical:** Grinds 440C. **Prices:** $100 to $200; some to $500. **Remarks:** Part-time maker; first knife sold in 1983. **Mark:** HAG

RENDON and MARK GRIFFIN, 9706 Cedardale, Houston, TX 77055/713-468-0436
Specialties: Working folding knives of their own designs. **Patterns:** Standard lockers and slip joints. **Technical:** Grind and forge; use 440C, 154CM, and their own Damascus. **Prices:** $185 to $300; some to $800. **Remarks:** Part-time makers; Rendon first knife sold in 1966; Mark's in 1974. **Mark:** Griffin in griffon logo

BEN GRIGSBY, Rt. 6 Box 510, Batesville, AR 72501/501-251-1367
Specialties: Working knives and period pieces. **Patterns:** Hunters, buckskinners, Bowies and daggers. **Technical:** Grinds 01, D2 and 440C. **Prices:** $65 to $175; some to $300. **Remarks:** Spare-time maker; first knife sold in 1976. **Mark:** GRIGSBY

JOHN D. (Butch) GRIGSBY, 5320 Circle Rd., Corryton, TN 37721/615-933-7802
Specialties: Miniature knife pins. **Patterns:** All patterns of using knives, including folding lockers, all in miniatures. **Technical:** Grinds 304 stainless and 440C. **Prices:** $10 to $100. **Remarks:** Part-time maker. **Mark:** Name

GRIZZLY FORGE (See Charles Bear)

W.W. GROSS, 325 Sherbrook Dr., High Point, NC 27260
Specialties: Working knives. **Patterns:** Hunters, boots, fighters. **Technical:** Grinds. **Prices:** Moderate. **Remarks:** Full-time maker. **Mark:** Name

KENNETH GUTH, 8 S. Michigan, 32nd Floor, Chicago, IL 60603/312-346-1760
Specialties: One-of-a-kind ornate straight and folding knives. **Patterns:** Flemish, Japanese and African-styled knives. **Technical:** Forges and grinds high carbon and 440C. Does brass and steel laminations, goldsmithing. **Prices:** Upscale. **Remarks:** Full-time goldsmith and knifemaker. **Mark:** Guth

GEORGE B. GUTHRIE, Rt. 3 Box 432, Bessemer City, NC 28016/704-629-3031
Specialties: Working knives—his design or yours. **Patterns:** Hunters, boots, fighters, locking folders, and slip joints in traditional styles. Techni-

cal: Grinds D2, 440C and 154CM. **Prices:** $85 to $300; some to $450. **Remarks:** Part-time maker; first knife sold in 1978. **Mark:** Name in state

BOB GWOZDZ, 71 Starr Ln., Attleboro, MA 02703/617-226-7475
Specialties: Fancy working straight knives. **Patterns:** Hunters, push knives, fighters and tantos. **Technical:** Grinds 440C. **Prices:** $120 to $250; some to $500. **Remarks:** Part-time maker; first knife sold in 1983. **Mark:** Name and serial number

PHILIP L. HAGEN, P.O. Box 58, Pelican Rapids, MN 56572/218-863-8503
Specialties: High-tech working straight and folding knives. **Patterns:** A wide variety of folders; makes defense-related straight knives. **Technical:** Forges and grinds; uses 440C, his own Damascus, others like Uddeholm UHB. **Prices:** $100 to $800; some to $3,000. **Remarks:** Part-time maker, first knife sold in 1975. **Mark:** DOC HAGEN in shield, knife, banner logo

GEORGE S. HAGGERTY, 414 Hammertown Road, Monroe, CT 06468/203-261-4626
Specialties: Working folding and straight knives. **Patterns:** Hunters, claws, camp and fish knives, and locking folders. **Technical:** Forges and grinds; uses W2, 440C and 154CM. **Prices:** $85 to $150. **Remarks:** Part-time maker; first knife sold in 1981; has taken over Anderson Cutlery, which is now Discount Steel and Handle. **Mark:** GSH

ROBERT J. HAJOVSKY, P.O. Box 21, Scotland, TX 76379/817-541-2219
Specialties: Working straight knives. **Patterns:** Fighters, tantos, daggers—all as heavy-duty knives. **Technical:** Grinds 440C, 154CM and ATS34; likes filework. **Prices:** $150 to $290; some to $500. **Remarks:** Part-time maker; first knife sold in 1973. **Mark:** Bob-Sky Knives or name, city, state

L. G. GREEN

J. GOTTAGE

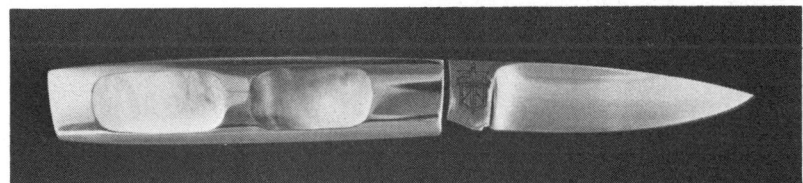

HAJOVSKY

HAGEN

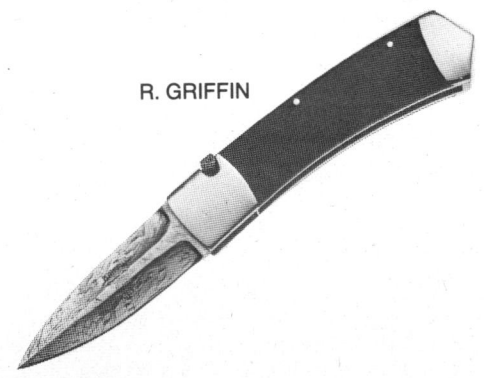

R. GRIFFIN

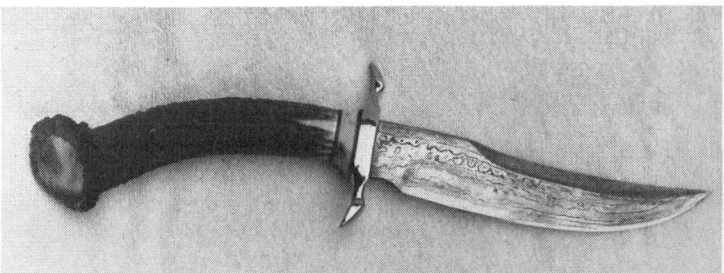

GOODWIN

EIGHTH ANNUAL EDITION 193

directory/custom knifemakers

JIM HAMMOND, P.O. Box 486, Arab, AL 35016/205-586-4151
Specialties: High-tech working straight knives. **Patterns:** Hunters in several patterns, fighters and boots. **Technical:** Grinds 440C and 154CM, very carefully. **Prices:** $200 to $975; some to $8,500. **Remarks:** Full-time maker; first knife sold in 1977. **Mark:** Full name, city, state in shield logo

HANGAS & SONS (See Ruana Knife Works)

ROBERT W. HANSEN, R.R. 2, Box 88, Cambridge, MN 55008/612-689-3242
Specialties: Straight and folding working knives. **Patterns:** From hunters to minis, camp knives to miniatures. Also makes folding lockers, slip joints in traditional styles. **Technical:** Grinds 01, 440C and 154CM; likes filework. **Prices:** $60 to $100; some to $550. **Remarks:** Part-time maker; first knife sold in 1983. **Mark:** Fish with H inside

HARBINGER (See Jimmy L. Fikes)

FRANK L. HARGIS, 321 S. Elm St., Flora, IL 62839/618-662-8281
Specialties: Fancy working knives. **Patterns:** Hunters, fighters, locking folders and Bowies. **Technical:** Grinds 440C, 154CM and ATS34; does filework. **Prices:** $90 to $1,000; some to $5,000. **Remarks:** Full-time maker; first knife sold in 1980. **Mark:** Name in logo

WALT HARLESS, P.O. Box 5913, Lake Worth, FL 33466-5913/305-964-3325
Specialties: Working straight knives in traditional style. **Patterns:** Does hunters, tantos, Bowies; has line of smaller scaled models for ladies. **Technical:** Grinds A2 and 440C; offers bone handles. **Prices:** $65 to $175; some to $300. **Remarks:** Full-time maker; sold first knife in 1978. **Mark:** A with arrow

LARRY W. HARLEY, Route 5, Box 37, Bristol, TN 37620/615-878-5368
Specialties: Period pieces and working knives. **Patterns:** Full range of straight knives, tomahawks, razors, buckskinners and hog spears. **Technical:** Forges and grinds; uses D2, 154CM and his own Damascus. All knives come very sharp. **Prices:** $50 to $500; some to $1,500. **Remarks:** Full-time maker; first knife sold in 1983; father is co-worker. **Mark:** Name, city and state in pine logo

ROBERT HARN, 228 Pensacola Rd., Venice, FL 33595/813-488-3418
Specialties: Folding period pieces. **Patterns:** Traditional lockback and slip joint folders. **Technical:** Grinds A2, 440C, and D2. **Prices:** $125 to $250; some double that. **Remarks:** Full-time maker; first knife sold in 1975. **Mark:** F. J. HARN

MIKE HARRINGTON, 408 S. Cedar, Abilene, KS 67410/913-263-3278
Specialties: Working straight knives. **Patterns:** Hunters, tantos and Bowies. **Technical:** Forges and grinds; uses 01, 440C and 154CM. **Prices:** $65 to $100; some $160. **Remarks:** Spare-time maker; first knife sold in 1981. **Mark:** MH connected

RALPH DEWEY HARRIS, P.O. Box 597, Grovetown, GA 30813/404-860-8719
Specialties: Straight working knives; some locking folders. **Patterns:** Combat knives, Bowies, tantos, and fish knives. **Technical:** Grinds 440C, D2, and ATS34. **Prices:** $80 to $200; some $500. **Remarks:** Full-time maker; first knife sold in 1978. **Mark:** HARRIS, or name and city

WILLIAM W. HARSEY, 82710 N. Howe Ln., Creswell, OR 97426/503-895-4941
Specialties: High-tech kitchen and outdoor knives. **Patterns:** Wide variety of straight knives; large display folders. **Technical:** Grinds, etches. **Prices:** $125 to $300; some up to $1,500. **Remarks:** Full-time maker; first knife sold in 1979. **Mark:** Name and date

ARLAN (LANNY) HARTMAN, 340 Ruddiman, N. Muskegon, MI 49445/616-744-3635
Specialties: Working straight knives. **Patterns:** Ultra-light drop point hunters, Bowies, and boots. **Technical:** Grinds D2 for working knives and 440C for display knives; flat grinds only. **Prices:** $100 to $150; some $400. **Remarks:** Part-time maker; first knife sold in 1982. **Mark:** HARTMAN

PHILL HARTSFIELD, 13095 Brookhurst St., Garden Grove, CA 92643/714-636-7633
Specialties: Working and heavy-duty straight knives. **Patterns:** Fighters, swords and survival knives, most in Japanese profile. **Technical:** Grinds 01, D2 and M2. Believes in sole authorship. **Prices:** $150 to $2,500. **Remarks:** Full-time maker; first knife sold about 1966. **Mark:** Initials, chiseled character

HARVEY MOUNTAIN KNIVES (See H. F. Wahlers)

MAX HARVEY, 14 Bass Rd., Bull Creek, Perth, 6155, WESTERN AUSTRALIA/09-332-7585
Specialties: Working straight knives, period and traditional, in heavy-duty weight. **Patterns:** Hunters, daggers, Bowies, tantos. **Technical:** Grinds 440C, 154CM, ATS34. **Prices:** $220 to $450; some to $1,500. **Remarks:** Part-time maker; first knife sold in 1981. **Mark:** M.C. HARVEY

HASTINGS (See Duayne Parrish)

RADE HAWKINS, P.O. Box H, Red Oak, GA 30272/404-964-1177
Specialties: Working knives to customer order. **Patterns:** Hunters, boots and camp knives; makes traditional folders. **Technical:** Grinds 154CM; 440C and D2. **Prices:** $140 to $400; some $1,200. **Remarks:** Part-time maker; first knife sold in 1972. **Mark:** Hawkins

CHAP HAYNES, R.R. #4, Tatamagouche, NS B0K 1V0, CANADA
Specialties: Working straight knives of his own designs. **Patterns:** Hunters, Bowies, tomahawks, swords, miniatures. **Technical:** Forges 01, his own Damascus, and laminates pure iron and nickel 200. **Prices:** $200 to $450; some to $1,500. **Remarks:** Part-time maker; first knife sold in 1985. **Mark:** Smith at anvil logo with HAYNES GREAT BLADES

WALTER F. HEDGECOCK, III, Box 175, Glen Daniel, WV 25844/304-934-6383
Specialties: Straight working knives in his design or yours. **Patterns:** Hunters, buckskinners, axes and tomahawks. **Technical:** Forges his own Damascus. **Prices:** $200 average. **Remarks:** Full-time maker; been smithing for 8 years. **Mark:** W.F.H. occasionally; SAXON FORGE

DON HEDRICK, 131 Beechwood Hills, Newport News, VA 23602/804-877-8100
Specialties: Working straight knives; period pieces and fantasy knives. **Patterns:** Hunters, boots, Bowies and miniatures. **Technical:** Grinds 440C and purchased Damascus. **Prices:** $150 to $550; some to $1,200. **Remarks:** Part-time maker; first knife sold in 1982. **Mark:** D. HEDRICK in oval logo

LOU HEGEDUS, JR., P.O. Box 441, Cave Spring, GA 30124
Specialties: Working straight and folding knives to customer order. **Patterns:** Full range of straight knives, folding lockers and slip joints. **Technical:** Grinds and forges; uses D2, 440C and his own Damascus. **Prices:** $75 to $250; some to $800. **Remarks:** Full-time maker; first knife sold in 1966. **Mark:** HEGEDUS

J. L. HEGWALD, 1106 Charles, Humboldt, KS 66748/316-473-3523
Specialties: Working straight knives, some fancy. **Patterns:** Makes Bowies, miniatures as well. **Technical:** Forges or grinds; uses 01, L6, 440C; mixes materials in handles. **Prices:** $35 to $200; some higher. **Remarks:** Part-time maker, sold first knife in 1983. **Mark:** JL

JOEL HEGWOOD, Rt. 4, Box 229, Summerville, GA 30747/404-397-8187
Specialties: High-tech working knives of his own design. **Patterns:** Hunters, boots and survival knives; locking folders, slip joints and interframes. **Technical:** Grinds A2, 01 and D2; uses 7075 aluminum in lightweight folder frames. **Prices:** $65 to $125; some to $200. **Remarks:** Part-time maker; first knife sold in 1979. **Mark:** Last name

RICHARD KARL HEHN, Karlsruhe Str. 7, D-7517 Waldbronn 1, WEST GERMANY/(07243) 61922
Specialties: High-tech working knives. **Patterns:** Hunters, fighters, Bowies, and locking folders. **Technical:** Grinds and forges 440C, CPM, and his own stainless Damascus; high-tech polishing for all steels; clean grinds; deluxe natural handles. **Prices:** $350 to $4,000; some $9,000. **Remarks:** Full-time maker; first knife sold in 1963. Has partner. **Mark:** Runic H in logo

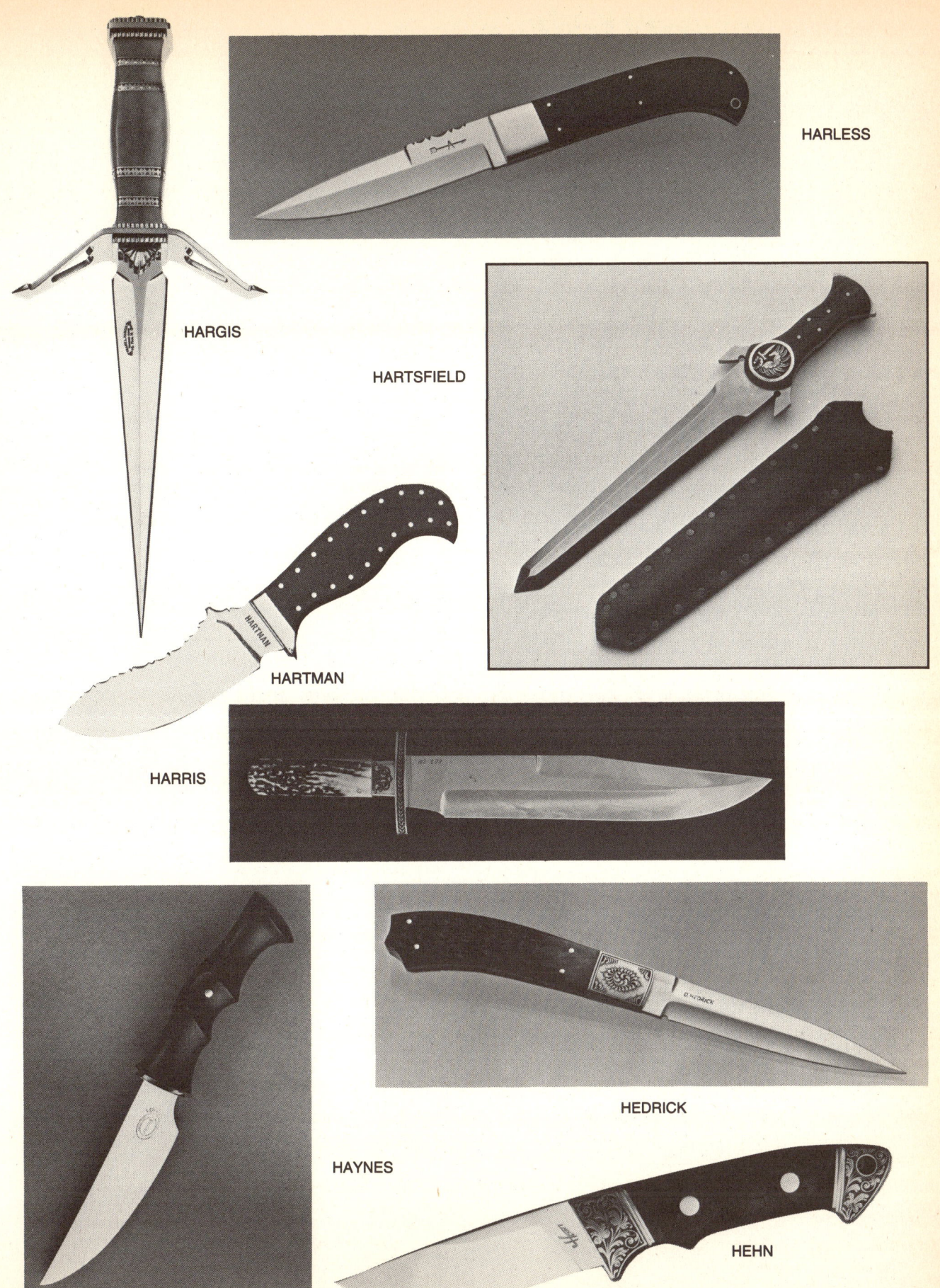

directory/custom knifemakers

RON HEMBROOK, P.O. Box 153, Neosho, WI 53059/414-625-3607
Specialties: Period pieces and straight working knives. **Patterns:** Hunters, buckskinners, tomahawks, fighters and Bowies. **Technical:** Grinds 01 and D2, and bought Damascus. **Prices:** $60 to $100; some to $350. **Remarks:** Part-time maker; first knife sold in 1970. **Mark:** Name with serial number

LORENZO "LARRY" HENDRICKS, 9919 E. Apache Trail, Mesa, AZ 85207/602-986-9252
Specialties: The Kangaroo design—a small knife piggybacked on a larger one. **Patterns:** All sizes, working and defense knives. **Technical:** Grinds 440C; uses gold, ivory, etc.; embellishes his own work. **Prices:** $550 to $1,600; some to $6,000. **Remarks:** Full-time maker; first knife sold in 1943. **Mark:** Name, town and state

E.J. (Jay) HENDRICKSON, 4204 Ballenger Creek Pike, Frederick, MD 21701/301-663-6923
Specialties: Working straight knives. **Patterns:** Bowies, hunters, camp knives, fighters in the Moran styles. **Technical:** Forges W2, 01, 1095, 5160; makes Damascus; does a lot of wire inlay. **Prices:** $200 to $900. **Remarks:** Full-time now; sold first knife in 1975. **Mark:** Name

D.E. HENRY, Star Route, Old Gulch Road, Mountain Ranch, CA 95246/209-754-4537
Specialties: Investor-class knives in standard patterns—premier maker of Sheffield-type Bowies. **Patterns:** Bowies of course, but also folding lockers, patent locks and push knives, even hunters. **Technical:** Grinds D2, D3 and 440C; finishes to immaculate line and grinds. **Prices:** $2,000 to $3,500. **Remarks:** Full-time maker; first knife sold in 1955. **Mark:** Name in Roman or Gothic lettering

PETER HENRY & SON, 332 Nine Mile Ride, Wokingham, Berkshire RG11 3NJ, ENGLAND/0734-734475
Specialties: Period pieces and working straight knives; will work to customer order. **Patterns:** Hunters to push knives, survival knives to boots; Sheffield-style a mainstay. **Technical:** Grind 01 and 154CM; make "faithful copies of Bowies, Scottish dirks and sgian dubhs." **Prices:** £20 to £100; some to £150. **Remarks:** Full-time maker; first knife sold in 1974. **Mark:** P. Henry & Son

WAYNE HENSLEY, P.O. Box 904, Conyers, GA 30207/404-483-8938
Specialties: Period pieces and fancy working knives. **Patterns:** Boots to Bowies, folding lockers to miniatures. Large variety of straight knives. **Technical:** Grinds D2, 440C, 154CM and commerical Damascus. **Prices:** $50 to $150; some to $800. **Remarks:** Part-time maker; first knife sold in 1974. **Mark:** Hensley

TIM HERMAN, 7721 Foster, Overland Park, KS 66204/913-649-3860
Specialties: Exceptionally ornate knives and period pieces in his own designs. **Patterns:** Boots, Bowies, daggers and push knives. **Technical:** Grinds D2, 440C and 154CM. Intricate handle designs, gold inlays; all knives fully embellished. **Prices:** $300 to $1,750; some to $3,000. **Remarks:** Part-time maker; first knife sold in 1978. **Mark:** Etched signature

WM. R. "BILL" HERNDON, c/o Jody Samson, 1834 W. Burbank, Burbank, CA 91506/213-840-8400
Specialties: Fancy working straight knives. **Patterns:** Hunters to tomahawks, miniatures to daggers and tantos to buckskinners. **Technical:** Grinds D2, 440C, 154CM. **Prices:** $90 to $185; some to $750. **Remarks:** Part-time maker; first knife sold in 1981. **Mark:** Signature or last name

GEORGE HERRON, Rt. 1, Box 24, Springfield, SC 29146/803-258-3914
Specialties: High-tech working straight knives; some folders. **Patterns:** Hunters, fighters, boots in personal style. **Technical:** Grinds 154CM, ATS34 and A2; builds knives to be used. **Prices:** $75 to $500; some $750. **Remarks:** Full-time maker; first knife sold in 1963. **Mark:** HERRON in script

DON HETHCOAT, Box 1764, Clovis, NM 88101/505-762-5721
Specialties: Straight working and folding knives. **Patterns:** Hunters, axes, fish knives, buckskinners and boots, and locking folders. **Technical:** Grinds D2, 440C and 154CM. **Prices:** $80 to $250; some $500. **Remarks:** Part-time maker; first knife sold in 1969. **Mark:** HETHCOAT, city, state

THOMAS S. HETMANSKI, 1107 William St., Trenton, NJ 08610/609-989-9371
Specialties: Working knives; some fantasy pieces. **Patterns:** Folding lockers and interframes; straight hunters, boots, fish knives. **Technical:** Grinds A2, 440C and commercial Damascus. **Prices:** $135 to $300; some to $400. **Remarks:** Part-time maker; first knife sold in 1982. **Mark:** Initials in monogram

DARYL HIBBEN, 1641 Domain Loop, Rio Rancho, NM 87124/505-892-5757
Specialties: Working straight knives, some fancy. **Patterns:** Simple hunters; complex fighters; Bowies and swords. **Technical:** Grinds 440C, 154CM; prefers hollow grind. **Prices:** $140 to $450; some to $3,000. **Remarks:** Full-time maker; first knife sold in 1979. **Mark:** Signature

GIL HIBBEN, 410 Production Court, Louisville, KY 40299/502-499-9097
Specialties: Working knives and fantasy pieces, made to customer order. **Patterns:** Full range of straight knives, including swords, axes, razors and miniatures. Does some locking folders. **Technical:** Grinds D2, 440C and 154CM. (Makes any kind of knife, welcomes one-of-a-kind designs.) **Prices:** $300 to $2,000; some $10,000. **Remarks:** Full-time maker; first knife sold in 1957. **Mark:** Name, city and state, or signature

VERNON W. HICKS, Rte. 1, Box 387, Bauxite, AR 72011/501-557-2813
Specialties: Working knives; some fancy pieces. **Patterns:** Folding lockers, slip joints in traditional styles; straight hunters, boots and Bowies. **Technical:** Grinds D2, 440C and 154CM. **Prices:** $75 to $300. **Remarks:** Sparetime maker; first knife sold in 1974. **Mark:** HICKS

TOM HIGH, 5474 S. 112.8 Rd., Alamoso, CO 81101/719-589-2108
Specialties: Hunter's knives, some fancy. **Patterns:** Drop-points in several shapes; some semi-skinners. **Technical:** Grinds 440C, 154CM; likes hollow grinds, mirror finishes; prefers scrimmable handles. **Prices:** $55 to $130; some to $350. **Remarks:** Full-time maker; first knife sold in 1965. Capable scrimshander; bowhunter. **Mark:** T and H connected

TOM HILKER, 4884 Harmony Lane, Santa Maria, CA 93455/805-937-5001
Specialties: Traditional straight and folding working knives. **Patterns:** Folding skinner in two sizes; Bowies, fork and knife sets, camp knives. **Technical:** Grinds D2, 440C, and ATS34. Does own heat-treating. **Prices:** $50 to $350; some $400. **Remarks:** Full-time maker; first knife sold in 1983. **Mark:** HILKER

HOWARD E. HILL, Box 3257, Polson, MT 59860/406-883-3405
Specialties: Working knives in personal designs, especially folders, fantasy pieces. **Patterns:** Locking folders, interframes; straight hunters and fighters. **Technical:** Grinds W2, 440C and 154CM; standard folder has grease ring joint. **Prices:** $100 to $300; some exceptional knives $5,000. **Remarks:** Part-time maker; first knife sold in 1981. **Mark:** Persuader

RICK HILL, 576 Clover Dr., Edwardsville IL, 62025/618-656-6850
Specialties: Working knives and period pieces; will fabricate to order. **Patterns:** Hunters, locking folders, fighters and daggers. **Technical:** Grinds D2, 440C and 154CM. **Prices:** $75 to $300; some to $1,500. **Remarks:** Part-time maker; first knife sold in 1983. Welcomes customer designs. **Mark:** Full name in hill shape logo

HARUMI HIRAYAMA, 4-5-13, Kitamachi, Warabi City, Saitama Pref., JAPAN #335/0484-43-2248
Specialties: High-tech working knives of her own design. Patterns: Folding lockers, interframes and straight gents knives. **Technical:** Grinds 440C or equivalent; uses natural handle materials and gold. **Prices:** $200 to $1,200; some to $5,000. **Remarks:** Part-time maker; first knife sold in 1985. **Mark:** H. Harumi

HOWARD HITCHMOUGH, 3 Highland Lodge, Fox Hill, London SE 19 2UJ, ENGLAND/01-653-6166
Specialties: Fancy working knives. **Patterns:** Fighters, boots and hunters, also folding lockers in traditional patterns. **Technical:** Grinds D2 and 154CM. Most knives in mirror finish. **Prices:** $140 to $300; some to $500. **Remarks:** Full-time maker; first knife sold in 1967. **Mark:** HITCHMOUGH, LONDON, ENGLAND

J.B. HODGE, 1100 Woodmont Ave. SE, Huntsville, AL 35801/205-536-8388
Specialties: Fancy folding working knives. **Patterns:** Lockers, slip joints, two-blades, fighters and traditional patterns. **Technical:** Grinds D2, 154CM and ATS34. Uses his own front lock on his folders. **Prices:** $150 to $300; some to $750. **Remarks:** Part-time maker; first knife sold in 1978. **Mark:** Name, city and state

JOHN HODGE, III, 422 S. 15th St., Palatka, FL 32077/904-328-3897
Specialties: Fancy folding and straight working knives. **Patterns:** Camp knives, boots, hunters and buckles. Makes folding lockers, slip joints and gents patterns. **Technical:** Forges 01, D1 and makes his own "Southern-style" Damascus. **Prices:** $200 to $600; some to $1,000. **Remarks:** Part-time maker; first knife sold in 1981. **Mark:** JH3 in logo

RICHARD J. HODGSON, 9081 Tahoe Lane, Boulder, CO 80301/303-666-9460
Specialties: Straight and folding knives in traditional styles. **Patterns:** High tech knives in various patterns. **Technical:** Grinds 440C, AEB-L, and CPM. **Prices:** $850 to $2,200. **Remarks:** Part-time maker. **Mark:** None

STEVE HOEL, P.O. Box 283, Pine, AZ 85544/602-476-4278
Specialties: Investor-class folders and period pieces in his own designs. **Patterns:** Folding interframes, both lockers and slip joints; straight Bowies, boots and daggers. **Technical:** Grinds 154CM, ATS34, and commercial Damascus. **Prices:** $450 to $750; some to $7,500. **Remarks:** Full-time maker of quality knives. **Mark:** SH logo with name and address

KEVIN L. HOFFMAN, 6392 Holly Ct., Lisle, IL 60532/312-983-8342
Specialties: High-tech working knives. **Patterns:** Fighters, tantos, claws, survival and push knives. **Technical:** Grinds 01, 440C and 154CM. Tantos with polished temper line and sandblasted finish. **Prices:** $100 to $300; some to $500. **Remarks:** Full-time maker; first knife sold in 1981. **Mark:** KLH

D'ALTON HOLDER, 3200 N. Carlton, Farmington, NM 87401/505-326-0611
Specialties: Deluxe working knives and high art hunters. **Patterns:** "My" knife is drop-point hunter most-sold, but makes fighters, Bowies, miniatures and locking folders. **Technical:** Grinds 440C and 154CM; uses amber and other materials in combination on stick tangs. **Prices:** $150 to $350; some to $1,000. **Remarks:** Full-time maker; first knife sold in 1970. **Mark:** D'HOLDER, city and state

DALE J. HOLLAND, 204 N.E. 82nd St., Kansas City, MO 64118/816-436-1493
Specialties: Fancy high-tech knives. **Patterns:** Locking folders, patent locks, and interframes. **Technical:** Grinds 440C, 154CM and ATS34. **Prices:** $120 to $350; some to $450. **Remarks:** Part-time maker; first knife sold in 1980. **Mark:** DJH

D. HIBBEN

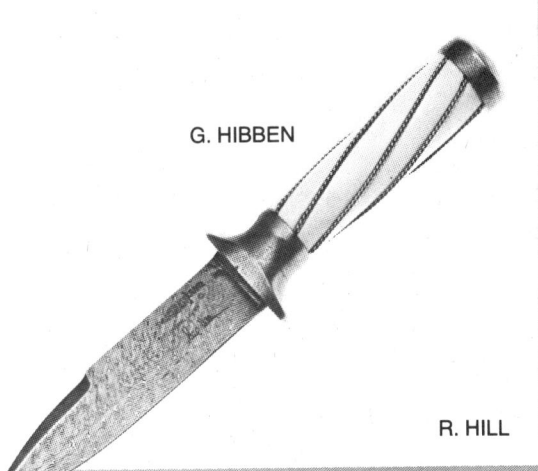
G. HIBBEN

R. HILL

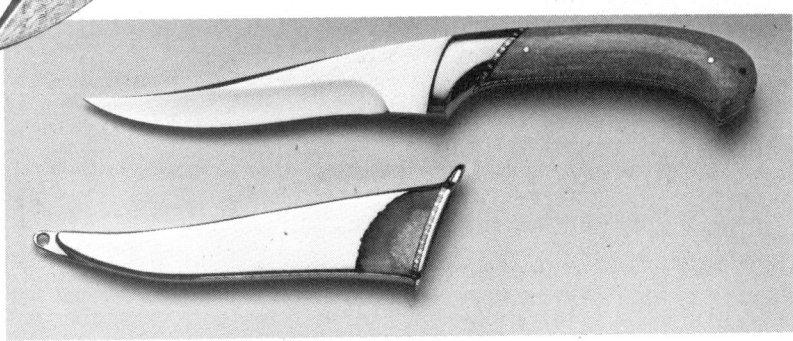
HERNDON

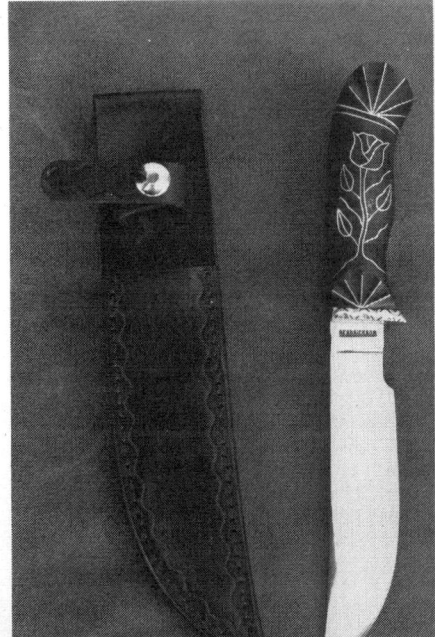
HENDRICKSON

directory/custom knifemakers

PAUL HOLLOWAY, 714 Burksdale Rd., Norfolk, VA 23518/804-588-7071
Specialties: Working straight and folding knives; will work to customer order. **Patterns:** Both lockers and slip joints; fighters and boots in straight knives; fish and push knives, from swords to miniatures. **Technical:** Grinds 154CM, 440C and ATS34. **Prices:** $95 to $230; some to $700. **Remarks:** Part-time maker; first knife sold in 1981. **Mark:** Holloway or name and city in logo

JESS HORN, 2850 Goodwater Ave., Redding, CA 96002/916-221-3681
Specialties: Investor-class working folders; some period pieces; famously collectible. **Patterns:** High-tech design and finish in locking folders; now offers traditional slip joints. **Technical:** Grinds 440C, 154CM and commercial Damascus. **Prices:** $400 to $700. **Remarks:** Full-time maker; first knife sold in 1968. **Mark:** Full name or Horn

GLEN HORNBY, P.O. Box 444, Glendale, CA 91209/818-244-1354
Specialties: Fancy working knives. **Patterns:** Bowies, fighters, hunters mainly; makes axes, minis, miniatures and push knives, too. **Technical:** Grinds ATS34, 154CM and 440C; likes big horn sheep handles. **Prices:** $95 to $175; some to $900. **Remarks:** Part-time maker. **Mark:** Script name under sheep horns

DURVYN M. HOWARD, Rt. 5, Box 77, Gadsden, AL 35903/205-492-5720
Specialties: Upscale working folders. **Patterns:** Folding lockers, gents, hunters, fighters, gent's dinner set—but folders only right now. **Technical:** Grinds 440C and D2; mirror finishes; natural handle materials; clean and careful work. **Prices:** $500 to $1,200; some to $2,500. **Remarks:** Full-time maker; now accepting orders. **Mark:** Name, very small

JOHN C. HOWSER, Rt. 9, Box 579, Bell Ln., Frankfort, KY 40601/502-875-3678
Specialties: Practical working knives. **Patterns:** Hunters and fighters of folding lockblades. **Technical:** Grinds D2, 440C and 154CM; clean crisp lines and mirror surface; natural materials. **Prices:** $85 to $125; some to $200. **Remarks:** Part-time maker; first knife sold in 1974. **Mark:** Signature

JIM HRISOULAS, 15258 Lakeside, Sylmar, CA 91342/818-362-5339
Specialties: Period pieces and straight working knives. **Patterns:** Swords, Bowies, tomahawks, daggers and sgian dubhs. **Technical:** Forges (only) 01, 1095, 5160, and makes his own Damascus. **Prices:** $85 to $175; some exceed $600. **Remarks:** Full-time maker; first knife sold in 1973. **Mark:** 8R in heart logo

ARTHUR J. HUBBARD, 574 Cutlers Farm Road, Monroe, CT 06468/203-268-3998
Specialties: Fancy working knives, his design or yours. **Patterns:** Hunters, fighters, boots, wood carving knives; folding lockers in traditional styles. **Technical:** Grinds and forges; uses W2, 440C and 154CM. **Prices:** $65 to $350; some to $1,000. **Remarks:** Full-time maker; first knife sold in 1976. **Mark:** Name, city and state

C. ROBBIN HUDSON, Rt. 1, Box 128B, Rock Hall, MD 21661/301-639-7273
Specialties: High art forged working knives. **Patterns:** Buckskinners, hunters, Bowies, fighters and push knives; folding lockers in traditional styles. **Technical:** Forges W2, 01 and his own Damascus; makes knives one at a time; ABS Master. **Prices:** $300 to $700; some to $5,000. **Remarks:** Full-time maker; first knife sold in 1970. **Mark:** Hudson and MS

CHUBBY HUESKE, 4808 Tamarisk Dr., Bellaire, TX 77401/713-667-0344
Specialties: Working knives, fancy and plain, with the hand of the maker easy to see. **Patterns:** Hunters, boots, fighters; folding lockers, slip joints and gents. **Technical:** Grinds D2. **Prices:** $100 to $225; some to $650. **Remarks:** Part-time maker every day; now making some specials like sesquicentennial Sam Houston and Yellow Rose knives; first knife sold in 1968. **Mark:** Name and Texas logo

STEVE HUEY, 27645 Snyder Rd. #38, Junction City, OR 97448/503-689-8362
Specialties: Straight working knives, some one of a kind. **Patterns:** Hunters, fighters, fish knives and kitchen cutlery. **Technical:** Hollow or flat grinds 1095, L6, 440C and D2. **Prices:** $75 to $600. **Remarks:** Part-time maker; first knife sold in 1981. **Mark:** HUEY in rectangle

DARYLE HUGHES, 10979 Leonard, Nunica, MI 49448/616-837-6623
Specialties: Working knives. **Patterns:** Buckskinners, hunters, camp knives, kitchen and fish knives. **Technical:** Grinds and forges; uses W2, 01 and D2. **Prices:** $40 to $100; some to $400. **Remarks:** Part-time maker, first knife sold in 1979. **Mark:** Name and town in logo

ED HUGHES, 280½ Holly Lane, Grand Junction, CO 81503/303-243-8547
Specialties: Working and miniature knives in traditional modes. **Patterns:** Bowies, push knives; has a pocketable straight knife he likes. **Technical:** Grinds stainless steels. **Prices:** $75 to $250; some to $600. **Remarks:** Full-time maker; sold first knife in 1978. **Mark:** Name or initials

LAWRENCE HUGHES, 207 W. Crestway, Plainview, TX 79072/806-293-5406
Specialties: Working and display knives. **Patterns:** Bowies, daggers, hunters, buckskinners and push knives. **Technical:** Grinds D2, 440C and 154CM. **Prices:** $50 to $125; some to $2,000. **Remarks:** Part-time maker; first knife sold in 1979. **Mark:** Name with buffalo skull in center

MICHAEL J. HULL, 2118 Obarr Pl., Apt. C, Santa Ana, CA 92701/714-541-2533
Specialties: Working knives and period pieces. **Patterns:** Fighters, Bowies and camp knives especially, but does boots, daggers and tantos. **Technical:** Grinds A2, 01 and 440C. **Prices:** $75 to $275; some to $700. **Remarks:** Full-time maker; first knife sold in 1983. **Mark:** Name, city, state

ROY HUMENICK, P.O. Box 494, Cupertino, CA 95015
Specialties: Working knives in his own style. **Patterns:** Hunters in traditional patterns; has Persian-handled drop point. **Technical:** Forges and grinds. Uses stainless; makes Damascus. **Prices:** $125 to $250; some to $600. **Remarks:** Part-time maker; first knife sold in 1984. **Mark:** Name, serial number

ROBERT E. HUNNICUTT, 2636 Magnolia Way, Forest Grove, OR 97116/503-357-3950
Specialties: Working knives and period pieces. **Patterns:** Fighters, boots and Bowies; also miniatures. **Technical:** Grinds D2 and 440C; prefers his rebated flat grind to standard designs. **Prices:** $150 to $400. **Remarks:** Full-time maker; first knife sold in 1979. **Mark:** Name plus production number

JEFF HURST, Rt. 1, Box 22-A, Rutledge, TN 37861/615-828-3909
Specialties: Straight working knives forged in his own designs. **Patterns:** Tomahawks, hunters, boots, and fighters. **Technical:** Forges W2, 01, and his own Damascus. **Prices:** $175 to $350; some $500. **Remarks:** Full-time maker; first knife sold in 1984. Marks partnered knives—with Newman L. Smith, handle artisan—SH in script. **Mark:** HURST

BILLY MACE IMEL, 1616 Bundy Ave., New Castle, IN 47362/317-529-1651
Specialties: High art working knives, period pieces and personal cutlery. **Patterns:** Daggers, fighters, hunters; folding lockers and slip joints with interframes; folding hunters. **Technical:** Grinds and forges D2, 440C and 154CM. **Prices:** $200 to $2,000; some to $4,000. **Remarks:** Part-time maker; first knife sold in 1973. **Mark:** Name in monogram

THE IRON DUCKLING (See John Sloan)

JACK KNIVES (See Jack Shedenhelm)

JIM JACKS, P.O. Box 2782, Covina, CA 91722/818-331-5665
Specialties: Straight working knives in traditional patterns. **Patterns:** Tantos, Bowies, fish and camp knives, even miniatures. **Technical:** Grinds Stellite 6K, 440C and 154CM. **Prices:** $100 to $250; some to $650. **Remarks:** Spare-time maker; first knife sold in 1980. **Mark:** JJ in diamond logo

JAGED (See Gregory H. Smith)

GERRY JEAN, 25B Cliffside Drive, Manchester, CT 06040/203-649-6449
Specialties: Working knives. **Patterns:** Folding lockers and butterflies. Straight hunters, survival and camp knives, some miniatures. **Technical:** Grinds A2, 440C and 154CM. Handle slabs applied in unique tongue-and-groove method. **Prices:** $125 to $250; some $450. **Remarks:** Spare-time maker; first knife sold in 1973. **Mark:** GJ and serial number

CARL A. JENSEN, JR., R.R. #2, Box 74B, Blair, NE 68008/402-426-3353
Specialties: Working knives and period pieces. **Patterns:** Hunters mainly, and fighters, boots and Bowies. Customer design. **Technical:** Grinds D2, 01 and 440C; does own heat treating. **Prices:** $50 to $150; some more than that. **Remarks:** Part-time maker; first knife sold in 1980. **Mark:** Bear's Cutlery

STEVE JERNIGAN, 298 Tunnel Rd., Milton, FL 32571/904-994-0802
Specialties: Fancy working knives; some one-of-a-kind knives. **Patterns:** Daggers and hunters; folding lockers and slip joints. **Technical:** Grinds D2, ATS34 and 440C. Uses "Italian Smalti" glass tiles for his unique mosaic handles. **Prices:** $150 to $350; some to $4,000. **Remarks:** Part-time maker; first knife sold in 1982. Not taking orders for folders. **Mark:** JERNIGAN

SID JIRIK, 11301 Patro St., Anchorage, AK 99516/907-346-2661
Specialties: Straight working knives. **Patterns:** Hunters, fighters and survival knives; distinctive variations on the standard themes. **Technical:** Grinds A2, D2 and 154CM; mirror finishes. **Prices:** $90 to $150; some to $1,000. **Remarks:** Full-time maker. **Mark:** Full name, city, state

BRAD JOHNSON, 3477 Running Deer Dr., El Paso, TX 79936/915-595-1035
Specialties: Traditional working straight knives. **Patterns:** For hunters and outdoorsmen; has capers and deep-bellied skinners. **Technical:** Grinds stainless steels; uses pins and not solder to install bolsters, etc. **Prices:** $50 to $150; some to $250. **Remarks:** Part-time maker; first knife sold in 1985; serving officer, U.S. Army. **Mark:** BNJ

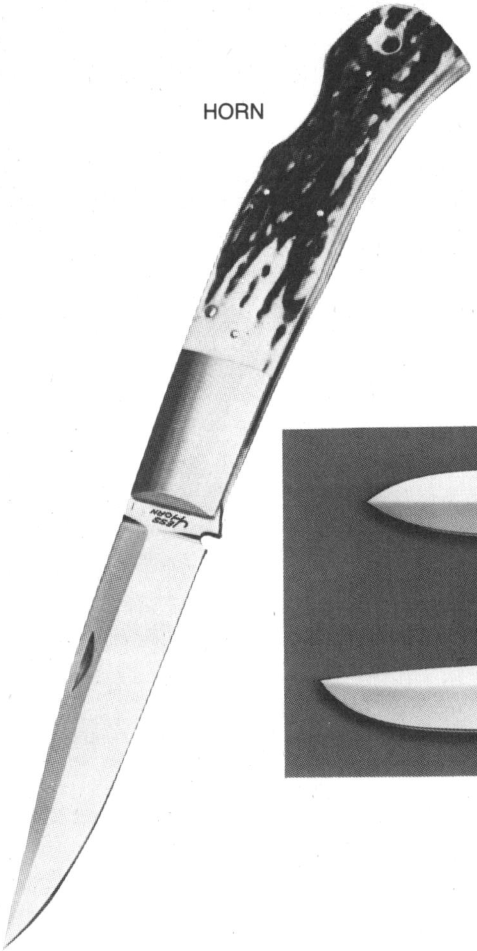

HORN

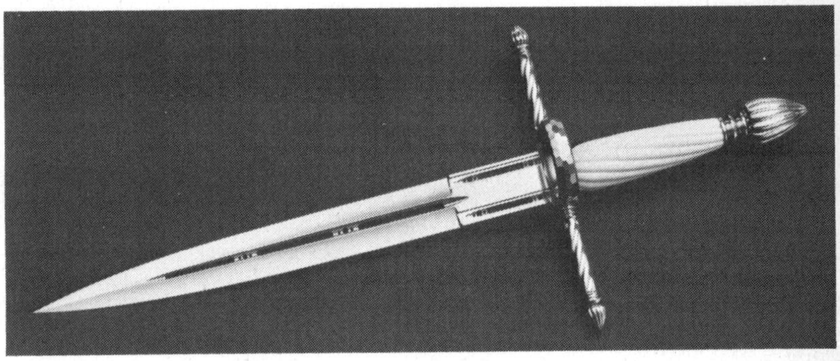

IMEL

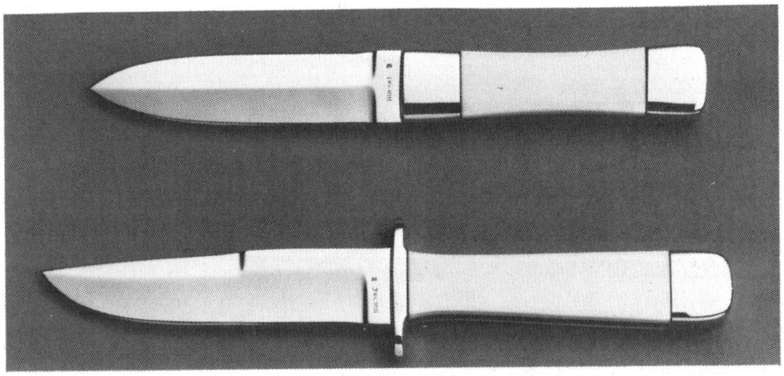

HUESKE

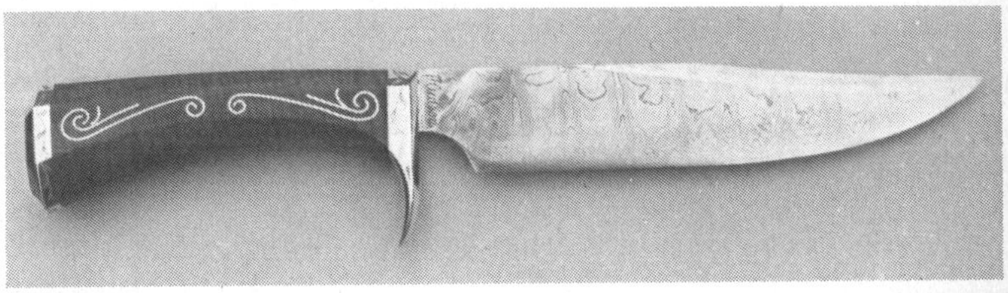

HUDSON

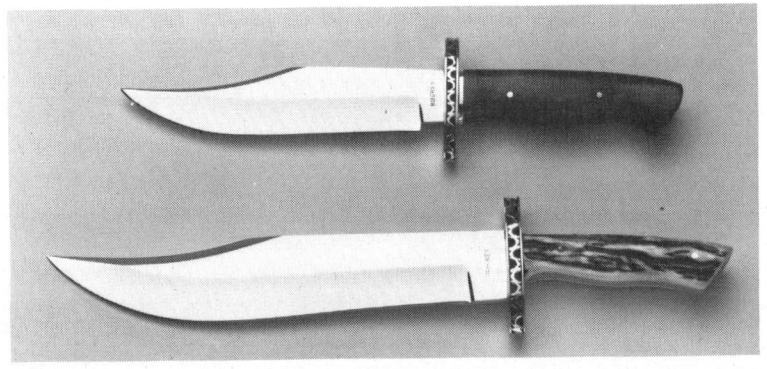

E. HUGHES

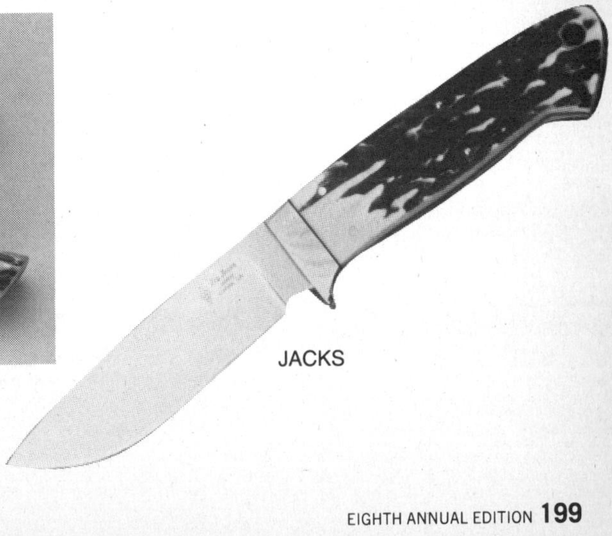

JACKS

EIGHTH ANNUAL EDITION 199

directory/custom knifemakers

C.E. "GENE" JOHNSON, 5648 Redwood Ave., Portage, IN 46368/219-762-5461
Specialties: Heavy-duty working knives of his own design. **Patterns:** Hunters, Bowies, survival knives and axes; locking folders. **Technical:** Grinds D2 and 440C; A18. **Prices:** $80 to $750; some to $1,000. **Remarks:** Part-time maker; first knife sold in 1975. **Mark:** Gene

GORDEN W. JOHNSON, 5426 Sweetbriar, Houston, TX 77017/713-645-8990
Specialties: Working knives and period pieces. **Patterns:** Hunters, boots and Bowies. **Technical:** Grinds 440C; all knives flat grind; most knives have narrow tang. **Prices:** $60 to $90; some to $300. **Remarks:** Full-time maker; first knife sold in 1974. **Mark:** Name, city, state

HAROLD "HARRY" C. JOHNSON, 1014 Lafayette Rd., Chickamauga, GA 30707/404-375-2321
Specialties: Working straight knives in "time-tested patterns and styles." **Patterns:** Mostly hunters, fighters and boots. **Technical:** Grinds 01, 440C, 154CM and commercial Damascus; keeps 50 woods in stock. **Prices:** $60 to $200; some $1,000. **Remarks:** Part-time maker; first knife sold in 1973; full-time gunsmith with retail store. **Mark:** H. JOHNSON, city, state in oval logo

RONALD B. JOHNSON, Box 11, Clearwater, MN 55320/612-558-6128
Specialties: Fancy working knives. **Patterns:** Hunters, fighters and tantos. Folding lockers, slip joints, all in traditional styles. **Technical:** Grinds 440C, 154CM and ATS34; uses no plastic; likes mastodon ivory. **Prices:** $90 to $250; some to $850. **Remarks:** Full-time maker; first knife sold in 1973. **Mark:** Signature; R.B. JOHNSON

RUFFIN JOHNSON, 215 LaFonda Dr., Houston, TX 77060/713-448-4407
Specialties: Working straight and folding knives. **Patterns:** Hunters, fighters and Bowies; folding lockers and slip joints. **Technical:** Grinds 440C and 154CM; hidden tangs and fancy handles. **Prices:** $165 to $325; some to $1,095. **Remarks:** Full-time maker; first knife sold in 1972. **Mark:** Wolf head logo and signature

STEVE R. JOHNSON, P.O. Box 5, 554 S. 500 E., Manti, UT 84642/801-835-7941
Specialties: Investor class working knives. **Patterns:** Hunters, fighters and boots in clean-lined contemporary patterns. **Technical:** Grinds ATS34, 154CM and 440C; buys Damascus. **Prices:** $225 to $1,000; some to $2,000. **Remarks:** Full-time maker; first knife sold in 1972. **Mark:** Name, city, state

W.C. "BILL" JOHNSON, 2242 N.W. 5th St., Okeechobee, FL 34972/813-467-4427
Specialties: Fancy working knives to order. **Patterns:** Hunters, fighters, tantos and push knives. He also makes folding lockers and slip joints. **Technical:** Grinds 440C, ATS34 and 154CM. **Prices:** $125 to $185; some to $500. **Remarks:** Fulltime maker; first time sold in 1979. **Mark:** W. C. Johnson

CHARLES JOKERST, 9312 Spaulding, Omaha, NE 68134/402-571-2536
Specialties: Working knives in standard patterns. **Patterns:** Hunters, fighters and Bowies; slip-joints, and miniatures. **Technical:** Grinds 440C, ATS34 and buys Damascus. **Prices:** $50 to $100; some $140. **Remarks:** Spare-time maker, first knife sold in 1984. **Mark:** Name and town

BOB JONES, 6219 Aztec N.E., Albuquerque, NM 87110/505-881-4472
Specialties: Fancy working knives of his own design. **Patterns:** Mountain-man/buckskinner types; folding lockers and slip joints. **Technical:** Grinds A2, 01, 1095 and commercial Damascus; uses no stainless steel. **Prices:** $75 to $300; some to $1,000. **Remarks:** Full-time maker; first knife sold in 1960. **Mark:** BJ on fixed blades; BJ encircled on folders

CHARLES ANTHONY JONES, 36 Broadgate Close, Bellaire Barnstaple, No. Devon E31 4AL, ENGLAND/0271-75328
Specialties: Working straight knives. **Patterns:** Simple hunters, boot and utility knives. **Technical:** Grinds 01 and D2. **Prices:** $60 to $100. **Remarks:** Spare-time maker; sold first knife in 1987. **Mark:** Circle T

ENOCH JONES, 4132 Novar Dr., Chantilly, VA 22021/703-378-0584
Specialties: Fancy straight working knives. **Patterns:** Hunters, fighters, boots and Bowies. **Technical:** Forges and grinds W2, 440C and commercial Damascus. **Prices:** $100 to $350; some to $1,000. **Remarks:** Part-time maker; first knife sold in 1982. **Mark:** ENOCH

JUDY (See J. Gottage)

JOSEPH F. KEESLAR, R #1, Box 252, Almo, KY 42020/502-753-7919
Specialties: Forged blades in traditional styles. **Patterns:** Period pieces—rifle knives, hunters, daggers. Forges small working knives from files. **Technical:** Forges 01, 1095, his own Damascus, and carbon files. **Prices:** $100 to $1,500; some over $2,000. **Remarks:** Full-time maker; first knife sold in 1976. **Mark:** KEESLAR with hammer/anvil logo and J.S. (Journeyman Smith with ABS)

WILLIAM L. KEETON, 4234 Lynnbrook Dr., Louisville, KY 40220/502-456-2378
Specialties: Plain and fancy working knives. **Patterns:** Hunters and fighters; folding lockers, and slip joints too. Names patterns for Derby winners. **Technical:** Grinds D2, 440C and 154CM; likes mirror finish. **Prices:** $75 to $475; some to $5,000. **Remarks:** Full-time maker; first knife sold in 1971. **Mark:** Logo of key

KELGIN KNIVES (See Ken Largin)

GARY KELLEY, 17485 S.W. Pheasant Lane, Aloha, OR 97006/503-649-7867
Specialties: Only miniature knives in exotic materials and designs. **Patterns:** Mostly miniature period pieces and fancy art knives. **Technical:** Forges and heat-treats 440C, purchased Damascus. **Prices:** $45 to $125; some to $500. **Remarks:** Part-time maker; first knife sold in 1969. **Mark:** Kelley in gold inlay

LANCE KELLY, 1824 Royal Palm Dr., Edgewater, FL 32032/904-423-4933
Specialties: Engraved folding and straight knives in the investor class. **Patterns:** Distinctly Kelly style in contemporary outlines. **Technical:** Grinds 01, D2 and 440C; engraves scroll in many patterns; inlays gold and silver. **Prices:** $600 to $3,500. **Remarks:** Full-time engraver/knifemaker; first knife sold in 1975. **Mark:** KELLY

KEMAL (Don Fogg and Murad Sayen), P.O. Box 127, Bryant Pond, ME 04219/207-665-2438
Specialties: High art straight knives; investor class one-of-a-kinds. **Patterns:** Fighters, daggers and tantos. **Technical:** Forges own Damascus. **Prices:** $3,500 to $6,500; some to $9,000. **Remarks:** Full-time makers; first knife sold in 1977. Fogg does blades; Sayen the handles and furniture. Not accepting orders. **Mark:** KEMAL and date.

BILL KENNEDY, JR., P.O. Box 850431, Yukon, OK 73085/405-354-9150
Specialties: Straight working knives. **Patterns:** Hunters, fighters, minis and fish knives. **Technical:** Grinds D2, 440C and 154CM. **Prices:** $80 to $250; some to $1,000. **Remarks:** Part-time maker; first knife sold in 1980. **Mark:** KENNEDY and year made

J.C. KENNELLEY, Box 145, Leon, KS 67074/316-745-3797
Specialties: Working straight knives; some fantasy pieces. **Patterns:** Hunters, fighters, skinners and fillet knives. **Technical:** Grinds D2 and 440C. **Prices:** $75 to $130; some to $450. **Remarks:** Part-time maker; first knife sold in 1982. **Mark:** Name logo

RALPH A. KESSLER, P.O. Box 202, Gary Goff Rd., Elgin, SC 29045/803-438-5360
Specialties: Working knives in standard patterns. **Patterns:** Hunters, fighters, kitchen knives. **Technical:** Grinds 154CM, D2 and ATS34; some scrimshaw. **Prices:** $75 to $200; some to $400. **Remarks:** Part-time maker; first knife sold in 1982. **Mark:** Name or name with logo

KESTREL TOOL (See Gregg Blomberg)

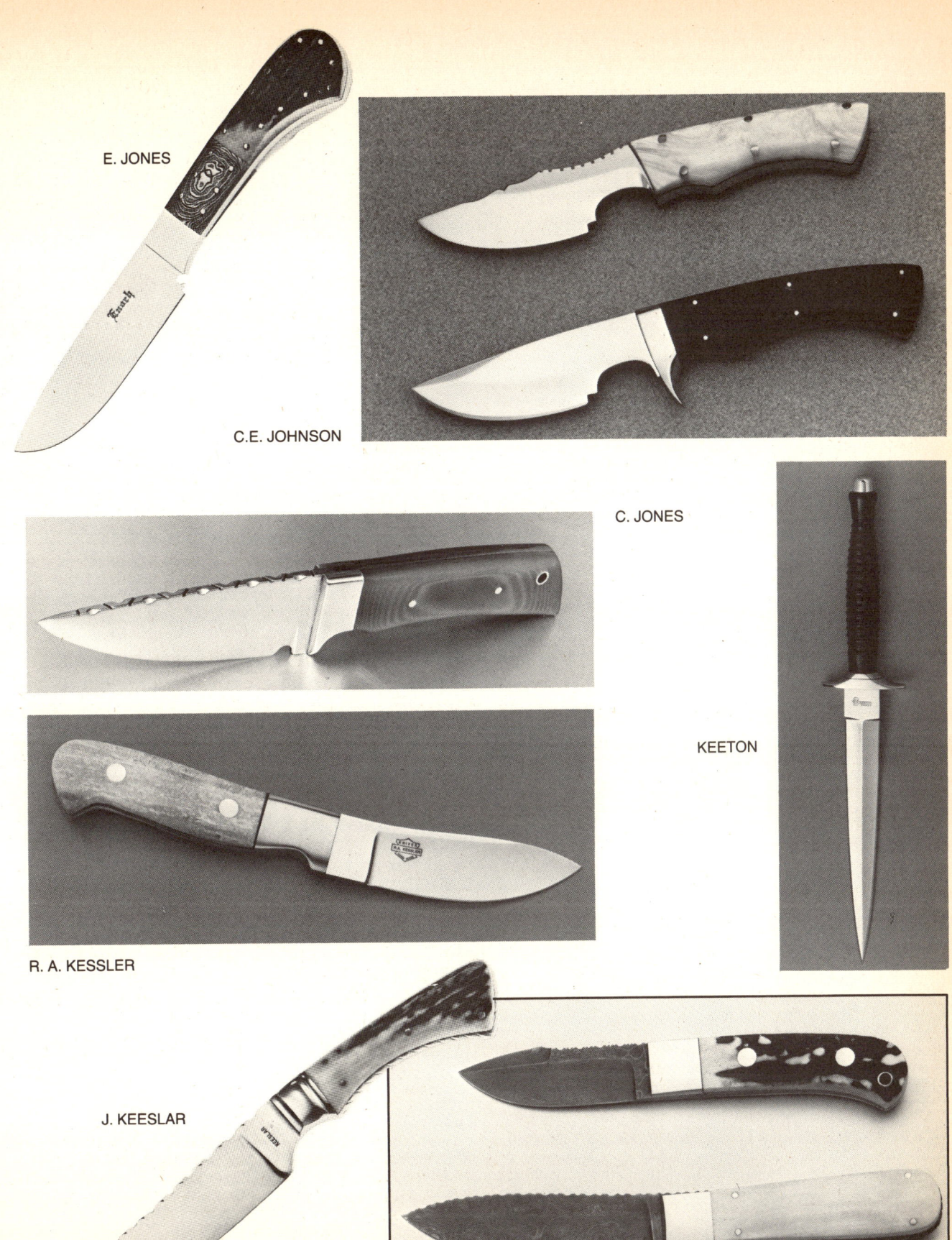

directory/custom knifemakers

JOT SINGH KHALSA, 368 Village St., Millis, MA 02054/617-376-8162
Specialties: High art knives in traditional patterns: **Patterns:** Full range of straight knives; mixes Sikh tradition and modern lines. **Technical:** Grinds and forges; uses W2, 440C and his own Damascus. **Prices:** $200 to $1,000; some very high. **Remarks:** Full-time maker; first knife sold in 1978. **Mark:** Crossed blade logo and name

SHIVA KI, 5222 Ritterman Ave., Baton Rouge, LA 70805/504-356-7274
Specialties: Fancy working straight and folding knives; welcomes customer designs. **Patterns:** Emphasis on defense styles in personal knives. Makes martial arts weapons. **Technical:** Forges and grinds; makes his own Damasucus; prefers natural handle materials. **Prices:** $135 to $850; some $1,800. **Remarks:** Full-time maker; first knife sold 1981. **Mark:** Name with logo

BILL KING, 14830 Shaw Road, Tampa, FL 33625/813-961-3455
Specialties: Fancy working knives; folding lockers in many varieties. **Patterns:** Straight hunters, boots and fish knives. **Technical:** Grinds 440C, 154CM, ATS34 and commercial Damascus. **Prices:** $135 to $250; some to $500. **Remarks:** Part-time maker; first knife sold in 1976. **Mark:** Name in crown

JOE KIOUS, Rt. 2, Box 232, Alamo, TX 78516/512-787-3178
Specialties: Fancy working knives in good contemporary styling. **Patterns:** Hunters, fighters, Bowies and miniatures; folders in traditional styles. **Technical:** Grinds D2, 440C and 154CM. **Prices:** $130 to $600; some to $5,000. **Remarks:** Full-time maker; first knife sold in 1969. **Mark:** KIOUS, city and state

GEORGE KIRTLEY, Salina Star Route, Boulder, CO 80302/303-443-1815
Specialties: Straight working knives. **Patterns:** Fighters, hunters, camp and kitchen knives. **Technical:** Forges and grinds W2, O1, and L6. **Prices:** $80 to $175; some $275. **Remarks:** Full-time maker; first knife sold in 1974. **Mark:** KIRTLEY

JERRY KITSMILLER, 62435 Gerry Rd., Montrose, CO 81401/303-249-4290
Specialties: Straight working knives in traditional patterns. **Patterns:** Hunters, boots and locking folders. **Technical:** Grinds D2, 440C and 154CM. **Prices:** $75 to $200; some to $300. **Remarks:** Spare-time maker; first knife sold in 1984. **Mark:** J&S Knives

K.K.K. CO. (See A.J. Collins)

W.K. KNEUBUHLER (See David Votaw)

KODAN (See B. Engnath)

ROBERT KOLITZ, W9342 Canary Rd., Beaver Dam, WI 53916/414-887-1287
Specialties: Working straight knives. **Patterns:** Hunters, boots and Bowies. **Technical:** Grinds O1 and 440C. **Prices:** $35 to $80; some to $400. **Remarks:** Spare-time maker; first knife sold in 1979. **Mark:** K

GEORGE KOUTSOPOULOS, 41491 Biggs Rd., La Grange, OH 44050/216-458-6464
Specialties: Heavy-duty working straight and folding knives. **Patterns:** Traditional hunters and skinners, lockbacks. **Technical:** Grinds 440C, 154CM, ATS34. **Prices:** $75 to $275; some higher. **Remarks:** Spare-time maker; first knife sold in 1976. **Mark:** GEK in diamond logo

MICHAEL T. KOVAL, 822 Busch Ct., Columbus, OH 43229/614-888-6486
Specialties: Period pieces and straight working knives of his own design. **Patterns:** Bowies, boots and daggers. **Technical:** Grinds D2, 440C and 154CM. **Prices:** $95 to $195; some $495. **Remarks:** Full-time knifemaker supply house, spare-time knifemaker. **Mark:** KOVAL

STEVE KRAFT, 315 S.E. 6th, Abilene, KS 67410/913-263-2198
Specialties: Working knives in traditional style. **Patterns:** Tantos, Bowies, fish knives. **Technical:** Grinds O1, L6, ATS34. **Prices:** $90 to $125; some to $300. **Remarks:** Part-time maker; sold first knife in 1984. **Mark:** SJK

TERRY L. KRANNING, 1900 West Quinn, #153, Pocatello, ID 83204/208-237-9047
Specialties: Miniature working and fantasy knives of his own design. **Patterns:** Miniature and some mini straight knives including razors, tomahawks, hunters, Bowies and fighters. **Technical:** Grinds 1095, 440C, purchased Damascus and nickel silver. Uses exotic materials, like meteorite. Makes cases for miniature sets made of brass or silver. **Prices:** $20 to $50; some to $250. **Remarks:** Part-time maker; first knife sold in 1978. **Mark:** K or TLK in eagle head logo

DONALD L. KREIBICH, 6082 Boyd Ct., San Jose, CA 95123/408-225-4719
Specialties: Straight working knives in standard patterns. **Patterns:** Bowies, boots and daggers; camp and fish knives in using finish. **Technical:** Grinds 440C, 154CM and ATS34; likes integrals. **Prices:** $100 to $200; some to $500. **Remarks:** Part-time maker; first knife sold in 1980. **Mark:** D.L. KREIBICH

JAMES J. KREIMER, Rt. 2, Box 280, Milan, IN 47031/812-654-2327
Specialties: Period pieces and working knives. **Patterns:** Hunters, fighters, tomahawks, buckskinners and camp knives. **Technical:** Forges 1095 and his own Damascus, and files. **Prices:** $35 to $200. **Remarks:** Part-time maker; first knife sold in 1978. **Mark:** JK connected

RAYMOND L. KREMZNER, 6620 Bonnie Ridge Dr., Baltimore, MD 21209-1940/301-653-1022
Specialties: Working straight knives in traditional styles, some fancy. **Patterns:** Hunters, fighters, Bowies and camp knives. **Technical:** Forges W2, O1, L6. **Prices:** $125 to $350. **Remarks:** Part-time maker; apprenticed to W.V. Fielder; sold first knife in 1987. **Mark:** Last name

D.F. KRESSLER, Lochhauser Strasse 86, 8039 Puchheim, WEST GERMANY/08142-30907
Specialties: High-tech working knives. **Patterns:** Hunters, fighters, daggers; follows Loveless style. **Technical:** Grinds new state-of-the-art steels; prefers natural handle materials. **Prices:** Upscale. **Mark:** Name in logo

PHILIP W. KRETSINGER, JR., Rt. #1, Box 158, Boonsboro, MD 21713/301-432-6771
Specialties: Period pieces in traditional and fancy styles. **Patterns:** Push knives, carvers, Bowies, camp knives. **Technical:** Forges W2 and 1095. **Prices:** $100 to $500; some to $1,500. **Remarks:** Full-time production. **Mark:** Name, city and state

AL KROUSE, 1903 Treble Drive #4A, Humble, TX 77338/713-446-5503
Specialties: Straight working knives in traditional patterns. **Patterns:** Bowies, hunters, skinners, and fish knives; some miniatures. **Technical:** Grinds O1, 440C and 154CM. Does own heat-treating and embellishments. **Prices:** $90 to $275; some to $750. **Remarks:** Full-time maker; first knife sold in 1981. **Mark:** KROUSE

MARTIN KRUSE, P.O. Box 487, Reseda, CA 91335/818-713-0172
Specialties: Period pieces and straight working knives. **Patterns:** Full line of straight knives, axes, tomahawks, razors, claws, and push knives. **Technical:** Grinds and forges W2, O1 and 1095; differential tempering. **Prices:** $60 to $450; some to $1,000. **Remarks:** Full-time maker; first knife sold in 1964. **Mark:** Initials

KUNI MITSU (See Michael Bell)

JIM KUYKENDALL, P.O. Box 539, Tulare, CA 93275/209-686-6130
Specialties: Fancy working knives. **Patterns:** Straight hunters, Bowies, buckskinners; developing full line in Japanese style. **Technical:** Grinds and forges A2, ATS34 and 440C. **Prices:** $75 to $240; some to $900. **Remarks:** Full-time maker; first knife sold in 1982. **Mark:** Name

JIM LADD, 1120 Helen, Deer Park, TX 77536/713-479-7286
Specialties: Period pieces and working knives. **Patterns:** Hunters, boots, Bowies and some other straight knives. **Technical:** Grinds D2, 440C and 154CM. **Prices:** $125 to $225; some to $550. **Remarks:** Part-time maker; first knife sold in 1965. **Mark:** J.S. Ladd

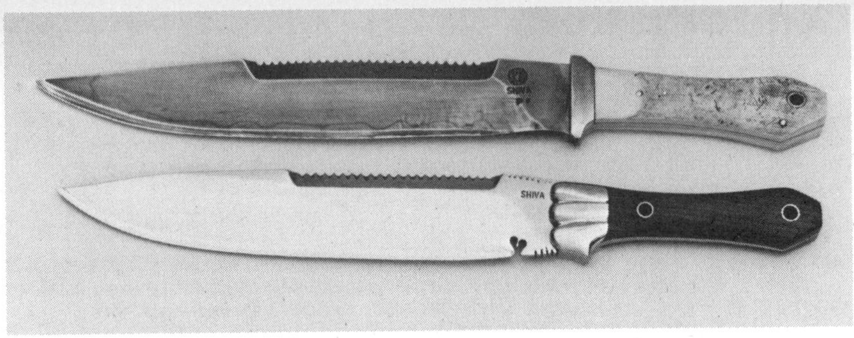

KI

KITSMILLER

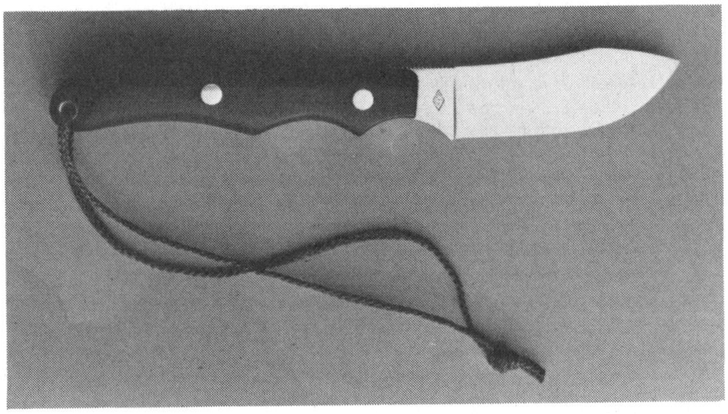

KOUTSOPOULOS

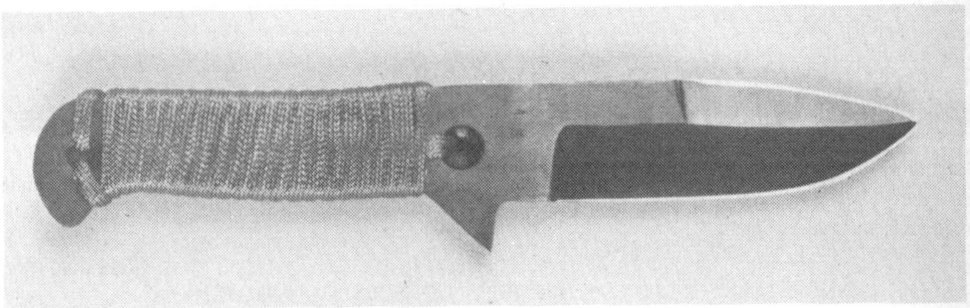

KRUSE

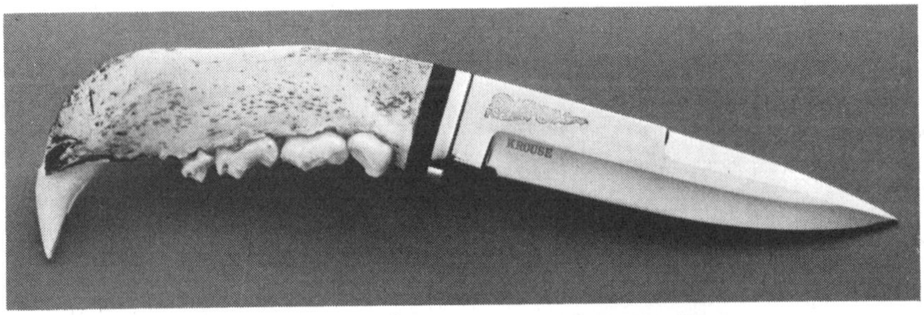

KROUSE

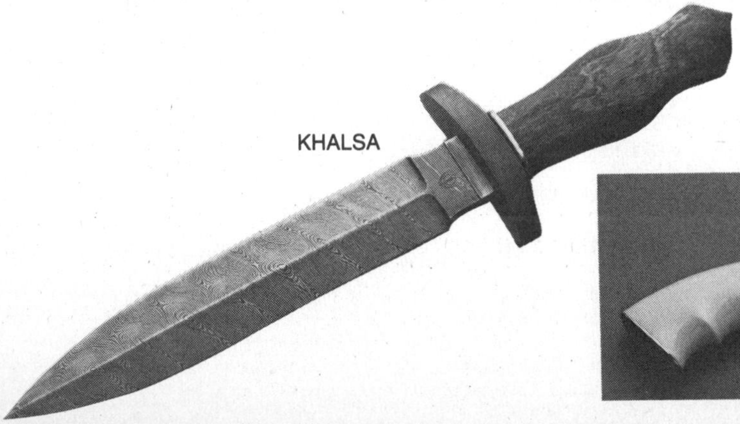

KHALSA

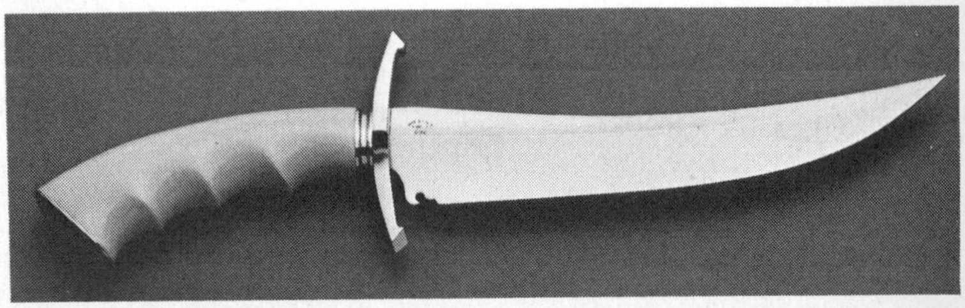

KIOUS

directory/custom knifemakers

RON LAKE, 123 East Park, Taylorville, IL 62568/217-824-2378
Specialties: High-tech working knives; inventor of the modern interframe folder. **Patterns:** Hunters, boots, other small straight knives; folding lockers. **Technical:** Grinds 154CM and ATS34; fine workmanship. Patented interframe with special lock release tab. **Prices:** $900 to $1,200; some to $4,000. **Remarks:** Full-time maker; first knife sold in 1968. **Mark:** LAKE

FRANK G. LAMPSON, 2052 I Rd., Fruita, CO 81521/303-858-7292
Specialties: Fancy working knives. **Patterns:** Full range of using designs, both straight and folding. **Technical:** Grinds A2, 440C and 154CM. **Prices:** $80 to $280; some to $2,500. **Remarks:** Full-time maker; first knife sold in 1971. **Mark:** Name in fish logo

ED LANE, 440 N. Topping, Kansas City, MO 64123/816-241-3217
Specialties: Fancy working knives to order. **Patterns:** Buckskinners, hunters, fighters, tantos and fish knives. **Technical:** Grinds 440C, 154CM, ATS34 and commercial Damascus; prefers knives very sharp. **Prices:** $65 to $350; some to $1,000. **Remarks:** Full-time maker; first knife sold in 1982. **Mark:** Signature

JERRY I. LANE, 1529 Stafford, Carbondale, IL 62901/618-549-2087
Specialties: Working straight knives. **Patterns:** Hunters, Bowies; does some tomahawks and buckle knives. **Technical:** Grinds 440C, 154CM and 01; makes knives to be used. **Prices:** $125 to $450; some to $3,000. **Remarks:** Full-time maker; first knife sold in 1970. **Mark:** J.I. LANE

GENE H. LANGLEY, Rt. 1, Box 204, Florence, SC 29501/803-669-3150
Specialties: Working knives in standard patterns. **Patterns:** Hunters, boots, fighters, folding lockers and slip joints. **Technical:** Grinds 440C, 154CM and ATS34. **Prices:** $70 to $110; some $400. **Remarks:** Spare-time maker; first knife sold in 1979. **Mark:** Name or Name, city and state

MICK LANGLEY, Box 1447, Weyburn, Sask. S4H 3J9, CANADA/306-842-3860
Specialties: Period pieces and working knives. **Patterns:** Fighters, tantos, boots, minis and miniatures; some folding lockers. **Technical:** Forges W2, 01 and his own Damascus. **Prices:** $150 to $1,000; some to $2,500. **Remarks:** Full-time maker; first knife sold in 1977. **Mark:** LANGLEY with M.S. (for ABS Master Smith)

SCOTT LANKTON, 8065 Jackson Rd., Ann Arbor, MI 48103/313-426-3735
Specialties: Krisses, Viking swords, the non-standard forged blade. **Patterns:** Generally one-of-a-kind in series; cloisoneé enameled handles were one such. **Technical:** Forges W2, L6 and his own Damascus. **Prices:** $300 to $900; some to $4,000. **Remarks:** Full-time maker; first knife sold in 1976. **Mark:** LANKTON logo

KEN LARGIN, 110 W. Pearl, Batesville, IN 47006/812-934-5938
Specialties: Working knives in standard patterns, some at low prices. **Patterns:** Hunters, tantos, swords, hatchets and folding butterflies. **Technical:** Grinds 01, 440C and buys Damascus; does filework. **Prices:** $49 to $150; some to $500. **Remarks:** Full-time maker; first knife sold in 1980. **Mark:** KELGIN or name

DON LAUGHLIN, 190 Laughlin Dr., Vidor, TX 77662/409-769-3390
Specialties: Working knives of his design. **Patterns:** Hunters, fighters, Bowies, folding lockers and two-blades. **Technical:** Grinds D2, 440C and 154CM. **Prices:** $75 to $200; some to $350. **Remarks:** Full-time maker; first knife sold in 1973. **Mark:** DEER or full name

STEPHEN M. LAWSON, 2638 Baker Rd., Placerville, CA 95667/916-626-1782
Specialties: Fancy working knives in his design or yours. **Patterns:** Cleavers, Bowies, fish and push knives; locking folders. **Technical:** Grinds 440C, 154CM and ATS34; engraves his own knives. **Prices:** $160 to $1,500; some to $2,500. **Remarks:** Full-time maker; first knife sold in 1978. **Mark:** S. LAWSON

L.J. LAY, 602 Mimosa Dr., Burkburnett, TX 76354/817-569-1329
Specialties: Working straight knives in traditional patterns, some period style. **Patterns:** Drop point hunters, some Bowies and fighters. **Technical:** Grinds ATS34 to mirror finish; likes linen Micarta. **Prices:** Moderate. **Remarks:** Part-time maker; sold first knife in 1985. **Mark:** Name and serial

MIKE J. LEACH, 5377 W. Grand Blanc Rd., Swartz Creek, MI 48473/313-655-4850
Specialties: Fancy working knives. **Patterns:** Hunters, fighters, Bowies, heavy-duty knives. Does slip joint folders and integral straight patterns. **Technical:** Grinds D2, 440C, 154CM; buys Damascus. **Prices:** $120 to $600; some to $2,500. **Remarks:** Part-time maker; first knife sold in 1952. **Mark:** LEACH

PAUL M. LeBATARD, 14700 Old River Rd., Vancleave, MS 39564/601-826-4137
Specialties: Straight and folding working knives. **Patterns:** Small game and fish knives, Bowies, camp and kitchen cutlery, folders, and slip joints. **Technical:** Grinds A2, 01, and ATS34. **Prices:** $50 to $160; some to $300. **Remarks:** Part-time maker; first knife sold in 1974. **Mark:** LEBATARD

HEINZ LEBER, Box 446, Hudson Hope, BC V0C 1V0, CANADA/604-783-5304
Specialties: Working straight and folding knives for use. **Patterns:** Personal hunter designs, kitchen knives, work knives for trappers. **Technical:** Grinds M2; uses some L6 and 01; likes moose antler for handles. **Prices:** $125 to $200; some to $500. **Remarks:** Full-time maker; sold first knife in 1975. **Mark:** HL connected

BRACY R. LEDFORD, 1917 Northgate St., Indianapolis, IN 46208/317-253-9740
Specialties: Working knives and some fantasy knives. **Patterns:** Bowies, locking folders and hunters. **Technical:** Files and sandpapers A2, D2, and 440C; no power tools used—all done by hand. **Prices:** $125 to $350; some to $500. **Remarks:** Part-time maker; first knife sold in 1983. **Mark:** B.R. LEDFORD

TOMMY LEE, Rt. 2, Box 392, Gaffney, SC 29340/803-489-6699
Specialties: Period pieces and working knives. **Patterns:** Fighters, boots, daggers and axes; folding lockers, slip joints in traditional styles. **Technical:** Forges and grinds; uses 440C, ATS34 and his own and commercial Damascus. **Prices:** $150 to $300; some to $1,500. **Remarks:** Full-time maker; first knife sold in 1974. **Mark:** LEE

BOB LEVINE, 3201 Iowa Drive, Anchorage, AK 99517/907-243-3878
Specialties: Working straight knives in traditional styles. **Patterns:** Full range of hunters, fighters, Bowies, tantos; makes all as miniatures as well. **Technical:** Grinds 440C, AEB-L, and ATS34; works backs. **Prices:** $85 to $135; some to $300. **Remarks:** Full-time maker; sold first knife in 1984. **Mark:** Name in logo

NORMAN LEVINE, Spring Valley Lake #7707, Victorville, CA 92392/619-245-1661
Specialties: Fancy working knives. **Patterns:** Hunters, boots, daggers, push knives; folding lockers and slip joints in gents and hunter patterns. **Technical:** Grinds 440C, 154CM, ATS34; provides ball bearing pivot in folders. **Prices:** $85 to $200; some to $1,500. **Remarks:** Full-time maker; first knife sold in 1974. **Mark:** Dragon on shield; sometimes name

TOM R. LEWIS, 1613 Standpipe Rd., Carlsbad, NM 88220/505-885-3616
Specialties: Traditional working straight knives. **Patterns:** Outdoors knives and tantos and Bowies. **Technical:** Grinds and forges; offers 440C and ATS34 and welded wire Damascus. **Prices:** $60 to $175; some to $300. **Remarks:** Part-time maker; sold first knife in 1980. **Mark:** TRL

LIL BEAR KNIVES (See Larry Berzas)

JIMMY (JAMES B.) LILE, Rt. 6, Box 27, Russellville, AR 72801/501-968-2011
Specialties: Creator of the original *First Blood* and *Rambo* survival knives. Makes fancy working knives. **Patterns:** Bowies and full line of straight knives and his own pattern in button-locking folders. **Technical:** Grinds D2 and 440C. **Prices:** $125 to $800; some "unlimited." **Remarks:** Full-time maker; first knife sold in 1944. **Mark:** Lile

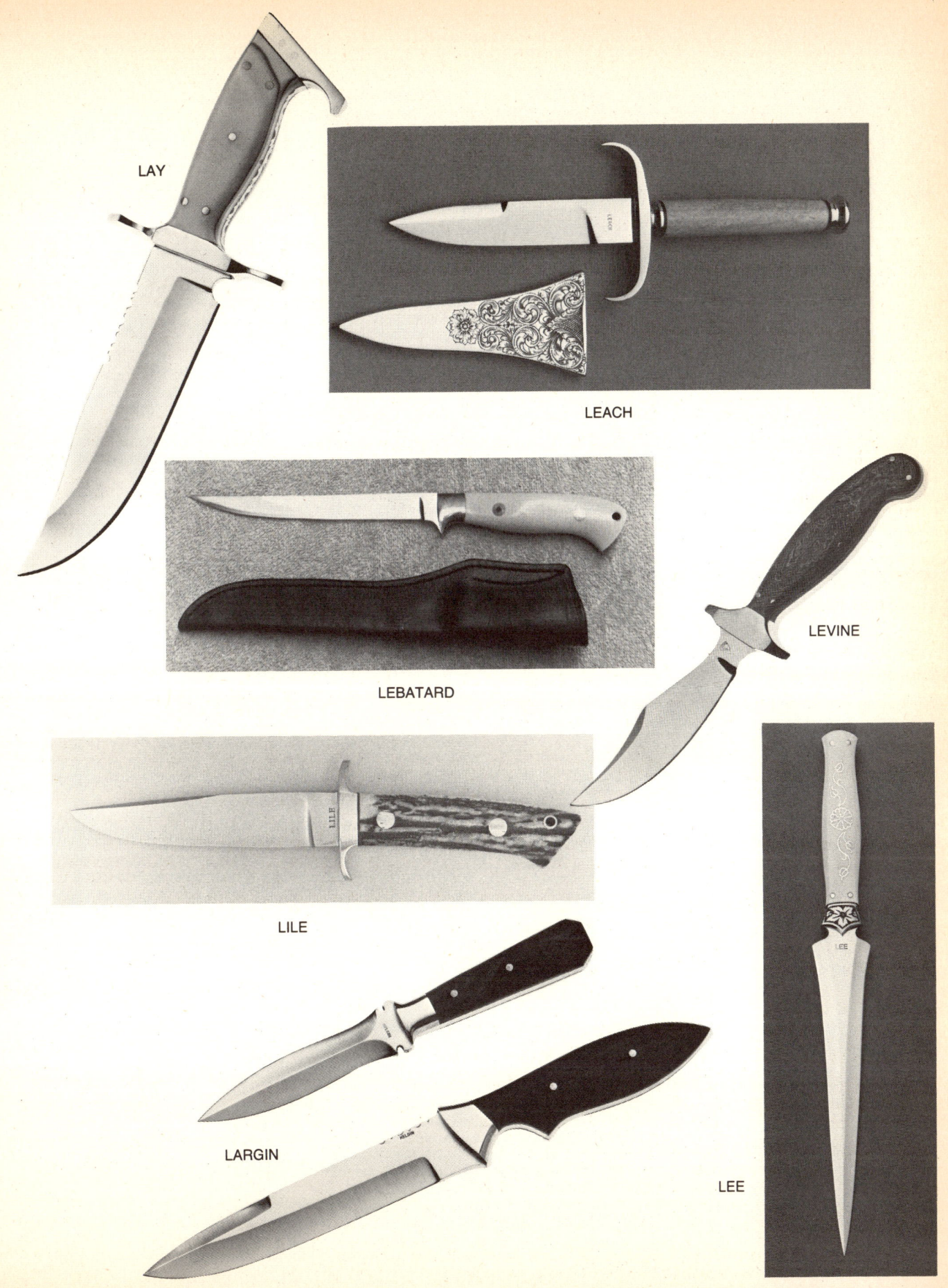

directory/custom knifemakers

CHRIS A. LINDSAY, 16237 Dyke Rd., La Pine, OR 97739/503-536-2386
Specialties: Working knives in standard patterns. **Patterns:** Hunters, kitchen and camp knives. **Technical:** Grinds D2, 440C and 154CM; brushed finishes, tapered tangs, hollow or flat ground. **Prices:** $65 to $130. **Remarks:** Part-time maker; first knife sold in 1980. **Mark:** Lindsay

GARY M. LITTLE, HC84 Box 10301, Broadbent, OR 97414-9801/503-572-2656
Specialties: Fancy working knives to order. **Patterns:** Hunters, tantos, Bowies, axes and buckskinners; folding lockers and interframes. **Technical:** Forges and grinds 01, L6, 1095 and makes his own Damascus; bronze fittings. **Prices:** $85 to $300; some to $2,500. **Remarks:** Full-time maker; first knife sold in 1979. **Mark:** Name, city and state

STERLING LOCKETT, 527 E. Amherst Dr., Burbank, CA 91504/818-846-5799
Specialties: Customer designs in working straight and folding knives. **Patterns:** Hunters and fighters. **Technical:** Grinds. **Prices:** Moderate. **Remarks:** Spare-time maker. **Mark:** Name, city with hearts

WOLFGANG LOERCHNER, P.O. Box 255, Bayfield, Ont. N0M 1G0, CANADA/519-565-2196
Specialties: Straight traditional knives, some fancy. **Patterns:** Bowies, swords, hunters, bird knives and miniatures; folding lockers and interframes. **Technical:** Grinds D2, 440C, and 154CM; all knives hand-filed and flat ground. **Prices:** $150 to $600; some to $3,000. **Remarks:** Part-time maker; first knife sold in 1983. **Mark:** WOLFE

BOB LOFLIN, 404 Burns Lane, Seymour, TN 37865/615-579-5378
Specialties: Fancy working knives in his own designs. **Patterns:** Hunters, fighters and camp knives; locking folders. **Technical:** Grinds D2, 440C and ATS34. **Prices:** $75 to $250; some to $700. **Remarks:** Part-time maker; first knife sold in 1983. **Mark:** Name, city and state

LONESOME PINE (See Larry W. Harley)

DAVE LONGWORTH, 151 McMurchy, Bethel, OH 45106/513-734-7719
Specialties: High-tech working knives in clean designs. **Patterns:** Folding lockers, interframes and straight and folding hunters and fighters. **Technical:** Grinds D2, 440C and buys Damascus. **Prices:** $150 to $300; some to $1,000. **Remarks:** Full-time maker; first knife sold in 1980. **Mark:** Longworth

A. C. LOVE, P.O. Box 334, Hearne, TX 77859/409-279-5265
Specialties: Period pieces and working knives. **Patterns:** Hunters, Bowies and camp knives; folding lockers, slip joints and two-blades. **Technical:** Forges mostly 01, 1095; uses 440C. **Prices:** $75 to $250. **Remarks:** Part-time maker; first knife sold in 1978. **Mark:** L or A.C.L.

ED LOVE, USACIL-Europe, APO NY, 09757-5272/06171-22820, Oberursel, W. Germany
Specialties: Fancy working knives in standard patterns. **Patterns:** Hunters, Bowies and fish knives. **Technical:** Grinds 440C, 154CM and ATS34. **Prices:** $75 to $140; some to $250. **Remarks:** Part-time maker; first knife sold in 1980. **Mark:** Name in oval logo

R.W. LOVELESS, P.O. Box 7836, Arlington Sta., Riverside, CA 92503/714-689-7800
Specialties: Master designer of working knives, fighters and hunters. **Patterns:** Hunters, fighters and boots in the contemporary line he originated. **Technical:** Grinds 154CM and ATS34. **Prices:** $500 to $1,850; some to $3,000. **Remarks:** Full-time maker; still working on orders. **Mark:** Name in logo

SCHUYLER LOVESTRAND, 325 Rolfe Dr., Apopka, FL 32703/305-886-0494
Specialties: Fancy working straight knives; welcomes designs from customers. **Patterns:** Hunters, fighters, Bowies and fish knives. **Technical:** Grinds 440C, ATS34 and commercial Damascus. **Prices:** $100 to $300; some to $450. **Remarks:** Part-time maker; first knife sold in 1982. **Mark:** LOVESTRAND

MIKE LOVETT, 3219E Rancier, Killeen, TX 76541/817-690-1122
Specialties: Working straight and folding knives. **Patterns:** Bowies, fighters, hunters; makes front release locking folders. **Technical:** Grinds D2 to mirror finish. **Prices:** $75 to $400. **Remarks:** Full-time maker; sold first knife in 1975. **Mark:** A chess knight with name

BILL LUCKETT, 10 Amantes Lane, Weatherford, TX 76086/817-599-4629
Specialties: Uniquely patterned robust straight knives. **Patterns:** Fighters, Bowies and tantos; making hunters now. **Technical:** Grinds 440C, 154CM and commercial Damascus; heavy knives, deep grinding, attention-getting work. **Prices:** $350 to $750; some to $2,000. **Remarks:** Part-time maker; first knife sold in 1975. **Mark:** Last name over Bowie logo

ROBERT W. LUM, 901 Travis Ave., Eugene, OR 97404/503-688-2737
Specialties: High art working knives of his own design. **Patterns:** Hunters, fighters and tantos. **Technical:** Grinds 440C, 154CM and ATS34; plans to forge soon. **Prices:** $175 to $500; some to $800. **Remarks:** Full-time maker; first knife sold in 1976. **Mark:** Chop with Lum underneath

ROBERT LUTES, 24878 U.S.6 (R.R. 1), Nappanee, IN 46550/219-773-4773
Specialties: Straight working knives—his design and standard patterns. **Patterns:** Hunters, fighters, boots and axes. **Technical:** Grinds 440C. **Prices:** $50 to $300; some to $800. **Remarks:** Part-time maker; first knife sold in 1980. Offers knives with stone handles. **Mark:** Lutes

ERNEST L. LYLE, III, 4501 Meadowbrook Ave., Orlando, FL 32808/305-299-7227
Specialties: Fancy period pieces in standard patterns. **Patterns:** Arabian/Persian influenced fighters, Bowies and swords. Offers minis and miniatures, too. **Technical:** Grinds D2, 440C and 154CM. **Prices:** $110 to $500; some to $1,400. **Remarks:** Part-time maker; first knife sold in 1972. **Mark:** LYLE

MW KNIVES (See Mark Wahlster)

M. W. KNIVES (See Mike Wesolowski)

MIKE MACRI, Box 222, Churchill, MB R0B 0E0, CANADA/204-675-2195
Specialties: Straight working knives in traditional patterns. **Patterns:** Arctic survival knives, tantos, Bowies, camp knives and locking folders. **Technical:** Grinds 440C, ATS34 and bought Damascus. Full-tapered tangs and hollow grinds. **Prices:** $100 to $500; some to $2,000. **Remarks:** Full-time maker; first knife sold in 1982. **Mark:** MACRI

J. M. "MICKEY" MADDOX, 63 Spring Circle, Ringgold, GA 30736/404-935-5082
Specialties: Working knives and traditional styles—all folders. **Patterns:** Lockers, slip joints in fighter, hunter and working shapes. **Technical:** Grinds D2, 440C and 154CM; prefers natural handle materials; engraves some. **Prices:** $100 to $500; some $1,000. **Remarks:** Part-time maker; first knife sold in 1976. **Mark:** Maddox

MADRONA KNIVES (See Adrienne Rice)

JACK MADSEN, 3311 Northwest Dr., Wichita Falls, TX 76305/817-322-4112
Specialties: Working straight knives in traditional patterns. **Patterns:** Bowies, hunters, swords, tomahawks and heavy-duty camp knives. Makes *hirschfanger* pattern. **Technical:** Forges W2, 01 and his own Damascus. **Prices:** $85 to $350; some to $1,000. **Remarks:** Full-time maker; first knife sold in 1975. **Mark:** Name and city

PETER A. MAESTRI, Rt. 1, Box 111, Spring Green, WI 53588/608-546-4481
Specialties: Straight working knives in traditional styles. **Patterns:** Camping and fishing knives, utility green-river styled. **Technical:** Grinds 440C, 154CM and 440A; professional cutler service to professional cutters. **Prices:** $5 to $25; some $150. **Remarks:** Full-time maker; first knife sold in 1981. **Mark:** CARISOLO or signature

JEFFREY G. MALITZKE, 4804 Lovers Lane, Wichita Falls, TX 76310/817-692-2604
Specialties: Straight knives. **Patterns:** Standard and traditional. **Technical:** Forges his own Damascus in precise patterns. **Mark:** Name

KENNETH MANEKER, R.R. 2, Galiano Island, B.C. V0N 1P0, CANADA/604-539-2084
Specialties: Period pieces and straight working knives. **Patterns:** Camp knives and hunters; French chef knives. **Technical:** Grinds 440C, 154CM and Vascowear. **Prices:** $50 to $200; some to $300. **Remarks:** Part-time maker; first knife sold in 1981. Water Mountain Knives label. **Mark:** Japanese Kanji, KM connected plus glyph

DAN MARAGNI, R.D. 1, Box 106, Georgetown, NY 13072/315-662-7490
Specialties: Heavy-duty working knives; some are investor class. **Patterns:** Hunters, fighters and camp knives; some Scottish types. **Technical:** Forges W2 and his own Damascus; gives toughness and edge holding a high priority. **Prices:** $125 to $500; some to $1,000. **Remarks:** Full-time maker; ABS Master; first knife sold in 1975. **Mark:** Celtic DM in circle

TOM MARINGER, 2306 S. Powell St., Springdale, AR 72764/501-751-9220
Specialties: High-tech and fantasy straight knives to order. Investor class work. **Patterns:** Swords, axes, daggers; state-of-the-art fighters; wire wrapped handles; Kydex sheaths. **Technical:** Grinds 01, D2 and 154CM; forges some. **Prices:** $350 to $3,000; some to $10,000. **Remarks:** Full-time maker; first knife sold 1975. **Mark:** Full name, serial number and year

CHRIS MARKS, Rt. 2 Box 879-R, Breaux Bridge, LA 70517/318-332-3930
Specialties: Traditional working knives; some period pieces. **Patterns:** Full range of straight knives, all the way to tomahawks. **Technical:** Forges W2, 1095 and his own Damascus. **Prices:** $165 to $400; some to $1,500. **Remarks:** Full-time maker; sold first knife in 1980. **Mark:** Name in anvil logo

GLENN MARSHALL, P.O. Box 1099 (305 Hofmann St.), Mason, TX 76856/915-347-6207
Specialties: Period pieces and working knives to order. **Patterns:** Straight and folding hunters, fighters and camp knives. **Technical:** Grinds and forges; uses 01, D2 and 440C. **Prices:** $90 to $150; some to $450. **Remarks:** Full-time maker; first knife sold in 1932. **Mark:** G. MARSHALL, city and state with anvil logo

PETER MARZITELLI, 14143 110A Ave., Surrey, BC V3R 2B2, CANADA/604-581-6759
Specialties: Straight working knives in traditional patterns. **Patterns:** Hunters, tantos, camp, kitchen and fish knives. **Technical:** Grinds 154CM. **Prices:** $100 to $350. **Remarks:** Part-time maker; first knife sold in 1984. **Mark:** Circular logo reads "Marz"

MASA.T (See Masao Takahashi)

BILL MASON, 1114 St. Louis, #33, Excelsior Springs, MO 64024/816-637-7335
Specialties: Combat knives; some folders. **Patterns:** Designs fighters to suit techniques in book Cold Steel. **Technical:** Grinds 01, 440C and ATS34. **Prices:** $115 to $250; some to $350. **Remarks:** Spare-time maker; first knife sold in 1979. **Mark:** BM connected

MAX'S GUNSHOP (See Max Mitchell)

LYNN MAXFIELD, 382 Colonial Ave., Layton, UT 84041/801-544-4176
Specialties: Working knives, some fancy. **Patterns:** Hunters, survival and fish knives; some folding lockers. **Technical:** Grinds D2, 440C and 154CM. **Prices:** $90 to $250; some to $600. **Remarks:** Full-time maker; first knife sold in 1979. **Mark:** Name, city and state

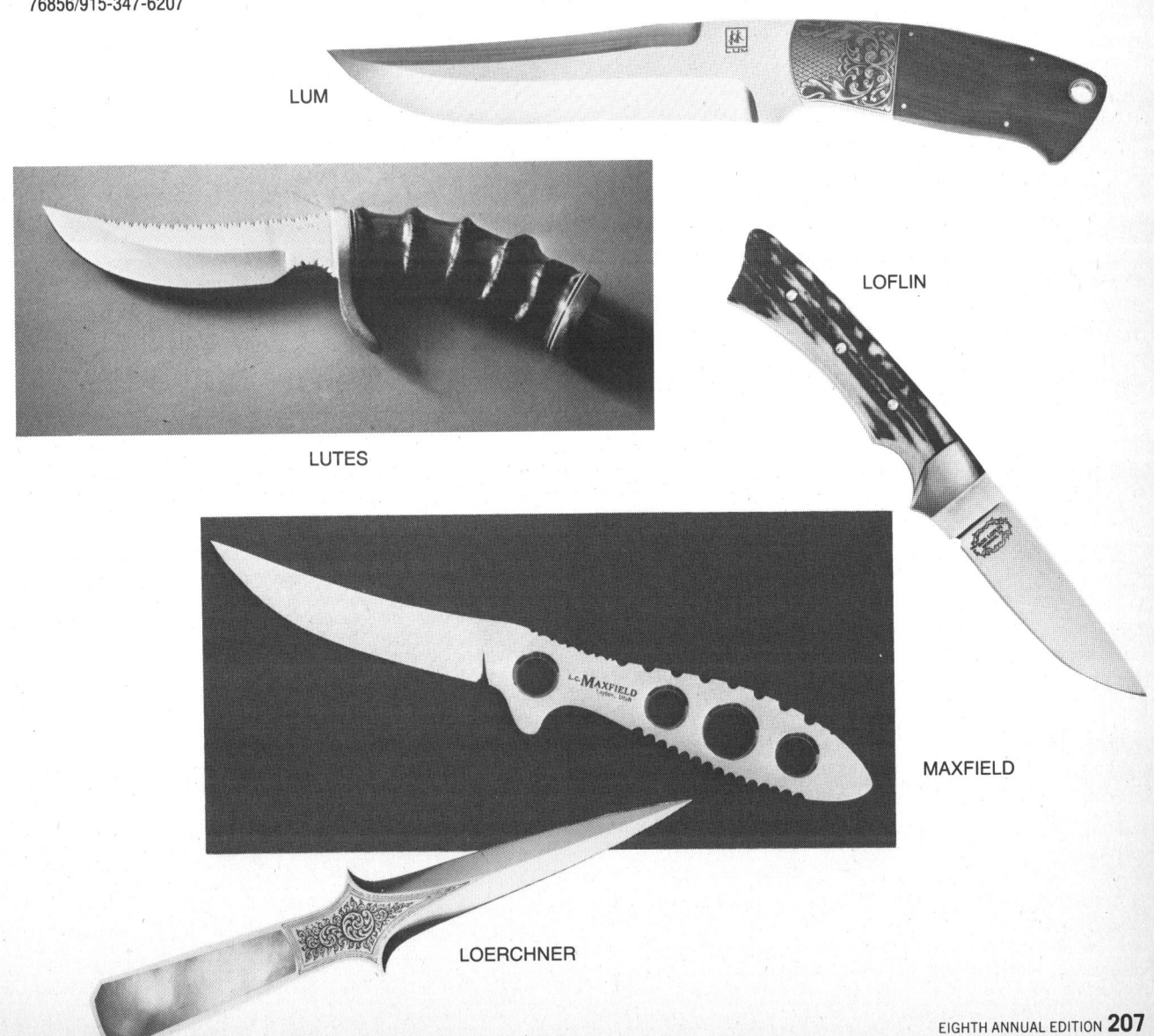

LUM

LOFLIN

LUTES

MAXFIELD

LOERCHNER

directory/custom knifemakers

JAMES E. MAY, Rt. 2, Box 191, Auxvasse, MO 65231/315-386-2910
Specialties: Working straight knives in his own designs. **Patterns:** Hunters, Bowies, fighters, boots. **Technical:** Grinds D2 and 440C. **Prices:** $45 to $250; some to $350. **Remarks:** Spare-time maker; first knife sold in 1978. **Mark:** J in pentagon

LARRY JOE MAYNARD, Box 85, Helen, WV 25853/304-774-0134
Specialties: Fancy and fantasy straight knives. **Patterns:** Big knives; makes a Bowie with full false edge. **Technical:** Grinds standard steels. **Prices:** $350 to $500; some to $1,000. **Remarks:** Full-time maker; sold first knife in 1986. **Mark:** State and knife logo

TOM MAYO, JR., 67-177 Kanoulu St., Waialua, HI 96791/808-637-6560
Specialties: Straight working knives. **Patterns:** Hunters, fighters, boots, locking folders and miniatures. **Technical:** Grinds D2, 440C and ATS34. **Prices:** $125 to $250; some to $500. **Remarks:** Part-time maker; first knife sold in 1983. **Mark:** Volcano logo with name and state

OSCAR L. MAYVILLE, 5660 Cooper Rd., Indianapolis, IN 46208/317-298-4912
Specialties: Period pieces and straight working knives. **Patterns:** Kitchen cutlery, Bowies, camp knives and hunters. **Technical:** Grinds A2, O1, and 440C. **Prices:** $50 to $350; some to $500. **Remarks:** Part-time maker; first knife sold in 1984. **Mark:** Initials in knife logo

HARVEY McBURNETTE, P.O. Box 227, Eagle Nest, NM 87718/505-377-6254
Specialties: Fancy working folders; some in customer designs. **Patterns:** Front-locking folders; traditional straight knives. **Technical:** Grinds D2, 440C and 154CM; engraves his own. **Prices:** $200 to $400; some to $1,200. **Remarks:** Full-time maker; first knife sold in 1972. **Mark:** McBURNETTE, city and state

JOHN McCARLEY, 1710 Keysville Rd. So., Keymar, MD 21757/301-775-2464
Specialties: Period pieces and working straight knives. **Patterns:** Hunters, Bowies, camp knives, miniatures; also throwing knives. **Technical:** Forges W2, O1, and his own Damascus. **Prices:** $150 to $300; some to $1,000. **Remarks:** Part-time maker; first knife sold in 1977. **Mark:** J.M. in script

HARRY McCARTY, 1121 Brough Ave., Hamilton, OH 45015/513-868-2290
Specialties: Period pieces and straight working knives. **Patterns:** Bowies, camp knives, daggers and buckskinner designs. **Technical:** Grinds and forges; uses O1 and D2. **Prices:** $75 to $350; some to $600. **Remarks:** Part-time maker; first knife sold in 1977. **Mark:** Name or initials

ZOLLAN McCARTY, 101½ Ave. E, Thomaston, GA 30286/404-647-6869
Specialties: Period pieces and working knives. **Patterns:** Wide variety of straight and folding knives; Scagel replicas; gut hook hatchets. **Technical:** Forges and grinds; uses 440C, 154CM and ATS34. **Prices:** $110 to $600. **Remarks:** Full-time maker; first knife sold in 1971. **Mark:** Z. McCARTY

CHARLES R. McCONNELL, 158 Genteel Ridge, Wellsburg, WV 26070/304-737-2015
Specialties: Straight working knives. **Patterns:** Hunters, Bowies, daggers, minis and push knives. **Technical:** Grinds 440C and 154CM; likes full tangs. **Prices:** $65 to $325; some to $800. **Remarks:** Part-time maker; first knife sold in 1977. **Mark:** Name

LOYD A. McCONNELL, JR., P.O. Box 7162, Odessa, TX 79760/915-366-9674
Specialties: Working straight and folding knives; some fancy. **Patterns:** Hunters, boots, Bowies, folding lockers and slip joints. Makes black-finish specials. **Technical:** Grinds A2, 154CM and commercial Damascus. **Prices:** $125 to $2,500; some to $4,000. **Remarks:** Full-time maker; first knife sold in 1978. **Mark:** Name, city and state in cactus logo

V. J. McCRACKIN and SON, 3720 Hess Rd., House Springs, MO 63051/314-376-4242
Specialties: Straight working knives in traditional patterns. **Patterns:** Hunters, Bowies, camp knives and tomahawks. **Technical:** Forges L6, 5160, and his own Damascus. **Prices:** $50 to $150; some $400. **Remarks:** Part-time maker; first knife sold in 1983. Son Kevin helps make the knives. **Mark:** McCRACKIN

LARRY E. McCULLOUGH, Route 4, Box 556, Mocksville, NC 27028/704-634-5632
Specialties: Straight working knives. **Patterns:** Hunters, boots, Bowies and push knives. **Technical:** Grinds D2, 440C and 154CM; scrims. **Prices:** $60 to $250; some to $500. **Remarks:** Spare-time maker; first knife sold in 1978. **Mark:** McCullough

DAVE McDEARMONT, 1618 Parkside Trail, Lewisville, TX 75067/214-436-4335
Specialties: High-tech working knives. **Patterns:** Hunters, buckskinners, fighters and boots. **Technical:** Grinds 440C; full tangs, mirror finishes. **Prices:** $125 to $300; some to $800. **Remarks:** Part-time maker; first knife sold in 1981. **Mark:** Name

KEN McFALL, P.O. Box 458, Lakeside, AZ 85929/602-537-2026
Specialties: Fancy working straight knives. **Patterns:** Daggers, boots, tantos, Bowies; some miniatures. **Technical:** Grinds D2, 154CM, and ATS34; does gold and silver inlay. **Prices:** $125 to $500; some $800. **Remarks:** Part-time maker; first knife sold in 1984. **Mark:** Name, city, and state

JOHN McGILL, P.O. Box 302, Blairsville, GA 30512/404-745-4686
Specialties: Working knives. **Patterns:** Traditional patterns; likes camp knives. **Technical:** Forges L6 and 9260; makes Damascus. **Prices:** $50 to $250; some to $500. **Remarks:** Full-time maker; first knife sold in 1982. **Mark:** XYLO

JIM McGOVERN, 31 Scenic Dr., Oak Ridge, NJ 07438/201-697-4558
Specialties: Working straight knives. **Patterns:** Hunters and boots. **Technical:** Grinds 440C, ATS34, in full tapered tang and hollow grind. **Prices:** Moderate. **Remarks:** Part-time maker; sold first knife in 1985. **Mark:** Name

TOMMY McKISSACK II, P.O. Box 991, Sonora, TX 76950/915-387-3253
Specialties: Working knives, some fancy, most heavy-duty. **Patterns:** CATTLE BARON LEATHER knives to Jerry Ardolino designs. **Technical:** Grinds D2, 154CM, ATS34, 440C; is commercial heat-treater. **Prices:** $65 to $700; some to $2,100. **Remarks:** Full-time maker; first knife sold in 1980. **Mark:** Name, town and state

THOMAS McLANE, 7 Tucson Terrace, Tucson, AZ 83745/602-623-6895
Specialties: Period pieces and display-class working knives. **Patterns:** Traditional tantos, daggers, swords and razors; folding lockers, interframes, two-blades. **Technical:** Forges O1, 1095 and his own Damascus. Uses old metalworking techniques, especially Japanese. **Prices:** $300 to $2,000; some to $8,000. **Remarks:** Full-time maker; first knife sold in 1979. **Mark:** Initials in a logo

JAMES McLEOD, 941 Thermalito Ave., Oroville, CA 95965/916-533-3539
Specialties: Scottish period pieces and working knives. **Patterns:** Dirks and sgian dubhs; buckskinners, boots and daggers. **Technical:** Grinds, and files, A2, 154CM, ATS34; hand-sanded finishes; full or tapered tangs. **Prices:** $150 to $450; some to $1,200. **Remarks:** Spare-time maker; first knife sold in 1983; a McLeod clansman, their motto "HOLD FAST." **Mark:** Name and clan badge

SEAN McWILLIAMS, 4334 C.R. 509, Bayfield, CO 81122/303-884-9854
Specialties: Period pieces and working knives. **Patterns:** Buckskinners blades, swords, Bowies and daggers; folding lockers. **Technical:** Forges only; uses CPM-T-440V, O1, 440C, ATS34 and his own Damascus; all knives individually tempered. **Prices:** $180 to $500; some to $1,500. **Remarks:** Full-time maker; first knife sold in 1979. **Mark:** Stylized bear paw

DARYL MEIER
R.R. 4
Carbondale, IL 62901/618-549-3234
Specialties: Damascus steel; buckskinner blades; swords. **Patterns:** Provides blades in collaboration; makes bars and forged blades for sale; makes production and high art tomahawks. **Technical:** Forges his own Damascus

W1 and A203E; W1 and Nickel 200. **Prices:** $250 to $450; some to $6,000. **Remarks:** Full-time smith and researcher since 1974; first knife sold in 1974. **Mark:** Name or circle/arrow symbol or SHAWNEE

HARRY E. MENDENHALL, 1848 Everglades Dr., Milpitas, CA 95035/408-263-0677
Specialties: Working straight knives. **Patterns:** Hunters, boots, buckskinners, and push knives. **Technical:** Grinds 440C, 154CM, and ATS34; engraving and scrimshaw available. **Prices:** $65 to $150; some $1,000. **Remarks:** Full-time maker; first knife sold in 1970. Business name is Thunderbird. **Mark:** Thunderbird with logo, or signature

TED MERCHANT, 7 Old Garrett Ct., White Hall, MD 21161/301-343-0380
Specialties: Working knives in traditional and period styles. **Patterns:** Makes using knives for hunters; some Bowies and camp knives. **Technical:** Forges W2 and 5160. **Prices:** $150 to $450; some to $600. **Remarks:** Full-time maker; sold first knife in 1985. **Mark:** Name

ROBERT L. MERZ III, 20219 Prince Creek Dr., Katy, TX 77450/713-492-7337
Specialties: Straight working knives, some fancy. **Patterns:** Hunters, skinners, fighters, folders and camp knives. Own designs. **Technical:** Grinds 440C, D2, O1, ATS34, and commercial Damascus. **Prices:** $70 to $200; some to $550. **Remarks:** Part-time maker; sold first knife in 1974. **Mark:** MERZ and serial number

CHRIS MILLER, JR., 3959 U.S. 27 South, Sebring, FL 33870/813-382-4402
Specialties: Fancy working straight knives. **Patterns:** Swords and large knives of all kinds, and a variety of working knives. **Technical:** Grinds D2, 440C, 154CM. **Prices:** $100 to $500. **Remarks:** Full-time maker; first knife sold in 1976. **Mark:** M on the blade

HANFORD J. MILLER, 5105 S. LeMaster Rd., Evergreen CO 80439/303-674-5263
Specialties: Period pieces and working knives in Moran style. **Patterns:** Bowies, fighters, camp knives and other large straight knives. **Technical:** Forges W2, 1095, 5160 and his own Damascus; differential tempers; wire inlay. **Prices:** $250 to $750; some to $1,500. **Remarks:** Part-time maker; first knife sold in 1968. **Mark:** Initials; name within Bowie logo

JAMES P. MILLER, 9024 Goeller Rd., R.R. 2, Fairbank, IA 50629/319-635-2294
Specialties: Period pieces and working knives. **Patterns:** Hunters, Bowies, camp knives and folding lockers. **Technical:** Forges and grinds; uses 1095, 440C, 5160 and his own Damascus. **Prices:** $75 to $350; some to $1,000. **Remarks:** Part-time maker; first knife sold in 1970. **Mark:** J. P. MILLER

MAYO — MENDENHALL — McGOVERN — McCONNELL — J.P. MILLER — McFALL

directory/custom knifemakers

RONALD T. MILLER, 12922 127th Ave. N., Largo, FL 33544/813-595-0378 (after 5 PM)
Specialties: Straight working knives in traditional patterns. **Patterns:** Combat and camp knives, tantos, and kitchen cutlery; locking folders and butterflies. **Technical:** Grinds D2, 440C and ATS34; offers brass inlays and scrimshaw. **Prices:** $35 to $125; some to $250. **Remarks:** Part-time maker; first knife sold in 1984. **Mark:** Name, city and state in palm tree logo

TED MILLER, P.O. Box 6328, Santa Fe, NM 87502/505-984-0338
Specialties: Carved antler display knives. **Patterns:** Hunters, swords, tomahawks and miniatures of his own designs. **Technical:** Grinds 440C. **Prices:** $110 to $350; some average $900. **Remarks:** Full-time maker; first knife sold in 1971. **Mark:** Initials and serial number

TERRY MILLER, 450 S. 1st, Seward, NE 68434/402-643-4726
Specialties: Working knives. **Patterns:** Hunters, tomahawks, fighters and Bowies; also makes folding lockers, slip joints and two-blades. **Technical:** Grinds 440C. **Prices:** $80 to $145; some $500. **Remarks:** Part-time maker; first knife sold in 1978. **Mark:** Stylized name in knife logo

ANDY MILLS, 316 W. Morse, Fredericksburg, TX 78624/512-997-8167
Specialties: Working straight and folding knives. **Patterns:** Hunter patterns, including folders. **Technical:** Grinds 440C, D2, A6. Does all—leatherwork, fabrication, heat treating. **Prices:** Moderate. **Remarks:** A Jim Barbee associate; full-time since 1984; sold first knife in 1980. **Mark:** Name

LOUIS G. MILLS (YASUTOMO), 3600 Rentz Rd., Ann Arbor, MI 48103/313-475-9796
Specialties: High art period pieces in Japanese mode. **Patterns:** Traditional tantos, daggers and swords. **Technical:** Makes own steel from iron; his own Damascus in traditional Japanese techniques. **Prices:** $900 to $2,000; some to $8,000. **Remarks:** Spare-time maker in partnership with Jim Kelso. **Mark:** Yasutomo in Japanese Kanji

JIM MINNICK, 144 N. 7th St., Middletown, IN 47356/317-354-4108
Specialties: Straight and folding knives in his own designs. **Patterns:** Daggers, hunters, folders and boots. **Technical:** Grinds stainless steels. Wife Joyce offers scrimshaw. **Prices:** Moderate. **Remarks:** Part-time maker. **Mark:** Name

JAMES A. MITCHELL, 1355 Autumnridge Dr., Columbus, GA 31904/404-322-8511
Specialties: Fancy working knives. Sells knives in sets. **Patterns:** Hunters, fighters, Bowies and folding lockers. **Technical:** Grinds D2, 440C and commercial Damascus. **Prices:** $100 to $400; some to $900. **Remarks:** Part-time maker; first knife sold in 1976. **Mark:** Signature and city

MAX and DEAN MITCHELL, 997 V.F.W. Road, Leesville, LA 71446/318-239-6416
Specialties: Period pieces and working knives. **Patterns:** Hunters, axes, tomahawks, buckskinners; makes hatchet-knife sets. **Technical:** Grinds 01, D2 and 440C. **Prices:** $120 to $200; some to $1,000. **Remarks:** Part-time makers; first knife sold in 1976. **Mark:** Max or Dean in oval logo

HARALD MOELLER, RR 3, Thornton, Ontario L0L 2N0, CANADA/705-424-6088
Specialties: Classy working straight knives. **Patterns:** Viper throwing knives. **Technical:** Grinds; mirror and sandblasted finishes in combination. **Prices:** Moderate. **Mark:** Name in logo

DELMAR R. MONTEGNA, P.O. Box 6261, Sheridan, WY 82801/307-672-2816
Specialties: Fancy working knives. **Patterns:** Hunters, boots and Bowies, as well as folding lockers. **Technical:** Grinds D2, 440C and 154CM; some knives embellished. **Prices:** $65 to $165. **Remarks:** Full-time maker. **Mark:** DELMAR Knives

CLAUDE MONTJOY, R.R. 2, Box 470C, Clinton, SC 29325/803-697-6160
Specialties: Fancy working knives. **Patterns:** Hunters, boots, fighters, folding lockers, slip joints and interframes. **Technical:** Grinds 440C, 154CM and ATS34; does filework. **Prices:** $75 to $125; some to $1,000. **Remarks:** Part-time maker; first knife sold in 1982. **Mark:** Montjoy

KEITH MOORBY, 63 Cawdor Rd., Sheffield, South Yorkshire S22EP, ENGLAND/0742-651400
Specialties: Working knives, many in Sheffield style. **Patterns:** Lockback folders, boots and daggers. **Technical:** Grinds and forges; prefers Damascus, SF67, D2 and 01; mirror finishes, except Damascus. **Mark:** Full name and address

JAMES B. MOORE, 1707 N. Gillis, Ft. Stockton, TX 79735/915-336-2113
Specialties: Straight and folding working knives. **Patterns:** Hunters, Bowies, tomahawks, folding lockers and camp knives. **Technical:** Grinds D2, 440C and 154CM. **Prices:** $85 to $135; some to $500. **Remarks:** Full-time maker; first knife sold in 1977. **Mark:** Name, town and state

TOM W. MOORE, JR., Rt. 7, Reece Church Rd., Columbia, TN 38401/615-381-2377
Specialties: Traditional straight working knives—his design or yours. **Patterns:** Bowies, tantos, hunters and fighters. **Technical:** Grinds 01, D2, and 440C. **Prices:** $50 to $320; some to $400. **Remarks:** Part-time maker; first knife sold in 1984. **Mark:** Rabbit Hill Custom Knives with signature

WM. F. MORAN, JR., P.O. Box 68, Braddock Heights, MD 21714/301-371-7543
Specialties: High art working knives of his own very well-known design. **Patterns:** Fighters, camp knives, Bowies, daggers, axes, tomahawks, push knives and miniatures. **Technical:** Forges W2, 5160 and his own Damascus; puts silver wire inlay on most handles; uses natural handle materials exclusively. **Prices:** $400 to $7,500; some to $9,000. **Remarks:** Full-time maker. ABS Master. **Mark:** W.F. MORAN M.S.

EMIL MORGAN, 2690 Calle Limonero, Thousand Oaks, CA 91360/805-492-6830
Specialties: Straight and folding working knives in his design or customers'. **Patterns:** Bowies, skinners, locking folders and fish knives. **Technical:** Forges and grinds L6, 1095 and 440C; makes horizontal sheaths. **Prices:** $90 to $225; some $500. **Remarks:** Part-time maker; first knife sold in 1980. **Mark:** Name and town

JEFF MORGAN, 9200 Arnaz Way, Santee, CA 92071/619-448-8430
Specialties: Fancy working straight knives. **Patterns:** Hunters, fighters, boots, miniatures and push knives. **Technical:** Grinds D2, 440C and 154CM; likes exotic handles. **Prices:** $90 to $140; some to $500. **Remarks:** Full-time maker; first knife sold in 1977. **Mark:** JM connected

JUSTIN MORGAN, 2690 Calle Limonero, Thousand Oaks, CA 91360/805-492-6830
Specialties: Working straight knives. **Patterns:** Hunters, boots and utility knives. **Technical:** Grinds 440C, 154CM and ATS34; mirror finishes. **Prices:** $85 to $200; some to $250. **Remarks:** Spare-time maker; first knife sold in 1983. **Mark:** Name in script

TOM MORGAN, 14689 Ellett Rd., Beloit, OH 44609/216-537-2023
Specialties: Period pieces and straight working knives. **Patterns:** Hunters, boots, daggers, presentation tomahawks. **Technical:** Grinds 01, 440C and 154CM. **Prices:** $45 to $125; some to $225. **Remarks:** Part-time maker; first knife sold in 1977. **Mark:** Morgan, date and steel

TOM MORLAN, 30635 S. Palm, Hemet, CA 92343/714-658-4113
Specialties: Fancy working knives in customer designs. **Patterns:** Bowies, tantos, fish knives, and locking folders. **Technical:** Grinds 440C, 154CM and ATS34. **Prices:** $75 to $250; some to $3,000. **Remarks:** Full-time maker; first knife sold in 1979. **Mark:** TM connected

C.H. MORRIS, 828 Meadow Dr., Atmore, AL 36502/205-368-2089
Specialties: Period pieces and working straight knives; some folders. **Patterns:** Hunters, fighters, Bowies and folding lockers. **Technical:** Grinds 440C. **Prices:** $50 to $160; some to $350. **Remarks:** Spare-time maker; first knife sold in 1973. **Mark:** C.H. Morris

MORSETH SPORTS EQUIP. CO. (See A.G. Russell)

GARY E. MOSSER, 15605 - 204th Ave. S.E., Renton, WA 98056/206-226-8949
Specialties: Working straight knives, some fancy. **Patterns:** Hunter types; some Bowies, camp knives, hatchets. **Technical:** Grinds stainless alloy steels; likes leather and concave grind. **Prices:** $75 to $150; some $250 and up. **Remarks:** Full-time maker; sold first knife in 1976. **Mark:** Name

MOUNTAIN FORGE (See Bill Buchman)

RUSS MOYER, 1622 Rich St., Havre, MT 59501/406-265-5116
Specialties: Working knives to order. **Patterns:** Hunters, Bowies, survival knives; folding lockers, too. **Technical:** Forges W2, 01 and D2. **Prices:** $100 to $250. **Remarks:** Part-time maker; first knife sold in 1976. **Mark:** RAM in logo

STEVE MULLIN, 500 W. Center Valley Rd., Sandpoint, ID 83864/208-263-7492
Specialties: Contemporary and period working knives. **Patterns:** Full range of folders, hunters, Bowies. Some buckskinner designs. **Technical:** Grinds and forges; uses 01, D2, 154CM and his own Damascus. **Prices:** $75 to $500; some to $1,200. **Remarks:** Full-time maker; first knife sold in 1975. **Mark:** Full name, city and state

PAUL MUNRO, RFD 1, Box 32, Franklin, ME 04634
Specialties: Working straight knives; some fancy pieces. **Patterns:** Standard hunters, fighters and daggers. **Technical:** Grinds 01, L6 and ATS34; offers Maine deer antler for handles. **Prices:** $70 to $125; some to $250. **Remarks:** Part-time maker; first knife sold in 1980. **Mark:** Munro clan badge

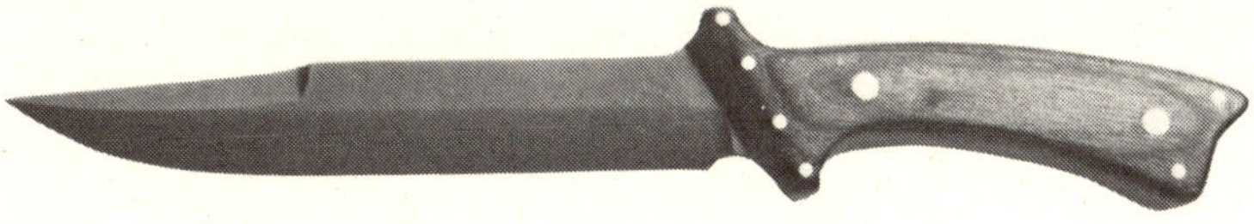

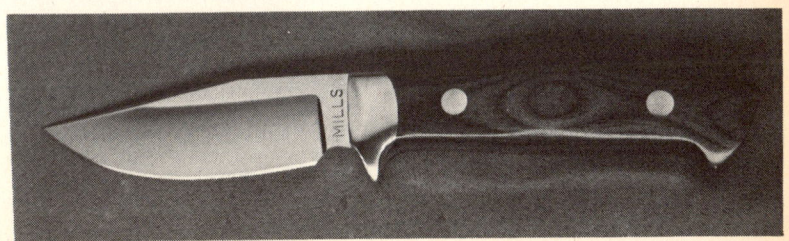

R. MILLER

MORLAN

MONTJOY

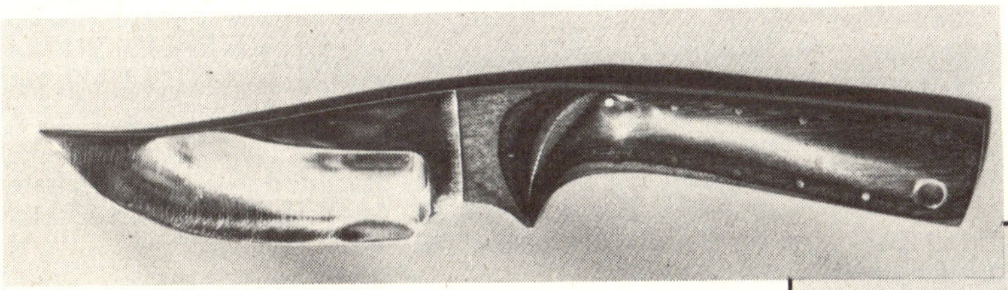

M. MITCHELL

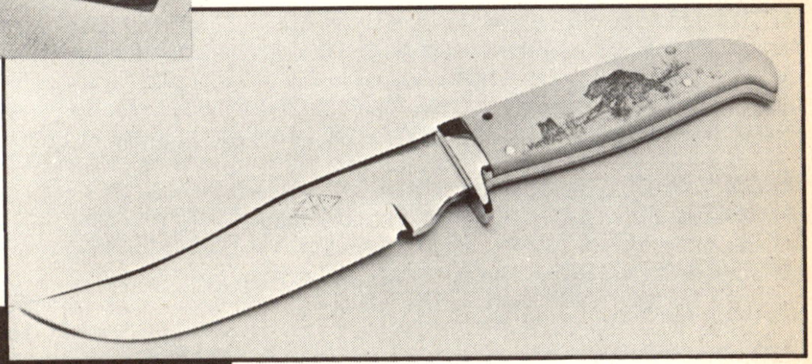

MOSSER

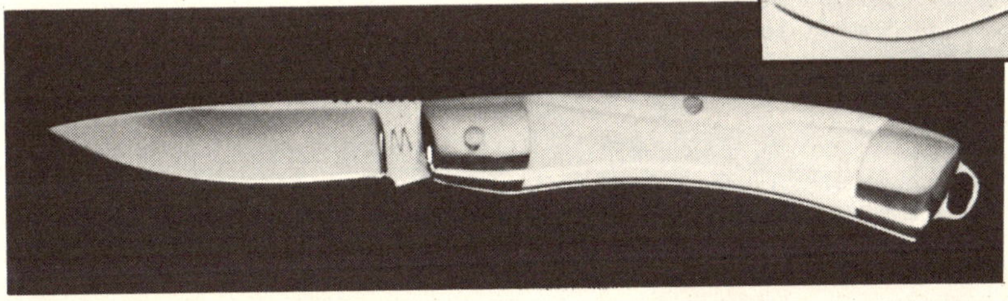

(Above and right) A. MILLS

directory/custom knifemakers

DAVE MURPHY, P.O. Box 256, Gresham, OR 97030/503-665-8634
Specialties: Fancy working knives in his own designs. **Patterns:** Hunters, fighters, boots. **Technical:** Grinds F-8 Silvanite and 154CM; likes narrow tangs, composite handles. **Prices:** $95 to $450; some to $3,900. **Remarks:** Full-time maker; first knife sold in 1940. **Mark:** Name, city and state

MEL MYERS, 611 Elmwood Drive, Spencer, IA 51301/712-262-3383
Specialties: Working hunters. **Patterns:** Hunters and small utilitarian knives. **Technical:** Uses 440C and no power tools except polisher. **Prices:** $75 to $150. **Remarks:** Spare-time maker; first knife sold in 1982. **Mark:** Signature

PAUL MYERS, 128 12th St., Wood River, IL 62095/618-254-2714
Specialties: Fancy working straight and folding knives. **Patterns:** Full range of folders, straight hunters, Bowies, tie tacks; knife and fork sets. **Technical:** Grinds D2, 440C and 154CM. **Prices:** $100 to $350; some to $3,000. **Remarks:** Full-time maker; first knife sold in 1974. **Mark:** P.M. with setting sun on front; name and number on back

WOODY NAIFEH, Rt. 13, Box 380, Tulsa, OK 74107/918-224-3943
Specialties: Working folding knives of his own design. **Patterns:** Folding patent lockers. **Technical:** Grinds 440C and Uddeholm "AEBL" stainless. **Prices:** $80 to $175. **Remarks:** Part-time maker, first knife sold in 1969. **Mark:** NAIFEH

JERRY C. NEAL, P.O. Box 12458, Winston-Salem, NC 27117/919-723-8747
Specialties: Fancy working straight and folding knives. **Patterns:** From hunters to axes; folding lockers to slip joints, tomahawks to claws, even miniatures. **Technical:** Grinds 01, D2, 440C and 154CM; does some chip finish like Indian Flint knives. **Prices:** $40 to $350; some to $1,500. **Remarks:** Full-time maker; first knife sold in 1970. **Mark:** J. NEAL

BUD NEALY, 822 Thomas St., Stroudsburg, PA 18360/717-421-4040
Specialties: Working knives of his own design. **Patterns:** Hunters, tantos and boots; carving sets. **Technical:** Forges and grinds D2, 440C and 154CM; and buys Damascus; mirror finishes; sharpens knives with "Moran edge." **Prices:** $75 to $300; some to $1,200. **Remarks:** Full-time maker; first knife sold in 1980. **Mark:** Name, city and state

VAUGHN NEELEY (See Timberline Knives)

KEITH A. NELSON, 18D Chughole Ln., Los Lunas, NM 87031/505-869-2228
Specialties: Straight working knives of his own designs. **Patterns:** Hunters, fighters and survival knives; some knives tailored to needs of elite military units. **Technical:** Grinds D2, 440C and 154CM. **Prices:** $125 to $175. **Remarks:** Spare-time maker; first knife sold in 1982. **Mark:** KN or stylized lion

ROGER S. NELSON, Box 294, Central Village, CT 06332/203-774-6749
Specialties: Working knives to order. **Patterns:** Hunters, fighters, camp knives, folding lockers, patent locks, butterflies. **Technical:** Grinds D2, 440C and 154CM. **Prices:** $90 to $140; some to $250. **Remarks:** Spare-time maker; first knife sold in 1975. **Mark:** R. NELSON

CORBIN NEWCOMB, 628 Woodland Ave., Moberly, MO 65270/816-263-4639
Specialties: Period pieces and working straight knives. **Patterns:** Hunters, axes, Bowies, buckskinner blades and boots. **Technical:** Hollow grinds D2, 440C and 154CM; prefers natural handle materials. **Prices:** $85 to $130; some to $350. **Remarks:** Full-time maker; first knife sold in 1982. **Mark:** CORBIN and serial number

R. KENT NICHOLSON, 615 Hollen Rd., Baltimore, MD 21212/301-323-6925
Specialties: Large using knives. **Patterns:** Bowies, camp knives, in the Moran style. **Technical:** Forges W2, 9260, 5160; makes Damascus. **Prices:** $295 to $595; some to $795. **Remarks:** Part-time maker; first knife sold in 1984. **Mark:** Name; Journeyman Smith with ABS

FRANK NIRO, Box 552, Mackenzie, BC V0J 2C0, CANADA/604-997-6975
Specialties: Comfortable working straight knives. **Patterns:** Hunters, Bowies, camp and kitchen knives; some axes. **Technical:** Grinds 01, L6, 440C; likes flat grind. **Prices:** $40 to $135; some to $175. **Remarks:** Part-time maker; first knife sold in 1983. **Mark:** NIRO

MELVIN S. NISHIUCHI, 45-006 Waikalua Rd., Kaneohe, HI 96744/808-235-1105
Specialties: Period pieces and straight working knives. **Patterns:** Chinese and Japanese-style blades, swords, Bowies and pole arms. **Technical:** Grinds and forges 5160, W2, and 440C; edge hardens carbon steels. **Prices:** $75 to $200; some $1,000. **Remarks:** Part-time maker; first knife sold in 1985. **Mark:** O, HAWAII

R.D. and GEORGE NOLEN, Box 2895, Estes Park, CO 80517/303-586-5814
Specialties: Working knives; many display pieces. **Patterns:** Wide variety of straight knives, folding lockers, butterflies and buckles. **Technical:** Grind D2, 440C and 154CM; filework on many knives; exotic handles nearly normal. **Prices:** $100 to $800; some very high. **Remarks:** Full-time makers; first knife sold in 1968. **Mark:** NK in oval logo

DON NORTON, 3206 Aspen Dr., Farmington, NM 87401/505-327-3604
Specialties: Working straight knives. **Patterns:** Hunters, Bowies and fish knives. **Technical:** Grinds D2, 440C and 154CM. **Prices:** $105 to $200; some to $1,000. **Remarks:** Full-time maker; first knife sold in 1980. **Mark:** D. Norton in logo

FRANK NORTON, 3964 Redwood Ct., Pleasanton, CA 94566/415-846-1784
Specialties: Period pieces and straight and folding working knives. **Patterns:** Hunters, fighters, folders, locking folders and push arms. **Technical:** Grinds D2, 440C and ATS34. **Prices:** $80 to $125; some to $350. **Remarks:** Part-time maker; first knife sold in 1979. **Mark:** NORTON, city and state

CHARLES F. OCHS, 124 Emerald Lane, Largo, FL 34641/813-536-3827
Specialties: Period pieces and working knives. **Patterns:** Hunters, fighters, Bowies, buckskinners and razors. **Technical:** Forges 01, 1095, SAE 5160 and his own Damascus; stag handles standard. **Prices:** $100 to $600; some to $1,000. **Remarks:** Full-time maker; first knife sold in 1978. **Mark:** OX Forge; Journeyman Smith with ABS.

KUZAN ODA, P.O. Box 2213, Hailey, ID 83333/208-788-2861
Specialties: High-tech in Japanese fashion; contemporary working knives. **Patterns:** Swords, fighters, hunters, spears and folding lockers. **Technical:** Forges and grinds; uses 154CM and Tamahagane, and his own Damascus; offers traditional and authentic Japanese sword-smithing and polishing. **Prices:** $200 to $600; some to $5,000. **Remarks:** Full-time maker; first knife sold in 1957. Not taking orders. **Mark:** KUZAN, variously

ROBERT G. OGG, Rt. 1, Box 345, Paris, AR 72855/501-963-2767
Specialties: Plain and fancy working knives. **Patterns:** Folding slip joints; daggers and kitchen knives. **Technical:** Grinds 440C, Sandvik 15LM and commercial Damascus. **Prices:** $60 to $85; some to $115. **Remarks:** Spare-time maker; first knife sold in 1964. **Mark:** Name

GORDON O'LEARY, 2566 Hearthside Dr., Ypsilanti, MI 48198/313-484-1230
Specialties: Period pieces and working straight knives. **Patterns:** Hunters, Bowies, boots and minis. **Technical:** Hollow grinds 440C; does full tangs and prefers natural handle materials. **Prices:** $100 to $200; some $300. **Remarks:** Spare-time maker; first knife sold in 1980. **Mark:** O'LEARY in script

MILFORD OLIVER, 3832 W. Desert Park Lane, Phoenix, AZ 85021/602-841-7038
Specialties: High-tech working knives. **Patterns:** Frontlock folders, slip joints, interframes; straight hunters, Bowies and camp knives. **Technical:** Grinds 440C, 154CM and ATS34. **Prices:** $225 to $450; some to $600. **Remarks:** Full-time maker; first knife sold in 1977. **Mark:** M.J. Oliver in logo

WAYNE C. OLSON, 11655 W. 35th Ave., Wheat Ridge, CO 80033/303-420-3415
Specialties: High-tech working knives. **Patterns:** Hunters to folding lockers; some integral designs. **Technical:** Grinds 440C, 154CM and ATS34; hand finish is standard; precision-fits stainless steel fittings—no solder, no nickel silver. **Prices:** $275 to $600; some to $3,000. **Remarks:** Full-time maker; first knife sold in 1979. **Mark:** WAYNE OLSON maker

ONE HANDER (See W.T. Fuller, Jr.)

WARREN OSBORNE, 111 Oak Lawn, Waxahachie, TX 75165/214-937-0899 **Specialties:** Working knives and fancy pieces. **Patterns:** Hunters, fighters, Bowies and folding lockers in traditional styles. **Technical:** Grinds D2, 440C and 154CM; does serrated bolsters. **Prices:** $175 to $285; some to $2,000. **Remarks:** Full-time maker; first knife sold in 1980. **Mark:** OSBORNE in boomerang logo

ANTHONY (Tony) L. OUTLAW, 1131 E. 24th Plaza, Panama City, FL 32405/904-769-7754 **Specialties:** Traditional straight knives in working styles. **Patterns:** Makes tantos, Bowies, camp knives—a full range. **Technical:** Grinds A2, W2, 01, L6, 1095 and stainless steels to mirror finish. **Prices:** $85 to $175; some to $300. **Remarks:** Part-time maker; sold first knife in 1984. **Mark:** OUTLAW

T.R. OVEREYNDER, 1800 S. Davis Dr., Arlington, TX 76013/817-277-4812 **Specialties:** Highly finished working knives. **Patterns:** Fighters, Bowies, daggers, folding lockers, slip joints and interframe folders. **Technical:** Grinds D2, 440C and 154CM. **Prices:** $250 to $550; some to $2,500. **Remarks:** Part-time maker; first knife sold in 1977. **Mark:** TRO KNIVES, city and state

DANNY OWENS, P.O. Box 284, Blacksburg, SC 29702/803-839-2287 **Specialties:** Traditional folders and straight knives, some fancy. **Patterns:** Full-sized and miniatures in hunter patterns. **Technical:** Grinds stainless steels and Damascus bars. **Prices:** $75 to $150; some to $400. **Remarks:** Full-time maker; sold first knife in 1982. **Mark:** DANO

OVEREYNDER

OUTLAW

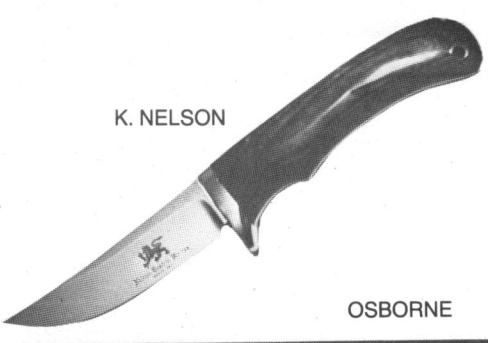

K. NELSON

D. NORTON

OSBORNE

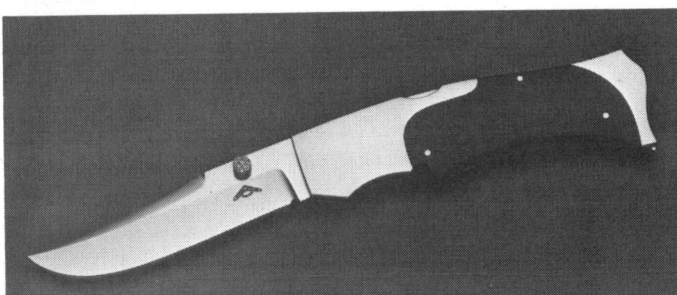

OCHS

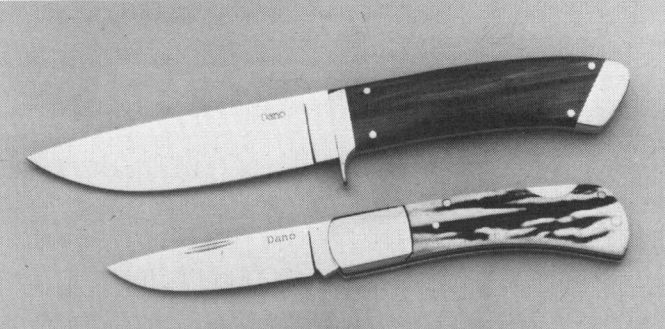

D. OWENS

directory/custom knifemakers

JOHN OWENS, 8755 S.W. 96th St., Miami, FL 33176
Specialties: Working straight knives in contemporary design; some period pieces. **Patterns:** Hunters, Bowies and camp knives. **Technical:** Grinds and forges; uses 440C and 154CM. **Prices:** $125; some to $350. **Remarks:** Spare-time maker. **Mark:** OWENS

OX FORGE (See Charles F. Ochs)

LOWELL R. OYSTER, RFD #1, Box 432, Kenduskeag, ME 04450/207-884-8663
Specialties: Working knives in his design or to customer order. **Patterns:** Hunters, minis, camp and fish knives; folding slip joints. **Technical:** Grinds 01; does own heat-treat. **Prices:** $30 to $100; some to $150. **Remarks:** Full-time maker; first knife sold in 1981. **Mark:** A clamshell

PACK RIVER KNIFE CO. (See Steve Mullin)

LARRY PAGE, 1494 Rolling Rock Rd., Aiken, SC 29801/803-648-0001
Specialties: Period pieces and working knives in his own design. **Patterns:** Hunters, boots, fighters and mini knives. **Technical:** Grinds 154CM and ATS34. **Prices:** $75 to $150; some $250. **Remarks:** Part-time maker; first knife sold in 1983. **Mark:** Name, city, state, in oval

PHILIP R. PANKIEWICZ, RFD #1, Waterman Rd., Lebanon, CT 06249
Specialties: Working straight knives. **Patterns:** Hunters, daggers, minis and fish knives. **Technical:** Grinds D2, 440C and 154CM. **Prices:** $60 to $125; some $250. **Remarks:** Spare-time maker; first knife sold in 1975. **Mark:** P in star

ROBERT "BOB" PAPP, P.O. Box 246, Elyria, OH 44036/216-458-8565
Specialties: High-tech working straight knives; some display knives. **Patterns:** Hunters, fighters, minis and boots; integral designs in all. **Technical:** Grinds D2, 440C and 154CM. **Prices:** $135 to $500; some to $2,500. **Remarks:** Full-time maker; first knife sold in 1964. **Mark:** Full name, city and state

MELVIN M. PARDUE, Rt. 1, Box 130, Repton, AL 36475/205-248-2686
Specialties: Fancy folding and straight knives. **Patterns:** Locking folders, large and small; makes folding tantos and krisses, too. Fighters, tantos and boots in straight patterns. Likes coffin handles. **Technical:** Grinds D2, 440C and 154CM; also UHB-A-EBL. **Prices:** $140 to $350. **Remarks:** Full-time maker; first knife sold in 1974. **Mark:** PARDUE

DUAYNE PARRISH, P.O. Box 181, Palestine, TX 75801/214-729-7319
Specialties: Traditional working straight knives. **Patterns:** Don Hastings hunters, Bowies, camp knives, fighters. **Technical:** Forges Damascus and 5160. **Prices:** $190 to $475; some to $650. **Remarks:** Full-time maker; sold first knife in 1984; has taken over for the late great Don Hastings. **Mark:** PARRISH one side; HASTINGS KNIFE WORKS the other.

ROBERT PARRISH, 1922 Spartanburg Hwy., Hendersonville, NC 28739/704-692-3466
Specialties: Heavy-duty working knives in his design or yours. **Patterns:** Survival and duty knives; hunters, fighters. **Technical:** Grinds 440C, D2, 01 and commercial Damascus. **Prices:** $200 to $300; some to $6,000. **Remarks:** Full-time maker; first knife sold in 1970. **Mark:** RP connected; sometimes with city and state

LLOYD D. PATE, 219 Cottontail Ln., Georgetown, TX 78626/512-863-7805
Specialties: Traditional working straight knives. **Patterns:** Hunters, fighters and Bowies, makes a special lady's knife. **Technical:** Grinds D2 and 440C; hollow-grinds and mirror-finishes. **Prices:** $85 to $165; some to $350. **Remarks:** Part-time maker; sold first knife in 1983. **Mark:** Name

CHUCK PATRICK, Rt. #1, Brasstown, NC 28902/NA
Specialties: Period knives in working patterns. **Patterns:** Hunters, camp knives, tomahawks; all pre-1860 styles. **Technical:** Forges all in 01, L6 or his own Damascus. **Prices:** $40 to $350 and up. **Remarks:** Full-timer who sold first knife in 1980. **Mark:** CP connected; knife; or eagle

HILL EVERETT PEARCE, III, Box 72, Gurley, AL 35748/205-776-3965
Specialties: High-art period pieces in his own design. **Patterns:** Folding lockers; straight Bowies, daggers and fighters. **Technical:** Forges W2, 01 and his own Damascus; does filework on all knives. **Prices:** $300 to over $600. **Remarks:** Full-time maker; first knife sold in 1982. Striving for sole authorship. **Mark:** Small script P

W.D. PEASE, Rt. 2 Box 13, Ewing, KY 41039/606-267-2304
Specialties: Display-quality working knives, folders and straight. **Patterns:** Fighters, tantos and boots; folding lockers and interframes. **Technical:** Grinds 440C, 154CM and commercial Damascus; has his own side release lock system. **Prices:** $300 to $500; some to $1,500. **Remarks:** Full-time maker; first knife sold in 1970. **Mark:** W.D. PEASE

LLOYD PENDLETON, 2116 Broadmore Ave., San Pablo, CA 94806/415-724-6104
Specialties: Contemporary working knives in standard patterns. **Patterns:** Hunters, fighters and boots. **Technical:** Grinds 154CM and ATS34; mirror finishes. **Prices:** $180 to $400; some to $1,300. **Remarks:** Full-time maker; first knife sold in 1973. **Mark:** L Pendleton logo, with city and state

ALFRED H. PENDRAY, Rt. 2, Box 1950, Williston, FL 32696/904-528-6124
Specialties: Period pieces and working knives. **Patterns:** Straight and folding fighters hunters. Also offers axes, camp knives and tomahawks. **Technical:** Forges Wootz steel; makes his own Damascus; does some traditional knives from old files and rasps. **Prices:** $125 to $1,000; some to $3,500. **Remarks:** Part-time maker; first knife sold in 1954. **Mark:** P in horseshoe logo

STEPHAN PEPIOT, General Delivery, Lancaster Park, Edmonton AB T0A 2H0, CANADA
Specialties: Working straight knives in standard patterns. **Patterns:** Hunters and camp knives. **Technical:** Grinds industrial hacksaw blades. **Prices:** $50 to $75. **Remarks:** Spare-time maker; first knife sold in 1982. **Mark:** "PEP"

PEPPER KNIVES (See J. Culpepper)

PERSUADER (See Howard Hill)

DAN L. PETERSEN, 327 N. Rim, Billings, MT 59102/406-252-5135
Specialties: Period pieces and straight working knives. **Patterns:** Hunters, Bowies, boots, fighters; does Persian/Northern India styles in Damascus steel. **Technical:** Forges 01, 1095 and his own Damascus. **Prices:** $125 to $400; some to $1,000. **Remarks:** Full-time maker; first knife sold in 1978. **Mark:** Stylized initials, DLP; JS for Journeyman Smith with the ABS

ELDON G. PETERSON, 260 Haugen Hts. Rd., Whitefish, MT 59937/406-862-2204
Specialties: Fancy working knives. **Patterns:** Folding lockers, interframes, two-blades and both straight and folding hunters. **Technical:** Grinds D2, 154CM and ATS34; uses no tracing mill for interframes—all done by hand. **Prices:** $185 to $300; some $1,200. **Remarks:** Full-time maker; first knife sold in 1974. **Mark:** Name, city and state

JACK PETERSON, 532 Duke St., Nanaimo, BC V9R 1K1, CANADA/604-753-0107
Specialties: Makes miniature folders. **Patterns:** Locking designs at 1 5/16-inch open; makes two-blade patterns, too. **Technical:** Grinds 1095 and 440C; makes cap and spring one piece and bolster and liner one-piece. **Prices:** $25 to $35; some to $100. **Remarks:** Part-timer; sold first knife in 1976. **Mark:** Name

JOHN PHILLIPS, 4021B Primavera, Santa Barbara, CA 93110/805-967-9464
Specialties: Traditional working knives; straight or folding. **Patterns:** Usual straight knives; both locking and slip-joint folders, including interframes in aluminum or titanium. **Technical:** Grinds D2, 154CM, ATS34. **Prices:** $75 to $250; some to $450. **Remarks:** Part-time maker; sold first knife in 1986. **Mark:** Name in dog head logo

RANDY PHILLIPS, P.O. Box 1303, Temple City, CA 91780/714-875-8105
Specialties: Straight working knives of his own design, some high art. **Patterns:** Hunters, boots, daggers, push knives and miniatures. **Technical:**

Grinds D2, 440C and 154CM; embellishes some. **Prices:** $95 to $1,000; some to $1,800. **Remarks:** Part-time maker; first knife sold in 1981. **Mark:** Name, city and state in eagle head

HAROLD L. PIERCE, 7150 Bronner Circle #10, Louisville, KY 40218/502-499-6615
Specialties: Working straight knives, some fancy. **Patterns:** Big fighters and Bowies. **Technical:** Grinds D2, 440C, 154CM; likes sub-hilts. **Prices:** $150 to $450; some to $1,200. **Remarks:** Full-time production; sold first knife in 1982. Police officer background **Mark:** Name

DAVID PITT, P.O. Box 7653, Klamath Falls, OR 97602/503-883-3430
Specialties: Working knives. **Patterns:** Straight knives for deer and elk hunters, including hatchets and cleavers. Small guthook hunters and capers big sellers. **Technical:** Grinds A2, 440C and 154CM. **Prices:** $100 to $200; some to $450. **Remarks:** Full-time maker; first knife sold in 1972. **Mark:** Bear Paw with name

LEON PITTMAN, Rt. 2, Box 2097, Pendergrass, GA 30567/404-654-2597
Specialties: Working folders, some very dressy. **Patterns:** Patent folding lockers and slip joints, interframes, two-blades and gents. **Technical:** Grinds D2, 440C and 154CM. **Prices:** $125 to $500; some $1,000 **Remarks:** Part-time maker; first knife sold in 1973. **Mark:** ''Worm'' and full name

JAMES POAG, RR 1, Box 213, New Harmony, IN 47631/812-682-3226
Specialties: Working knives and period pieces, straight or folding. **Patterns:** Does Bowies and camp knives, lockers and slip joints. **Technical:** Grinds and forges stainless steels and others; provides serious leather. **Prices:** $65 to $180; some to $800. **Remarks:** Full-time maker; sold first knife in 1967. **Mark:** Name

LARRY POGREBA, Box 861, Lyons, CO 80540/303-823-6691
Specialties: Working straight knives. **Patterns:** Hunters and fighters, tomahawks and axes, camp knives; pole arms. **Technical:** Forges and grinds W2, 154CM, and his own Damascus. **Prices:** $150 to $350; some to $1,000. **Remarks:** Full-time maker; first knife sold in 1976. **Mark:** Rocking Lazy LP brand

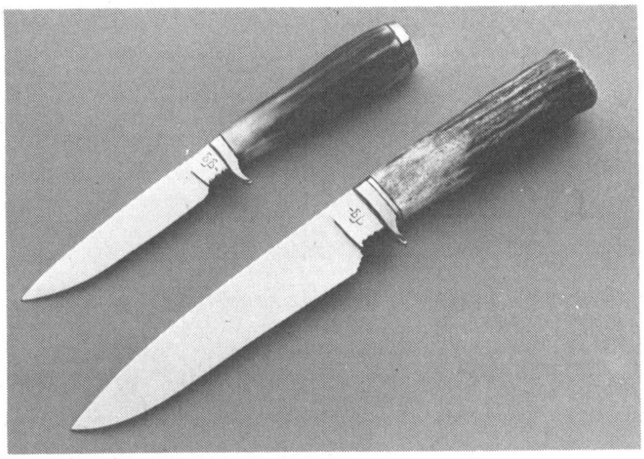

D. PETERSON

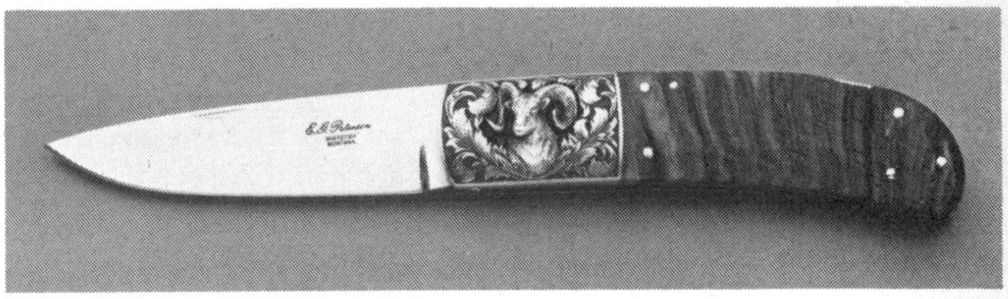

E. G. PETERSON

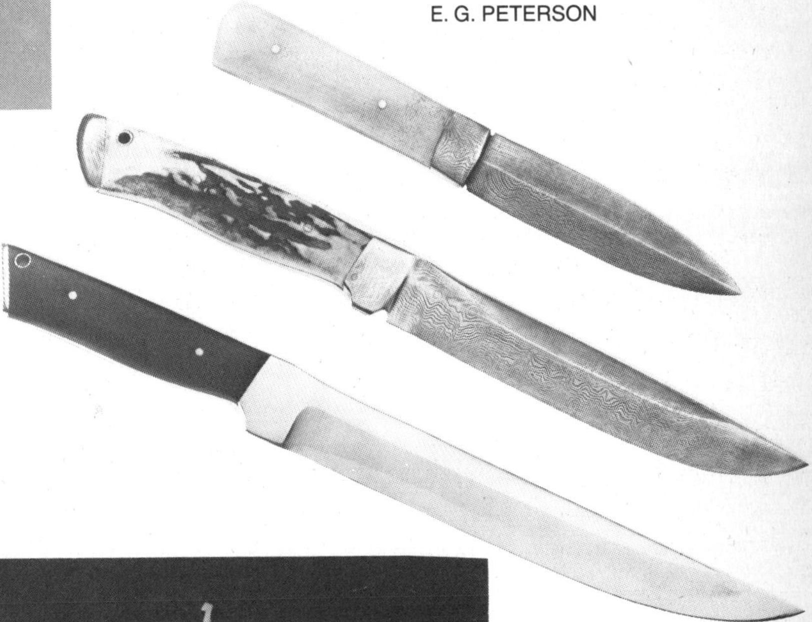

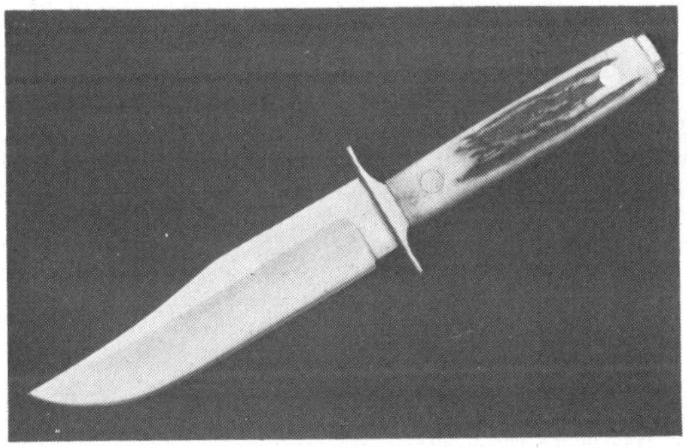

PATE

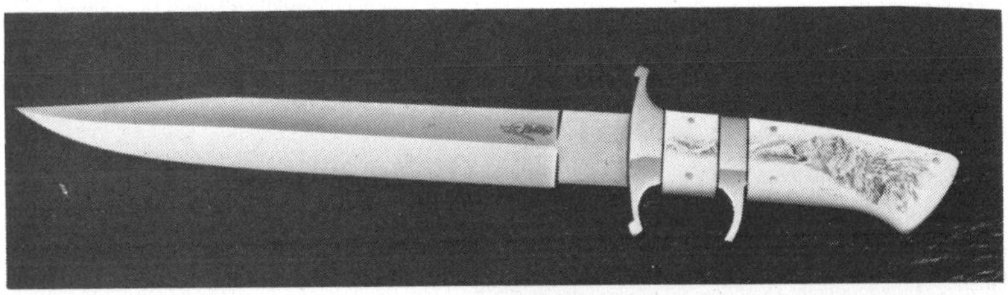

R. PHILLIPS

PEASE

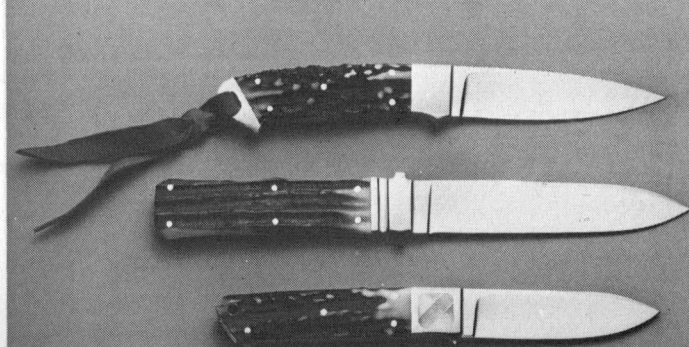

directory/custom knifemakers

CLIFTON POLK, 3526 Eller St., Ft. Smith, AR 72904/501-782-1396
Specialties: Fancy working folders and straight knives. **Patterns:** Folding lockers, slip joints, and two-blades; straight hunters, Bowies, hatchets and kitchen cutlery. **Technical:** Grinds 440C and forges D2 and his own Damascus. **Prices:** $100 to $300; some to $3,000. **Remarks:** Full-time maker; accepts mail for son Rusty. **Mark:** Name

RUSTY POLK (See Clifton Polk)

JAMES L. POPLIN, Rt.2, Box 191A, Washington, GA 30673/404-678-2729
Specialties: Contemporary patterns for hunters. **Patterns:** Hunters, a few boots. **Technical:** Very clean work, deep hollow grinds. **Prices:** Reasonable. **Mark:** POP

JAMES E. PORTER, P.O. Box 2583, Bloomington, IN 47402/812-824-4703
Specialties: Straight knives as period pieces or working blades. **Patterns:** Outdoors knives; some Bowies and miniatures **Technical:** Forges 01 and 1095; makes pattern-welded and welded-wire Damascus; likes integral pommels. **Prices:** $50 to $175; some to $375. **Remarks:** Part-time maker; sold first knife in 1986. **Mark:** JP connected

ALVIN POSTON, 1813 Old Colony Rd., Columbia, SC 29209/803-776-2589
Specialties: Straight working knives. **Patterns:** Hunters, Bowies and fish knives; some miniatures. **Technical:** Grinds 154CM and ATS34. **Prices:** $80 to $125; some to $250. **Remarks:** Part-time maker; first knife sold in 1979. **Mark:** POSTON

ROBERT PREUSS, P.O. Box 65, Cedar, MN 55011
Specialties: Straight working knives in traditional patterns. **Patterns:** Bowies, swords, hunters, and fish knives. **Technical:** Grinds 440C, 440A, and 154CM. **Prices:** $65 to $135; some to $500. **Remarks:** Full-time maker; first knife sold in 1982. Business name is Sharp Custom Knives. **Mark:** RP connected

JERRY L. PRICE, P.O. Box 782, Springdale, AR 72764
Specialties: Straight working knives in standard patterns. **Patterns:** Fighters, boots and Bowies. **Technical:** Grinds A2, 440C and 154CM; offers Kydex sheaths, matte black oxide finish on fighters. **Prices:** $60 to $200; some to $400. **Remarks:** Full-time maker; first knife sold in 1975. **Mark:** J. PRICE

JOEL HIRAM PRICE, Rt. 1, Box 3067, Palatka, FL 32077/904-325-5621
Specialties: Working straight knives to customer order. **Patterns:** Wide variety of straight knives, all with filework. **Technical:** Forges and grinds W2, 01, D2 and 440C—customer choice. Buys Damascus, too. **Prices:** $50 to $250; some over $750. **Remarks:** Full-time maker; first knife sold in 1984. **Mark:** HIRAM Knives in script

STEVE PRICE, 899 Ida Lane, Kamloops, BC V2B 6V2, CANADA/604-579-8932
Specialties: Working knives and fantasy pieces—your design or his. **Patterns:** Hunters, axes, tantos, survival knives, folding lockers and some miniatures. **Technical:** Grinds D2, 440C and ATS34. **Prices:** $90 to $350; some to $1,200. **Remarks:** Full-time maker; first knife sold in 1982. **Mark:** S. PRICE

RON PRITCHARD, 613 Crawford Ave., Dixon, IL 61021/815-284-6005
Specialties: Plain or fancy working knives. **Patterns:** Wide variety of straight knives, locking folders, interframes and miniatures. **Technical:** Grinds 440C, 154CM and commercial Damascus. **Prices:** $100 to $200; some to $1,500. **Remarks:** Part-time maker; first knife sold in 1979. **Mark:** Name and town

JOSEPH D. PROVENZANO, 3024 Ivy Place, Chalmette, LA 70043/504-279-3154
Specialties: Straight working knives in traditional patterns. **Patterns:** Hunters with hollow grinds, Bowies, camp and fish knives. **Technical:** Grinds D2, 440C, and 154CM. **Prices:** $60 to $300; some $500. **Remarks:** Full-time maker; first knife sold in 1980. **Mark:** Joe-Pro

JIM PUGH, P.O. Box 711, Azle, TX 76020/817-444-2679
Specialties: High art knives in working styles of his own designs. **Patterns:** Hunters, Bowies and fighters; some commemoratives; designs animal heads for buttcaps and paws or claws for guards. **Technical:** Grinds 440C, ASP23, ASP60; casts guards in bronze, silver or gold, all finish-engraved by hand. **Prices:** $500 to $5,500; some to $20,000. **Remarks:** Full-time maker; first knife sold in 1970. **Mark:** Pugh

MARTIN PULLEN, 813 Broken Bow WHH, Granbury, TX 76048/817-573-1784
Specialties: Period pieces and straight working knives. **Patterns:** Fighters, Bowies and daggers; folding lockers. **Technical:** Grinds D2, 440C and 154CM. **Prices:** $100 to $300; some to $600. **Remarks:** Spare-time maker; first knife sold in 1978. **Mark:** PULLEN

MORRIS C. PULLIAM, Rt. 7, Box 272, Shelbyville, KY 40065/502-633-2261
Specialties: Period pieces and working knives. **Patterns:** Hunters, tomahawks and buckskinner knives, boots and Bowies; makes folding slip joints in old patterns. **Technical:** Forges 01, L6 and 1095; his own wire-welded Damascus. **Prices:** $160 to $450; some $550. **Remarks:** Full-time maker; first knife sold in 1974. **Mark:** PULLIAM or P

AARON PURSLEY, Box 1037, Big Sandy, MT 59520/406-378-3200
Specialties: Fancy working knives. **Patterns:** Folding lockers, straight hunters and daggers in individual style. **Technical:** Grinds 01 and D2; all knives are engraved by Pursley. **Prices:** $350 to $450; some to $900. **Remarks:** Full-time maker; first knife sold in 1975. **Mark:** AP connected, with year

BARR QUARTON, P.O. Box 2211, Hailey, ID 83333/208-788-2529
Specialties: Plain and fancy working knives and period pieces. **Patterns:** Hunters, tantos and swords. **Technical** Grinds and forges; uses 154CM, ATS34 and his own Damascus. **Prices:** $180 to $450; some to $3,500. **Remarks:** Full-time maker; first knife sold in 1978. **Mark:** Barr with bear logo

WARNER QUENTON, P.O. Box 607, Peterstown, WV 24963
Specialties: Small using knives in high-tech style. **Patterns:** Personal designs exclusively, non-traditional. **Technical:** Grinds stainless steel only; prefers bevel edges. **Prices:** $25 to $200. **Remarks:** Spare-time maker; sold first knife in 1985. **Mark:** WQ

GEORGE QUINN, P.O. Box 692, Julian, CA 92036/619-765-1415
Specialties: Contemporary daggers; integral designs. **Patterns:** Hunters, fighters and daggers. **Technical** Grinds mostly 440C, some 154CM and ATS34; elaborate filework; all knives scrimmed or engraved by Mrs. Quinn. **Prices:** $100 to $600; some to $1,500. **Remarks:** Full-time maker; first knife sold in 1982. **Mark:** QUINN in script

RP KNIVES (See Robert Parrish)

JERRY F. RADOS, R.R. 1, Box 151, Grant Park, IL 60940/815-472-3350
Specialties: Deluxe knives in period designs. **Patterns:** Hunters, fighters, locking folders, daggers and camp knives. **Technical:** Forges and grinds; uses 01, L6 and his own Damascus. Makes own pattern-welded Turkish Damascus. Sells own Damascus commercially. **Prices:** $300 to $1,550; some to $5,000. **Remarks:** Full-time maker; first knife sold in 1981. **Mark:** JR connected; sometimes in diamond logo

RICHARD RAINVILLE, 126 Cockle Hill Rd., Salem, CT 06415/203-859-2776
Specialties: Traditional working straight knives. **Patterns:** Outdoors knives, including fish knives. **Technical:** Grinds 01, L6, D2; heat treats; custom-fits handles. **Prices:** $85 to $165; some to $250. **Remarks:** Part-time maker; sold first knife in 1982. **Mark:** RJR

MARSHALL F. RAMEY, P.O. Box 2589, West Helena, AR 72390/501-572-5256
Specialties: Working knives of traditional types. **Patterns:** Designs military combat knives; makes butterfly folders, camp knives, miniatures. **Technical:** Grinds D2 and 440C. **Prices:** $100 to $200; some to $300. **Remarks:** Full-time maker; sold first knife in 1978. **Mark:** Name with Ram's head

W.D. and GARY T. RANDALL, Box 1988, Orlando, FL 32802/305-855-8075
Specialties: Straight working knives; a standard. **Patterns:** Hunters, fighters and Bowies. **Technical:** Forges and grinds 01 and 440B. **Prices:** $30 to

$250; some to $350. **Remarks:** Full-time maker; first knife sold in 1937; leader in the field. **Mark:** Randall, city, state in scimitar logo

STEVEN J. RAPP, 3437 Crestfield Dr., Salt Lake City, UT 84119/801-966-5595
Specialties: Period pieces and fancy hunter straight knives. **Patterns:** Gold Rush era cutlery. **Technical:** Grinds 440C and Damascus bars. **Prices:** $125 to $300; some to $1,000. **Remarks:** Part-time maker; sold first knife in 1981. **Mark:** Name and state

RICHARD RAPPAZZO, 217 Troy-Schenectady Rd., Latham, NY 12110/518-783-6843
Specialties: Folders and straight knives, traditional or fancy. **Patterns:** Standard types, and tantos and both locking and slip-joint folders. **Technical:** Forges W2, 01, his own Damascus; does filework; prefers natural handles. **Prices:** $250 to $500; some to $800. **Remarks:** Full-time maker; sold first knife in 1985. **Mark:** Name, date, serial

A.D. RARDON, Rt. 1, Box 79, Polo, MO 64671/816-354-2330
Specialties: Working knives; some fancy. **Patterns:** Hunters, buckskinners, Bowies and daggers; some folders. **Technical:** Grinds 01, D2 and 440C, some ATS34. **Prices:** $100 to $500; some to $1,000. **Remarks:** Part-time maker; first knife sold in 1954. **Mark:** Name, address in fox logo

MICHAEL RAY, 533 W. 36th North, Wichita, KS 67204/316-838-4844
Specialties: High-tech working straight and folding knives. **Patterns:** Hunters, fighters and survival knives; gents and hunters in folders. **Technical:** Grinds A2, 440C and ATS34. **Prices:** $80 to $350; some to $500. **Remarks:** Part-time maker. **Mark:** RAY, city and state

CHARLES V. RECE, Rt. 2, Box 477, Albemarle, NC 28001/704-982-2572
Specialties: Working straight knives. **Patterns:** Does hunters, tantos, Bowies. **Technical:** Grinds 01, D2, 440C; prefers flat grind. **Prices:** $25 to $125; some to $250. **Remarks:** Part-time maker; sold first knife in 1986. **Mark:** Name with snake

DAVID REE, 816 Main St., Van Buren, AR 72956/501-474-3198
Specialties: Fancy working knives. **Patterns:** Hunters, folding lockers and boots. **Technical:** Grinds 01, D2 and 440C; prefers exotic and unusual handle materials. **Prices:** $90 to $250; some to $600. **Remarks:** Full-time maker; first knife sold in 1982. **Mark:** REE

CHRIS REEVES, 6433 Frederick Rd., Baltimore, MD 21228
Specialties: Straight working knives in his own designs. **Patterns:** Hollow-handle integral survival and combat knives; lightweight backpackers and bird and trout knives. **Technical:** Grinds, mills and bores D2. **Prices:** $150 to $259. **Remarks:** Full-time maker; first knife sold in 1984. **Mark:** CR connected

WINFRED M. REEVES, P.O. Box 315, West Union, SC 29696/803-638-6121
Specialties: Working straight knives; some elaborate pieces. **Patterns:** Hunters, tantos, fish knives. **Technical:** Grinds D2, 440C and ATS34. No solder joints, no buffer unless requested. **Prices:** $75 to $150; some to $300. **Remarks:** Part-time maker; first knife sold in 1975. **Mark:** Reeves, Walhalla, S.C.

BILL REH, 4610 South Ave. W., Missoula, MT 59801/406-721-2883
Specialties: Straight working knives; some to order. **Patterns:** Hunters, boots, daggers. **Technical:** Grinds D2, 440C and buys Damascus; does his own scrimshaw. **Prices:** $70 to $140; some to $250. **Remarks:** Full-time maker; first knife sold in 1982. **Mark:** REH in sun ray logo

JOHN C. REYNOLDS, Box 119, Mica Court, Gillette, WY 82716/307-682-6076
Specialties: Working knives, some fancy. **Patterns:** Hunters, Bowies, tomahawks and buckskinners; some folders. **Technical:** Grinds D2, 440C and commerical Damascus; scrims his own. **Prices:** $75 to $320; some to $500. **Remarks:** Spare-time maker; first knife sold in 1969. **Mark:** REYNOLDS

DAVID RHEA, Rt. 1, Box 272, Lynnville, TN 38472/615-363-5993
Specialties: High art and fantasy knives. **Patterns:** Fighters, Bowies, survival knives; folding lockers. **Technical:** Grinds and forges; uses D2, 440C and 154CM; makes bronze or silver blades for custom orders; does all embellishing himself. **Prices:** $45 to $300; some to $1,000. **Remarks:** Full-time maker; first knife sold in 1982. **Mark:** D. RHEA, year in circle

DOUGLAS RIAL, Rt. 2, Box 117A, Greenfield, TN 38230/901-235-3994
Specialties: Period pieces and working knives, some to order. **Patterns:** Hunters, fighters, boots, folding lockers, slip joints and miniatures. **Technical:** Grinds D2, 440C and 154CM. **Prices:** $60 to $100; some to $250. **Remarks:** Spare-time maker; first knife sold in 1978. **Mark:** Name and hometown

ADRIENNE RICE, Rt. 1, Box 1744, Lopez Island, WA 98261/206-468-2522
Specialties: Straight knives, either working or fantasy. **Patterns:** Hunters and daggers, women's knives; "power objects" and ceremonial knives. **Technical:** Forges and grinds 01, D2, 440C; also works in bronze. **Prices:** $90 to $150; some to $650. **Remarks:** Full-time production; sold first knife in 1981. **Mark:** AR connected in Madrona logo with date

RICE

RAPP

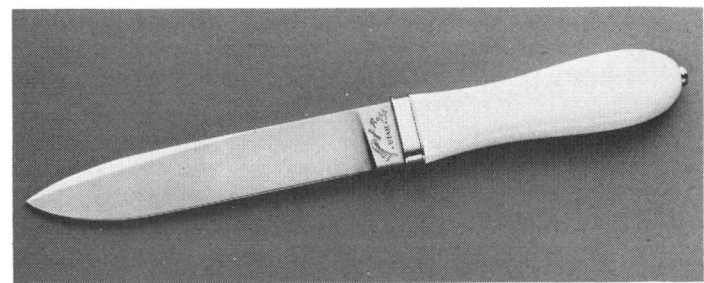

PULLIAM

directory/custom knifemakers

SAM RICHARDS, c/o Post Office, Olinda, Victoria 3788, AUSTRALIA/03-751-1673
Specialties: Fancy working knives of his own designs. **Patterns:** Hunters, folding lockers, camp and kitchen knives. **Technical:** Grinds 01 and 440C. **Prices:** $100 to $400; some to $1,200. **Remarks:** Spare-time maker; first knife sold in 1982. **Mark:** Stylized SR

DAVE RICKE, 1209 Adams, West Bend, WI 53095/414-334-5739
Specialties: Period pieces and working knives. **Patterns:** Hunters, boots, Bowies and buckskinners; folding lockers and slip joints. **Technical:** Grinds A2, 440C and 154CM. **Prices:** $75 to $260; some to $500; some to $450. **Remarks:** Part-time maker; first knife sold in 1976. **Mark:** RICKE

WILLIE RIGNEY, R.R. 3, Box 404, Shelbyville, IN 46176/317-398-4151
Specialties: High-style period pieces and fancy working knives. **Patterns:** Fighters, boots, daggers and push knives. **Technical:** Grinds 440C and 154CM; most knives with embellished surfaces. **Prices:** $150 to $1,500; some to $10,000. **Remarks:** Full-time maker; first knife sold in 1978. **Mark:** W. RIGNEY

THE RINGING CIRCLE (See Dennis M. Fitzgerald)

RIO VERDE BLADES (See V.E. Harrison)

DEAN ROATH, 3050 Winnipeg Dr., Baton Rouge, LA 70819/504-272-5562
Specialties: Classic styling in working straight knives. **Patterns:** Hunters, fighters and camp knives. **Technical:** Grinds D2, 440C and 154CM; clean lines and profiles. **Prices:** $150 to $400; some to $1,500. **Remarks:** Part-time maker; first knife sold in 1978. **Mark:** Name, city and state

HOWARD P. ROBBINS, 875 Rams Horn Rd - Moraine Rt., Estes Park, CO 80517/303-586-8755
Specialties: Working knives; some fancy. **Patterns:** Hunters, boots, fish knives and minis. **Technical:** Grinds 440C. **Prices:** $70 to $150; some to $500. **Remarks:** Full-time maker; first knife sold in 1982. **Mark:** Name, city and state

RON ROBERTSON, 6708 Lunar Dr., Anchorage, AK 99504/903-338-3686
Specialties: Working straight knives of traditional type. **Patterns:** Hunters, tantos, Bowies, camp and fish knives. **Technical:** Grinds 440C and ATS34; likes some guardless designs. **Prices:** $120 to $250; some to $400. **Remarks:** Part-time maker; sold first knife in 1983. **Mark:** Talon in eagle logo

MICHAEL R. ROCHFORD, Trollhaugen Ski Area, P.O. Box 607, Dresser, WI 54009/715-755-3520
Specialties: Straight working knives in standard patterns. **Patterns:** Bowies, fishing and camp knives, miniatures. **Technical:** Grinds and forges W2, 440C, 154CM and his own Damascus. **Prices:** $80 to $250; some to $500. **Remarks:** Full-time maker; first knife sold in 1984. **Mark:** Name

ROCKET (See Rob Davidson)

FRED D. ROE, Jr., 4009 Granada Dr., Huntsville, AL 35802/205-881-6847
Specialties: Period pieces and highly finished working knives of his own designs. **Patterns:** Hunters, fighters and survival knives; folding lockers; specialty designs like divers' knives. **Technical:** Grinds D2, 154CM and ATS34; field-tests his own blades. **Prices:** $125 to $250; some to $700. **Remarks:** Part-time maker; first knife sold in 1980. **Mark:** ROE

ROBERT P. ROGERS, JR., 3979 South Main St., Acworth, GA 30101/409-974-9982
Specialties: Working knives in traditional modes. **Patterns:** Hunter types; has a 4-inch trailing point he likes. **Technical:** Grinds D2, 154CM, ATS34; likes ironwood and ivory Micarta. **Prices:** $65 to $85; some to $125. **Remarks:** Spare-time maker; sold first knife in 1975. **mark:** Name

FRED ROHN, W7615 Clemetson Rd., Coeur d'Alene, ID 83814/208-667-0774
Specialties: Straight working knives, some unusual. **Patterns:** Hunters, fighters, a unique Bowie design, and folding lockers. **Technical:** Grinds 440C and 154CM; stainless steel pins, bolsters and guards on all knives. **Prices:** $65 to $200; some over $450. **Remarks:** Part-time maker. **Mark:** Name in logo and each knife with serial number.

STEVE ROLLERT, P.O. Box 65, Keenesburg, CO 80643/303-732-4858
Specialties: Highly finished affordable working knives. **Patterns:** Full range of straight knives, including kitchen cutlery; also folding lockers and slip joints. **Technical:** Forges and grinds W2, 1095, 440C and his own Damascus. **Prices:** $75 to $250; some to $2,000. **Remarks:** Full-time maker; first knife sold in 1980; Dove Knives label. **Mark:** Rollert in script

MARK H. ROPER, Jr., 206 Plymouth Rd., Martinez, GA 30907/404-863-2972
Specialties: Working knives and some fantasy pieces. **Patterns:** Hunters, fighters and boots, also folding lockers. **Technical:** Grinds 440C, 154CM and ATS34. **Prices:** $90 to $350; some to $600. **Remarks:** Part-time maker; first knife sold in 1980. **Mark:** Name in arc

ALEX ROSE, 3624 Spring Valley Dr., New Port Richey, FL 33552/813-376-5059
Specialties: Miniatures of a wide variety. **Patterns:** Miniature tantos, Bowies, Mid-East styles, and push knives. **Technical:** Grinds 440C, 154CM, and bought Damascus; carving, scrimshaw and inlay on handles. **Prices:** $75 to $125; some $350. **Remarks:** Spare-time maker; first knife sold in 1981. **Mark:** Name with rose logo

STEWART G. ROWE, 56 Baildon St., Kangaroo Point, Bris. 4169, AUSTRALIA/393-1192
Specialties: Japanese tools, working knives, tantos and katanas. **Patterns:** Wide variety of draw knives, adzes, and carving and sculptural chisels. **Technical:** Forges and forge-welds a very wide variety of high carbon steel; works in both modern and traditional styles. **Prices:** $60 to $1,200, or more. **Remarks:** Full-time maker; sold first knife in 1969. **Mark:** Kogatana

RUANA KNIFE WORKS, Box 520, Bonner, MT 59823/406-258-5368
Specialties: Working knives and period pieces in their unique style. **Patterns:** Full range of straight knives, mostly as Rudy made them. **Technical:** 5160 chrome alloy for Bowies and 1095. **Prices:** $60 to $240; some over $300. **Remarks:** Full-time maker; first Ruana knife sold in 1938; Victor N. Hangas now in charge; no quality change in fine knives. **Mark:** Name

JAMES A. RUBLEY, R.R. 3, Box 682, Angola, IN 46703/219-833-1255
Specialties: Pre-Industrial Revolution knives for buckskinners and others. **Patterns:** Anything authentic, barring folders—dirks, Bowies, rifle knives and smaller pieces. **Technical:** Iron fittings, natural materials; forges files and buggy seat springs; does it the old ways. **Prices:** $125 to $350; some to $2,500. **Remarks:** Museum consultant and two decades a blacksmith. **Mark:** Lightning bolt

RUNNING RIVER KNIVES (See Steve Allen)

A.G. RUSSELL, 1705 Hwy. 471 N., Springdale, AR 72764/501-751-7341
Specialties: Morseth Knives; contemporary working knives. **Patterns:** Hunters, Bowies, personal utility knives in Morseth line; drop-points and boots in Russell line. **Technical:** Morseth laminated blades; modern stainless in Russell name; classic shapes. **Prices:** Moderate. **Remarks:** Old name still at work. **Mark:** MORSETH or A.G. RUSSELL

CHARLES C. RUST, P.O. Box 374, Palermo, CA 95968/916-533-9389
Specialties: Period pieces and working knives, some fancy. **Patterns:** Hunters, Bowies, buckskinners, sets. **Technical:** All handwork; low production. **Prices:** $125 to $2,000; some to $3,500; no orders. **Remarks:** Full-time maker; first knife sold in 1972. **Mark:** Rustway in logo

RUSTWAY (See Charles C. Rust)

SF MADE KNIVES (See Shiro Furukawa)

SUZANNE ST. AMOUR, Oldstore House R.R. 1, Hillsburgh, Ont. N0B 1Z0, CANADA/519-855-6494
Specialties: Fine art and fantasy; fancy working knives. **Patterns:** Knives as art, hunters, kitchen cutlery and camp knives. **Technical:** Grinds D2, 440C and 154CM; embellishes most knives; trained as a jeweler. **Prices:** $85 to $500; some to $1,000. **Remarks:** Full-time maker. **Mark:** St. Amour in script

SALAMANDER ARMOURY (See Jim Hrisoulas)

JOHN D. SALLEY, 3965 Frederick-Ginghamsburg Rd., Tipp City, OH 45371/ 513-698-4588
Specialties: Fancy working knives. **Patterns:** Hunters, survival knives and butterfly folding knives; some swords. **Technical:** Grinds D2, 440C; buys Damascus. **Prices:** $75 to $500; some to $3,000. **Remarks:** Part-time maker; first knife sold in 1979. **Mark:** J. Salley

BOB SALPAS, P.O. Box 117, Homewood, CA 95718/916-525-6833
Specialties: Fancy working straight knives. **Patterns:** Hunters, Bowies, tantos, push knives and miniatures. **Technical:** Grinds 440C, ATS34 and AEB-L. **Prices:** $100 to $160; some $450. **Remarks:** Full-time maker; first knife sold in 1981. **Mark:** SALPAS

SAM ENTERPRISES (See George Cooper)

LYNN SAMPSON, Rt. 2, Box 283, Jonesboro, TN 37659/615-753-2090
Specialties: Highly finished working knives, mostly folders. **Patterns:** Folding lockers, slip-joints, interframes and two-blades, all with extensive filework. **Technical:** Grinds D2, 440C and ATS34. **Prices:** $200 to $400 and higher. **Remarks:** Full-time maker; first knife sold in 1982. **Mark:** Name and town in logo

JOSEPH D. SAMS, 10640 Prince George Lane, El Paso, TX 79924/915-821-2705
Specialties: Heavy-duty straight knives, some fancy. **Patterns:** Hunters, fighters, boots. **Technical:** Grinds D2, 440C and 154CM; builds knives to perform. **Prices:** $50 to $250; some to $650. **Remarks:** Part-time maker; first knife sold in 1978. **Mark:** Name, city, state and serial number

JODY SAMSON, 1834 W. Burbank Blvd., Burbank, CA 91506/818-843-4006
Specialties: Straight knives, some fancy, some fantasy—his design or yours. **Patterns:** Hunters, Bowies, swords, axes and camp knives. Does movie props. **Technical:** Grinds 5160, 440C and bought Damascus. **Prices:** $200 to $800; some to $4,500. **Remarks:** Full-time maker; first knife sold in 1970. **Mark:** Lion logo with name

BILL SANDERS (See Timberline Knives)

MICHAEL M. SANDERS, P.O. Box 1106, Ponchatoula, LA 70454/504-294-3601
Specialties: Working straight knives; some deluxe. **Patterns:** Hunters, fighters, survival and Bowies. **Technical:** Grinds 01, D2 and 440C. **Prices:** $75 to $150; some to $350. **Remarks:** Part-time maker; first knife sold in 1967. **Mark:** Name and state

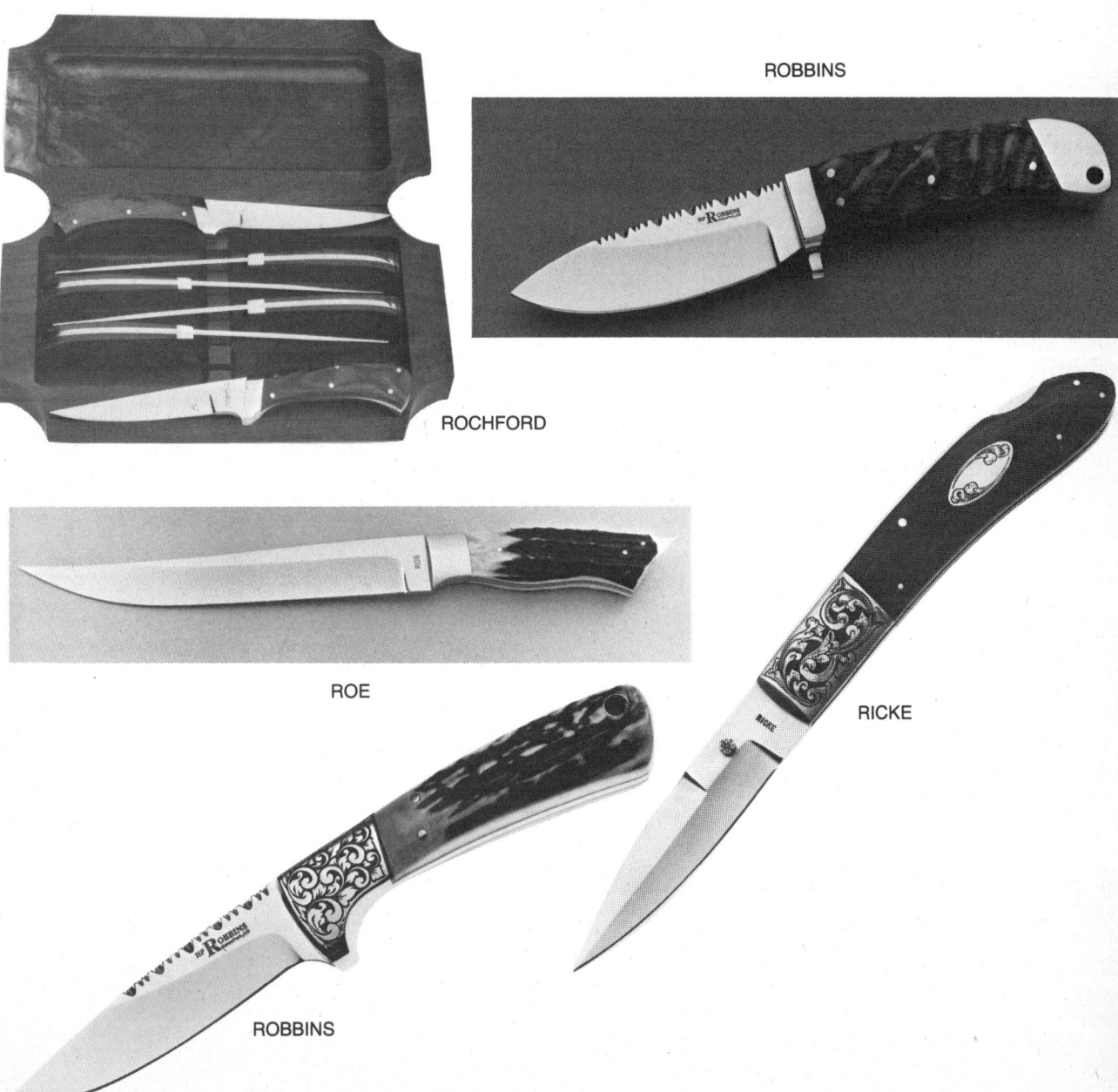

directory/custom knifemakers

SCOTT SAWBY, 500 W. Center Valley Rd., Sand Point, ID 83864/208-263-4171
Specialties: High-tech working folders. **Patterns:** Folding lockers, patent locking systems and interframes. **Technical:** Grinds 440C, 154CM and ATS34. **Prices:** $250 to $350; some to $500. **Remarks:** Full-time maker; first knife sold in 1974. **Mark:** SAWBY, city and state

MURAD SAYEN (See Kemal)

WILL SCARROW, P.O. Box 147, San Gabriel, CA 91775/818-286-6069
Specialties: Working straight knives in traditional patterns or customer designs. **Patterns:** Hunters, skinners, swords and Bowies. Will attempt any design. **Technical:** Grinds and forges; uses W2, 440C and Uddeholm AEB-L. **Prices:** $95 to $200; some to $600. **Remarks:** Part-time maker; first knife sold in 1983. **Mark:** SC in arrow logo

JACK SCHEDENHELL, P.O. Box 307, Superior, MT 59872/406-822-4415
Specialties: Straight working knives in customer design. **Patterns:** Hunters, buckskinners, fighters and tantos. **Technical:** Grinds 440C. **Prices:** $30 to $60; some to $150. **Remarks:** Full-time maker; first knife sold in 1985. **Mark:** Jack Knives

MAGGIE SCHEID, P.O. Box 8059, W. Webster, NY 14580/716-671-8137
Specialties: Straight and simple working knives. **Patterns:** Kitchen and utility knives; some miniatures. **Technical:** Forges 5160 high carbon steel. **Prices:** $100 to $200. **Remarks:** Part-time smith; sold first knife in 1986. **Mark:** Full name

GEORGE B. SCHEPERS, Box 83, Chapman, NE 68827/308-986-2444
Specialties: Fancy period pieces in his own designs. **Patterns:** Bowies, swords, tomahawks; also folding lockers and miniatures. **Technical:** Grinds W1, W2 and his own Damascus; etches some knives. **Prices:** $125 to $600; some more. **Remarks:** Full-time maker; first knife sold in 1981. **Mark:** Schep

JAMES A. SCHMIDT, R.D. 3, Eastern Ave., Ballston Lake, NY 12019/518-882-9322
Specialties: High art Damascus in folders and collector-quality period pieces—sole authorship. **Patterns:** Schmidt patterns in folders; variety of investor-class straight knives. **Technical:** Forges W2 and his own Damascus; elaborate file work and etching, and exotic handle materials. **Prices:** $900 to $2,200; some to $5,000. **Remarks:** Full-time maker; first knife sold in 1975; an ABS Master. **Mark:** SCHMIDT

HERMAN J. SCHNEIDER, 24296 Via Aquara, Laguna Niguel, CA 92677/714-495-4589
Specialties: Investor-class straight knives and fantasies. **Patterns:** Hunters, daggers, fighters and push knives, all personal designs, fully finished. **Technical:** Grinds and forges; uses 154CM, ATS34 and his own Damascus; exotic materials, even rare and expensive materials, a specialty. **Prices:** $800 to $5,000; some to $12,000. **Remarks:** Full-time maker; first knife sold in 1972. **Mark:** H.J. Schneider

MATTHEW A. SCHOENFELD, RR #1, Galiano Island, B.C. V0N 1P0, CANADA/604-539-2806
Specialties: Working knives in distinctly personal style. **Patterns:** All his own in kitchen cutlerly, camp knives, hunters, even swords. **Technical:** Grinds 440C, ATS34; buys Damascus. **Prices:** $85 to $200; some to $500 and up. **Remarks:** Full-time maker; first knife sold in 1978. **Mark:** Signature, Galiano Is. B.C., and date

JOHN J. SCHWARZ, 41 Fifteenth St., Wellsburg, WV 26070
Specialties: Working knives. **Patterns:** Folding lockers, hunters, Bowies and buckskinner knives. **Technical:** Hand forges O1 blades in a coal fire; uses D2 and 440C, also. **Prices:** $50 to $125; some to $200. **Remarks:** Part-time maker; first knife sold in 1939. **Mark:** JS

STEPHEN SCHWARZER, 2119 Westover Dr., Palatka, FL 32077/904-328-3316
Specialties: Fancy forged working knives. **Patterns:** Hunters, fighters, folding lockers, axes and buckskinners—all personally expressed. **Technical:** Forges W2, O1, Wootz steel and his own Damascus; all knives have carving or filework. **Prices:** $800 to $1,800; some $6,000. **Remarks:** Full-time maker; first knife sold in 1976; ABS Master. **Mark:** Name over anvil

WINSTON SCOTT, Rt. 2, Box 62, Huddleston, VA 24104/703-297-6130
Specialties: Working knives. **Patterns:** Hunters, fighters, tantos and mini knives. **Technical:** Grinds D2, 440C and 154CM; likes full tangs, natural materials, sterling silver guards. **Prices:** $100 to $150; some to $200. **Remarks:** Part-time maker; first knife sold in 1984. **Mark:** *SCOTT*

JIM SERVEN, 6153 Third St., Mayville, MI 48744/517-843-6539
Specialties: Highly finished unique folders. **Patterns:** Most known for his fancy working folders; does axes, miniatures and razors, but not many straight knives. **Technical:** Grinds 440C; forges his own Damascus. **Prices:** $150 to $800; some to $1,500. **Remarks:** Full-time maker; first knife sold in 1971. **Mark:** Name in map logo

ROBERT G. SHARP, 17540 St. Francis Blvd., Anoka, MN 55303/612-753-2858
Specialties: Working straight knives. **Patterns:** Hunters, Bowies, daggers and push knives; some axes. **Technical:** Grinds 440C and 154CM. **Prices:** $75 to $175; some to $450. **Remarks:** Full-time maker; first knife sold in 1978. **Mark:** Signature

PHILIP S. SHARPE, 483 Landmark Way S.W., Austell, GA 30001/404-944-9276
Specialties: Pre-1845 straight knives, distressed to appear old. **Patterns:** Hunters, rifle knives, some daggers and Bowies. **Technical:** Grinds D2. **Prices:** $65 to $150; some to $260. **Remarks:** Part-time maker; first knife sold in 1978; nicknamed "Pasquinel;" sells only at rendezvous. **Mark:** Fancy P

ROBERT A. SHEARER, 2121 Avenue T, Huntsville, TX 77340/409-295-0779
Specialties: Working straight knives in traditional patterns. **Patterns:** Fighters, survival knives, and Bowies. **Technical:** Grinds 440C, and 154CM. **Prices:** $50 to $250; some $400. **Remarks:** Part-time maker; first knife sold in 1972. **Mark:** SHEARER

SCOTT SHOEMAKER, 316 S. Main St., Miamisburg, OH 45342/513-859-1935
Specialties: Heavy duty knives, fantasy swords. **Patterns:** Fighters in full tang, Bowies, one-of-a-kinds. **Technical:** Grinds A6 and S7; buys Damascus. **Prices:** $100 to $300; swords to $2,000. **Remarks:** Part-time maker; first knife sold in 1984. **Mark:** Name or Warrior Elite; Angel wings with an S

RICK SHUFORD, 431 Hillcrest Dr., Statesville, NC 28677/704-873-0633
Specialties: Fancy working knives in customer design. **Patterns:** Hunters, buckskinners, camp and fish knives, and miniatures. **Technical:** Grinds and forges; uses O1, D2 and 440C. **Prices:** $75 to $150; some to $250. **Remarks:** Part-time maker; first knife sold in 1981. **Mark:** SHUFORD and 3 dots

CORBET R. SIGMAN, Rte. 1, Box 212-A, Liberty, WV 25124/304-586-9131
Specialties: Collectible working straight knives, highly evolved. **Patterns:** Hunters, fighters, boots, camp knives and exotics like sgian dubhs—distinctly Sigman lines. **Technical:** Grinds D2, 154CM, plain carbon tool steel and ATS34; fine craftsmanship, clean lines. **Prices:** $60 to $800; some to $4,000. **Remarks:** Full-time maker; first knife sold in 1970. **Mark:** Name or initials

ROB SIMONICH, P.O. Box 278, Clancy, MT 59634/406-933-8274
Specialties: Working knives in standard patterns. **Patterns:** Skinners, hunters, hatchets, and some locking folders. **Technical:** Grinds O1, L6, and 154CM; file work on most knives. **Prices:** $50 to $250; some $600. **Remarks:** Full-time maker; first knife sold in 1984. **Mark:** Simonich in buffalo logo

BILL SIMONS, P.O. Box 311, Highland City, FL 33846/813-646-3783
Specialties: Working folding knives. **Patterns:** Folding lockers, slip joints in hunters; some straight camp knives and boots. **Technical:** Grinds D2, 440C and ATS34. **Prices:** $50 to $300. **Remarks:** Full-time maker; first knife sold in 1970. **Mark:** Simons, city and state

BOB SIMS, P.O. Box 772, Meridian, TX 76665/817-435-6240
Specialties: Working straight and folding knives in traditional patterns. **Patterns:** Enjoys locking folders and multi-bladed folding knives. Also offers hunters and boot straight knives. **Technical:** Grinds L6, D2, and 440C. Does file work on some knives. **Prices:** $85 to $175; some over $300. **Remarks:** Spare-time maker; first knife sold in 1978. **Mark:** The division sign

CLESTON S. SINYARD, Rt. 2, Box 634, Elberta, AL 36530/205-986-7984
Specialties: Working straight knives in his designs. **Patterns:** Hunters, buckskinner knives, Bowies, daggers and fighters. **Technical:** Forges 01, D2 and his own Damascus; forges "forefinger pad" into hunters and skinners. **Prices:** In Damascus: $450 to $1,500; some to $2,500. **Remarks:** Full-time maker; first knife sold in 1980. **Mark:** SINYARD. U.S.A. in anvil

JIM SISKA, 6 Highland Ave., Westfield, MA 01085/413-568-9787
Specialties: Traditional types of working knives, straight or folding. **Patterns:** Outdoors knives, some Bowies and interframes; best seller is a troutbird knife. **Technical:** Grinds D2, 154CM, ATS34; likes ivory and stag. **Prices:** $120 to $350; some much higher. **Remarks:** Part-time maker; sold first knife in 1983. **Mark:** Name

SHOEMAKER

SINYARD

SCHNEIDER

SHOEMAKER

SIGMAN

SCHOENFELD

SAWBY

EIGHTH ANNUAL EDITION **221**

directory/custom knifemakers

SAMUEL SKIRCHAK, JR., RD #1, Lisbon Rd., Midland, PA 15059/412-495-3948
Specialties: Straight and folding working knives in traditional types. **Patterns:** Full range of standard and survival knives, including multi-blade folders; does miniatures. **Technical:** Grinds 01, 440C and 154CM; will try customer designs. **Prices:** $75 to $300; some to $600. **Remarks:** Part-time maker; sold first knife in 1983. **Mark:** Name

FRED SLEE, 9 John St., Morganville, NJ 07751/201-591-9047
Specialties: Straight working knives; some fancy. **Patterns:** Hunters, fighters, boots, minis and push knives; welcomes customer designs. **Technical:** Grinds D2, 440C and 154CM. **Prices:** $90 to $250; some to $600. **Remarks:** Part-time maker; first knife sold in 1980. **Mark:** SLEE

JOHN SLOAN, P.O. Box 486, Foxboro, MA 02035
Specialties: Affordable working knives of his own design; some whimsical. **Patterns:** Hunters, fighters and kitchen cutlery. **Technical:** Forges 01, D2 and his own Damascus. **Prices:** $20 to $40; some to $300. **Remarks:** Full-time maker; first knife sold in 1978. **Mark:** Iron duckling

SHANE SLOAN, Rt. 1, Box 17, Newcastle, TX 76372/817-846-3290
Specialties: Working straight and folding knives, some fancy. **Patterns:** Does tantos, Bowies, lockers, slip-joints; makes fancy fighters. **Technical:** Grinds D2, 440C, 154CM; tempers 440Cs to be tough; mixes mirror and satin finishes. **Prices:** $85 to $175; some to $185. **Remarks:** Full-time maker; sold first knife in 1985. **Mark:** Name in logo with eagle

ED SMALL, Rt. 1, Box 178-A, Keyser, WV 26726/304-298-4254
Specialties: Period pieces and working knives of his own designs. **Patterns:** Hunters, daggers, buckskinners and camp knives; likes one-of-a-kinds. **Technical:** Forges and grinds W2, L6, and his own Damascus. Uses no solder joint at guard or spacing material. **Prices:** $150 to $600. **Remarks:** Part-time maker; first knife sold in 1978. Business name is Iron Mountain Forge Works. **Mark:** Script ES connected

JIM SMALL, P.O. Box 67, Madison, GA 30650/404-342-4707
Specialties: Fancy working knives in his design or yours. **Patterns:** Bowies, camp and fish knives, hunters and locking folders. **Technical:** Grinds D2, 440C, 154CM and ATS34; offers engraving on his knives or others. **Prices:** $75 to $185; some to $1,000. **Remarks:** Full-time maker; first knife sold in 1970. **Mark:** SMALL

DAVID LYNN SMITH, P.O. Box 36, Duchesne, UT 84021/801-738-2582
Specialties: Working straight knives in traditional styles. **Patterns:** All steel wallet knives; fighters, Bowies and camp knives in modern treatment. **Technical:** Flat grinds 01 and 154CM. **Prices:** $50 to $200; some to $300. **Remarks:** Part-time maker; first knife sold in 1983. **Mark:** D. LYN

GREGORY H. SMITH, 8607 Coddington Ct., Louisville, KY 40299/502-425-3005
Specialties: Traditional straight working knives; some fantasy knives; likes customer design work. **Patterns:** Fighters and modified Bowies; some camp knives and swords. **Technical:** Grinds 01, 440C, commercial Damascus bars. **Prices:** $55 to $300. **Remarks:** Part-time maker; sold first knife in 1985. **Mark:** JAGED, plus signature

HARRY R. SMITH, 2105 So. 27th Ave., Missoula, MT 59801/406-549-5940
Specialties: Working knives, some fancy. **Patterns:** Hunters, Bowies, folding lockers; some swords and axes. **Technical:** Forges and grinds 01, D2, and 154CM. **Prices:** $75 to $135; some $650. **Remarks:** Part-time maker; first knife sold in 1941. **Mark:** H. SMITH

JAMES B. "RED" SMITH, Jr., Rt. 2, Box 199, Morven, GA 31638/912-775-2844
Specialties: Folding and straight working knives. **Patterns:** Hunters, camp knives, machetes, and folding lockers. **Technical:** Grinds ATS34, 440C, and D2. **Prices:** $90 to $150; some $250. **Remarks:** Full-time maker; first knife sold in 1985. **Mark:** GA RED in cowboy hat

NEWMAN L. SMITH, Rt. 1, Box 119A, Glades Rd., Gatlinburg, TN 37738/615-428-0811 (evenings)
Specialties: Working knives, some fancy, both straight and folding. **Patterns:** Hunters and slip-joint folders; some miniatures. **Technical:** Grinds 01 and 440C; makes extra-fancy sheaths. **Prices:** $85 to $450; some to $800. **Remarks:** Full-time production; sold first knife in 1984. Partners part-time to handle Damascus blades by Jeff Hurst and marks these SH connected. **Mark:** NLS

RALPH L. SMITH, P.O. Box 395, Greer, SC 29652/803-877-7580
Specialties: Affordable working knives. **Patterns:** Hunters, fighters, boots, folding lockers; some axes and push knives. **Technical:** Grinds 440C, 154CM and ATS34. **Prices:** $100 to $225; some to $500. **Remarks:** Part-time maker; first knife sold in 1971. **Mark:** Smith in map logo

W.F. "RED" SMITH, P.O. Box 6, Gatlinburg, TN 37738/615-436-3520
Specialties: Straight working knives; some fancy. **Patterns:** Hunters, fighters, daggers, tomahawks. Some commemorative series. **Technical:** Grinds and forges; offers 440C and his own Damascus. **Prices:** $150 to $600; some to $3,500. **Remarks:** Full-time maker; first knife sold in 1975. **Mark:** RED SMITH

W.J. SONNEVILLE, 1050 Chalet Dr. W., Mobile, AL 36608/205-342-5447
Specialties: Working straight knives. **Patterns:** Hunters, fighters, Bowies in heavy duty styles. **Technical:** Grinds and forges; uses 1095 and 440C. **Prices:** $130 to $250; some $750. **Remarks:** Full-time maker; first knife sold in 1965. **Mark:** SONNEVILLE, city and state

G. DOUGLAS SONTHEIMER, 1705 Chester Mill Road, Silver Spring, MD 20906/301-924-3657
Specialties: Working straight knives to his own images. **Patterns:** Fighters, backpackers, claws, straight edges. **Technical:** Grinds. **Price:** $275 to $900; some to $1,500. **Remarks:** Spare-time maker; sold first knife in 1976. **Mark:** LORD

JIM SORNBERGER, 5675 Meridian Ave., San Jose, CA, 95118/408-267-7180
Specialties: Collectible straight knives, highly finished. **Patterns:** Fighters, daggers, Bowies; some folding lockers and miniatures; some hunters. **Technical:** Grinds 440C, 154CM and ATS34; does his own engraving, carving and other embellishment. **Prices:** $500 to $1,500; some to $3,500. **Remarks:** Full-time maker; first knife sold in 1970. **Mark:** SORNBERGER U.S.A.

BERNARD SPARKS, Box 73, Dingle, ID 83233/208-847-1883
Specialties: Original designs in straight and folding working knives. **Patterns:** Hunters, fighters, folding lockers, camp knives and miniatures. **Technical:** Grinds and forges; offers 440C, 154CM, Vascowear and his own Damascus. **Prices:** $100 to $500; some to $1,000. **Remarks:** Full-time maker; first knife sold in 1966. **Mark:** SPARKS

JOHN E. SPENCER, Box 582-B—Star Rt., Harper, TX 78631/512-864-4216
Specialties: Straight working knives. **Patterns:** Hunters, fighters and survival knives; locking folders; some axes. **Technical:** Grinds 01, D2 and 440C; commercial Damascus. **Prices:** $60 to $300; some $500. **Remarks:** Full-time maker; first knife sold in 1982. **Mark:** SPENCER

RICHARD SPINALE, 3415 Oakdale Ave., Lorain, OH 44055/216-246-5344
Specialties: High art working knives of individual designs. **Patterns:** Hunters, fighters, daggers and folding lockers. **Technical:** Grinds 440C and 07; all knives are engraved by this maker; offers gold bolsters, other deluxe treatments. **Prices:** $125 to $800; some to $2,000. **Remarks:** Spare-time maker; first knife sold in 1976. **Mark:** Name, address, year and model number

JEFFERSON SPIVEY, P.O. Box 60584, Oklahoma City, OK 73146/405-282-1802
Specialties: Heavy-duty straight knives. **Patterns:** Personal designs only; his horseman's Sabertooth at first, now similar profiles in a couple of sizes. **Technical:** Grinds chrome-moly steel. **Prices:** $225 up. **Remarks:** Sold first knives in 1977; is a famous long-distance rider. **Mark:** Varies, but includes name and patent number.

RICHARD STAFFORD, 104 Marcia Ct., Warner Robins, GA 31088/912-923-6372

Specialties: Working knives, some fancy. **Patterns:** Hunters, fighters, tantos and mini knives. **Technical:** Grinds D2, 440C and 154CM; favors bolsters and satin finishes. **Prices:** $75 to $250; some to $600. **Remarks:** Full-time maker; first knife sold in 1983. **Mark:** STAFFORD

HARRY L. STALTER, R.R. 1, Box 60, Trivoli, IL 61569/309-362-2306
Specialties: Working knives; some period pieces. **Patterns:** Hunters, fighters and Bowies; locking folders. Now making a rifle stock handle model. **Technical:** Grinds 440C, D2 and 154CM. **Prices:** $80 to $160; some to $300. **Remarks:** Full-time maker; first knife sold in 1980. **Mark:** H. STALTER, city and state

CHUCK STAPEL, Box 1617, Glendale, CA 91209/213-662-5954
Specialties: Original approaches to working knife design. **Patterns:** A full range of straight knives, individually patterned—tantos, hunters, folders, utility knives. **Technical:** Grinds D2, 440C, AEB-L and his own Damascus. **Prices:** $125 to $400; some to $1,500. **Remarks:** Full-time maker; first knife sold in 1974. **Mark:** STAPEL

CRAIG STAPEL, Box 1617, Glendale, CA 91209/213-668-2669
Specialties: Working knives. **Patterns:** Hunters, tantos, fish knives. **Technical:** Grinds 440C and AEB-L. **Prices:** $80 to $100; some $150. **Remarks:** Spare-time maker; first knife sold in 1981. **Mark:** C.C. STAPEL

JOHN STAPLETON, 37 Ernest Cres., Happy Valley, SOUTH AUSTRALIA 5159/08-381-7587
Specialties: Period pieces and working knives. **Patterns:** Hunters, fighters, Bowies; some folding lockers. **Technical:** Grinds 01, D2 and 440C. **Prices:** $180 to $320; some to $500. **Remarks:** Part-time maker; first knife sold in 1979. **Mark:** Gothic S

RANDY STEFANI, 2393 Mayfield Ave., Montrose, CA 91020/818-957-4204
Specialties: Working straight knives in traditional models. **Patterns:** Hunters, fighters, tantos, Bowies; makes small utility knives. **Technical:** Grinds 440C, 154CM, ATS34. **Prices:** $75 to $250; some to $500. **Remarks:** Part-time maker; sold first knife in 1983. **Mark:** Last name

KEITH STEGALL, 3206 Woodland Pk. Dr., Anchorage, AK 99517/907-243-2001
Specialties: Miniature straight knives in traditional working styles. **Patterns:** Most patterns. **Technical:** Grinds 440C, 154CM; tries for clean lines, good detail. **Prices:** Around $100. **Remarks:** Spare-time maker; sold first knife in 1987. **Mark:** Name, state, with anchor

AL STEINBERG, 2499 Trenton Dr., San Bruno, CA 94066/415-583-8281
Specialties: Fancy straight working knives in customer designs. **Patterns:** Hunters, Bowies, fish and camp knives; some push knives. **Technical:** Grinds 01, 440C and 154CM. **Prices:** $60 to $125; some to $300. **Remarks:** Full-time maker; first knife sold in 1972. **Mark:** Signature, city and state

KELLY LEE STEPHENS, 4235 78th Ln. N., St. Petersburg, FL 33709
Specialties: Working knives and period pieces, some fancy. **Patterns:** Straight and folding hunters; centerline Bowies; some swords. **Technical:** Grinds stainless steels. **Mark:** name

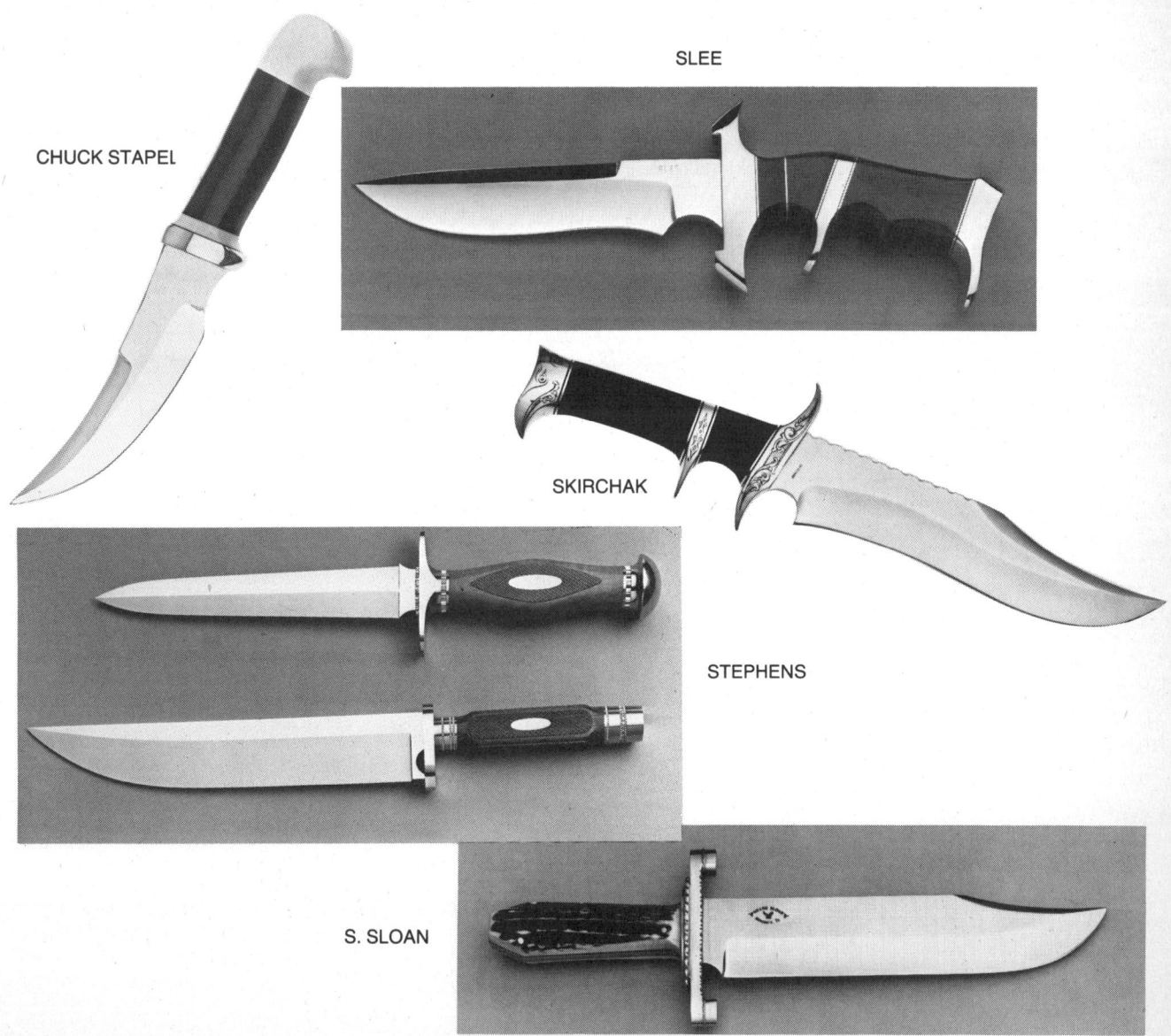

CHUCK STAPEL

SLEE

SKIRCHAK

STEPHENS

S. SLOAN

directory/custom knifemakers

STEVES KNIVES (See Steve Davenport)

CHARLES (CHUCK) STEWART, P.O. Box 514, 2996 Walmsley Circle, Lake Orion, MI 48035/313-391-2289
Specialties: Working knives, personally designed. **Patterns:** Makes exotic opening mechanisms for his designs of folders; also straight knives, some fancy. **Technical:** Forges and grinds 440C, 154CM and ATS34; offers finishes from gold to blueing. **Prices:** $200 to $800; some to $9,500. **Remarks:** Full-time maker; first knife sold in 1968. **Mark:** Stylized initials

KAY STITES, 4931 Rands Rd., Bloomfield Hills, MI 48013/313-251-7336
Specialties: Working straight knives in traditional patterns. **Patterns:** Hunters and fish knives. **Technical:** Grinds D2, O1, and 440C. **Prices:** $75 to $225; some to $500. **Remarks:** Spare-time maker; first knife sold in 1986. **Mark:** Stites

W.B. "BILL" STODDART, 917 Smiley, Forest Park, OH 45240/513-851-1543
Specialties: Sportsmen's working knives. **Patterns:** Hunters, camp and fish knives; folding lockers in traditional styles. **Technical:** Grinds A2, 440C and ATS34; makes sheaths to match handle material. **Prices:** $80 to $150; some $400. **Remarks:** Full-time maker; first knife sold in 1976. **Mark:** Name, city and state

G.W. STONE and JIM ERICKSON, 610 No. Glenville Dr., Richardson, TX 75081/214-231-0970
Specialties: Working knives in standard patterns built for heavy duty. **Patterns:** Hunters, fighters and kitchen cutlery and locking folders. **Technical:** Grinds D2, 440C, and ASP-23. **Prices:** $100 to $300; some to $600. **Remarks:** Veteran full-time maker; first knife sold in 1964. **Mark:** Name

JOHNNY STOUT, 1514 Devin, Braunfels, TX 78130/512-629-1011
Specialties: Working knives, some fancy. **Patterns:** Hunters, Bowies, fishing knives and folding lockers. **Technical:** Grinds D2, 440C and ATS34; satin and mirror finishes; uses local woods for handles—mesquite, cat claw, cedar. **Prices:** $100 to $250; some to $1,500. **Remarks:** Part-time maker; first knife sold in 1983. **Mark:** Name, and city in logo; serial number

SCOTT STRONG, 2138 Oxmoor Dr., Beaver Creek, OH 45431/513-426-9290
Specialties: Working knives, some deluxe. **Patterns:** Hunters, fighters, survival knives and folding lockers. **Technical:** Forges and grinds O1, D2, 440C, and his own wire-welded Damascus. **Prices:** $40 to $185; some $350. **Remarks:** Spare-time maker; first knife sold in 1983. **Mark:** STRONG KNIVES

GEORGE STUMPFF, JR., P.O. Box 2, Glorieta, NM 87535/505-757-6036
Specialties: Traditional working straight and folding knives, some fancy. **Patterns:** Tantos and Bowies; lockers and slip-joints in the old style. Does fancy pin and file work. **Technical:** Grinds A2, O1, ATS34; triple flat-grinds some blades. **Prices:** $70 to $250; some to $500. **Remarks:** Full-time production; sold first knife in 1975. **Mark:** GWS in logo

HARLAN SUEDMEIER, RFD2, Nebraska City, NE 68410/402-873-4372
Specialties: Working straight knives. **Patterns:** Hunters, fighters and Bowies. **Technical:** Grinds A2, D2 and 440C. **Prices:** $65 to $120; some to $200. **Remarks:** Part-time maker; first knife sold in 1982. **Mark:** H. Suedmeier

ROD SWAIN, 1020 Avon Place, South Pasadena, CA 91030/818-799-7666
Specialties: Working straight knives, some fancy. **Patterns:** Outdoors patterns, and Bowies and push knives; likes his utility drop-point. **Technical:** Grinds O1, 440C, AEB-L; takes on some customer designs. **Prices:** $60 to $200; some to $400. **Remarks:** Part-time maker; sold first knife in 1981. **Mark:** Last name in logo

CHUCK SYSLO, 3418 South 116 Ave., Omaha, NE 68144/402-333-0647
Specialties: High-tech working straight knives. **Patterns:** Hunters, daggers, survival knives; some folding lockers. **Technical:** Grinds D2, 440C and 154CM; hand polishes only; flat ground only. **Prices:** $175 to $375; some to $1,000. **Remarks:** Part-time maker; first knife sold in 1978. **Mark:** CISCO in logo

ANTONIO J. TAGLIENTI, P.O. Box 221, Darlington, PA 16115/412-846-5259
Specialties: Straight working knives in traditional style. **Patterns:** Hunters—likes forefinger radius; also makes Bowies, tantos, camp knives. **Technical:** Grinds D2, 440C, 154CM; does full tangs only; fancy filework on most knives. **Prices:** $85 to $200; some to $350. **Remarks:** Part-time maker; sold first knife in 1985. **Mark:** Last name

MASAO TAKAHASHI, Umemoto-so, 2-28 Chihaya-cho, Toshima-Ku, Tokyo 171, JAPAN/03-959-6087
Specialties: Highly finished working knives. **Patterns:** Hunters, fishing knives and miniatures. **Technical:** Grinds ATS34. **Prices:** $80 to $145; some to $300. **Remarks:** Part-time maker; first knife sold in 1982. **Mark:** M. TAKAHASHI

TALON KNIVES (See Ron Robertson)

MICHAEL TAMBOLI, 12447 N. 49 Ave., Glendale, AZ 85304/602-978-4308
Specialties: Miniature straight knives. **Patterns:** Full range of models, but miniatures only. **Technical:** Grinds O1, 440C and Damascus bars; heat-treats blades properly. **Prices:** $35 to $75; some to $150. **Remarks:** Part-time maker; sold first knife in 1978. **Mark:** MT

SEIICHI TASAKI, 2-17-8, Shiba-Tsukahara, Kawaguchi-City, Saitama 332, JAPAN/0482-61-0517
Specialties: Does high-tech and traditional folding and straight knives. **Patterns:** Full range of types—hunters, miniatures, interframe folders, and more. **Technical:** Grinds and forges; uses 440C and carbon steel. **Prices:** $230 to $850; some to $5,000. **Remarks:** Full-time maker; sold first knife in 1984. **Mark:** ST connected

C. GRAY TAYLOR, 137 Lana View Dr., Kingsport, TN 37664/615-288-5969
Specialties: Period pieces and high art display knives. **Patterns:** Fighters, Bowies, daggers, folding lockers, and interframes. **Technical:** Grinds 440C, 154CM and ATS34. **Prices:** $200 to $3,000; some to $7,000. **Remarks:** Part-time maker; first knife sold in 1975. **Mark:** Name, city and state

DAVID TAYLOR, 137 Lana View Dr., Kingsport, TN 37664/615-288-5969
Specialties: High-tech working knives. **Patterns:** Hunters, fighters, boots and locking folders. **Technical:** Grinds 440C, 154CM and ATS34. **Prices:** $80 to $200; some to $750. **Remarks:** Part-time maker; first knife sold in 1981. Now serving in the armed forces full time; not taking any orders. **Mark:** Name, city state

MICKEY TEDDER, Rt. 2, Box 22, Conover, NC 28613/704-464-9002
Specialties: Working folders. **Patterns:** Lockers in hunter, fighter and boot designs. **Technical:** Grinds D2, 440C and 154CM; makes gold miniatures as jewelry. **Prices:** $150 to $300; some to $1,500. **Remarks:** Part-time maker. **Mark:** TEDDER

LOU TEICHMOELLER, P.O.B. 282, Dolores, CO 81323
Specialties: Working knives, straight and folding. **Patterns:** Hunters, fighters, boots and slip-joint pocketknives. **Technical:** Grinds and forges; uses O1, W2, 1095, and his own Damascus. **Prices:** $75 to $150; some to $250. **Remarks:** Spare-time maker; first knife sold in 1980. **Mark:** TEICHMOELLER

STEPHEN TERRILL, 908 S. Magnolia, Lindsay, CA 93247/209-562-4395
Specialties: Deluxe working straight and folding knives. **Patterns:** Fighters, tantos, boots, folding lockers and axes. Oriental patterns done in traditional manner. **Technical:** Grinds and forges; uses A2, 440C and his own Damascus; clean lines. **Prices:** $80 to $550; some to $4,000. **Remarks:** Part-time maker; first knife sold in 1972; not taking orders. **Mark:** Name, city, state in logo

ROBERT TERZUOLA, Route 6, Box 83A, Santa Fe, NM 87501/505-473-1002
Specialties: Period pieces and working knives in his own designs. **Patterns:** Hunters, fighters and tantos—high-tech style and substance in mostly defense knives. **Technical:** Grinds D2, 440C and buys Damascus; working knives with Kydex sheath. **Prices:** $175 to $300; some to $3,000. **Remarks:** Full-time maker; first knife sold in 1980. **Mark:** Mayan dragon head and name, city and state

BRUCE LEE THOMPSON, 4101 W. Union Hills Dr., Glen Dale, AZ 85308
Specialties: Working straight knives in traditional patterns. **Patterns:** Bowies, skinners, swords, tomahawks, and butterfly knives. **Technical:** Grinds 01, 440C and 154CM; file work on most knives. **Prices:** $75 to $250; some to $300. **Remarks:** Part-time maker; first knife sold in 1979. **Mark:** Clasped hands

LEON THOMPSON, 1735 Leon Drive, Forest Grove, OR 97116/503-357-2573
Specialties: Period pieces and working knives. **Patterns:** Hunters, Bowies, folding lockers, fishing knives and miniatures. **Technical:** Grinds D2, 440C and 154CM. **Prices:** $125 to $250; some to $600. **Remarks:** Part-time maker; first knife sold in 1976. **Mark:** THOMPSON

DANNY THORNTON, P.O. Box 334, Fort Mill, SC 29715/803-547-6341
Specialties: Working straight knives. **Patterns:** Small boots—the Vindicator—and hunters, plus the Quicksilver, a hollow-handled defense-survival knife system. **Technical:** Grinds. **Prices:** Moderate. **Remarks:** Clean designs. **Mark:** Name

MICHAEL W. THOUROT, T814RR1, RD 11, Napoleon, OH 43545/419-533-6832
Specialties: Working straight knives in customer designs. **Patterns:** Fish and fillet knives; Bowies, tantos and hunters. **Technical:** Grinds 01, D2, and 440C. **Prices:** $200 to $325; some to $1,500. **Remarks:** Part-time maker; first knife sold in 1969. **Mark:** MWT

ED THUESEN, 10649 Haddington, Suite 190, Houston, TX 77043/713-461-8632
Specialties: Working straight knives. **Patterns:** Hunters, fighters and survival knives. **Technical:** Grinds D2, 440C and 154CM. **Prices:** $85 to $250; some to $600. **Remarks:** Full-time maker; first knife sold in 1979; runs knifemaker supply business. **Mark:** THUESEN

KEVIN THUESEN, 10649 Haddington, Suite 190, Houston, TX 77043/713-461-8632
Specialties: Working straight knives. **Patterns:** Hunters, including upswept skinners; also makes custom walking sticks. **Technical:** Grinds D2, 440C, 154CM and ATS34. **Prices:** $85 to $125; some to $200. **Remarks:** Part-time maker; sold first knife in 1985. **Mark:** KAT on slant

THUNDERBOLT ARTISANS (See Thomas N. Hilker)

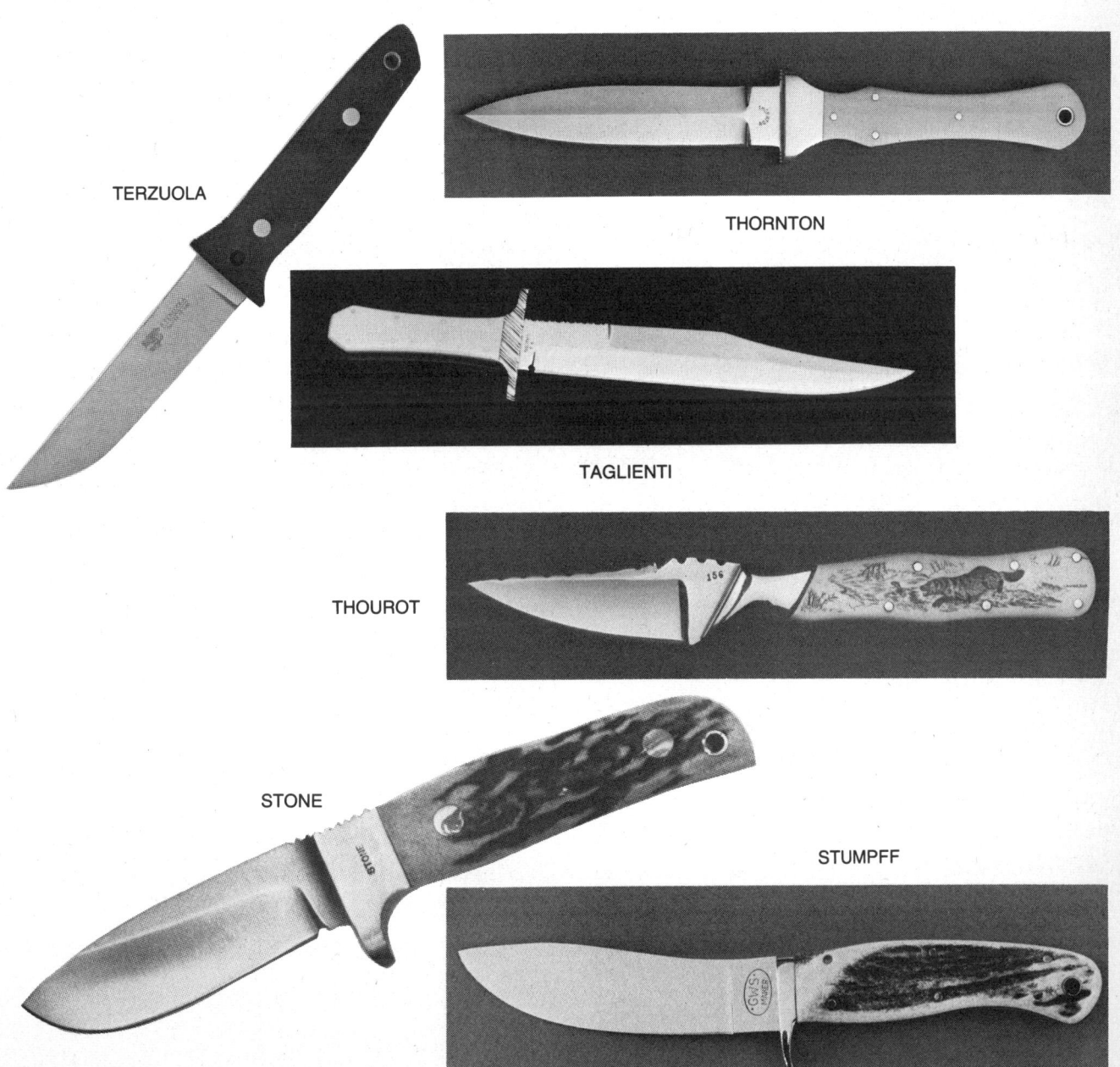

TERZUOLA

THORNTON

TAGLIENTI

THOUROT

STONE

STUMPFF

directory/custom knifemakers

TIMBERLINE KNIVES, P.O. Box 36, Mancos, CO 81328/303-533-7006
Specialties: High-tech straight and folding working knives. **Patterns:** Survival knives in complete systems; stag hunters—high-tech approaches; locking folders and interframes. **Technical:** Grinds 440C, D2, and 154CM. **Prices:** Moderate. **Remarks:** Full-time makers. Partnership of V. Neeley and W. Sanders since 1982. **Mark:** Timberline

THE TINKER (See Jim Ladd)

CAROLYN D. TINKER, P.O. Box 5123, Whittier, CA 90607/213-696-9202
Specialties: Working straight knives in her own designs. **Patterns:** Hunters, kitchen and fish knives; small tools. **Technical:** Grinds D2, 440C and 154CM. **Prices:** $85 to $125. **Remarks:** Full-time maker; first knife sold in 1974. **Mark:** Name and city in logo

TKM (TENNESSEE KNIFE MAKER) (See W.C. Ward)

DANIEL TOKAR, Box 1776, Shepherdstown, WV 25443
Specialties: Period pieces and working knives. **Patterns:** Hunters, camp knives, buckskinner blades; also axes, swords and battle gear. **Technical:** Forges L6, 1095 and his own Damascus. Makes mokume, Japanese alloys and bronze daggers; restores old edged weapons. **Prices:** $125 to $400; some to $1,500. **Remarks:** Full-time maker; first knife sold in 1979. **Mark:** Arrow over rune and date

P.J. TOMES, P.O. Box 37268, Jacksonville, FL 32236/904-786-1731
Specialties: Period pieces and plain and fancy working knives. **Patterns:** Boots, daggers, Bowies; folding lockers; simple lightweight hunters and household cutlery. **Technical:** Grinds and forges; uses D2, ATS34 and his own Damascus. **Prices:** $75 to $500; some to $2,000. **Remarks:** Full-time maker. **Mark:** TOMES

DAN TOMPKINS, 310 N. Second St., Peotone, IL 60468/312-258-3620
Specialties: Working knives, some deluxe. **Patterns:** Hunters, boots, daggers and push knives. **Technical:** Grinds D2, 440C and 154CM; buys Damascus. **Prices:** $85 to $150; some to $400. **Remarks:** Part-time maker; first knife sold in 1975. **Mark:** TOMPKINS, city and state

DWIGHT L. TOWELL, Rt. 1, Box 66, Midvale, ID 83645/208-355-2419
Specialties: Solid and elegant working knives. **Patterns:** Hunters, Bowies, daggers; folders in several weights. **Technical:** Grinds 154CM; some knives engraved. **Prices:** $250 to $800; some over $3,500. **Remarks:** Part-time maker; first knife sold in 1970. **Mark:** TOWELL

R.W. TRABBIC, 4550 N. Haven, Toledo, OH 43612/419-478-9578
Specialties: Working knives. **Patterns:** Hunters, Bowies; locking hunters and springbacks in standard patterns. **Technical:** Grinds D2, 440C and 154CM. **Prices:** $80 to $250. **Remarks:** Part-time maker; first knife sold in 1973. **Mark:** R. W. TRABBIC

TERRY A. TREUTEL, P.O. Box 187, Hamilton, MT 59840/406-363-4142
Specialties: Working straight knives in his designs and traditional patterns. **Patterns:** Hunters, skinners, camp and fish knives; roached back short hunters. **Technical:** Grinds D2, 154CM, and 440C on request basis; does own heat-treating. **Prices:** $107 to $180; some $450. **Remarks:** Full-time maker; first knife sold in 1983. **Mark:** Name

TRO KNIVES (See Overeynder)

THOMAS A. TRUJILLO, 2905 Arctic Blvd., Anchorage, AK 99503/907-563-2738
Specialties: Working knives. **Patterns:** Hunters, Bowies, daggers, folding lockers. **Technical:** Grinds 01, ATS34, and commercial Damascus. **Prices:** $150 to $900; some to $3,000. **Remarks:** Full-time maker; first knife sold in 1976. **Mark:** Alaska Knife

JON J. TSOULAS, 1 Home St., Peabody, MA 01960/617-532-3163
Specialties: Fancy straightworking knives of his own design. **Patterns:** Hunters, fighters, and Bowies. **Technical:** Grinds D2, 440C, and 154CM; high polish grinds, and likes wood handles. **Prices:** $75 to $225; some $450. **Remarks:** Part-time maker; first knife sold in 1984. **Mark:** TSOULAS

RALPH A. TURNBULL, 5722 Newburg Rd., Rockford, IL 61108/815-398-3799
Specialties: Plain or fancy working knives. **Patterns:** Hunters, fighters, boots, folders and Bowies. **Technical:** Grinds 440C, 154CM and CPM; does wood into wood inlay handles. **Prices:** $100 to $300; some to $2,000. **Remarks:** Full-time maker; first knife sold in 1973. **Mark:** Signature

TWIG (See K.M. Davis)

WAYNE VALACHOVIC, RFD #1 Box 215B, Hillsboro, NH 03244/603-464-5773
Specialties: Fighters and folders in his own designs. **Patterns:** Persian-influenced fighters, a number of robust folding designs; camp knives. **Technical:** Forges own Damascus; most knives have filework. **Prices:** $100 to $850; some to $2,000. **Remarks:** Full-time maker. **Mark:** V with cross; ABS Master Smith

A. DANIEL VALOIS, 4299 Hawthorne Rd., Orefield, PA 18069/215-767-0213
Specialties: Big knives for rough duty. **Patterns:** Fighters in survival packs; sturdy working knives; belt buckle knives; military styling. **Technical:** Forges and grinds A2, 01 and 440C; likes full tangs. **Prices:** $65 to $240; some to $600. **Remarks:** Full-time maker; first knife sold in 1969. **Mark:** Initials, anvil logo

FRANS VAN ELDIK, Ho Flaan 3, 3632 BT Loenen, NETHERLANDS/02943-3095
Specialties: Fancy working knives in his own designs. **Patterns:** Hunters, fighters, boots. **Technical:** Grinds and forges; uses D2, 154CM and Damascus from Germany. **Prices:** $225 to $1,750; some to $2,500. **Remarks:** Spare-time maker; first knife sold in 1979. **Mark:** Lion with F.V.E. Amsterdam

MICHAEL VEIT, Rt. 1, 3070 E. Fifth Rd., LaSalle, IL 61301/815-223-3538
Specialties: Period pieces and fancy straight knives. **Patterns:** Fighters, Bowies and daggers. **Technical:** Forges his own Turkish Damascus, 01 and L6. All hidden tang knives have complete disassembly. **Prices:** $200 to $650; some to $1,200. **Remarks:** Full-time maker; first knife sold in 1985. **Mark:** Name in script

H.J. VIELE, 88 Lexington Ave., Westwood, NJ 07675/201-666-2906
Specialties: Clean design in straight knives of distinctive shapes, often Oriental. **Patterns:** Tantos, daggers, utility and personal knives; now swagger sticks and canes with blades. **Technical:** Grinds 440C, ATS34. **Prices:** $300 to $350; some to $1,200. **Remarks:** Part-time maker; first knife sold in 1973. **Mark:** VIELE with Japanese crane

DAVID P. VOTAW, Box 327, Pioneer, OH 43554/419-737-2774
Specialties: Period pieces as working knives. **Patterns:** Hunters, Bowies, camp knives, buckskinners, tomahawks to W-K's traditional standards. **Technical:** Grinds 01 and D2. **Prices:** $75 to $200; some to $500. **Remarks:** Part-time maker; took over for the late Walter Kneubuehler. **Mark:** WK with V inside anvil

FRANK VOUGHT, JR., 115 Monticello Dr., Hammond, LA 70401/504-345-0278
Specialties: Distinctive working knives. **Patterns:** Bowies, hunters, survival knives; daggers and swords; folding lockers. **Technical:** Grinds and forges; offers D2, 440C, 154CM and ATS34; has new "field grade" Outfitter line. **Prices:** $50 to $350; some $1,500. **Remarks:** Full-time maker; first knife sold in 1973. **Mark:** Signature with fleur-de-lis, or Outfitter

ROBERT "BOB" VUNK, 4408 Buckeye Ct., Orlando, FL 32804/305-628-3970
Specialties: Working knives, some fancy or period pieces. **Patterns:** Tantos in many flavors; some swords and camp knives. **Technical:** Grinds 01, 440C, ATS34; provides mountings, cases, stands. **Prices:** $35 to $500; some to $1,000. **Remarks:** Part-time maker; sold first knife in 1985. **Mark:** RV and date

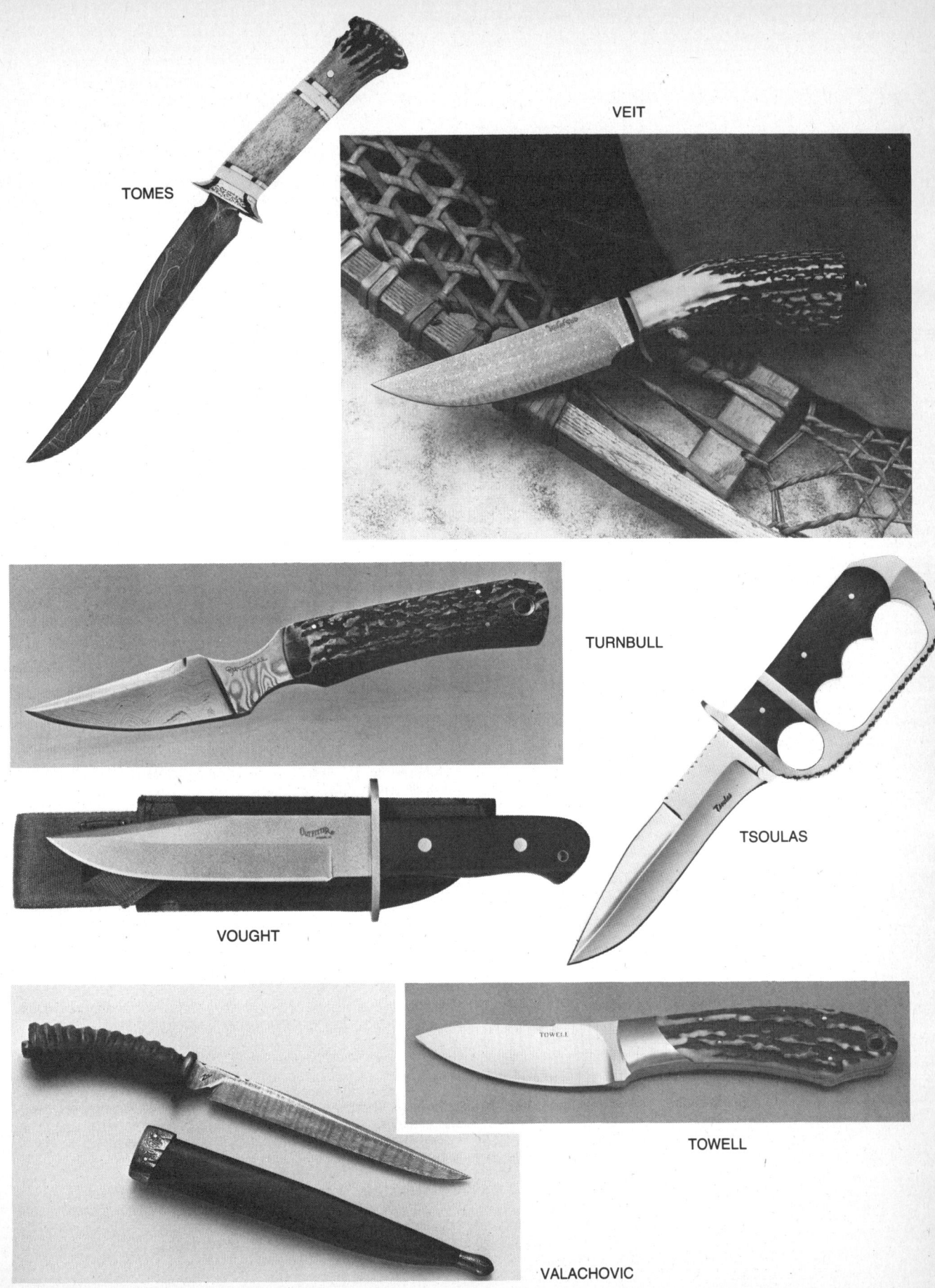

directory/custom knifemakers

JAMES M. WADE, Rt. 1, Box 56, Wade, NC 28395/919-483-3548
Specialties: Straight working knives. **Patterns:** Hunters, fighters and boots. **Technical:** Grinds D2, 440C, 154CM and ATS34. **Prices:** $100 to $450; some to $1,000. **Remarks:** Spare-time maker; first knife sold in 1982. **Mark:** Name and serial number

JOHN K. WAGAMAN, 903 Arsenal Ave., Fayetteville, NC 28305/919-485-7860
Specialties: Fancy working knives. **Patterns:** Bowies, miniatures, hunters, fighters, boots. **Technical:** Grinds D2, 440C and 154CM, and bought Damascus; inlays mother-of-pearl. **Prices:** $80 to $340; some to $800. **Remarks:** Part-time maker, first knife sold in 1975. **Mark:** WAGAMAN

HERMAN F. WAHLERS, Star Route Box 1, Austerlitz, NY 12017/518-392-3570
Specialties: Straight working knives of his own design. **Patterns:** Bowies, hunters and camp knives; favors clip-point for general use. **Technical:** Grinds D2, 440C and 154CM. **Prices:** $75 to $150; some $200. **Remarks:** Full-time maker; first knife sold in 1983. **Mark:** H.W.

MARK DAVID WAHLSTER, 6108 Radiant Dr. N.E., Salem, OR 97303/503-393-5430
Specialties: Working knives and period pieces. **Patterns:** Hunters, boots, Bowies, daggers; makes lots of buckskinner gear; some folders; miniatures. **Technical:** Grinds and forges; offers 01, L6, 440C, ATS34 and buys Damascus. **Prices:** $75 to $375; some to $2,000. **Remarks:** Full-time maker; first knife sold in 1981. **Mark:** Name and place

MARK WALDROP, P.O. Box 129, Lady Lake, FL 32659/904-821-2530
Specialties: Period pieces and working knives. **Patterns:** Folding lockers, hunters, Bowies and daggers. **Technical:** Forges W2, 01 and his own Damascus; forges ribbed blades. **Prices:** $175 to $800. **Remarks:** Part-time maker; first knife sold in 1978. **Mark:** WALDROP

GEORGE A. WALKER, Star Route, Alpine, WY 83128/307-883-2372
Specialties: Deluxe working knives in partnership. **Patterns:** Folding lockers, hunters, boots, Bowies and tomahawks. **Technical:** Grinds and forges; offers 440C, 154CM, ATS34 and his own welded-wire Damascus; engraving, scrimshaw, sheaths all in the Walker family. **Prices:** $125 to $750; some to $1,000. **Remarks:** Full-time maker; first knife sold in 1979. **Mark:** Fish with signature, or name, city and state

JOHN W. WALKER, Rt. 2, Box 376, Bon Aqua, TN 37025/615-670-4754
Specialties: Working straight knives in standard patterns. **Patterns:** Hunters, boots, push knives and miniatures. **Technical:** Grinds 440C, 154CM and ATS34. **Prices:** $85 to $200; some to $450. **Remarks:** Full-time maker; first knife sold in 1982. **Mark:** Hohenzollern Eagle below name

MICHAEL L. WALKER, Box 2343, Taos, NM 87571/505-758-0233
Specialties: High-tech folders of original design and execution. **Patterns:** Folding lockers, patent locks, interframes—engraved, scrimmed, anodized in titanium colors, furnished with rich materials. **Technical:** Grinds AEB-L, 6K, commercial Damascus; most knives a team effort with Patricia Walker. **Prices:** $475 to $1,800; some to $4,500. **Remarks:** Full-time maker; first knife sold in 1980. **Mark:** Walker's Lockers by M.L. Walker, or initials

A.F. WALTERS, 609 E. 20th St., Tifton, GA 31794/912-382-1282
Specialties: Working knives; some to order. **Patterns:** Folding lockers; fixed hunters, fish and survival knives. **Technical:** Grinds D2, 154CM and 13C26. **Prices:** $85 on up. **Remarks:** Part-time maker. Label: "The jewel knife." **Mark:** J in diamond and knife logo

BRIAN K. WALTERS, P.O. Box 2124, Des Moines, IA 50310/515-255-4699
Specialties: Straight working knives, some deluxe. **Patterns:** Hunters to survival knives. **Technical:** Flat grinds; D2, 440C and 154CM; hand polishes. **Prices:** $100 to $300; some to $1,000. **Remarks:** Spare-time maker, first knife sold in 1978. **Mark:** W in circle

KEN WARD, 3401 Becerra Wy., Sacramento, CA 95821/916-482-9650
Specialties: Working knives, some to custom design. **Patterns:** Hunters, folding and fixed; axes, Bowies, buckskinners and miniatures. **Technical:** Grinds 440C, 154CM and ATS34. **Prices:** $80 to $125; some to $180. **Remarks:** Full-time maker; first knife sold in 1977. **Mark:** KW

W.C. WARD, Rte. 6, Lynn Rd, Box 184-B, Clinton, TN 37716/615-457-3568
Specialties: Straight working knives, and some period pieces. **Patterns:** Hunters, Bowies, swords and kitchen cutlery. **Technical:** Grinds 01. **Prices:** $65 to $135; some $300. **Remarks:** Part-time maker; first knife sold in 1969; styled the Tennessee Knife Maker. **Mark:** TKM

DAVE WARDMAN, 9910 U.S.-23, Ossineke, MI 49766/517-471-2090
Specialties: Straight working knives to order. **Patterns:** Hunters, minis, boots and survival knives. **Technical:** Hollow grinds D2, 440C and 154CM. **Prices:** $55 to $150. **Remarks:** Spare-time maker; first knife sold in 1977. **Mark:** Wardman

BUSTER WARENSKI, P.O. Box 214, Richfield, UT 84701/801-896-5319
Specialties: Investor-class design and execution in straight knives. **Patterns:** Daggers, swords, fighters and Bowies. **Technical:** Grinds; does own engraving and inlays; surface treatments. **Prices:** Upscale. **Remarks:** Full-time maker. Not taking orders. **Mark:** Buster or Warenski

AL WARREN, 63664 High Standard, Bend, OR 97701/503-389-3299
Specialties: Straight working knives, some quite fancy. **Patterns:** Hunter patterns, some Bowies; incorporates intact fossil ivory artifacts. **Technical:** Grinds D2, 440C and F8 (a high carbon, high tungsten steel); laminates $1/16$-inch ivory over ebony or koa; brass-wraps all full tangs. **Prices:** $195 to $850; some to $1,500. **Remarks:** Full-time maker; sold first knife in 1978. **Mark:** NAME, serial

DALE WARTHER, 164 West St., Box 265, Bolivar, OH 44612/216-343-7513
Specialties: Period pieces and working knives. **Patterns:** Kitchen cutlery, daggers, hunters and some folders. **Technical:** Grinds and forges; uses 01, D2 and 440C. **Prices:** $100 to $350; some to $5,000. **Remarks:** Full-time maker; first knife sold in 1967. Taking orders only at shows or personal interviews at shop. **Mark:** WARTHER ORIGINALS

STANLEY WARZOCHA, 32540 Wareham Dr., Warren, MI 48092/313-939-9344
Specialties: Straight working knives; some period pieces. **Patterns:** Hunters, buckskinners; fighters and fish knives. **Technical:** Grinds 01, 440C and 154CM. **Prices:** $80 to $140; some to $300. **Remarks:** Spare-time maker; first knife sold in 1978. **Mark:** WARZOCHA

WATER MOUNTAIN KNIVES (See Kenneth Maneker)

DANIEL and BILL WATSON, 350 Jennifer Ln., Driftwood, TX 78619/512-847-9679
Specialties: Fancy working knives and swords. **Patterns:** Hunters, daggers and swords. **Technical:** Hand forges 01 and his own Damascus; uses leaf springs, too. **Prices:** $90 to $4,000; swords to $10,000. **Remarks:** Full-time maker; Daniel sold his first knife in 1979. Bill sold his in 1982. **Mark:** "Angel Sword"

FREDDIE WATT, III, P.O. Box 1372, Big Spring, TX 79721/915-263-6629
Specialties: Straight and folding working knives; some fancy. **Patterns:** Hunters, fighters, Bowies; some folders. **Technical:** Grinds D2, 440C and ATS34; likes mirror finishes. **Prices:** $150 to $220; some to $500. **Remarks:** Full-time maker; first knife sold in 1979. **Mark:** WATT, city, state

FRED E. WEBER, 517 Tappan St., Forked River, NJ 08731/609-693-0452
Specialties: Working knives in standard patterns. **Patterns:** Hunters, fighters, Bowies, boots and daggers. **Technical:** Grinds D2, 154CM and CPM. **Prices:** $110 to $250; some $500. **Remarks:** Full-time maker; first knife sold in 1973. **Mark:** F.E. WEBER

DEL WEDDLE, Jr., Box 10, Stewartsville, MO 64490/816-669-3478
Specialties: Working knives; some period pieces. **Patterns:** Hunters, fighters, folding lockers; makes push knives. **Technical:** Grinds D2 and 440C; can provide precious metals and set gems. **Prices:** $80 to $250; some to $2,000. **Remarks:** Full-time maker; first knife sold in 1972. **Mark:** Signature with last name and date

RUDY WEHNER, 2713 Riverbend Dr., Violet, LA 70092/504-682-3168
Specialties: Working straight knives in traditional patterns. **Patterns:** Full-size to miniature Bowies of various styles, skinners, camp knives. **Technical:** Grinds D2, 440C, and 154CM. **Prices:** $60 to $125; some up to $450. **Remarks:** Part-time maker; first knife sold in 1975. **Mark:** Full name, city and state

J. REESE WEILAND, JR., 14919 Nebraska Ave., Tampa, FL 33612/813-971-5378 (M-F 7:30-5:00)
Specialties: Straight and folding working knives of traditional types. **Patterns:** Hunters, tantos, Bowies, butterflies, some swords; distinctive bird-shaped handle on some models. **Technical:** Grinds 440C, ATS34 and Damascus bars. **Prices:** $100 to $250; some higher. **Remarks:** Full-time production; sold first knife in 1983. **Mark:** RW slant

DONALD E. WEILER, P.O. Box 1576, Yuma, AZ 85364/602-782-1159
Specialties: Period pieces and straight working knives. **Patterns:** Dirks, daggers, fighters, survival knives; scramasax; likes Norse designs. **Technical:** Grinds and forges; uses 01, W1 and D2. **Prices:** $60 to $200; some to $750. **Remarks:** Part-time maker; first knife sold in 1952. **Mark:** WEILER, YUMA

GEROME W. WEINAND, Box 385, Lolo, MT 59847/406-273-6553
Specialties: Straight working knives. **Patterns:** Bowies, fish and camp knives; large special hunters. **Technical:** Grinds 01, 440C, and L6. Does own heat-treating. **Prices:** $25 to $50; some $250. **Remarks:** Full-time maker; first knife sold in 1982. **Mark:** Name, city and state

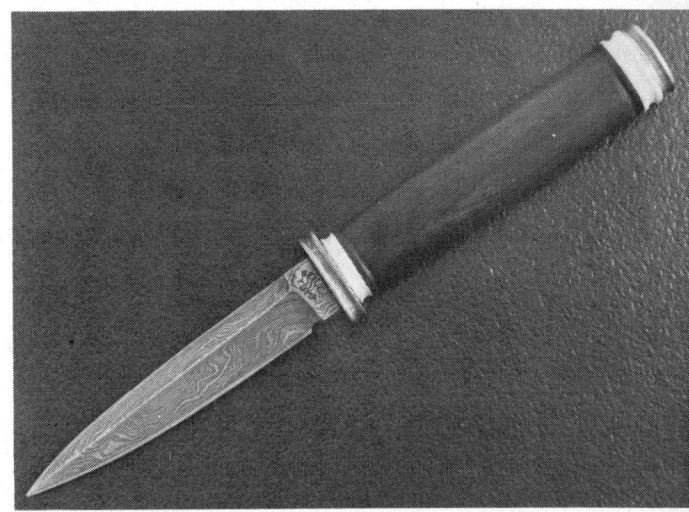
WEILER

WEINAND

WAHLSTER

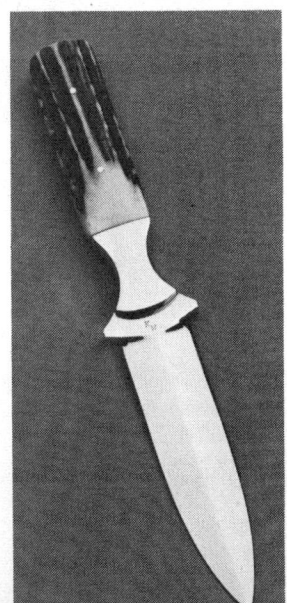
K. WARD

WARREN

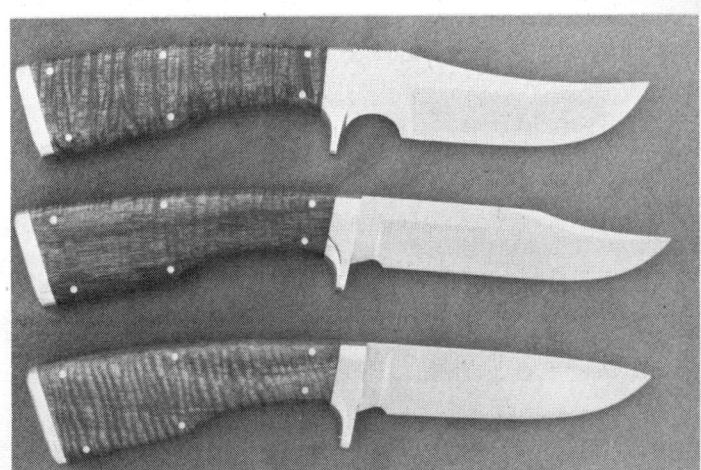

EIGHTH ANNUAL EDITION **229**

directory/custom knifemakers

CHARLES L. WEISS, 18847 N. 13th Ave., Phoenix, AZ 85027/602-869-0425 **Specialties:** Deluxe period pieces; high art straight knives. **Patterns:** Daggers, fighters, boots, push knives and miniatures. **Technical:** Grinds 440C, 154CM and ATS34. **Prices:** $300 to $1,200; some to $2,000. **Remarks:** Full-time maker; first knife sold in 1975. **Mark:** Name and town

WILLIAM H. WELCH, 5226 Buell Drive, Fort Wayne, IN 46807/219-745-0411
Specialties: Working knives and deluxe period pieces. **Patterns:** Hunters, tantos, Bowies, locking folders and spears. **Technical:** Grinds A2, D2 and 440C. **Prices:** $80 to $400; some to $1,000. **Remarks:** Part-time maker; first knife sold in 1976. **Mark:** WELCH

GEORGE W. WERTH, 9010 Cary Rd., Cary, IL 60013/312-639-9308 **Specialties:** Period pieces, some fancy. **Patterns:** Straight knives in hunters, fighters, daggers, Bowies and miniatures. **Technical:** Forges and grinds 01, 1095 and his own Damsacus in mosaic patterns. **Prices:** $200 to $650; some much more. **Remarks:** Full-time production. **Mark:** Name in logo or GWW connected

CODY WESCOTT, 5610 Hanger Lake Ln., Las Cruces, NM 88001/505-382-5008
Specialties: Fancy working knives. **Patterns:** Hunters, buckskinners, Bowies, fighters and folders. **Technical:** Hollow grinds and forges; offers D2, 440C and commercial Damascus; all knives extensively fileworked. **Prices:** $50 to $240; some to $700. **Remarks:** Full-time maker; first knife sold in 1982. **Mark:** C. WESCOTT

JIM WESCOTT, 4225 Elks Dr., Las Cruces, NM 88005/505-526-8926 **Specialties:** Working knives. **Patterns:** Bowies, hunters and locking folders. **Technical:** Grinds D2 and 440C. **Prices:** $90 to $170; some to $300. **Remarks:** Part-time maker; first knife sold in 1982. **Mark:** Wescott

MIKE WESOLOWSKI, 902-A Lohrman Lane, Petaluma, CA 94952/707-762-7564
Specialties: Working knives; display Bowies. **Patterns:** Hunters, utility and using knives, and miniatures. **Technical:** Flat grinds; finger placement choils. Uses D2, 440C, and 154CM. **Prices:** $90 to $200; some $500. **Remarks:** Part-time maker; first knife sold in 1973. **Mark:** M.W., city and state in knife logo

WHISKERS (See Mike Allen)

GENE E. WHITE, 5415 Taney Ave., Alexandria, VA 22304/703-751-1833 **Specialties:** Working knives; period pieces to order. **Patterns:** Simple guardless hunters and utility knives; makes fighters to order. **Technical:** Grinds; uses stainless steels. **Prices:** $60 to $150; some to $300. **Remarks:** Part-time maker; first knife sold in 1971. **Mark:** Last name

ROBERT J. "BOB" WHITE, RR 1, Gilson, IL 61436/309-289-4487 **Specialties:** Working knives; some quite deluxe. **Patterns:** Bird and trout knives, hunters, survival knives and folding lockers. **Technical:** Grinds and forges A2, D2 and 440C; commercial Damascus. Does own heat-treating. **Prices:** $95 to $185; some to $600. **Remarks:** Full-time maker; first knife sold in 1976. **Mark:** White in script

ROBERT J. "BUTCH" WHITE, JR., R.R. 1, Gilson, IL 61436/309-289-4487 **Specialties:** Fixed and folding working knives. **Patterns:** Hunters, fighters and boots and Damascus miniatures. **Technical:** Grinds and forges; offers D2, 440C and his own Damascus. **Prices:** $75 to $200. **Remarks:** Full-time maker; first knife sold in 1980. **Mark:** WHITE in block letters

WHITEFISH SPORTSMAN (See Pete Forthofer)

JAMES D. WHITEHEAD, P.O. Box 540, Durham, CA 95938/916-894-3938 **Specialties:** Highly detailed straight and folding miniatures. **Patterns:** Traditional and fancy. **Technical:** Forges and grinds 01 and bought Damascus. **Prices:** $75 to $300. **Remarks:** Part-time maker; first knife sold in 1985. **Mark:** JDW

JIM WHITMAN, SR3 Box 5387, Chugiak, AK 99567/907-688-4575 **Specialties:** Working straight knives in traditional modes. **Patterns:** Hunters, especially skinners, Bowies, camp knives. **Technical:** Grinds A2, 440C, ABL-SWD in "semi-flat" grind for good edge-holding. **Prices:** $75 to $145; some to $750. **Remarks:** Part-time maker; sold first knife in 1983. **Mark:** Name, city, state

EARL T. WHITMIRE, 725 Colonial Dr., Rock Hill, SC 29730/803-324-8384 **Specialties:** Working straight knives, some to order. **Patterns:** Hunters, fighters, fish knives; some fantasy pieces. **Technical:** Grinds D2, 440C and 154CM. **Prices:** $40 to $200; some to $250. **Remarks:** Full-time maker; first knife sold in 1967. **Mark:** Name, city, state in oval logo

KEN J. WHITWORTH, 41667 Tetley Ave., Sterling Heights, MI 48078/313-739-5720
Specialties: Straight and folding working knives. **Patterns:** Locking folders and slip joints, hunters and tantos. **Technical:** Grinds 440C, 154CM and D2. **Prices:** $100 to $170; some to $300. **Remarks:** Part-time maker; first knife sold in 1976. **Mark:** WHITWORTH

HORACE WIGGINS, 203 Herndon, Box 152, Mansfield, LA 71502/318-872-4471 (evenings)
Specialties: Fancy working knives. **Patterns:** Hunters, fixed and folding. **Technical:** Grinds 01, D2 and 440C. **Prices:** $90 to $275. **Remarks:** Part-time maker; first knife sold in 1970. **Mark:** Name, city, state in diamond logo

JAMES C. WIGGINS, 1540 W. Pleasant Rd., Hammond, LA 70403/504-345-0454
Specialties: Folding and straight working knives in standard patterns: **Patterns:** Hunters, camp knives and locking folders. **Technical:** Grinds D2, 440C and 154CM. **Prices:** $75 to $150; some to $600. **Remarks:** Part-time maker; first knife sold in 1981. **Mark:** Full name

WILD BILL & SONS (See Bill Caldwell)

GERI L. WILLEY, Rt. 1, Box 235-B, Greenwood, DE 19950/302-349-4070 **Specialties:** Straight working knives of her own design. **Patterns:** Hunters. **Technical:** Grinds 440C. **Prices:** $45 to $75; some $90. **Remarks:** Spare-time maker; daughter of W.G. Willey. Has worked in his shop for five years. **Mark:** Willey in diamond logo

W.G. WILLEY, R.D. 1, Box 235-B, Greenwood, DE 19950/302-349-4070 **Specialties:** Fancy working straight knives. **Patterns:** Small game knives, Bowies and throwing knives. **Technical:** Grinds 440C and 154CM. **Prices:** $225 to $600; some to $1,500. **Remarks:** Part-time maker; first knife sold in 1975. Has retail store. **Mark:** WILLEY inside map logo

SHERMAN A. WILLIAMS, 1709 Wallace St., Simi Valley, CA 93065/805-583-3821
Specialties: Straight working knives in standard patterns. **Patterns:** Hunters, boots, utility knives, also unusual trail knives. **Technical:** Grinds and forges; uses ATS34, 1095, DA and A2. **Prices:** $45 to $250. **Remarks:** Part-time maker; first knife sold in 1983. **Mark:** SHERMAN in crow logo

THE WILLOW FORGE (See Daniel Tokar)

WILSONHAWK (See James G. Wilson)

JAMES G. WILSON, Moraine Rt. UC 2004, Estes Park, CO 80517/303-586-3944
Specialties: The Bronze Age first; the 20th century second. **Patterns:** Bronze knives and swords and battle axes. Bowies and boots. **Technical:** Casts bronze; grinds D2, 440C and 154CM. **Prices:** $65 to $250; some to $1,200. **Remarks:** Part-time maker; first knife sold in 1975. **Mark:** WilsonHawK

R.W. WILSON, P.O. Box 2012, Weirton, WV 26062/304-723-2771 **Specialties:** Period pieces; working knives. **Patterns:** Straight working knives; Bowies and tomahawks and patch knives. **Prices:** $85 to $175; some $1,000. **Technical:** Grinds 440C; scrimshaw. **Remarks:** Part-time maker; first knife sold in 1966. Knifemaker supplier. **Mark:** Name in tomahawk

MICHAEL WINE, 66 Westview Ln., Cocoa Beach, FL 32931/305-784-2187
Specialties: Straight and folding traditional working knives. **Patterns:** Does some fish knives; has a bareheaded, linerless, mid-release locking folder. **Technical:** Grinds 440C, 154CM and Stellite. **Prices:** $100 to $175; some to $350. **Remarks:** Spare-time maker; sold first knife in 1971. **Mark:** M. WINE with palm tree

TRAVIS A. WINN, 558 E. 3065 So., Salt Lake City, UT 84106/801-467-5957
Specialties: Fancy working knives and customer designs. **Patterns:** Hunters, fighters and fancy daggers; some miniatures. **Technical:** Grinds 01, D2 and 440C. **Prices:** $80 to $200; some to $1,000. **Remarks:** Part-time maker; first knife sold in 1976. **Mark:** TRAV stylized

EARL WITSAMAN, 1975 Echo Rd., Stow, OH 44224/216-688-4208
Specialties: Miniatures of straight knives and fantasy pieces. **Patterns:** Wide variety—Randall to D-guard Bowie. **Technical:** Grinds 01, 440C and 300 stainless; commercial Damascus; mirror finishes; greatly detailed. **Prices:** $35 to $50; some to $100. **Remarks:** Full-time maker; first knife sold in 1974. **Mark:** EW

W-K Knives (See Votaw)

BARRY W. WOOD, 38 S. Venice Blvd., Venice, CA 90291/213-823-5637
Specialties: High-tech working knives in their designs. **Patterns:** Patent Wood folder and interframes in wide variety. **Technical:** Grind 154CM and ATS34; Sharon saw steel. **Prices:** $150 to $600; some to $2,500. **Remarks:** Full-time maker; first knife sold in 1969. **Mark:** bw in script within triangle

LARRY B. WOOD, 6945 Fishburg Rd., Huber Heights, OH 45424/513-233-6751
Specialties: Fancy working knives in his own designs. **Patterns:** Hunters, buckskinners, Bowies, tomahawks, folding lockers and Damascus miniatures. **Technical:** Forges 1095, file steel, and his own Damascus. **Prices:** $125 to $500; some to $2,000. **Remarks:** Full-time maker; first knife sold in 1974. **Mark:** Variations of Wood, sometimes with blacksmith logo

OWEN DALE WOOD, P.O. Box 515, Honeydew 2040 (Transvaal), SOUTH AFRICA/International + 2711 + 795-1050
Specialties: Fancy working knives. **Patterns:** Hunters and fighters; big knives of many types; sword canes. **Technical:** Forges and grinds 440C, 154CM and his own Damascus. Uses rare African handle materials. **Prices:** $280 to $450; some to $3,000. **Remarks:** Full-time maker; first knife sold in 1976. **Mark:** An O encircling a W

WEBSTER WOOD, 4726 Rosedale, Clarkston, MI 48016/313-394-0351
Specialties: Fancy working knives. **Patterns:** Hunters, survival knives, folding lockers and slip joints. **Technical:** Grinds 01, 440C and 154CM; does all engraving and scrimming. **Prices:** $100 to $500; some to $3,000. **Remarks:** Full-time maker; first knife sold in 1980. **Mark:** Initials inside shield and name

WILLIAM W. WOOD, P.O. Box 877, Vera, TX 76383/817-888-5832
Specialties: Exotic working knives with Middle-East flavor. **Patterns:** Fighters, boots; some utility knives. **Technical:** Grinds D2, 440C and buys Damascus; hand rubbed satin finish; only natural handle materials. **Prices:** $300 to $600; some to $2,000. **Remarks:** Full-time maker; first knife sold in 1977. **Mark:** Name, city, state

HAROLD E. WOODWARD, Rt 3, Box 64A, Woodbury, TN 37190/615-563-4619
Specialties: Period pieces and working knives. **Patterns:** Hunters, Bowies, swords, sword canes and tomahawks. **Technical:** Grinds A2, D2 and 440C; does his own engraving. **Prices:** $75 to $350; some much more. **Remarks:** Full-time maker; first knife sold in 1972. **Mark:** WOODWARD

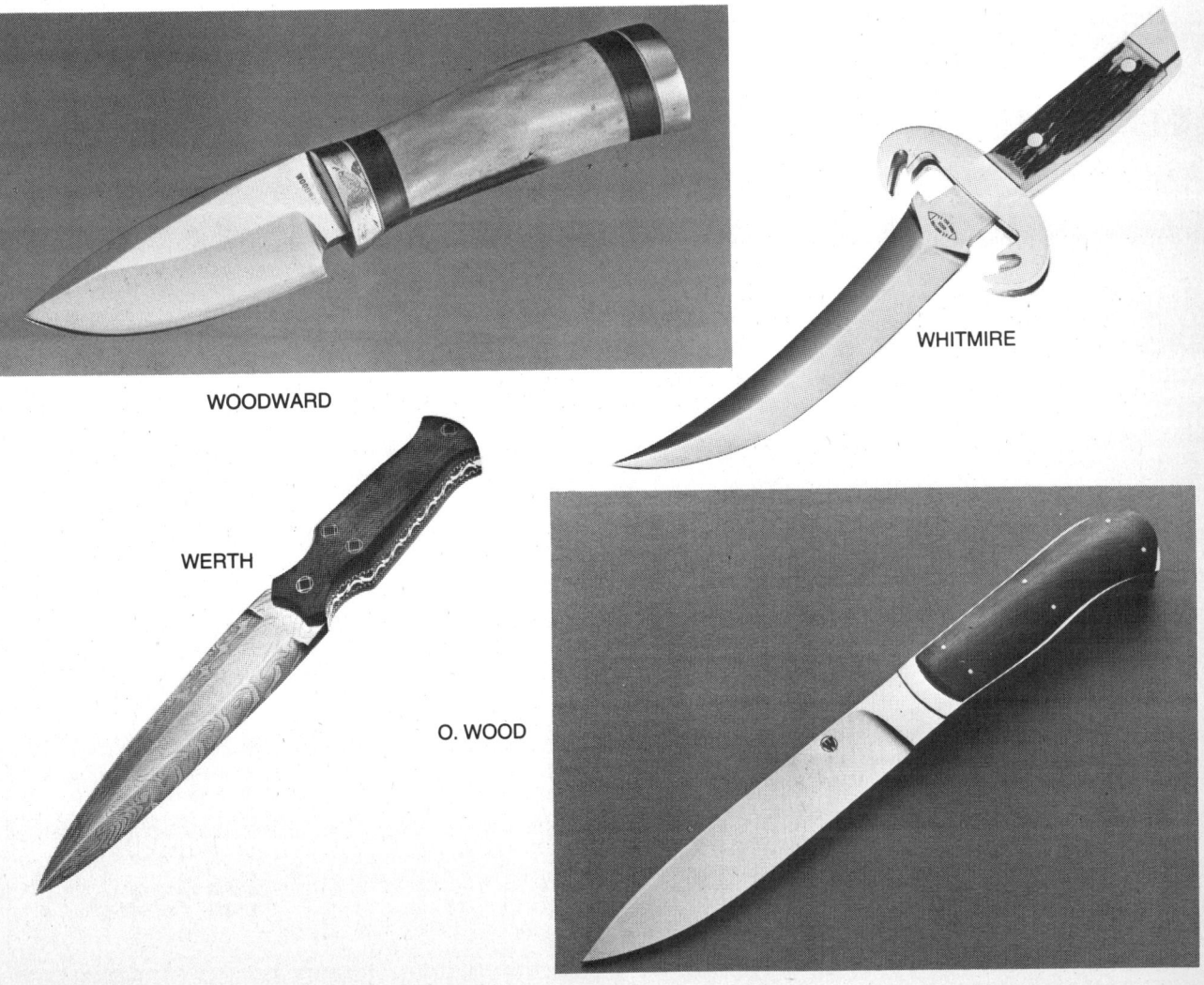

WOODWARD

WHITMIRE

WERTH

O. WOOD

directory/custom knifemakers

AL WOODWORTH, 4420 State Route 316 W., Ashville, OH 43103/614-983-3880
Specialties: Working straight knives and fantasies in his personal designs. **Patterns:** Bowies, camp knives, daggers, some butterflies. **Technical:** Grinds 01, D2, 440C; uses natural handles, 416 SS for fittings. **Prices:** $125 to $250; some to $450. **Remarks:** Full-time maker; sold first knife in 1987. **Mark:** AW with cross, Libra sign

JOE WOREL, 3040 N. LaPorte, Melrose Park, IL 60164/312-455-8243
Specialties: Straight working knives, some fancy. **Patterns:** Hunters, Bowies and survival knives. **Technical:** Grinds 1095, 440C and F8. **Prices:** $80 to $225; some to $500. **Remarks:** Full-time maker; first knife sold in 1937. **Mark:** WOREL

WORM (See Pittman)

HAROLD C. WRIGHT, 1710 Bellwood Drive, Centerville, TN 37033/615-729-4444
Specialties: Straight working knives. **Patterns:** Hunters, buckskinners, Bowies and tantos. **Technical:** Grinds 01, 440C and 154CM; likes hollow grinds and filework. **Prices:** $40 to $100; some $150. **Remarks:** Spare-time maker; first knife sold in 1982. **Mark:** Name and town (Grinders Switch is the home of Minnie Pearl)

KEVIN WRIGHT, 671 Leland Valley Rd. W, Quilcene, WA 98376-9517/206-765-3589
Specialties: Fancy working knives in standard patterns. **Patterns:** Hunters, boots, buckskinners, daggers, swords, even miniatures. **Technical:** Forges and grinds; offers 1095, 440C and his own Damascus. **Prices:** $50 to $300; some to $1,000. **Remarks:** Part-time maker; first knife sold in 1978. **Mark:** W in anvil

TIMOTHY WRIGHT, 4100 W. Grand Ave., Chicago, IL 60651/312-489-4436/4186
Specialties: High-tech working folders; high-tech household knives. **Patterns:** Folding lockers in interframes; fixed hunters and kitchen cutlery. **Technical:** Grinds A2, ATS34 and M4-CPM; works with new steels, careful grinds; makes folders to disassemble, furnishes parts, tools. **Prices:** $75 to $300; some to $1,000. **Remarks:** Full-time maker; first knife sold in 1975. **Mark:** WRIGHT

YASUTOMO (See Louis G. Mills)

DAVID C. YORK, P.O. Box 1342, Crested Butte, CO 81224/303-349-5826
Specialties: Working knives, both folding and fixed. **Patterns:** Prefers small hunters and skinners. Offers folding lockers, buckskinner and survival knives. **Technical:** Grinds D2, 440C; buys Damascus. **Prices:** $75 to $300; some to $600. **Remarks:** Part-time maker; first knife sold in 1975. **Mark:** YORK

BUD YOUNG, Box 336, Port Hardy, BC V0N 2P0, CANADA/604-949-6478
Specialties: Working straight knives, some fancy. **Patterns:** Hunters from drop-points to skinners. **Technical:** Grinds 01, L6, 1095; uses 154CM and ATS34 when available; likes mirror polish, natural handles. **Prices:** $200 to $400; some higher. **Remarks:** Spare-time maker; sold first knife in 1985. **Mark:** Name

CLIFF YOUNG, R.R.#1, Cotnams Island, Pembroke, Ont. K8A 6WZ, CANADA/613-735-6401
Specialties: Working knives for users; some display pieces. **Patterns:** Hunters, fighters, locking folders, and fish knives. **Technical:** Grinds mostly; some forging; offers D2, 440C and 154CM. **Prices:** $165 to $350; some to $800. **Remarks:** Part-time maker; first knife sold in 1980. **Mark:** Name, city, province

ERROL YOUNG, 4826 Storey Land, Alton, IL 62002/618-466-4707
Specialties: Straight and folding working knives in traditional styles. **Patterns:** Wide range, including tantos and Bowies, miniatures and multi-blade folders. **Technical:** Grinds D2, 440C, and ATS34. **Prices:** $75 to $650; some to $800. **Remarks:** Part-time maker; sold first knife in 1987. **Mark:** Last name with arrow

YAMIL R. YUNES, P.O. Box 573, Roma, TX 78584/512-849-1001
Specialties: Folding and straight knives in traditional patterns. **Patterns:** Folding lockers, slip joints, hunters, fighters and utility knives. **Technical:** Grinds 440C, 01 and D2. Has patented cocking design for folders. **Prices:** $45 to $140; some to $300. **Remarks:** Part-time maker; first knife sold in 1975. **Mark:** YUNES

MIKE YURCO, 260 E. Laclede Ave., Youngstown, OH 44507/216-788-7310
Specialties: Working straight knives. **Patterns:** Hunters, utility knives; some Bowies and push knives; makes buckle knives and other hideouts. **Technical:** Grinds 440C; likes mirror finishes and Pakkawood. **Prices:** $35 to $150; some higher. **Remarks:** Part-time maker; sold first knife in 1983. **Mark:** NAME, steel, serial number

Z CUSTOM KNIVES (See Zollan McCarty)

DON ZACCAGNINO, P.O. Box 583, Pahokee, FL 33476/305-924-7844
Specialties: Working knives and some period pieces in his own style. **Patterns:** Heavy-duty hunters, axes, Bowies, daggers and fantasy miniatures. **Technical:** Grinds 440C and 17-4-PH—highly finished in complex handle and blade treatments. **Prices:** $150 to $500; some to $1,000. **Remarks:** Full-time maker; first knife sold in 1969. **Mark:** ZACK, city and state

DENNIS J. ZELLER, 1791 South West Lilyben Ave., Gresham, OR 97030/503-667-7869
Specialties: Working knives. **Patterns:** Daggers and fighters and boots are first; survival knives and such second. **Technical:** Grinds L6, 440C and A514. **Prices:** $125 to $475; some to $875. **Remarks:** Full-time maker; first knife sold in 1984. **Mark:** Zeller

JOE ZEMITIS, 14 Currawong Rd., Cardiff Hts./2285 Newcastle, AUSTRALIA/049-549907
Specialties: Traditional working straight knives. **Patterns:** Hunters, Bowies, tantos, camp knives, all in heavy-duty construction. **Technical:** Grinds 01, D2, 440C. **Prices:** $65 to $500. **Remarks:** Part-time maker; sold first knife in 1983. **Mark:** Name

TIM ZOWADA, 23583 Church Rd., Battle Creek, MI 49017/616-965-3461
Specialties: Working knives, some fancy. **Patterns:** Hunters, camp knives, boots, fighters and tantos, and locking folders. **Technical:** Forges 01, L6 and his own Damascus. **Prices:** $180 to $600; some to $2,000. **Remarks:** Full-time maker; first knife sold in 1980. **Mark:** Lower case gothic letters "tz"

MICHAEL ZSCHERNY, 2512 "N" Ave. NW, Cedar Rapids, IA 52405/319-396-3659
Specialties: Fancy working knives in standard patterns. **Patterns:** Hunters, tantos, boots, push knives and razors. **Technical:** Grinds 440C and 154CM; prefers natural handle materials. **Prices:** $150 to $1,000; some to $1,700. **Remarks:** Part-time maker. **Mark:** ZSCHERNY

We have lost touch with these knifemakers:

BILL BAGWELL	EDWARD LAWLESS
RODERICK CHAPPEL	ANTHONY LOUIS, JR.
DANNY COURTNEY	C.O. McCLUNG
JIM CUNNINGHAM	JERRY POLETIS
STEVE DAVENPORT	WILLIAM J. RICHARDSON
ROBERT ORR DODGE	G. ROCHA
ROGER GLEASON	HAROLD F. ROLLINS
CHARLES W. GRAHAM	JIM SASSER
LLOYD A. HALE	ADAM SMITH
V.E. "GENE" HARRISON	JOHN T. SMITH
DON & RON ISAACS	KEN STEIGERWALT
DON KARLIN	WELDON WHITLEY
KIOSHI KATO	ART WIMAN
JON KIRK	BRUCE WOOD
KURT LANG	RICHARD WORTHEN
GARY LANGLEY	

Knifemakers
State-By-State

Here is a very special list, prepared exclusively for readers of KNIVES '88. Below you will find all the knifemakers from the Directory listed alphabetically by state. Also shown are the towns where you may find them. Address details, of course, are to be found in our Directory.

ALABAMA
Bell, Frank	(Huntsville)
Bryan, Jack and Morgan	(Gardendale)
Conn, C.T., Jr.	(Attalla)
Dorough, Dick	(Gadsden)
Edwards, Fain	(Jacksonville)
Fuller, Jim	(Burnwell)
Fuller, W.T. Jr.	(East Gadsden)
Gilbreath, Randall	(Dora)
Hammond, Jim	(Arab)
Hodge, J.B.	(Huntsville)
Howard, Durvyn M.	(Gadsden)
Morris, C.H.	(Atmore)
Pardue, Melvin M.	(Repton)
Pearce, Hill Everett, III	(Gurley)
Roe, Red D. Jr.	(Huntsville)
Sinyard, Cleston S.	(Elberta)
Sonneville, W.J.	(Mobile)

ALASKA
Amoureux, A.W.	(Anchorage)
Breuer, Wayne	(Wasilla)
Broome, Thomas A.	(Kenai)
Bucholz, Mark A.	(Chugiak)
Chamberlin, John A.	(Anchorage)
Dempsey, Gordon W.	(N. Kenai)
DuFour, Arthur J.	(Anchorage)
Grebe, Gordon S.	(Anchorage)
Jirik, Sid	(Anchorage)
Levine, Bob	(Anchorage)
Robertson, Ron	(Anchorage)
Stegall, Keith	(Anchorage)
Trujillo, Thomas A.	(Anchorage)
Whitman, Jim	(Chugiak)

ARIZONA
Beaver, Devon	(Phoenix)
Bloomfield, L.H.	(Kingman)
Brunckhorst, C. Lyle	(Kingman)
Cheatham, Bill	(Phoenix)
Dagget, Dan	(Flagstaff)
Edwards, Thomas W.	(Phoenix)
Goo, Tai	(Tempe)
Hendricks, Lorenzo Lee	(Mesa)
Hoel, Steve	(Pine)
McFall, Ken	(Lakeside)
McLane, Thomas	(Tucson)
Oliver, Milford	(Phoenix)
Poletis, Jerry	(Scottsdale)
Thompson, Bruce Lee	(Glen Dale)
Weiler, Donald E.	(Yuma)
Weiss, Charles L.	(Phoenix)

ARKANSAS
Crawford, Pat	(West Memphis)
Crowell, James L.	(Mountain View)
Duvall, Fred	(Benton)
Ferguson, Lee	(Hindsville)
Fisk, Jerry	(Lockesburg)
Flournoy, Joe	(El Dorado)
Foster, Al	(Dogpatch)
Grigsby, Ben	(Batesville)
Hicks, Vernon G.	(Bauxite)
Kirk, Jon W.	(Fayetteville)
Lile, James B.	(Russellville)
Maringer, Tom	(Springdale)
Ogg, Robert G.	(Paris)
Polk, Clifton	(Ft. Smith)
Price, Jerry I.	(Springdale)
Ramey, Marshall F	(West Helena)
Ree, David	(Van Buren)
Russell, A.G.	(Springdale)

CALIFORNIA
Bear, Charles	(Sebastopo)
Bell, Michael	(San Francisco)
Benson, Don	(Escalon)
Besic, Leroy	(Hemet)
Blum, Chuck	(Brea)
Bochman, Bruce	(El Granada)
Breshears, Clint	(Redondo Beach)
Browne, Rick	(Upland)
Brown, L.E. Red	(Lakewood)
Brown, Ted	(Downey)
Casey, Dennis E.	(Redwood City)
Chelquist, Cliff	(Arroyo Grande)
Cohen, Terry A.	(Santa Cruz)
Collins, A.J.	(Burbank)
Detloff, Larry	(Santa Cruz)
Dias, Jack	(Palermo)
Dillon, Earl E.	(Arleta)
Dion, Greg	(Oxnard)
Dion, Malcom C.	(Goleta)
Donovan, Patrick	(San Jose)
Doolittle, Mike	(Novato)
Eaton, Al	(Clayton)
Engnath, Bob	(Glendale)
Faulkner, Al	(Marysville)
Ferdinand, Don	(San Rafael)
Fisher, Ted	(Montague)
Foust, Roger	(Modesto)
Freeman, Arthur F.	(Citrus Heights)
Funderburg, Joe	(Los Osos)
Gamble, Frank	(Gilroy)
George, Tom	(Magalia)
Gofourth, Jim	(Santa Paula)
Goodwin, Butch	(Vista)
Hartsfield, Phil	(Garden Grove)
Henry, D.E.	(Mountain Ranch)
Herndon, Wm. R. Bill	(Burbank)
Hilker, Tom	(Santa Maria)
Hornby, Glen	(Glendale)
Horn, Jess	(Redding)
Hrisoulas, Jim	(Sylmar)
Hull, Michael J.	(Santa Ana)
Humenick, Roy	(Cupertino)
Jacks, Jim	(Covina)
Kreibich, Donald L.	(San Jose)
Kruse, Martin	(Reseda)
Kuykendall, Jim	(Tulare)
Lawson, Stephan M.	(Placerville)
Levine, Norman	(Victorville)
Lockett, Sterling	(Burbank)
Loveless, R.W.	(Riverside)
McLeod, James	(Oroville)
Mendenhall, Harry E.	(Milpitas)
Morgan, Emil	(Thousand Oaks)
Morgan, Jeff	(Santee)
Morgan, Justin	(Thousand Oaks)
Morlan, Tom	(Hemet)
Norton, Frank	(Pleasanton)
Pendleton, Lloyd	(San Pablo)
Phillips, John	(Santa Barbara)
Phillips, Randy	(Temple City)
Quinn, George	(Julian)
Rust, Charles C.	(Palermo)
Salpas, Bob	(Homewood)
Samson, Jody	(Burbank)
Scarrow, Will	(San Gabriel)
Schneider, Herman J.	(Laguna Niguel)
Sornberger, Jim	(San Jose)
Stapel, Chuck	(Glendale)
Stapel, Craig	(Glendale)
Stefani, Randy	(Montrose)
Steinberg, Al	(San Bruno)
Swain, Rod	(South Pasadena)
Tamboli, Michael	(Glendale)
Terrill, Stephan	(Lindsay)
Tinker, Carolyn D.	(Whittier)
Ward, Ken	(Sacramento)
Wesolowski, Mike	(Petaluma)
Whitehead, James D.	(Durham)
Williams, Sherman A.	(Simi Valley)
Wood, Barry W.	(Venice)

COLORADO
Appleton, Ray	(Byers)
Barminski, Tom and William	(Loveland)
Belk, Jack	(Marble)
Brock, Kenneth L.	(Allinspark)
Campbell, Dick	(Conifer)
Davis, Don	(Loveland)
Dawson, Dane and Barry	(Marvel)
Dennehy, Dan	(Del Norte)
Genge, Roy E.	(Eastlake)
High, Tom	(Alamoso)
Hodgson, Richard J.	(Boulder)
Hughes, Ed	(Grand Junction)
Kirtley, George	(Boulder)
Kitsmiller, Jerry	(Montrose)
Lampson, Frank G.	(Fruita)
McWilliams, Sean	(Bayfield)
Miller, Hanford J.	(Evergreen)
Nolen, R.D. and George	(Estes Park)
Olson, Wayne C.	(Wheat Ridge)
Pogreba, Larry	(Lyons)
Robbins, Howard P.	(Estes Park)
Rollert, Steve	(Keenesburg)
Teichmoeller, Lou	(Dolores)
Timberline Knives	(Mancos)
Wilson, James G.	(Estes Park)
York, David C.	(Crested Butte)

CONNECTICUT
Granquist, William R.	(Bristol)
Haggerty, George S.	(Monroe)
Hubbard, Arthur J.	(Monroe)
Jean, Gerry	(Manchester)
Nelson, Roger S.	(Central Village)
Pankiewicz, Philip R.	(Lebanon)
Rainville, Richard	(Salem)

DELAWARE
Willey, Geri L.	(Greenwood)
Willey, W.G.	(Greenwood)

FLORIDA
Barry, James J.	(West Palm Beach)
Blackton, Andrew	(Bayonet Point)
Brown, E.H.	(Eustis)
Brown, Harold E.	(Arcadia)
Burns, Dave	(Boynton Beach)
Centofante, Frank and Mark	(Tampa)
Cox, Colin J.	(Apopka)
Daniels, Alex	(Lynn Haven)
Ellerbe, W.B.	(Geneva)
Enos, Thomas M. III	(Orlando)
Garner, William O. Jr.	(Pensacola)
Griffin, Howard A. Jr.	(Davie)
Harless, Walt	(Lake Worth)
Harn, Robert	(Venice)
Hodge, John III	(Palatka)
Jernigan, Steve	(Milton)
Johnson, W.C. Bill	(Okeechobee)
Kelly, Lance	(Edgewater)

King, Bill (Tampa)
Lovestrand, Schuyler (Apopka)
Lyle, Ernest L. III (Orlando)
Miller, Chris Jr. (Sebring)
Miller, Robert T. (Largo)
Ochs, Charles F. (Largo)
Outlaw, Anthony L. (Panama City)
Owens, John (Miami)
Pendray, Alfred H. (Williston)
Price, Joel Hiram (Palatka)
Randall, W.D. and Gary T. (Orlando)
Rose, Alex (New Port Richey)
Schwarzer, Stephen (Palatka)
Simons, Bill (Highland City)
Stephens, Kelly Lee (St. Petersburg)
Tomes, P.J. (Jacksonville)
Vunk, Robert Bob (Orlando)
Waldrop, Mark (Lady Lake)
Weiland, J. Reese Jr. (Tampa)
Wine, Michael (Cocoa Beach)
Zaccagnino, Don (Pahokee)

GEORGIA
Bradley, Dennis (Blairsville)
Buckner, Jimmie H. (Putney)
Cheatham, Don E. (Savannah)
Crockford, Jack (Chamblee)
Dearhart, Richard (Lula)
Ford, Allen (Rosewell)
Fuller, John W. (Douglasville)
Harris, Ralph Dewey (Grovetown)
Hawkins, Rade (Red Oak)
Hegedus, Lou Jr. (Cave Spring)
Hegwood, Joel (Summerville)
Hensley, Wayne (Conyers)
Johnson, Harold Harry C. (Chickamauga)
Maddox, J.M. Mickey (Ringgold)
McGill, John (Blairsville)
Mitchell, James A. (Columbus)
Poplin, James L. (Washington)
Rogers, Robert P. Jr. (Acworth)
Roper, Mark H. Jr. (Martinez)
Sharpe, Philip S. (Austell)
Small, Jim (Madison)
Smith, James B. Red Jr. (Morven)
Stafford, Richard (Warner Robins)
Walters, A.F. (Tifton)

HAWAII
Evans, Vincent K. (Honolulu)
Fujisaka, Stanley (Kaneohe)
Mayo, Thomas H. Jr. (Waialua)
Nishiuchi, Melvin S. (Kaneohe)

IDAHO
Andrews, Don (Coeur D'Alene)
Kranning, Terry L. (Pocatello)
Mullin, Steve (Sandpoint)
Oda, Kuzan (Hailey)
Quarton, Barr (Hailey)
Rohn, Fred (Coeur d'Alene)
Sawby, Scott (Sand Point)
Sparks, Bernard (Dingle)
Towell, Dwight L. (Midvale)

ILLINOIS
Atkinson, Dick (Decatur)
Bridgnardello, E.D. (Beecher)
Guth, Kenneth (Chicago)
Hargis, Frank L. (Flora)
Hill, Rick (Edwardsville)
Hoffman, Kevin L. (Lisle)
Lake, Ron (Taylorville)
Lane, Jerry I. (Carbondale)
Meier, Daryl (Carbondale)
Pritchard, Ron (Dixon)
Rados, Jerry F. (Grant Park)
Robert J. Bob White, Jr. (Gilson)
Stalter, Harry L. (Trivoli)
Tompkins, Dan (Peotone)
Turnbull, Ralph A. (Rockford)
Veit, Michael (LaSalle)
Werth, George W. (Cary)
White, Robert J. Bob (Gilson)
Worel, Joe (Melrose Park)

Wright, Timothy (Chicago)
Young, Errol (Alton)

INDIANA
Birt, Sid (Nashville)
Brewer, Jack (Lafayette)
Fitzgerald, Dennis (Fort Wayne)
Imel, Billy Mace (New Castle)
Johnson, C.E. Gene (Portage)
Kreimer, James J. (Milan)
Largin, Ken (Batesville)
Ledford, Bracy R. (Indianapolis)
Lutes, Robert (Nappanee)
Mayville, Oscar (Indianapolis)
Minnick, Jim (Middletown)
Poag, James (New Harmony)
Porter, James E. (Bloomington)
Rigney, Willie (Shelbyville)
Rubley, James A. (Angola)
Welch, William H. (Fort Wayne)

IOWA
Brower, Max (Boone)
Miller, James P. (Fairbank)
Myers, Mel (Spencer)
Walters, Brian K. (Des Moines)
Zscherny, Michael (Cedar Rapids)

KANSAS
Chard, Gordon R. (Iola)
Courtney, Eldon (Wichita)
Dugger, Dave (Westwood)
Dunn, Melvin T. (Rossville)
Green, L.G. (Prairie Village)
Harrington, Mike (Abilene)
Hegwald, J.L. (Humboldt)
Herman, Tim (Overland Park)
Kennelley, J.C. (Leon)
Kraft, Steve (Abilene)
Ray, Michael (Wichita)

KENTUCKY
Baskett, Lee Gene (Elizabethtown)
Brandstetter, Larry (Paducah)
Bugden, John (Murray)
Carson, Harold J. Kit (Radcliff)
Clay, J.D. (Greenup)
Downing, Larry (Bremen)
Fister, Jim (Finchville)
Hibben, Gil (Louisville)
Howser, John C. (Frankfort)
Keeslar, Joseph F. (Almo)
Keeton, William L. (Louisville)
Pease, W.D. (Ewing)
Pierce, Harold L. (Louisville)
Pulliam, Morris C. (Shelbyville)
Smith, Gregory H. (Louisville)

LOUISIANA
Berzas, Larry (Cut Off)
Blaum, Roy (Covington)
Caldwell, Bill (West Monroe)
Culpepper, John (Monroe)
Douglas, Dale (Ponchatoula)
Faucheaux, Howard J. (Loreauville)
Ki, Shiva (Baton Rouge)
Marks, Chris (Breaux Bridge)
Mitchell, Max and Dean (Leesville)
Provenzano, Joseph D. (Chalmette)
Roath, Dean (Baton Rouge)
Sanders, Michael M. (Ponchatoula)
Vought, Frank Jr. (Hammond)
Wehner, Rudy (Violet)
Wiggins, Horace (Mansfield)
Wiggins, James C. (Hammond)

MAINE
Bohrmann, Bruce (Yarmouth)
Fuegen, Larry (Wiscasset)
Kemal (D. Fogg & M. Sayen) (Bryant Pond)
Munro, Paul (Franklin)
Oyster, Lowell R. (Kenduskeag)

MARYLAND
Antonio, William J. (Warwick)

Barnes, Gary L. (New Windsor)
Bauchop, Peter (Hunt Valley)
Beers, Ray (Monkton)
Fielder, William V. (Westminster)
Freiling, Albert J. (Finksburg)
Hendrickson, E.J. (Jay) (Frederick)
Hudson, Robbin C. (Rock Hall)
Kremzner, Raymond L. (Baltimore)
Kretsinger, Philip W. Jr. (Boonsboro)
McCarley, John (Keymar)
Merchant, Ted (White Hall)
Moran, Wm. F. (Braddock Heights)
Nicholson, Kent R. (Baltimore)
Reeves, Chris (Baltimore)
Sontheimer, Douglas G. (Silver Spring)

MASSACHUSETTS
Dailey, G.E. (Seekonk)
Fikes, Jimmy L. (Orange)
Gaudette, Linden L. (Wilbraham)
Gwozdz, Bob (Attleboro)
Khalsa, Jot Singh (Millis)
Siska, Jim (Westfield)
Sloan, John (Foxboro)
Tsoulas, Jon J. (Peabody)

MICHIGAN
Beckwith, Michael R. (New Baltimore)
Buckbee, Donald M. (Warren)
Cousino, George (Woodhaven)
Dilluvio, Frank J. (Warren)
Enders, Robert (Cement City)
Erickson, Walter E. (Warren)
Gottage, Dante and Judy (St. Clair Shores)
Hartman, Arlan (N. Muskegon)
Hughes, Daryle (Nunica)
Lankton, Scott (Ann Arbor)
Leach, Mike J. (Swartz Creek)
Mills, Louis G. (Yasutomo) (Ann Arbor)
O'Leary, Gordon (Ypsilanti)
Serven, Jim (Mayville)
Stewart, Charles (Chuck) (Lake Orion)
Stites, Kay (Bloomfield Hills)
Wardman, Dave (Ossineke)
Warzocha, Stanley (Warren)
Whitworth, Ken J. (Sterling Heights)
Wood, Webster (Clarkston)
Zowada, Tim (Battle Creek)

MINNESOTA
Goltz, Warren L. (Ada)
Hagen, Philip L. (Pelican Rapids)
Hansen, Robert W. (Cambridge)
Johnson, Robert B. (Clearwater)
Preuss, Robert (Cedar)
Sharp, Robert G. (Anoka)

MISSISSIPPI
Davis, Jesse W. (Walls)
LeBatard, Paul M. (Vancleave)

MISSOURI
Bolton, Charles B. (Jonesburg)
Cover, Raymond A. (Mineral Point)
Craig, James H. (Manchester)
Davis, W.C. (Raymore)
Driskill, Beryl (Braggadocio)
Duvall, Larry E. (Gallatin)
Gilmore, Jon (St. Louis)
Glaser, Ken (Purdy)
Holland, Dale J. (Kansas City)
Lane, Ed (Kansas City)
Mason, Bill (Excelsior Springs)
May, James E. (Auxvasse)
McCrackin and Son, V.J. (House Springs)
Newcomb, Corbin (Moberly)
Rardon, A.D. (Polo)
Weddle, Del Jr. (Stewartsville)

MONTANA
Anderson, Charles B. (Polson)
Brooks, Steve R. (Big Timber)
Crowder, Robert (Thompson Falls)
Dunkerley, Rick (Cameron)
Ellefson, Joel (Bozeman)

Fassio, Melvin G. (Missoula)
Forthofer, Pete (Whitefish)
Frank, Heinrich H. (Whitefish)
Moyer, Russ (Havre)
Peterson, Dan L. (Billings)
Peterson, Eldon G. (Whitefish)
Pursley, Aaron (Big Sandy)
Reh, Bill (Missoula)
Ruana Knife Works (Bonner)
Schedenhell, Jack (Superior)
Simonich, Bob (Clancy)
Smith, Harry R. (Missoula)
Treutel, Terry A. (Hamilton)
Weinand, Gerome W. (Lolo)

NEBRASKA
Brown, David B. (Doniphan)
Jensen, Carl A. Jr. (Blair)
Jokerst, Charles (Omaha)
Miller, Terry (Seward)
Schepers, George B. (Chapman)
Suedmeier, Harlan (Nebraska City)
Syslo, Chuck (Omaha)

NEVADA
Duff, Bill (Virginia City)

NEW HAMPSHIRE
Valachovic, Wayne (Hillsboro)

NEW JERSEY
Defeo, Robert A. (Mays Landing)
Hetmanski, Thomas S. (Trenton)
McGovern, Jim (Oak Ridge)
Slee, Fred (Morganville)
Viele, H.J. (Westwood)
Weber, Fred E. (Forked River)

NEW MEXICO
Coleman, Keith E. (Los Lunas)
Cordova, Joseph G. (Bosque Farms)
Digangi, Joseph M. (Santa Cruz)
Hethcoat, Don (Clovis)
Hibben, Daryl (Rio Rancho)
Holder, D'Alton (Farmington)
Jones, Bob (Albuquerque)
Lewis, Tom R. (Carlsbad)
McBurnette, Harvey (Eagle Nest)
Miller, Ted (Santa Fe)
Nelson, Keith A. (Los Lunas)
Norton, Don (Farmington)
Stumpff, George Jr. (Glorieta)
Terzuola, Robert (Santa Fe)
Walker, Michael (Taos)
Wescott, Cody (Las Cruces)
Wescott, Jim (Las Cruces)

NEW YORK
Anderson, Edwin (New Hyde Park)
Coleman, Ken (Brooklyn)
Cumming, R.J. (New York)
Cute, Thomas (Cortland)
Davis, Barry L. (Castleton)
Love, Ed (APO New York)
Maragni, Dan (Georgetown)
Rappazzo, Richard (Latham)
Scheid, Maggie (W. Webster)
Schmidt, James A. (Ballston Lake)
Wahlers, Herman F. (Austerlitz)

NORTH CAROLINA
Addison, Ed (Asheboro)
Bonner, Jeremy (Weaverville)
Busfield, John (Roanoke Rapids)
Fox, Paul (Valdese)
Garlits, Chuck K. (Rosman)
Gross, W.W. (High Point)
Guthrie, George B. (Bessemer City)
McCullough, Larry E. (Mocksville)
Neal, Jerry C. (Winston-Salem)
Parrish, Robert (Hendersonville)
Patrick, Chuck (Brasstown)
Rece, Charles V. (Albemarle)
Shuford, Rick (Statesville)
Tedder, Mickey (Conover)

Wade, J.M. (Wade)
Wagaman, John K. (Fayetteville)

OHIO
Busse, Jerry (Wauseon)
Collins, Lynn M. (Elyria)
Darby, Rick (Youngstown)
Downing, Tom (Cortland)
Franklin, Mike (Aberdeen)
Glover, Ron (Cincinnati)
Hill, Howard E. (Columbus)
Koutsopoulos, George (La Grange)
Koval, Michael T. (Columbus)
Longworth, Dave (Bethel)
McCarty, Harry (Hamilton)
Morgan, Tom (Beloit)
Papp, Robert Bob (Elyria)
Salley, John D. (Tipp City)
Shoemaker, Scott (Miamisburg)
Spinale, Richard (Lorain)
Stoddart, W.B. Bill (Forest Park)
Strong, Scott (Beaver Creek)
Thourot, Michael W. (Napoleon)
Trabbic, R.W. (Toledo)
Underwood, W.L. (East Liverpool)
Votaw, David P. (Pioneer)
Warther, Dale (Bolivar)
Witsaman, Earl (Stow)
Woodworth, Al (Ashville)
Wood, Larry B. (Huber Heights)
Yurco, Mike (Youngstown)

OKLAHOMA
Baker, Ray (Sapulpa)
England, Mike (Enid)
Englebretson, George (Oklahoma City)
Kennedy, Bill Jr. (Yukon)
Naifeh, Woody (Tulsa)
Spivey, Jefferson (Oklahoma City)

OREGON
Alverson, Tim (Keno)
Anderson, Virgil W. (Portland)
Buchman, Bill (Bend)
Buchner, Bill (Idleyld Park)
Corrado, Jim (Glide)
Davis, Terry (Sumpter)
Dowell, T.M. (Bend)
Goddard, Wayne (Eugene)
Harsey, William W. (Creswell)
Huey, Steve (Junction City)
Hunnicutt, Robert E. (Forest Grove)
Kelley, Gary (Aloha)
Lindsay, Chris A. (La Pine)
Little, Gary M. (Broadbent)
Lum, Robert W. (Eugene)
Murphy, Dave (Gresham)
Pitt, David (Klamath Falls)
Thompson, Leon (Forest Grove)
Wahlster, Mark David (Salem)
Warren, Al (Bend)
Zeller, Dennis J. (Gresham)

PENNSYLVANIA
Bartrug, Hugh E. (Elizabeth)
Candrella, Joe (Warminster)
Clark, D.E. Lucky (Mineral Point)
Frey, W. Fredrick Jr. (Milton)
Gottchalk, Gregory J. (Carnegie)
Nealy, Bud (Stroudsburg)
Skirchak, Samuel Jr. (Midland)
Taglienti, Antonio J. (Darlington)
Valois, A. Daniel (Orefield)

RHODE ISLAND
Allen, Steve (Riverside)
Bardsley, Norman P. (Pawtucket)

SOUTH CAROLINA
Barefoot, Joe W. (Easley)
Beatty, Gordon H. (Seneca)
Beck, P.F. (Barnwell)
Brend, Walter J. (Walterboro)
Bridwell, Richard A. (Taylors)

Burnette, Skip (Spartanburg)
Cannady, Daniel L. (Allendale)
Davis Brothers Knives (Camden)
Davis, Dixie (Clinton)
Defreest, William G. (Barnwell)
Easler, Russell O. Jr. (Woodruff)
Fecas, Stephan J. (Clemson)
Gaston, Ron (Woodruff)
Gillenwater, E.E. Dick (Aiken)
Gregory, Michael (Belton)
Herron, George (Springfield)
Kessler, Ralph A. (Elgin)
Langley, Gene H. (Florence)
Lee, Tommy (Gaffney)
Montjoy, Claude (Clinton)
Owens, Danny (Blacksburg)
Page, Larry (Aiken)
Poston, Alvin (Columbia)
Reeves, Winfred M. (West Union)
Smith, Ralph L. (Greer)
Whitmire, Earl T. (Rock Hill)

TENNESSEE
Bartlow, John (Norris)
Canter, Ronald E. (Jackson)
Cargill, Bob (Oldfort)
Casteel, Douglas (Hillsboro)
Clay, Wayne (Pelham)
Conley, Bob (Jonesboro)
Coogan, Robert (Smithville)
Copeland, George A. Steve (Alpine)
Corby, Harold (Johnson City)
Crisp, Harold (Cleveland)
Grigsby, John D. Butch (Corryton)
Harley, Larry W. (Bristol)
Hurst, Jeff (Rutledge)
Loflin, Bob (Seymour)
Moore, Tom W. Jr. (Columbia)
Rhea, David (Lynnville)
Rial, Douglas (Greenfield)
Sampson, Lynn (Jonesboro)
Smith, Newman L. (Gatlinburg)
Smith, W.F. Red (Gatlinburg)
Taylor, C. Gray (Kingsport)
Taylor, David (Kingsport)
Walker, John W. (Bon Aqua)
Ward, W.C. (Clinton)
Woodward, Harold E. (Woodbury)
Wright, Harold C. (Centerville)

TEXAS
Allen, Mike Whiskers (Malakoff)
Bagwell, Bill (Marietta)
Barbee, Jim (Ft. Stockton)
Barr, A.T. (Denton)
Birch, Robert F. (Huntsville)
Broadwell, David (Wichita Falls)
Brooks, Michael (Littlefield)
Carter, Fred (Wichita Falls)
Cellum, Tom S. (Spring)
Champion, Robert (Amarillo)
Chase, John E. (Aledo)
Connor, Michael (Winters)
Costa, Scott (Spicewood)
Crain, Jack W. (Weatherford)
Crawford, Larry (Rosenberg)
Davidson, Rob (Lubbock)
Davis, Syd (Richmond)
DiTomaso, Larry (Longview)
Donaghey, John (Garland)
Finger, L.C. (Weatherford)
Fischer, Clyde E. (Nixon)
Gartman, M.D. (Gatesville)
Gault, Clay (Lexington)
Green, Roger M. (Joshua)
Griffin, Rendon and Mark (Houston)
Hajovsky, Robert J. (Scotland)
Hipp, Charles (Bone Knife Co.) (Lubbock)
Hueske, Chubby (Bellaire)
Hughes, Lawrence (Plainview)
Johnson, Brad (El Paso)
Johnson, Gorden W. (Houston)
Johnson, Ruffin (Houston)
Kious, Joe (Alamo)
Krouse, Al (Humble)
Ladd, Jim (Deer Park)

Laughlin, Don	(Vidor)
Lovett, Mike	(Killeen)
Love, A.C.	(Hearne)
Luckett, Bill	(Weatherford)
Madsen, Jack	(Wichita Falls)
Malitzke, Jeffrey G.	(Wichita Falls)
Marshall, Glenn	(Mason)
McConnell, Charles R. Jr.	(Odessa)
McConnell, Loyd A. Jr.	(Odessa)
McDearmont, Dave	(Lewisville)
McKissack, Tommy II	(Sonora)
Merz, Robert L. III	(Katy)
Mills, Andy	(Fredricksburg)
Moore, James B.	(Ft. Stockton)
Osborne, Warren	(Waxahachie)
Overeynder, T.R.	(Arlington)
Parrish, Duayne	(Palestine)
Pate, Lloyd D.	(Georgetown)
Pugh, Jim	(Azle)
Pullen, Martin	(Granbury)
Sams, Joseph D.	(El Paso)
Shearer, Robert A.	(Huntsville)
Sims, Bob	(Meridian)
Sloan, Shane	(Newcastle)
Spencer, John E.	(Harper)
Stone, G.W.	(Richardson)
Stout, Johnny	(New Braunfels)
Thuesen, Ed	(Houston)
Thuesen, Kevin	(Houston)
Watson, Daniel and Bill	(Driftwood)
Wood, William W.	(Vera)
Yunes, Yamil R.	(Roma)

UTAH
Black, Earl	(Salt Lake City)
Bryner, Barry R.	(Price)
Ence, Jim	(Richfield)
Erickson, Curt	(Ogden)
Erickson, L.M.	(Liberty)
Johnson, Steve R.	(Manti)
Maxfield, Lynn	(Layton)
Rapp, Steven J.	(Salt Lake City)
Smith, David Lynn	(Duchesne)
Warenski, Buster	(Richfield)
Winn, Travis A.	(Salt Lake City)

VIRGINIA
Barber, Robert E.	(Virginia Beach)
Blakley, William E. II	(Fredricksburg)
Callahan, Errett	(Lynchburg)
Davidson, Edmund	(Goshen)
Frazier, Ron	(Powhatan)
Goldenberg, T.S.	(Herndon)
Hedrick, Don	(Newport News)
Holloway, Paul	(Norfolk)
Jones, Enoch	(Chantilly)
Scott, Winston	(Huddleston)
White, Gene E.	(Alexandria)

WASHINGTON
Baldwin, Phillip	(Snohomish)
Ber, Dave	(Nooksack)
Blomberg, Gregg	(Lopez)
Boguszewski, Phil	(Tacoma)
Chappel, Roderick C.	(Edmonds)
Conti, Jeffrey D.	(Bremerton)
Davis, K.M. Twig	(Monroe)
Goertz, Paul S.	(Renton)
Mosser, Gary E.	(Renton)
Rice, Adrienne	(Lopez Island)
Wright, Kevin	(Quilcene)

WEST VIRGINIA
Bowen, Tilton and James	(Baker)
Cantini, Don	(Weirton)
Dent, Douglas M.	(South Charleston)
Hedgecock, Walter R.	(Glen Daniel)
Maynard, Larry Joe	(Helen)
Quenton, Warner	(Peterstown)
Schwarz, John J.	(Wellsburg)
Sigman, Corbet R.	(Liberty)
Small, Ed	(Keyser)
Tokar, Daniel	(Shepherdstown)
Wilson, R.W.	(Weirton)

WISCONSIN
Brandsey, Edward P.	(Edgerton)
Brdlik, Dan E.	(Prescott)
Dahl, Cris	(Lake Geneva)
DeYong, Clarence	(Racine)
Hembrook, Ron	(Neosho)
Kolitz, Robert	(Beaver Dam)
Maestri, Peter A.	(Spring Green)
Ricke, Dave	(West Bend)
Rochford, Michael R.	(Dresser)

WYOMING
Alexander, Darrel	(Big Piney)
Ankrom, W.E.	(Cody)
Fowler, Ed A.	(Riverton)
Friedly, Dennis	(Cody)
Montegna, John C.	(Sheridan)
Reynolds, John C.	(Gillette)
Walker, George A.	(Alpine)

FOREIGN COUNTRIES
AFRICA
Burger, Pon	(Zimbabwe)

AUSTRALIA
Brown, Peter	(Ryde)
Butler, Gary	(Perth)
Harvey, Max	(Perth)
Richards, Sam	(Victoria)
Rowe, Stewart G.	(Kangaroo Point)
Stapleton, John	(Happy Valley)
Zemitis, Joe	(Cardiff Hts.)

CANADA
Downie, James T.	(Thedford)
Dublin, Dennis	(Enderby)
Grenier, Roger	(Saint Hubert)
Haynes, Chap	(Tatamagouche)
Langley, Mick	(Weyburn)
Leber, Heinz	(Hudson Hope)
Loerchner, Wolfgang	(Bayfield)
Macri, Mike	(Churchill)
Maneker, Kenneth	(Galiano Island)
Marzitelli, Peter	(Surrey)
Moeller, Harald	(Thornton)
Pepiot, Stephan	(Edmonton)
Peterson, Jack	(Nanaimo)
Price, Steve	(Kamloops)
Schoenfeld, Matthew A.	(Galiano Island)
St. Amour, Suzanne	(Hillsburgh)
Wood, Bruce	(Truro)
Young, Bud	(Port Hardy)
Young, Cliff	(Pembroke)

ENGLAND
Henry, Peter and Son	(Wokingham)
Hitchmough, Howard	(London)
Jones, Charles Anthony	(No. Devon)
Moorby, Keith	(South Yorkshire)

JAPAN
Aida, Yoshihito	(Tokyo)
Fujimoto, Yasuhiro	(Tokyo)
Furukawa, Shiro	(Tokyo)
Hirayama, Harumi	(Warabi City)
Takahashi, Masao	(Tokyo)
Tasaki, Seiichi	(Kawaguchi-City)

NETHERLANDS
Van Eldik, Frans	(Loenen)

SOUTH AFRICA
Owen Wood	(Honeydew)

WALES
Elliott, Marcus	(Llandudno)

WEST GERMANY
Hehn, Richard Karl	(Waldbronn)
Kressler, D.F.	(Puchheim)

Official Knifemakers Membership Lists

Not all knifemakers are organization types, but those listed here are in good standing with these organizations.

Knifemakers Guild
1987 Voting Membership

R. V. Alverson, Ed Anderson, W.E. Ankrom, Dick Atkinson.
Phillip Baldwin, Norman Bardsley, Joe Barefoot, Gary Barnes, Gene Baskett, Butch Beaver, Raymond Beers, Leslie Berryman, Leroy Besic, Sid Birt, Paul Bizal, Earl Black, Andrew Blackton, Philip Boguszewski, Jeremy Bonner, Edward Brandsey, Walter Brend, Clint Breshears, Richard Bridwell, Ed Brignardello, Tim Britton, David Broadwell, David Brown, Rick Browne, John Busfield.
Bill Caldwell, Ronald Canter, Don Cantini, Bob Cargill, Fred Carter, Frank & Mark Centofante, Gordon Chard, Wayne Clay, Gerald Click, Keith Coleman, Vernon Coleman, Walter Collins, Bob Conley, C. T. Conn, Harold Corby, Joe Cordova, Leonard Corlee, Jim Corrado, Eldon Courtney, George Cousino, Raymond Cover, Colin Cox, Jack Crain, Pat Crawford, James Crowell.
Dan Dagget, Cris Dahl, Alex Daniels, Barry Davis, Jesse Davis, W.C. Davis, Douglas Dent, Robert Dodge, Patrick Donovan, Dick Dorough, T.M. Dowell, Larry Downing, Tom Downing, Bill Duff, Melvin Dunn, Larry Duvall.
Russell Easler, Fain Edwards, Joel Ellefson, Jim Ence, Robert Enders, Curt Erickson, L. M. Erickson, Walter Erickson.
Allen Faulkner, Stephen Fecas, Lee Ferguson, Joe Flournoy, Pete Forthofer, Paul Fox, Henry Frank, Ron Frazier, Dennis Friedly, Tak Fukuta, John Fuller.

Frank Gamble, Ronald Gaston, Clay Gault, Roy Genge, Randall Gilbreath, E.E. (Dick) Gillenwater, Kenneth Glaser, R. G. Glover, Wayne Goddard, Warren Goltz, Dante & Judith Gottage, Larry Green, Michael Gregory, Rendon & Mark Griffin.
Doc Hagen, Robert Hajovsky, Jim Hammond, Frank Hargis, Rade Hawkins, Richard Hehn, Larry Hendricks, Wayne Hensley, Tim Herman, George Herron, Don Hethcoat, Gil Hibben, Vernon Hicks, Howard Hill, Harumi Hirayama, J.B. Hodge, Richard Hodgson, Steve Hoel, Kevin Hoffman, D'Alton Holder, Dale Holland, Jess Horn, Glen Hornby, Arthur Hubbard, Chubby Hueske.
Bill Imel.
Jim Jacks, Steve Jernigan, Gorden Johnson, Ronald Johnson, Ruffin Johnson, Steve Johnson, William Johnson, Robert Jones.
Don Karlin, William Keeton, Gary Kelley, Kemal (Sayen-Fogg), Bill Kennedy, J. C. Kennedy, Jot Khalsa, Shiva Ki, Bill King, Joe Kious, Mike Koval, D.F. Kressler.
Ron Lake, Frank Lampson, Ed Lane, Gene Langley, Scott Lankton, Don Laughlin, M. Leach, Tommy Lee, Norman Levine, James Lile, Dave Longworth, Ed Love, William Luckett, Robert Lum, Ernest Lyle.
Mickey Maddox, Dan Maragni, Tom Maringer, Bill Mason, James May, Harvey McBurnette, Charles McConnell, Loyd McConnell, Sean McWilliams, Chris Miller, James Miller, Terry Miller, Louis Mills & Jim Kelso, Jim Minnick, Claude Montjoy, William Moran, Jeff Morgan, Steven Mullin, Paul Myers.
Woody Naifeh, Corbin Newcomb, R.D. Nolen.
Kuzan Oda, Gordon O'Leary, Milford Oliver, Wayne Olson, Warren Osborne, T.R. Overeynder.
Robert Papp, Melvin Pardue, W.D. Pease, Lloyd Pendleton, Alfred Pendray, Eldon Peterson, Randy Phillips, David Pitt, Leon Pittman, Clifton Polk, James Poplin, Stephen Price, Joe Prince, Ron Pritchard, Jim Pugh, Martin Pullen, Morris Pulliam.
Barr Quarton, George Quinn.
Jerry Rados, A. D. Rardon, David Ree, Winfred Reeves, Bill Reh, John Reynolds, Douglas Rial, Ron Richard, David Ricke, Willie Rigney, Dean Roath, Howard Robbins, Fred Roe, Mark Roper, A.G. Russell.
Masaki Sakakibara, John Salley, Scott Sawby, George Schepers, James Schmidt, Herman Schneider, Matthew Schoenfeld, Maurice & Alan Schrock, Steve Schwarzer, James Serven, Corbet Sigman, Norman Simons, Fred Slee, Ralph Smith, Jim Sornberger, Harry Stalter, Ken Steigerwalt, Charles Stewart, Charles Syslo.
Gray Taylor, J.M. Tedder, Stephen Terrill, Robert Terzuola, Leon Thompson, Danny Thornton, Timberline Knives, Carolyn Tinker, Pat Tomes, Dan Tompkins, Dwight Towell, Ralph Turnbull.
Wayne Valachovic, Frans Van Eldik, Howard Viele, Frank Vought.
George Walker, Michael Walker, Brian Walters, Kenneth Ward, Buster Warenski, Dale Warther, Del Weddle, Charles Weiss, Mike Wesolowski, Robert White, Weldon Whitley, Ken Whitworth, Horace Wiggins, R.W. Wilson, Webster Wood, William W. Wood, Harold Woodward, Joe Worel, Tim Wright.
Michael Zscherny.

1986 Probationary Members eligible for Voting Membership 1988
Franz Becker, Robert Engnath, Shiro Furukawa, Kenneth Guth, Enoch Jones, Ralph Kessler, Schuyler Lovestrand, David McDearmont, Jim Siska, Seiichi Tasaki, Michael Veit, Tim Zowada.

1987 Probationary Members eligible for Voting Membership in 1989
Chuck Anderson, Steven Rapp.

Alaska Knifemakers Association

A. W. Amoureux, Robert Ball, J. D. Biggs, Lonnie Brewer, Tom Broom, Mark Bucholz, John Chamberlin, Bill Chatwood, Bob Cunningham, Gordon S. Dempsey, Art Dufour, Brad Estelle, Gordon Grebe, Bob Levine, John Palowski, Scott Reymiller, Ron Robertson, Steve Robertson, Red Rowell, Keith Stegall, Jim Stow, Thomas Trujillo, John Warner, Ulys Whalen, Jim Whitman, Bob Willis.

American Bladesmith Society

Gary D. Anderson, Norman B. Anderson, Marvin C. Arneson.
Bill Bagwell, Aubrey G. Barnes, Gary L. Barnes, Hugh Bartrug, Charles Bear, Dave Ber, Tom Berry, W. T. Biskamp, Leon E. Borgman, Jimmy Buckner, Jay Burger.
Tommy S. Cellum, Dave Chrishlom, Joseph Cordova, Barry Crandall, James L. Crowell.
Terry Davis, Gary Davidson, Harvey Dean, Ray Demers, Gordon S. Dempsey, Mike de Punté, Ted M. Dowell.
Bill Fielder, Jerry Fisk, Edward A. Fowler, Wendell Fox, Larry Fuegen, Jack Fuller.
Mark Gardner, Ray Garrison, Mike Gillenigan, Sal Glesser, Wayne L. Goddard, Frank Gunn.
P.L. (Doc) Hagen, Larry W. Harley, Chris Hawthorne, Chap Haynes, Lou Hegedus, Jay Hendrickson, Bill Hicks, Roger Hockwalt, C. Robert Hudson, Daryle J. Hughes, Carl Hunkle, Jimmy Hyde.
C.R. Johnson.
Joseph F. Keeslar, Dick Kimberley, Philip Kretsinger Jr.
Donald G. Lange, Mick Langley, David L. Lassio, Nick Leone III, A.C. Love.
Dan Maragni, Joe Mark, Harry McCarty, Kevin McCrackin, Victor J. McCrackin, Walter McCrum, Henry "Ted" Merchant, Hanford J. Miller, William F. Moran Jr., Russell A. Moyer, Jack Muse.
Bruce Nelson, R. Kent Nicholson, Robert Nicholson.
Charles F. Ochs III, Randy W. Ogden, Rodney Olsen, Lee Osberg, Michael Osbourne.
Joseph Page, Dwayne Parrish, Alfred H. Pendray, Dan L. Peterson, James Porter, Morris C. Pulliam.
Jerry Rados, W.D. "Bo" Randall, Scott Reymiller, James D. Rhodes, Michael R. Rochford II.
Margaret R. Scheid, Norman F. Schenk, James A. Schmidt, Stephen C. Schwarzer, Malcolm Tiki Shewan, Mark O. Shogar, Cleston Sinyard, Patrick M. Small, Arthur Swyhart.
Lou Teichmoeller, John Teslow, Thomas Theill, Robert Timm, Lester A. Twigg.
Wayne Valachovic, Michael Veit.
Mark Waldrop, Bill Walker, Roger Wallace, Daniel Watson, Ferris Watson, E.A. "Buddy" Wehman Jr., Donald E. Weiler, James F. West, Ray R. Wheelington, Daniel J. White, Charles E. Williams, David Williamson, Wayne Willson, David Wilson.
William H. Zeanon.

California Knifemakers Assn.*

Arnie Abegg, Elmer Art.
John Beavans, Leory Besic, Bruce Bochman, Donald Breier, Clint Breshears.
Lock Cameron.
Dean Davidson, Mal Dion.
Richard Eaton, Bob Engnath.
Ted Fisher.
Jay Harris, William Herndon, Glen Hornby, Jim Hrisoulas, Eppy Huertas.
Jim Jacks, Ann Jensen.
John Knapp, John Kray, Don Kreibich, Martin Kruse, Jim Kuykendall.
Leo Mason, Tom Mayo, Rick Mecchi, Harry Mendenhall, Jim Merritt, Emil Morgan, Jeff Morgan.
Thomas Orth.
Leroy Reamer, Mark Redmon, Bob Roberts, Thomas Ross.
Will Scarrow, Herman Schneider, Ray Shepard, James Sornberger, Al Steinberg.
Steve Terrill, Carolyn Tinker.
Greg Whitteg, Sherman Williams, Harold Wilson, Barry Wood.

Arizona Knifemakers Association

D. "Butch" Beaver, Jack Busfield, Bill Cheatham, Dan Dagget, Tom Edwards, Anthony Goddard, Larry Hendricks, Steve Hoel, Ken McFall, Milford Oliver, Jerry Poletis, Merle Poteet, Mike Quinn, Elmer Sams, Jim Sornberger, Glen Stockton, Bruce Thompson, Sandy Tudor, Charles Weiss.

The New England Bladesmith's Guild

Jimmy Fikes, Don Fogg, Dan Maragni, Louis Mills, Jim Schmidt.

South Carolina Association of Knifemakers

Joe Barefoot, Walter Brend, Richard Bridwell, Tony Bryant, Bob Burdette, Ship Burnette, Dan Cannady, Charles Cox, Davis Bros., Dixie Davis, William DeFreest, Russell Easler, Steve Fecas, Hal Gainey, Ron Gaston, Dick Gillenwater, Mike Gregory, George Herron, Ralph Kessler, Gene Langley, Tommy Lee, Claude Montjoy, Larry Page, Alvin Poston, Joe Prince, Winfred Reeves, Terry Roberts, Duncan Rutherfurd, Pat Schwallie, Ralph Smith.

Tennessee Knifemakers Association

John Bartlow, Doug Casteel, Harold Crisp, Larry Harley, John W. Walker, Harold Woodward, Harold Wright.

---

*CAL-Knives

Knife Photo Index
To Previous Editions

As a service to readers, we have here compiled an alphabetical guide to photos of handmade knives, listed according to their makers. THIS INDEX DOES NOT INCLUDE KNIVES PUBLISHED IN THIS ISSUE.

A

Ed Addison: K'86:103
Yoshihito Aida: K'82:74; **K'85**:114; **K'86**:64,67; **K'87**:51,109
Mike Allen: K'87:69,89
Steve Allen: K'87:96
A.W. Amoureux: K'84:92
Charles B. Anderson: K'86:60,170; **K'87**:121,233
Edwin Anderson: K'83:85,149; **K'84**:69,173; **K'85**:157; **K'86**:229
E.R. (Russ) Andrews, II: K'81:18,71,102
W.E. Ankrom: K'81:36,37,94; **K'82**:77,90; **K'83**:149; **K'86**:63,229; **K'7**:171
William J. Antonio, Jr.: K'83:149; **K'85**:157; **K'87**:58,97,107
Ray Appleton: K'87:117
Dick Atkinson: K'81:39; **K'82**:71,93,97; **K'83**:66,75,149; **K'84**:Cover, 173; **K'86**:87,229; **K'87**:52

B

Bill Bagwell: K'81:123; **K'82**:103; **K'83**:117; **K'84**:85,173; **K'85**:100
Ray Baker: K'87:171
Phill Baldwin: K'82:123; **K'83**:108; **K'84**:73,121,134; **K'85**:157; **K'86**:54,118; **K'87**:92
James Barbee: K'83:149; **K'84**:130
Norman P. Bardsley: K'83:44,138,149; **K'84**:136; **K'85**:69; **K'86**:110; **K'87**:49,113,119,171
Joe W. Barefoot: K'84:67,173; **K'85**:49,73; **K'87**:171
John Barlow: K'86:120
Tom Barminski: K'84:173; **K'85**:55
Mike Barna: K'87:130
Gary L. Barnes: K'82:104; **K'83**:112,115; **K'84**:55,56,77,111,119; **K'85**:Cover, 79,125; **K'86**:78,107,151,229; **K'87**:71,73,77,121,132
Richard W. Barney: K'82:46,61,81,123
A.T.Barr: K'82:97,123
Jack Barrett: K'81:30,123; **K'85**:159
James J. Barry: K'82:46,123; **K'83**:41,87,105; **K'84**:57,84,99,175; **K'85**:66,101; **K'87**:155,173
John Bartlow: K'87:121
Hugh Bartrug: Cover, 109,140
Lee Gene Baskett: K'84:175; **K'85**:56,118,159; **K'86**:92; **K'87**:54,101
John Bassney: K'81:125; **K'82**:55,91
Bear Claw (See B.R. Bryner.)
Norman Beardsley: K'85:75
Devon (Butch) Beaver: K'82:24,52; **K'83**:39,63,67,86,90; **K'84**:Cover, 56,62,70,82,89,95,116,145,175; **K'85**:54,72,133,159; **K'86**:56; **K'87**:91,125,148,173
Judy Beaver: K'87:125
P.F. Beck: K'81:125; **K'82**:96; **K'83**:74
Michael R. Beckwith: K'84:93,175
Ray Beers: K'81:22,125; **K'82**:72,78; **K'83**:55,90,151; **K'84**:72,97,110; **K'85**:72,159; **K'86**:148,152; **K'87**:49,121,173
Jack Belk: K'82:78,112,125 **K'83**:76
Frank Bell: K'87:82, 109
Michael Bell: K'85:71,159; **K'86**:54,229; **K'87**:112,173
William N. Bennett: K'82:45,125; **K'83**:77,151; **K'84**:66; **K'85**:90
Andrew G. Berendt: K'82:56
Leslie L. Berryman: K'81:18; **K'85**:112
Leroy Besic: K'85:161; **K'86**:55; **K'87**:52
Sid Birt: K'82:102; **K'83**:105,106,111,112,116,151; **K'84**:89; **K'85**:50,79,94,161; **K'86**:70,113,117
Paul W. Bizal: K'83:41
Earl Black: K'84:55; **K'85**:161; **K'86**:254; **K'87**:92,175
Black Oak (See KEMAL.)
Andrew Blackton: K'82:46,80,125; **K'83**:83,151; **K'84**:67,177; **K'85**:115; **K'86**:59
Roy Blaum: K'82:125; **K'84**:177; **K'87**:60,123
Block: K'85:140
Gregg Blomberg: K'87:34,35
Bob-Sky (See Hajovsky.)
Phil Boguszewski: K'85:108,161
Bruce Bohrmann: K'85:113
Bone Knife Co., Inc.: K'81:64,75,99,125; **K'82**:41,45,51,61,79,125; **K'83**:153; **K'86**:62
Jeremy Bonner: K'85:45; **K'86**:51,52
Lew Booth: K'81:125
James and Talon Bowen: K'85:99,161
Tilton and James Bowen: K'87:175
Dennis Bradley: K'85:163; **K'86**:72,80; **K'87**:69,175
Edward Brandsey: K'85:62,163; **K'86**:122,244; **K'87**:108
Larry Brandstetter: K'81:63;110; **K'82**:90,127; **K'86**:77
Dan Bradlik: K'87:53,107
Walter J. Brend: K'83:88,153; **K'85**:132,163; **K'86**:229
Clint Breshears: K'85:163; **K'86**:59,229

Brian: K'85:139
Richard A. Bridwell: K'82:74,84,94,119; **K'83**:47,53,58; **K'84**:79,143,177
E.D. Brignardello: K'82:44; **K'83**:83,153; **K'84**:91,177; **K'85**:67,163; **K'86**:147
G.M. (Tim) Britton: K'81:81,127; **K'82**:94; **K'83**:52,76
David Broadwell: K'85:73; **K'86**:100,253; **K'87**:113,175
Dennis Brooker: K'81:38,40,113,127; **K'82**:112
Steve Brooks: K'87:155
Mark Brower: K'87:175
David B. Brown: K'83:30,87,153; **K'85**:163
E.H. Brown: K'85:163
Floyd E. Brown: K'82:127; **K'83**:130,146; **K'84**:179
Harold E. Brown: K'86:171; **K'87**:123,177
L.E. "Red" Brown: K'81:127; **K'82**:45; **K'84**:179
Rick Browne: K'81:100; **K'83**:63; **K'84**:96,179; **K'85**:77,165; **K'86**:57
Barry R. Bryner: K'84:179; **K'86**:75; **K'87**:177
Bill Buchner: K'83:128; **K'84**:75,85,133,179; **K'85**:71
R.E. Buebendorf: K'83:153; **K'85**:165
John Bugden: K'87:49,105
Skip Burnette: K'87:177
Dave Burns: K'85:254
John Busfield: K'82:97,127; **K'83**:56; **K'84**:76,139; **K'86**:82,144; **K'87**:61,67,146,177
Jerry Busse: K'87:50

C

Bill Caldwell: K'85:56; **K'86**:89; **K'87**:96,179
Dick Campbell: K'81:Cover, 61,93,97,127; **K'82**:48,57,98,127; **K'84**:67,88
Joe Cndrella: K'87:179
Daniel L. Cnnady: K'87:179
Ronald E. Canter: K'81:127; **K'82**:81; **K'84**:179
Bob Cargill: K'81:85,92,93,127; **K'83**:44,56,77,155; **K'84**:78,134,179; **K'85**:108,143,151,165; **K'86**:93,94,95,123,161,162
W.R. Carnes: K'84:138
Fred Carter: K'81:6,16,47,48,50,53,63,70,73,96,116,118,119,121,129; **K'82**:Cover, 41,50,64; **K'83**:40,41,64,65,134,155; **K'84**:81,91,114,140; **K'85**:40,43,94,142,165; **K'86**:61,98
Frank and Mark Centofante: K'81:29,120,129; **K'82**:129; **K'83**:Cover, 35,36,61; **K'84**:181; **K'85**:136; **K'86**:144; **K'87**:Cover, 68,149
Gordon Chard: K'86:57,177; **K'87**:85,148,179
John E. Chase: K'81:129; **K'82**:109; **K'83**:155; **K'84**:51; **K'86**:56,124
Bill Cheatham: K'81:22,129; **K'82**:56,61,93,129; **K'83**:122,145; **K'84**:133,181; **K'85**:76,141
D.W. Childress: K'82:83,119
D.E. (Lucky) Clark: K'81:129; **K'82**:129
J.D. Clay: K'82:64,75,78,86,129; **K'85**:107,113,167
Wayne Clay: K'83:50,75,155; **K'84**:64,181; **K'85**:167; **K'86**:57; **K'87**:31,70,105
Keith E. Coleman: K'84:181; **K'85**:49,57,73; **K'87**:181
Ken Coleman: K'87:119
A.J. Collins: K'82:87,93,129; **K'84**:85,97,100,181; **K'85**:87,89,90; **K'87**:119
Lynn M. Collins: K'84:93,181; **K'85**:133
Michael Collins: K'82:119
Walter "Blackie" Collins: K'81:171; **K'82**:95,173; **K'83**:40; **K'85**:151
Paul E. Compton: K'81:25,129; **K'83**:84,129; **K'84**:183
Bob Conley: K'85:106,114,167; **K'86**:76,230
C.T. Conn, Jr.: K'83:155; **K'84**:70,105,183; **K'85**:167; **K'86**:79,124,229
Michael Connor: K'81:6,25,84; **K'82**:67,103,129; **K'84**:81; **K'85**:115,167
Robert Coogan: K'86:51; **K'87**:73,79,121,181
George J. Cooper: K'82:56
Harold Corby: K'81:69,74,130; **K'82**:62,118; **K'83**:35,36,47,157; **K'84**:95,144; **K'85**:95,169; **K'87**:181
Joseph G. Cordova: K'82:67,73,85; **K'84**:92; **K'85**:76
Leonard Corlee: K'81:17,92,130; **K'82**:41,52,62; **K'83**:43,157; **K'84**:77,183
Jim Corrado: K'83:Cover 2,30,50,59,111,114,115; **K'84**:83
Danny Courtney Jr.: K'83:157
Eldon Courtney: K'81:130; **K'82**:45,63,80,92,131; **K'83**:40,61,157; **K'84**:85,183; **K'85**:54,63,130,169; **K'86**:90,112; **K'87**:181
George Cousino: K'83:143; **K'84**:183; **K'85**:141,169; **K'86**:230; **K'87**:181
A.E. Cover: K'81:24,29,78,131; **K'82**:62,131; **K'83**:78; **K'84**:111,183
Ray Cover: K'86:149
Colin J. Cox: K'83:157; **K'85**:55,73,107; **K'86**:121; **K'87**:53,95,101,143
Sam Cox: K'87:250 James H. Craig: K'83**: 157; **K'84**: 185
Jack W. Crain: K'83:157; **K'84**:93,153,185; **K'85**:53,98,142,167; **K'86**:91,230; **K'87**:94,95,135,181
Larry Crawford: K'87:81
Pat Crawford: K'81:36,37,62,73,75,78,79,82,93,131; **K'82**:44,131; **K'83**:90,120,123,127,129,157; **K'84**:86,115; **K'85**:49,118; **K'86**:78,80,122,142; **K'87**:73,137
Harold Crisp: K'82:131; **K'84**:91,101,134,152; **K'85**:82,115,169

238 KNIVES '88

Jack Crockford: K'82:71; K'83:53,157; K'84:67,185; K'86:79
W.W. Cronk: K'81:110
James L. Crowell: K'83:113,116,117,147; K'84:71,185; K'85:41,71,78,171; K'86:110,118
W. Daniel Cullity: K'82:119
John Culpepper: K'81:131
R.J. Cumming: K'83:41; K'84:116,185; K'85:139,171
Jim Cunningham: K'81:131; K'83:159

D

Dan Dagget: K'81:85,86,103,115,132; K'82:52,53,75,111; K'83:Cover, 64,159; K'84:83,185; K'85:66,104; K'86:99,230
Cris Dahl: K'84:185; K'86:147; K'87:105
George Dailey: K'85:85; K'86:113; K'87:90,183
Alex Daniels: K'85:171; K'87:55,105,183
Art A. Darakis: K'81: Cover, 32,34,56,132; K'82:117; K'83:143,159; K'84:75,115,187
Rick Darby: K'83:81,159; K'84:110,187
Steve Davenport: K'82:133; K'83:51; K'84:187; K'87:62,183
Rob Davidson: K'85:97,121,135; K'86:118; K'87:85
Davis Brothers Knives: K'82:133; K'83:159; K'84:110; K'85:171; K'87:183
Davis Custom Knives: K'81:22,46,47,50,67,133
Barry Davis: K'84:68,79,81,187; K'85:171; K'86:61,71,78; K'87:81,183
Dixie Davis: K'85:171
K.M. "Twig" Davis: K'82:Cover; K'83:44,159; K'84:67,187
Syd Davis: K'84:105
W.C. Davis: K'81:93; K'82:75,133; K'83:114,159; K'84:79,88,103,187; K'86:Cover, 77,85
Dane and Barry Dawson: K'82:133; K'83:121,159; K'84:105
Richard Dearhart: K'82:133
Robert DeFeo: K'86:101; K'87:185
William G. DeFreest: K'82:60,61,83,119,133; K'83:79; K'85:100,173
Frank D'Elia: K'83:40,161
George S. Dempsey: K'85:98,173
Dan Dennehy: K'86:101
Douglas M. Dent: K'82:135; K'85:173
Larry Detloff: K'82: 114; K'83:145,161; K'84:66,141; K'85:88
Carl Dillon: K'87:70
Malcolm Dion: K'86:58; K'87:59,79,185
Jack Dias: K'84:189; K'85:173
Robert Orr Dodge: K'84:83,106
Patrick Donovan: K'86:99,144
Dick Dorough: K'81:34,135; K'82:51,135; K'83:55; K'84:75; K'87:146
T.M. Dowell: K'81:13,17,37,41,55,65,67,71,78,96,103,112,135; K'82:Cover, 39,48,79; K'83:134,137,138,139; K'84:52,94,117,150; K'85:31,97,116,175; K'86:24; K'87:109,185
Larry Downing: K'83:47,161; K'84:84,87,105,109,111,189; K'85:Cover, 48,89; K'86:83
T.M. Downing: K'86:56,181; K'87:50,58,82
Dubba (See E.W. Schulenberg.)
Bill Duff: K'81:135; K'82:87; K'86:145,230; K'87:187
Dave Dugger: K'84:189; K'85:48,135,175; K'86:59
Roy Dunlap: K'83:95
Melvin T. Dunn: K'83:209; K'84:61,189; K'85:57; K'86:66
Larry Duvall: K'86:109

E

R.O. Easler: K'83:161; K'84:189; K'85:106,175; K'86: 84,230
Al Eaton: K'87:85,95,109,148,187
Rick Eaton: K'87:187
Fain E. Edwards: K'82:51,135; K'83:87,90,116; K'84:73,116,191; K'85:60,61
Tom Edwards: K'86:126; K'87:87
Joel Ellefson: K'83:161; K'84:93,191; K'85:140; K'86:121; K'87:187
W.B. Ellerbe: K'85:175
Marcus Elliott: K'84:191
Don Ellison: K'83:48,61,161; K'84:103
Brad Embry: K'81:135
Jim Ence: K'81:53,54,55,58,65,76; K'82:25,48,49,66; K'83:43,84,86,163; K'84:Cover, 185; K'86:63,185
Robert Enders: K'86:79; K'87:187
Mike England: K'82:74; K'83:94,131,163; K'85:46,54,79,83,177; K'86:88,121
Virgil England: K'82:87
George Englebretson: K'85:115,177
Bob Engnath: K'86:54,128,129,132,133; K'87:109,112
Thomas M. Enos III: K'82:135; K'83:96,163
Curt Erickson: K'84:56,191; K'85:177; K'86:61,67,99,169; K'87:110,149,187
L.M. Erickson: K'84:191; K'86:230
Walter Erickson: K'86:122,255; K'87:72

F

Melvin Fassio: K'86:80; K'87:62,68,189
Howard J. Faucheaux: K'84:136; K'85:67; K'87:189
Al Faulkner: K'86:67
Stephen H. Fecas: K'82:60,96,119,137; K'83:84,94,163; K'84:115; K'85:75,177; K'86:79,186
Vince Feragotti: K'81:21,135; K'84:65
Lee Ferguson: K'85:177; K'86:109
William V. Fielder: K'84:76; K'86:118
Jimmy L. Fikes: K'83:111; K'84:86,119,121,133,136; K'85:64,78,115; K'86:140
L.C. Finger: K'83:Cover, 129; K'84:193; K'87:75
Clyde E. Fischer: K'82:87,137; K'85; 31; K'87:72
Jim Fister: K'87:81,189
Joe Flournoy: K'82:63; K'84:193; K'86:231; K'87:189

Don Fogg (See Kemal)
Allen Ford: K'85:179
Pete Forthofer: K'85:108; K'86:82; K'87:53,64
Roger Foust: K'83: 87,163; K'84:193; K'85: 56,61,83,91,179; K'86: 105
Ed A. Fowler: K'83:79; K'84:193; K'85:179; K'86:231
J. Paul Fox: K'81:85,93,136; K'82:137; K'83:50; K'85:108,179; K'86:78,106,231; K'87:66,116
Wendell Fox: K'87:130
Ed Fowler: K'87:130,189
Heinrich H. Frank: K'81:136; K'82:117,137; K'83:138; K'84:149; K'85:109; K'86:74; K'87:71
Andrew Frankland: K'84:116; K'87:93,136
Mike Franklin: K'81:136; K'82:73,95; K'83:35,36
Ron Frazier: K'81:7,67,137; K'82:48; K'84:53,81,193; K'85:72; K'87:152
Art Freeman: K'85:68,114
A.J. Freiling: K'83:50,107; K'85:64,139
Dennis Friedly: K'85:98,129; K'86:100
Yasuhiro Fujimoto: K'86:79; K'87:118
S.M. Fujisaka: K'86:57; K'87:52,78,191
Burt Fuller and Hall: K'81:25,80
Jim Fuller: K'86:Cover, 104; K'87:32,76
John W. Fuller: K'81:30,137; K'82:72,137; K'83:105,165; K'85:179
W.T. Fuller, Jr.: K'81:30,137; K'82:137; K'83:54,165; K'85:179
R. Fulton: K'85:181
Joe Funderburg: K'82:25,26; K'83:43,139; K'86:64
Shiro Furukawa: K'84:195; K'87:63

G

Frank Gamble: K'82:80,97; K'84:96; K'85:74,102,181
Chuck Garlitz: K'87:56,191
Willard O. Garner: K'87:107,191
Ron Gaston: K'83:82; K'84:195; K'85:181; K'86:124; K'87:54
Clay Gault: K'81:36,139; K'83:74,165; K'84:195; K'85:112; K'86:58,75,143; K'87:61,72,103,111
Roy E. Genge: K'82:139; K'83:165; K'84:195
Rick Genovese: K'81:12,139; K'83:165
Randall Gilbreath: K'85:181; K'86:75; K'87:49,63,95,191
E.E. "Dick" Gillenwater: K'82:78,119,139; K'83:35,36,79; K'84:195; K'85:Cover; K'87:77,103,152,191
Jon Gilmore: K'87:Cover, 75,193
Ken Glaser: K'86:90; K'87:193
Roger Gleason: K'84:131
Ron Glover: K'84:65,95,195; K'85:68,109; K'86:231; K'87:155
Wayne Goddard: K'82:79; K'83:35,36,165; K'84:62; K'85:61,69,181; K'86:136,137; K'87:130
Jim Gofourth: K'87:61
T.S. Goldenberg: K'85:181
Tai Goo: K'83:117,165; K'84:197; K'85:91; K'86:139; K'87:137,141,193
Butch Goodwin: K'87:110,129
Gordon (See DeFreest)
Butch Gordon: K'87:58
Dante and/or Judy Gottage: K'83:167; K'84:78,197; K'85:73,83,107,183; K'86:82,189; K'87:104,193,65
Greg Gottschalk: K'85:183; K'87:Cover, 109,151
Charles W. Graham: K'81:42
William R. Granquist: K'83:167
G. Green: K'82:139; K'83:47,51,167; K'84:76; K'85:108,183; K'86:55,145; K'87:68
Michael Gregory: K'83:41,73; K'84:61,109,197; K'85:114,183
Roger Grenier: K'84:103,197; K'87:151,153
Mark Griffin: K'85:183
Rendon Griffin: K'81:6,17,19,52,93,139; K'82:75; K'83:52,121,122,167; K'84:66,77,136; K'85:107,110; K'87:61
Larry Grigg: K'86:147
George B. Guthrie: K'83:81,167; K'84:197; K'85:185
Bob Gwozdz: K'85:132,185; K'86:125

H

Phillip L. (Doc) Hagen: K'83:45,167; K'84:197; K'85:62,185; K'86:83; K'87:65,195
George S. Haggerty: K'84:67,108,199; K'85:90; K'86:60; K'87:69,104,195
Robert J. Hajovsky: K'81:12,61,69,73,74; K'82:61,66; K'83:44,46,88,129; K'84:72,199
Lloyd A. Hale: K'81:47,52,65,79; K'83:Cover, 35,36,167; K'85:31; K'86:66,117
Joe R. Hales: K'82:77
Jim Hammond: K'81:8,14,55,74,78,98,105,139; K'82:64,119; K'83:65,79,131,169; K'84:61,96; K'85:185; K'86:91,145,231; K'87:59
Royal H. Hanson: K'82:139; K'83:44,51,142; K'85:108,137
Jim Hardenbrook: K'81:6,48,65,141; K'82:48,50,52; K'83:41,44,169; K'84:63,81,151; K'85:14,66
Frank L. Hargis: K'83:86,169; K'84:94,199; K'85:98,103,185; K'86:Cover; K'87:195
Larry W. Harley: K'85:185; K'87:54,83,87,121,195
Ralph Dewey: K'87:61,111
V.E. "Gene" Harrison: K'84:68; K'85:84; K'87:137
William W. Harsey: K'85:35,136; K'87:106,130
Allan (Lanny) Hartman: K'87:195
Phill Hartsfield: K'81:8; K'82:44,68,141; K'83:98,169; K'85:37,187; K'87:49,59,92
M.C. Harvey: K'86:89
Don Hastings: K'81:66,70,75,84,102; K'82:103; K'83:112; K'84:49,51,52,68,199; K'85:97,187; K'86:62,90
Rade Hawkins: K'81:141; K'83:86,169; K'84:106; K'87:103,195
Chap E. Haynes: K'87:107,135,140
Don Hedrick: K'84:60; K'85:187; K'86:65,106; K'87:54,86,135
Lou Hegedus: K'84:68,199; K'86:90,140; K'87:59

EIGHTH ANNUAL EDITION 239

Richard Karl Hehn: **K'87**:61,83,139,147,197
Lorenzo "Larry" Hendricks: **K'81**:38; **K'82**:141; **K'83**:107,169; **K'84**:151; **K'87**:147
D.E. Henry: **K'81**:65; K'83: 80,84,85,124; **K'84**: 12,13,14,15,16,17,18,19; K'87: 110
Wayne Hensley: **K'81**:62,141; **K'83**:45,83,130,169; **K'86**:141
Tim Herman: **K'82**:55,141; **K'83**:66,113,169; **K'84**:51,88; **K'85**:49,109,155,187
Bill Herndon: **K'87**:76,115,125
George Herron: **K'81**:76; **K'82**:79,119,141; **K'83**:35,36; **K'84**:63,201; **K'85**:124; **K'86**:57,81
Don Hethcoat: **K'83**:171; **K'84**:63,93,201; **K'87**:57
Thomas S. Hetmanski: **K'85**:109,189; **K'86**:122,126; **K'87**:86,101,197,238
Daryl Hibben: **K'87**:56,197
Gil Hibben: **K'81**:43,93; **K'82**:42,54,68,77,141; **K'83**:35,36,91,108,171; **K'84**:Cover, 56,57,58; **K'85**:55,76,86,102,103,118; **K'86**:55,106,122; **K'87**:56,89,90,121,137
Vernon W. Hicks: **K'81**:31,34,141; **K'83**:56,121,171; **K'84**:201
Howard E. Hill: **K'83**:57; **K'84**:101,109,201; **K'85**:117; **K'86**:69,191; **K'87**:97,197
Rick Hill: **K'87**:90,197
Harumi Hirayama: **K'86**:51
Howard Hitchmough: **K'82**:118; **K'8**:55,126,142,171; **K'84**:64,141,145,201; **K'85**:97,189
J.B. Hodge: **K'81**:19,28,30,85,100,141; **K'82**:114; **K'83**:51; **K'84**:139; **K'85**:134; **K'87**:Cover
John Hodge (III): **K'84**:134,201
Steve Hoel: **K'81**:34,35; **K'82**:49; **K'83**:55; **K'84**:75,201; **K'85**:110,189; **K'86**:84; **K'87**:146
Donald B. Hoffmann: **K'82**:Cover
Kevin L. Hoffman: **K'83**:80,130,171; **K'84**:70,89,92,203; **K'85**:39,50,68,76,115,189; **K'86**:101; **K'87**:59,78,96
D'Alton Holder: **K'81**:16,54,64,77,84,104,109,114,143; **K'82**:25,26; **K'83**:35,36,47,66,142,171,202; **K'84**:68,122,203; **K'85**:Cover, 44,50,121; **K'86**:62,71,231
Dale J. Holland: **K'85**:110; **K'86**:82
Paul Holloway: **K'85**:67,90,93,189; **K'86**:113; **K'87**:51,110,120,199
Ron Holstrom: **K'85**:39,189; **K'86**:145,231; **K'87**:105,143,199
M.E. Holze and R.K. Hehn: **K'82**:85,143
Jess Horn: **K'81**:28; **K'82**:69,77,87,98; **K'83**:54,61,108,134,171; **K'84**:51,79; **K'85**:136,141; **K'86**:77,79; **K'87**:146,151
Glen Hornby: **K'82**:44,143; **K'83**:143,171; **K'84**:203; **K'85**:57; **K'86**:63,88,116,120,121
Durvyn M. Howard: **K'82**:69,143; **K'83**:54,60; **K'84**:88; **K'85**:191
David M. Howie: **K'81**:16,26,29,55,79; **K'82**:95,143; **K'83**:173; **K'84**:203
John Howser: **K'86**:64
Arthur J. Hubbard: **K'81**:143; **K'82**:63,143; **K'83**:42,64,173; **K'84**:86,203; **K'85**:74,91,117,132,191; **K'86**:90,100,125; **K'87**:67,81,83,123,143,199
C. Robbin Hudson: **K'84**:85,203; **K'85**:93; **K'87**:55
Chubby Hueske: **K'81**:15,114; **K'82**:84; **K'83**:35,36,40,173; **K'84**:78; **K'86**:60,63,80; **K'87**:121
Lawrence Hughes: **K'84**:203; **K'85**:191; **K'87**:154,155
Roy Humenick: **K'87**:199
Bob Hunnicutt: **K'86**:63,142

I

Billy Mace Imel: **K'81**:22,27,57,73,143; **K'82**:60,91,143; **K'83**:53,60,74,122,138,139,173; **K'84**:144,150; **K'85**:103,106,121,191; **K'86**:196; **K'87**:33,137

J

Gerry Jean: **K'82**:95,145; **K'83**:102,129,139,140; **K'85**:193; **K'87**:59
Steve Jernigan: **K'85**:79; **K'86**:197
Sid Jirik: **K'83**:80; **K'85**:75,98,193; **K'86**:60,232
Robert Job (See Wootz Int'l.)
S.R. Jobs: **K'81**:67,143
Gorden W. Johnson: **K'81**:144; **K'83**:81,173
Harold "Harry" C. Johnson: **K'83**:175
Ronald B. Johnson: **K'83**:143,173; **K'85**:193; **K'86**:149
Ruffin Johnson: **K'81**:11,25,68,70,71,105,112,113; **K'82**:68,145; **K'83**:173; **K'84**:104,153,205; **K'87**:126,137,141,201
S.R. Johnson: **K'81**:Cover, 13,62,78,144; **K'82**:67,85,91,115,120,145; **K'83**:43,83,95,175; **K'85**:193; **K'86**:63,231; **K'87**:149
W.C. "Bill" Johnson: **K'83**:41,77,142; 1 **K'84**:205; **K'85**:112,193; **K'86**:147; **K'87**:83,201
Bob Jones: **K'84**:111,205; **K'85**:63; **K'86**:80; **K'87**:66

K

Robert A. Kapela: **K'81**:44,92,144
Lee Karkruff: **K'84**:114
Don Karlin: **K'81**:42,103; **K'82**:145; **K'83**:175; **K'86**:100,125
Kioshi Kato: **K'82**:104; **K'84**:95,119
Joseph F. Keeslar: **K'87**:55,140,203
William L. Keeton: **K'81**:15,33,42,145; **K'82**:78,92,145; **K'84**:62,64,85; **K'85**:69; **K'86**:67,81; **K'87**:32,51,110,201
Gary Kelley: **K'81**:51; **K'84**:56,86,98,99,113,136,205; **K'85**:86; **K'86**:103,126; **K'87**:84,86,87,201
Lance Kelly: **K'81**:33,56,57,86,92,120,145; **K'82**:117; **K'83**:121,143; **K'84**:141,207; **K'85**:137; **K'86**:Cover, 61; **K'87**:201
Jim Kelso: **K'85**:Cover, 71,86,203; **K'86**:55
Kemal: **K'81**:41,48,71,81,103,119,144; **K'82**:102,147; **K'83**:90,113,127; **K'84**:52,71,81,114,123; **K'85**:43,73,78; **K'86**:70,98; **K'87**:108,139
Bill Kennedy, Jr.: **K'85**:117; **K'87**:85
J.C. Kennelley: **K'86**:125
Jot Singh Khalsa: **K'81**:21,51,70,71,75,145; **K'82**:45,63,66,90; **K'83**:Cover, 99,106,127,175; **K'84**:84,94; **K'85**:95,195; **K'86**:89,232; **K'87**:91,92
Shiva Ki: **K'84**:207; **K'85**:56,72,74,195; **K'86**:65,78,100,151,198; **K'87**:47,77,113

Bill King: **K'82**:147; **K'83**:175; **K'86**:75; **K'87**:69
Joe Kious: **K'82**:50,52,115; **K'83**:60,66,122,175; **K'84**:122,207; **K'85**:44,95,97,106; **K'86**:75,98,232; **K'87**:155
Jon W. Kirk: **K'81**:147; **K'83**:175; **K'84**:207
George Kirtley: **K'83**:175; **K'84**:91
K.K.K. Co. (See A.J. Collins.)
W. Kneubuehler: **K'85**:61,63
George Koutsopoulos: **K'85**:195; **K'86**:116; **K'87**:73,203
Michael T. Koval: **K'81**:60,62,63,65,66,147; **K'82**:86,93,147; **K'84**:84,207
Terry L. Kranning: **K'85**:82,83; **K'87**:86,87,203
D.F. Kressler: **K'84**:60,207; **K'86**:59,64; **K'87**:51,106,116
Martin Kruse: **K'87**:50,90,203
Jim Kuykendall: **K'85**:195; **K'86**:55

L

Ron Lake: **K'85**:107,112; **K'86**:25,57,77,231; **K'87**:64,146
Frank G. Lampson: **K'83**:177; **K'84**:66,137,139,207; **K'85**:139; **K'87**:203
Ed Lane: **K'83**:177
Kurt Lang: **K'83**:63,101,109,115; **K'84**:51; **K'86**:52
Gary Langley: **K'84**:209; **K'86**:80,232
Mick Langley: **K'87**:205
Scott Lankton: **K'84**:132; **K'85**:79,85,87,121,122,197; **K'87**:91,135,140,141
Ken Largin: **K'83**:95,177; **K'84**:99,106; **K'85**:74,81,89,197; **K'86**:67,71,114,115; **K'87**:58,93,205
Milo J. (Mike) Leach: **K'81**:64,93; **K'82**:42,92,147; **K'83**:46,146; **K'84**:209; **K'85**:109,197; **K'86**:60,88
Tommy Lee: **K'81**:15,27,64,69,80,81,106,107,121,147; **K'82**:109,119,147; **K'83**:135,177; **K'84**:83,209; **K'86**:62,92; **K'87**:108,121
Charles Lejcek: **K'87**:73,140
E. Lenaz: **K'84**:139; **K'85**:135
Norman Levine: **K'82**:42,96; **K'83**:94,121,130; **K'84**:56,89,144,209; **K'85**:139,197; **K'87**:205
Wendell Liggett: **K'85**:82,83
Jimmy Lile: **K'81**:31,55,56,57,61,82,84,110,147; **K'83**:50,61,64,83,94; **K'84**:52,114,143; **K'85**:31,46,53,197; **K'86**:91,116,120; **K'87**:64,101,107,119
Chris A. Lindsay: **K'87**:205
Gary M. Little: **K'85**:113,197; **K'86**:58; **K'87**:111
Wolfgang Loerchner: **K'87**:52,59,89,149,205
Bob Lofgren: **K'81**:54; **K'84**:114
Dave Longworth: **K'84**:209; **K'85**:50; **K'86**:76,200; **K'87**:Cover, 68
Tony Louis: **K'84**:56,209; **K'85**:199; **K'86**:63,91,112,119
A.C. Love: **K'84**:209
Ed Love: **K'83**:87,88,177; **K'84**:62; **K'85**:113,199,237
R.W. Loveless: **K'81**:12,73,96,170; **K'82**:Cover, 79,120; **K'83**:103; **K'86**:22,24; **K'87**:Cover 2,14-17,19
Schuyler Lovestrand: **K'86**:64; **K'87**:152,207
Bill Luckett: **K'82**:42,67,149; **K'83**:67,105,177; **K'84**:58,72,122,211; **K'85**:74,102,137
Robert W. Lum: **K'81**:40,147; **K'82**:64,97; **K'83**:Cover 2,79,80,98,130,179; **K'84**:63,72; **K'85**:71,77; **K'86**:56,139; **K'87**:53,79,126
Robert Lutes: **K'87**:150,207
Ernest L. Lyle: **K'82**:149; **K'83**:179; **K'86**:232

M

Mike Macri: **K'87**:51,113,207
J.M. "Mickey" Maddox: **K'81**:147; **K'83**:53,60
Jack Madsen: **K'83**:98,117; **K'87**:91
Jeffrey G. Malitzke: **K'85**:93
Mike Manrow: **K'81**:10,45,46,57,74,83,92,93,97,118; **K'83**:42,45; **K'85**:103
Dan Maragni: **K'82**:102,149; **K'83**:179; **K'84**:82; **K'85**:93,129; **K'86**:71,89,151; **K'87**:126,207
Tom Maringer: **K'81**:43,49; **K'82**:54,149; **K'83**:39,89,90,91,129,179; **K'84**:73,135; **K'85**:75,85,87,103,117,199; **K'86**:Cover 2,101,109,110, 111,116,126,142; **K'87**:93,126
Glenn Marshall: **K'83**:94,179; **K'84**:211; **K'85**:90,113,199; **K'86**:72; **K'87**:105,143
Bill Mase: **K'82**:149
Lynn Maxfield: **K'84**:211; **K'87**:137,207
Tom Mayo: **K'85**:99,201; **K'87**:79,82,123
Harvey McBurnette: **K'81**:21,36,93,98,149; **K'82**:51,69,116,151; **K'83**:52,121,126,179; **K'84**:79,89; **K'85**:136,201; **K'86**:76; **K'87**:62,66,121,147
Harry McCarty: **K'85**:62
Zollan McCarty: **K'84**:106
C.O. "Mac" McClung: **K'81**:106; **K'82**:151
Loyd A. McConnell, Jr.: **K'82**:151; **K'84**:145; **K'85**:91,201; **K'86**:56,64; **K'87**:49,120,209
Larry E. McCullough: **K'84**:211
Dave McDearmont: **K'85**:201; **K'87**:209
Ken McFall: **K'87**:209
Thomas McLane: **K'82**:97,151; **K'83**:98,127; **K'84**:71; **K'85**: 78
John McLeod: **K'86**:72; **K'87**:148,209
Sean McWilliams: **K'85**:89,94,115,141,201; **K'86**:71,99,109; **K'87**:93,104
John Meeks: **K'85**:49,118,201
Daryl Meier: **K'84**:83; **K'86**:139
Harry E. Mendenhall: **K'87**:209
Larry B. Merical: **K'83**:202
Chris Miller, Jr.: **K'81**:81,92,149; **K'82**:66,68; **K'84**:93; **K'85**:100; **K'86**:232; **K'87**:59
Hanford J. Miller: **K'83**:181; **K'84**:63,82,96; **K'85**:85,129,203; **K'86**:65; **K'87**:55,81,111
J.P.Miller: **K'83**:117,181; **K'84**:119; **K'87**:149
Terry Miller: **K'82**:43,111,151; **K'83**:181; **K'84**:213; **K'85**:203; **K'86**:124; **K'87**:97
Louis G. Mills (Yasutomo): **K'84**:71,135; **K'85**:Cover, 71,86,203; **K'86**:54;

K'87:112,116,154
Jim Minnick: K'81:85; K'82:50,86,151; K'83:79; K'85:135
Max Mitchell: K'84:53,100,106,213; K'85:60,82,108,203; K'86:91,103,115,232; K'87:87
Harald Moeller: K'84:213; K'85:203
Claude Montjoy: K'84:213; K'85:102,139,203; K'86:83,148; K'87:63
Keith Moorby: K'84:213; K'85:203
James B. Moore: K'85:205; K'87:211
Tom Moore: K'87:121
Wm. F. Moran, Jr.: K'81:Cover, 59; K'82:28,29,30,31,32,33,34, 68,77,101,120,153; K'83:33,34,92,100,101,102,103,111; K'84:82,127,150; K'85:43,68,77; K'86:120; K'87:Cover 2,55,80,106,111,120
Emil Morgan: K'85:205; K'87:106,211
Jeff Morgan: K'84:145; K'85:137,205; K'86:203; K'87:123,148,211
Tom Morgan: K'85:63; K'86:118; K'87:86,211
Tom Morland: K'84:139
Morseth (See A.G. Russell.)
Steve Mullin: K'83:107,189; K'84:105,215; K'85:109,205; K'86:74,83; K'87:62,70,108
Dave Murphy: K'83:22,23,24,25,26; K'84:215; K'85:Cover; K'87:141
John Myakowa: K'87:110
Mel Myers: K'85:205
Paul Myers: K'81:32,93; K'85:82,86,205; K'86:80,148; K'87:86,150,153

N

Woody Naifeh: K'82:153; K'85:110
Jerry Neal: K'85:91,205; K'86:124
Budd Nealey: K'84:215
Keith Nelson: K'86:91,122,207,234
R. Kent Nicholson: K'87:81
R.D. and Roger Nolen: K'81:24,28,33,40,44,55,56,93,109,118,151; K'82:55; K'83:67,126; K'84:96,215; K'85:207,239; K'86:109,112,233; K'87:155,213

O

Charles Ochs: K'87:108,135,136,213
Robert O. Ogg: K'85:137
Robert Oleson: K'81:48,84,92,98,151; K'82:74
Gordon O'Leary: K'86:233; K'87:53,148,213
Milford Oliver: K'84:100; K'86:83
Wayne C. Olson: K'85:114; K'86:145,208
Warren Osborne: K'86:58,76,100,232; K'87:213
T.R. Overeynder: K'82:114,153; K'83:145,183; K'84:145,217; K'85:207; K'86:76,84,144; K'87:71,87
Lowell Oyster: K'86:104; K'87:123

P

Larry Page: K'85:207; K'86:58
Robert "Bob" Papp: K'82:60,153; K'83:43,63,139; K'84:140,217; K'85:207; K'86:233; K'87:88,215
Melvin M. Pardue: K'81:22,93,117; K'82:98,115; K'83:52,54,80,183; K'84:66,140; K'85:76; K'86:144
Robert Parrish: K'85:56; K'86:120; K'87:95,101
W.C. Pass: K'83:39
Hill Pearce: K'83:Cover 2,43,65,183; K'84:121; K'85:78; K'87:125,126,215
W.D. Pease: K'81:14,36,84,93,115,151; K'82:67,75; K'83:53,120,183; K'84:53,114,217; K'86:209; K'87:146
Lloyd Pendleton: K'81:16,114; K'82:60,92,94,155; K'83:78,183; K'84:52; K'85:99; K'87:50
Alfred H. Pendray: K'84:112,217; K'86:81
Stephan Pepiot: K'87:215
Pepper Knives (See J. Culpepper.)
Eldon G. Peterson: K'81:18,29; K'83:55,66; K'84:217; K'86:80,209; K'87:64,66,72,215
Harold "Bud" Phillips: K'82:72
Randy Phillips: K'85:209; K'86:99,121,233; K'87:108
Larry Pickering: K'84:92,152,217; K'85:40
David Pitt: K'86:116
Leon Pittman: K'81:20,93; K'82:Cover; K'83:60,185; K'87:65,73
Paul W. Poehlmann: K'81:171; K'84:77,219
Jerry Poletis: K'81:23,66,82,153; K'82:56,155; K'83:185
Clifton Polk: K'82:155; K'83:51,202; K'84:103,111; K'85:209; K'86:115; K'87:72
Rusty Polk: K'84:219
L.T. Pomykalski: K'86:102,104
James L. Poplin: K'81:20,79,95,97,153; K'82:83; K'83:185; K'84:143
Alvin Poston: K'84:219; K'85:209
J. Merle Poteet: K'85:211
Jerry L. Price: K'83:129,185
Joel Hiram Price: K'87:82,106,215
Steve Price: K'86:55,155; K'87:96,217
Joe M. Prince: K'82:119; K'84:79,219; K'85:211
Ron Pritchard: K'82:155; K'83:39,77,185; K'84:219; K'87:139,217
Jim Pugh: K'81:21,50,81,121,153; K'82:55,56; K'85:104,142; K'87:127,217
Morris C. Pulliam: K'85:211; K'86:65,81,139; K'87:62,107,132
Aaron Pursley: K'82:116; K'83:122,133; K'84:75; K'85:211; K'87:121,217

Q

Barr Quarton: K'83:44,46,63,76,185; K'85:211; K'87:111,113
George Quinn: K'85:211; K'86:99,212

R

Jerry F. Rados: K'83:41,75,187; K'84:221; K'85:49,103,130,211; K'86:110,139,233; K'87:66,140
W.D. and (Bo) Gary T. Randall: K'81:23,58,64,69,102,117,153; K'82:41,71,92,120,157; K'83:93; K'85:54; K'86:22,126,149; K'87:Cover 2
Steve Rapp: K'87:154
Rick Rappazzo: K'87:68,217
Michael Ray: K'81:153; K'82:60,61,84,91,157; K'84:53,144,221; K'85:213
Mike Ream: K'82:88
Chris Reeves: K'87:96
Winfred M. Reeves: K'83:79; K'84:70
Bill Reh: K'84:65,221; K'85:213; K'87:52,123
John Reynolds: K'86:233
David Rhea: K'86:107
Ron Richard: K'84:76,221
Sam Richards: K'86:52
Dave Ricke: K'83:187; K'84:137,140; K'86:74
Willie Rigney: K'84:84; K'85:67,94,213; K'86:65,98,233
Dean Roath: K'81:14,40,82,106,107,108,155; K'82:64,86; K'83:187; K'84:139
J.B. Robbins: K'86:212
G. Rocha: K'84:112; K'85:113,121
Fred D. Roe, Jr.: K'83:74,187; K'84:63,109,221; K'85:213; K'86:88; K'87:83,68
Fred Rohn: K'81:15,80,112,113,114,155; K'82:157; K'83:78,94,187; K'85:213
Steve Rollert: K'86:126
Harold F. Rollins: K'82:49; K'84:221
Mark H. Roper, Jr.: K'83:187; K'84:61,93; K'85:105,215
Alex Rose: K'84:101,223; K'87:85,219
Rudolph H. Ruana: K'83:93; K'86:22,24
A.G. Russell: K'81:23,149,171; K'82:72,97,120; K'83:39,88; K'84:61; K'85:48; K'86:60,117,147; K'87:76
Roger J. Russell: K'81:72,110,113,155,171; K'82:51,53,80,96,157; K'83:123,134,189; K'85:215
Charles C. Rust: K'83:189,202; K'85:215

S

Suzanne St. Amour: K'86:51,52
John D. Salley: K'83:142; K'84:110,223; K'85:57,86,215; K'86:110; K'87:Cover, 77,90,219
Bob Salpas: K'85:141,215; K'86:56
Lynn J. Sampson: K'85:114; K'86:234; K'87:63
Jody Samson: K'84:223; K'85:67,215; K'87:50,92,151,219
Bill Sanders (See Timberline Knives.)
Michael M. Sanders: K'87:219
Jim Sasser: K'81:32; K'82:44,159; K'83:93,102,105; K'84:106
Scott Sawby: K'83:107,189; K'85:217; K'86:81,144
Murad Sayen (See Kemal.)
Will Scarrow: K'87:122,126
George Schepers: K'86:118,234
Carl Schlieper: K'87:455
James A. Schmidt: K'81:49,50,51,52,62,76,101,102,115,155; K'82:99,101,159; K'83:102,113,114,116,126; K'84:Cover, 75,223; K'85:44,50,94; K'86:84,97
Herman J. Schneider: K'81:46,48,61,157; K'82:24,53,118,159; K'83:35,36; K'84:57,115,151; K'85:104,134,217; K'87:120
Matthew A. Schoenfeld: K'81:38,41; K'82:54; K'83:189; K'84:57,97,225; K'85:74,129,217; K'87:58,219
Maurice and Alan Schrock: K'81:40
Stephen Schwarzer: K'82:104,105; K'83:101,102,107,112,114,127; K'84:82,114,137,225; K'85:63,66,110,217; K'86:116,140
Jim Serven: K'81:20,42,72,85,92,157; K'82:50,73,159; K'83:52,191; K'84:88,225; K'85:106,217; K'86:77,234; K'87:67
Robert G. Sharp: K'82:80,161; K'83:53,88,191; K'84:109,225; K'85:217
Phil Sharpe: K'85:62,217
David L. Shaw: K'81:79,157; K'82:51,58,63,113,161; K'83:191
Scott Shoemaker: K'87:55,89,92,131
William E. Shulenberger: K'82:161; K'83:191
Corbet R. Sigman: K'81:19,99,105,108,109,114,117,157; K'82:73,79,97,120,161; K'83:35,36,42,65,74,191; K'84:Cover 2, 62,64,110,126; K'86:139; K'87:52,107
Cleston S. Sinyard: K'85:60,92,217; K'86:90,101; K'87:50,219
Jim Siska: K'85:140; K'87:58,97,152,219
David Sites: K'81:157
Fred Slee: K'86:233
John Sloan: K'83:77,108,191
Ed Small: K'85:60; K'86:118; K'87:81
Jim Small: K'82:161; K'84:112,121,225; K'87:145,223
Adam Smith: K'81:83; K'83:191; K'84:227
Harry Smith: K'86:74
John T. Smith: K'81:14,28,39,159; K'82:67,98; K'83:193
Ralph L. Smith: K'82:96,110,119; K'83:76,193; K'84:78,92,227; K'87:63,69
W.F. (Red) Smith: K'83:86,193
W.J. Sonneville: K'81:159
Jim Sornberger: K'81:14,45,59,66,159; K'82:49,53,87,117,163; K'83:48,63,85,106,142,193; K'84:83; K'85:Cover, 77,100,132,219; K'86:111; K'87:81,136,143
Bernard Sparks: K'81:23,79,159
John Spencer: K'85:219; K'87:103
Dale Spendlove: K'84:78,227
Richard Spinale: K'82:117,163; K'83:143; K'84:75,115; K'85:221; K'87:71
Richard Stafford: K'85:98; K'87:53,223
Harry L. Stalter: K'87:136,152,223
Chuck Stapel: K'82:96,163; K'83:39,42,85,129,193; K'84:65,72,112,125,144,152,227; K'85:75,151,221; K'86:121; K'87:58,70,136
Craig Stapel: K'87:223
Richard S. Staples: K'82:41,62,85,163; K'83:193; K'84:65
John Stapleton: K'85:99,221
Harry L. Statler: K'86:145
Ken Steigerwalt: K'83:193; K'84:227; K'85:221; K'86:74,214; K'87:64,67

Kelly Lee Stephens: K'82:42,60,67
Charles (Chuck) Stewart: K'83:41,57,75; K'84:55,89,227; K'85:57,76,107,221; K'86: 77,98; K'87:65,70,169
G.W. Stone: K'82:119
Johnny Stout: K';86:59
Scott Strong: K'86:59; K'87:133,219
Stud (Custom Knives Ltd.): K'82:176
Rod Swain: K'85:221
Chuck Syslo: K'84:229; K'85:223

T

Masao Takahashi: K'85:114; K'86:50; K'87:109
C. Gray Taylor: K'81:47,63,82,159; K'82:49,50; K'83:Cover, 46,134,195; K'84:83,93,110; K'85:32,94,104,223; K'86:82; K'87:72
David Taylor: K'83:107; K'84:86,110,229; K'85:223; K'86:81,85; K'87:65
Mickey Tedder: K'85:48
Lou Teichmoeller: K'82:43,104,163
Stephen Terrill: K'83:195; K'84:91,229; K'85:100,136,223; K'86:67; K'87:51,225
Robert Terzuola: K'83:195; K'84:64,91; K'85:72,99,223; K'87:91,112,136,225
David Thompson: K'87:130
Leon Thompson: K'81:13,27,64,84,161; K'83:56,61,84,195; K'84:64,76,229; K'87:68,225
Danny Thornton: K'81:161; K'83:93; K'84:111
Timberline Knives: K'84:63,229
Carolyn D. Tinker: K'81:12,99,107,161; K'83:78,195; K'84:229; K'86:55
Robert E. Tison: K'81:37,100,161
Pat Tomes: K'82:98; K'83:76,84,116; K'85:97,223; K'87:91,155,225
Dan Tompkins: K'84:67,231; K'85:223; K'86:151
Dwight L. Towell: K'81:Cover, 161; K'83:35,36,86,99,195; K'84:62,76,94,231; K'85:66,225; K'86:66; K'87:125,225
R.W. Trabbic: K'81:19,36; K'82:46,165; K'84:231; K'85:225
Terry A. Treutel: K'87:104
TRO Knives (See Overeynder.)
Thomas A. Trujillo: K'87:82
Ralph A. Turnbull: K'81:86,122; K'82:43,69,86,98,115; K'83:57,197; K'84:Cover, 94; K'85:110,112,121; K'86:77,219; K'87:54,113,227
Twig (See K.M. Davis.)

U

W.L. Underwood: K'84:231

V

Wayne Valachovic: K'82:91,105,165; K'83:58,114; K'84:88,231; K'85:67,77,93,225; K'86:84,221; K'87:32,66,83,121,125,126
A. Daniel Valois: K'85:58
Frans Van Eldik: K'84:103; K'85:225; K'86:58; K'87:51,119
Michael Veit: K'87:139,227
H.J. Viele: K'81:22,39,40,82,83,85,86,98,99,161; K'82:49,96,165; K'83:98,99; K'84:96; K'85:69,143; K'86:149
David Votaw: K'83:106,197; K'85:225
Frank Vought, Jr.: K'82:43,62,78,165; K'84:61,110,231; K'85:50,79,85,132,225; K'86:92,107,112,142,234; K'87:Cover, 227

W

J.M. Wade: K'84:231; K'85:225
John K. Wagaman: K'85:225; K'86:66; K'87:56,82,97,227
Mark Wahlster: K'87:115
Mark Waldrop: K'84:78,86; K'85:97,110,225; K'86:75; K'87:90
George A. Walker: K'82:74,110,165; K'83:197; K'84:75,104,141; K'86:74,125; K'87:63,129,147
John Walker: K'87:123
Michael L. Walker: K'83:123,197; K'84:70,75,77,105,111,140,231; K'85:122,227; K'86:Cover 2,85,141; K'87:61,67,79,121,147,227
David Wardman: K'83:93,197; K'85:227
J.D. Ware: K'84:60
Buster Warenski: K'81:12,47,50,54,55,66,67; K'82:23,26,52,57,83,167; K'83:35,36,83,219; K'84:149; K'85:44,150,227
Stanley Warzocha: K'83:197; K'85:227
Daniel Watson: K'86:109; K'87:89,93,120
Freddie Watt III: K'85:227; K'86:62,234
Fred E. Weber: K'82:66,84,95; K'83:41,133,197; K'85:98
Donald E. Weiler: K'81:108; K'82:167; K'83:103,199; K'84:233; K'85:129,227; K'86:69; K'87:55,78,229
Charles L. Weiss: K'81:46,48,49,70,163; K'82:54; K'85:95,99; K'86:Cover, 151; K'87:229
William H. Welch: K'81:13,39,80,163; K'83:97; K'84:233; K'85:68,227; K'86:234
Cody Wescott: K'86:76
Mike Wesolowski: K'81:13,62,163; K'85:81
Gene E. White: K'85:136
Bob White, Jr.: K'87:86
Robert J. "Bob" White: K'82:72; K'83:56,75; K'84:89,109,143; K'85:90,229; K'86:49,56,83,92; K'87:100,123,229
Weldon Whitley: K'81:24; K'82:119; K'83:199; K'84:233
Ken Whitworth: K'82:86,115,167; K'83:45,61,199; K'84:78,94,233; K'85:107,229
James C. Wiggins: K'84:60,233; K'85:106,229
H.L. Wiggins: K'87:123
L.R. Wilding: K'81:78,163
Gery L. Willey: K'87:231 W.G. Willey: K'82: 112,167; K'83: 199; K'86: 234; K'87: 231
W.C. Williams: K'81:20,33,34,163; K'82:119
Lowell Wills: K'83:130,199
James G. Wilson: K'87:109

R.W. Wilson: K'82:114
Art Wiman: K'83:56,199; K'86:115
Bill Winn: K'81:18,21,164
Travis A. Winn: K'84:235; K'85:75,104,112; K'86:101; K'87:155,231
Earl Witsaman: K'82:56; K'83:106,199; K'84:99; K'85:81; K'86:126; K'87:86
W-K Knives (See Votaw)
B.B. Wood: K'83:131; K'86:81
Bruce Wood: K'84:235; K'85:100
Owen Wood: K'83:55,85,201; K'87:152,231
Webster Wood: K'83:201; K'84:73; K'85:55; K'86:78,85; K'87:83
William W. Wood: K'81:41,81,100,165; K'82:64,169; K'83:201; K'85:78,231; K'86:222; K'87:124
Harold E. Woodward: K'85:231; K'87:121
Wootz International: K'83:118
Joe Worel: K'85:231; K'86:66
Worm (See L. Pittman.)
Richard Worthen: K'85:75
Harold Wright: K'87:103,104 Kevin Wright: K'85: 89; K'87: 87,231
Timothy Wright: K'82:85,94,168; K'83:122,201; K'84:77; K'86:Cover 2,141

X,Y,Z

T.J. and Ann Yancey: K'81:17,50,72,97,112,114,165; K'82:111,169; K 83:201,203
Cliff Young: K'83:201; K'84:66,92,235; K'85:100
Yamil R. Yunes: K'86:76,226; K'87:53,64
Z Custom Knives (See Zellon McCarty.)
Zack (See D. Zaccagnino.)
Don Zaccagnino: K'81:24,46,61,119,165; K'83:35,36,84,201; K'85:255; K'86:227; K'87:82,232
Tim Zowoda: K'85:72,93; K'86:70; K'87:70,136
Michael Zscherny: K'83:45,201; K'84:65,97,112; K'85:48,118,231; K'86: 234

ENGRAVERS

Sam Alfanoi: K'84:60,139; K'85:135,136
Ralph Alpin: K'87:107
Billy Bates: K'84:63,139; K'85:134; K'86:145
Tim Bina: K'87:147
Gary Blanchard: K'86: 55,77
Carl Bleile: K'82:114; K'83:139; K'84:140
C. Roger Bleile: K'84:140
Dale Boster: K'87:61
Gary Bouchard: K'84:60
Rudolph Bochenski: K'85:135
Dennis R. Brooker: K'82:112; K'85:117,135
Byron Burgess: K'82:114; K'84:66,141; K'85:88; K'86:145; K'87:148
Martin Butler: K'86:144; K'87:Cover, 52,89,149
Frank Clark: K'85:135
Fred Clark: K'87:154,155
Larry Cole: K'87:111
Lester Davis: K'82:45
Melissa Dibben: K'85:135; K'86:55,82
W.R. Dilling: K'87:149
Rick Eaton: K'87:148
Ken Eyster: K'86:Cover
Terry Flowers: K'87:148
Firmo Fracassi: K'82:113
Foster: K'83:51
Fred A. Harrington: K'82:50,86,115; K'83:143; K'84:83,88,89,94,140; K'85:39; K'86:74,145; K'87:123
Fred D. Henderson: K'82:114; K'83:51; K'84:138
Frank Hendricks: K'86:75,143; K'87:103
Tim Herman: K'85:135; K'86:85,98; K'87:148
Benno Heune: K'86:145
Domingos Joaquim: K'87:96
Bill Johns: K'87:150
Lancy Kelly: K'81:33,56,57,86,92,120,145; K'82:117; K'83:121,143; K'84:57,141,207; K'85:137; K'86:72
Jim Kelso: K'82:Cover; K'83:104,111; K'84:82; K'85:Cover, 71,136; K'87:154
Max Kissler: K'83:51
Joe Kosteinik: K'87:151
John M. Kudlas: K'83:143
Harry Limings, Jr.: K'83:82,221; K'84:140; K'85:49; K'86:Cover, 67,113; K'87:54,148
Steve Lindsay: K'82:49,115; K'84:75,139; K'85:110,141; K'86:82,144; K'87:61,67,146,149
Simon M. Lytton: K'84:141; K'85:136; K'86:144; K'87:146
Robert Maki: K'84:137,140
George Marek: K'85:90,140
Franz Marktl: K'82:27
Lynton McKenzie: K'81:52,54,55,65,66; K'82:50,115; K'84:139,149,151; K'85:110; K'86:84
Mitchell Moschetti: K'86:145
F. Oberndorfer: K'87:139,147
Marcello Pedini: K'82:53
Wayne Potts: K'81:Cover, 93
Aaron Pursley: K'86:75
Martin Rabeno: K'85:98; K'86:145; K'87:146
Andrew Raftis: K'85:137; K'86:145; K'87:146
Bob Rosser: K'87:146
E. Seifert: K'87:61
Bruce Shaw: K'83:143; K'84:139; K'85:135; K'87:61,70,149
George Sherwood: K'81:Cover, 54,93; K'82:Cover, 115; K'83:142; K'84:114; K'85:137; K'87:110

Ben Shostle: **K'82**:50; **K'85**:135,137,140
W.P. Sinclair: **K'82**:118; **K'83**:142; **K'84**:64,145
R.E. Skaggs: **K'81**:50,55; **K'82**:Cover, 24,48,118; **K'84**:84,150,151; **K'85**:134; **K'86**:61,144; **K'87**:149
Robert Skaggs: **K'87**:92
Ralph Smith: **K'87**:71
Ron Smith: **K'82**:114; **K'83**:67; **K'84**:145; **K'85**:137; **K'86**:143
Jim Sornberger: **K'85**:100
James Stewart: **K'81**:55,56,57
Shigetoshi Takeuchi: **K'85**:114; **K'86**:67
Robert Valade: **K'81**:170; **K'84**:57
George Vartanian: **K'85**:135
George Walker: **K'87**:149
Patricia Walker: **K'83**:123; **K'84**:70,75,77,140,143; **K'85**:140; **K'86**:Cover 2,85; **K'87**:61,67,147
Buster Warenski: **K'87**:110
Kenneth W. Warren: **K'87**:123
Claus Willig: **K'82**:115,190
H. Wood: **K'86**:77,98
Mel Wood: **K'81**:45,56,57,59,66; **K'82**:25,26,61,115; **K'83**:66,67; **K'84**:Cover, 62,83,137,139; **K'85**:137; **K'87**:123

SCRIMSHANDERS

John Alward: **K'83**:67,142
Terry Jack Anderson: **K'81**:58; **K'82**:108
C.M. Barringer: **K'82**:110
Connie Bellet: **K'84**:143; **K'85**:140
R. Bochenski: **K'85**:139
Benita Bonshire: **K'85**:137,140
Rick Bowles: **K'86**:65,106,147; **K'87**:152
Sandra Brady: **K'86**:56; **K'87**:108
Bob Burdette: **K'82**:108,109; **K'84**:65; **K'85**:69
Mary Gregg Byrne: **K'84**:144
Jerry Cable: **K'82**:108
Lynda Capocci: **K'86**:147
Michael Collins: **K'82**:119; **K'84**:61,96
Andy Cook: **K'85**:139
Ray Cover: **K'86**:149
Jean Curtis: **K'85**:141; **K'86**:60
Guy Dahl: **K'86**:147
Georgia Davenport (Gigi): **K'82**:108; **K'83**:145; **K'84**:144; **K'87**:151
Richard DeMarzo: **K'86**:147
Jean E. DeSavage: **K'85**:141; **K'87**:126
Joni Elbourn: **K'86**:149; **K'87**:151,153
Bob Engnath: **K'86**:148; **K'87**:151
Linda Erickson: **K'85**:67
Rick Evans: **K'84**:64
Rick B. Fields: **K'83**:142; **K'84**:144; **K'86**:148,149; **K'87**:152
Dale Fisk: **K'87**:153
Adam Funmaker: **K'81**:54,55; **K'83**:145
Jim Gullette: **K'82**:110; **K'84**:143
Charles Hargraves: **K'85**:139,141

Stan Hawkins: **K'86**:148
Bob Hergert: **K'87**:86
H. Harve Hildebrand: **K'82**:107; **K'83**:65; **K'86**:70
Alan Jiramek: **K'87**:119
Ann Jordan: **K'83**:145
Patty Kosteinick: **K'87**:151
John Land: **K'82**:107
Ben Lane, Jr.: **K'83**:142
George Marek: **K'87**:152
Berni McFadden: **K'86**:144
Gayle McGrath: **K'87**:150
Tommy McKissack, II: **K'87**:153
Carole McWilliams: **K'85**:141; **K'87**:86
Anita Miller: **K'82**:111
Joyce Minnick: **K'82**:50,111
J.B. Moore: **K'85**:140
Don Myrer: **K'86**:100
Vaughn Parrish: **K'84**:65
Larry Peck: **K'83**:145; **K'84**:Cover
Lou Peterson: **K'84**:143
Bob Purdy: **K'82**:107
Tom Radant: **K'84**:94
Joe Rundell: **K'81**:58; **K'82**:109; **K'83**:146
Bob Satre: **K'86**:148
Pat Schwallie: **K'86**:148; **K'87**:63
George Seymour: **K'82**:109
Larry Seymour: **K'84**:143
Patricia Schwallie: **K'85**:139,140,141; **K'87**:63
Laura Schwarz: **K'84**:144,145; **K'86**:147
Peggy Smith: **K'85**:139
John Stahl: **K'82**:107,108; **K'87**:152
Harry Stalter: **K'87**:152
Glen Stearns: **K'81**:58; **K'82**:110
Don Swasey: **K'85**:139
Oranda Tahl: **K'86**:71
Mary Austin Talley: **K'86**:148,149; **K'87**:150,153
Gerald Tisdale: **K'81**:58; **K'82**:109; **K'85**:139
Karen Walker: **K'86**:146

ETCHERS/CARVERS

Mary Ann Eubanks: **K'87**:155
Dennis Holland: **K'87**:154,155
Leonard Leibowitz: **K'86**:151; **K'87**:155
Shaw-Leibowitz: **K'81**:57,65,85; **K'82**:58,91; **K'83**:141; **K'84**:114

HANDLE ARTISANS

John Alward: **K'86**:151
R. Hill: **K'85**:140,141
Mike Ochonicky: **K'84**:142
Tom Patterson: **K'83**:146
Chris Reed: **K'86**:127,151
Robert Schaber: **K'82**:46; **K'83**:146
Steve Schwarzer: **K'86**:150
Gary Vann Ausdle: **K'84**:137; **K'85**:119,132; **K'87**:155

Specialty Cutlers

The firms listed here are special in the sense that they make or market special kinds of knives made in facilities they own or control either in the U.S. or overseas, or because the knives are special because of unique design, or function.

B&D TRADING COMPANY
3935 Fair Hill Rd.
Fair Oaks, CA 95628
Phone: 916-965-0555

Specialties: Carries the full line of Executive Edge—Brazil's locking folders.

BAUSKA MANUFACTURING CORP.
P.O. Box 2270
Kalispell, MT 59903-2270
Phone: 406-752-8080

Specialties: Sportsmen knives in Bowies, hunters, skinners, and utility styles. Offered custom or semi-custom made.

BECKER KNIFE and TOOL CO.
255 Newton Rd.
Cincinnati, OH 45244
Phone: 513-231-9710

Specialties: The Machax, a kukri-shaped machete intended to do light ax work.

BENCHMARK KNIVES (See Gerber/General Cutlers)

BERETTA U.S.A. CORP.
17601 Indian Head Highway
Accokeek, MD 20607
Phone: 301-283-2191

Specialties: A variety of Beretta-only designs, including their Classic Daggers, and folders.

BROWNING
Rt. 1
Morgan, UT 84050
Phone: 801-543-3200

Specialties: Has its own name on sports knives of all kinds, all in Browning finish.

BRUNTON/LAKOTA
620 E. Monroe
Riverton, WY 82501
Phone: 307-856-6559

Specialties: Heavy-duty sports knives, straight and folding, on a distinctive design theme.

CATTLE BARON LEATHER
P.O. Box 100724, Dept. K8
San Antonio, TX 78201
Phone: 512-697-8900

Specialties: Adventure knives from overseas; others made to Jerry Ardolino's design by Tommy McKissack.

CHARTER ARMS CORP.
430 Sniffens Lane
Stratford, CT 06497
Phone: 203-377-8080

Specialties: Makes the Skatchet, a special hunter's belt tool that can chop, gut and skin.

COLD STEEL, INC.
2128 Knoll Dr., Unit D
Ventura, CA 93003
Phone: 805-656-5191/800-255-4716

Specialties: Variety of urban survival instruments—big in tantos. Outdoorsman series and a new Bowie.

CONDOR (See Hoffman)

CROSMAN BLADES
250 N. St. Francis
Wichita, KS 67201
Phone: 316-261-3211

Specialties: Crosman Airguns in the sports knife business.

EK COMMANDO KNIFE CO.
601 North Lombardy St.
Richmond, VA 23230
Phone: 804-257-7272/800-468-5575

Specialties: Military fighting and survival knives, combat proven in three wars. All made in USA.

H&B FORGE CO.
Rte. 2, Geisinger Rd.
Shiloh, OH 44878
Phone: 419-895-1856

Specialties: Tomahawks and throwing knives.

HOFFMAN DESIGN
5341A Derry Ave.
Agoura Hills, CA 91301
Phone: 818-991-5291

Specialties: The Condor upscale sports knives now on the market.

KERSHAW CUTLERY CO.
25300 S.W. Parkway
Wilsonville, OR 97070
Phone: 503-682-1966

Specialties: Former Gerber designer's heavy-duty sports knives made overseas; also smaller "pocket jewelry;" handsome scrimshaw; new designs in using knives.

LAKER KNIFE WORKS
P.O. Box 216
Taylorville, IL 62568
Phone: 217-287-1322

Specialties: Fillet knife designed for production by Ron Lake—piercing point, handle features, etc. Offers now Hip-mate model with mortised style handle construction.

LAKOTA CORP. (See Brunton)

LEATHERMAN TOOL GROUP, INC.
10300 N.E. Marx St.
P.O. Box 20595
Portland, OR 97220
Phone: 503-253-7826

Specialties: All-in-one pocket tool; has two sizes.

LEE BENCH MADE
P.O. Box 1777
Gaffney, SC 29342
Phone: 803-489-6699

Specialties: Fighters, boots and hunters, made at bench by group of craftsmen; offers knives in American Damascus steel in several standard models.

LIFEKNIFE
Box 771
Santa Monica, CA 90406
Phone: 213-821-6192

Specialties: Popular-priced knife survival systems; a trend-setter.

AL MAR KNIVES, INC.
5755 SW Jean Rd., Suite 101
Lake Oswego, OR 97034
Phone: 503-635-9229

Specialties: Designer in production oversees foreign manufacture of his own knives—first class in all respects.

MORTY THE KNIFE MAN
60 Otis St., Unit C
West Babylon, NY 11704
Phone: 516-491-5764

Specialties: Everything for the fish trade; own make and both U.S. and import brands; includes many working knives not easily found, as well as chain mesh protection gloves and aprons.

MOTENG INTERNATIONAL, INC.
549 S. Fairfax Ave.
Los Angeles, CA 90036
Phone: 213-933-5900

Specialties: Kitchen and outdoors cutlery; markets Stapel's Outside Knife; U.S. Bali-Song knives, other high ticket survival gear.

MUSEUM REPLICAS LTD.
915 Center St.
Conyers, GA 30207
Phone: 800-241-3664 to order

Specialties: Authentic edged weapons of the ages, battle-ready—over 20 models; subsidiary of Atlanta Cutlery; catalog $1.

MYERCHIN MARINE CLASSICS
P.O. Box 911
Rialto, CA 92376
Phone: 714-875-3592

Specialties: The Myerchin Offshore. System—a quality cutlery package for the yachtsman or deep water sailor.

OLSON INDUSTRIES, INC./HANK ROBERTS
4550 Jackson St.
Denver, CO 80216
Phone: 303-399-4623

Specialties: Walton's Thumb—a multi-tool folder, and a line of hunter knives.

PILTDOWN PRODUCTIONS
Errett Callahan
Cliffside
2 Fredonia Ave.
Lynchburg, VA 24503
Phone: 804-528-3444

Specialties: Makes obsidian scalpels and knives; replicates Stone Age tools and weapons—all types—for museums and for academia. $3 for catalog.

RIGID KNIVES
P.O. Box 186, Hwy. 290E
Lake Haminton, AR 71951
Phone: 501-525-1377

Specialties: Rugged styling and size in mostly full-tang straight knives and big folders made in Arkansas.

SANTA FE STONEWORKS, INC.
1209 Calle de Comercio
Sante Fe, NM 87501
Phone: 800-257-7625/505-471-3953

Specialties: Knives handled in gem stones and exotic woods in jewelry fashion.

SIMMONS OUTDOOR CORP.
14205 Southwest 119th Ave.
Miami, FL 33186
Phone: 305-252-0477

Specialties: "Old Ern" sports knives.

SPYDERCO, INC.
P.O. Box 800
Golden, CO 80402
Phone: 303-279-8383/800-525-7770

Specialties: Clipit folding knives; sharpening gear.

TEKNA DESIGN GROUP
101 Twin Dolphin Drive
Redwood City, CA 94065
Phone: 415-593-1410

Specialties: Flashlight maker with several slick boot knife systems.

TRU-BALANCE KNIFE CO.
2155 Tremont Blvd., N.W.
Grand Rapids, MI 49504
Phone: 616-453-3679

Specialties: Harry McEvoy's full line of throwers—a design for any throwing job.

WENOKA CUTLERY/SEASTYLE
1134-53rd Ct. N.
West Palm Beach, FL 33407
Phone: 305-845-6155

Specialties: First a full line of divers' knives, and now a beefy folder.

WYOMING KNIFE CORP.
101 Commerce Drive
Ft. Collins, CO 80524
Phone: 303-224-3454

Specialties: A tool for dealing with game animals—gutting and skinning. Also makes a short folding saw, and the Powder River folders.

General Cutlers

These are, plain and simple, knife factories. Some are giants; some not so big; some are a century old; some just two decades in existence. All market very complete lines of knives, generally through standard mercantile channels.

ALCAS CUTLERY CORPORATION
1116 E. State St.
P.O. Box 810
Olean, NY 14760
Phone: 716-372-3111

Specialties: Broad line of knives includes high quality household knives, as well as hunting and pocketknives. Brands are Cutco and Wearever; has Solution and Solution's spirit.

BUCK KNIVES
P.O. Box 1267
El Cajon, CA 92022
Phone: 619-449-1100

Specialties: Creators of the belt folder syndrome; sturdy, solid working knives widely sold.

CAMILLUS CUTLERY CO.
52-54 W. Genesee St.
Camillus, NY 13031-0038
Phone: 315-672-8111

Specialties: Long-time competitor in all phases of cutlery, military knife contractor, some neat pocketknife designs.

W.R. CASE & SONS CUTLERY CO.
Owens Way
Bradford, PA 16701
Phone: 814-368-4123 or 24

Specialties: Big Daddy for pocketknife collectors, but makes full line of sports and commercial cutlery. Handsome knives.

CHICAGO CUTLERY CO.
5420 N. County Rd. #18
Minneapolis, MN 55428
Phone: 612-533-0472

Specialties: Solid utility knives, branching into sports knives.

COLEMAN-WESTERN CUTLERY
1800 Pike Rd.
P.O. Box 1539
Longmont, CO 80501
Phone: 303-772-5900

Specialties: Working pocket and belt knives. Upgraded Westmark belt knives. New locking folders.

COLONIAL KNIFE CO. INC.
P.O. Box 3327
Providence, RI 02909
Phone: 401-421-1600

Specialties: Commercial pocketknives for competitive pricing; some belt knives. Offering six new models this year; also has new logo.

FISKARS MANUFACTURING CORP.
7811 West Stewart Ave.
Wausau, WI 54401
Phone: 715-842-2091

Specialties: Best known for their scissors—now have cutlery and sharpening devices within their sheaths. In 1987 Fiskars bought Gerber Legendary Blades.

GERBER LEGENDARY BLADES
14200 S.W. 72nd St.
Portland, OR 97223
Phone: 503-639-6161

Specialties: Clean design and good function and imaginative promotion; was sold to Fiskars this year.

IMPERIAL SCHRADE CORP.
1776 Broadway
New York, NY 10019
Phone: 212-757-1814

Specialties: Probably the biggest; owns Imperial and Schrade. Sells many labels in several brands, U.S. made and imported.

IMPERIAL KNIFE COMPANY, INC.
60 King St.
Providence, RI 02909
Phone: 401-861-4700

Specialties: Pocket and hunting knives; Jackmaster; Diamond Edge; Frontier Double Eagle; others.

KA-BAR CUTLERY, INC.
5777 Grant Ave.
Cleveland, OH 44105
Phone: 216-271-4000/800-321-1630

Specialties: Makes working sports cutlery and always has. Made the first WW II Marine Corps knife, a design still in service. Imports Khyber knives.

KA-BAR KNIVES, COLLECTORS DIVISION
434 No. 9th St.
Olean, NY 14760
Phone: 716-372-5611

Specialties: Commemoratives and special models are this KA-BAR branch's business.

ONTARIO KNIFE COMPANY
P.O. Box 145
Franklinville, NY 14737
Phone: 716-676-5527/800-222-5233

Specialties: Some pocketknives; many styles of utility knives for household and restaurant use. Brands, both Hickory and Colonial Forge. Excellent values.

QUEEN CUTLERY
P.O. Box 500
Franklinville, NY 14737
Phone: 800-222-5233

Specialties: Old name. The line is shorter than once, but there are good Queen knives to be had.

SCHRADE CUTLERY CORP.
Rte. 209 North
Ellenville, NY 12428
Phone: 914-647-7600

Specialties: Widely sold pocketknives in several degrees of finish; slick own designs in belt knives. Old name.

SPORTING IMAGES
P.O. Box 8391
8659 Olive St. Dr.
St. Louis, MO 63132
Phone: 314-432-3565

Specialties: They offer all steel construction pen knives with wildlife scenes etched—some colored etched on slab.

UTICA CUTLERY COMPANY
820 Noyes St.
Utica, NY 13503
Phone: 315-733-4663/800-448-9246

Specialties: Nice line of pocketknives, including Barlows and hunters and working pattern knives. Brands: Kutmaster, Walco.

WESTERN CUTLERY (See Coleman)

Importers & Foreign Cutlers

Knives are imported these days by almost every sort of commercial cutler, but the names here are those whose specialty is importing, whether it be their own brand, famous overseas brands, or special knives for special purposes best made overseas. Every effort is made to keep the list up to date, but importing is sometimes an uncertain endeavor.

ATLANTA CUTLERY CORP.
Box 839 XV
Conyers, GA 30207
Phone: 404-922-3700/800-241-3595

Specialties: Carefully chosen inventory from all over the world; selected Indian, Pakistani, Spanish, Japanese, German, English and Italian knives; often new ideas—now a principal source for kukris, kindjals and Khyber knives.

B&D TRADING CO.
P.O. Box 1023; 3935 Fair Hill Rd.
Fair Oaks, CA 95628
Phone: 916-965-0555 or 967-9366

Specialties: The Executive Edge, a folder made in Brazil, and importers of Zakharov knives.

BOKER USA, INC.
14818 W. 6th Ave. #17A
Golden, CO 80401
Phone: 303-279-5997

Specialties: Tree Brand knives and a host of new knives in the Boker USA label.

CAM III ENTERPRISES
425-A Merchant St.
Vacaville, CA 95688
Phone: 707-448-5827

Specialties: Sports folders and straight knives in modern designs; utility belt buckle; knife kits and pouches.

CATOCTIN CUTLERY
P.O. Box 188; 17 S. Main St.
Smithsburg, MD 21783
Phone: 301-824-7416

Specialties: Full line of Aitor knives from Spain, others from Italy, Germany and the Philippines.

CHARLTON LTD. (See Damascus U.S.A.)

CHINA IM/EX
Steven Schneider
69 Rockaway Ave.
San Francisco, CA 94127
Phone: 415-665-5857

Specialties: Specializes in sports cutlery from the Far East.

COLUMBIA PRODUCTS COMPANY
P.O. Box 1333
Sialkot-1. PAKISTAN
Phone: (0432)86921
U.S. Branch:
P.O. Box 1481
Flushing, NY 11354
Phone: 718-939-5331

Specialties: Lockblade and slip-joint folders in old and new U.S.-style patterns; heavy-duty belt knives; all at very low prices.

COMPASS INDUSTRIES, INC.
104 E. 25th St.
New York, NY 10010
Phone: 212-473-2614

Specialties: Imports for dealer trade from all over at many price and quality levels; two hot brands are Silver Falcon and Sportster.

CONSOLIDATED CUTLERY CO., INC.
696 NW Sharpe St.
Port St. Lucie, FL 33452
Phone: 305-878-6139; effective 4/88: 407-878-6139

Specialties: Hunting knives, woodcarving tools, stag handled steak/carving sets, camping axes, knife sharpening steels.

CRAZY COW TRADING POST
P.O. Box 314
Denison, TX 75020
Phone: 214-463-1366

Specialties: Mountain men cutlery and fixings.

DAMASCUS U.S.A.
Suite B
243 Glendora
Long Beach, CA 90803
Phone: 213-439-2801

Specialties: Finished forged Damascus knives in period styles and replicas of American patterns; military sgian dubhs and dirks; some swords.

EXECUTIVE EDGE (See B&D Co.)

R.H. FORSCHNER CO., INC.
14 Progress Dr.
Shelton, CT 06484
Phone: 203-929-6391

Specialties: Imports professional cutlery by Victorinox, Solingen special-orders; Sheffield butcher steels, many other specialties, Sabinox cutlery from France.

FREDIANI COLTELLI FINLANDESI
Via Lago Maggiore 41
I-21038 Leggiuno, ITALY
Phone: 00332/647362

Specialties: Purveyors from Italy of fine Finnish knives, some with Italian decorative touches.

GASTINNE RENETTE, INC.
225 Industrial Drive
P.O. Box 3395 College Station
Fredericksburg, VA 22401
Phone: 703-898-1524

Specialties: French sports cutlery.

GOODWIN ENTERPRISES
P.O. Box 4124
Chattanooga, TN 37405
Phone: 615-267-5071

Specialties: Imports German cutlery, including exclusive Red Stag pocketknives—jigged bone, etched blades in colors, and more.

GUTMANN CUTLERY CO., INC.
120 S. Columbus Ave.
Mt. Vernon, NY 10553
Phone: 914-699-4044/800-CUTLERY

Specialties: Puma, Edge Mark, Explorer, Hen & Rooster, Opinel and Russell Green River are the leading names in a selection of over 300 knives sold through retail stores and through the mail.

J.A. HENCKELS ZWILLINGSWORK, INC.
9 Skyline Dr., Box 253
Hawthorne, NY 10532
Phone: 914-592-7370

Specialties: U.S. office of world-famous Solingen cutlers—high quality pocket and sportsman's knives with the "twin" logo.

HOFFRITZ
515 W. 24th St.
New York, NY 10011
Phone: 212-924-7300

Specialties: Selected chef's kitchen and carving cutlery; elegant gentlemen's pocketknives; sports knives of all kinds, most with Hoffritz's own name; all sold in Hoffritz stores and through catalog.

C.A.S. IBERIA INC./Muela
54 Patricia La.
So. Setauket, NY 11720
Phone: 516-698-9349

Specialties: Knives made in Spain by people with an eye on U.S. custom makers.

INTCO (Intl. Netting Co., Inc.)
P.O. Box 2180
Paso Robles, CA 93447
Phone: 805-238-6702

Specialties: Full line of sports cutlery—dozens of models—with Zest trademark in 440-A steel.

JET-AER CORP.
100 Sixth Ave.
Paterson, NJ 07524
Phone: 201-278-8300

Specialties: Specialists in mass-marketing practical sports cutlery, most often blisterpacked, at low prices. Marks much of this G-96; has own designs, some pretty special.

JOY ENTERPRISES
801 Broad Ave; P.O. Box 314
Ridgefield, NJ 07657
Phone: 201-943-5920

Specialties: Martial arts, sporting and combat-style cutlery under the Fury label—full range.

KEN'S FINN KNIVES
P.O. Box 126
Republic, MI 49879
Phone: 906-376-2132

Specialties: Puukkos and other Finnish knives.

KNIFE IMPORTERS, INC.
P.O. Box 2122
Austin, TX 78768
Phone: 512-282-6860/800-531-5301

Specialties: Eye Brand cutlery.

KRIS CUTLERY (Formerly Cecil Quirino)
P.O. Box 133
Pinole, CA 94564
Phone: 415-758-9912

Specialties: Importer and designer of Philippine edged weapons.

LIBERTY ORGANIZATION INC.
P.O. Box 306
Montrose, CA 91020
Phone: 800-423-2666, Ext. 24

Specialties: Wide range of Spain, Finland, Brazil, Japanese and German imports. Sells to dealers. Has hundreds of models.

MARTTIINI KNIVES
P.O. Box 44
96101 Rovaniemi 10, FINLAND
Phone: 358-91-21751

Specialties: Finnish knives straight from Finland's biggest cutler. Includes fancy Finn-type hunters. Line has been repriced.

MATTHEWS CUTLERY
4401 Sentry Dr.
Tucker, GA 30084
Phone: 404-939-6915

Specialties: Are wholesalers only. Carries all major brands which include over 2000 patterns.

MID-EAST MFG., INC.
2817 Cameron St.
Melbourne, FL 32901
Phone: 305-724-1477

Specialties: Scots dirks in deluxe finish; Indian-made swords, kukris, daggers in Damascus steel.

MILITARY REPLICA ARMS INC.
P.O. Box 360006
Tampa, FL 33673
Phone: 813-237-0764

Specialties: Ron Hickox picks out dandies to copy Ames naval cutlasses, Krag Bowie bayonets, a wide variety of U.S. sabers and such—and prices them pretty low.

MIRANDA IMPORTS and EXPORTS
1524 E. Santa Clara St.
San Jose, CA 95116
Phone: 408-923-6894

Specialties: Working cutlery and sports knives in Iberian traditions.

MUELA (See C.A.S. Iberia Inc.)

MUSEUM REPLICAS LIMITED
Box 840 XV
Conyers, GA 30207
Phone: 404-922-3703/800-241-3664

Specialties: Battle ready hand forged edged weapons. They carry swords, daggers, halberds, dirks and axes. Catalog $1.

MUSKETEER (See Liberty Organization)

NEW PATHS, INC.
1272 Washington St.
Denver, CO 80203
Phone: 303-830-7942

Specialties: Direct importers of Norwegian cutlery, including folding Norseax hatchet, deluxe dress knives, more.

NORMARK CORP.
1710 E. 78th St.
Minneapolis, MN 55423
Phone: 612-869-3291

Specialties: Scandinavian-made sturdy knives for fishermen; puuko-style belt knives for hunters; filet knives. Good stainless steel.

PARKER CUTLERY
2837 Hickory Valley Rd.; P.O. Box 22668
Chattanooga, TN 37422
Phone: 615-894-1782

Specialties: Collector quality pocketknives.

PRECISE INTERNATIONAL
3 Chestnut St.
Suffern, NY 10901
Phone: 914-357-6200

Specialties: Wenger Swiss Army knives; many American patterns in current style with Precise name; fish and marine knives—in all, hundreds of knives.

PRIMA KNIVES USA, INC.
4000 Kruse Way Place #2-225
Lake Oswego, OR 97034
Phone: 503-697-3175

Specialties: Pocketknives, outdoors specialty knives; private labels and OEM production knives manufactured in Hong Kong.

PROFESSIONAL CUTLERY
9712 Washburn Road
Downey, CA 90241
Phone: 213-803-8778

Specialties: Wholesale only. Imports historical medieval and samurai swords; armor and weapons, over 100 different models.

CECIL QUIRINO (See Kris Cutlery)

A.G. RUSSELL CO.
1705 Highway 471 North
Springdale, AR 72764
Phone: 501-751-7341

Specialties: Russell-marked special designs, as the "Woods Walker," Sting, CIA letter opener.

STAR SALES CO., INC.
1803 N. Central St.; P.O. Box 1503
Knoxville, TN 37901
Phone: 615-524-0771

Specialties: New collector pocketknives; imports Star knives and Kissing Crane knives.

SUOMI SHOP
Rte. 2
Fergus Falls, MN 56537
Phone: 218-739-9013

Specialties: A full and complete Finnish cutlery line, including the Puukko cutlery line.

SWISS ARMY KNIVES, INC.
P.O. Box 846
Shelton, CT 06484
Phone: 203-929-6391

Specialties: This is the Victorinox headquarters in the U.S.; all current production comes through here; manages service center also.

TAYLOR CUTLERY MFG. CO.
806 E. Center St., P.O. Box 1638
Kingsport, TN 37662
Phone: 615-247-2406

Specialties: Taylor-Seto folders and butterfly and straight knives, plus the Elk Horn brand.

TOLEDO ARMAS S.A.
302 Ponce de Leon Blvd.
St. Augustine, FL 32084
Phone: 904-829-9671

Specialties: Spanish-made finished cutlery and blades.

UNITED CUTLERY CORP.
P.O. Box 586, Hwy. 66
Sevierville, TN 37862
Phone: 615-428-2532

Specialties: Full lines of knives at wholesale.

VALOR CORPORATION
5555 N.W. 36th Ave.
Miami, FL 33142
Phone: 305-633-0127

Specialties: Emphasizes lockback folders from overseas in popular styles. Over 100 knife models imported.

RUDOLF WEBER, JR.
P.O. Box 160106
D-565 Solingen 16
WEST GERMANY
Phone: 0212/592136

Specialties: Hunting and sports knives.

ZAKHAROV KNIVES (See B&D Trading Co.)

Knifemaking Supplies

The firms listed here specialize in furnishing knifemaker supplies in small amounts. Knifemakers—professionals—have their own sources for much of what they use, but often patronize some of these firms. All have catalogs. Send self-addressed and stamped envelope for information.

We list firms in this category upon request. New firms may be listed upon receipt of catalogs or the like. We cannot guarantee their performance. Several charge for their catalogs.

AC ENTERPRISES (See Damascus U.S.A.)

ANDERSON CUTLERY & SUPPLY CO.
Shepard Hill, Box 383
Newtown, CT 06470
Phone: 203-426-8623

Specialties: A complete selection of knifemaking supplies and equipment; $2 for catalog.

ART JEWEL ENTERPRISES, LTD.
421-A Irmen Dr.
Addison, IL 60101
Phone: 312-628-6220; 800-323-6144 (orders only)

Specialties: Handles—stag, ivory, pearl, horn, rosewood, ebony.

ATLANTA CUTLERY CORPORATION
Box 839XV
Conyers, GA 30207
Phone: 404-922-3700/800-241-3595

Specialties: Many blades and fixings to choose from; occasional special buys in cutlery handles, pocketknife blades, and the like; complete kits for buckskinner knives, small pocket knives. Catalog. $1.50.

BDL ENTERPRISES (R.M. Garrison)
68-487 E. Palm Canyon Dr., Suite 56
Cathedral City, CA 92234
Phone: 619-328-3354

Specialties: 2001 blade sharpener.

BOONE TRADING CO., INC.
562 Coyote Rd.
Brinnon, WA 98320
Phone: 206-796-4330

Specialties: Exotic handle materials including elephant, fossil walrus, mastodon, warthog and hippopotamus ivory. Also sambar stag, oosik, impala and sheep horn.

CHARLTON, LTD. (See Damascus U.S.A.)

E. CHRISTOPHER FIREARMS
Rt. #128, Ferry St.
Miamitown, OH 45041
Phone: 513-353-1321

Specialties: Blades and supplies, including modern guthook hunters; classic Bowies.

CUSTOM KNIFEMAKER'S SUPPLY
Bob Schrimsher
P.O. Box 308
Emory, TX 75440
Phone: 214-473-3330

Specialties: Big catalog full of virtually everything for knifemaking. In business a long time.

DAMASCUS U.S.A.
Suite B
243 Glendora
Long Beach, CA 90803
Phone: 213-439-2801

Specialties: Imports forged-to-shape Damascus blades and steel billets. (Formerly Charlton Ltd.)

DAN'S WHETSTONE CO., INC.
207 Remington Dr.
Hot Springs, AR 71913
Phone: 501-767-9598

Specialties: Traditional sharpening materials.

DIAMOND MACHINING TECH., INC.
85 Hayes Memorial Dr.
Marlborough, MA 01752
Phone: 617-481-5944

Specialties: Sophisticated sharpening gear.

DIXIE GUN WORKS, INC.
P.O. Box 130
Union City, TN 38261
Phone: 901-885-0700/800-238-6785 (Orders only)

Specialties: Knife supplies for buckskinners; much early American hardware; blades; catalog.

EZE-LAP DIAMOND PRODUCTS
15164 Weststate St.; P.O. Box 2229
Westminster, CA 92683
Phone: 714-847-1555

Specialties: Diamond-coated sharpening instruments, various sizes.

RICK B. FIELDS
230 No. Durango Ave.
Ocoee, FL 32761
Phone: 305-877-2339

Specialties: Ancient ivories—fossilized mastodon, etc.

FLITZ INTERNATIONAL, LTD.
821 Mohr Ave.
Waterford, WI 53185
Phone: 414-534-5898

Specialties: General line of polishers.

FORTUNE PRODUCTS, INC.
P.O. Box 1308
Friendswood, TX 77546
Phone: 713-996-0729

Specialties: "Accu-sharp" sharpeners.

GILMER WOOD CO.
2211 N.W. St. Helens Rd.
Portland, OR 97210
Phone: 503-274-1271

Specialties: They list 112 varieties of natural woods.

GOLDEN AGE ARMS CO.
Box 283; 14 W. Winter St.
Delaware, OH 43015
Phone: 614-369-6513

Specialties: Blades, many types; stag for handles; cast items—much for the buckskinner. Catalog $3.

HOLT-SORNBERGER
1253 Birchwood Dr., Unit F
Sunnyvale, CA 94089
Phone: 408-745-0306

Specialties: Special buys on steel; complete furnishings for the trade; heat treaters; catalog $3.

HOUSE OF MUZZLELOADING
1019 East Palmer; P.O. Box 6217
Glendale, CA 91205
Phone: 818-241-0455

Specialties: Full line of supplies and equipment, including excellent selection of tropical woods. Does big business in custom-ground heat-treated blades in dozens of shapes.

INDIAN RIDGE TRADERS
Box 869
Royal Oak, MI 48068
Phone: 313-399-6034

Specialties: Wide selection of blades for modern or old-style knives.

JOHNSON WOOD PRODUCTS
Route 1
Strawberry Point, IA 52076
Phone: 319-933-4930

Specialties: Midwestern woods, including black ash burl, walnut burl and the like.

STANLEY A. JONES
7702 E. Hopi
Mesa, AZ 85208
Phone: 602-986-4822

Specialties: Quality iron wood.

KNIFE AND GUN FINISHING SUPPLIES
P.O. Box 13522; 624 E. Abram
Arlington, TX 76013
Phone: 817-274-1282

Specialties: Complete line of machine and materials for knifemaking and metal finishing. Specializing in rare and exotic handle materials—oosic, ivory, rare hard woods, horn, stag. Catalog $2.

KOVAL KNIVES
P.O. Box 14130; 822 Busch Ct.
Columbus, OH 43229
Phone: 614-888-6486

Specialties: Full range Micarta, other materials for handles; brass, nickel-silver, steels; machines and supplies for all knife making; some knife kits; catalog.

KWIK-SHARP
350 N. Wheeler St.
Ft. Gibson, OK 74434
Phone: 918-478-2443

Specialties: Ceramic rod knife sharpeners.

LAKEVIEW GUN SHOP
1018 Lloyd Ave.
Latrobe, PA 15650
Phone: 412-539-9221

Specialties: Manufactures parts—mostly guards—for knives.

CHRIS A. LINDSAY
16237 Dyke Rd.
La Pine, OR 97739
Phone: 503-536-2386

Specialties: Handle materials; abrasives; grinders. Catalog 50¢.

LOG CABIN SPORTS SHOP, INC.
8010 Lafayette Rd.; P.O. Box 275
Lodi, OH 44254
Phone: 216-948-1082

Specialties: Muzzle-loading-style blades and fixings, to include tomahawk heads and handles.

MASECRAFT SUPPLY CO.
P.O. Box 423, 902 Old Colony Rd.
Meriden, CT 06450
Phone: 203-238-3049/800-682-5489

Specialties: Handle materials.

MID-EAST MFG., INC.
2817 Cameron St.
Melbourne, FL 32901
Phone: 305-724-1477

Specialties: Damascus blades and axe heads hardened and blemish free.

MOTHER OF PEARL CO.
P.O. Box 445
Franklin, NC 28734
Phone: 704-524-6842

Specialties: Dave Culpepper's knife handle supplies.

MOUNTAIN STATE MUZZLELOADING SUPPLIES, INC.
Rt. 2, Box 154-1
Williamstown, WV 26187
Phone: 304-375-7842

Specialties: Buckskinner stuff.

OPTRONICS, INC. (See Kwik-Sharp)

OZARK KNIFE & STONE
3607 So. Brunswick
Springfield, MO 65804
Phone: 417-887-2635

Specialties: Shining Wave Damascus steel billets, U.S.-made in two patterns.

JIM PUGH
P.O. Box 711, 917 Carpenter St.
Azle, TX 76020
Phone: 817-444-2679

Specialties: Leather hides.

PURDY'S, INC.
2505 Canterbury Rd.
Hays, KS 67601
Phone: 913-628-3043

Specialties: All kinds of ivory.

R & R SALES
P.O. Box 498
Sycamore, IL 60178
Phone: 815-895-4995

Specialties: Makes soft zip knife cases in several sizes.

RAMCO
Box 175
Portage, MI 49081
Phone: 616-323-3570

Specialties: Wood products makers; make exotic woods knife handle scales.

SANDPAPER, INC. OF ILLINOIS
838 Hill Ave.
Glen Ellyn, IL 60137
Phone: 312-469-3320

Specialties: Coated abrasives in belts, sheets, rolls, discs or any coated abrasive specialty.

SCHEP'S FORGE
Box 83
Chapman, NE 68827
Phone: 308-986-2444

Specialties: Damascus steel made in Nebraska.

SHEFFIELD'S KNIFEMAKER'S SUPPLY
P.O. Box 141
Deland, FL 32720
Phone: 904-775-6453

Specialties: Wood, stones, steel, brass, Micarta and more; catalog $2.

SHINING WAVE METALS
Box 563
Snohomish, WA 98290
Phone: 206-334-5569

Specialties: Phil Baldwin makes and sells mokume, Damascus and a variety of Japanese alloys (for furniture, not blades) either to order or from stock.

SMITH WHETSTONE, INC.
1500 Sleepy Valley Rd.
Hot Springs, AR 71901
Phone: 501-321-2244/800-221-4156 (orders only)

Specialties: Sharpeners of every kind, ceramic sharpeners, oils, kits and polishing creams.

TEXAS KNIFEMAKERS SUPPLY
10649 Haddington, Suite 190
Houston, TX 77043
Phone: 713-461-8632

Specialties: Bar stock, factory blades, much handle material; they offer heat-treating; catalog $1.50.

THE TINKER SHOP
1120 Helen
Deer Park, TX 77536
Phone: 713-479-7286

Specialties: Factory blades, and all needs to finish them.

TRU-GRIT
11231 Thienes Ave.
So. El Monte, CA 91733
Phone: 818-444-5192

Specialties: Complete selection of 3M, Norton, Klingspor and Hermes belts and discs for grinding and polishing, also excellent line of machines for knifemakers.

R.W. WILSON
P.O. Box 2012
Weirton, WV 26062
Phone: 304-723-2771

Specialties: Full range of supplies, but sells nothing he doesn't use himself.

J. WOLFE'S KNIFE WORKS
Box 1056
Larkspur, CA 94939
Phone: NA

Specialties: Advertises full range of products for knifemaking.

A WORLD OF KNIVES
3376 Kietzke Lane
Reno, NV 89502
Phone: 702-826-9300

Specialties: Blades, blade material, handle materials and knife parts.

YAUN FORGE
31240 Highway 43
Albany, LA 70711
Phone: 504-567-2187

Specialties: Damascus steel in at least five patterns from a fourth generation smith.

Mail-Order Sales

The firms listed here are the firms that have come to our attention over a period of years. All publish lists or catalogs. Their specialties are shown; it's a good idea to send a self-addressed and stamped envelope for information. We will list firms in this category upon request. New firms may be listed upon receipt of catalogs or the like. We cannot guarantee their performance.

A&J ENTERPRISES
P.O. Box 1343 S.S.S.; 3221 S. Scenic
Springfield, MO 65805
Phone: 417-882-9543

Specialties: Buy, sell, trade collector-grade knives by mail and at major shows.

AMERICAN HISTORICAL FOUNDATION
1142 West Grace St.
Richmond, VA 23220
Phone: 804-353-1812

Specialties: Limited editions of replica military knives in collector and presentation grades; serve as headquarters for the Military Knife and Bayonet Collectors Club International.

ATLANTA CUTLERY
Box 839XV
Conyers, GA 30207
Phone: 404-922-3700/800-241-3595

Specialties: Catalog on request; wide selection of types; aims to provide working quality knives and give good value; showroom.

BALLARD CUTLERY
1495 Brummel Ave.
Elk Grove Village, IL 60007
Phone: 312-228-0070

Specialties: Special-purchase knives, all types. Tries for good buys.

BLUE RIDGE KNIVES
Rte. 5, Box 311B
Marion, VA 24354
Phone: 703-783-6143

Specialties: Wholesale only; top brand knives.

BOONE TRADING CO., INC.
562 Coyote Rd.
Brinnon, WA 98320
Phone: 206-796-4330

Specialties: Ivory, catalog features scrimshawed and carved ivory-handled knives.

CARMEL CUTLERY
Dolores & 6th; P.O. Box 1346
Carmel, CA 93921
Phone: 408-624-6699

Specialties: Knife retailer

CASANOVA GUNS, INC.
1601 W. Greenfield Ave.
Milwaukee, WI 53204
Phone: 414-672-3040

Specialties: Factory and handmade collector knives; make Kydex sheaths. Has list.

CATOCTIN CUTLERY
P.O. Box 188, 17 Main St.
Smithsburg, MD 21783
Phone: 301-824-7416

Specialties: Wholesaler. Popular lines of domestic cutlery to dealers, as well as many import brands.

CRAZY CROW TRADING POST
P.O. Box 314
Denison, TX 75020
Phone: 214-463-1366

Specialties: Knife blades, books, knifemaking supplies; $3 for catalog.

CREATIVE SALES & MFG.
Box 556
Whitefish, MT 59937
Phone: 406-862-5533

Specialties: Patent knife sharpeners.

CUTLERY SHOPPE
404 S. 8th St.
Boise, ID 83702
Phone: 208-343-7640/800-231-1272

Specialties: Discounts; custom and unusual Bali-Songs; fighting and military type knives: catalog $1.

MAUREEN DEVLET (CUSTOM PURVEYORS)
P.O. Box 886
Fort Lee, NJ 07024
Phone: 201-886-0196

Specialties: Overseas: 23 Elvaston Mews, London SW7, England (01-584-1441). Dealers in best-grade custom knife collections; generally have a big selection.

ED'S ENGRAVING
121 East Main St.
Statesboro, GA 30458
Phone: 912-764-4409

Specialties: Broker for Randall-made knives, as well as Buck, Puma, Gerber and Case.

FALCON SUPPLY
28 Halsey St.; P.O. Box 1056
Trumansburg, NY 14886
Phone: 607-387-6666

Specialties: Victorinox and Henckels.

FROST CUTLERY CO.
4639 Shallowford
Chattanooga, TN 37421
Phone: 615-894-6079

Specialties: Discontinued domestic and imported cutlery, especially folders and pocketknives.

INTERNATIONAL CUTLERY CORP.
3902 Croporex Pk. Dr., Suite 550
Tampa, FL 33619
Phone: 813-626-0028/800-624-3545

Specialties: Name brands.

INTERNATIONAL CUTLERY PURVEYORS
P.O. Box 1525
Royal Oak, MI 48068
Phone: 313-547-5699

Specialties: Dealer in Randalls and specialize in custom-made folders. Publish lists three times a year, $2 per list.

KEN'S FINN KNIVES
P.O. Box 126
Republic, MI 49879
Phone: 906-376-2132

Specialties: Puuko and Finnish-made knives. Brochures and price lists available to readers on request.

DOUG KENEFICK
19 Leander St.
Danielson, CT 06239
Phone: 203-774-8929

Specialties: Excellent selection of Randall Made knives, and custom knives at list prices; catalog on request.

KNIFE-AHOLICS UNANIMOUS
P.O. Box 831
Cockeysville, MD 21030
Phone: 301-628-6262

Specialties: David Cohen—purveyor of custom knives, as well as exclusive agent for Gary Barnes knives. They sell posters of custom knives as well.

KNIFE & GUN FINISHING SUPPLIES
P.O. Box 13522; 624 E. Abram
Arlington, TX 76013
Phone: 817-274-1282

Specialties: Complete line of machine and materials for knifemaking and metal finishing. Specializing in rare and exotic handle materials—oosic, ivory, rare hard woods, horn, stag. Catalog $2.

KNIFE WORLD, INC. (JOE DAVIS)
5152 So. Broadway
Englewood, CO 80110
Phone: 303-781-0322

Specialties: Custom knives for collectors.

LANDERDALL'S KNIFE CITY
Rt. 1, Box 269
Castalian Springs, TN 37031
Phone: 615-374-3824

Specialties: Old and new collector knives, some foreign. Mostly pocketknives. Call PM.

LOG CABIN SPORTS SHOP INC.
8010 Lafayette
Lodi, OH 44254
Phone: 216-948-1082

Specialties: Buckskinner knives in proper style, including Mexican type, ready to go.

JEFF MARNELL'S KNIVES
52 Edmund Ave.
Uniontown, PA 15401
Phone: 412-437-3931

Specialties: Survival, discounted major brands; catalog $2.

MORTY THE KNIFE MAN
60 Otis St.
West Babylon, NY 11704
Phone: 516-491-5764/800-247-2511

Specialties: The world's fish knives—all of them.

NORDIC KNIVES
1634CZ Copenhagen Dr.
Solvang, CA 93463
Phone: 805-688-3612

Specialties: Custom and Randall knives; custom catalog $3; Randall catalog $2; both catalogs $4.

NORTH AMERICAN KNIFE ASSOC., LTD. (See International Cutlery Purveyors)

PARKER CUTLERY
2837 Hickory Valley Road
P.O. Box 22668
Chattanooga, TN 37422
Phone: 615-894-1782

Specialties: Collector quality pocket knives and a new line of American-made knives.

PLAZA CUTLERY INC.
333 Bristol, South Coast Plaza
Costa Mesa, CA 92626
Phone: 714-549-3932

Specialties: List ($1) of custom knives for collectors, many top names every time. Other knives, too, of course, at two stores.

R&C KNIVES AND SUCH
P.O. Box 32631
San Jose, CA 95152
Phone: 408-923-5728

Specialties: Custom knives for collectors. Wide variety. Send stamps; can call anytime. Catalog $2.

R&R SALES
P.O. Box 498
Sycamore, IL 60178
Phone: 815-895-4995

Specialties: Hand-made soft zip knife cases in several sizes.

A.G. RUSSELL CO.
1705 Hiway 471N
Springdale, AR 72764
Phone: 501-751-7341

Specialties: Regularly lists custom knives by all makers; sold on consignment; also commemoratives, Russell and Morseth knives.

SAN DIEGO KNIVES
P.O. Box 326; 11280 Posthill Rd.
Lakeside, CA 92040
Phone: 619-561-5900

Specialties: All brand names, most all types; most all discounted. Further volume discounts, each order. Lists.

SAN FRANCISCO COLLECTOR KNIVES
624 Stanyan St.
San Francisco, CA 94117
Phone: 415-668-3360

Specialties: High-tech collector Wolf Schulz-Tattenpach will share his goodies with qualified buyers—Paul, Walker, Appleton are some of the names.

SHOFNER'S WORLD OF KNIVES
2104 Prestonwood Ctr.
Dallas, TX 75240
Phone: 214-661-2298

Specialties: Collector grade custom knives at two Dallas stores.

SHOFNER'S WORLD OF KNIVES
2501 West Memorial Road
Oklahoma City, OK 73134
Phone: 405-752-1447

Specialties: Collector grade knives.

SMOKY MOUNTAIN KNIFE WORKS
Hwy. 66, P.O. Box 430
Sevierville, TN 37862
Phone: 615-453-5871

Specialties: Retail and wholesale all kinds of knives and supplies.

SPORTS HUT
1311 Bell Ridge Dr.
Kingsport, TN 37665
Phone: 615-247-3987 or 378-3232

Specialties: Discounts all major brands of pocket knives and military-related cutlery.

UNITED STATES CUTLERY
P.O. Box 418
Wyckoff, NJ 07481-0418
Phone: 800-345-0710

Specialties: Top line of Precise knives.

A WORLD OF KNIVES
3376 Kietzke Lane
Reno, NV 89502
Phone: 702-826-9300

Specialties: Major brands, imported and domestic, and RANDALL MADE knives.

Knife Services

Engravers

SAM ALFANO
Rt. 1, Box 365
Pearl River, LA 70452
Phone: 504-863-3364

GARY ALLARD
Creek Side
Fishers Hill, VA 22626
Phone: 703-465-3903

BILLY BATES
2905 Lynnwood Circle S.W.
Decatur, AL 35603
Phone: 205-355-3690

JAMES P. BINA
P.O. Box 6532
Evanston, IL 60204
Phone: 312-475-6377

LAWRENCE T. BLAKESLEE
1650 El Cerrito Court
San Luis Obispo, CA 93401
Phone: 805-544-5182
(After 5 PM PCT)

GARY BLANCHARD
720 Holly Ave.
P.O. Box 1123
Burney, CA 96013
Phone: 916-335-5343

C. ROGER BLEILE
5040 Ralph Ave.
Cincinnati, OH 45238
Phone: 513-251-0249

BENITA BONSHIRE
1121 Burlington
Muncie, IN 47302
Phone: 317-282-9073

BRYAN BRIDGES
6350 E. Paseo San Andres
Tucson, AZ 85710
Phone: 602-886-9146

DENNIS B. BROOKER
502 Hwy 92
Prole, IA 50229
Phone: 515-961-8200

BYRON BURGESS
710 Bella Vista Dr.
Morro Bay, CA 93442
Phone: 805-772-3974

MARTIN BUTLER
P.O. Box 167
Mt. Brydges, Ont.
CANADA NOL 1WO

FRANK CLARK
3714 - 27th St.
Lubbock, TX 79410
Phone: 806-799-1187

LARRY R. COLE
P.O. Box 104
Ione, WA 99139
Phone: 509-442-3072

JIM DASHWOOD
255 Barkham Road
Wokingham
Berkshire RG11 4BY
ENGLAND
Phone: 0734-781761

ED DeLORGE
2231 Hwy. 308
Thibodaux, LA 70301
Phone: 504-447-1633

ROD DILLING
105 N. Ridgewood Dr.
Sebring, FL 33870
Phone: 813-385-0647

RICK EATON
448 Winslow St.
Crockett, CA 94525
Phone: 415-787-2539

KEN EYSTER
Heritage Gunsmiths Inc.
6441 Bishop Rd.
Centerburg, OH 43011
Phone: 614-625-6131

TERRY FLOWERS
P.O. Box 96
Midland, OR 97634
Phone: 503-882-1323

FRED A. HARRINGTON
2107 W. Frances Road
Mt. Morris, MI 48458
Phone: 313-686-3008

FRED D. HENDERSON
569 Santa Barbara Dr.
Forest Park, GA 30050
Phone: 404-968-4866

BENNO HUENE
934 Jack London Dr.
Santa Rosa, CA 95405
Phone: 707-539-1747

RALPH W. INGLE
#4 Missing Link
Rossville, GA 30741
Phone: 404-866-5589

BILL JOHNS
1113 Nightingale
McAllen, TX 78504
Phone: 512-682-6606

LANCE KELLY
1824 Royal Palm Dr.
Edgewater, FL 32032
Phone: 904-423-4933

JIM KELSO
RD 1, Box 5300
Worcester, VT 05682
Phone: 802-229-4254

JOE and PATTY KOSTELNIK
RD #4, Box 323
Greensburg, PA 15601
Phone: 412-832-0365

JOHN M. KUDLAS
622 - 14th St. S.E.
Rochester, MN 55901
Phone: 507-288-5579

FRANZ LETSCHNIG
210 Chemin Marieville
Richelieu, P. Que. J3L 3V8
CANADA
Phone: 514-658-5616

HARRY LIMINGS, JR.
5030 Patrick Rd.
Sunbury, OH 43074
Phone: 614-965-3272

STEVE LINDSAY
RR2 Cedar Hills
Kearney, NE 68847
Phone: 308-236-7885

SIMON M. LYTTON
19 Pinewood Gardens
Hemel Hempstead
Herts. HP1 1TN
ENGLAND
Phone: UK# 04442-55542

ROBERT E. MAKI
P.O. Box 947
Northbrook, IL 60065
Phone: 312-724-8238

GEORGE MAREK
P.O. Box 213
Westfield, MA 01086
Phone: 413-568-9816
(Evenings)

LYNTON McKENZIE
6940 N. Alvernon Way
Tucson, AZ 85718
Phone: 602-299-5090

DAVID A. MORTON
1110 W. 21st St.
Lorain, OH 44052
Phone: 216-245-3419

MITCH MOSCHETTI
P.O. Box 27065
Denver, CO 80227
Phone: 303-936-1184

OLD DOMINION HAND ENGRAVERS
Brett Irby, David Perdue,
Jon Robyn, Lisa Tomlin
10119 Timberlake Rd.
Lynchburg, VA 24502
Phone: 804-239-1067/4928

JON POULAKIS
Rt. 11, Box 260, Pinehaven Dr.
Sevierville, TN 37862
Phone: 615-453-1311

MARTIN RABENO
Box 37F, RD #1
Ellenville, NY 12428
Phone: 914-647-4567

ANDREW RAFTIS
2743 N. Sheffield
Chicago, IL 60614
Phone: 312-871-6699

CHRIS REED
4399 Bonny Mede Ct.
Jackson, MI 49201
Phone: 517-764-4387

J.J. ROBERTS
166 Manassas Dr.
Manassas Park, VA 22111
Phone: 703-361-4513

BOB ROSSER
162 Ramsey Dr.
Albertville, AL 35950
Phone: 205-878-5388

LEWIS B. SANCHEZ
11711 Gillette St.
Tampa, FL 33617
Phone: 813-988-2772

BRUCE SHAW
P.O. Box 545
Pacific Grove, CA 93950
Phone: 408-646-1937

GEORGE SHERWOOD
Box 735
Winchester, OR 97495
Phone: 503-672-3159

BEN SHOSTLE
1121 Burlington
Muncie, IN 47302
Phone: 317-282-9073

W.P. SINCLAIR
46 Westbury Road
Edington, Wiltsh. BA13 4PG
ENGLAND
Phone: U.K. Code then
(0380) 830494

R.E. SKAGGS
P.O. Box 34, 114 Miles Court
Princeton, IL 61356
Phone: 815-875-8207

RON SMITH
3601 West 7th St.
Ft. Worth, TX 76107
Phone: 817-732-4623

ROBERT VALADE
931 - 3d Ave.
Seaside, OR 97138
Phone: 503-738-7672

GEORGE A. WALKER
Star Route
Alpine, WY 83128
Phone: 307-883-2372

PATRICIA WALKER
P.O. Box 2343
Taos, NM 87571
Phone: 505-758-0233

KENNETH WARREN
c/o Mountain States Engraving
8333 E. San Sebastian Dr.
Scottsdale, AZ 85258
Phone: 602-991-5035

CLAUS WILLIG
Siedlerweg 17
8720 Schweinfurt
WEST GERMANY
Phone: 09721-41446

MEL WOOD
P.O. Box 1255
Sierra Vista, AZ 85636
Phone: 602-455-5541

Scrimshanders

JOHN ALWARD
879 Watkins Road
Allen, MI 49227
Phone: 517-869-2454

TERRY JACK ANDERSON
430 E. 1st North
Richfield, UT 84701
Phone: 802-896-6803

ART OF SCRIMSHAW
(See Gil Velasquez)

DUANE BAKER
1656 Vilardo Lane
Columbus, OH 43227
Phone: 614-236-0915

C.M. BARRINGER
244 Lakeview Terr.
Palm Harbor, FL 33563
Phone: 813-785-0088

CONNIE BELLET
P.O. BOX 111
Ringling, MT 59642
Phone: 406-547-2272

BENITA BONSHIRE
1121 Burlington
Muncie, IN 47302
Phone: 317-282-9073

BOONE TRADING CO., INC.
562 Coyote Rd.
Brinnon, WA 98320
Phone: 206-796-4330

JUDY BOUCHARD
1808 W. Pleasant Ridge Rd.
Hammond, LA 70401
Phone: 504-345-2456

SANDRA BRADY
9608 Monclova Rd.
P.O. Box 104
Monclova, OH 43542
Phone: 419-866-0435

BOB BURDETTE
4908 Maplewood Dr.
Greenville, SC 29615
Phone: 803-288-0976

MARY GREGG BYRNE
P.O. Box 2394
Bellingham, WA 98227
Phone: 206-676-1413

JERRY CABLE
332 Main St.
Mt. Pleasant, PA 15666
Phone: 412-547-8282

LYNDA CAPOCCI
Rt. 1, Box 144, Lukens Lake
Roann, IN 46974
Phone: 317-833-4771

LYLE CAUDILL
720 W. Walnut St.
Felicity, OH 45120
Phone: 513-876-2212

MICHAEL COLLINS
Rte. 4, Batesville Rd.
Woodstock, GA 30188
Phone: 404-475-7410

RAYMOND A. COVER, JR.
Rt. 1, Box 194
Mineral Point, MO 63660
Phone: 314-749-3783

BARBARA CRICCHIO
P.O. Box 656
Ringwood, NJ 07456
Phone: 201-962-6674

JEAN E. CURTIS
2809 Midwood
Lansing, MI 48910
Phone: 517-393-9316

GUY M. DAHL
Box 308
Horsefly, BC VOL 1LO
CANADA
Phone: 604-620-3349

MARY E. DAVIDSON
2419-25th St.
Lubbock, TX 79411
Phone: 806-762-1901

JEAN E. DeSAVAGE
9168 Redwood
Fontana, CA 92335
Phone: 714-822-6050

RICHARD DiMARZO
2357 Center Place
Birmingham, AL 35205
Phone: 205-252-3331

JONI ELBOURN
P.O. Box 404, Hudson P.O.
Hudson, Que. JOP 1HO
CANADA
Phone: 514-458-2663

BOB ENGNATH
1217 B Crescent Dr.
Glendale, CA 91205
Phone: 818-241-3629

RICK M. EVANS
2717 Arrowhead Dr.
Abilene, TX 79606
Phone: 915-698-2620

RICK B. FIELDS
320 No. Durango Ave.
Ocoee, FL 32761
Phone: 305-877-2339

DALE FISK
Box 252
Council, ID 83612
Phone: 208-253-4582

TERRY FLOWERS
(See Engravers)

W.C. FRAZIER
1029 Kavanaugh St.
Mansfield, LA 71052
Phone: 318-872-1732

GIGI
P.O. Box 624
Clovis, CA 93613
Phone: 209-298-0685

JIM GULLETTE
Rte. 8, Box 265
Greer, SC 29651
Phone: 803-877-7727

CHARLES HARGRAVES
1839 Kingston Rd.
Scarborough, Ont., M1N 1T3
Canada
Phone: 416-699-6791

STAR HARLESS
P.O. Box 5913
Lake Worth, FL 33466-5913
Phone: 305-964-3325

FRED HARRINGTON
(See "Engravers")

STAN HAWKINS
2230 El Capitan
Arcadia, CA 91006
Phone: 818-445-3054

TOM HIGH
5474 S. 112.8 Rd.
Alamosa, CO 81101
Phone: 719-589-2108

DENNIS K. HOLLAND
4908-17th Place
Lubbock, TX 79416
Phone: 806-799-8427

HARVEY HOOVER
1263 Nunneley Rd.
Paradise, CA 95969
Phone: 916-872-1154

IMAGES IN IVORY
(See John Stahl)

ALAN JIRANEK
9065 Van Emmon Rd.
Yorkville, IL 60560
Phone: 312-553-0302

ANN JORDAN
733 Santa Lucia
Los Osos, CA 93402
Phone: 805-528-7398

LINDA K. KARST
P.O. Box 171
Coppell, TX 75019
Phone: 214-462-9006

JIM KELSO
(See "Engravers")

JOE and PATTY KOSTELNIK
(See "Engravers")

JOHN W. LAND
P.O. Box 917
Wadesboro, NC 28170
Phone: 704-694-5141
Home: 704-694-2001

ERIK LOVESTRAND
325 Rolfe Dr.
Apopka, FL 32703
Phone: 305-886-0494

GEORGE MAREK
(See "Engravers")

LARRY E. McCULLOUGH
Rte. 4, Box 556
Mocksville, NC 27028
Phone: 704-634-5632

BERNI McFADDEN
2524 N. 16th
Coeur d'Alene, ID 83814
Phone: 208-664-2686

LOU McLARAN
603 Powers St.
Waco, TX 76705
Phone: 817-799-2234

CAROLE McWILLIAMS
4334 C.R. 509
Bayfield, CO 81122
Phone: 303-884-9854

ANITA MILLER
450 S. 1st
Seward, NE 68434
Phone: 402-643-4726

PETRIA MITCHELL
R.D. 1, Box 244
Brattleboro, VT 05301
Phone: 802-257-4021

MICHELLE OCHONICKY
4059 Toenges Ave.
St. Louis, MO 63116
Phone: 314-351-2612

BELLE OCHS
124 Emerald Lane
Largo, FL 34641
Phone: 813-536-3827

VAUGHN PARISH
103 Cross St.
Monaca, PA 15061
Phone: 412-495-3024

LARRY H. PECK
14 Patricia Lane
Hannibal, MO 63401
Phone: 314-221-5994

LOU PETERSON
514 S. Jackson St.
Gardner, IL 60424
Phone: 815-237-8432

TRENA POLK
3526 Eller St.
Fort Smith, AR 72904
Phone: 501-782-1396

JON POULAKIS
(See Engravers)

BOB PURDY
2505 Canterbury Rd.
Hays, KS 67601
Phone: 913-628-3043

NANCY QUINN
P.O. Box 692
Julian, CA 92036
Phone: 619-765-1415

CHARLES V. RECE
Rt. 2, Box 477
Albemarle, NC 28001
Phone: 704-982-2572

J.J. ROBERTS
(See "Engravers")

JOE RUNDELL
6198 Frances Rd.
Clio, MI 48420
Phone: 313-687-0559

ROBERT SATRE
518-3rd Ave. N.W.
Weyburn, Sask. S4H 1R1
CANADA
Phone: 306-842-3051

ROBERT SCHABER
3710 No. Palm
Sebastian, FL 32958
Phone: 305-589-8609

PATRICIA SCHWALLIE
217 Parliament Rd.
Greenville, SC 29615
Phone: 803-268-0182

LURA SCHWARZ
8033 Sunset Blvd., Suite 233
Hollywood, CA 90046
Phone: 805-251-0400

GEORGE SHERWOOD
(See "Engravers")

R.E. SKAGGS
(See "Engravers")

PEGGY SMITH
Rt. 1, Box 119A Glades Rd.
Gatlinburg, TN 37738
Phone: 615-428-0811

RON SMITH
(See "Engravers")

JOHN STAHL
2049 Windsor Rd.
Baldwin, NY 11510
Phone: 516-223-5007

HARRY L. STALTER
RR 1, Box 60
Trivoli, IL 61569
Phone: 309-362-2306

MARY AUSTIN TALLEY
2499 Countrywood Parkway
Cordova, TN 38018
Phone: 901-372-2263

GERALD TISDALE
6 Aurora St.
Laredo, TX 78041
Phone: 512-723-2549

GIL VELASQUEZ
7120 Madera Dr.
Goleta, CA 93117
Phone: 805-968-7787

KAREN WALKER
Star Route
Alpine, WY 83128
Phone: 307-883-2372

PATRICIA WALKER
(See "Engravers")

BECKY WILSON
8080 Greenwood Ct.
Denver, CO 80221
Phone: 303-650-6338

MARY YOUNG
4826 Storeyland Dr.
Alton, IL 62002
Phone: 618-466-4707

Leatherwork

DON BAKER
1656 Vilardo Lane
Columbus, OH 43227
Phone: 614-236-0915

JOHN BUCKELEW
P.O. Box 5913
Lake Worth, FL 33466-5913
Phone: 305-964-3325

CATTLE BARON LEATHER CO.
P.O. Box 100724, Dept. K8
San Antonio, TX 78201
Phone: 512-697-8900

GRANT CHERAMIE
4260 West Main
Rt. 3, Box 940
Cut Off, LA 70345
Phone: 504-632-5770

CHINA IM/EX
Steven Schneider
69 Rockaway Ave.
San Francisco, CA 94127
Phone: 415-665-5857

CHAS. CLEMENTS
1741 Dallas St.
Aurora, CO 80010
Phone: 303-364-0403

COW CATCHER LEATHERWORKS
(See W. Barry Wilder)

JOE DAVIS
5152 S. Broadway
Englewood, CO 80110
Phone: 303-781-0322

J.R. EDMONDSON
13424 Abinger Drive
Little Rock, AR 72212
Phone: 501-225-4698

TOM HARRIS
617 S. 1st St.
Mount Vernon, WA 98273
Phone: 206-336-2413

BRIAN KATZ
2043 Hoyne
Chicago, IL 60647
Phone: 312-235-5518

TIM KENNEDY
1428 S. Morningside Dr.
Melbourne, FL 32901
Phone: 305-676-2396

CHRIS KRAVETT
Tree Stump Leather
18 State St.
Ellsworth, ME 04605
Phone: NA

JIM LAYTON
2710 Gilbert Ave.
Portsmouth, OH 45662
Phone: 614-353-6179

GEORGE S. NOONE
THE ASTORIAN LTD.
8533 Gray Ct.
Arvada, CO 80003-1337
Phone: 303-429-4132

JIM PUGH
P.O. Box 711-L
917 Carpenter
Azle, TX 76020
Phone: 817-444-2679

RAVON INC.
P.O. Box 670
311 N. Locust
Denton, TX 76201
Phone: 817-382-1831

NORM RINEY
6212 S. Marion Way
Littleton, CO 80121
Phone: 303-794-1731

RUIZ INDUSTRIES INC.
3829 San Fernando Rd.
Glendale, CA 91204
Phone: 213-242-4131

ROBERT G. SCHRAP
7024 W. Wells St.
Wauwatosa, WI 53213
Phone: 414-771-6472

SHERMAN CUSTOM LEATHER
Landon Hill Rd.
Chestertown, NY 12817
Phone: 518-494-2057

JESSEE W. SMITH SADDLERY
No. 307 Haven St.
Spokane, WA 99202
Phone: 509-534-3229

JOHN R. STUMPF
John's Custom Leather
525 So. Liberty St.
P.O. Box 402
Blairsville, PA 15717
Phone: 412-459-6802

MIKE TIERNEY
447 Rivercrest Dr.
Woodstock, ON N4S 5W5
Phone: 519-539-8859

SYLVIA VAUGHAN
332 Joha Loop
Los Alamos, NM 87544
Phone: 505-672-9133

GIL VELASQUEZ
7120 Madera Dr.
Goleta, CA 93117
Phone: 805-968-7787

WALT WHINNERY
1947 Meadow Creek Dr.
Louisville, KY 40218
Phone: 502-458-4361

W. BARRY WILDER
3006 Industrial Dr.
Raleigh, NC 27609
Phone: 919-833-8262

TAMI WORTHINGTON
86 Ensenada
Los Alamos, NM 87544
Phone: 505-672-3309

Photographers

PETER L. BLOOMER
Horizons West
427 S. San Francisco
Flagstaff, AZ 86001
Phone: 602-779-1014

STEVEN BRADLEY
Integrated Arts
P.O. Box 3252
Taos, NM 87571
Phone: 505-758-1281

DEAN R. BROWN
Diamond Portrait Gallery
423 S. Buchanan
Edwardsville, IL 62025
Phone: 618-656-4338

BYRON BURGESS
710 Bella Vista Dr.
Morro Bay, CA 93442
Phone: 805-772-3974

ART CARTER
818 Buffin Bay Rd.
Columbia, SC 28210
Phone: 802-772-2148

JOHN D. CATALANO
56 Kingston Ave.
Hicksville, NY 11801
Phone: 516-938-1356

JOHN E. CHASE
("See Heat Treaters")

ROBERT COMBS
1386 Rambling Rd.
Ypsilanti, MI 48197
Phone: 313-482-6629

BILL DeSAVAGE
9168 Redwood Ave.
Fontana, CA 92335
Phone: 714-822-6050

DAVID EVERETT
White Lotus Studio
12 Jefferson Ave.
West Hartford, CT 06110
Phone: 203-236-5783

DAN FITZGERALD
P.O. Box 198
Beverly Hills, CA 90213
Phone: 213-255-3457

BOB GLADSTONE
6623 Sedan Ave.
Canoga Park, CA 91307
Phone: 818-348-9255

RONALD E. GODBY
204 Seven Hollys Dr.
Yorktown, VA 23692
Phone: 804-898-4445

JOHN HANUSIN
3306 Commercial
Northbrook, IL 60062
Phone: 312-564-2706

JIM HAYS
7118 McGee
Kansas City, MO 64114
Phone: 816-363-1344

DAVID HUTSON
8120 Juniper
Prairie Village, KS 66208
Phone: 913-383-1123

C.A. JONES
36 Broadgate Close
Bellaire
Barnstaple, N. Devon
EX 31 4AL, England
Phone: 0271-75328

ERIC KLINEFELTER
10963 Hickory Ridge Rd.
Columbia, MD 21044
Phone: 301-964-0273

LENZ PHOTOGRAPHY
2810 S. 24th St., Suite 111
Phoenix, AZ 85034
Phone: 602-275-1005

GARY W. LONG
Rt. 2, Box 169
Hillsboro, TN 37342
Phone: 615-596-2275

JIM MOAKE
18 Council Ave.
Aurora, IL 60504
Phone: 312-898-7184

RICHARD OWLETT
P.O. Box 169
Trumansburg, NY 14886
Phone: 607-387-5202

C. H. PIPES
718 Alpine Dr.
Sevierville, TN 37862
Phone: 615-453-4595

ERIC L. RASMUSSEN
5735 N. 4700 W.
Bear River, UT 84301
Phone: 801-279-8578

TIM RICE
P.O. Box 85
Whitefish, MT 59937
Phone: 406-862-5416

TOM RUBY
Holiday Inn University
11200 E. Goodman Rd.
Olive Branch, MS 38654
Phone: 601-895-2941

DAVID V. SCADLOCK
P.O. Box 1702
Lacrosse, WI 54602-1702
Phone: 608-787-6126

CHARLES SEMMER
7885 Cyd Dr.
Denver, CO 80221
Phone: 303-429-6947

RANDALL SMITH
1720 Oneco Ave.
Winter Park, FL 32789
Phone: 305-628-5447

MARK SURLES
Route 1 Box 70-A
Wade, NC 28395
Phone: 919-483-8814

ALLAN I. TEGER
248 Tremont St.
Newton, MA 02158
Phone: 617-527-0798

THIRD EYE PHOTOS
140 E. Sixth Ave.
Helena, MT 59601
Phone: 406-443-4688

BILL THOMAS
412 B 6th Ave.
Salt Lake City, UT 84103
Phone: 801-364-7153

TONY TOCCI
41 Ellwood Rd.
East Brunswick, NJ 08816
Phone: 201-238-2289

STEVEN L. TOWELL
Rt. 2, Fern Lane
Wilder, ID 83676
Phone: 208-482-7703

CYNTHIA VANNOY-RHOADES
Box 195
Clearmont, WY 82835
Phone: 307-758-4460

WEYER PHOTO SERV., INC.
Mail: 333 14th St.
Shpg.: 324 15th St.
Toledo, OH 43624
Phone: 419-241-5454

HOLLY WORLEY
6545 S. Balsom Ct.
Littleton, CO 80123
Phone: NA

Heat Treaters

JIM BARBEE
P.O. Box 1173
Fort Stockton, TX 79753
Phone: 915-336-2882

BAY STATE METAL TREATING CO.
6 Jefferson Ave.
Woburn, MA 01801
Phone: 617-935-4100

PAUL BOS
1900 Weld Blvd.
El Cajon, CA 92020
Phone: (Shop) 619-562-2370
(Home) 619-445-4740

RICHARD BRIDWELL
801 Milford Ch. Rd.
Taylors, SC 29687
Phone: 803-895-1715

JOHN E. CHASE
217 Walnut
P.O. Drawer H
Aledo, TX 76008
Phone: 817-441-8331

EL MONTE STEEL
2456 N. Rosemead Blvd.
El Monte, CA 91733
Phone: 213-575-1234

HAUNI RICHMOND INC
2800 Charles City Rd.
Richmond, VA 23231
Phone: 804-222-5262

HOLT-SORNBERGER
1253 Birchwood Dr., Unit-F
Sunnyvale, CA 94089
Phone: 408-745-0306

METAL TREATING
710 Burns St.
Cincinnati, OH 45204
Phone: 513-921-2300

TEXAS KNIFEMAKER SUPPLY
10649 Haddington, Suite 190
Houston, TX 77043
Phone: 713-461-8632

THE TINKER SHOP
1120 Helen
Deer Park, TX 77536
Phone: 713-479-7286

R.W. WILSON
P.O. Box 2012
Weirton, WV 26062
Phone: 304-723-2771

JIM PUGH
P.O. Box 711-H
917 Carpenter St.
Azle, TX 76020
Phone: 817-444-2679

MISCELLANEOUS

Etching

ATS INDUSTRIAL, INC.
1901 East Madison St.
Tempe, AZ 85281
Phone: 602-231-0107
602-956-4373

AURUM ETCHINGS
601 E. Walnut Circle
Garland, TX 75040
Phone: 214-276-8551

BARON TECHNOLOGY, INC.
62 Spring Hill Rd.
Trumbull, CT 06611
Phone: 203-452-0515

FOUNTAIN PRODUCTS
492 Prospect Ave.
West Springfield, MA 01089
Phone: 413-781-4651

LEONARD LEIBOWITZ
1202 Palto Alto St.
Pittsburgh, PA 15212
Phone: 412-231-5388

SHAW-CULLEN, INC.
212 East 47th St.
New York, NY 10017
Phone: 212-759-8460

Custom Handle Artisans

JOHN ALWARD
(See "Scrimshanders")

JAMES M. COOPER
2148 Cook Place
Ramona, CA 92065
Phone: NA

RICHARD DI MARZO
2357 Center Pl. So.
Birmingham, AL 35205
Phone: 205-252-3331

ED HARRISON
10125 Palestine
Houston, TX 77029
Phone: 713-673-6893

RUSSELL S. HILL
2384 Second Ave.
Grand Island, NY 14072
Phone: 716-773-0084

DENNIS K. HOLLAND
(See Scrimshanders)

BRIAN KATZ
(See Leatherworkers)

JIM KELSO
Rt. 1, Box 5300
Worcester, VT 05682
Phone: 802-229-4254

MEL KEMP
c/o Scottsdale Casting Inc.
3949 N. Buckboard Trail
Scottsdale, AZ 85251
Phone: 602-941-4938

ROBERT SATRE
(See Scrimshanders)

SHAW-CULLEN, INC.
(See Etching)

GLENN L. SMITH
1307 Custer Ave.
Billings, MT 59102
Phone: 406-252-4064

GARY VANN AUSDLE
R.R. 1, Box 50
Wingina, VA 24599
Phone: 804-263-5303

Other

BILL'S CUSTOM CASES
Wm. C. Mittelman
P.O. Box 555
Boyes Hot Springs, CA 95416
Phone: 707-996-5091
(knife cases)

NELSON GIMBERT
P.O. Box 787
Clemmons, NC 27012
Phone: 919-766-5216
(custom display chests)

THE LONG ISLAND SUTLERS
38 Willis Ave.
Mineola, NY 11501
Phone: 516-781-5515
(display boxes)

CHARLES R. (DICK) McDONALD
1918 Leavenworth
Manhatten, KS 66502
Phone: 913-539-9572
(custom made knife cases)

FRANCES OLIVER
3832 W. Desert Park Lane
Phoenix, AZ 85021
Phone: 602-841-7038
(pouches for folding knives)

Custom Grinders

BOB ENGNATH
1217 B Crescent Dr.
Glendale, CA 91205
Phone: 818-241-3629

KELGIN KNIVES
Ken Largin
110 W. Pearl
Batesville, IN 47
Phone: 812-934-5938

Organizations/Publications

KNIFEMAKERS GUILD
c/o Fred Carter, President
5219 Deer Creek Rd.
Wichita Falls, TX 76302
Phone: 817-723-4020

This continues to be the big one. The times have been sometimes tough and the atmosphere strained, but the Guild has prospered, as have its members. It screens prospects to ensure they are serious craftsmen; and it runs a big show (heretofore in Kansas City, now in Dallas) each July where over 250 Guild members show their best work, all in one room. Not all good knifemakers belong; some have joined and later left for their own reasons; the Guild drops some for cause now and again. The Knifemakers Guild is an organization with a function. A list of Guild members appears on pages 236-237.

AMERICAN BLADESMITH SOCIETY
c/o William F. Moran, Jr.
P.O. Box 68
Braddock Heights, MD 21714
Phone: 301-371-7543

If you're interested in the forged blade, you are welcome here. The Society has a teaching program, East and West, and awards stamps to Journeymen and Master Smiths after they pass tests—tough tests at a hot forge. You don't have to make knives to belong. A list of knifemaker members appears on pages 236-237.

REGIONAL ASSOCIATIONS

There are an increasing number of state and regional associations with goals possibly more directly realted to promotion of their members' sales than the Guild and the ABS. Among these known to us are the Arizona Knifemakers Association; the California Knifemakers Association; south Carolina Association of Knifemakers; the Midwest Knifemakers Association; Professional Knifemakers Assn; New England Bladesmiths Guild; and the Association of Southern Knifemakers. Lists of members of most of these may be found on pages 236-237.

CANADA

One umbrella organization—the Canadian Knife Collectors Club—serves collectors and craftsmen alike. The CKCC holds its own shows and has a semi-annual newsletter. Address CKCC president W. C. White, 148 Islington Ave., Apt. 208, Toronto, ON M8V 3B6, Canada or telephone 416-251-4552.

AMERICAN CUTLERY MFRS. ASSOCIATION
1133 15th St. N.W.
Washington, DC 20005
Phone: 202-429-9440

The ACMA does for its over three dozen member firms what manufacturers associations of many kinds do—provide neutral ground for meetings between competitors, legitmately combined interests for representation to government and provide a forum for the sharing of technical information. It is in no sense a public association; membership is held by companies, not individuals.

THE BLADE MAGAZINE
P.O. Box 22007-K8
Chattanooga, TN 37422
Phone: 615-894-0339

Editor/Publisher: Bruce Voyles. Six Times. Special show, fishing, hunting issues. Official magazine of the Knifemakers Guild. $15.99 per year, includes EDGES, a tabloid published periodically, and membership in the American Blade Collectors Assn.

KNIFE WORLD
P.O. Box 3395
Knoxville, TN 37927
Phone: 615-523-3339

Editor and Publisher: Houston Price. Monthly. Tabloid size on newsprint. Covers custom knives, knifemakers, collecting, old factory knives, etc. General coverage for the knife enthusiast. Subscr. $10 year.

NATIONAL KNIFE MAGAZINE
7201 Shallowford Rd.
Chattanooga, TN 37421
Phone: 615-899-9456

Editor and Publisher: James V. Allday. Monthly. Four-color cover. For members, National Knife Collectors Association. Lots of ads. Emphasis on pocketknife collecting, but has broadened coverage to include all phases of knife interest. Membership $15 year.